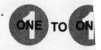 **TO** ON

Bilingual Dictionary

English-Thai
Thai-English
Dictionary

Compiled by

Suwan Kaewkongpan

STAR Foreign Language BOOKS

© Publishers

ISBN : 978 1 908357 94 6

First Edition   : 2012
Second Edition : 2018

Published by

STAR Foreign Language BOOKS

a unit of
ibs BOOKS (UK)

56, Langland Crescent
Stanmore HA7 1NG, U.K.
info@starbooksuk.com
www.starbooksuk.com

Printed in India at
Star Print-O-Bind, New Delhi-110 020

About this Dictionary

Developments in science and technology today have narrowed down distances between countries, and have made the world a small place. A person living thousands of miles away can learn and understand the culture and lifestyle of another country with ease and without travelling to that country. Languages play an important role as facilitators of communication in this respect.

To promote such an understanding, STAR **Foreign Language** BOOKS has planned to bring out a series of bilingual dictionaries in which important English words have been translated into other languages, with Roman transliteration in case of languages that have different scripts. This is a humble attempt to bring people of the word closer through the medium of language, thus making communication easy and convenient.

Under this series of *one-to-one dictionaries*, we have published almost 50 languages, the list of which has been given in the opening pages. These have all been compiled and edited by teachers and scholars of the relative languages.

Publishers

Bilingual Dictionaries in this Series

English-Afrikaans / Afrikaans-English	Abraham Venter
English-Albanian / Albanian-English	Theodhora Blushi
English-Amharic / Amharic-English	Girun Asanke
English-Arabic / Arabic-English	Rania-al-Qass
English-Bengali / Bengali-English	Amit Majumdar
English-Bosnian / Bosnian-English	Boris Kazanegra
English-Bulgarian / Bulgarian-English	Vladka Kocheshkova
English-Cantonese / Cantonese-English	Nisa Yang
English-Chinese (Mandarin) / Chinese (Mandarin)-Eng	Y. Shang & R. Yao
English-Croatian / Croatain-English	Vesna Kazanegra
English-Czech / Czech-English	Jindriska Poulova
English-Dari / Dari-English	Amir Khan
English-Dutch / Dutch-English	Lisanne Vogel
English-Estonian / Estonian-English	Lana Haleta
English-Farsi / Farsi-English	Maryam Zaman Khani
English-French / French-English	Aurélie Colin
English-Gujarati / Gujarati-English	Sujata Basaria
English-German / German-English	Bicskei Hedwig
English-Greek / Greek-English	Lina Stergiou
English-Hindi / Hindi-English	Sudhakar Chaturvedi
English-Hungarian / Hungarian-English	Lucy Mallows
English-Italian / Italian-English	Eni Lamllari
English-Korean / Korean-English	Mihee Song
English-Latvian / Latvian-English	Julija Baranovska
English-Levantine Arabic / Levantine Arabic-English	Ayman Khalaf
English-Lithuanian / Lithuanian-English	Regina Kazakeviciute
English-Nepali / Nepali-English	Anil Mandal
English-Norwegian / Norwegian-English	Samuele Narcisi
English-Pashto / Pashto-English	Amir Khan
English-Polish / Polish-English	Magdalena Herok
English-Portuguese / Portuguese-English	Dina Teresa
English-Punjabi / Punjabi-English	Teja Singh Chatwal
English-Romanian / Romanian-English	Georgeta Laura Dutulescu
English-Russian / Russian-English	Katerina Volobuyeva
English-Serbian / Serbian-English	Vesna Kazanegra
English-Sinhalese / Sinhalese-English	Naseer Salahudeen
English-Slovak / Slovak-English	Zuzana Horvathova
English-Slovenian / Slovenian-English	Tanja Turk
English-Somali / Somali-English	Ali Mohamud Omer
English-Spanish / Spanish-English	Cristina Rodriguez
English-Swedish / Swedish-English	Madelene Axelsson
English-Tagalog / Tagalog-English	Jefferson Bantayan
English-Tamil / Tamil-English	Sandhya Mahadevan
English-Thai / Thai-English	Suwan Kaewkongpan
English-Turkish / Turkish-English	Nagme Yazgin
English-Ukrainian / Ukrainian-English	Katerina Volobuyeva
English-Urdu / Urdu-English	S. A. Rahman
English-Vietnamese / Vietnamese-English	Hoa Hoang
English-Yoruba / Yoruba-English	O. A. Temitope

More languages in print

STAR Foreign Language BOOKS

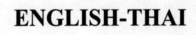

ENGLISH-THAI

ENGLISH-THAI

A

a *a.* หนึ่ง neung
aback *adv.* ตกตะลึง toktaleung
abaction *n* การลักต้อนปศุสัตว์ ganlaktonpasusat
abactor *n* ผู้ลักต้อนปศุสัตว์ pulaktonpasusat'
abandon *v.t.* ทอดทิ้ง todting
abase *v.t.* ถ่อมตัว tomtua
abasement *n* การถ่อมตัว gantomtua
abash *v.t.* ทำให้อับอาย tamhai-ab-ai
abate *v.t.* บรรเทา bantao
abatement *n.* การบรรเทา ganbantao
abbey *n.* สำนักสงฆ์ samnaksong
abbreviate *v.t.* ย่อคำ yawkam
abbreviation *n* คำย่อ kamyaw
abdicate *v.t,* สละอำนาจ sala-umnad
abdication *n* การสละอำนาจ gansala-umnad
abdomen *n* ท้อง tong
abdominal *a.* ส่วนท้อง suantong
abduct *v.t.* ลักพาตัว lakpatua
abduction *n* การลักพาตัว ganlakpatua
abed *adv.* บนเตียง bontiang
aberrance *n.* การเบี่ยงเบนจากภาวะปกติ ganbiangbein-akpawapagati
abet *v.t.* ยุยงให้ทำผิด yuyonghaitampid
abetment *n.* การยุยงให้ทำผิด ganyuyonghaitampid
abeyance *n.* การระงับชั่วคราว ganra-gnabchuakrao
abhor *v.t.* เกลียด gliad
abhorrence *n.* ความเกลียดชัง kwamgliadchang
abide *v.i* อดทน odton
abiding *a* ทนทาน tontan
ability *n* ความสามารถ kwamsamad
abject *a.* น่าเวทนา nawetana
ablaze *adv.* โชติช่วง chodchuang
ablactate *v. t* หย่านม yanom

ablactation *n* การหย่านม ganyanom
able *a* สามารถ samad
ablepsy *n* ความมืดบอด kwammeudbod
ablush *adv* หน้าแดง nadeang
ablution *n* การชำระล้าง ganchamralang
abnegate *v. t* ละทิ้ง lating
abnegation *n* การละทิ้ง ganlating
abnormal *a* ผิดปกติ pidpagati
aboard *adv* ขึ้นเครื่อง keunkreuang
abode *n* บนยานพาหนะ bonyanpahana
abolish *v.t* เลิกล้ม leuklom
abolition *v* การเลิกล้ม ganleuklom
abominable *a* น่าชัง nachang
aboriginal *a* พื้นเมือง peunmeuang
aborigines *n. pl* ชาวพื้นเมือง chaopeunmeuang
abort *v.i* แท้ง taeng
abortion *n* การทำแท้ง gantamtaeng
abortive *adv* ไร้ผล raipon
abound *v.i.* ชุก chuk
about *adv* ประมาณ praman
about *prep* เกี่ยวกับ giawgab
above *adv* เหนือกว่า neuakwa
above *prep.* ข้างบน kangbon
abreast *adv* เคียงข้าง kiangkang
abridge *v.t* ตัดทอน tadton
abridgement *n* การตัดทอน gantadton
abroad *adv* แพร่หลาย praelai
abrogate *v. t.* ยกเลิก yokleuk
abrupt *a* ทันที tanti
abruption *n* การเกิดขึ้นในทันที gangeudkeunnaitanti
abscess *n* ฝี fee
absonant *adj* ไม่ปรองดอง maiprongdong
abscond *v.i* หลบหนี lopni
absence *n* การไม่เข้าร่วม ganmaikaoruam
absent *a* หายไป haipai
absent *v.t* ไม่เข้าร่วม maikaoruam
absolute *a* แน่นอน naenon
absolutely *adv* อย่างแน่นอน yangnaenon
absolve *v.t* ให้อภัย hai-a-pai
absorb *v.t* ดูดกลืน dudgleun

abstain *v.i.* ละเว้น lawen
abstract *a* นามธรรม nammatam
abstract *n* บทคัดย่อ bodkadyaw
abstract *v.t* ถอน tawn
abstraction *n.* สิ่งที่เป็นนามธรรม
singtipennamatam
absurd *a* ไร้สาระ raisara
absurdity *n* ความไร้สาระ kwamraisara
abundance *n* ความสมบูรณ์
kwamsomboon
abundant *a* มาก mak
abuse *v.t.* ข่มเหง komheng
abuse *n* การข่มเหง gankomheng
abusive *a* เหยียดหยาม yiadyam
abutted *v* ติดกับ tidgab
abyss *n* เหวลึก hewleuk
academic *a* ด้านวิชาการ danwichagan
academy *n* สำนักวิชาการ
samnakwichagan
acarpous *adj.* ไม่ออกผล mai-awkpon
accede *v.t.* ยอมทำตาม yomtamtam
accelerate *v.t* เร่ง reng
acceleration *n* การเร่งความเร็ว
ganreingkwamrew
accent *n* สำเนียง samniang
accent *v.t* ออกเสียง auk-siang
accept *v* ยอมรับ yomrab
acceptable *a* ยอมรับได้ yomrabdai
acceptance *n* การยอมรับ ganyomrab
access *n* เข้าถึง kaoteung
accession *n* การเข้าถึง gankaoteung
accessory *n* เครื่องประดับ kreuangpradab
accident *n* อุบัติเหตุ u-bathed
accidental *a* โดยบังเอิญ doeybang-eun
accipitral *adj* เหมือนเหยี่ยว meuanyiaw
acclaim *v.t* ชื่นชม cheunchom
acclaim *n* การชื่นชม gancheunchom
acclamation *n* การโห่ร้องชื่นชม
ganhorongcheunchom
acclimatise *v.t* ชินกับสภาพอากาศ
chingabsapab-a-gad
accommodate *v.t* จัดหาที่อยู่ jadhatiyu

accommodation *n.* ที่อยู่ tiyu
accompaniment *n* สิ่งเพิ่มเติม
singpeumteum
accompany *v.t.* ติดตาม tidtam
accomplice *n* ผู้สมรู้ร่วมคิด
pusomruruamkid
accomplish *v.t.* ทำสำเร็จ tamsamred
accomplished *a* สำเร็จ samred
accomplishment *n.* ความสำเร็จ
kwamsamred
accord *v.t.* ตกลง toklong
accord *n.* ข้อตกลง kawtoklong
accordingly *adv.* ตามนั้น tamnan
account *n.* บัญชี banchi
account *v.t.* ทำบัญชี tambanchi
accountable *a* มีความรับผิดชอบ
mikwamrabpidchob
accountancy *n.* การบัญชี ganbanchi
accountant *n.* นักบัญชี nakbanchi
accredit *v.t.* แต่งตั้ง taengtang
accrementition *n* การแตกตัวของเซล
gantaektuakongsell
accrete *v.t.* เพิ่มขึ้น peumkeun
accrue *v.i.* เพิ่มขึ้น peumkeun
accumulate *v.t.* สะสม sasom
accumulation *n* การสะสม gansasom
accuracy *n.* ความถูกต้อง kwamtooktong
accurate *a.* ถูกต้อง tooktong
accursed *a.* ถูกสาป tooksab
accusation *n* การกล่าวหา ganglaoha
accuse *v.t.* กล่าวหา glaoha
accused *n.* ผู้ถูกกล่าวหา putookglaoha
accustom *v.t.* ทำให้คุ้นเคย
tamhaikunkeuy
accustomed *a.* คุ้นเคย kunkeuy
ace *n* หนึ่งแต้ม neungtam
acentric *adj* ไม่อยู่ตรงกลาง
maiyutrongglang
acephalous *adj.* ไร้หัว raihua
acephalus *n.* ทารกไร้หัว tarokraihua
acetify *v.* เปลี่ยนเป็นกรด plianpengrod
ache *n.* อาการปวด a-ganpuad

ache *v.i.* ปวด puad

achieve *v.t.* ทำสำเร็จ tamsamred

achievement *n.* ความสำเร็จ kwamsamred

achromatic *adj* ไม่มีสี maimisi

acid *a* ภาวะเป็นกรด pawapengrod

acid *n* กรด grod

acidity *n.* สภาพเป็นกรด sapabpengrod

acknowledge *v.* ยอมรับ yomrab

acknowledgement *n.* การยอมรับ ganyomrab

acne *n* สิว siew

acorn *n.* ผลต้นโอ๊ก ponton-oak

acoustic *a* เกี่ยวกับเสียง giawgabsiang

acoustics *n.* ศาสตร์เกี่ยวกับเสียง sadgiawgabsiang

acquaint *v.t.* คุ้นเคย kunkeuy

acquaintance *n.* ความคุ้นเคย kwamkunkeuy

acquest *n* ทรัพย์สินที่หามาได้ subsintihamadai

acquiesce *v.i.* ยอมตาม yomtam

acquiescence *n.* การยอมตาม ganyomtam

acquire *v.t.* ได้มา daima

acquirement *n.* การได้มา gandaima

acquisition *n.* การหามาได้ ganhamadai

acquit *v.t.* ปล่อยตัว ploytua

acquittal *n.* การปล่อยตัว ganploytua

acre *n.* เอเคอร์ acre

acreage *n.* พื้นที่เป็นเอเคอร์ peuntipenacre

acrimony *n* ความรุนแรง kwamroonraeng

acrobat *n.* นักกายกรรม nakgaiyagam

across *adv.* ตลอด talod

across *prep.* ข้าม kam

act *n.* กฎหมาย godmai

act *v.i.* กระทำ gratam

acting *n.* การแสดง gansadeang

action *n.* การกระทำ gangratam

activate *v.t.* กระตุ้น gratoon

active *a.* คล่อง klong

activity *n.* กิจการ gidjagan

actor *n.* นักแสดงชาย naksadeangchai

actress *n.* นักแสดงหญิง naksadeangying

actual *a.* จริง jing

actually *adv.* ตามจริง tamjing

acumen *n.* ฉลาด chalad

acute *a.* เฉียบพลัน chiabplan

adage *n.* ภาษิต pasit

adamant *a.* แน่วแน่ naewnae

adamant *n.* หินแข็ง hinkaeng

adapt *v.t.* ปรับตัว prabtua

adaptation *n.* การปรับตัว ganprabtua

adays *adv* สมัยนี้ samaini

add *v.t.* เพิ่ม peum

addict *v.t.* ติด tid

addict *n.* ผู้ติดยา putidya

addiction *n.* การติดยา gantidya

addition *n.* การเพิ่ม ganpeum

additional *a.* เพิ่มเติม peumteum

addle *adj* เน่า now

address *v.t.* ปราศรัย prasai

address *n.* ที่อยู่ tiyu

addressee *n.* ผู้รับ purab

adduce *v.t.* อ้างอิง ang-ing

adept *n.* ผู้ชำนาญการ puchamnangan

adept *a.* ชำนาญ chamnan

adequacy *n.* ความพอเพียง kwampawpiang

adequate *a.* พอเพียง pawpiang

adhere *v.i.* ติด tid

adherence *n.* การยึดมั่น ganyeudman

adhesion *n.* การติดแน่น gantidnaen

adhesive *n.* กาว gao

adhesive *a.* ติดแน่น tidnaen

adhibit *v.t.* ยอมให้เข้า yomhaikao

adieu *n.* การจากลา ganjakla

adieu *interj.* ลา la

adjure *v.t.* สั่ง sang

adjacent *a.* ติดกัน tidgan

adjective *n.* คำคุณศัพท์ kamkunnasab

adjoin *v.t.* ติด tid

adjourn *v.t.* เลื่อน leuan

adjournment *n.* การเลื่อน ganleuan

adjudge *v.t.* ตัดสิน tadsin

adjunct *n.* ผู้ช่วย puchuay
adjuration *n* การร้องขอ ganrongkaw
adjust *v.t.* ปรับแก้ prabgae
adjustment *n.* การปรับแก้ ganprabgae
administer *v.t.* บริหาร borihan
administration *n.* การบริหาร ganborihan
administrative *a.* เกี่ยวกับการบริหาร
  giawgabganborihan
administrator *n.* ผู้บริหาร puborihan
admirable *a.* น่าชื่นชม nacheunchom
admiral *n.* นายพลเรือ naiponreua
admiration *n.* การชื่นชม gancheunchom
admire *v.t.* นับถือ nabteu
admissible *a.* ยอมรับได้ yomrabdai
admission *n.* การรับ ganrab
admit *v.t.* รับ rab
admittance *n.* การอนุญาต gan-a-nuyad
admonish *v.t.* ตักเตือน takteuan
admonition *n.* การตักเตือน gantakteuan
adnascent *adj.* เติบโตบนสิ่งอื่น
  teubtobonsing-eun
ado *n.* อุปสรรค u-pasak
adobe *n.* อิฐ eid
adolescence *n.* วัยรุ่น wairoon
adolescent *a.* ช่วงวัยรุ่น chuangwairoon
adopt *v.t.* รับเลี้ยงเป็นบุตร rabliangpenbud
adoption *n* การรับบุตรบุญธรรม
ganrabbudboontam
adorable *a.* ชื่นชม cheunchom
adoration *n.* ความชื่นชม
  kwamcheunchom
adore *v.t.* รัก rak
adorn *v.t.* ตกแต่ง toktaeng
adscititious *adj* เพิ่ม peum
adscript *adj.* เขียนตามหลัง kiantamlang
adulation *n* การยกยอ ganyokyaw
adult *a* วัยผู้ใหญ่ waipuyai
adult *n.* ผู้ใหญ่ puyai
adulterate *v.t.* เจือปน jeuapon
adulteration *n.* การเจือปน ganjeuapon
adultery *n.* การคบชู้ gankobchu
advance *v.t.* ก้าวหน้า gaona

advance *n.* เคลื่อนไปข้างหน้า
  kleuanpaikangna
advancement *n.* การพัฒนา ganpatana
advantage *n.* ความได้เปรียบ
  kwamdaipriab
advantage *v.t.* ได้เปรียบ daipriab
advantageous *a.* เป็นประโยชน์ penprayod
advent *n.* การมาถึงของสิ่งสำคัญ
  ganmateungkongsingsamkan
adventure *n* การผจญภัย ganpajonpai
adventurous *a.* น่าตื่นเต้น nateunten
adverb *n.* คำวิเศษณ์ kamwised
adverbial *a.* เกี่ยวกับคำวิเศษณ์
  giawgabkamwised
adversary *n.* ศัตรู sattru
adverse *a* มีผลในทางลบ miponnaitanglob
adversity *n.* เคราะห์กรรม krawgam
advert *v.* เรียกความสนใจ riakkwamsonjai
advertise *v.t.* ลงโฆษณา longkodsana
advertisement *n* การโฆษณา gankodsana
advice *n* คำแนะนำ kamnaenam
advisable *a.* เหมาะสม mawsom
advisability *n* ความสามารถในการแนะนำ
  kwamsamadnaigannaenam
advise *v.t.* แนะนำ naenam
advocacy *n.* การสนับสนุน
  gansanabsanoon
advocate *n* ทนาย tanai
advocate *v.t.* สนับสนุน sanabsanoon
aerial *a.* เกี่ยวกับอากาศ giawgab-a-gad
aerial *n.* เสาอากาศ sao-a-gad
aeriform *adj.* เหมือนอากาศ meuan-a-gad
aerify *v.t.* อัดอากาศเข้า ad-a-gadkao
aerodrome *n* สนามบินเล็ก sanambinlek
aeronautics *n.pl.* วิชาการบิน wichaganbin
aeroplane *n.* เครื่องบิน kreuangbin
aesthetic *a.* สวยงาม suay-ngam
aesthetics *n.pl.* สุนทรียศาสตร์
  soontariyasad
aestival *adj* แห่งฤดูร้อน haenggreuduron
afar *adv.* ห่างไกล hangklai
affable *a.* สุภาพ supab

affair n. งาน ngan

affect v.t. ผลกระทบ pongratob

affectation n การเสแสร้ง gansesaeng

affection n. ความรัก kwamrak

affectionate a. รักใคร่ rakkrai

affidavit n พยานหลักฐาน payanlaktan

affiliation n. ความผูกพัน kwampukpan

affinity n ความเกี่ยวดอง kwamgiawdong

affirm v.t. ยืนยัน yeunyan

affirmation n การยืนยัน ganyeunyan

affirmative a ยืนยันว่าจริง yeunyanwajing

affix v.t. ผูก puk

afflict v.t. ทำให้เจ็บป่วย tamhaijebpuay

affliction n. โรคภัย rokpai

affluence n. ความร่ำรวย kwamramruay

affluent a. รวย ruay

afford v.t. สามารถหาได้ samadhadai

afforest v.t. ทำให้เป็นป่า tamhaipenpa

affray n การทะเลาะวิวาท kantarawwiwat

affront v.t. ดูถูก dutook

affront n การดูถูก gandutook

afield adv. ในทุ่งนา naitungna

aflame adv. ลุกเป็นไฟ lukpenfai

afloat adv. ลอย loy

afoot adv. ดำเนินไป damneunpai

afore prep. ก่อน gon

afraid a. กลัว glua

afresh adv. ใหม่ mai

after prep. หลัง lang

after adv ภายหลัง pailang

after conj. ต่อมา tawma

after a หลังจาก langjak

afterwards adv. หลังจากนั้น langjaknan

again adv. อีกครั้ง eik-krang

against prep. ต้าน tan

agamist n คนที่ต่อต้านการแต่งงาน kontitawtangantaeng-gnan

agape adv., อ้าปากค้าง a-pakkang

agaze adv จ้องเขม็ง jongkameng

age n. อายุ a-yu

aged a. มีอายุ mi-a-yu

agency n. หน่วยงาน nuay-ngan

agenda n. วาระ wara

agent n ตัวแทน tuatan

aggravate v.t. ยั่วยุ yuayu

aggravation n. การทำให้รุนแรง gantamhairoonraeng

aggregate v.t. รวบรวม ruabruam

aggression n การรุกราน ganrukran

aggressive a. ก้าวร้าว gaorao

aggressor n. ผู้รุกราน purukran

aggrieve v.t. เศร้าโศก saosok

aghast a. ตกตะลึง toktaleung

agile a. คล่องแคล่ว klongklaew

agility n. ความคล่องแคล่ว kwamklongklaew

agitate v.t. ปลุกปั่น plukpan

agitation n การปลุกปั่น ganplukpan

agist v.t. พาสัตว์ไปเล็มหญ้า pasatpailemya

aglow adv. สว่าง sawang

agnus n แกะ gae

ago adv. ที่ผ่านมา tipanma

agog adj. ตื่นเต้น teunten

agonist n ตัวทำการ tuatamgan

agonize v.t. เจ็บปวด jebpuad

agony n. ความเจ็บปวด kwamjebpuad

agronomy n. ปฐพีศาสตร์ patapisat

agoraphobia n. ความกลัวที่โล่ง kwamkluatilong

agrarian a. ที่ทำการเกษตร titamgangased

agree v.i. ตกลง toklong

agreeable a. เห็นด้วย henduay

agreement n. ความตกลง kwamtoklong

agricultural a ทางการเกษตร tanggangased

agriculture n เกษตรกรรม gasedtagam

agriculturist n. เกษตรกร gasedtagon

ague n อาการสั่น a-gansan

ahead adv. ขึ้นหน้า keunna

aheap adv แน่น soomnaen

aid n ความช่วยเหลือ kwamchuayleua

aid v.t ช่วยเหลือ chuayleua

aigrette n ขนนกประดับ konnokpradab

ail *v.t.* ป่วย puay
ailment *n.* อาการป่วย a-ganpuay
aim *n.* ความตั้งใจ kwamtangjai
aim *v.i.* ตั้งใจ tangjai
air *n* อากาศ a-gad
aircraft *n.* เครื่องบิน kreuangbin
airy *a.* บนอากาศ bon-a-gad
ajar *adv.* แง้มอยู่ ngaemyu
akin *a.* เกี่ยวดอง giawdong
alacrious *adj* กระตือรือร้น grateureuron
alacrity *n.* ความกระตือรือร้น
    kwamgrateureuron
alamort *adj.* เศร้าโศก saosok
alarm *n* สัญญาณเตือน sanyanteuanpai
alarm *v.t* เตือนภัย teuanpai
alas *interj.* อนิจจา a-nidja
albeit *conj.* แม้ว่า maewa
albion *n* อังกฤษ ang-glid
album *n.* อัลบั้ม album
albumen *n* ไข่ขาว kaikao
alchemy *n.* การแปรธาตุ ganpraetat
alcohol *n* อัลกอฮอล์ alcohol
ale *n* เหล้ามอลต์ laomalt
alegar *n* น้ำส้มสายชูจากเหล้ามอลต์
    namsomsaichujaklaomalt
alert *a.* ตื่นตัว teuntua
alertness *n.* ความตื่นตัว kwamteuntua
algebra *n.* พีชคณิต pichakanid
alias *n.* ฉายา chaya
alias *adv.* มีฉายาว่า michayawa
alibi *n.* ข้อแก้ตัว kawkaetua
alien *a.* ต่างด้าว tangdao
alienate *v.t.* หมางเมิน mangmeun
aliferous *adj.* มีปีก mipeek
alight *v.i.* ลงจอด longjod
align *v.t.* จัดแนว jadnaew
alignment *n.* การวางแนว ganwangnaew
alike *a.* คล้ายกัน klaikan
alike *adv* เช่นเดียวกัน chaindiaogan
aliment *n.* อาหาร a-han
alimony *n.* ค่าเลี้ยงดู kaliangdu
alien *adj* ต่างด้าว tangdao

aliquot *n.* ตัวหารจำนวนเต็ม
    tuahanjamnuantem
alive *a* มีชีวิตชีวา michiwitchiwa
alkali *n* ด่าง dang
all *a.* ทุกๆ tuktuk
all *n* จำนวนทั้งหมด jamnuantangmod
all *adv* ทั้งหมด tangmod
all *pron* ทุกคน tookkon
allay *v.t.* บรรเทา bantao
allegation *n.* ข้อกล่าวหา kawklaoha
allege *v.t.* กล่าวหา glaoha
allegiance *n.* ความจงรักภักดี
    kwamjongrakpakdi
allegorical *a.* เชิงเปรียบเทียบ
    cheungpriabtiab
allegory *n.* การสมมติเปรียบเทียบ
    gansommudpriabtiab
allergy *n.* อาการแพ้ a-ganpae
alleviate *v.t.* บรรเทา bantao
alleviation *n.* การบรรเทา ganbantao
alley *n.* ตรอก trok
alliance *n.* แนวร่วม naewruam
alligator *n* จระเข้ jarake
alliterate *v.* ออกเสียงพยางค์แรกซ้ำ
    awksiangpayanraeksam
alliteration *n.*
    การออกเสียงซ้ำของพยางค์แรก
    ganawksiangpayangraeksam
allocate *v.t.* จัดสรร jadsan
allocation *n.* การจัดสรร ganjadsan
allot *v.t.* แบ่งสรร baengsan
allotment *n.* การแบ่งสรร ganbaengsan
allow *v.t.* อนุญาต a-nuyad
allowance *n.* การอนุญาต gan-a-nuyad
alloy *n.* โลหะผสม lohapasom
allude *v.i.* พูดเป็นนัย pudpennai
alluminate *v.t.* ส่องสว่าง songsawang
allure *v.t.* จูงใจ jungjai
allurement *n* การจูงใจ ganjungjai
allusion *n* การอ้างถึง gan-angteung
allusive *a.* อ้างอิงถึง ang-ingteung
ally *v.t.* เข้ากลุ่ม kaoglum

ally *n.* พันธมิตร pantamit
almanac *n.* ปฏิทินโหราศาสตร์
 patitinhorasad
almighty *a.* ยิ่งใหญ่ yingyai
almond *n.* อัลมอนด์ almond
almost *adv.* เกือบ geuab
alms *n.* ของบริจาค kongborijak
aloft *adv.* สูงขึ้นไป soongkeunpai
alone *a.* ลำพัง lampang
along *adv.* ด้วย duay
along *prep.* ขนานกันไป kananganpai
aloof *adv.* ห่างไกล hangglai
aloud *adv.* ดัง dang
alp *n.* เทือกเขาแอลป์ teuakkao-alp
alpha *n* จุดเริ่ม judreum
alphabet *n.* ตัวอักษร tua-akson
alphabetical *a.* เรียงตามตัวอักษร
 riangtamtua-akson
alpinist *n* นักปีนเขา nakpinkao
already *adv.* เรียบร้อย riabroy
also *adv.* ด้วย duay
altar *n.* แท่น tan
alter *v.t.* แก้ gae
alteration *n* การแก้ไข gangaekai
altercation *n.* การวิวาท ganwiwad
alternate *a.* สลับกันได้ salabgandai
alternate *v.t.* สำรอง samrong
alternative *n.* ทางเลือก tangleuak
alternative *a.* เลือกได้ leuakdai
although *conj.* แม้ว่า maewa
altimeter *n* เครื่องมือวัดความสูง
 kreuangmeuwadkwamsoong
altitude *n.* ความสูง kwamsoong
altivalent *adj* บินสูง binsung
alto *n* ชั้นกลาง changlang
altogether *adv.* ด้วยกัน duaygan
aluminium *n.* อัลลูมิเนียม aluminium
alumna *n* ศิษย์เก่าหญิง sidgaoying
always *adv* เสมอ sameu
alveary *n* รังผึ้ง rangpeung
alvine *adj.* เกี่ยวกับท้อง giawgabtong
am เป็น pen

amalgam *n* สารอุดฟัน san-udfun
amalgamate *v.t.* รวมกัน ruamgan
amalgamation *n* การควบรวม
 gankuabruam
amass *v.t.* รวบรวม ruabruam
amateur *n.* มือสมัครเล่น meusamaklen
amatory *adj* แสดงความรัก
 sadaengkwamrak
amauriosis *n* ตาบอด tabod
amaze *v.t.* แปลกใจ plaekjai
amazement *n.* ความประหลาดใจ
 kwampraladjai
ambassador *n.* ทูต toot
amberite *n.* ดินปืน dinpeun
ambient *adj.* โดยรอบ doeyrob
ambiguity *n.* ความกำกวม kwamgamguam
ambiguous *a.* กำกวม gamguam
ambition *n.* ความทะเยอทะยาน
 kwamtayeutayan
ambitious *a.* ทะเยอทะยาน tayeutayan
ambry *n.* ตู้ tu
ambulance *n.* รถพยาบาล rodpayaban
ambulant *adj* เคลื่อนที่ไปมา
 kleuantipaima
ambulate *v.t* เดิน deun
ambush *n.* การโจมตี ganjomti
ameliorate *v.t.* ดีขึ้น dikeun
amelioration *n.* การทำให้ดีขึ้น
 gantamhaidikeun
amen *interj.* อาเมน amen
amenable *a* ยอมรับฟัง yomrabfang
amend *v.t.* แก้ไข gaekai
amendment *n.* การแก้ไข gangaekai
amends *n.pl.* การแก้ไข gangaekai
amenorrhoea *n* ภาวะไร้ประจำเดือน
 pawaraiprajamdeuan
amiability *n.* ความเป็นเพื่อน
 kwampenpeuan
amiable *a.* เป็นมิตร penmit
amicable *adj.* เป็นมิตร penmit
amid *prep.* ท่ามกลาง tamglang
amiss *adv.* ไม่ถูกต้อง maitooktong

amity *n.* มิตรภาพ mitrapab
ammunition *n.* เครื่องกระสุน
keuanggrasoon
amnesia *n* ความจำเสื่อม kwamjamseuam
amnesty *n.* การนิรโทษกรรม
ganniratodsagam
among *prep.* ท่ามกลาง tamglang
amongst *prep.* ท่ามกลาง tamglang
amoral *a.* ไร้ศีลธรรม raisilatam
amount *n* จำนวนรวม jamnuanruam
amount *v.i* ผลรวม ponruam
amount *v.* รวมเป็น ruampen
amorous *a.* ด้วยความรัก duaykwamrak
amour *n* ความรัก kwamrak
ampere *n* แอมป์ amp
amphibious *adj* สะเทินน้ำสะเทินบก
sateunnamsateunbok
amphitheatre *n* อัฒจรรย์ asajan
ample *a.* มาก mak
amplification *n* การขยายความ
gankayaikwam
amplifier *n* เครื่องขยายเสียง
kreungkayaisiang
amplify *v.t.* ขยาย kayai
amuck *adv.* อาละวาด a-lawad
amulet *n.* เครื่องราง kreungrang
amuse *v.t.* ทำให้สนุกสนาน
tamhaisanooksanan
amusement *n* ความสนุกสนาน
kwamsanooksanan
an *art* หนึ่ง neung
anabaptism *n* ลัทธิ latti
anachronism *n* การผิดสมัย ganpidsamai
anaclisis *n* การพึ่งพาผู้อื่น ganpeungpapu-
eun
anadem *n* มาลัยครอบศีรษะ malaikrobsisa
anaemia *n* โรคโลหิตจาง roklohidjang
anaesthesia *n* อาการสลบ a-gansalob
anaesthetic *n.* ยาสลบ yasalob
anal *adj.* ทางทวาร tangtawan
analogous *a.* คล้ายกัน klaigan
analogy *n.* ความคล้ายกัน kwamklaigan

analyse *v.t.* วิเคราะห์ wikraw
analysis *n.* การวิเคราะห์ ganwikraw
analyst *n* นักวิเคราะห์ nakwikraw
analytical *a* เชิงวิเคราะห์ cheungwikraw
anamnesis *n* ประวัติการป่วย
prawatganpuay
anamorphous *adj* ก่อตัวขึ้นอีกครั้ง
gawtuakeun-eik-krang
anarchism *n.* ลัทธิอนาธิปไตย latti-a-
natipatai
anarchist *n* ผู้นิยมอนาธิปไตย puniyom-
latti-a-natipatai
anarchy *n* อนาธิปไตย anatipatai
anatomy *n.* กายวิภาค gaiwipak
ancestor *n.* บรรพบุรุษ banpaburud
ancestral *a.* สืบต่อมาจากบรรพบุรุษ
seubtawmajakbanpaburud
ancestry *n.* วงศ์ตระกูล wongtragoon
anchor *n.* สมอเรือ samawreua
anchorage *n* ที่ทอดสมอ titodsamawreua
ancient *a.* โบราณ boran
ancon *n* ข้อศอก kawsok
and *conj.* และ lae
androphagi *n.* ผู้กินเนื้อคน puginneuakon
anecdote *n.* เกร็ด gred
anemometer *n* มาตรวัดความเร็วลม
madwatkwamrewlom
anew *adv.* อีกครั้ง eik-krang
anfractuous *adj* วกวน wokwon
angel *n* นางฟ้า nangfa
anger *n.* ความโกรธ kwamgrot
angina *n* หลอดเลือดหัวใจตีบ
lawdleuadhuajaitib
angle *n.* มุม moom
angle *n* มุมมอง moommong
angry *a.* โกรธ grot
anguish *n.* ความทุกข์ kwamtook
angular *a.* เกี่ยวกับมุม giawgabmoom
anigh *adv.* ใกล้ glai
animal *n.* สัตว์ sat
animate *v.t.* เคลื่อนไหวได้ kleuanwaidai
animate *a.* เหมือนมีชีวิต meuanmichiwit

 งภาพเคลื่อนไหว
nwai
ลียดชัง
จ kwamtangjai
ศ kreuangted
vtao
gamlaitao
เหตุการณ์ประจำปี
nprajampi
ยเหตุ jodmaihed
ต่อ cheuamtaw
ak
นวก ganpanuak
ทำลาย tamlai
n การทำลายล้าง
ailang
ersary n. การฉลองครบรอบปี
ganchalongkrobrobpi
nnounce v.t. ประกาศ pragad
nnouncement n. คำประกาศ kampragad
noy v.t. น่ารำคาญ naramkan
noyance n. ความรำคาญ kwamramkan
nual a. ประจำปี prajampi
annuitant n ผู้รับเงินประจำปี purab-ngeunprajampi
annuity n. เงินรายปี ngeunraipi
annul v.t. ทำให้เป็นโมฆะ tamhaipenmoka
annulet n วงแหวนเล็ก wongwaenlek
anoint v.t. ทาน้ำมัน tanamman
anomalous a ผิดธรรมดา pidtammada
anomaly n ความผิดปกติ kwampidpagati
anon adv. ทันที tanti
anonymity n. การปิดบังชื่อ ganpidbangcheu
anonymity n. ความไม่มีลักษณะเฉพาะ kwammaimilaksanachapaw
anonymous a. นิรนาม niranam
another a สิ่งอื่น sing-eun
answer n คำตอบ kamtob
answer v.t ตอบ tob
answerable a. ตอบได้ tobdai

ant n มด mod
antacid adj. สารลดกรด sanlodgrod
antagonism n การเป็นปฏิปักษ์ ganpenpatipak
antagonist n. ผู้เป็นปฏิปักษ์ pupenpatipak
antagonize v.t. เป็นปฏิปักษ์ penpatipak
antarctic a. ใกล้กับขั้วโลกใต้ glaigabkualoktai
antecede v.t. เกิดก่อน geudgon
antecedent n. ตัวแปรต้น tuapraeton
antecedent a. มีมาก่อนหน้า mimagonna
antedate n ลงวันที่ก่อนวันจริง longwantigonwanjing
antelope n. ละมั่ง lamang
antenatal adj. ก่อนเกิด gongeud
antennae n. เสาอากาศ sao-a-gad
antenuptial adj. ก่อนแต่งงาน gontaeng-gnan
anthem n เพลงชาติ plaingchat
anthology n. การรวบรวมบทประพันธ์ ganruabruambodprapan
anthropoid adj. คล้ายมนุษย์ klaimanud
anti pref. ต่อต้าน tawtan
anti-aircraft a. ต่อต้านอากาศยาน tawtan-a-gadsayan
antic n การเล่นตลก ganlentalok
anticardium n ช่องท้อง chongtong
anticipate v.t. คาดการณ์ kadgan
anticipation n. การคาดการณ์ gankadgan
antidote n. ยาถอนพิษ yatawnpid
antinomy n. ข้อความที่ขัดแย้งกัน kawkwamtikadyanggan
antipathy n. ความเกลียดชัง kwamgliadchang
antiphony n. การขับร้องสลับกัน gankabrongsalabgan
antipodes n. สิ่งตรงข้ามกัน singtrongkamgan
antiquarian a. เกี่ยวกับโบราณวัตถุ giawgabboranwattu
antiquarian n ผู้ศึกษาโบราณวัตถุ puseuksaboranwattu

antiquary *n.* ผู้ชำนาญด้านโบราณวัตถุ puchamnandanboranwattu

antiquated *a.* เก่าแก่ gaogae

antique *a.* วัตถุโบราณ wattuboran

antiquity *n.* สมัยโบราณ samaiboran

antiseptic *n.* ยาฆ่าเชื้อโรค yakacheuarok

antiseptic *a.* ปราศจากเชื้อโรค prasajakcheuarok

antithesis *n.* สิ่งที่ตรงกันข้าม singtitronggankam

antitheist *n* ผู้ต่อต้านลัทธิเทวนิยม putawtanlattitewaniyom

antler *n.* เขากวาง kaogwang

antonym *n.* คำที่มีความหมายตรงข้าม kamtimikwammaitrongkam

anus *n.* ทวารหนัก tawannak

anvil *n.* ทั่ง tang

anxiety *a* ความกังวล kwamgangwon

anxious *a.* กังวล gangwon

any *a.* ใดๆ daidai

any *adv.* บ้าง bang

anyhow *adv.* ทั้งนี้ tangni

apace *adv.* อย่างเร็ว yangrew

apart *adv.* นอกเหนือ nawkneua

apartment *n.* อพาร์ตเมนต์ apartment

apathy *n.* ไร้อารมณ์ rai-a-rom

ape *n* ผู้เลียนแบบ purianbaeb

ape *v.t.* เลียนแบบ lianbaeb

aperture *n.* ช่อง chong

apex *n.* ปลายสุด plaisud

aphorism *n* คำพังเพย kampangpei

apiary *n.* รังผึ้ง rangpeung

apiculture *n.* การเลี้ยงผึ้ง ganliangpeung

apish *a.* คล้ายมนุษย์ klaimanud

apnoea *n* การหยุดหายใจชั่วคราว ganyudhaijaichuakrao

apologize *v.i.* ขอโทษ kawtod

apologue *n* นิทานแฝงคติ nitanfaengkati

apology *n.* คำขอโทษ kamkawtod

apostle *n.* สาวกของพระคริสต์ sawokkongprakris

apostrophe *n.* เครื่องหม kreuangmaiwakton

apotheosis *n.* การนับถือ gannabteuhaipenpraj

apparatus *n.* เครื่องมือ

apparel *n.* เสื้อผ้า seua

apparel *v.t.* แต่งกาย ta

apparent *a.* ชัดเจน cha

appeal *n.* คำอุทธรณ์ ka

appeal *v.t.* อุทธรณ์ u-t

appear *v.i.* ปรากฏ pra

appearance *n* การปรา

appease *v.t.* ปลอบ p

appellant *n.* ผู้อุทธรณ์ p

append *v.t.* เชื่อมต่อ cheuan

appendage *n.* ส่วนผนวก suan

appendicitis *n.* ไส้ติ่งอักเสบ sait

appendix *n.* ไส้ติ่ง saiting

appendix *n.* ภาคผนวก pakpanuak

appetence *n.* ความต้องการ kwamtongga

appetent *adj.* อยากอาหาร yak-a-han

appetite *n.* ความอยากอาหาร kwamyak han

appetite *n.* ความอยาก kwamyak

appetizer *n* อาหารเรียกน้ำย่อย a-hanriaknamyoi

applaud *v.t.* ปรบมือ probmeu

applause *n.* การปรบมือ ganprobmeu

apple *n.* แอปเปิ้ล apple

appliance *n.* เครื่องใช้ kreuangchai

applicable *a.* เหมาะ maw

applicant *n.* ผู้สมัคร pusamak

application *n.* การสมัคร gansamak

apply *v.t.* สมัคร samak

appoint *v.t.* นัดหมาย nadmai

appointment *n.* การนัดหมาย gannadmai

apportion *v.t.* แจกจ่าย jaekjai

apposite *adj* เหมาะ maw

apposite *a.* เกี่ยวข้อง giawkong

appositely *adv* อย่างเหมาะสม yangmawsom

approbate *v.t* เห็นด้วย henduay

appraise v.t. ประเมิน prameun

appreciable a. พอประเมินค่าได้
pawprameunkadai

appreciate v.t. ชื่นชม cheunchom

appreciation n. ความชื่นชม
kwamcheunchom

apprehend v.t. เข้าใจ kaojai

apprehension n. ความเข้าใจ kwamkaojai

apprehensive a. เข้าใจได้ kaojaidai

apprentice n. ผู้ฝึกงาน pufeuk-gnan

apprise v.t. แจ้ง jaeng

approach v.t. เข้าใกล้ kaoglai

approach n. การเข้าใกล้ gankaoglai

approbation n. การยินยอม ganyinyom

appropriate v.t. กันไว้ ganwai

appropriate a. เหมาะสม mawsom

appropriation n. การจัดสรร ganjadsan

approval n. การอนุมัติ gan-a-numad

approve v.t. อนุมัติ a-numad

approximate a. ประมาณ praman

apricot n. แอปริคอต apricot

appurtenance n ส่วนเสริม suanseum

apron n. ผ้ากันเปื้อน paganpeuan

apt a. เฉลียวฉลาด chaliawchalad

aptitude n. ความถนัด kwamtanad

aquarium n. ตู้ปลา tupla

aquarius n. ราศีกุมภ์ rasigoom

aqueduct n สะพานส่งน้ำ sapansongnam

arable adj เหมาะแก่การเพาะปลูก
mawgaeganpawpruk

arbiter n. ผู้ตัดสิน putadsin

arbitrary a. โดยพลการ doeyparagan

arbitrate v.t. ตัดสินชี้ขาด tadsinchikad

arbitration n. อนุญาโตตุลาการ a-
nuyatotulagan

arbitrator n. ผู้ตัดสินชี้ขาด
putadsinchikad

arc n. ส่วนโค้ง suankong

arcade n ทางเดินที่มีหลังคาโค้ง
tangdeuntimilangkakong

arch n. ซุ้มประตูโค้ง soompratukong

arch v.t. ทำให้โค้ง tamhaikong

arch a รูปโค้ง roobkong

archaic a. โบราณ boran

archangel n หัวหน้าทูตสวรรค์
huanatudsawan

archbishop n. หัวหน้าบาทหลวง
huanabatluang

archer n ผู้ยิงธนู puyingtanu

architect n. สถาปนิก satapanik

architecture n. การออกแบบ gan-aukbaeb

archives n.pl. จดหมายเหตุ jobmaihed

Arctic n ใกล้กับขั้วโลกเหนือ
glaigabkualokneua

ardent a. กระตือรือร้น grateureuron

ardour n. ความกระตือรือร้น
kwamgrateureuron

arduous a. ยากลำบาก yaklambak

area n พื้นที่ peunti

areca n ผลหมาก ponmak

arefaction n การเจือจาง ganjeuajang

arena n สนามกีฬา sanamgila

argil n เนื้อดิน neuadin

argue v.t. โต้แย้ง toyang

argument n. ข้อโต้แย้ง kawtoyang

argute adj หลักแหลม laklaem

arid adj. แห้งแล้ง haenglaeng

aries n ราศีเมษ rasimed

aright adv ถูกต้อง tooktong

aright adv. อย่างถูกต้อง yangtooktong

arise v.i. เกิดขึ้น geudkeun

aristocracy n. ชนชั้นสูง chonchansoong

aristocrat n. ผู้ดี pudi

aristophanic adj เกี่ยวข้องกับนักกวีตลก
giawkonggabnakkawitalok

arithmetic n. คณิตศาสตร์ kanitsat

arithmetical a. เกี่ยวกับคณิตศาสตร์
giawgabkanitsat

ark n เรือโนอา reuano-a

arm n. อาวุธ a-wut

arm v.t. ติดอาวุธ tid-a-wut

armada n. กองเรือรบ gongreuarob

armament n. กำลังทหาร gamlangtahan

armature n. เกราะ graw

18

armistice n. การพักรบ ganpakrob
armlet a ปลอกแขน plawkkaen
armour n. เสื้อเกราะ seuagraw
armoury n. คลังอาวุธ klang a-wut
army n. กองทัพ gongtab
around prep. ประมาณ praman
around adv ใกล้ๆ glaiglai
arouse v.t. กระตุ้น gratoon
arraign v. กล่าวหา glaoha
arrange v.t. จัดการ jadgan
arrangement n. การจัดการ ganjadgan
arrant n. อย่างมาก yangmak
array v.t. แต่งกาย taenggai
array n. เครื่องแต่งกาย kreuangtaenggai
arrears n.pl. เงินค้างชำระ
   ngeunkangchamra
arrest v.t. จับกุม jabgoom
arrest n. การจับกุม ganjabgoom
arrival n. การมาถึง ganmateung
arrive v.i. มาถึง mateung
arrogance n. ความหยิ่ง kwamying
arrogant a. หยิ่ง ying
arrow n ธนู tanu
arrowroot n. มันสาคู mansaku
arsenal n. คลังอาวุธ klang a-wut
arsenic n สารหนู sannu
arson n การวางเพลิง ganwangpleung
art n. ศิลปะ silapa
artery n. หลอดเลือดแดง lawdleuaddaeng
artful a. ฉลาด chalad
arthritis n โรคปวดข้อ rokpuadkaw
artichoke n. อาติโช๊ค atichoke
article n บทความ bot-kwam
articulate a. ชัดเจน chad-jen
artifice n. อุบาย u-bai
artificial a. ปลอม plom
artillery n. ปืนใหญ่ peunyai
artisan n. ช่างฝีมือ changfeemeu
artist n. ศิลปิน silapin
artistic a. มีศิลปะ misilapa
artless a. ไม่มีศิลปะ maimisilapa
as adv. พอๆ กัน pawpawgan

as conj. ขณะที่ kanati
as pron. ในฐานะ naitana
asafoetida n. ยางไม้ yangmai
asbestos n. แร่ใยหิน raeyaihin
ascend v.t. ปีนขึ้น pinkeun
ascent n. การปีนขึ้น ganpinkeun
ascertain v.t. ทำให้แน่ใจ tamhainaejai
ascetic n. ผู้บำเพ็ญตบะ pubampentaba
ascetic a. เข้มงวด kem-nguad
ascribe v.t. เขียนโดย kiandoey
ash n. เถ้าถ่าน taotan
ashamed a. ละอาย la-ai
ashore adv. เทียบฝั่ง tiabfang
aside adv. ข้างๆ kangkang
aside n. พูดป้องปาก pudpongpak
asinine adj. โง่ ngo
ask v.t. ถาม tam
asleep adv. ง่วง nguang
aspect n. มุมมอง noommong
asperse v. ใส่ร้าย sairai
aspirant n. ผู้มีความปรารถนา
   pumikwampratana
aspiration n. ความปรารถนา kwampratana
aspire v.t. มีความปรารถนา
   mikwampratana
ass n. กัน gon
assail v. จู่โจม jujom
assassin n. ผู้สังหาร pusanghan
assassinate v.t. สังหาร sanghan
assassination n การลอบสังหาร
   ganlobsanghan
assault n. การทำร้าย gantamrai
assault v.t. ทำร้าย tamrai
assemble v.t. ประกอบ pragob
assembly n. การประชุม ganprachum
assent v.i. เห็นด้วย henduay
assent n. การยอมรับ ganyomrab
assert v.t. ยืนยัน yeunyan
assess v.t. ประเมิน prameun
assessment n. การประเมิน ganprameun
asset n. ทรัพย์สิน sabsin

assibilate v. ออกเสียงตามไรฟัน awksiangtamraifan

assign v.t. มอบหมาย mobmai

assignee n. ผู้รับโอน purab-on

assimilate v. ทำให้คล้ายกัน tamhaiklaigan

assimilation n ผสมกลมกลืน pasomglomgleun

assist v.t. ช่วยเหลือ chuayleua

assistance n. ความช่วยเหลือ kwanchuayleua

assistant n. ผู้ช่วย puchuay

associate v.t. รวมกลุ่ม ruamglum

associate a. ที่สัมพันธ์กัน tisampangan

associate n. ผู้ร่วมงาน puruamngan

association n. สมาคม samakom

assoil v.t. ยกโทษ yoktod

assort v.t. แยกประเภท yaekpraped

assuage v.t. บรรเทา buntao

assume v.t. ทึกทัก teuktak

assumption n. สมมติฐาน sommutitan

assurance n. การรับรอง ganrabrong

assure v.t. รับรอง rabrong

astatic adj. ไม่แน่นอน mainaenon

asterisk n. เครื่องหมายดอกจัน kreuangmaidawkjan

asterism n. กลุ่มดาว glumdao

asteroid adj. คล้ายดาว klaidao

asthma n. โรคหอบ rokhawb

astir adv. เคลื่อนไหวไปมา kleuanwaipaipa

astonish v.t. แปลกใจ plaekjai

astonishment n. ความแปลกใจ kwamplaekjai

astound v.t ทำให้งง tamhai-ngong

astray adv., หลงทาง longtang

astrologer n. นักโหราศาสตร์ nakhorasat

astrology n. โหราศาสตร์ horasat

astronaut n. นักบินอวกาศ nakbin-a-wagad

astronomer n. นักดาราศาสตร์ nakdarasat

astronomy n. ดาราศาสตร์ darasat

asunder adv. แตกออก taek-awk

asylum n ที่ลี้ภัย tilipai

at prep. ที่ ti

atheism n อเทวนิยม a-tewaniyom

atheist n ผู้ไม่เชื่อในพระเจ้า pumaicheuanai-prajao

athirst adj. กระหายน้ำ grahainam

athlete n. นักกีฬา nakgila

athletic a. ด้านกีฬา dangela

athletics n. การกีฬา gangila

athwart prep. ขวาง kwang

atlas n. แผนที่ paenti

atmosphere n. บรรยากาศ banyagad

atoll n. เกาะที่เกิดจากหินปะการัง gawtigeudjakhinpagarang

atom n. อะตอม a-tom

atomic a. เกี่ยวกับอะตอม giawgab-a-tom

atone v.i. ไถ่โทษ taitod

atonement n. การไถ่โทษ gantaitoad

atrocious a. โหดร้าย hodrai

atrocity n ความโหดร้าย kwamhodrai

attach v.t. ติด tid

attache n. ผู้ช่วยทูต puchuaytut

attachment n. การอายัดทรัพย์ gan-a-yadsab

attack n. การจู่โจม ganjujom

attack v.t. จู่โจม jujom

attain v.t. บรรลุผล banlupon

attainment n. การบรรลุผล ganbanlupon

attaint v.t. เพิกถอนสิทธิ peuktonsit

attempt v.t. พยายาม payayam

attempt n. ความพยายาม kwampayayam

attend v.t. เข้าร่วม kaoruam

attendance n. การเข้าร่วม gankaoruam

attendant n. ผู้เข้าร่วม pukaoruam

attention n. ความสนใจ kwamsonjai

attentive a. ใส่ใจ saijai

attest v.t. ยืนยัน yeunyan

attire n. เครื่องแต่งกาย kreuangtaenggai

attire v.t. แต่งกาย taenggai

attitude n. ทัศนคติ tasanakati

attorney n. ทนาย tanai

attract v.t. ดึงดูด deungdud

attraction *n.* การดึงดูด gandeungdud
attractive *a.* น่าดึงดูด nadeungdud
attribute *v.t.* ถือว่า teuwa
attribute *n.* คุณลักษณะ kunnalaksana
auction *n* การประมูล ganpramoon
auction *v.t.* ประมูล pramoon
audible *a* ได้ยิน daiyin
audience *n.* ผู้ฟัง pufang
audit *n.* การตรวจสอบบัญชี
gantruadsobbanchi
audit *v.t.* ตรวจสอบบัญชี truadsobbanchi
auditive *adj.* เกี่ยวกับการได้ยิน
giawgabgandaiyin
auditor *n.* ผู้ตรวจสอบบัญชี
putruadsobbanchi
auditorium *n.* หอประชุม hawprachum
auger *n.* สว่าน sawan
aught *n.* สิ่งใดๆ singdaidai
augment *v.t.* เพิ่ม peum
augmentation *n.* การเพิ่มขึ้น
ganpeumkeun
August *n.* สิงหาคม singhakom
august *n* สง่างาม sa-nga-ngam
aunt *n.* ป้า pa
auriform *adj.* รูปร่างคล้ายหู
roobrangklaihu
aurilave *n.* ไม้แคะหู maikaehu
aurora *n* แสงทอง sangtong
auspicate *v.t.* ทำพิธีเปิด tampitipeud
auspice *n.* ฤกษ์ดี reukdi
auspicious *a.* เป็นมงคล penmongkon
austere *a.* เคร่งครัด kreingkrad
authentic *a.* แท้ tae
author *n.* ผู้เขียน pukian
authoritative *a.* ซึ่งมีอำนาจ seungmi-um-
nad
authority *n.* อำนาจ um-nad
authorize *v.t.* ให้อำนาจ hai-umnad
autobiography *n.* อัตชีวประวัติ
attachiwaprawat
autocracy *n* อัตาธิปไตย atta-tipatai

autocrat *n* ผู้มีอำนาจเด็ดขาด pumi-
umnarddedkad
autocratic *a* เผด็จการ padedgan
autograph *n.* ลายเซ็นต์ laisen
automatic *a.* อัตโนมัติ attanomat
automobile *n.* รถยนต์ rodyon
autonomous *a* ปกครองตนเอง
pokkrongton-eng
autumn *n.* ฤดูใบไม้ร่วง reudubaimairuang
auxiliary *a.* เสริม seum
auxiliary *n.* กริยาช่วย gariyachuay
avale *v.t.* ลง long
avail *v.t.* ใช้ประโยชน์ chaiprayod
available *a* ใช้ประโยชน์ได้ chaiprayoddai
avarice *n.* ความโลภ kwamlob
avenge *v.t.* แก้แค้น gaekaen
avenue *n.* ถนน tanon
average *n.* ค่าเฉลี่ย kachalia
average *a.* โดยเฉลี่ย doeychalia
average *v.t.* หาค่าเฉลี่ย hakachalia
averse *a.* รังเกียจ ranggiad
aversion *n.* การรังเกียจ ganranggiad
avert *v.t.* เบนสายตา bensaita
aviary *n.* กรงนกขนาดใหญ่
grongnokkanadyai
aviation *n.* การบิน ganbin
aviator *n.* นักบิน nakbin
avid *adj.* โลภ lob
avidity *adv.* ความโลภ kwamlob
avidly *adv* ด้วยความโลภ duaykwamlob
avoid *v.t.* หลีกเลี่ยง leekliang
avoidance *n.* การหลีกเลี่ยง ganleekliang
avow *v.t.* ยืนยัน yeunyan
avulsion *n.* การฉีกขาด gancheekkad
await *v.t.* รอ raw
awake *v.t.* ตื่น teun
awake *a* ตื่นตัว teuntua
award *v.t.* มอบรางวัล mobrangwan
award *n.* รางวัล rangwan
aware *a.* ตระหนัก tranak
away *adv.* ไม่อยู่ maiyu

awe *n.* ความน่าเกรงขาม kwamnagreingkam

awful *a.* แย่มาก yaemak

awhile *adv.* ชั่วครู่ chuakru

awkward *a.* งุ่มง่าม ngum-ngam

axe *n.* ขวาน kwan

axis *n.* เส้นแกน sengaen

axle *n.* แกน gaen

B

babble *n.* การพูดพล่าม ganpudplam

babble *v.i.* พูดพล่าม pudplam

babe *n.* ทารก tarok

babel *n* เสียงคุยอื้ออึง siengkui-eu-eung

baboon *n.* ลิง ling

baby *n.* ทารก tarok

bachelor *n.* หนุ่มโสด noomsod

back *n.* หลัง lang

back *adv.* ข้างหลัง kanglang

backbite *v.t.* นินทาลับหลัง nintalablang

backbone *n.* กระดูกสันหลัง gradooksanlang

background *n.* ภูมิหลัง poomlang

backhand *n.* แบกแฮนด์ backhand

backslide *v.i.* ย้อนกลับ yawnglab

backward *a.* สมองช้า samongcha

backward *adv.* ถอยกลับ toyglab

bacon *n.* เบคอน bacon

bacteria *n.* แบคทีเรีย bacteria

bad *a.* เลว lew

badge *n.* เครื่องหมายแสดงตัว kreuangmaisadaengtua

badger *n.* แบดเจอร์ badger

badly *adv.* แย่ yae

badminton *n.* แบดมินตัน badminton

baffle *v. t.* ทำให้สับสน tamhaisabson

bag *n.* ถุง tung

bag *v. i.* ใส่ถุง saitung

baggage *n.* กระเป๋าเดินทาง grapaodeuntang

bagpipe *n.* ปี่สก็อต pisagot

bail *n.* การประกันตัว ganpragantua

bail *v. t.* ประกันตัว pragantua

bailable *a.* ให้ประกันตัวได้ haipragantuadai

bailiff *n.* เจ้าพนักงานศาล jaopanakngansan

bait *n* เหยื่อ yeua

bait *v.t.* ล่อเหยื่อ lawyeua

bake *v.t.* อบ aob

baker *n.* คนทำขนมปัง kontamkanompang

bakery *n* ร้านขายขนมปัง rankaikanompang

balance *n.* ความสมดุล kwamsomdoon

balance *v.t.* ทำให้สมดุล tamhaisomdoon

balcony *n.* ระเบียง rabiang

bald *a.* หัวล้าน hualan

bale *n.* บรรจุภัณฑ์ banjupan

bale *v.t.* บรรจุหีบห่อ banjuheephaw

baleful *a.* ร้ายกาจ raigad

baleen *n.* ซี่กรอง sigrong

ball *n.* บอล ball

ballad *n.* ลำนำนิทาน lamnamnitan

ballet *sn.* บัลเลต์ ballet

balloon *n.* บอลลูน ballon

ballot *n* บัตรลงคะแนน batlongkanan

ballot *v.i.* หย่อนบัตรลงคะแนน yonbatlongkanaen

balm *n.* ขี้ผึ้ง kipeung

balsam *n.* ขี้ผึ้ง kipeung

bam *n.* เสียงดัง siangdang

bamboo *n.* ไม้ไผ่ maipai

ban *v.* ห้าม ham

ban *n* คำสั่งห้าม kamsangham

banal *a.* น่าเบื่อ nabeua

banana *n.* กล้วย gluay

band *n.* วงดนตรี wongdontri

bandage *~n.* ผ้าพันแผล papanpae

bandage *v.t* พันแผล panpae

bandit *n.* โจร jon

bang *v.t.* ฟาด fad

bang *n.* เสียงระเบิด siangrabeud

bangle *n.* กำไล gamlai
banish *v.t.* เนรเทศ nerated
banishment *n.* การเนรเทศ gannerated
banjo *n.* แบนโจ banjo
bank *n.* ธนาคาร tanakan
bank *v.t.* ฝากเงิน fak-ngeun
banker *n.* นายธนาคาร naitanakan
bankrupt *n.* ล้มละลาย lomlalai
bankruptcy *n.* การล้มละลาย ganlomlalai
banner *n.* ธง tong
banquet *n.* งานเลี้ยง nganliang
banquet *v.t.* ร่วมงานเลี้ยง ruam-nganliang
bantam *n.* ไก่แจ้ gaijae
banter *v.t.* แหย่ yae
banter *n.* มุขตลก mooktalok
bantling *n.* ทารก tarok
banyan *n.* ต้นไทร tonsai
baptism *n.* พิธีล้างบาป pitilangbab
baptize *v.t.* รับศีลจุ่ม rabsinjoom
bar *n.* ลูกกรง lookgrong
bar *v.t* ห้าม ham
barb *n.* ลวดหนาม luadnam
barbarian *a.* ป่าเถื่อน pateuan
barbarian *n.* คนป่าเถื่อน konpateuan
barbarism *n.* ความป่าเถื่อน kwampateuan
barbarity *n* ความป่าเถื่อน kwampateuan
barbarous *a.* ป่าเถื่อน pateuan
barbed *a.* ตะขอ takaw
barber *n.* ช่างตัดผม changtadpom
bard *n.* กวี gawi
bare *a.* เปลือยเปล่า pleuayplao
bare *v.t.* เผย peuy
barely *adv.* น้อยมาก noimak
bargain *n.* การต่อรอง gantawrong
bargain *v.t.* ต่อรอง tawrong
barge *n.* เรือบรรทุก reuabantook
bark *n.* เสียงเห่า sianghao
bark *v.t.* เห่า hao
barley *n.* ข้าวบาร์เลย์ kaobarley
barn *n.* โรงนา rongna
barnacles *n* เพรียง prieng
barometer *n* บาโรมิเตอร์ barometer

barouche *n.* รถม้า rotma
barrack *n.* ค่ายทหาร kaitahan
barrage *n.* การโจมตี ganjomti
barrator *ns.* ผู้กระทำผิดกฎหมาย
pugratampidgodmai
barrel *n.* กระบอกสูบ graboksoob
barren *n* แห้งแล้ง haenglaeng
barricade *n.* ด่าน dan
barrier *n.* เครื่องกีดขวาง
kreuanggidkwang
barrister *n.* ทนาย tanai
barter1 *v.t.* แลกเปลี่ยน lakplian
barter2 *n.* การแลกเปลี่ยนสินค้า
ganlakpliansinka
barton *n.* ฟาร์ม farm
basal *adj.* พื้นฐาน peuntan
base *n.* ฐานที่มั่น tantiman
base *a.* ต่ำช้า tamcha
base *v.t.* ประจำการ prajamgan
baseless *a.* ไม่มีมูลความจริง
maimimoonkwamjing
basement *n.* ชั้นใต้ดิน chantaidin
bashful *a.* ขี้อาย ki-ai
basial *n.* การจูบ ganjoob
basic *a.* พื้นฐาน peuntan
basil *n.* ใบกระเพรา baigraprao
basin *n.* อ่าง ang
basis *n.* รากฐาน raktan
bask *v.i.* อาบแดด abdad
basket *n.* ตะกร้า tagra
baslard *n.* มีดสั้น meetsan
bass *n.* ปลาตะเพียน platapian
bastard *n.* ลูกนอกกฎหมาย
looknawkgodmai
bastard *a* ไม่ถูกกฎหมาย maitookgodmai
bat *n* ค้างคาว kangkao
bat *n* กระบอง grabong
bat *v. i* กระพริบตา grapribta
batch *n* อาหารและเครื่องดื่ม a-
hanlaekreuangdeum
bath *n* การอาบน้ำ gan-ab-nam
bathe *v. t* อาบน้ำ abnam

baton *n* ไม้สั้นของวาทยากร maisankongwaitayagon

batsman *n.* ผู้ตีลูกบอล putilookbon

battalion *n* กองทหาร gongtahan

battery *n* การโจมตี ganjomti

battle *n* สนามรบ sanamrob

battle *v. i.* สู้รบ surob

bawd *n.* แม่เล้า maelao

bawl *n.i.* การตะโกน gantagoan

bawn *n.* กำแพงสูง gampangsoong

bay *n* อ่าว owl

bayard *n.* ม้าในนิยาย manainiyai

bayonet *n* ดาบปลายปืน dabplaipeun

be *v.t.* อยู่ yu

be *pref.* ตลอด talod

beach *n* ชายหาด chaihad

beacon *n* สัญญาณไฟนำทาง sanyanfainamtang

bead *n* ลูกปัด lookpad

beadle *n.* ผู้นำพิธีการ punampitigan

beak *n* จงอยปากนก ja-ngoypaknok

beaker *n* แก้วที่ใช้ในห้องทดลอง gaewtichainaihongtodlong

beam *n* ลำแสง lamsaeng

beam *v. i* แผ่รังสี paerangsi

bean *n.* ถั่ว tua

bear *n* หมี mi

bear *v.t* ทน ton

beard *n* เครา krao

bearing *n* ตลับลูกปืน talablookpeun

beast *n* สัตว์ร้าย satrai

beastly *a* น่ารังเกียจ naranggiad

beat *v. t.* เต้นเป็นจังหวะ tenpenjangwa

beat *n* จังหวะ jangwa

beautiful *a* สวย suay

beautify *v. t* ตกแต่ง toktaeng

beauty *n* ความงาม kwam-ngam

beaver *n* บีเวอร์ beaver

because *conj.* เพราะว่า prawwa

beck *n.* จงอยปาก ja-ngoypak

beckon *v.t.* ส่งสัญญาณเรียก songsanyanriak

become *v. i* กลายเป็น glaipen

becoming *a* เหมาะสม mawsom

bed *n* เตียง tiang

bedevil *v. t* รบกวน robguan

bedding *n.* เครื่องนอน kreuangnon

bedight *v.t.* แต่งตัว taengtua

bed-time *n.* เวลานอน welanon

bee *n.* ผึ้ง peung

beech *n.* พืชชนิดหนึ่ง peudchanidneung

beef *n* เนื้อวัว neuawua

beehive *n.* รังผึ้ง rangpeung

beer *n* เบียร์ beer

beet *n* หัวบีท huabeet

beetle *n* เต่าทอง taotong

befall *v. t* เกิดขึ้น geudkeun

before *prep* อยู่หน้า yuna

before *adv.* ก่อนหน้านี้ gonnani

before *conj* ก่อน gon

beforehand *adv.* ก่อนหน้า gonna

befriend *v. t.* เป็นเพื่อน penpeuan

beg *v. t.* ขอ kaw

beget *v. t* ก่อให้เกิด gawhaigeud

beggar *n* ขอทาน kawtan

begin *v,* เริ่ม reum

beginning *n.* จุดเริ่ม judreum

begird *v.t.* ล้อมรอบ lomrob

beguile *v. t* ล่อลวง lawluang

behalf *n* ในนามของ nainamkong

behave *v. i.* วางตัว wangtua

behaviour *n* ความประพฤติ kwamprapeud

behead *v. t.* ตัดหัว tadhua

behind *adv* ช้า cha

behind *prep* ข้างหลัง kanglang

behold *v. t* จ้องมอง jongmong

being *n* สิ่งมีชีวิต singmichiwit

belabour *v. t* พูดตอกย้ำ pudtokyam

belated *adj.* ล่าช้า lacha

belch *v. t* เรอ reu

belch *n* การเรอ ganreu

belief *n* ความเชื่อ kwamcheua

believe *v. t* เชื่อ cheua

bell *n* กระดิ่ง grading

belle *n* ความงาม kwam-ngam

bellicose *a* พร้อมต่อสู้ promtawsu

belligerency *n* ภาวะสงคราม pawa-
songkram

belligerent *a* เป็นปฏิปักษ์ penpatipak

belligerent *n* คู่สงคราม ku-songkram

bellow *v. i* แผดเสียง paed-siang

bellows *n.* เสียงคำราม siangkamram

belly *n* ท้อง tong

belong *v. i* เป็นของ pen-kong

belongings *n.* สมบัติส่วนตัว
sombatsuantua

beloved *a* เป็นที่รัก pentirak

beloved *n* ที่รัก tirak

below *adv* ข้างล่าง kanglang

below *prep* ใต้ tai

belt *n* เข็มขัด kemkat

belvedere *n* หอทัศนา haw-tasana

bemask *v. t* ปกปิด pokpid

bemire *v. t* ทำให้เปื้อนโคลน tamhai-
peuan-clone

bemuse *v. t* ทำให้สับสน tamhaisabson

bench *n* ม้านั่ง ma-nang

bend *n* ทางโค้ง tang-kong

bend *v. t* โค้ง kong

beneath *adv* ข้างใต้ kangtai

beneath *prep* ต่ำกว่า tamgwa

benefaction *n.* การทำความดี
gantamkwamdi

benefice *n* ตำแหน่งบาทหลวง
tamnaengbatluang

beneficial *a* เป็นประโยชน์ penprayod

benefit *n* ผลประโยชน์ ponprayod

benefit *v. t.* ได้ประโยชน์ daiprayod

benevolence *n* การกุศล ganguson

benevolent *a* ใจบุญ jaiboon

benight *v. t* ปิดบัง pidbang

benign *adj* ไม่รุนแรง mairoonraeng

benignly *adv* อย่างไม่รุนแรง
yangmairoonrang

benison *n* คำอวยพร kam-uaypon

bent *n* ความชำนาญ kwamchamnan

bequeath *v. t.* ยกมรดกให้ yokmoradokhai

bereave *v. t.* สูญเสีย soonsia

bereavement *n* การสูญเสีย gansoonsia

berth *n* ที่นอน tinon

beside *prep.* ข้างๆ kangkang

besides *prep* นอกจากนี้ nawkjakni

besides *adv* นอกจากนี้ nawkjakni

beslaver *v. t* เปื้อนน้ำลาย peuannamlai

besiege *v. t* รุมล้อม rumlom

bestow *v. t* มอบให้ mobhai

bestrew *v. t* โปรย proey

bet *v.i* พนัน panan

bet *n* การพนัน ganpansuan

betel *n* ใบพลู baiplu

betray *v.t.* ทรยศ torayod

betrayal *n* การทรยศ gantorayod

betroth *v. t* หมั้น man

betrothal *n.* การหมั้นหมาย ganmanmai

better *a* ดีกว่า dikwa

better *adv.* ดีขึ้น dikeun

better *v. t* ทำให้ดีขึ้น tamhaidikeun

betterment *n* การดีขึ้น gandikeun

between *prep* ระหว่าง rawang

beverage *n* เครื่องดื่ม kreuangdeum

bewail *v. t* เสียใจ siajai

beware *v.i.* ระวัง rawang

bewilder *v. t* สับสน sabson

bewitch *v.t* ทำให้หลงเสน่ห์
tamhailongsanae

beyond *prep.* เหนือกว่า neuakwa

beyond *adv.* ไกลออกไป klai-awkpai

bi *pref* สอง song

biangular *adj.* มีสองมุม misongmoom

bias *n* อคติ a-kati

bias *v. t* มีอคติ mi-a-kati

biaxial *adj* แกนคู่ gaenku

bibber *n* คนขี้เมา konkimao

bible *n* ไบเบิ้ล bible

bibliography +*n* บรรณานุกรม
bannanugrom

bibliographer *n* บรรณารักษ์ bannarak

bicentenary *adj* ครบรอบสองร้อยปี krobrobsongroypi

biceps *n* กล้ามเนื้อแขน glamneuakaen

bicker *v. t* โต้เถียง totiang

bicycle *n.* จักรยาน jakgayan

bid *v.t* ประมูล pramoon

bid *n* การประมูล ganpramoon

bidder *n* ผู้ประมูล pupramoon

bide *v. t* คอย koy

biennial *adj* เกิดขึ้นทุกสองปี geudkeuntooksongpi

bier *n* ที่ตั้งศพ titangsob

big *a* ใหญ่ yai

bigamy *n* การมีคู่ครองพร้อมกันสองคน ganmikukrongpromgansongkon

bight *n* เว้ง weung

bigot *n* คนหัวดื้อ konhuadeu

bigotry *n* ความดื้อรั้น kwamdeuran

bile *n* น้ำดี namdi

bilingual *a* สองภาษา song-pasa

bill *n* บิล bill

billion *n* พันล้าน panlan

billow *n* คลื่นใหญ่ kleuanyai

billow *v.i* ทำให้พอง tamhai-pong

biliteral *adj* ใช้อักษรสองตัว chai-ak-son-songtua

bilk *v. t.* โกง gong

bimensuel *adj* รายปักษ์ raipak

bimonthly *adj.* รายปักษ์ raipak

binary *adj* ระบบฐานสอง rabobtansong

bind *v.t* มัด mad

binding *a* ผูกมัด pookmad

binocular *n.* กล้องส่องทางไกล glongsongtangglai

biographer *n* ผู้เขียนชีวประวัติ pukianchiwaprawat

biography *n* อัตชีวประวัติ attachiwaprawat

biologist *n* นักชีววิทยา nakchiwawittaya

biology *n* ชีววิทยา chiwawittaya

bioscope *n* กล้องจุลทรรศน์ glongjunlatad

biped *n* สัตว์สองเท้า satsongtao

birch *n.* ต้นไม้ชนิดหนึ่ง tonmaichanidneung

bird *n* นก nok

birdlime *n* กาวดักนก gaodaknok

birth *n.* การเกิด gangeud

biscuit *n* บิสกิต biscuit

bisect *v. t* แบ่งครึ่ง baengkreung

bisexual *adj.* ที่มีลักษณะสองเพศ timilaksanasongped

bishop *n* บิชอป bishop

bison *n* กระทิง grating

bisque *n* น้ำซุปข้น namsoupkon

bit *n* ชิ้นส่วนเล็กๆ chinsuanleklek

bitch *n* สุนัขตัวเมีย sunaktuamia

bite *v. t.* กัด gad

bite *n* รอยกัด roygad

bitter *a* ขม kom

bi-weekly *adj* รายปักษ์ raipak

bizarre *adj* ประหลาด pralad

blab *v. t. & i* ปากเปราะ pakpraw

black *a* ดำ dam

blacken *v. t.* ทำให้มืด tamhaimeud

blackmail *n* การขู่เปิดโปง gankupeidpong

blackmail *v.t* ขู่ ku

blacksmith *n* ช่างตีเหล็ก changtilek

bladder *n* กระเพาะปัสสาวะ grapawpatsawa

blade *n.* ใบมีด baimid

blain *n* อาการปวดบวม a-ganpuadbuam

blame *v. t* กล่าวหา glaoha

blame *n* การกล่าวหา ganglaoha

blanch *v. t. & i* ซีด seed

bland *adj.* ไม่มีรสชาติ maimirodchat

blank *a* ว่างเปล่า wangplao

blank *n* ช่องว่าง chongwang

blanket *n* ผ้าห่ม pahom

blare *v. t* ส่งเสียงดัง songsiangdang

blast *n* การระเบิด ganrabeud

blast *v.i* ระเบิด rabeud

blaze *n* เปลวไฟ plaewfai

blaze *v.i* ลุกโพลง lookplong

bleach *v. t* ฟอกสี foksi

blear v. t ทำให้มัว tamhaimua

bleat n เสียงป่น siangbon

bleat v. i ป่น bon

bleb n เม็ดพอง medpong

bleed v. i เลือดออก leuad-awk

blemish n ตำหนิ tamni

blend v. t ผสม pasom

blend n การผสม ganpasom

bless v. t อวยพร uay-pon

blether v. i พูดเรื่อยเปื่อย pudreuaypeuay

blight n โรคใบไหม้ rokbaimai

blind a ตาบอด tabod

blindage n ที่คลุมสนามเพลาะ tiklumsanamplaw

blindfold v. t ผ้าปิดตา papidta

blindness n ความมืดบอด kwammeudbod

blink v. t. & i กระพริบตา grapribta

bliss n ความสุข kwamsook

blister n แผลพุพอง plaepupong

blizzard n พายุหิมะ payuhima

bloc n กลุ่ม glum

block n สิ่งกีดขวาง singgidkwang

block v.t กีดขวาง gidkwang

blockade n การปิดล้อม ganpidlom

blockhead n คนโง่ kon-ngo

blood n เลือด leuad

bloodshed n การนองเลือด gannongleuad

bloody a เปื้อนเลือด peuanleuad

bloom n การออกดอก gan-awkdawk

bloom v.i. เบ่งบาน bengban

blossom n ดอกไม้ dawkmai

blossom v.i ออกดอก awk-dawk

blot n. รอยเปื้อน roypeuan

blot v. t ทำให้เปื้อน tamhaipeuan

blouse n เสื้อสตรี seuasatri

blow v.i. พัด pat

blow n ลมแรง lomraeng

blue n สีฟ้า sifa

blue a เศร้า sao

bluff v. t แกล้ง glaeng

bluff n การแกล้ง ganglaeng

blunder n ความสะเพร่า kwamsaprow

blunder v.i สะเพร่า saprao

blunt a ทื่อ teu

blur n ความพร่ามัว kwampramua

blurt v. t พูดโพล่ง pudplong

blush n อาการหน้าแดง a-gan-na-daeng

blush v.i หน้าแดง nadaeng

boar n หมูป่า moo-pa

board n กระดาน gradan

board v. t. ขึ้น keun

boast v.i โม้ mo

boast n การคุยโม้ gankuimo

boat n เรือ reua

boat v.i เดินเรือ deunreua

bodice n เสื้อรัดรูป seuaradroob

bodily a ทางร่างกาย tangranggai

bodily adv. ทั้งร่ายกาย tangranggai

body n ร่างกาย ranggai

bodyguard n. ผู้คุ้มกัน pukumgan

bog n ห้วย huay

bog v.i ติดปลัก tidplug

bogle n ผี pi

bogus a หลอก lawk

boil n การต้ม gantom

boil v.i. ต้ม tom

boiler n หม้อน้ำ mawnam

bold a. กล้า gla

boldness n ความกล้า kwamgla

bolt n กลอนประตู glonpratu

bolt v. t ใส่กลอน saiglon

bomb n ลูกระเบิด lookrabeud

bomb v. t ระเบิด rabeud

bombard v. t โจมตีด้วยระเบิด jomti-duay-ra-beud

bombardment n การโจมตีด้วยระเบิด ganjomtiduayrabeud

bomber n เครื่องบินทิ้งระเบิด kreungbintingrabeud

bonafide adv จริงใจ jingjai

bonafide a แท้ tae

bond n พันธะ panta

bondage n พันธนาการ pantanagan

bone n. กระดูก gradook

bonfire *n* กองไฟ gongfai

bonnet *n* ฝากระโปรงเครื่อง fagraprongrod

bonus *n* โบนัส bonus

book *n* หนังสือ nangseu

book *v. t.* จอง jong

book-keeper *n* นักบัญชี nakbanchi

book-mark *n.* ที่คั่นหนังสือ tikannangseu

book-seller *n* คนขายหนังสือ
   konkainangseu

book-worm *n* หนอนหนังสือ nonnangseu

bookish *n.* หนอนหนังสือ nonnangseu

booklet *n* อนุสาร a-nusan

boon *n* สิ่งที่เป็นประโยชน์ singtipenprayod

boor *n* คนชั้นต่ำ konchantam

boost *n* การส่งเสริม gansongseum

boost *v. t* ส่งเสริม songseum

boot *n* รองเท้าบูต rongtawboot

booth *n* คูหา kuha

booty *n* ของโจร kongjon

booze *v. i* ดื่มเหล้า deumlao

border *n* เขตแดน ketdan

border *v.t* สร้างแนวเขต sangnaewket

bore *v. t* เบื่อ beua

bore *n* ความเบื่อ kwambeua

born *v.* เกิด geud

born rich *adj.* รวยตั้งแต่เกิด
   ruaytangtaegeud

borne *adj.* เป็นพาหะ penpaha

borrow *v. t* ยืม yeum

bosom *n* อก auk

boss *n* เจ้านาย jaonai

botany *n* พฤกษศาสตร์ pruksasad

botch *v. t* ทำผิดพลาด tampidplad

both *a* ทั้งคู่ tangku

both *pron* ทั้งคู่ tangku

both *conj* เหมือนๆ กัน meuanmeuangan

bother *v. t* รบกวน robguan

botheration *n* การรบกวน ganrobguan

bottle *n* ขวด kuad

bottler *n* ผู้สูญเสียความมั่นใจ
   pusoonsiakwammanjai

bottom *n* ก้น gon

bough *n* กิ่งไม้ gingmai

boulder *n* หินขนาดใหญ่ hinkanadyai

bouncer *n* คนเฝ้าหน้าร้าน konfaonaran

bound *n.* ผูกพัน pukpan

boundary *n* ขอบเขต kobket

bountiful *a* ใจบุญ jaiboon

bounty *n* ความใจบุญ kwamjaiboon

bouquet *n* ช่อดอกไม้ chawdawkmai

bout *n* การประลองฝีมือ
   ganpralongfeemeu

bow *v. t* คำนับ kamnab

bow *n* การคำนับ gankamnab

bow *n* คันธนู kantanu

bowel *n.* ลำไส้ lamsai

bower *n* ร่มไม้ rommai

bowl *n* ชาม cham

bowl *v.i* ชนล้ม chonlom

box *n* กล่อง glong

boxing *n* การชกมวย ganchokmuay

boy *n* เด็กชาย dekchai

boycott *v. t.* คว่ำบาตร kwambat

boycott *n* การคว่ำบาตร gankwambat

boyhood *n* วัยเด็ก waidek

brace *n* ที่รั้ง tirang

bracelet *n* สร้อยคอ soikaw

brag *v. i* โม้ mo

brag *n* การโอ้อวด gan-o-uad

braille *n* อักษรเบรล aksonbraille

brain *n* สมอง samong

brake *n* เครื่องห้ามล้อ kreunghamlaw

brake *v. t* ห้ามล้อ hamlaw

branch *n* สาขา saka

brand *n* ยี่ห้อ yihaw

brandy *n* บรั่นดี brandy

brangle *v. t* เถียง tiang

brass *n.* ทองเหลือง tongleuang

brave *a* กล้า gla

bravery *n* ความกล้า kwamgla

brawl *v. i. & n* การวิวาท ganwiwad

bray *n* เสียงแตร siangtrae

bray *v. i* เป่าแตร paotrae

breach *n* การผิดสัญญา ganpidsanya

bread *n* ขนมปัง kanompang
breaden *v. t. & i* ทำขนมปัง
   tamkanompang
breadth *n* ความกว้าง kwamkwang
break *v. t* หยุด yud
break *n* ช่วงพัก chuangpak
breakage *n* รอยแตก roytaek
breakdown *n* การเสีย gansia
breakfast *n* อาหารเช้า a-hanchao
breakneck *n* การล้มคอหัก ganlomkawhak
breast *n* หน้าอก na-oak
breath *n* ลมหายใจ lomhaijai
breathe *v. i.* หายใจ haijai
breeches *n.* กางเกงขี่ม้า ganggengkima
breed *v.t* ผสมพันธุ์ pasompan
breed *n* การผสมพันธุ์ ganpasompan
breeze *n* ลมอ่อนๆ lom-on-on
breviary *n.* หนังสือสวดมนต์
   nangseusuadmon
brevity *n* การสรุป gansaroob
brew *v. t.* กลั่น glan
brewery *n* โรงกลั่นเหล้า rongglanlao
bribe *n* สินบน sinbon
bribe *v. t.* ให้สินบน haisinbon
brick *n* อิฐ eid
bride *n* เจ้าสาว jaosao
bridegroom *n.* เจ้าบ่าว jaobao
bridge *n* สะพาน sapan
bridle *n* บังเหียน banghian
brief *a.* สรุป saloop
brigade *n.* กองพลน้อย gongponnoy
brigadier *n* พลจัตวา ponjatawa
bright *a* สว่าง sawang
brighten *v. t* ทำให้สว่าง tamhaisawang
brilliance *n* ความสว่าง kwamsawang
brilliant *a* แพรวพราว praewpraow
brim *n* ขอบ kob
brine *n* น้ำเกลือ namgleua
bring *v. t* นำ nam
brinjal *n* มะเขือเปราะ ma-keua-praw
brink *n.* ขอบ kob
brisk *adj* ไว wai

bristle *n* ขนแข็ง konkang
british *adj* คนอังกฤษ kon-anglid
brittle *a.* เปราะ praw
broad *a* กว้าง gwang
broadcast *n* การกระจายเสียง
   gangrajaisiang
broadcast *v. t* กระจายเสียง grajaisiang
brocade *n* ผ้ายก payok
broccoli *n.* บร็อคโคลี่ broccoli
brochure *n* แผ่นพับ paenpub
broker *n* นายหน้า naina
brood *n* พันธุ์ pan
brook *n.* ห้วย huay
broom *n* ไม้กวาด maigwad
bronze *n. & adj* ทองแดง tongdaeng
broth *n* ซุป soup
brothel *n* ช่อง song
brother *n* พี่หรือน้องชาย pireunongchai
brotherhood *n* ความเป็นพี่น้อง
   kwampenpinong
brow *n* คิ้ว kew
brown *a* สีน้ำตาล sinamtan
brown *n* สีน้ำตาล sinamtan
browse *n* การอ่านคร่าวๆ gan-an-kraokrao
bruise *n* รอยช้ำ roycham
bruit *n* ข่าวลือ kaoleu
brush *n* แปรง prang
brustle *v. t* ทำเสียงดัง tamsiangdang
brutal *a* ทารุณ taroon
brute *n* สัตว์ป่า satpa
bubble *n* ฟอง fong
bucket *n* ถัง tang
buckle *n* หัวเข็มขัด huakemkat
bud *n* ต้นอ่อน ton-on
budge *v. i. & n* ขยับ kayab
budget *n* งบประมาณ ngob-praman
buff *n* สีน้ำตาลอมเหลือง sinamtan-om-
   leuang
buffalo *n.* ควาย kwai
buffoon *n* ตัวตลก tautalok
bug *n.* แมลง malaeng
bugle *n* แตรเดี่ยว traediaw

build *v. t* สร้าง sang
build *n* โครงร่าง krongrang
building *n* อาคาร a-kan
bulb *n.* หลอดไฟฟ้า lawdfaifa
bulk *n* ความจุ kwamju
bulky *a* เลอะเทอะ leuteu
bull *n* วัว wua
bulldog *n* สุนัขพันธุ์หนึ่ง sunakpanneung
bull's eye *n* ใจกลางเป้า jaiglangpao
bullet *n* กระสุน grasoon
bulletin *n* สิ่งตีพิมพ์ singtipim
bullock *n* วัวหนุ่ม wuanoom
bully *n* อันธพาล an-tapan
bully *v. t.* รังแก ranggae
bulwark *n* ป้อมปราการ pompragan
bumper *n.* กันชน gunchon
bumpy *adj* ขรุขระ krukra
bunch *n* ช่อ chaw
bundle *n* พวง puang
bungalow *n* บังกาโล bangalow
bungle *v. t* ซุ่มซ่าม sumsam
bungle *n* ความซุ่มซ่าม kwamsumsam
bunk *n* ที่นอน tinon
bunker *n* หลุมหลบภัย loomlobpai
buoy *n* ทุ่น toon
buoyancy *n* การลอย ganloy
burden *n* ภาระ para
burden *v. t* รับภาระ rabpara
burdensome *a* เป็นภาระ penpara
bureau *n.* สำนักงาน samnak-ngan
Bureacuracy *n.* ระบบราชการ
    rabobratchagan
bureaucrat *n* ข้าราชการ karachagan
burglar *n* นักย่องเบา nakyongbao
burglary *n* การย่องเบา ganyongbao
burial *n* การฝังศพ ganfangsob
burke *v. t* ลอบสังหาร lobsanghan
burn *v. t* ไหม้ mai
burn *n* การเผาไหม้ ganpaomai
burrow *n* โพรง prong
burst *v. i.* ระเบิด rabeud
burst *n* การระเบิด ganrabeud

bury *v. t.* ฝัง fang
bus *n* รถบัส rodbus
bush *n* พุ่มไม้ poommai
business *n* ธุรกิจ turagid
businessman *n* นักธุรกิจ nakturagid
bustle *v. t* พลุกพล่าน plukplan
busy *a* ยุ่ง yung
but *prep* ยกเว้น yokwen
but *conj.* แต่ tae
butcher *n* คนขายเนื้อ konkaineua
butcher *v. t* ฆ่าสัตว์ขาย kasatkai
butter *n* เนย neuy
butter *v. t* ทาเนย taneuy
butterfly *n* ผีเสื้อ piseua
buttermilk *n* นมเปรี้ยว nompriaw
buttock *n* สะโพก sapok
button *n* กระดุม gradoom
button *v. t.* ติดกระดุม tidgradoom
buy *v. t.* ซื้อ seu
buyer *n.* ผู้ซื้อ puseu
buzz *v. i* กดออด kod-awd
buzz *n.* เสียงหึ่ง siangheung
by *prep* โดย doey
by *adv* ก่อนเวลาที่กำหนด
    gonwelatigamnod
bye-bye *interj.* ลาก่อน lagon
by-election *n* เลือกตั้งซ่อม leuaktangsom
bylaw, bye-law *n* กฎหมายท้องถิ่น
    godmaitongtin
bypass *n* บายพาส bypass
by-product *n* ผลพลอยได้ ponploydai
byre *n* คอกวัว kokwua
byword *n* คำคม kamkom

C

cab *n.* รถรับจ้าง rodrabjang
cabaret *n.* คาบาเร่ย์ cabaret
cabbage *n.* กระหล่ำปลี gralampli
cabin *n.* กระท่อมไม้ gratommai
cabinet *n.* ตู้เก็บของ tugebkong

cable *n.* สายเคเบิ้ล saicable
cable *v. t.* ส่งสัญญาณผ่านสายเคเบิ้ล
song-sanyanpansai-cable
cache *n* ที่เก็บของ tigebkong
cachet *n* สัญลักษณ์ sanyalak
cackle *v. i* หัวเราะ huaraw
cactus *n.* ตะบองเพชร tabongped
cad *n* ชายที่มีความประพฤติไม่ดี
chaitimikamprapreudmaidi
cadet *n.* นักเรียนนายร้อย nakriannairoy
cadge *v. i* ขอ kaw
cadmium *n* แคดเมียม cadmium
cafe *n.* ร้านกาแฟ rangafae
cage *n.* กรง grong
cain *n* ค่าเช่า kachao
cake *n.* เค้ก cake
calamity *n.* เหตุร้าย hedrai
calcium *n* แคลเซียม calcium
calculate *v. t.* คำนวณ kamnuan
calculator *n* เครื่องคิดเลข kreuangkidlek
calculation *n.* การคำนวณ gankamnuan
calendar *n.* ปฏิทิน patitin
calf *n.* ลูกวัว lookwua
call *v. t.* เรียก riak
call *n.* การเรียก ganriak
caller *n* ผู้เรียก puriak
calligraphy *n* ศิลปะการคัดลายมือ
silapagankadlaimeu
calling *n.* การเรียกร้อง ganriakrong
callow *adj* ไร้ประสบการณ์ raiprasobgan
callous *a.* ใจดำ jaidam
calm *n.* ความสงบ kwamsa-ngob
calm *v. t.* ทำให้สงบ tamhaisa-ngob
calmative *adj* มีฤทธิ์ระงับประสาท miridra-
ngabprasad
calorie *n.* แคลอรี่ calorie
calumniate *v. t.* ใส่ร้าย sairai
camel *n.* อูฐ ud
camera *n.* กล้อง glong
camlet *n* ผ้าขนสัตว์ pakonsat
camp *n.* แคมป์ camp
camp *v. i.* ตั้งแคมป์ tangcamp

campaign *n.* การรณรงค์ ganronnarong
camphor *n.* การบูร garaboon
can *n.* กระป๋อง grapong
can *v. t.* บรรจุกระป๋อง banjukrapong
can *v.* สามารถ samad
canal *n.* คลอง klong
canard *n* เรื่องเท็จ reuangted
cancel *v. t.* ยกเลิก yokleuk
cancellation *n* การยกเลิก ganyokleuk
cancer *n.* มะเร็ง mareing
candidate *n.* ผู้สมัครแข่งขัน
pusamakkaengkan
candle *n.* เทียนไข tiankai
candour *n.* การเปิดเผย ganpeudpeuy
candy *n.* ลูกกวาด lookgwad
candy *v. t.* เชื่อม cheuam
cane *n.* ไม้เท้า maitao
cane *v. t.* โบย boey
canister *n.* กระป๋อง grapong
cannon *n.* ปืนใหญ่ peunyai
cannonade *n. v. & t* การระดมยิงปืนใหญ่
ganradomyingpeunyai
canon *n* หลักการ lakgan
canopy *n.* ปะรำ param
canteen *n.* โรงอาหาร rong-a-han
canter *n* การวิ่ง ganwing
canton *n* เขตปกครอง kedpokkrong
cantonment *n.* ค่ายทหาร kaitahan
canvas *n.* ผ้าใบ pabai
canvass *v. t.* สำรวจความเห็น
samruadkwamhen
cap *n.* ฝาครอบ fakrob
cap *v. t.* ครอบ krob
capability *n.* ความสามารถ kwamsamad
capable *a.* สามารถ samad
capacious *a.* มีเนื้อที่บรรจุได้มาก
mineuatibanjudaimak
capacity *n.* ความสามารถที่จะรับได้
kwamsamadtijarabdai
cape *n.* ถ้ำ tam
capital *n.* เมืองหลวง meuangluang
capital *a.* สำคัญ samkan

capitalist n. ผู้ลงทุน pulongtun

capitulate v. t ยอมตาม yomtam

caprice n. การเปลี่ยนใจกะทันหัน ganplianjaigatanhan

capricious a. มีแนวโน้มจะเปลี่ยนใจ minaewnomjaplianjai

capsicum n พริกขี้หนู prikkinu

capsize v. i. คว่ำ kwam

capsular adj เกี่ยวกับถุงหุ้ม giawgabtunghoom

captain n. กัปตัน gabtan

captaincy n. ตำแหน่งกัปตัน tamnaenggabtan

caption n. คำบรรยายใต้ภาพ kambanyaitaipab

captivate v. t. หว่านเสน่ห์ wansanae

captive n. นักโทษ naktod

captive a. ถูกกักขัง tookgakkang

captivity n. การถูกกักขัง gantookgakkang

capture v. t. จับกุม jabgoom

capture n. การจับเป็นเชลย ganjabpenchaleoy

car n. รถยนต์ rodyon

carat n. สัญลักษณ์ sanyalak

caravan n. กองคาราวาน gongkarawan

carbide n. สารประกอบคาร์บอน sanprakobcarbon

carbon n. คาร์บอน carbon

card n. การ์ด card

cardamom n. กระวาน grawan

cardboard n. กระดาษแข็ง gradadkaeng

cardiac adj เกี่ยวกับหัวใจ giawgabhuajai

cardinal a. สำคัญ samkan

cardinal n. พระราชาคณะ prarachakana

care n. การดูแล gandulae

care v. i. ดูแล dulae

career n. อาชีพ a-chib

careful a รอบคอบ robkob

careless a. ไม่รอบคอบ mairobkob

caress v. t. สัมผัส sampad

cargo n. สินค้า sinka

caricature n. ภาพล้อเลียน pablawlian

carious adj ผุ pu

carl n บุคคลธรรมดา bukkontammada

carnage n การสังหาร gansanghan

carnival n งานคาร์นิวัล ngan-carnival

carol n เพลงสวด plengsuad

carpal adj เกี่ยวกับกระดูกข้อมือ giawgabgradookkawmeu

carpenter n. ช่างไม้ changmai

carpentry n. งานไม้ ngan-mai

carpet n. พรม prom

carriage n. ตู้โดยสารรถไฟ tudoeysanrodfai

carrier n. คนส่งเอกสาร konsong-ekgasan

carrot n. แครอท carrot

carry v. t. บรรทุก bantook

cart n. รถลาก rodlak

cartage n. การขับรถม้า gankabrodma

carton n กล่อง glong

cartoon n. การ์ตูน cartoon

cartridge n. ปลอกกระสุน plawkkasoon

carve v. t. แกะสลัก gaesalak

cascade n. น้ำตก namtok

case n. คดี kadi

cash n. เงินสด ngeunsod

cash v. t. ขึ้นเงินสด keun-ngeunsod

cashier n. แคชเชียร์ cashier

casing n. กรอบ grob

cask n ถังไม้ tangmai

casket n หีบศพ hibsob

cassette n. ตลับเทป talabtape

cast v. t. เข้าเฝือก kaofeuak

cast n. เฝือก feuak

caste n ชนชั้น chonchan

castigate v. t. ลงโทษ longtod

casting n การคัดเลือกนักแสดง gankadleuaknaksadaeng

cast-iron n เหล็กแข็ง lekkaeng

castle n. ปราสาท prasad

castor oil n. น้ำมันละหุ่ง nammanlahoong

castrol adj คาสตรอล castrol

casual a. ไม่เป็นทางการ maipentanggan

casualty n. อุบัติเหตุ u-bathed

cat *n.* แมว maew
catalogue *n.* แคตาล็อก catalogue
cataract *n.* ต้อ taw
catch *v. t.* จับ jab
catch *n.* การจับ ganjab
categorical *a.* แน่ชัด naechad
category *n.* หมวด muad
cater *v. i* จัดหา jadha
caterpillar *n* หนอนผีเสื้อ nonpiseua
cathedral *n.* โบสถ์ bod
catholic *a.* แคธอลิก catholic
cattle *n.* ปศุสัตว์ pasusat
cauliflower *n.* ดอกกระหล่ำ dawkgralam
causal *adj.* เป็นมูลเหตุ penmoonhed
causality *n* เหตุและผล hedlaepon
cause *n.* สาเหตุ sahed
cause *v.t* ทำให้เกิด tamhaigeud
causeway *n* ทางหลวง tangluang
caustic *a.* กัดกร่อน gadgron
caution *n.* การตักเตือน gantakteuan
caution *v. t.* เตือน teuan
cautious *a.* รอบคอบ robkob
cavalry *n.* ทหารม้า tahanma
cave *n.* ถ้ำ tam
cavern *n.* ถ้ำ tam
cavil *v. t* ตำหนิ tamni
cavity *n.* โพรง prong
caw *n.* เสียงร้องของกา siangrongkongga
caw *v. i.* ร้องกาๆ ronggaga
cease *v. i.* หยุด yud
ceaseless ~*a.* ไม่สิ้นสุด maisinsud
cedar *n.* ต้นสน tonson
ceiling *n.* เพดาน pedan
celebrate *v. t. & i.* ฉลอง chalong
celebration *n.* การฉลอง ganchalong
celebrity *n* ผู้มีชื่อเสียง pumicheusiang
celestial *adj* เกี่ยวกับสวรรค์ giawgabsawan
celibacy *n.* การเป็นโสด ganpensod
celibacy *n.* การละเว้นจากการร่วมเพศ
　ganlawenjakganruamped
cell *n.* เซล sell
cellar *n* ห้องใต้ดิน hongtaidin

cellular *adj* เกี่ยวกับเซล giawgabsell
cement *n.* ปูน poon
cement *v. t.* ฉาบ chab
cemetery *n.* สุสาน susan
cense *v. t* จุดธูป judtoob
censer *n* กระถางธูป gratangtoob
censor *n.* ผู้ตรวจแก้ putruadgae
censor *v. t.* ตรวจสอบ truadsob
censorious *adj* วิจารณ์อย่างรุนแรง
　wijanyangroonraeng
censorship *n.* การตรวจสอบ gantruadsob
censure *n.* การตำหนิ gantamni
censure *v. t.* ตำหนิ tamni
census *n.* การสำรวจประชากร
　gansamruadprachagon
cent *n* เซนต์ cent
centenarian *n* ผู้มีอายุร้อยปีขึ้นไป pumi-a-
　yuroipikeunpai
centenary *n.* การครบรอบหนึ่งร้อยปี
　gankrobrobneungroypi
centennial *adj.* ครบรอบร้อยปี
　krobrobroypi
center *n* ศูนย์กลาง soonglang
centigrade *a.* หน่วยวัดความร้อน
　nuaywatkwamron
centipede *n.* ตะขาบ takab
central *a.* กลาง glang
centre *n* ศูนย์กลาง soonglang
centrifugal *adj.* หนีศูนย์กลาง nisoonglang
centuple *n. & adj* ร้อยเท่า roytao
century *n.* ศตวรรษ satawat
ceramics *n* เครื่องเคลือบดินเผา
　kreuangkreuabdinpao
cerated *adj.* เคลือบด้วยขี้ผึ้ง
　kreuabduaykipeung
cereal *n.* ธัญพืช tanyapeud
cereal *a* เกี่ยวกับธัญญาหาร
　giawgabtanyahan
cerebral *adj* เกี่ยวกับสมอง
　giawgabsamong
ceremonial *a.* เป็นทางการ pentanggan
ceremonious *a.* เป็นพิธีการ penpitigan

ceremony *n.* พิธีการ pitigan

certain *a* แน่นอน naenon

certainly *adv.* อย่างแน่นอน yangnaenon

certainty *n.* ความแน่นอน kwamnaenon

certificate *n.* ประกาศนียบัตร
pragasaniyabat

certify *v. t.* รับรอง rabrong

cerumen *n* ขี้หู kihu

cesspool *n.* บ่อพักน้ำเสีย bawpaknamsia

chain *n* โซ่ so

chair *n.* เก้าอี้ gao-i

chairman *n* ประธาน pratan

chaise *n* รถม้า rodma

challenge *n.* ความท้าทาย kwamtatai

challenge *v. t.* ท้าทาย tatai

chamber *n.* ห้อง hong

chamberlain *n* ผู้ดูแลงานภายในวัง
pudulae-nganpainaiwang

champion *n.* ผู้ชนะเลิศ puchanaleud

champion *v. t.* ชนะเลิศ chanaleud

chance *n.* โอกาส o-gad

chancellor *n.* รัฐมนตรี rattamontri

chancery *n* ศาลชั้นต้น sanchanton

change *v. t.* เปลี่ยนแปลง plianplaeng

change *n.* การเปลี่ยนแปลง
ganplianplaeng

channel *n* ช่องทาง chongtang

chant *n* การร้องเพลง ganrongpleing

chaos *n.* ความวุ่นวาย kwanwunwai

chaotic *adv.* วุ่นวาย wunwai

chapel *n.* ห้องสวดมนต์ hongsuadmon

chapter *n.* บท bod

character *n.* บุคลิกลักษณะ
bukkaliklaksana

charge *v. t.* กล่าวหา glaoha

charge *n.* ข้อกล่าวหา kawklaoha

chariot *n* รถม้า rodma

charitable *a.* ใจบุญ jaiboon

charity *n.* การกุศล ganguson

charm1 *n.* เสน่ห์ sanae

charm2 *v. t.* ทำให้หลงเสน่ห์
tamhailongsanae

chart *n.* ตาราง talang

charter *n* กฎบัตร gotbad

chase1 *v. t.* ไล่ตาม laitam

chase2 *n.* การไล่ตาม ganlaitam

chaste *a.* บริสุทธิ์ borisud

chastity *n.* การรักษาพรมจรรย์
ganraksapromajan

chat *n.* การพูดคุย ganpudkui

chat2 *v. i.* คุย kui

chatter *v. t.* ช่างพูด changpud

chauffeur *n.* คนขับรถ konkabrod

cheap *a* ถูก took

cheapen *v. t.* ทำให้ราคาถูก
tamhairakatook

cheat *v. t.* โกง gong

cheat *n.* การโกง gangong

check *v. t.* ตรวจสอบ truadsob

check *n* การตรวจสอบ gantruadsob

checkmate *n* การรุกจนแต้ม
ganrookjontam

cheek *n* แก้ม gaem

cheep *v. i* ร้องเสียงแหลม rongsianglaem

cheer *n.* ความรื่นเริงยินดี
kwamreunreungyindi

cheer *v. t.* โห่ร้องยินดี horongyindi

cheerful *a.* รื่นเริง reunreung

cheerless *a* ไม่รื่นเริง maireunreung

cheese *n.* ชีส cheese

chemical *a.* ทางเคมี tangkemi

chemical *n.* สารเคมี sankemi

chemise *n* เสื้อชั้นในสตรี seuachannaisatri

chemist *n.* นักเคมี nakkemi

chemistry *n.* วิชาเคมี wichakemi

cheque *n.* เช็ค cheque

cherish *v. t.* ชื่นชม cheunchom

cheroot *n* บุหรี่ buri

chess *n.* หมากรุก makrook

chest *n* อก oak

chestnut *n.* เกาลัด gaolad

chew *v. t* เคี้ยว kiaw

chevalier *n* ทหารม้า tahanma

chicken *n.* ไก่ gai

chide v. t. ดุ du
chief a. สำคัญ samkan
chieftain n. หัวหน้าเผ่า haunapao
child n เด็ก dek
childhood n. วัยเด็ก waidek
childish a. ไร้เดียงสา raidiangsa
chill n. ความหนาวเย็น kwamnaoyen
chilli n. พริก prik
chilly a หนาว nao
chiliad n. หนึ่งพันปี neungpanpi
chimney n. ปล่องไฟ plongfai
chimpanzee n. ลิง ling
chin n. คาง kang
china n. ประเทศจีน pratedjeen
chirp v.i. นกร้อง nokrong
chirp n เสียงนกร้อง siangnokrong
chisel n สิ่ว siew
chisel v. t. สกัด sagad
chit n. ใบเสร็จ bai-sed
chivalrous a. กล้าหาญ glahan
chivalry n. ความกล้าหาญ kwamglahan
chlorine n คลอรีน chlorine
chloroform n ยาสลบ yasalob
choice n. ทางเลือก tang-leuak
choir n งาน ngan
choke v. t. สำลักอาหร samlak-a-han
cholera n. อหิวาต์ a-hiwa
chocolate n ช็อกโกแลต chocolate
choose v. t. เลือก leuak
chop v. t สับ sab
chord n. ผสมผสาน pasompasan
choroid n เยื่อหุ้มลูกตา yeuahoomlookta
chorus n. การร้องประสานเสียง ganrong-prasan-siang
Christ n. พระเยซู pra-yesu
Christendom n. คริสต์จักร kris-tajak
Christian n คริสตศาสนิกชน krisasanigachon
Christian a. เกี่ยวกับศาสนาคริสต์ giawgabsasanakrit
Christianity n. ศาสนาคริสต์ sasanakrit
Christmas n วันคริสต์มาส wanchristmas

chrome n แผ่นเคลือบโครเมียม paenkleuabchromium
chronic a. เรื้อรัง reuarang
chronicle n. เหตุการณ์ในอดีต hedgannai-a-did
chronology n. ศาสตร์ในการลำดับเหตุการณ์ sadnaiganlamdabhedgan
chronograph n นาฬิกาจับเวลา narikajabwela
chuckle v. i หัวเราะ huaraw
chum n เพื่อน peuan
church n. โบสถ์ bod
churchyard n. ลานโบสถ์ lanbod
churl n คนหยาบคาย konyabkai
churn v. t. & i. ปั่น pan
churn n. เครื่องปั่น kreuangpan
cigar n. ซิการ์ cigar
cigarette n. บุหรี่ buri
cinema n. โรงหนัง rongnang
cinnabar n ชาด chad
cinnamon n ซินนามอน cinnamon
cipher, cipher n. ศูนย์ soon
circle n. วงกลม wongglom
circuit n. วงจร wongjon
circumfluence n. การล้อมรอบ ganlomrob
circumspect adj. รอบคอบ robkob
circular a ที่เคลื่อนเป็นวงกลม tikleuanpenwongglom
circular n. หนังสือเวียน nangseuwian
circulate v. i. หมุนเวียน moonwian
circulation n การหมุนเวียน ganmoonwian
circumference n. เส้นรอบวง senrobwong
circumstance n สิ่งแวดล้อม singwaedrom
circus n. โรงละครสัตว์ ronglakonsat
cist n กล่อง glong
citadel n. ป้อมปราการ pompragan
cite v. t อ้างถึง angteung
citizen n พลเมือง ponlameuang
citizenship n ความเป็นพลเมือง kwampenponlameuang
citric adj. เป็นกรด pengrod

city *n* เมือง meuang

civic *a* เกี่ยวกับพลเมือง giawgabponlameuang

civics *n* วิชาหน้าที่พลเมือง wichanatiponlameuang

civil *a* เกี่ยวกับพลเมือง giawgabponlameuang

civilian *n* พลเรือน ponlareuan

civilization *n.* อารยธรรม a-rayatam

civilize *v. t* มีอารยธรรม mi-a-rayatam

clack *n. & v. i* ทำเสียงแหลม tamsianglaem

claim *n* การเรียกร้อง ganriakrong

claim *v. t* เรียกร้อง riakrong

claimant *n* ผู้เรียกร้อง puriakrong

clamber *v. i* ปีนด้วยความลำบาก pindauykwamlambak

clamour *n* โห่ร้อง horong

clamour *v. i.* เสียงอึกทึก siang-eukgateuk

clamp *n* คีบ keep

clandestine *adj.* ลับ lab

clap *v. i.* ปรบมือ probmeu

clap *n* การปรบมือ ganprobmeu

clarify *v. t* ชี้แจง chijang

clarification *n* การชี้แจง ganchijang

clarion *n.* แตรโบราณ traeboran

clarity *n* ความชัดเจน kwamchadjen

clash *n.* การชน ganchon

clash *v. t.* ชน chon

clasp *n* จับแน่น jabnaen

class *n* ชนชั้น chonchan

classic *a* มีระดับ miradab

classic *n* ศิลปะคลาสสิก silapaclassic

classical *a* เกี่ยวกับศิลปะคลาสสิก giawgabsilapaclassic

classification *n* การจัดประเภท ganjadpraped

classify *v. t* แยกประเภท yaekpraped

clause *n* ข้อกำหนด kawgamnod

claw *n* กรงเล็บ grongleb

clay *n* ดิน din

clean *a* สะอาด sa-ad

clean *v. t* ทำความสะอาด tamkwamsa-ad

cleanliness *n* การรักษาความสะอาด ganraksakwamsa-ad

cleanse *v. t* ทำความสะอาด tamkwamsa-ad

clear *a* ชัดเจน chadjen

clear *v. t* ทำให้ชัดเจน tamhaichadjen

clearance *n* การกำจัด gangamjad

clearly *adv* อย่างชัดเจน yangchadjen

cleft *n* ร่อง rong

clergy *n* นักบวช nakbuad

clerical *a* เกี่ยวกับงานศาสนา giawgab-ngansasana

clerk *n* เสมียน samian

clever *a.* ฉลาด chalad

clew *n.* กลุ่มด้าย glumdai

click *n.* ดีดนิ้ว didnew

client *n..* ลูกค้า lookka

cliff *n.* หน้าผา napa

climate *n.* บรรยากาศ banyagad

climax *n.* จุดสุดยอด judsudyod

climb1 *n.* การปีน ganpin

climb *v.i* ปีน pin

cling *v. i.* ยึดติด yeudtid

clinic *n.* คลินิก clinic

clink *n.* เสียงดัง siangdang

cloak *n.* เสื้อคลุม seuaklum

clock *n.* นาฬิกา naliga

clod *n.* ดิน din

cloister *n.* วัด wat

close *n.* การยุติ ganyuti

close *a.* ใกล้ชิด glaichid

close *v. t* ปิด pid

closet *n.* ห้องเล็ก honglek

closure *n.* การจบ ganjob

clot *n.* ลิ่ม lim

clot *v. t* จับตัวเป็นลิ่ม jabtuapenlim

cloth *n* เสื้อผ้า seuapa

clothe *v. t* สวมเสื้อผ้า suamseuapa

clothes *n.* เสื้อผ้า seuapa

clothing *n* เครื่องนุ่งห่ม kreuangnunghom

cloud *n.* เมฆ mek

cloudy *a* ปกคลุมด้วยเมฆ
pokklumduaymek

clove *n* กานพลู ganplu

clown *n* ตัวตลก tautalok

club *n* สโมสร samoson

clue *n* เบาะแส bawsae

clumsy *a* ซุ่มซ่าม sumsam

cluster *n* กลุ่ม glum

cluster *v. i.* รวมกลุ่ม ruamglum

clutch *n* คลัตช์ clutch

clutter *v. t* ความยุ่งเหยิง kwamyungyeung

coach *n* โค้ช coach

coachman *n* คนขับรถม้า konkabrodma

coal *n* ถ่านหิน tanhin

coalition *n* รัฐบาลผสม ratabanpasom

coarse *a* หยาบ yab

coast *n* ชายฝั่ง chaifang

coat *n* เสื้อโค้ท seuacoat

coating *n* การเคลือบ gankleuab

coax *v. t* เกลี้ยกล่อม gliaglom

cobalt *n* โคบอลต์ cobalt

cobbler *n* ช่างซ่อมรองเท้า
changsomrongtaw

cobra *n* งูเห่า ngu-how

cobweb *n* ใยแมงมุม yaimaengmoom

cocaine *n* โคเคน cocaine

cock *n* ไก่ gai

cocker *v. t* ตามใจ tamjai

cockle *v. i* หด hod

cock-pit *n.* ห้องคนขับ hongkonkab

cockroach *n* แมลงสาบ malaengsab

coconut *n* มะพร้าว mapraw

code *n* รหัส rahad

co-education *n.* สหศึกษา sahaseuksa

coefficient *n.* สัมประสิทธิ์ samprasit

co-exist *v. i* อยู่ร่วมกัน yuruamgan

co-existence *n* การอยู่ร่วมกัน
ganyuruamgan

coffee *n* กาแฟ gafae

coffin *n* โรงศพ rongsob

cog *n* ซี่ล้อ silaw

cogent *adj.* หว่านล้อม wanlom

cognate *adj* สัมพันธ์กันทางสายเลือด
sampangantangsaileuad

cognizance *n* การรับรู้ ganrabru

cohabit *v. t* การอยู่ร่วมกันโดยไม่แต่งงาน
ganyuruamgandoeymaitaeng-ngan

coherent *a* สอดคล้องกัน sodklonggan

cohesive *adj* ติดกัน tidgan

coif *n* หมวก muak

coin *n* เหรียญ rian

coinage *n* การผลิตเหรียญ ganpalidrian

coincide *v. i* เกิดขึ้นพร้อมกัน
geudkeunpromgan

coir *n* ใยมะพร้าว yaimaprao

coke *v. t* เผาไหม้ paomai

cold *a* เย็น yen

cold *n* ไข้หวัด kaiwad

collaborate *v. i* ร่วมมือ ruammeu

collaboration *n* ความร่วมมือ
kwamruammeu

collapse *v. i* ล้ม lom

collar *n* ปลอกคอ plawkkaw

colleague *n* เพื่อนร่วมงาน peuanruam-
ngan

collect *v. t* สะสม sasom

collection *n* การสะสม gansasom

collective *a* เป็นกลุ่ม pengloom

collector *n* นักสะสม naksasom

college *n* วิทยาลัย wittayalai

collide *v. i.* ปะทะกัน patagan

collision *n* การปะทะกัน ganpatagan

collusion *n* การสมรู้ร่วมคิด
gansomruruamkid

colon *n* เครื่องหมาย kreuangmai

colon *n* ลำไส้ใหญ่ lamsaiyai

colonel *n.* พันเอก pan-ek

colonial *a* เป็นอาณานิคม pen-a-nanikom

colony *n* อาณานิคม a-nanikom

colour *n* สี si

colour *v. t* ทาสี tasi

colter *n* ลิ่ม lim

column *n* แถว taew

coma *n.* โคม่า coma

comb *n* หวี wi
combat1 *n* การต่อสู้ gantawsu
combat *v. t.* ต่อต้าน tawtan
combatant1 *n* นักรบ nakrob
combatant *a.* ชอบต่อสู้ chobtawsu
combination *n* การรวมกัน ganruamgan
combine *v. t* รวม ruam
come *v. i.* มา ma
comedian *n.* นักแสดงตลก
naksadaengtalok
comedy *n.* ละครตลก lakontalok
comet *n* ดาวหาง daohang
comfit *n.* ขนม kanom
comfort *n.* ความสบาย kwamsabai
comfort *v. t* อำนวยความสะดวก umnuaykwamsaduak
comfortable *a* สบาย sabai
comic *a* ตลก talok
comic *n* ตัวตลก tuatalok
comical *a* ตลก talok
comma *n* เครื่องหมายวรรคตอน
kreuangmaiwakton
command *n* คำสั่ง kamsang
command *v. t* สั่ง sang
commandant *n* ผู้บัญชาการ pubanchagan
commander *n* ผู้บัญชาการ pubanchagan
commemorate *v. t.* ระลึกถึง raleukteung
commemoration *n.* การระลึกถึง
ganrareukteung
commence *v. t* เริ่ม reum
commencement *n* การเริ่ม ganreum
commend *v. t* แนะนำ naenam
commendable *a.* น่ายกย่อง nayokyong
commendation *n* คำแนะนำ kamnaenam
comment *v. i* ให้ความเห็น haikwamhen
comment *n* ความเห็น kwamhen
commentary *n* คำวิจารณ์ kamwijan
commentator *n* ผู้วิจารณ์ puwijan
commerce *n* การค้า ganka
commercial *a* ทางการค้า tangganka
commiserate *v. t* ทำให้เศร้า tamhaisao

commission *n.* คณะกรรมการ
kanagammagan
commissioner *n.* ผู้ตรวจการ putruadgan
commissure *n.* ตะเข็บ takeb
commit *v. t.* ให้คำมั่น haikamman
committee *n* คณะกรรมการ
kanagammagan
commodity *n.* สินค้า sinka
common *a.* สามัญ saman
commoner *n.* สามัญชน samanchon
commonplace *a.* สามัญ saman
commonwealth *n.* เครือจักรภพ
kreuajaggapob
commotion *n* ความสับสน kwamsabsom
commove *v. t* ชักจูง chakjung
communal *a* สาธารณะ satarana
commune *v. t* คุยกันอย่างสนิทสนม
kuiganyangsanidsanom
communicate *v. t* สื่อสาร seusan
communication *n.* การสื่อสาร ganseusan
communiqué *n.* คำแถลงการณ์
kamtalaenggan
communism *n* ลัทธิคอมมิวนิสต์
lattikommunit
community *n.* ประชาคม prachakom
commute *v. t* เดินทางไปมา
deuntangpaima
compact *a.* ที่อัดแน่น ti-adnaen
compact *n.* ข้อตกลง kawtoklong
companion *n.* เพื่อน peuan
company *n.* บริษัท borisat
comparative *a* เชิงเปรียบเทียบ
cheuangpriabtiab
compare *v. t* เปรียบเทียบ priabtiab
comparison *n* การเปรียบเทียบ
ganpriabtiab
compartment *n.* การแบ่ง ganbaeng
compass *n* เข้าใจ kaojai
compassion *n* ความเห็นใจ kwamhenjai
compel *v. t* บังคับ bangkab
compensate *v.t* ชดเชย chodcheuy
compensation *n* ค่าชดเชย kachodcheuy

compete v. *i* ทำให้สมบูรณ์
tamhaisomboon
competence *n* ความสามารถ kwamsamad
competent *a.*มีความสามารถ
mikwamsamad
competition *n.* การแข่งขัน gankaengkan
competitive *a* แข่งขันกันได้
kaengkangandai
compile v. *t* รวบรวม ruabruam
complacent *adj.* พอใจ pawjai
complain v. *i* ร้องทุกข์ rongtook
complaint *n* คำร้องทุกข์ kamrongtook
complaisance *n.* การทำให้พอใจ
gantamhaipawjai
complaisant *adj.* ทำให้พอใจ
tamhaipawjai
complement *n* คำชม kamchom
complementary *a* ซึ่งทำให้สมบูรณ์
seungtamhaisomboon
complete *a* ที่เสร็จสิ้น tisedsin
complete v. *t* ทำให้ครบถ้วน
tamhaikrobtuan
completion *n* การทำให้ครบถ้วน
gantamhaikrobtuan
complex *a* ซับซ้อน sabson
complex *n* ปมด้อย pomdoy
complexion *n* สีผิว sipew
compliance *n.* การยอมทำตาม
ganyomtamtam
compliant *adj.* ซึ่งยินยอม seungyinyom
complicate v. *t* ทำให้ยุ่งยาก
tamhaiyungyak
complication *n.* ความยุ่งยาก
kwamyungyak
compliment *n.* คำชม kamchom
compliment v. *t* ชม chom
comply v. *i* ยอมตาม yomtam
component *adj.* ที่เป็นส่วนเสริม
tipensuanseum
compose v. *t* ประกอบด้วย pragobduay
composition *n* การจัดวางองค์ประกอบ
ganjatwang-ongpragob

compositor ผู้จัดวางองค์ประกอบ
pujatwang-ongpragob
compost *n* การผสมผสาน ganpasompasan
composure *n.* ความสงบ kwamsa-ngob
compound *n* คำประสม kamprasom
compound *a* ซึ่งประกอบกัน
seungpragobgan
compound *n* สารประกอบ sanpragob
compound v. *i* ผสม pasom
compounder *n.* ผู้ประกอบ pupragob
comprehend v. *t* เข้าใจ kaojai
comprehension *n* ความเข้าใจ
kwamkaojai
comprehensive *a* ครอบคลุม krobklum
compress v. *t.* บีบอัด beeb-ad
compromise *n* ความประนีประนอม
kwampranipranom
compromise v. *t* ประนีประนอม
pranipranom
compulsion *n* การบังคับ ganbangkab
compulsory *a* ที่บังคับ tibangkab
compunction *n.* ความสำนึกผิด
kwamsamneukpid
computation *n.* การคำนวณ gankamnuan
compute v.t. คำนวณ kamnuan
comrade *n.* สหาย sahai
conation *n.* ภาวะจิต pawajid
concave *adj.* เว้า wao
conceal v. *t.* ปกปิด pokpid
concede v.t. ยอมรับ yomrab
conceit *n* ความคิด kwamkid
conceive v. *t* รับรู้ rabru
concentrate v. *t* ตั้งใจ tanggai
concentration *n.* ความตั้งใจ kwamtangjai
concept *n* แนวคิด naewkid
conception *n* การรับรู้ ganrabru
concern v. *t* กังวล gangwon
concern *n* ความกังวล kwamgangwon
concert *n.* คอนเสิร์ต concert
concert2 v. *t* แสดงคอนเสิร์ต
sadaengconcert
concession *n* สัมปทาน sampatan

conch *n.* เปลือกหอย pleuakhoy
conciliate *v.t.* ทำให้เป็นมิตร tamhaipenmit
concise *a* กระชับ grachab
conclude *v. t* สรุป saloop
conclusion *n.* ข้อสรุป kawsalub
conclusive *a* สุดท้าย sudtai
concoct *v. t* ประกอบ pragob
concoction *n.* การประกอบ ganpragob
concord *n.* ความกลมเกลียว
kwamglomgliaw
concrescence *n.* การเกิดร่วมกัน
gangeudruamgan
concrete *n* คอนกรีต concrete
concrete *a* รูปธรรม roobpatam
concrete *v. t* ทำจากคอนกรีต
tamjakconcrete
concubinage *n.*
การอยู่ร่วมกันโดยไม่แต่งงาน
ganyuruamgandoeymaitaeng-ngan
concubine *n* ภรรยาน้อย panrayanoy
conculcate *v.t.* เหยียบย่ำ yiabyam
condemn *v. t.* ประณาม pranam
condemnation *n* การประณาม ganpranam
condense *v. t* ย่อ yaw
condite *v.t.* ดอง dong
condition *n* เงื่อนไข ngeuankai
conditional *a* ซึ่งเป็นเงื่อนไข seungpen-
ngeuankai
condole *v. i.* แสดงความเสียใจ
sadaengkwamsiajai
condolence *n* การแสดงความเสียใจ
gansadaengkwamsiajai
condonation *n.* การให้อภัย ganhai-a-pai
conduct *n* ความประพฤติ kwamprapeud
conduct *v. t* ควบคุม kuabkum
conductor *n* ผู้ควบคุม pukuabkum
cone *n.* กรวย gruay
confectioner *n* คนขายขนม konkaikanom
confectionery *n* ร้านขายขนม
rankaikanom
confer *v. i* สนทนา sontana
conference *n* การประชุม ganprachum

confess *v. t.* สารภาพ sarapab
confession *n* การสารภาพ gansarapab
confidant *n* คนที่ไว้ใจได้ kontiwaijaidai
confide *v. i* ปรึกษาความลับ
preuksakwamlab
confidence *n* ความลับ kwamlab
confident *a.* มั่นใจ manjai
confidential *a.* ลับ lab
confine *v. t* จำกัด jamgad
confinement *n.* การจำกัด ganjamgad
confirm *v. t* ยืนยัน yeunyan
confirmation *n* การยืนยัน ganyeunyan
confiscate *v. t* ยึดทรัพย์ yeudsab
confiscation *n* การยึดทรัพย์ ganyeudsab
conflict *n.* ความขัดแย้ง kwamkadyaeng
conflict *v. i* ขัดแย้ง kadyaeng
confluence *n* ฝูงชน foongchon
confluent *adj.* ที่ไหลไปด้วยกัน
tilaipaiduaygan
conformity *n.* ความสอดคล้อง
kwamsodklong
confraternity *n.* ความเป็นพี่น้อง
kwampenpinong
confrontation *n.* การเผชิญหน้า
ganpacheunna
confuse *v. t* ทำให้สับสน tamhaisabson
confusion *n* ความสับสน kwamsabson
confute *v.t.* พิสูจน์ว่าทำผิด pisudwatampid
conge *n.* การอำลา gan-umla
congenial *a* แต่กำเนิด taegamnued
conglutinate *v.t.* ทำให้รวมกัน
tamhairuamgan
congratulate *v. t* แสดงความยินดี
sadaengkwamyindi
congratulation *n* การแสดงความยินดี
gansadaengkwamyindi
congress *n* สภาคองเกรส sapacongress
conjecture *n* การคาดเดา gankaddao
conjecture *v. t* คาดเดา kaddao
conjugal *a* เกี่ยวกับการสมรส
giawgabgansomrod
conjugate *v.t. & i.* จับคู่ jabku

conjunct *adj.* ที่รวมกัน tiruamgan
conjunctive *n.* คำเชื่อม kamcheuam
conjuncture *n.* การรวมกัน ganruamgan
conjure *v.t.* ขอร้อง kawrong
conjure *v.i.* ร่ายเวทมนตร์ raiwedmon
connect *v. t.* เชื่อมโยง cheuamyong
connection *n* ความเกี่ยวข้อง kwamgiawkong
connivance *n.* การรู้เห็นเป็นใจ ganruhenpenjai
conquer *v. t* ชนะ chana
conquest *n* ชัยชนะ chaichana
conscience *n* สติสัมปชัญญะ satisampachanya
conscious *a* มีสติ misati
consecrate *v.t.* อุทิศตนให้กับ u-thidtonhaigab
consecutive *adj.* ต่อเนื่อง tawneuang
consecutively *adv* อย่างต่อเนื่อง yang-taw-neuang
consensus *n.* ประชามติ prachamati
consent *n.* การยินยอม gan-yinyom
consent *v. i* เห็นด้วย henduay
consent3 *v.t.* ยินยอม yinyom
consequence *n* ผลลัพธ์ ponlab
consequent *a* ผลที่ตามมา ponti-tamma
conservative *a* เชิงอนุรักษ์นิยม cheung-a-nurakniyom
conservative *n* ผู้มีแนวคิดอนุรักษ์นิยม puminaewkid-a-nurakniyom
conserve *v. t* ถนอมอาหาร tanom-a-han
consider *v. t* พิจารณา pijarana
considerable *a* สำคัญ samkan
considerate *a.* เกรงใจ greinggai
consideration *n* การพิจารณา ganpijarana
considering *prep.* เกี่ยวกับ giawgab
consign *v.t.* ส่งของ songkong
consign *v. t.* มอบหมาย mobmai
consignment *n.* จำนวนสินค้าที่ส่ง jamnuamsinkatisong
consist *v. i* ประกอบด้วย pragobduay

consistency *n.* ความต่อเนื่อง kwamtawneuang
consistent *a* สอดคล้องกัน sodklonggan
consolation *n* การปลอบใจ ganplobjai
console *v. t* ปลอบใจ plobjai
consolidate *v. t.* ผนึกกำลัง paneukgamlang
consolidation *n* การรวมกลุ่ม ganruamglum
consonance *n.* ความสอดคล้อง kwamsodklong
consonant *n.* พยัญชนะ payanchana
consort *n.* คู่สมรส kusomrod
conspectus *n.* การสำรวจ gansamruad
conspicuous *a.* ชัดเจน chadjen
conspiracy *n.* การสมรู้ร่วมคิด gansomruruamkid
conspirator *n.* ผู้สมรู้ร่วมคิด pusomruruamkid
conspire *v. i.* สมรู้ร่วมคิด somruruamkid
constable *n* ตำรวจ tamruad
constant *a* แน่นอน naenon
constellation *n.* กลุ่ม glum
constipation *n.* ท้องผูก tongpuk
constituency *n* เขตเลือกตั้ง ket-leuaktang
constituent *n.* ผู้มีสิทธิเลือกตั้ง pumisitleuaktang
constituent *adj.* สำคัญ samkan
constitute *v. t* ประกอบด้วย pragobduay
constitution *n* รัฐธรรมนูญ ratatammanoon
constrict *v.t.* กดแน่น godnaen
construct *v. t.* ก่อสร้าง gawsang
construction *n* การก่อสร้าง gangangwsang
consult *v. t* หารือ hareu
consultation *n* การหารือ ganhareu
consume *v. t* บริโภค boripok
consumption *n* การบริโภค ganboripok
consumption *n* วัณโรคปอด wannarokpod
contact *n.* การติดต่อ gantidtaw
contact *v. t* ติดต่อ tidtaw
contagious *a* ติดต่อกันได้ tidtawgandai
contain *v.t.* บรรจุ banju

contaminate v.t. เปื้อน peuan
contemplate v. t พิจารณา pijarana
contemplation n การพิจารณา ganpijarana
contemporary a ร่วมสมัย ruamsamai
contempt n การดูหมิ่น gandumin
contemptuous a เป็นการดูหมิ่น pengandumin
contend v. i ต่อสู้ tawsu
content a. พอใจ pawjai
content v. t ทำให้พอใจ tamhaipawjai
content n ความพอใจ kwampawjai
content n. เนื้อหา neuaha
contention n การแข่งขัน gankaengkan
contentment n ความพอใจ kwampawjai
contest v. t แข่งขัน kengkan
contest n. การแข่งขัน gankaengkan
context n บริบท boribod
continent n ทวีป tawib
continental a เกี่ยวกับแผ่นดินใหญ่ giawgabpaendinyai
contingency n. ความบังเอิญ kwambangeun
continual adj. ต่อเนื่อง tawneuang
continuation n. ความต่อเนื่อง kwamtawneuang
continue v. i. ทำต่อเนื่อง tamtawneuang
continuity n ความต่อเนื่อง kwamtawneuang
continuous a ต่อเนื่อง tawneuang
contour n เส้นขอบ senkob
contra pref. ตรงข้าม trongkam
contraception n. ยาคุมกำเนิด yakumgamneud
contract n สัญญา sanya
contract v. t ทำสัญญา tamsanya
contrapose v.t. วางตรงกันข้าม wangtronggankam
contractor n ผู้รับเหมา purabmao
contradict v. t ขัดแย้ง kadyaeng
contradiction n ความขัดแย้ง kwamkadyaeng
contrary a ตรงข้าม trongkam

contrast v. t แตกต่าง taektang
contrast n ความแตกต่าง kwamtaektang
contribute v. t บริจาค borijak
contribution n การบริจาค ganborijak
control n การควบคุม gankuabkum
control v. t ควบคุม kwuab-kum
controller n. ผู้ควบคุม pukuabkum
controversy n ความขัดแย้ง kwamkadyaeng
contuse v.t. ฟกช้ำ fokcham
conundrum n. ปริศนา prisana
convene v. t เรียกประชุม riekprachum
convener n ผู้เรียกประชุม puriekprachum
convenience n. ความสะดวก kwamsaduak
convenient a สะดวก saduak
convent n สำนักชี samnakchi
convention n. การประชุม ganprachum
conversant a คุ้นเคย kunkeuy
conversant adj. รอบรู้ robru
conversation n การสนทนา gansontana
converse v.t. สนทนา sontana
conversion n การเปลี่ยนแปลง ganplianplang
convert v. t เปลี่ยน plian
convert n การเปลี่ยนศาสนา ganpliansasana
convey v. t. สื่อสาร seusan
conveyance n. การขนส่ง gankonsong
convict v. t. ตัดสินว่าผิด tadsinwapid
convict n นักโทษ naktod
conviction n การพิพากษาลงโทษ ganpipaksa-longtod
convince v. t ชักชวน chakchuan
convivial adj. ชอบสังสรรค์ chobsangsan
convocation n. การเรียกประชุม ganriekprachum
convoke v.t. เรียกประชุม riekprachum
convolve v.t. ม้วนเข้าด้วยกัน muankaoduaygan
coo n เสียงร้องของนกเขา siangrongkongnokkao
coo v. i ขัน kan

cook *v. t* ทำอาหาร tam-a-han
cook *n* คนทำอาหาร kontam-a-han
cooker *n* ภาชนะทำอาหาร pachanatam-a-han
cool *a* ใจเย็น jaiyen
cool *v. i.* คลาย klai
cooler *n* ตู้แช่ tuchae
coolie *n* กุลี guli
co-operate *v. i* ร่วมมือ ruammeu
co-operation *n* การร่วมมือ ganruammeu
co-operative *a* ร่วมมือกัน ruammeugan
co-ordinate *a.* ขนานกัน kanangan
co-ordinate *v. t* ประสานงาน prasan-ngan
co-ordination *n* การประสานงาน ganprasan-ngan
coot *n.* คนแปลก konplaek
co-partner *n* ผู้ร่วมงาน puruamngan
cope *v. i* จัดการ jadgan
coper *n.* บาร์ลอยน้ำ barloynam
copper *n* ทองแดง tongdaeng
coppice *n.* ป่าละเมาะ palamaw
coprology *n.* ความหยาบโลน kwamyalon
copulate *v.i.* มีเพศสัมพันธ์ mipedsampan
copy *n* สำเนา samnao
copy *v. t* ทำสำเนา tamsamnao
coral *n* ปะการัง pagarang
cord *n* เชือก cheuak
cordial *a* เป็นมิตร penmit
corbel *n.* คานรับ kanrab
cordate *adj.* รูปหัวใจ roobhuajai
core *n.* แกน gaen
coriander *n.* ผักชี pakchi
Corinth *n.* ชื่อเมืองในกรีซ cheumeuangnaigreece
cork *n.* จุกไม้ก๊อก jookmaikok
cormorant *n.* คนโลภ konlob
corn *n* ข้าวโพด kaopod
cornea *n* กระจกตา grajokta
corner *n* มุม moom
cornet *n.* แตรทองเหลือง traetongleuang
cornicle *n.* เขาเล็กๆ kao-lek-lek
coronation *n* การสถาปนา gansatapana

coronet *n.* รัดเกล้า radglao
corporal *a* เกี่ยวกับร่างกาย giawgabranggai
corporate *adj.* เกี่ยวกับบริษัท giawgabborisat
corporation *n* บริษัท borisat
corps *n* กองกำลังทหาร gonggamrangtahan
corpse *n* ศพ sob
correct *a* ถูกต้อง tooktong
correct *v. t* ทำให้ถูกต้อง tamhaitooktong
correction *n* ความถูกต้อง kwamtooktong
correlate *v.t.* มีความสัมพันธ์กัน mikwamsampangan
correlation *n.* ความสัมพันธ์ kwamsampan
correspond *v. i* โต้ตอบ totob
correspondence *n.* การโต้ตอบ gantotob
correspondent *n.* ผู้สื่อข่าว puseukao
corridor *n.* ระเบียง rabiang
corroborate *v.t.* ยืนยัน yeunyan
corrosive *adj.* กัดกร่อน gadgron
corrupt *v. t.* ให้สินบน haisinbon
corrupt *a.* ทุจริต tujarit
corruption *n.* การทุจริต gantujarit
cosier *n.* ช่างเย็บผ้า changyebpa
cosmetic *a.* ใช้เพื่อความงาม chaipeuakwam-ngam
cosmetic *n.* เครื่องสำอาง kreuangsam-ang
cosmic *adj.* กว้างใหญ่ gwangyai
cost *v.t.* มีมูลค่า mimoonlaka
cost *n.* ต้นทุน ton-toon
costal *adj.* เกี่ยวกับซี่โครง giawgabsikrong
cote *n.* เพิง peung
costly *a.* แพง paeng
costume *n.* เสื้อผ้า seuapa
cosy *a.* อบอุ่น ob-aun
cot *n.* เตียงพับ tiangpab
cottage *n* กระท่อม gra-tom
cotton *n.* ฝ้าย fai
couch *n.* เก้าอี้ยาว gao-ii-yao
cough *n.* อาการไอ a-gan-ai
cough *v. i.* ไอ ai

council *n.* สภา sapa
councillor *n.* สมาชิกสภา samachiksapa
counsel *n.* ข้อเสนอแนะ kawsaneunae
counsel *v. t.* ให้คำปรึกษา haikampreuksa
counsellor *n.* ทนาย tanai
count *n.* การนับ gannab
count *v. t.* นับ nab
countenance *n.* สีหน้า sina
counter *n.* เคาน์เตอร์ counter
counter *v. t* พูดแย้ง pudyaeng
counteract *v.t.* ตอบโต้ tobto
countercharge *n.* การฟ้องแย้ง
ganfongyaeng
counterfeit *a.* ปลอม plom
counterfeiter *n.* ผู้ปลอมแปลง
puplomplaeng
countermand *v.t.* ยกเลิก yokleuk
counterpart *n.* คู่ฉบับ kuchabab
countersign *v. t.* ลงนามร่วม longnamruam
countess *n.* ภรรยาขุนนาง panrayakunnang
countless *a.* นับไม่ถ้วน nabmaituan
country *n.* ประเทศ prated
county *n.* เขตปกครอง kesprokkrong
coup *n.* การยึดอำนาจ ganyeud-um-nard
couple *n* คู่สามีภรรยา kusamipanlaya
couple *v. t* เชื่อมต่อ cheuamtaw
couplet *n.* คู่เหมือน kumeuan
coupon *n.* คูปอง kupong
courage *n.* ความกล้า kwamgla
courageous *a.* กล้าหาญ glahan
courier *n.* ผู้ส่งสาร pusongsan
course *n.* แนวปฏิบัติ naewpatibat
court *n.* ศาล san
court *v. t.* จีบ jib
courteous *a.* สุภาพ supab
courtesan *n.* โสเภณี sopeni
courtesy *n.* ความมีมารยาท
kwammimarayad
courtier *n.* คนประจบสอพลอ
konprajobsawplaw
courtship *n.* การจีบ ganjeeb
courtyard *n.* ลานบ้าน lanban

cousin *n.* ญาติ yat
covenant *n.* ข้อตกลง kawtoklong
cover *v. t.* ปกปิด pokpid
cover *n.* การปกปิด ganpokpid
coverlet *n.* ผ้าคลุมเตียง paklumtiang
covet *v.t.* อยากได้ของผู้อื่น yakdaikongpu-
eun
cow *n.* วัว wua
cow *v. t.* ขู่ ku
coward *n.* คนขี้ขลาด konkiklad
cowardice *n.* ความขี้ขลาด kwamkiklad
cower *v.i.* ตกใจกลัว tokjaiglua
cozy *a* เป็นกันเอง pengan-eng
crab *n* ปู pu
crack *n* รอยแตก roytaek
crack *v. i* แตกร้าว taekrao
cracker *n* ขนมปังกรอบ kanompang
crackle *v.t.* ทำเสียงดัง tamsiangdang
cradle *n* เปลเด็ก playdek
craft *n* งานฝีมือ ngan-feemeu
craftsman *n* ผู้ทำงานฝีมือ putam-
nganfeemeu
crafty *a* มีเล่ห์เหลี่ยม milayliam
cram *v. t* กินอย่างตะกละ ginyangtagla
crambo *n.* การทายคำสัมผัส
gantaikamsampad
crane *n* ปั้นจั่น panjan
crankle *v.t.* ทำให้ย่น tamhaiyon
crash *v. i* ชน chon
crash *n* การชนกัน ganchongan
crass *adj.* โง่ ngo
crate *n.* ลังไม้ langmai
crave *v.t.* ปรารถนา pratana
craw *n.* กระเพาะอาหารของสัตว์ grapraw-
a-hankongsat
crawl *v. t* คลาน klan
crawl *n* การคลาน ganklan
craze *n* ความคลั่งใคล้ kwamklangklai
crazy *a* คลั่ง klang
creak *v. i* ทำเสียงดัง tamsiangdang
creak *n* เสียงดัง siangdang
cream *n* ครีม cream

crease *n* รอยย่น royyon
create *v. t* สร้าง sang
creation *n* การสร้าง gansang
creative *adj.* สร้างสรรค์ sangson
creator *n* ผู้สร้าง pusang
creature *n* สัตว์ sat
credible *a* น่าเชื่อถือ nacheuateu
credit *n* เครดิต credit
creditable *a* น่าเชื่อถือ nacheuateu
creditor *n* เจ้าหนี้ jaoni
credulity *adj.* หูเบา hubao
creed *n.* ลัทธิความเชื่อ lattikwamcheua
creek *n.* ลำธาร lamtan
creep *v. i* คลาน klan
creeper *n* ไม้เลื้อย maileuay
cremate *v. t* เผา pao
cremation *n* การเผาศพ ganpaosob
crest *n* ยอด yawd
crevet *n.* กุ้ง gung
crew *n.* ลูกเรือ look-reua
crib *n.* เปลเด็ก playdek
cricket *n* คริกเก็ต cricket
crime *n* คดีอาญา kadi-a-ya
crimp *n* การทำให้เป็นลอน gantamhaipenlon
crimple *v.t.* ทำให้เป็นลอน tamhaipenlon
criminal *n* ผู้ร้าย purai
criminal *a* ทางอาญา tang-a-ya
crimson *n* สีแดงเข้ม sidaengkem
cringe *v. i.* นอมน้อม nobnom
cripple *n* คนพิการ konpigan
crisis *n* วิกฤตการณ์ wigrittagan
crisp *a* กรอบ grob
criterion *n* เกณฑ์ gain
critic *n* นักวิจารณ์ nakwijan
critical *a* สำคัญ samkan
criticism *n* การวิจารณ์ ganwijan
criticize *v. t* วิจารณ์ wijan
croak *n.* การปน ganbon
crockery *n.* เครื่องเคลือบดินเผา kreuangkleuabdinpao
crocodile *n* จระเข้ jarake

croesus *n.* มหาเศรษฐ์ mahasedti
crook *a* โค้งงอ kong-ngaw
crop *n* พืช peud
cross *v. t* ข้าม kam
cross *n* การข้าม gankam
cross *a* ตรงข้าม trongkam
crossing *n.* จุดตัดกัน judtadgan
crotchet *n.* ตะขอ takaw
crouch *v. i.* ก้มศีรษะ gomsisa
crow *n* กา ga
crow *v. i* ขัน kan
crowd *n* ฝูงชน foongchon
crown *n* มงกุฎ monggut
crown *v. t* สวมมงกุฎ suammonggut
crucial *adj.* สำคัญ samkan
crude *a* ดิบ dip
cruel *a* โหดร้าย hodrai
cruelty *n* ความโหดร้าย kwamhodrai
cruise *v.i.* ล่องเรือ longreua
cruiser *n* เรือนำเที่ยว reaunamtiaw
crumb *n* เศษเล็กเศษน้อย sedleksednoy
crumble *v. t* แตกละเอียด taekra-iad
crump *adj.* เปราะ praw
crusade *n* สงครามศาสนา songkramsasana
crush *v. t* บีบอัด bib-ad
crust *n.* ขนมปังป่น kanompangpon
crutch *n* ไม้เท้า maitao
cry *n* การร้องไห้ ganronghai
cry *v. i* ร้องไห้ ronghai
cryptography *n.* การเข้ารหัสลับ gankaorahadlab
crystal *n* คริสตัล crystal
cub *n* กระบอง grabong
cube *n* ก้อน gon
cubical *a* เป็นลูกบาศก์ penlookbat
cubiform *adj.* ที่มีรูปร่างคล้ายลูกบาศก์ timiroobrangklailookbat
cuckold *n.* สามีที่ภรรยามีชู้ samitipanrayamichu
cuckoo *n* คนแปลก konplaek
cucumber *n* แตงกวา taengkwa
cudgel *n* ไม้กระบอง maigrabong

cue *n* แถว taew
cuff *n* กุญแจมือ goonjaemeu
cuff *v. t* ใส่กุญแจมือ saigoonjaemeu
cuisine *n.* อาหาร a-han
cullet *n.* เศษแก้ว sedgaew
culminate *v.i.* ทำให้ถึงจุดสูงสุด
 tamhaiteungjudsungsud
culpable *a* น่าตำหนิ natamni
culprit *n* ผู้กระทำผิด pugratampid
cult *n* ลัทธิ latti
cultivate *v. t* เพาะปลูก pawpruk
cultrate *adj.* แถบกว้าง taebkwang
cultural *a* ทางวัฒนธรรม tangwattanatam
culture *n* วัฒนธรรม wattanatam
culvert *n.* ท่อใต้ดิน tawtaidin
cunning *a* เจ้าเล่ห์ jaolay
cunning *n* ความเจ้าเล่ห์ kwamjaolay
cup *n.* ถ้วย tuay
cupboard *n* ตู้เก็บของ tugebkong
Cupid *n* คิวปิด cupid
cupidity *n* ความโลภ kwamlob
curable *a* รักษาได้ raksadai
curative *a* รักษาได้ raksadai
curb *n* ขอบทาง kobtang
curb *v. t* ควบคุม kuabkum
curcuma *n.* ขมิ้น kamin
curd *n* นมข้น nomkon
cure *n* การรักษา ganraksa
cure *v. t.* รักษา raksa
curfew *n* เคอร์ฟิว curfew
curiosity *n* ความอยากรู้ kwamyakru
curious *a* อยากรู้ yakru
curl *n.* เกลียว gliaw
currant *n.* องุ่นแห้ง a-ngunhaeng
currency *n* สกุลเงิน sagoon-ngeun
current *n* กระแสเงิน grasae-ngeun
current *a* ปัจจุบัน patjuban
curriculum *n* หลักสูตร laksut
curse *n* คำแช่ง kamchaeng
curse *v. t* แช่ง chaeng
cursory *a* คร่าวๆ kraokrao
curt *a* หยาบ yab

curtail *v. t* ย่อ yaw
curtain *n* ม่าน man
curve *n* เส้นโค้ง senkong
curve *v. t* ทำให้โค้ง tamhaikong
cushion *n* เบาะ baw
cushion *v. t* รองเบาะ rongbaw
custard *n* คัสตาร์ด custard
custodian *n* ผู้คุ้มครอง pukumkrong
custody *v* การคุ้มครอง gankumkrong
custom *n.* ประเพณี prapeni
customary *a* คุ้นเคย kunkeuy
customer *n* ลูกค้า lookka
cut *v. t* ตัด tad
cut *n* การตัด gantad
cutis *n.* ผิวหนัง pewnang
cuvette *n.* หลอดแก้ว lawdgaew
cycle *n* วงโคจร wongkojon
cyclic *a* เกี่ยวกับวงโคจร
 giawgabwongkojon
cyclist *n* นักปั่นจักรยาน nakpanjaggayan
cyclone *n.* พายุไซโคลน payucyclone
cyclostyle *n* การลอกลายฉลุ
 ganlawklaichalu
cyclostyle *v. t* ลอกลายฉลุ loklaichalu
cylinder *n* กระบอกสูบ graboksub
cynic *n* ผู้ถากถาง putaktang

D

dabble *v. i.* ทำเล่นๆ tamlenlen
dacoit *n.* โจร jon
dacoity *n.* แกงค์ปล้น gangplon
dad, daddy *n* พ่อ paw
daffodil *n.* ดอกแดฟโฟดิล dawkdaffodil
daft *adj.* โง่ ngo
dagger *n.* กริช grid
daily *a* ประจำวัน prajamwan
daily *adv.* ทุกวัน tookwan
daily *n.* หนังสือพิมพ์รายวัน
 nangseupimraiwan
dainty *a.* อร่อย a-roi

dainty *n.* อาหารเลิศรส a-hanleudrod

dairy *n* ผลิตภัณฑ์จากนม palidtapanjaknom

dais *n.* เวที weti

daisy *n* ดอกเดซี่ dawkdaisy

dale *n* หุบเขา hoobkao

dam *n* เขื่อน keuan

damage *n.* ความเสียหาย kwamsiahai

damage *v. t.* ทำให้เสียหาย tamhaisiahai

dame *n.* คุณหญิง kunying

damn *v. t.* ฉิบหาย chibhai

damnation *n.* การแช่ง ganchaeng

damp *a* ชื้น cheun

damp *n* ความชื้น kwamcheun

damp *v. t.* ทำให้ชื้น tamhaicheun

damsel *n.* หญิงพรมจรรย์ yingprommajan

dance *n* การเต้นรำ gantenram

dance *v. t.* เต้นรำ tenram

dandelion *n.* ต้นไม้ชนิดหนึ่ง tonmaichanidneung

dandle *v.t.* เล่นหัว lenhua

dandruff *n* รังแค rangkae

dandy *n* ผู้ชายสำรวย puchaisamruay

danger *n.* ความอันตราย kwamantarai

dangerous *a* อันตราย an-tarai

dangle *v. t* ห้อย hoy

dank *adj.* เปียกชื้น piakcheun

dap *v.i.* ตกปลา tokpla

dare *v. i.* ท้า ta

daring *n.* ความกล้าหาญ kwamglahan

daring *a* กล้าหาญ glahan

dark *a* มืด meud

dark *n* ความมืด kwammeud

darkle *v.i.* มืด meud

darling *n* คนรัก konrak

darling *a* ที่รัก tirak

dart *n.* ลูกดอก lookdawk

dash *v. i.* กระแทก grataek

dash *n* การกระแทก gangrataek

date *n* วันที่ wanti

date *v. t* ลงวันที่ longwanti

daub *n.* โคลน clone

daub *v. t.* เปื้อน peuan

daughter *n* ลูกสาว looksao

daunt *v. t* ทำให้กลัว tamhaiglua

dauntless *a* ไม่กลัว maiglua

dawdle *v.i.* ชักช้า chakcha

dawn *n* รุ่งเช้า rungchao

dawn *v. i.* เริ่มขึ้น reumkeun

day *n* วัน wan

daze *n* ความงุนงง kwam-ngun-ngong

daze *v. t* ทำให้งง tamhai-ngong

dazzle *n* แสงจ้า saengja

dazzle *v. t.* ทำให้ตาพร่า tamhaitapra

deacon *n.* ผู้ช่วยบาทหลวง puchuaybatluang

dead *a* ตาย tai

deadlock *n* ความล้มเหลว kwamlomlew

deadly *a* ถึงตายได้ teungtaidai

deaf *a* หูหนวก hunuak

deal *n* การซื้อขาย ganseukai

deal *v. i* จัดการ jadgan

dealer *n* ผู้ค้า puka

dealing *n.* การติดต่อ gantidtaw

dean *n.* คณบดี kanabodi

dear *a* แพง paeng

dearth *n* ความขาดแคลน kwamkadklan

death *n* ความตาย kwamtai

debar *v. t.* ตัดสิทธิ์ tadsit

debase *v. t.* ทำให้เสื่อม tamhaiseuam

debate *n.* การอภิปราย gan-a-piprai

debate *v. t.* โต้แย้ง toyaeng

debauch *v. t.* ล่อลวงให้ทำผิด lawluanghaitampid

debauch *n* การล่อลวงให้ทำผิด ganlawluanghaitampid

debauchee *n* ผู้ล่อลวงให้ทำผิด pulawluanghaitampid

debauchery *n* ความเสเพล kwamseplay

debility *n* ความอ่อนเพลีย kwam-onplia

debit *n* รายการเงินที่ถูกหักจากบัญชี raigan-ngeuntitookhakjakbanchi

debit *v. t* หักบัญชี hakbanchi

debris *n* ซากปรักหักพัง sakparakhakpang

debt *n* หนี้ ni

debtor *n* เจ้าหนี้ jaoni

decade *n* ทศวรรษ tosawat

decadent *a* เสื่อมโทรม seuamsom

decamp *v. i* หลบหนี lopni

decay *n* การย่อยสลาย ganyoisalai

decay *v. i* ย่อยสลาย yoisalai

decease *n* ความตาย kwamtai

decease *v. i* ตาย tai

deceit *n* การหลอกลวง ganlokluang

deceive *v. t* หลอกลวง lokluang

december *n* ธันวาคม tanwakom

decency *n* ความประพฤติดี kwamprapeuddi

decennary *n.* ระยะเวลาสิบปี rayawelasippi

decent *a* เหมาะสม mawsom

deception *n* การหลอกลวง ganlokluang

decide *v. t* ตัดสินใจ tadsinjai

decillion *n.* จำนวนนับมหาศาล jamnuannabmahasan

decimal *a* ตำแหน่งทศนิยม tamnaengtodsaniyom

decimate *v.t.* ทำลาย tamlai

decision *n* การตัดสินใจ gantadsinjai

decisive *a* เด็ดเดี่ยว deddiaw

deck *n* ดาดฟ้าเรือ dadfareua

deck *v. t* ตกแต่ง toktaeng

declaration *n* คำประกาศ kampragad

declare *v. t.* ประกาศ pragad

decline *n* การปฏิเสธ ganpatised

decline *v. t.* ปฏิเสธ patised

declivous *adj.* ค่อยๆ ลดลง koykoylodlong

decompose *v. t* สลายตัว salaitua

decomposition *n.* การสลายตัว gansalaitua

decontrol *v.t.* ไม่ควบคุม maikuabkum

decorate *v. t* ตกแต่ง toktaeng

decoration *n* การตกแต่ง gantoktaeng

decorum *n* มารยาท marayat

decrease *v. t* ลดลง lodlong

decrease *n* การลดลง ganlodlong

decree *n* กฤษฎีกา grisadiga

decree *v. i* ประกาศกฤษฎีกา pragadgrisadiga

decrement *n.* การลดลง ganlodlong

dedicate *v. t.* อุทิศตัว u-tidtua

dedication *n* การอุทิศตัว gan-u-tidtua

deduct *v.t.* หักออก hak-awk

deed *n* การกระทำ gangratam

deem *v.i.* คิดว่า kidwa

deep *a.* ลึก leuk

deer *n* กวาง gwang

defamation *n* การใส่ร้าย gansairai

defame *v. t.* ใส่ร้าย sairai

default *n.* การผิดสัญญา ganpidsanya

defeat *n* ความพ่ายแพ้ kwampaipae

defeat *v. t.* เอาชนะ ao-chana

defect *n* ความบกพร่อง kwambokprong

defence *n* การป้องกัน ganponggan

defend *v. t* ป้องกัน ponggan

defendant *n* จำเลย jamleuy

defensive *adv.* อย่างป้องกันได้ yangponggandai

deference *n* การเชื่อฟัง gancheuafang

defiance *n* การขัดขวาง gankadkwang

deficit *n* การขาดดุล gankaddun

deficient *adj.* ขาดแคลน kadklan

defile *n.* ช่องแคบ chongkaeb

define *v. t* นิยาม niyam

definite *a* แน่นอน naenon

definition *n* คำนิยาม kamniyam

deflation *n.* ภาวะเงินฝืด pawa-ngeunfeud

deflect *v.t. & i.* เบนความสนใจ benkwamsonjai

deft *adj.* คล่องแคล่ว klongklaew

degrade *v. t* ลดค่า lodka

degree *n* ระดับ radab

dehort *v.i.* ห้ามปราม ham-pram

deist *n.* ผู้นับถือพระเจ้า punabteuprajao

deity *n.* เทพ teb

deject *v. t* ทำให้ผิดหวัง tamhaipidwang

dejection *n* ความผิดหวัง kwampidwang

delay *v.t. & i.* ทำให้ล่าช้า tamhailacha

delibate *v.t.* ชิม chim
deligate1 *n* มัดไว้ madwai
delegate *v. t* มอบหมาย mobmai
delegation *n* ผู้แทน putaen
delete *v. t* ลบ lob
deliberate *v. i* ไตร่ตรอง traitrong
deliberate *a* รอบคอบ robkob
deliberation *n* ความรอบคอบ kwamrobkob
delicate *a* ละเอียดอ่อน la-iad-on
delicious *a* อร่อย a-roy
delight *n* ความยินดี kwamyindi
delight *v. t.* ยินดี yindi
deliver *v. t* ส่ง song
delivery *n* การนำส่ง gannamsong
delta *n* ดินดอนสามเหลี่ยม dindonsamliam
delude *v. t.* ลวงตา luangta
delusion *n.* ภาพลวงตา pabluangta
demand *n* การเรียกร้อง ganriakrong
demand *v. t* เรียกร้อง riakrong
demarcation *n.* การแบ่งเขต ganbaengket
dement *v.t* ทำให้บ้า tamhaiba
demerit *n* ข้อบกพร่อง kawbokprong
democracy *n* ประชาธิปไตย prachatipatai
democratic *a* เป็นประชาธิปไตย penprachatipatai
demolish *v. t.* ทำลาย tamlai
demon *n.* ปีศาจ pisad
demonetize *v.t.* ถอนเงิน tawn-ngeun
demonstrate *v. t* ประท้วง pratuang
demonstration *n.* การประท้วง ganpratuang
demoralize *v. t.* ทำให้เสื่อม tamhaiseuam
demur *n* การคัดค้าน gankadkan
demur *v. t* คัดค้าน kadkan
demurrage *n.* ค่าเสียเวลา kasiawela
den *n* ถ้ำ tam
dengue *n.* ไข้เลือดออก kaileuad-awk
denial *n* การปฏิเสธ ganpatised
denote *v. i* บ่งชี้ bongchi
denounce *v. t* ประนาม pranam
dense *a* ขุ่น kun

density *n* ความหนาแน่น kwamnanaen
dentist *n* ทันตแพทย์ tantapaed
denude *v.t.* เปลือย pleuay
denunciation *n.* การประจาน ganprajan
deny *v. t.* ปฏิเสธ patised
depart *v. i.* จาก jak
department *n* กรมกอง gromgong
departure *n* การจาก ganjak
depauperate *v.t.* แกร็น graen
depend *v. i.* พึ่งพา peung-pa
dependant *n* ผู้อยู่ในอุปการะ puyunai-u-pagara
dependence *n* การพึ่งพา ganpeungpa
dependent *a* ขึ้นอยู่กับ keunyugab
depict *v. t.* พรรณนา panana
deplorable *a* น่าตำหนิ natamni
deploy *v.t.* เคลื่อนกำลัง kleuangamlang
deponent *n.* ผู้ให้การเป็นพยาน puhaiganpenpayan
deport *v.t.* เนรเทศ nerated
depose *v. t* ถอดถอน todtawn
deposit *n.* การฝากเงิน ganfak-ngeun
deposit *v. t* ฝากเงิน fak-nguen
depot *n* คลังสินค้า klangsinka
depreciate *v.t.i.* ลดค่า lodka
depredate *v.t.* ปล้น plon
depress *v. t* ทำให้หดหู่ tamhaihodhu
depression *n* อาการเศร้าหดหู่ a-gansaohodhu
deprive *v. t* ยึดทรัพย์ yeudsab
depth *n* ความลึก kwamleuk
deputation *n* การแต่งตั้งผู้แทน gantaengtangputaen
depute *v. t* แต่งตั้งผู้แทน taengtangputaen
deputy *n* ผู้รักษาการแทน puraksagan
derail *v. t.* ตกราง tokrang
derive *v. t.* ได้มาจาก daimajak
descend *v. i.* สืบทอด seubtod
descendant *n* ผู้สืบสกุล puseubsagoon
descent *n.* การสืบสกุล ganseubsagoon
describe *v. t* บรรยาย banyai
description *n* คำบรรยาย kambanyai

descriptive *a* เป็นการบรรยาย penganbanyai

desert *v. t.* ทอดทิ้ง todting

desert *n* ทะเลทราย talaysai

deserve *v. t.* สมควรได้รับ somkuandairab

design *v. t.* ออกแบบ awkbaeb

design *n.* การออกแบบ gan-awkbaeb

desirable *a* เป็นที่พึงปรารถนา pentipeungpratana

desire *n* ความปรารถนา kwampratana

desire *v.t* ปรารถนา pratana

desirous *a* เป็นที่พึงปรารถนา pentipeungpratana

desk *n* โต๊ะ to

despair *n* ความสิ้นหวัง kwamsinwang

despair *v. i* สิ้นหวัง sinwang

desperate *a* ซึ่งหมดหวัง seungmodwang

despicable *a* เลวทราม lewsam

despise *v. t* ชิงชัง chingchang

despot *n* ผู้กดขี่ pugodki

destination *n* จุดหมาย judmai

destiny *n* โชคชะตา chokchata

destroy *v. t* ทำลาย tamlai

destruction *n* การทำลาย gantamlai

detach *v. t* แยกออก yaek-awk

detachment *n* การแยกออก ganyaek-awk

detail *n* รายละเอียด raila-iad

detail *v. t* ให้รายละเอียด hairaila-iad

detain *v. t* กักขัง gakkang

detect *v. t* สืบหา seubha

detective *a* เกี่ยวกับการสืบ giawgabganseub

detective *n.* นักสืบ nakseub

determination *n.* การตัดสินใจ gantadsinjai

determine *v. t* ตัดสินใจ tadsinjai

dethrone *v. t* ปลดอำนาจ plod-umnad

develop *v. t.* พัฒนา pattana

development *n.* การพัฒนา ganpattana

deviate *v. i* เบี่ยงเบน biangbein

deviation *n* การเบี่ยงเบน ganbiangbein

device *n* เครื่องมือ kreuangmeu

devil *n* ปีศาจ pisad

devise *v. t* คิดขึ้นใหม่ kidkeunmai

devoid *a* ขาดแคลนมาก kadklaenmak

devote *v. t* มอบให้ mobhai

devotee *n* ผู้อุทิศตัว pu-u-tidtua

devotion *n* การอุทิศตัว gan-u-tidtua

devour *v. t* กินอย่างตะกละ ginyangtakla

dew *n.* น้ำค้าง namkang

diabetes *n* โรคเบาหวาน rokbaowan

diagnose *v. t* วินิจฉัยโรค winichairok

diagnosis *n* การวินิจฉัยโรค ganwinichairok

diagram *n* แผนภาพ paenpab

dial *n.* หน้าปัด napad

dialect *n* ภาษาถิ่น pasatin

dialogue *n* บทสนทนา bodsontana

diameter *n* เส้นผ่าศูนย์กลาง senpasoonglang

diamond *n* เพชร ped

diarrhoea *n* อาการท้องร่วง a-gantongruang

diary *n* ไดอารี่ diary

dice *n.* ลูกเต๋า looktao

dice *v. i.* ทอยลูกเต๋า toylooktao

dictate *v. t* ควบคุม kuabkum

dictation *n* การควบคุม gankuabkum

dictator *n* ผู้เผด็จการ pupadedgan

diction *n* สำนวน samnuan

dictionary *n* พจนานุกรม pojananugrom

dictum *n* สุภาษิต supasit

didactic *a* ชอบสั่งสอน chobsangson

die *v. i* ตาย tai

die *n* แม่พิมพ์ maepim

diet *n* การควบคุมอาหาร gankwuabkum-a-han

differ *v. i* แตกต่าง taektang

difference *n* ความแตกต่าง kwamtaektang

different *a* ต่างกัน tanggan

difficult *a* ยาก yak

difficulty *n* ความยาก kwamyak

dig *n* การขุด gankud

dig *v.t.* ขุด kud

digest *v. t.* ย่อย yoi
digest *n.* ฉบับย่อ chababyaw
digestion *n* การย่อย ganyoi
digit *n* ตัวเลข tualek
dignify *v.t* ทำให้สง่างาม tamhaisa-nga-ngam
dignity *n* สง่างาม sa-nga-ngam
dilemma *n* สภาวะลำบาก sapawalambak
diligence *n* ความขยัน kwamkayan
diligent *a* ขยัน kayan
dilute *v. t* ทำให้เจือจาง tamhaijeuajang
dilute *a* ซึ่งเจือจาง seungjeuajang
dim *a* สลัว salua
dim *v. t* ทำให้สลัว tamhaisalua
dimension *n* ขอบเขต kobked
diminish *v. t* ลดลง lodlong
din *n* เสียงอึกทึก siang-eukgateuk
dine *v. t.* ทาน tan
dinner *n* อาหารเย็น a-hanyen
dip *n.* การจุ่ม ganjoom
dip *v. t* จุ่ม joom
diploma *n* ประกาศนียบัตร pragasaniyabat
diplomacy *n* การทูต gantut
diplomat *n* นักการทูต nakgantut
diplomatic *a* ทางการทูต tanggantut
dire *a* เลวร้าย lewrai
direct *a* ตรง trong
direct *v. t* ชี้ทาง chitang
direction *n* ทิศทาง tidtang
director *n.* ผู้กำกับ pugamgab
directory *n* สมุดรายนาม samudrainam
dirt *n* ความสกปรก kwamsokgaprok
dirty *a* สกปรก sokgaprok
disability *n* ความพิการ kwampigan
disable *v. t* ทำให้ไร้ความสามารถ
  tamhairaikwamsamad
disabled *a* พิการ pigan
disadvantage *n* การเสียประโยชน์
  gansiaprayod
disagree *v. i* ไม่เห็นด้วย maihenduay
disagreeable *a.* ซึ่งไม่เห็นด้วย
  seungmaihenduay

disagreement *n.* ความไม่เห็นด้วย
  kwammaihenduay
disappear *v. i* หายไป haipai
disappearance *n* การหายไป ganhaipai
disappoint *v. t.* ผิดหวัง pidwang
disapproval *n* ความไม่เห็นด้วย
  kwammaihenduay
disapprove *v. t* ไม่เห็นด้วย maihenduay
disarm *v. t* ปลดอาวุธ plod-a-wut
disarmament *n.* การปลดอาวุธ ganplod-a-
  wut
disaster *n* ความหายนะ kwamhaiyana
disastrous *a* หายนะ haiyana
disc *n.* ดิสก์ disc
discard *v. t* ละทิ้ง lating
discharge *v. t* ปลด plod
discharge *n.* การพ้นจากตำแหน่ง
  ganponjaktamnaeng
disciple *n* ศิษย์ sid
discipline *n* หลักการ lakgan
disclose *v. t* เปิดเผย peudpeuy
discomfort *n* ความไม่สะดวกสบาย
  kwammaisaduaksabai
disconnect *v. t* ตัดขาด tadkad
discontent *n* ความไม่พอใจ
  kwammaipawjai
discontinue *v. t* ไม่ต่อเนื่อง maitawneuang
discord *n* ความไม่ลงรอยกัน
  kwammailongroygan
discount *n* การลดราคา ganlodraka
discourage *v. t.* ทำให้หมดกำลังใจ
  tamhaimodgamrangjai
discourse *n* วาทกรรม watagam
discourteous *a* ไม่สุภาพ maisupab
discover *v. t* ค้นพบ konpob
discovery *n.* การค้นพบ gankonpob
discretion *n* ดุลยพินิจ dunpinid
discriminate *v. t.* แบ่งแยก baengyaek
discrimination *n* การแบ่งแยก
  ganbaengyaek
discuss *v. t.* หารือ hareu
disdain *n* การดูถูก gandutook

disdain *v. t.* ดูถูก dutook

disease *n* โรค rok

disguise *n* การปลอมตัว ganplomtua

disguise *v. t* ปลอมตัว plomtua

dish *n* จาน jan

dishearten *v. t* ทำให้หมดกำลังใจ tamhaimodgamrangjai

dishonest *a* ไม่ซื่อสัตย์ maiseusat

dishonesty *n.* ความไม่ซื่อสัตย์ kwammaiseusat

dishonour *v. t* ไม่ให้เกียรติ maihaigiat

dishonour *n* ความไม่ให้เกียรติ kwammaihaigiat

dislike *v. t* ไม่ชอบ maichob

dislike *n* ความไม่ชอบ kwammaichob

disloyal *a* ไม่ซื่อสัตย์ maiseusat

dismiss *v. t.* ไล่ออก lai-awk

dismissal *n* การไล่ออก ganlai-awk

disobey *v. t* ไม่เชื่อฟัง maicheuafang

disorder *n* ความวุ่นวาย kwamwunwai

disparity *n* ความแตกต่าง kwamtaektang

dispensary *n* ร้านขายยา rankaiya

disperse *v. t* กระจาย grajai

displace *v. t* ขับไล่ kablai

display *v. t* แสดง sadaeng

display *n* การแสดง gansadaeng

displease *v. t* ไม่พอใจ maipawjai

displeasure *n* ความไม่พอใจ kwammaipawjai

disposal *n* การกำจัด gangamjad

dispose *v. t* กำจัด gamjad

disprove *v. t* พิสูจน์ว่าผิด pisudwapid

dispute *n* ความขัดแย้ง kwamkadyaeng

dispute *v. i* ขัดแย้ง kadyaeng

disqualification *n* การขาดคุณสมบัติ gankadkunasombat

disqualify *v. t.* ไม่มีคุณสมบัติ maimikunasombat

disquiet *n* ความไม่สงบ kwammaisa-ngob

disregard *n* ความไม่สนใจ kwammaisonjai

disregard *v. t* ไม่สนใจ maisonjai

disrepute *n* การเสียชื่อเสียง gansiacheusiang

disrespect *n* ความไม่เคารพ kwammaikaorob

disrupt *v. t* ทำให้ยุ่ง tamhaiyung

dissatisfaction *n* ความไม่พอใจ kwammaipawjai

dissatisfy *v. t.* ไม่พอใจ maipawjai

dissect *v. t* ชำแหละ chamlae

dissection *n* การชำแหละ ganchamlae

dissimilar *a* ไม่เหมือนกัน maimeuangan

dissolve *v.t* ละลาย lalai

dissuade *v. t* ห้ามปราม hampram

distance *n* ระยะทาง rayatang

distant *a* ห่างไกล hangglai

distil *v. t* กลั่น glan

distillery *n* โรงกลั่นสุรา rongglansura

distinct *a* แตกต่าง taektaeng

distinction *n* ความโดดเด่น kwamdodden

distinguish *v. i* แยกแยะความแตกต่าง yaekyaekwamtaektang

distort *v. t* บิดเบือน bidbeuan

distress *n* ความเศร้า kwamsao

distress *v. t* ทำให้เสียใจ tamhaisiajai

distribute *v. t* แจกจ่าย jaekjai

distribution *n* การแจกจ่าย ganjaekjai

district *n* เขต ket

distrust *n* ความไม่ไว้ใจ kwammaiwaijai

distrust *v. t.* ไม่ไว้ใจ maiwaijai

disturb *v. t* รบกวน robguan

ditch *n* คูน้ำ kunam

ditto *n.* สิ่งที่เหมือนกัน singtimeuangan

dive *v. i* ดำน้ำ damnam

dive *n* การดำน้ำ gandamnam

diverse *a* หลากหลาย laklai

divert *v. t* เบี่ยงเบน biengben

divide *v. t* แบ่ง baeng

divine *a* เกี่ยวกับสวรรค์ giawgabsawan

divinity *n* พระเจ้า prajao

division *n* การแตกแยก gantaekyaek

divorce *n* การหย่า ganya

divorce *v. t* หย่า ya

divulge *v. t* เปิดเผยความลับ
  peudpeuykwamlab
do *v. t* ทำ tam
docile *a* เชื่อง cheuang
dock *n.* ท่าเรือ tareua
doctor *n* หมอ maw
doctorate *n* ปริญญาเอก parinya-ek
doctrine *n* ลัทธิ latti
document *n* เอกสาร ek-gasan
dodge *n* การหลบ ganlobni
dodge *v. t* หลบ lob
doe *n* กวางตัวเมีย gwangtuamia
dog *n* สุนัข sunak
dog *v. t* ไล่ตาม laitam
dogma *n* หลักความเชื่อ lakkwamcheua
dogmatic *a* หัวดื้อ huadeu
doll *n* ตุ๊กตา tookgata
dollar *n* ดอลลาร์ dollar
domain *n* อาณาเขต a-naket
dome *n* หลังคากลม langkaglom
domestic *a* เกี่ยวกับบ้าน giawgabban
domestic *n* คนรับใช้ konrabchai
domicile *n* ถิ่นที่อยู่ tintiyu
dominant *a* เด่น den
dominate *v. t* ปกครอง pokkrong
domination *n* การครอบงำ gankrob-ngam
dominion *n* ประเทศในเครือจักรภพ
  pratednaikreuajakgapob
donate *v. t* บริจาค borijak
donation *n.* การบริจาค ganborijak
donkey *n* ลา la
donor *n* ผู้บริจาค puborijak
doom *n* คำตัดสิน kamtadsin
doom *v. t.* ตัดสิน tadsin
door *n* ประตู pratu
dose *n* ปริมาณยา parimanya
dot *n* จุด jud
dot *v. t* ใส่จุด saijud
double *a* สองเท่า songtao
double *v. t.* ทำเป็นสองเท่า tampensongtao
double *n* จำนวนสองเท่า jamnuamsongtao
doubt *v. i* สงสัย songsai

doubt *n* ข้อสงสัย kawsongsai
dough *n* แป้งขนมปัง paengkanompang
dove *n* นกพิราบ nokpirab
down *adv* ข้างล่าง kanglang
down *prep* ลงไป longpai
down *v. t* ทำให้ตกลงมา tamhaitoklongma
downfall *n* ความตกต่ำ kwamtoktam
downpour *n* ฝนตกหนัก fontoknak
downright *adv* โดยสิ้นเชิง
  doeysincheuang
downright *a* จริงจัง jingjang
downward *a* ลดต่ำลง lodtamlong
downward *adv* ลงต่ำ longtam
downwards *adv* ลงต่ำ longtam
dowry *n* สินสอด sinsod
doze *n.* การสัปหงก gansappa-ngok
doze *v. i* สัปหงก sappa-ngok
dozen *n* หนึ่งโหล neunglo
draft *v. t* ร่าง rang
draft *n* ภาพร่าง pabrang
draftsman *a* คนร่างแบบ konrangbaeb
drag *n* การลาก ganlak
drag *v. t* ลาก lak
dragon *n* มังกร mangkon
drain *n* ท่อระบายน้ำ tawrabainam
drain *v. t* ระบาย rabai
drainage *n* การระบายน้ำ ganrabainam
dram *n* หน่วยน้ำหนัก neuynamnak
drama *n* ละคร lakon
dramatic *a* เกี่ยวกับละคร giawgablakon
dramatist *n* นักเขียนบทละคร
  nakkianbodlakon
draper *n* คนขายผ้า konkaipa
drastic *a* รุนแรง roonraeng
draught *n* ลมเย็น lomyen
draw *v.t* วาด wad
draw *n* การวาด ganwad
drawback *n* ข้อเสียเปรียบ kawsiapriab
drawer *n* ลิ้นชัก linchak
drawing *n* การวาดรูป ganwadroob
drawing-room *n* ห้องวาดรูป
  hongwadroob

dread *n* ความน่ากลัว kwamnaglua
dread *v.t* กลัว glua
dread *a* น่ากลัว naglua
dream *n* ความฝัน kwamfun
dream *v. i.* ฝัน fun
drench *v. t* ทำให้ชุ่ม tamhaichum
dress *n* การแต่งตัว gantaengtua
dress *v. t* แต่งตัว taengtua
dressing *n* น้ำสลัด namsalad
drill *n* การฝึกฝน ganfeukfon
drill *v. t.* ฝึกฝน feukfon
drink *n* เครื่องดื่ม kreuangdeum
drink *v. t* ดื่ม deum
drip *n* หยดน้ำ yodnam
drip *v. i* ทำให้หยด tamhaiyod
drive *v. t* ขับ kab
drive *n* แรงขับ raengkab
driver *n* คนขับ konkab
drizzle *n* ฝนตกปรอยๆ fontokployploy
drizzle *v. i* ตกปรอยๆ tokployploy
drop *n* การทิ้ง ganting
drop *v. i* ตก tok
drought *n* ความแห้งแล้ง
  kwamhaenglaeng
drown *v.i* จมน้ำ jomnam
drug *n* ยา ya
druggist *n* เภสัชกร peisachagon
drum *n* กลอง glong
drum *v.i.* ตีกลอง tiglong
drunkard *n* คนเมา konmao
dry *a* แห้ง haeng
dry *v. i.* ทำให้แห้ง tamhaihaeng
dual *a* คู่ ku
duck *n.* เป็ด ped
duck *v.i.* ดำน้ำ damnam
due *a* ถึงกำหนด teunggamnod
due *n* เงินที่ต้องชำระ ngeuntitongchamla
due *adv* โดยตรง doeytrong
duel *n* การแข่งขันระหว่างสองคน
  gankaengkanrawaengsongkon
duel *v. i* แข่งขันระหว่างสองคน
  kaengkanrawangsongkon

duke *n* ดยุค duke
dull *a* มัว mua
dull *v. t.* ทำให้มัว tamhaimua
duly *adv* ไม่มีชีวิตชีวา maimichiwitchiwa
dumb *a* โง่ ngo
dunce *n* คนโง่ konngo
dung *n* มูลสัตว์ moonsat
duplicate *a* เหมือนกัน meuangan
duplicate *n* การทำซ้ำ gantamsam
duplicate *v. t* ทำซ้ำ tamsam
duplicity *n* การหลอกลวง ganlawkluang
durable *a* ทนทาน tontan
duration *n* ระยะเวลา rayawela
during *prep* ระหว่าง rawang
dusk *n* สนธยา sontaya
dust *n* ฝุ่น foon
dust *v.t.* ปัดฝุ่น padfoon
duster *n* ที่ปัดฝุ่น ti-padfoon
dutiful *a* รับผิดชอบต่อหน้าที่
  rabpidchobtawnati
duty *n* หน้าที่ nati
dwarf *n* คนแคระ konkrae
dwell *v. i* อาศัย a-sai
dwelling *n* ที่อยู่อาศัย tiyu-a-sai
dwindle *v. t* ลดลง lodlong
dye *v. t* ย้อม yom
dye *n* สีย้อม siyom
dynamic *a* พลวัตร ponlawat
dynamics *n.* พลศาสตร์ ponlasat
dynamite *n* ระเบิด rabeud
dynamo *n* ไดนาโม dynamo
dynasty *n* ราชวงศ์ rachawong
dysentery *n* โรคบิด rokbid

E

each *a* แต่ละ taela
each *pron.* แต่ละคน taelakon
eager *a* กระตือรือร้น grateureuron
eagle *n* นกอินทรีย์ nok-insi
ear *n* หู hu

early *adv* แต่เช้า taechao
early *a* เช้า chao
earn *v. t* ได้รับ dairab
earnest *a* จริงจัง jingjang
earth *n* พื้นดิน peundin
earthen *a* เครื่องดินเผา kreuangdinpao
earthly *a* เกี่ยวกับโลกมนุษย์
  giawgablokmanud
earthquake *n* แผ่นดินไหว paendinwai
ease *n* ความสุขสบาย kwamsooksabai
ease *v. t* ผ่อนคลาย ponklai
east *n* ทิศตะวันออก tidtawan-awk
east *adv* ทางทิศตะวันออก tangtidtawan-
  awk
east *a* ทางทิศตะวันออก tangtidtawan-awk
easter *n* เทศกาลอีสเตอร์ teidsagan-easter
eastern *a* ทางตะวันออก tangtawan-awk
easy *a* ง่าย ngai
eat *v. t* กิน gin
eatable *n.* สิ่งที่กินได้ singtigindai
eatable *a* กินได้ gindai
ebb *n* การลดลง ganlodlong
ebb *v. i* ลดลง lodlong
ebony *n* ไม้มะเกลือ maimagleua
echo *n* เสียงสะท้อน siang-saton
echo *v. t* สะท้อน saton
eclipse *n* สุริยุปราคา suriyubparaka
economic *a* ทางเศรษฐกิจ tangsetagid
economical *a* ประหยัด prayad
economics *n.* เศรษฐศาสตร์ setasad
economy *n* ความประหยัด kwamprayad
edge *n* ขอบ kob
edible *a* กินได้ gindai
edifice *n* อาคาร a-kan
edit *v. t* แก้ไข gaekai
edition *n* ฉบับพิมพ์ chababpim
editor *n* บรรณาธิการ bannatigan
editorial *a* เกี่ยวกับการแก้ไข
  giawgabgangaekai
editorial *n* บทบรรณาธิการ bodbannatigan
educate *v. t* ให้การศึกษา haigansuksa
education *n* การศึกษา gansuksa

efface *v. t* ลบออก lob-awk
effect *n* ผลกระทบ pongratob
effect *v. t* กระทบ gratob
effective *a* มีผลกระทบ mipongratob
effeminate *a* อ่อนแอ้น on-aen
efficacy *n* ความมีประสิทธิภาพ
  kwammiprasitipab
efficiency *n* ความมีประสิทธิภาพ
  kwammiprasitipab
efficient *a* มีผลกระทบ mipongratob
effigy *n* หุ่นจำลอง hoonjamlong
effort *n* ความพยายาม kwampayayam
egg *n* ไข่ kai
ego *n* อัตตา atta
egotism *n* ความมีอัตตา kwammi-atta
eight *n* แปด paed
eighteen *a* สิบแปด sibpaed
eighty *n* แปดสิบ paedsib
either *a.,* อย่างใดอย่างหนึ่ง
  yangdaiyangneung
either *adv.* เช่นกัน chaingan
eject *v. t.* ดันออกมา dan-awkma
elaborate *v. t* อธิบายเพิ่มเติม a-
  tibaipeuamteum
elaborate *a* ละเอียด la-iad
elapse *v. t* ผ่านไป panpai
elastic *a* ยืดหยุ่น yeudyoon
elbow *n* ศอก sok
elder *a* แก่กว่า gaegwa
elder *n* ผู้อาวุโส pu-a-wuso
elderly *a* สูงวัย soongwai
elect *v. t* เลือกตั้ง leuaktang
election *n* การเลือกตั้ง ganleuaktang
electorate *n* ผู้มีสิทธิเลือกตั้ง
  pumisitleuaktang
electric *a* เกี่ยวกับไฟฟ้า giawgabfaifa
electricity *n* ไฟฟ้า faifa
electrify *v. t* อัดไฟ ad-fai
elegance *n* ความสง่างาม kwamsa-nga-
  ngam
elegant *adj* สง่างาม sa-nga-ngam
elegy *n* บทกวีไว้อาลัย bodgawiwai-a-lai

element *n* องค์ประกอบ ong-pragob
elementary *a* เบื้องต้น beuangton
elephant *n* ช้าง chang
elevate *v. t* ยกระดับ yokradab
elevation *n* การยกให้สูงขึ้น
ganyokhaisoongkeun
eleven *n* สิบเอ็ด sib-ed
elf *n* เอลฟ์ elf
eligible *a* มีสิทธิ์เลือกตั้ง misidleuaktang
eliminate *v. t* กำจัด gamjad
elimination *n* การกำจัด gangamjad
elope *v. i* หนีตาม nitam
eloquence *n* การพูดอย่างมีวาทศิลป์
ganpudyangmiwatasin
eloquent *a* มีวาทศิลป์ miwatasin
else *a* อื่น eun
else *adv* อย่างแตกต่าง yangtaektang
elucidate *v. t* ชี้แจง chijang
elude *v. t* หลบหลีก loblik
elusion *n* การหลบหลีก ganloblik
elusive *a* หลบหลีกได้ loblikdai
emancipation *n.*
การปลดปล่อยให้เป็นอิสระ
ganplodployhaipen-issara
embalm *v. t* ดองศพ dongsob
embankment *n* เขื่อน keuan
embark *v. t* ขึ้นเครื่องบิน keunkreungbin
embarrass *v. t* ทำให้อาย tamhai-ai
embassy *n* สถานทูต satantut
embitter *v. t* ทำให้ขมขื่น tamhaikomkeun
emblem *n* สัญลักษณ์ sanyalak
embodiment *n* การรวมตัว ganruamtua
embody *v. t.* รวมรวม ruabruam
embolden *v. t.* ทำให้กล้า tamhaigla
embrace *v. t.* โอบกอด ob-god
embrace *n* การโอบกอด gan-obgod
embroidery *n* การเย็บปักถักร้อย
ganyebpaktakroy
embryo *n* ตัวอ่อน tua-on
emerald *n* มรกต mora-got
emerge *v. i* โผล่ออกมา plo-awkma

emergency *n* สถานการณ์ฉุกเฉิน
satanaganchukcheuan
eminance *n* ความโดดเด่น kwamdodden
eminent *a* โดดเด่น dodden
emissary *n* ผู้แทนทางการทูต
putantanggantut
emit *v. t* ปล่อยออกมา ploy-awkma
emolument *n* เงินรายได้ ngeunraidai
emotion *n* อารมณ์ a-rom
emotional *a* ทางอารมณ์ tang-a-rom
emperor *n* จักรพรรดิ์ jakgapad
emphasis *n* การเน้น gannen
emphasize *v. t* เน้น nen
emphatic *a* สำคัญ samkan
empire *n* อาณาจักร a-najak
employ *v. t* จ้าง jang
employee *n* ลูกจ้าง lookjang
employer *n* นายจ้าง naijang
employment *n* การจ้างงาน ganjang-ngan
empower *v. t* ให้อำนาจ hai-umnad
empress *n* จักรพรรดินี jakgapaddini
empty *a* ว่างเปล่า wangplao
empty *v* ทำให้ว่าง tamhaiwang
emulate *v. t* เลียนแบบ lianbaeb
enable *v. t* สามารถ samad
enact *v. t* ออกกฎหมาย awkgodmai
enamel *n* สารเคลือบฟัน sankleuabfun
enamour *v. t* ทำให้หลงใหล tamhailonglai
encase *v. t* ห่อหุ้ม haw-hoom
enchant *v. t* ทำให้หลงใหล tamhailonglai
encircle *v. t.* ล้อมรอบ lomrob
enclose *v. t* ล้อมรอบ lomrob
enclosure *n.* การล้อมรอบ ganlomrob
encompass *v. t* ล้อมรอบ lomrob
encounter *n.* การเผชิญหน้า
ganpacheunna
encounter *v. t* เผชิญหน้า pacheunna
encourage *v. t* ให้กำลังใจ haigamlangjai
encroach *v. i* ล่วงล้ำ luanglam
encumber *v. t.* กีดขวาง gidkwang
encyclopaedia *n.* สารานุกรม saranugrom
end *v. t* สิ้นสุด sinsud

end *n.* การสิ้นสุด gansinsud

endanger *v. t.* ตกอยู่ในอันตราย tokyunai-antarai

endear *v.t* ทำให้เป็นที่รัก tamhaipentirak

endearment *n.* การทำให้เป็นที่รัก gantamhaipentirak

endeavour *n* ความพยายาม kwampayayam

endeavour *v.i* พยายาม payayam

endorse *v. t.* สนับสนุน sanabsanoon

endow *v. t* บริจาค borijak

endurable *a* ทนทานได้ tontandai

endurance *n.* ความทนทาน kwamtontan

endure *v.t.* ทนทาน tontan

enemy *n* ศัตรู sadtru

energetic *a* กระตือรือร้น grateureuron

energy *n.* พลังงาน palang-ngan

enfeeble *v. t.* ตัดกำลัง tadgamlang

enforce *v. t.* เสริมกำลัง seumgamlang

enfranchise *v.t.* ให้สิทธิ์เลือกตั้ง haisitleuaktang

engage *v. t* หมั้น man

engagement *n.* การหมั้น ganman

engine *n* เครื่องยนต์ kreuangyon

engineer *n* วิศวกร witsawagon

English *n* ภาษาอังกฤษ pasa-anglid

engrave *v. t* สลัก salak

engross *v.t* หมกมุ่น mokmoon

engulf *v.t* ปกคลุม pokklum

enigma *n* ปริศนา prissana

enjoy *v. t* สนุกสนาน sanooksanan

enjoyment *n* ความสนุกสนาน kwamsanooksanan

enlarge *v. t* ขยาย kayai

enlighten *v. t.* รู้แจ้ง rujaeng

enlist *v. t* สมัครเป็นทหาร samakpentahan

enliven *v. t.* ทำให้มีชีวิตชีวา tamhaimichiwitchiwa

enmity *n* ความเป็นศัตรู kwampensattru

ennoble *v. t.* ทำให้สูงส่ง tamhaisoongsong

enormous *a* ใหญ่ yai

enough *a* พอเพียง pawpiang

enough *adv* พอเพียง pawpiang

enrage *v. t* ทำให้โมโห tamhaimoho

enrapture *v. t* ทำให้ดีใจ tamhaidijai

enrich *v. t* ทำให้ดีขึ้น tamhaidikeun

enrol *v. t* สมัคร samak

enshrine *v. t* บูชา bucha

enslave *v.t.* กดขี่ godki

ensue *v.i* มีผลตามมา mipontamma

ensure *v. t* ทำให้แน่ใจ tamhainaejai

entangle *v. t* พัวพัน puapan

enter *v. t* เข้า kao

enterprise *n* วิสาหกิจ wisahagit

entertain *v. t* ให้ความบันเทิง haikwambanteung

entertainment *n.* ความบันเทิง kwam-banteung

enthrone *v. t* ให้ขึ้นครองราชย์ haikeunkrongrad

enthusiasm *n* ความกระตือรือร้น kwamgrateureuron

enthusiastic *a* กระตือรือร้น grateureuron

entice *v. t.* ล่อใจ lawjai

entire *a* ทั้งหมด tangmod

entirely *adv* โดยสิ้นเชิง doeysincheung

entitle *v. t.* ตั้งชื่อ tangcheu

entity *n* ธาตุแท้ tadtae

entomology *n.* วิชาว่าด้วยแมลง wichawaduaymalaeng

entrails *n.* เครื่องใน kreuangnai

entrance *n* ทางเข้า tangkao

entrap *v. t.* ทำให้ติดกับ tamhaitidgab

entreat *v. t.* ร้องขอ rongkaw

entreaty *n.* การร้องขอ ganrongkaw

entrust *v. t* ไว้ใจ waijai

entry *n* ทางเข้า tangkao

enumerate *v. t.* แจกแจง jaekjaeng

envelop *v. t* ห่อ haw

envelope *n* ซอง song

enviable *a* น่าอิจฉา na-idcha

envious *a* อิจฉา id-cha

environment *n.* สิ่งแวดล้อม singwaedlom

envy *v* ความอิจฉา kwam-id-cha

envy v. t อิจฉา id-cha

epic n มหากาพย์ mahagab

epidemic n การระบาด ganra-bad

epigram n คำคม kamkom

epilepsy n โรคลมบ้าหมู roklombamu

epilogue n บทส่งท้าย botsongtai

episode n ตอน ton

epitaph n คำจารึกบนหลุมฝังศพ kamjareukbonloomfangsob

epoch n ช่วงเวลาสำคัญในอดีต chuangwelasamkannai-a-did

equal a เท่าเทียม taotiam

equal v. t ทำให้เท่ากัน tamhaitaogan

equal n คนที่มีคุณสมบัติเท่าเทียมกัน kontimikunsombattaotiamgan

equality n ความเท่าเทียม kwamtaotiam

equalize v. t. ทำให้เท่ากัน tamhaitaogan

equate v. t ทำให้เท่ากัน tamhaitaogan

equation n ความเท่าเทียม kwamtaotiam

equator n เส้นศูนย์สูตร seinsoonsut

equilateral a มีด้านเท่ากันทุกด้าน midantaogantookdan

equip v. t จัดหาให้ jadhahai

equipment n อุปกรณ์ ooppagon

equitable a เที่ยงตรง tiangtrong

equivalent a เท่ากัน taogan

equivocal a กำกวม gamguam

era n ยุค yuk

eradicate v. t กำจัด gamjad

erase v. t ลบ lob

erect v. t ทำให้ตั้งขึ้น tamhaitangkeun

erect a ตั้งตรง tangtrong

erection n การตั้งชัน gantangchan

erode v. t กร่อน gron

erosion n การกัดกร่อน gangadgron

erotic a กระตุ้นความรู้สึกทางเพศ gratoonkwamruseuktangped

err v. i ทำผิด tampid

errand n งาน ngan

erroneous a ไม่ถูกต้อง maitooktong

error n ความผิดพลาด kwampidplad

erupt v. i ปะทุ patu

eruption n การปะทุ ganpatu

escape n การหลบหนี ganlobni

escape v.i หลบหนี lobni

escort n การคุ้มกัน gankoomgan

escort v. t คุ้มกัน kumgan

especial a พิเศษ pised

essay n. ความพยายาม kwam-payayam

essay v. t. ทดสอบ todsob

essayist n ผู้ทดสอบ putodsob

essence n เนื้อหา neuaha

essential a สำคัญ samkan

establish v. t. สร้าง sang

establishment n การก่อตั้ง gangawtang

estate n ที่ดิน tidin

esteem n ความเคารพ kwamkaorob

esteem v. t เคารพ kaorob

estimate n. การตีราคา gantiraka

estimate v. t ตีราคา tiraka

estimation n การคาดการณ์ gankadgan

etcetera อื่นๆ eun-eun

eternal ที่ไม่สิ้นสุด timaisinsud

eternity n นิรันดร nirandon

ether n อีเธอร์ ether

ethical a ตามหลักจริยธรรม tamlakjariyatam

ethics n. จริยธรรม jariyatam

etiquette n มารยาท marayat

etymology n. นิรุกติศาสตร์ nirooktisat

eunuch n ขันที kanti

evacuate v. t อพยพ obpayob

evacuation n การอพยพ gan-obpayob

evade v. t หลบหลีก loblik

evaluate v. t ประเมิน prameun

evaporate v. i ระเหย raheuy

evasion n การหลีกเลี่ยง ganlikliang

even a เท่ากัน taogan

even v. t ทำให้เท่ากัน tamhaitaogan

even adv แม้กระทั่ง maegratang

evening n เวลาเย็น welayen

event n เหตุการณ์ hedgan

eventually adv. ในที่สุด naitisud

ever adv เคย keuy

evergreen *a* เขียวชอุ่มตลอดปี kiawcha-umtalawdpi

evergreen *n* ต้นไม้ที่เขียวชอุ่มตลอดปี tonmaitikiawcha-umtalodpi

everlasting *a.* ตลอดกาล talodgan

every *a* ทุก took

evict *v. t* ขับไล่ kablai

eviction *n* การขับไล่ gankablai

evidence *n* หลักฐาน laktan

evident *a.* ชัดเจน chadjen

evil *n* ปีศาจ pisad

evil *a* ชั่วร้าย chuarai

evoke *v. t* ทำให้ปรากฏ tamhaipragod

evolution *n* วิวัฒนาการ wiwattanagan

evolve *v.t* เกี่ยวข้อง giawkong

ewe *n* แกะตัวเมีย gaetuamia

exact *a* แม่นยำ maenyam

exaggerate *v. t.* พูดเกินจริง pudgeunjing

exaggeration *n.* การพูดเกินจริง ganpudgeunjing

exalt *v. t* ยกระดับ yokradab

examination *n.* การทดสอบ gantodsob

examine *v. t* ทดสอบ todsob

examinee *n* ผู้ถูกทดสอบ putooktodsob

examiner *n* ผู้สอบ pusob

example *n* ตัวอย่าง tuayang

excavate *v. t.* ขุดค้น kudkon

excavation *n.* การขุดค้น gankudkon

exceed *v.t* เกิน geun

excel *v.i* เก่ง geng

excellence *n.* ความเป็นเลิศ kwampenleud

excellency *n* พณฯ ท่าน panatan

excellent *a.* ยอดเยี่ยม yodyiam

except *v. t* เว้น wen

except *prep* ยกเว้น yokwen

exception *n* ข้อยกเว้น kawyokwein

excess *n* จำนวนมากเกินไป jamnuanmakgeunpai

excess *a* มากเกินไป makgeunpai

exchange *n* การแลกเปลี่ยน ganlaekplian

exchange *v. t* แลกเปลี่ยน laekplian

excise *n* ภาษีอากร pasi-a-gon

excite *v. t* ตื่นเต้น teuntein

exclaim *v.i* อุทาน u-tan

exclamation *n* คำอุทาน kam-u-tan

exclude *v. t* แยกออก yaek-awk

exclusive *a* เฉพาะ chapaw

excommunicate *v. t.* ไล่ออกจากกลุ่ม lai-awkjakglum

excursion *n.* การเดินทาง gandeuntang

excuse *v.t* แก้ตัว gaetua

excuse *n* ข้อแก้ตัว kawgaetua

execute *v. t* ประหาร prahan

execution *n* โทษประหาร todprahan

executioner *n.* ผู้ประหารชีวิต puprahanchiwit

exempt *v. t.* ยกเว้น wokwen

exempt *a* ได้รับการยกเว้น dairabganyokwen

exercise *n.* การออกกำลัง gan-awkgamlanggai

exercise *v. t* ออกกำลัง awk-gamlanggai

exhaust *v. t.* เหนื่อย neuay

exhibit *n.* ของที่จัดแสดง kongtijadsadaeng

exhibit *v. t* จัดแสดง jadsadaeng

exhibition *n.* การจัดแสดง ganjadsadaeng

exile *n.* การเนรเทศ gannerated

exile *v. t* เนรเทศ nerated

exist *v.i* อยู่ yu

existence *n* การคงอยู่ gankongyu

exit *n.* ทางออก tang-awk

expand *v.t.* ขยาย kayai

expansion *n.* การขยาย gankayai

ex-parte *a* โดยฝ่ายเดียว doeyfaidiaw

ex-parte *adv* โดยฝ่ายเดียว doeyfaidiaw

expect *v. t* คาดหวัง kadwang

expectation *n.* ความคาดหวัง kwamkadwang

expedient *a* เหมาะสม mawsom

expedite *v. t.* เร่ง reng

expedition *n* การเตรียมพร้อม gantriamprom

expel *v. t.* ขับไล่ kablai

expend *v. t* จ่าย jai
expenditure *n* ค่าใช้จ่าย kachaijai
expense *n.* ค่าใช้จ่าย kachaijai
expensive *a* แพง paeng
experience *n* ประสบการณ์ prasobgan
experience *v. t.* มีประสบการณ์
   miprasobgan
experiment *n* การทดลอง gantodlong
expert *a* เชี่ยวชาญ chiawchan
expert *n* ผู้เชี่ยวชาญ puchiawchan
expire *v.i.* หมดอายุ mod-a-yu
expiry *n* วันหมดอายุ wanmod-a-yu
explain *v. t.* อธิบาย a-tibai
explanation *n* การอธิบาย gan-a-tibai
explicit *a.* ชัดเจน chadjen
explode *v. t.* ระเบิด rabeud
exploit *n* การตักตวง gantaktuang
exploit *v. t* ตักตวง taktuang
exploration *n* การสำรวจ gansamruad
explore *v.t* สำรวจ samruad
explosion *n.* การระเบิด ganrabeud
explosive *n.* วัตถุระเบิด watturabeud
explosive *a* ระเบิดได้ rabeuddai
exponent *n* ผู้สนับสนุน pusanabsanoon
export *n* การส่งออก gansong-awk
export *v. t.* ส่งออก song-awk
expose *v. t* เปิดเผย peudpeuy
express *v. t.* แสดง sadaeng
express *a* ด่วน duan
express *n* รถด่วน rodduan
expression *n.* ความประทับใจ
   kwampratabjai
expressive *a.* ประทับใจ pratabjai
expulsion *n.* การขับไล่ gankablai
extend *v. t* ขยาย kayai
extent *n.* ขอบเขต kobket
external *a* ภายนอก painok
extinct *a* สูญพันธุ์ soonpan
extinguish *v.t* ดับไฟ dabfai
extol *v. t.* ยกย่อง yokyong
extra *a* เป็นพิเศษ penpised
extra *adv* อย่างพิเศษ yangpised

extract *n* การตัดตอน gantadton
extract *v. t* ตัดตอน tadton
extraordinary *a.* ผิดธรรมดา pidtammada
extravagance *n* ความฟุ่มเฟือย
   kwamfumfeuay
extravagant *a* ฟุ่มเฟือย fumfeuay
extreme *a* ที่สุด tisud
extreme *n* ความสูงสุด kwamsoongsud
extremist *n* คนหัวรุนแรง
   konhuaroonraeng
exult *v. i* ยินดี yindi
eye *n* ตา ta
eyeball *n* ลูกตา lookta
eyelash *n* ขนตา konta
eyelet *n* รูร้อยเชือก ruroycheuak
eyewash *n* การล้างตา ganrangta

F

fable *n.* นิทาน nitan
fabric *n* ผ้า pa
fabricate *v.t* แต่งเรื่อง taengreuang
fabrication *n* การแต่งเรื่อง
   gantaengreuang
fabulous *a* เยี่ยม yiam
facade *n* ด้านหน้าอาคาร danna-a-kan
face *n* หน้า na
face *v.t* เผชิญหน้า pacheunna
facet *n* เหลี่ยมมุม liammoom
facial *a* เกี่ยวกับใบหน้า giawgabbaina
facile *a* คล่องแคล่ว klongklaew
facilitate *v.t* อำนวยความสะดวก
   umnuaykwamsaduak
facility *n* สิ่งอำนวยความสะดวก sing-
   umnuaykwamsaduak
fac-simile *n* โทรสาร torasan
fact *n* ข้อเท็จจริง kawtedjing
faction *n* สัดส่วน sadsuan
factious *a* เล่นพรรคเล่นพรรค
   lenpaklenpuak
factor *n* ปัจจัย patjai

factory *n* โรงงาน rong-ngan
faculty *n* คณะ kana
fad *n* แฟชั่น fashion
fade *v.i* จางหาย jang-hai
faggot *n* เศษเหล็ก sedlek
fail *v.i* ล้มเหลว lomlew
failure *n* ความล้มเหลว kwamlomlew
faint *a* หน้ามืด nameud
faint *v.i* รู้สึกหน้ามืด ruseuknameud
fair *a* ยุติธรรม yutitam
fair *n.* ความยุติธรรม kwamyutitam
fairly *adv.* อย่างยุติธรรม yangyutitam
fairy *n* เทพนิยาย tebniyai
faith *n* ความศรัทธา kwamsatta
faithful *a* มีความศรัทธา mikwamsatta
falcon *n* เหยี่ยว yiaw
fall *v.i.* ล้ม lom
fall *n* การล้ม ganlom
fallacy *n* ความคิดที่ไม่ถูกต้อง
    kwamkidtimaitooktong
fallow *n* ไม่กระฉับกระเฉง
    maigrachabgracheng
false *a* ผิด pid
falter *v.i* พูดตะกุกตะกัก pudtakuktakak
fame *n* ชื่อเสียง cheusiang
familiar *a* คุ้นเคย kunkeuy
family *n* ครอบครัว krobkrua
famine *n* ความอดอยาก kwam-od-yak
famous *a* มีชื่อเสียง micheusiang
fan *n* พัดลม padlom
fanatic *a* คลั่งใคล้ klanglai
fanatic *n* ผู้คลั่งใคล้ puklangklai
fancy *n* จินตนาการ jintanagan
fancy *v.t* จินตนาการ jintanagan
fantastic *a* เยี่ยม yiam
far *adv.* ห่างไกล hangglai
far *a* ไกล glai
farce *n* ละครตลก lakontalok
fare *n* ค่าโดยสาร kadoeysan
farewell *n* การเลี้ยงอำลา ganliang-umla
farewell *interj.* ลาก่อน lagon
farm *n* ฟาร์ม farm

farmer *n* ชาวนา chaona
fascinate *v.t* ทำให้หลงใหล tamhailonglai
fascination *n.* ความหลงใหล kwamlonglai
fashion *n* แฟชั่น fashion
fashionable *a* ทันสมัย tansamai
fast *a* เร็ว rew
fast *adv* เร็ว rew
fast *n* การอดอาหาร gan-od-a-han
fast *v.i* อดอาหาร od-a-han
fasten *v.t* รัดเข็มขัด radkemkad
fat *a* อ้วน auan
fat *n* ไขมัน kaiman
fatal *a* อันตราย antarai
fate *n* โชคชะตา chokchata
father *n* พ่อ paw
fathom *v.t* ลึก leuk
fathom *n* ความลึก kwamleuk
fatigue *n* ความเหนื่อย kwamneuy
fatigue *v.t* เหนื่อย neuay
fault *n* ความผิด kwampid
faulty *a* มีข้อผิดพลาด mikawpidplad
fauna *n* ช่วงชีวิตของสัตว์
    chuangchiwitkongsat
favour1 *n* ความช่วยเหลือ kwamchuayleua
favour *v.t* ช่วยเหลือ chuayleua
favourable *a* เห็นด้วย henduay
favourite *a* โปรดปราน prodpran
favourite *n* ของโปรด kongprod
fear *n* ความกลัว kwamglua
fear *v.i* กลัว glua
fearful *a.* น่ากลัว naglua
feasible *a* เป็นไปได้ penpaidai
feast *n* งานเลี้ยง nganliang
feast *v.i* จัดงาน jad-ngan
feat *n* ความสำเร็จ kwamsamred
feather *n* ขนนก konnok
feature *n* ลักษณะเฉพาะ laksanachapaw
February *n* กุมภาพันธ์ goompapan
federal *a* สหพันธ์ sahapan
federation *n* สหพันธรัฐ sahapantarat
fee *n* ค่าธรรมเนียม katamniam
feeble *a* อ่อนแรง on-raeng

feed *v.t* ให้อาหาร hai-a-han

feed *n* อาหาร a-han

feel *v.t* รู้สึก ru-seuk

feeling *n* ความรู้สึก kwamruseuk

feign *v.t* แสร้งทำ saengtam

felicitate *v.t* แสดงความยินดี sadaengkwamyindi

felicity *n* ความสุข kwamsook

fell *v.t* ล้ม lom

fellow *n* เพื่อน peuan

female *a* เกี่ยวกับสตรี giawgabsatri

female *n* สตรี satri

feminine *a* เกี่ยวกับสตรี giawgabsatri

fence *n* รั้ว rua

fence *v.t* ล้อมรั้ว lomrua

fend *v.t* ป้องกัน ponggan

ferment *n* เชื้อหมัก cheuamak

ferment *v.t* ทำให้บูด tamhaibud

fermentation *n* การหมัก ganmak

ferocious *a* ดุร้าย durai

ferry *n* เรือข้ามฟาก reuakamfak

ferry *v.t* ส่งข้ามฟาก songkamfak

fertile *a* อุดมสมบูรณ์ u-domsomboon

fertility *n* ความอุดมสมบูรณ์ kwam-u-domsomboon

fertilize *v.t* ใส่ปุ๋ย saipui

fertilizer *n* ปุ๋ย pui

fervent *a* แรงกล้า raenggla

fervour *n* ความรู้สึกท่วมท้น kwamruseuktuamton

festival *n* งานรื่นเริง ngan-reunreung

festive *a* เกี่ยวกับการฉลอง giawgabganchalong

festivity *n* การเฉลิมฉลอง ganchaleumchalong

festoon *n* พวงมาลัย puangmalai

fetch *v.t* รับมา rabma

fetter *n* โซ่ตรวน sotruan

fetter *v.t* ดีตรวน titruan

feud *n.* ความอาฆาต kwam-a-kat

feudal *a* เกี่ยวกับระบบศักดินา giawgabrabobsakdina

fever *n* การเป็นไข้ ganpenkai

few *a* เล็กน้อย leknoy

fiasco *n* ความล้มเหลว kwamlomlew

fibre *n* เส้นใย senyai

fickle *a* แปรปรวน praepruan

fiction *n* นิยาย niyai

fictitious *a* ลวง luang

fiddle *n* ซอ saw

fiddle *v.i* สีซอ sisaw

fidelity *n* ความซื่อสัตย์ kwamseusat

fie *interj* คำอุทานแสดงความไม่พอใจ kam-u-tansadaengkwammaipawjai

field *n* ทุ่งนา tungna

fiend *n* ปีศาจ pisad

fierce *a* ดุร้าย durai

fiery *a* ลุกเป็นไฟ lookpenfai

fifteen *n* สิบห้า sibha

fifty *n.* ห้าสิบ hasib

fig *n* ผลมะเดื่อ ponmadeua

fight *n* การต่อสู้ gantawsu

fight *v.t* ต่อสู้ tawsu

figment *n* สิ่งที่กุขึ้น singtigukeun

figurative *a* อุปมาอุปไมย u-pama-u-pamai

figure *n* รูปร่าง roobrang

figure *v.t* จินตนาการ jintanagan

file *n* แฟ้มเอกสาร faem-ekkasan

file *v.t* จัดแฟ้ม jadfaem

file *n* ตะไบ tabai

file *v.t* ตะไบ tabai

file *n* สำนวนความ samnuankwam

file *v.i.* ยื่นฟ้อง yeunfong

fill *v.t* เติม teum

film *n* ภาพยนตร์ pabpayon

film *v.t* ถ่ายภาพยนตร์ taipabpayon

filter *n* เครื่องกรอง kreunggrong

filter *v.t* กรอง grong

filth *n* ความสกปรก kwamsokgaprok

filthy *a* สกปรก sokgaprok

fin *n* ครีบปลา kribpla

final *a* สุดท้าย sudtai

finance *n* การเงิน gan-ngeun

finance *v.t* จัดหาเงินทุน jadha-ngeuntun
financial *a* ทางการเงิน tang-gan-nguen
financier *n* นักการเงิน nak-gan-nguen
find *v.t* พบ pob
fine *n* ค่าปรับ kaprab
fine *v.t* ปรับ prab
fine *a* ดี di
finger *n* นิ้ว new
finger *v.t* แตะด้วยนิ้ว taeduaynew
finish *v.t* จบ job
finish *n* ตอนจบ tawnjob
finite *a* มีขอบเขต mikobket
fir *n* ต้นสน tonson
fire *n* ไฟ fai
fire *v.t* จุดไฟ judfai
firm *a* แข็ง kaeng
firm *n.* บริษัท borisat
first *a* คนแรก konraek
first *n* หนึ่ง neung
first *adv* อย่างแรก yangraek
fiscal *a* ทางการเงิน tang-gan-nguen
fish *n* ปลา pla
fish *v.i* ตกปลา tokpla
fisherman *n* ชาวประมง chaopramong
fissure *n* รอยแตก roytaek
fist *n* กำปั้น gampan
fistula *n* ฝีคัณฑสูตร feekannasut
fit *v.t* ใส่ได้พอดี saidaipawdi
fit *a* พอดี pawdi
fit *n* ความพอดี kwampawdi
fitful *a* ไม่ต่อเนื่อง maitawneuang
fitter *n* ช่างฟิต changfit
five *n* ห้า ha
fix *v.t* แก้ไข gaekai
fix *n* การแก้ไข gangaekai
flabby *a* อ่อนแรง on-raeng
flag *n* ธง tong
flagrant *a* ชัดแจ้ง chadjaeng
flame *n* เปลวไฟ plewfai
flame *v.i* ลุกไหม้ lookmai
flannel *n* ผ้าสักหลาด pasakkarad
flare *v.i* ลุกเป็นไฟ lookpenfai

flare *n* เปลวไฟ plewfai
flash *n* แสงไฟวาบ saengfaiwab
flash *v.t* วาบ wab
flask *n* ขวดแก้ว kuadgaew
flat *a* ราบ rab
flat *n* ที่ราบ tirab
flatter *v.t* ยกยอ yokyaw
flattery *n* คำยกยอ kamyokyaw
flavour *n* รสชาติ rodchat
flaw *n* ข้อผิดพลาด kawpidplad
flea *n.* หมัด mad
flee *v.i* หนี ni
fleece *n* ขนแกะ kongae
fleece *v.t* ตัดขน tadkon
fleet *n* กองเรือรบ gongreuarob
flesh *n* เนื้อ neua
flexible *a* ยืดหยุ่น yeudyoon
flicker *n* เปลวไฟริบหรี่ plewfairibri
flicker *v.t* ริบหรี่ ribri
flight *n* การต่อสู้ gantawsu
flimsy *a* บาง bang
fling *v.t* ขว้าง kwang
flippancy *n* ความตลกคะนอง
  kwamtalokkanong
flirt *n* การจีบ ganjib
flirt *v.i* จีบ jib
float *v.i* ลอย loy
flock *n* ฝูงชน foongchon
flock *v.i* รวมตัว ruamtua
flog *v.t* โบย boey
flood *n* น้ำท่วม namtuam
flood *v.t* ท่วม tuam
floor *n* พื้น peun
floor *v.t* ล้มคู่ต่อสู้ lomkutawsu
flora *n* พืช peud
florist *n* คนขายดอกไม้ konkaidawkmai
flour *n* แป้ง paeng
flourish *v.i* รุ่งเรือง rungreung
flow *n* การไหล ganlai
flow *v.i* ไหล lai
flower *n* ดอกไม้ dawkmai

flowery *a* เต็มไปด้วยดอกไม้ tempaiduaydawkmai

fluent *a* คล่อง klong

fluid *a* เป็นของเหลว penkonglew

fluid *n* ของเหลว konglew

flush *v.i* ทำให้หน้าแดง tamhainadaeng

flush *n* หน้าแดง nadaeng

flute *n* ขลุ่ย kluy

flute *v.i* เป่าขลุ่ย paokluy

flutter *n* การเต้นรัวของหัวใจ gantenruakonghuajai

flutter *v.t* เต้นรัว tenrua

fly *n* แมลงวัน malaengwan

fly *v.i* บิน bin

foam *n* ฟอง fong

foam *v.t* ทำให้เกิดฟอง tamhaigeudfong

focal *a* เฉพาะจุด chapawjud

focus *n* จุดสนใจ judsonjai

focus *v.t* สนใจ sonjai

fodder *n* อาหารสัตว์ a-han-sat

foe *n* ศัตรู sadtru

fog *n* หมอก mok

foil *v.t* ขัดขวาง kadkwang

fold *n* รอยพับ roypab

fold *v.t* พับ pab

foliage *n* ใบไม้ baimai

follow *v.t* ติดตาม tidtam

follower *n* ผู้ติดตาม putidtam

folly *n* ความเขลา kwamklao

foment *v.t* ประคบ prakob

fond *a* ด้วยความรักใคร่ duaykwamrakkrai

fondle *v.t* ลูบไล้ loop-lai

food *n* อาหาร a-han

fool *n* คนโง่ kon-ngo

foolish *a* โง่ ngo

foolscap *n* กระดาษ gradad

foot *n* เท้า tao

for *prep* เพื่อ peua

for *conj.* เนื่องจาก neuangjak

forbid *v.t* ห้าม ham

force *n* กำลัง gamlang

force *v.t* บังคับ bangkab

forceful *a* มีกำลัง migamlang

forcible *a* โดยการบังคับ doeyganbangkab

forearm *n* แขนท่อนล่าง kaentonlang

forearm *v.t* จัดเตรียม jadtriam

forecast *n* การพยากรณ์ ganpayakon

forecast *v.t* พยากรณ์ payakon

forefather *n* บรรพบุรุษ banpaburud

forefinger *n* นิ้วชี้ newchi

forehead *n* หน้าผาก napak

foreign *a* แปลกปลอม plaekplom

foreigner *n* ชาวต่างชาติ chaotangchat

foreknowledge *n.* การรู้ล่วงหน้า ganruluangna

foreleg *n* ขาหน้า kana

forelock *n* ผมที่ปรกหน้าผาก pomtiproknapak

foreman *n* หัวหน้าคนงาน huanakon-ngan

foremost *a* สำคัญที่สุด samkantisud

forenoon *n* เวลาก่อนเที่ยง welagontiang

forerunner *n* ผู้บุกเบิก pubukbeuk

foresee *v.t* รู้ล่วงหน้า ruluangna

foresight *n* การรู้ล่วงหน้า ganruluangna

forest *n* ป่า pa

forestall *v.t* ป้องกัน ponggan

forester *n* พนักงานรักษาป่าไม้ panak-nganraksapamai

forestry *n* วนศาสตร์ wanasat

foretell *v.t* ทำนาย tamnai

forethought *n* การคิดล่วงหน้า gankidluangna

forever *adv* ตลอดไป talodpai

forewarn *v.t* เตือนล่วงหน้า teuanluangna

foreword *n* กองหน้า gongna

forfeit *v.t* ยึด yeud

forfeit *n* การถูกปรับ gantookprab

forfeiture *n* การยึดทรัพย์ ganyeudsab

forge *n* โรงตีเหล็ก rongtilek

forge *v.t* ปลอมแปลง plomplaeng

forgery *n* การปลอมแปลง ganplomplaeng

forget *v.t* ลืม leum

forgetful *a* ขี้ลืม kileum

forgive *v.t* ให้อภัย hai-a-pai

forgo *v.t* ละทิ้ง lating

forlorn *a* เหงา ngao

form *n* รูปร่าง roobrang

form *v.t.* ทำให้เป็นรูปร่าง tamhaipenroobrang

formal *a* ทางการเงิน tanggan-nguen

format *n* รูปแบบ roobbaeb

formation *n* การสร้างแบบ gansangbaeb

former *a* ก่อน gon

former *pron* อันแรก an-raek

formerly *adv* แต่ก่อน taegon

formidable *a* น่ากลัว naglua

formula *n* สูตร sut

formulate *v.t* กำหนด gamnod

forsake *v.t.* ละทิ้ง lating

forswear *v.t.* ให้การเท็จ haiganted

fort *n.* ป้อมปราการ pompragan

forte *n.* จุดแข็ง judkaeng

forth *adv.* ไปข้างหน้า paikangna

forthcoming *a.* ที่จะมาถึง tijamateung

forthwith *adv.* ทันที tanti

fortify *v.t.* ปลุกใจ plukjai

fortitude *n.* ความอดทน kwam-od-ton

fort-night *n.* สองสัปดาห์ songsabda

fortress *n.* ป้อมปราการ pompragan

fortunate *a.* โชคดี chokdi

fortune *n.* โชค chok

forty *n.* สี่สิบ sisib

forum *n.* เวที weti

forward *a.* ข้างหน้า kangna

forward *adv* ก้าวหน้า gaona

forward *v.t* ส่งต่อ songtaw

fossil *n.* ฟอสซิล fossil

foster *v.t.* ดูแล dulae

foul *a.* สกปรก sokgaprok

found *v.t.* สร้าง sang

foundation *n.* การก่อตั้ง gangawtang

founder *n.* ผู้ก่อตั้ง pugawtang

foundry *n.* โรงหล่อ ronglaw

fountain *n.* น้ำพุ nampu

four *n.* สี่ si

fourteen *n.* สิบสี่ sibsi

fowl *n.* สัตว์ปีก satpik

fowler *n.* นักล่านก naklanok

fox *n.* หมาป่า mapa

fraction *n.* เศษส่วน sedsuan

fracture *n.* รอยแตก roytaek

fracture *v.t* แตก taek

fragile *a.* เปราะ praw

fragment *n.* ส่วนที่แตกออก suantitaek-awk

fragrance *n.* น้ำหอม namhom

fragrant *a.* หอม hom

frail *a.* เปราะ praw

frame *v.t.* กรอบ grob

frame *n* ความมีชื่อเสียง kwammicheusiang

frachise *n.* แฟรนไชส์ franchise

frank *a.* จริงใจ jingjai

frantic *a.* ลนลาน lonlan

fraternal *a.* แฝดต่าง faedtang

fraternity *n.* สมาคม samakom

fratricide *n.* การฆ่าพี่น้อง gankapinong

fraud *n.* การฉ้อโกง ganchawgong

fraudulent *a.* ฉ้อโกง chawgong

fraught *a.* เต็มไปด้วย tempaiduay

fray *n* การทะเลาะวิวาท gantalawwiwat

free *a.* อิสระ isala

free *v.t* ปล่อยเป็นอิสระ ploypen-isala

freedom *n.* ความเป็นอิสระ kwampen-issara

freeze *v.i.* ทำให้แข็ง tamhaikaeng

freight *n.* สินค้าที่ขนส่ง sinkatikonsong

French *a.* เกี่ยวกับฝรั่งเศส giawgabfarangsed

French *n* คนฝรั่งเศส konfarangsed

frenzy *n.* ความบ้าคลั่ง kwambaklang

frequency *n.* ความถี่ kwamti

frequent *n.* ความถี่ kwamti

fresh *a.* สด sod

fret *n.* ความไม่สบายใจ kwammaisabaijai

fret *v.t.* ไม่สบายใจ maisabaijai

friction *n.* แรงเสียดทาน raengsiadtan

Friday *n.* วันศุกร์ wansook

fridge n. ตู้เย็น tuyen
friend n. เพื่อน peuan
fright n. ความกลัว kwamglua
frighten v.t. ทำให้กลัว tamhaiglua
frigid a. แข็ง kaeng
frill n. พู่ห้อย puhoi
fringe n. ตะเข็บ takeb
fringe v.t ใส่ตะเข็บ saitakeb
frivolous a. ไม่น่าสนใจ mainasonjai
frock n. เสื้อนอก seuanok
frog n. กบ gob
frolic n. ความสนุกสนาน
   kwamsanooksanan
frolic v.i. เล่นสนุก lensanook
from prep. จาก jak
front n. ด้านหน้า danna
front a ข้างหน้า kangna
front v.t เผชิญหน้า pacheunna
frontier n. ชายแดน chaidaen
frost n. น้ำค้างแข็ง namkangkaeng
frown n. การทำหน้าบึ้ง gantamnabeung
frown v.i ทำหน้าบึ้ง tamnabeung
frugal a. มัธยัสถ์ mattayad
fruit n. ผลไม้ ponlamai
fruitful a. อุดมสมบูรณ์ u-domsomboon
frustrate v.t. สับสน sabson
frustration n. ความสับสน kwamsabson
fry v.t. ทอด tod
fry n มันฝรั่งทอด manfarang
fuel n. เชื้อเพลิง cheuapleung
fugitive a. หลบหนี lobni
fugitive n. ผู้ลี้ภัย pulipai
fulfil v.t. สมหวัง somwang
fulfilment n. ความสมหวัง kwamsomwang
full a. เต็ม tem
full adv. สมบูรณ์ somboon
fullness n. ความสมบูรณ์ kwamsomboon
fully adv. อย่างเต็มที่ yangtemti
fumble v.i. ซุ่มซ่าม sumsam
fun n. ความสนุก kwansanook
function n. หน้าที่ nati
function v.i ทำหน้าที่ tamnati

functionary n. เจ้าหน้าที่ jaonati
fund n. เงินทุน ngeuntoon
fundamental a. พื้นฐาน peuntan
funeral n. งานศพ ngansob
fungus n. เชื้อรา cheuara
funny n. เรื่องขบขัน reuang-kobkan
fur n. ขนสัตว์ konsat
furious a. โกรธ grot
furl v.t. ม้วน muan
furlong n. มาตรวัดระยะทาง
   matwadrayatang
furnace n. เตาผิง taoping
furnish v.t. ตกแต่ง toktaeng
furniture n. เฟอร์นิเจอร์ furniture
furrow n. ร่องดิน rongdin
further adv. เพิ่มขึ้น peumkeun
further a เพิ่มขึ้น peumkeun
further v.t ส่งเสริม songseum
fury n. ความเดือดดาล kwamdeuaddan
fuse v.t. เชื่อมต่อ cheuamtaw
fuse n ฟิวส์ fuse
fusion n. การหลอมละลาย ganlomlalai
fuss n. ความวุ่นวาย kwamwunwai
fuss v.i วุ่นวาย wunwai
futile a. เป็นหมัน penman
futility n. การไร้ประโยชน์ ganraiprayod
future a. ในอนาคต nai-a-nakod
future n อนาคต a-nakod

G

gabble v.i. พูดพล่าม pudplam
gadfly n. ผู้ก่อความรำคาญ
   pukawkwamramkan
gag v.t. พูดตลก pudtalok
gag n. มุขตลก mooktalok
gaiety n. ความรื่นเริง kwamreunreung
gain v.t. ได้รับ dairab
gain n ผลประโยชน์ ponprayod
gainsay v.t. ปฏิเสธ patised
gait n. ท่าเดิน tadeun

galaxy *n.* กาแล็กซี่ galaxy
gale *n.* ลมแรง lomraeng
gallant *a.* กล้าหาญ glahan
gallant *n* คนกล้าหาญ konglahan
gallantry *n.* ความกล้าหาญ kwamglahan
gallery *n.* แกลเลอรี่ gallery
gallon *n.* แกลลอน gallon
gallop *n.* การควบม้า gankuabma
gallop *v.t.* ควบม้า kuabma
gallows *n.* . ที่แขวนคอนักโทษ
    tikwaenkawnaktod
galore *adv.* มากมาย makmai
galvanize *v.t.* ชุบโลหะ chubloha
gamble *v.i.* พนัน ganpanan
gamble *n* การพนัน ganpanan
gambler *n.* คนเล่นพนัน konlenpanan
game *n.* การแข่งขัน gankaengkan
game *v.i* พนัน panan
gander *n.* ห่านตัวผู้ hantuapu
gang *n.* แก๊ง gang
gangster *n.* นักเลง nakleng
gap *n* ช่องว่าง chongwang
gape *v.i.* อ้าปากค้าง a-pakkang
garage *n.* โรงรถ rongrod
garb *n.* เครื่องแต่งตัว kreuangtaengtua
garb *v.t* แต่งตัว taengtua
garbage *n.* ขยะ kaya
garden *n.* สวน suan
gardener *n.* คนทำสวน kontamsuan
gargle *v.i.* กลั้วคอ gluakaw
garland *n.* พวงมาลัย puangmalai
garland *v.t.* ร้อยมาลัย roymalai
garlic *n.* กระเทียม gratiam
garment *n.* เสื้อผ้า seuapa
garter *n.* สายรัดถุงเท้า sairadtungtao
gas *n.* แก๊ส gas
gasket *n.* ปะเก็น pagen
gasp *n.* การอ้าปากค้าง gan-a-pakkang
gasp *v.i* อ้าปากค้าง a-pak-kang
gassy *a.* ท้องเฟ้อ tongfeu
gastric *a.* เกี่ยวกับกระเพาะอาหาร
    giawgabgrapaw-a-han

gate *n.* ประตูรั้ว praturua
gather *v.t.* รวมตัว ruamtua
gaudy *a.* ฉูดฉาด chudchad
gauge *n.* มาตรวัด madwat
gauntlet *n.* ถุงมือยาว tungmeuyao
gay *a.* เกย์ gay
gaze *v.t.* เพ่ง peng
gaze *n* การเพ่งมอง ganpengmong
gazette *n.* หนังสือพิมพ์ nangseupim
gear *n.* เกียร์ gear
geld *v.t.* ตอน tawn
gem *n* อัญมณี an-yamani
gender *n.* เพศ ped
general *a.* ทั่วไป tuapai
generally *adv.* โดยทั่วไป doeytuapai
generate *v.t.* ก่อกำเนิด gawgamneud
generation *n.* ยุคสมัย yuksamai
generator *n.* เครื่องกำเนิดไฟฟ้า
    keuanggamneudfiafa
generosity *n.* ความใจดี kwamjaidi
generous *a.* ใจดี jaidi
genius *n.* คนฉลาด konchalad
gentle *a.* อ่อนโยน on-yon
gentleman *n.* สุภาพบุรุษ supabburut
gentry *n.* ผู้ดี pudi
genuine *a.* แท้ tae
geographer *n.* นักภูมิศาสตร์ nakpumisad
geographical *a.* เกี่ยวกับภูมิศาสตร์
    giawgabpumisad
geography *n.* ภูมิศาสตร์ pumisad
geological *a.* ทางธรณีวิทยา
    tangtoraniwittaya
geologist *n.* นักธรณีวิทยา
    naktawraniwittaya
geology *n.* ธรณีวิทยา tawraniwittaya
geometrical *a.* ทางเรขาคณิต
    tangrekakanit
geometry *n.* เรขาคณิต rekakanit
germ *n.* เชื้อโรค cheuarok
germicide *n.* ยาฆ่าเชื้อโรค yakacheuarok
germinate *v.i.* แตกหน่อ taeknaw
germination *n.* การแตกหน่อ gantaeknaw

gerund *n.* อาการนาม a-ganranam

gesture *n.* ท่าทาง tatang

get *v.t.* ได้รับ dairab

ghastly *a.* น่ากลัว naglua

ghost *n.* ผี pi

giant *n.* ยักษ์ yak

gibbon *n.* ชะนี chani

gibe *v.i.* เยาะเย้ย yawyei

gibe *n* คำเยาะเย้ย kamyawyei

giddy *a.* น่าวิงเวียน nawingwian

gift *n.* ของขวัญ kongkwan

gifted *a.* มีพรสวรรค์ miponsawan

gigantic *a.* ใหญ่ yai

giggle *v.i.* หัวเราะ huaraw

gild *v.t.* เคลือบทอง kleuabtong

gilt *a.* ฉาบด้วยทอง chabdeuytong

ginger *n.* ขิง king

giraffe *n.* ยีราฟ giraffe

gird *v.t.* พัน pan

girder *n.* นั่งร้าน nangran

girdle *n.* ผ้ารัดเอว parad-eiw

girdle *v.t* พัน pan

girl *n.* เด็กสาว deksao

girlish *a.* เหมือนเด็กผู้หญิง
    meuandekpuying

gist *n.* ใจความสำคัญ jaikwamsamkan

give *v.t.* ให้ hai

glacier *n.* ธารน้ำแข็ง tannamkaeng

glad *a.* ดีใจ dijai

gladden *v.t.* ทำให้ดีใจ tamhaidijai

glamour *n.* ความมีเสน่ห์ kwammisanei

glance *n.* การชำเลือง gan-chamleuang

glance *v.i.* ชำเลือง chamleuang

gland *n.* ความใหญ่โต kwamyaito

glare *n.* แสงจ้า sangja

glare *v.i* เปล่งแสง plengsaeng

glass *n.* แก้ว gaew

glaucoma *n.* ต้อหิน tawhin

glaze *v.t.* เคลือบ kleuab

glaze *n* การเคลือบ gankleuab

glazier *n.* ช่างกระจก changgrajok

glee *n.* ความสนุก kwamsanook

glide *v.t.* ร่อน ron

glider *n.* เครื่องร่อน kreuangron

glimpse *n.* การชำเลือง ganchamreuang

glitter *v.i.* ระยิบระยับ rayibrayab

glitter *n* แสงระยิบระยับ saengrayibrayab

global *a.* ทั่วโลก tualok

globe *n.* โลก lok

gloom *n.* ความมืด kwammeud

gloomy *a.* มืดมัว meudmua

glorification *n.* การเชิดชู gancheudchu

glorify *v.t.* ยกย่อง yokyong

glorious *a.* รุ่งเรือง rungreuang

glory *n.* ความรุ่งเรือง kwamrungreuang

gloss *n.* ความแวววาว kwamwaewwao

glossary *n.* อภิธานศัพท์ a-pitansab

glossy *a.* เป็นมันวาว penmanwow

glove *n.* ถุงมือยาว tungmeuyao

glow *v.i.* เปล่งแสง plengsaeng

glow *n* แสงแวววาว saengwaewwao

glucose *n.* กลูโคส glucose

glue *n.* กาว gao

glut *v.t.* กินอิ่มเกินไป gin-imgeunpai

glut *n* การกินอิ่มเกินไป gangin-im-geunpai

glutton *n.* คนตะกละ kontagla

gluttony *n.* นิสัยตะกละ nisaitagla

glycerine *n.* กลีเซอไลน์ glycerine

go *v.i.* ไป pai

goad *n.* สิ่งกระตุ้น singgratoon

goad *v.t* กระตุ้น gratoon

goal *n.* เป้าหมาย paomai

goat *n.* แพะ pae

gobble *n.* รีบกิน ribgin

goblet *n.* แก้วเหล้า gaewlao

god *n.* พระเจ้า(ชาย) prajao (chai)

goddess *n.* พระเจ้า(หญิง) prajao (ying)

godhead *n.* พระเจ้า prajao

godly *a.* ศักดิ์สิทธิ์ saksit

godown *n.* โกดัง godang

godsend *n.* สิ่งที่พระเจ้าประทานให้
    singtiprajaopratanhai

goggles *n.* แว่นตากันฝุ่น waentaganfoon

gold *n.* ทอง tong

golden *a.* สีทอง sitong

goldsmith *n.* ช่างทอง changtong

golf *n.* กอล์ฟ golf

gong *n.* ฆ้อง kong

good *a.* ดี di

good *n* ความดี kwamdi

good-bye *interj.* ลาก่อน lagon

goodness *n.* ความดี kwamdi

goodwill *n.* ไมตรีจิต maitrijit

goose *n.* ห่าน han

gooseberry *n.* ต้นไม้ tonmai

gorgeous *a.* สวย suay

gorilla *n.* ลิง ling

gospel *n.* คำสอนของพระเยซู kamsonkongprayesu

gossip *n.* การนินทา ganninta

gourd *n.* บวบ buab

gout *n.* โรคเกาต์ rokgout

govern *v.t.* ปกครอง pokkrong

governance *n.* การปกครอง ganpokkrong

governess *n.* ผู้ปกครองหญิง pupokkrongying

government *n.* รัฐบาล rattaban

governor *n.* นายกเทศมนตรี nayoktedsamontri

gown *n.* เสื้อกราวน์ seuagao

grab *v.t.* คว้า kwa

grace *n.* ความสง่างาม kwamsa-nga-ngam

grace *v.t.* ทำให้งดงาม tamhai-ngod-ngam

gracious *a.* งดงาม ngod-ngam

gradation *n.* การเปลี่ยนแปลงช้าๆ ganplianplaengchacha

grade *n.* ระดับ radab

grade *v.t* แบ่งระดับ baengradab

gradual *a.* ทีละน้อย tilanoi

graduate *v.i.* เรียนจบ rianjob

graduate *n* ผู้สำเร็จการศึกษา pusamredganseuksa

graft *n.* การปลูกถ่ายอวัยวะ ganpluktai-a-waiyawa

graft *v.t* ปลูกถ่ายเนื้อเยื่อ pluktaineuayeua

grain *n.* เมล็ดข้าว maledkao

grammar *n.* ไวยากรณ์ waiyagon

grammarian *n.* นักไวยากรณ์ nakwaiyagon

gramme *n.* กรัม gram

gramophone *n.* เครื่องเล่นแผ่นเสียง kreuanglenpansiang

granary *n.* ยุ้งฉาง yungchang

grand *a.* ใหญ่ yai

grandeur *n.* ความสง่างาม kwamsa-nga-ngam

grant *v.t.* ให้ hai

grant *n* เงินช่วยเหลือ ngeunchuayleua

grape *n.* องุ่น a-ngun

graph *n.* กราฟ graph

graphic *a.* เกี่ยวกับภาพ giawgabpab

grapple *n.* ตะขอ takaw

grapple *v.i.* จับ jab

grasp *v.t.* จับ jab

grasp *n* การจับ ganjab

grass *n* หญ้า ya

grate *n.* ตะแกรง tagraeng

grate *v.t* ขูด kud

grateful *a.* เป็นบุญคุณ penboonkun

gratification *n.* ความพึงพอใจ kwampeungpawjai

gratis *adv.* ให้เปล่า haiplao

gratitude *n.* ความสำนึกในบุญคุณ kwamsamneuknaiboonkun

gratuity *n.* เงินรางวัล ngeunrangwan

grave *n.* หลุมฝังศพ lomfangsob

grave *a.* ร้ายแรง rairaeng

gravitate *v.i.* ดูดเข้าหากัน dudkaohagan

gravitation *n.* แรงโน้มถ่วง raengnomtuang

gravity *n.* แรงโน้มถ่วง raengnomtuang

graze *v.i.* เล็มหญ้า lemya

graze *n* การขูด gankud

grease *n* น้ำมันหล่อลื่น nammanlawleun

grease *v.t* หยอดน้ำมัน yodnamman

greasy *a.* ลื่น leun

great *a* ยิ่งใหญ่ yingyai

greed *n.* ความโลภ kwamlob

greedy *a.* โลภ lob

Greek *n.* คนกรีก kongreek
Greek *a* เกี่ยวกับกรีก giawgabgreek
green *a.* เขียว kiaw
green *n* สีเขียว sikiaw
greenery *n.* เขียวขจี kiawkaji
greet *v.t.* ทักทาย taktai
grenade *n.* ลูกระเบิด lookrabeud
grey *a.* ผมขาว pomkao
greyhound *n.* สุนัข sunak
grief *n.* ความเสียใจ kwamsiajai
grievance *n.* ความเสียใจ kwamsiajai
grieve *v.t.* เสียใจ siajai
grievous *a.* ทุกข์ใจ tookjai
grind *v.i.* บด bod
grinder *n.* เครื่องบด keuangbod
grip *v.t.* จับ jab
grip *n* การจับยึด ganjabyeud
groan *v.i.* คราง krang
groan *n* เสียงคราง siangkrang
grocer *n.* คนขายของชำ konkaikongcham
grocery *n.* ร้านขายของชำ
   rankaikongcham
groom *n.* เจ้าบ่าว jaobao
groom *v.t* เตรียมพร้อม triamprom
groove *n.* ป่าโกงกาง pagonggang
groove *v.t* ร่อง rong
grope *v.t.* คลำ klam
gross *n.* รายได้รวม raidairuam
gross *a* ทั้งหมด tangmod
grotesque *a.* พิลึก pileuk
ground *n.* พื้น peun
group *n.* กลุ่ม glum
group *v.t.* จับกลุ่ม jabglum
grow *v.t.* เติบโต teubto
grower *n.* ผู้ปลูกต้นไม้ pupluktonmai
growl *v.i.* คำราม kamram
growl *n* เสียงคำราม siangkamram
growth *n.* การเติบโต ganteubto
grudge *v.t.* เกลียด gliad
grudge *n* ความเกลียด kwamgliad
grumble *v.i.* บ่น bon
grunt *n.* เสียงคำราม siangkamram

grunt *v.i.* คำราม kamram
guarantee *n.* การรับรอง ganrabrong
guarantee *v.t* รับรอง rabrong
guard *v.i.* คุ้มกัน kumgan
guard ผู้คุ้มกัน pukumgan
guardian *n.* ผู้ดูแล pudulae
guava *n.* ฝรั่ง falang
guerilla *n.* ลิง ling
guess *n.* การคาดเดา gankaddao
guess *v.i* เดา dao
guest *n.* แขก kaek
guidance *n.* คำแนะนำ kamnaenam
guide *v.t.* แนะนำ naenam
guide *n.* ไกด์ guide
guild *n.* สมาคม samakom
guile *n.* ความหลอกลวง kwamlokluang
guilt *n.* ความผิด kwampid
guilty *a.* รู้สึกผิด ruseukpid
guise *n.* ลักษณะภายนอก laksanapainok
guitar *n.* กีตาร์ guitar
gulf *n.* อ่าว aow
gull *n.* นกนางนวล noknangnuan
gull *n* คนถูกหลอก kontooklok
gull *v.t* หลอกลวง lawkluang
gulp *n.* การกลืน gangleun
gum *n.* เหงือก ngeuak
gun *n.* ปืน peun
gust *n.* ลมแรง lomraeng
gutter *n.* รางน้ำ rangnam
guttural *a.* แหบแห้ง haebhaeng
gymnasium *n.* โรงยิม rongyim
gymnast *n.* นักยิมนาสติก nakgymnastic
gymnastic *a.* เกี่ยวกับยิมนาสติก
   giawgabgymnastic
gymnastics *n.* ยิมนาสติก gymnastic

habeas corpus *n.*
   หมายส่งตัวผู้คุมขังมาศาล
   maisongtuapukumkangmasan

habit *n.* นิสัย nisai

habitable *a.* พออยู่ได้ pawyudai

habitat *n.* ถิ่นที่อยู่ tintiyu

habitation *n.* ที่อยู่อาศัย tiyu-a-sai

habituate *v. t.* ทำให้เคยชิน tamhaikeuychin

hack *v.t.* โค่น kon

hag *n.* ตม tom

haggard *a.* ซูบผอม soobpom

haggle *v.i.* ต่อรองราคา tawrongraka

hail *n.* ลูกเห็บ lookheb

hail *v.i* ลูกเห็บตก lookhebtok

hail *v.t* ทักทาย taktai

hair *n* ผม pom

hale *a.* กระชุ่มกระชวย grachumgrachuay

half *n.* ครึ่ง kreung

half *a* ครึ่ง kreung

hall *n.* ห้องโถง hongtong

hallmark *n.* เครื่องหมายรับรองคุณภาพ kreuangmairabrongkunnapab

hallow *v.t.* ทำให้ศักดิ์สิทธิ์ tamhaisaksit

halt *v. t.* หยุด yud

halt *n* การหยุดชั่วคราว ganyudchuakrao

halve *v.t.* แบ่งครึ่ง baengkreung

hamlet *n.* หมู่บ้านขนาดเล็ก mubankanadlek

hammer *n.* ค้อน kon

hammer *v.t* ตอก tok

hand *n* มือ meu

hand *v.t* ส่ง song

handbill *n.* ใบปลิว baiplew

handbook *n.* คู่มือ kumeu

handcuff *n.* กุญแจมือ goonjaemeu

handcuff *v.t* ใส่กุญแจมือ saigoonjaemeu

handful *n.* เต็มมือ temmeu

handicap *v.t.* ทำให้พิการ tamhaipigan

handicap *n* คนพิการ konpigan

handicraft *n.* งานฝีมือ ngan-feemeu

handiwork *n.* งานฝีมือ ngan-feemeu

handkerchief *n.* ผ้าเช็ดหน้า pachedna

handle *n.* ที่จับ tijab

handle *v.t* จัดการ jadgan

handsome *a.* หล่อ law

handy *a.* สะดวก saduak

hang *v.t.* แขวน kwaen

hanker *v.i.* อยากได้ yakdai

haphazard *a.* โดยบังเอิญ doeybang-eun

happen *v.t.* เกิดขึ้น geudkeun

happening *n.* เหตุการณ์ hedgan

happiness *n.* ความสุข kwamsook

happy *a.* ความสุข kwamsook

harass *v.t.* ข่มขู่ komku

harassment *n.* การข่มขู่ gankomku

harbour *n.* ท่าเรือ tareua

harbour *v.t* จอดเรือ jawdreua

hard *a.* แข็ง kaeng

harden *v.t.* ทำให้แข็ง tamhaikaeng

hardihood *n.* ความกล้าหาญ kwamglahan

hardly *adv.* ไม่ค่อยจะ maikoyja

hardship *n.* ความทุกข์ยาก kwamtookyak

hardy *adj.* อดทน odton

hare *n.* กระต่ายป่า grataipa

harm *n.* ความเสียหาย kwamsiahai

harm *v.t* ทำให้เสียหาย tamhaisiahai

harmonious *a.* กลมเกลียว glomgliaw

harmonium *n.* ออร์แกนเล็ก organlek

harmony *n.* ความสามัคคี kwamsamakki

harness *n.* บังเหียน banghian

harness *v.t* ควบคุม kwaubkum

harp *n.* ฮาร์พ harp

harsh *a.* กระด้าง gradang

harvest *n.* การเก็บเกี่ยว gangebgiaw

havester *n.* ผู้เก็บเกี่ยว pugebgiaw

haste *n.* ความรีบเร่ง kwamribreng

hasten *v.i.* รีบเร่ง ribreng

hasty *a.* รีบเร่ง ribreng

hat *n.* หมวก muak

hatchet *n.* ขวาน kwan

hate *n.* ความเกลียด kwamgliad

hate *v.t.* ชิงชัง chingchang

haughty *a.* ทะนง tanong

haunt *v.t.* หลอน lawn

haunt *n* สถานที่ที่ไปบ่อย satantitipaiboy

have *v.t.* มี mi

haven *n.* ที่หลบภัย tilobpai

havoc *n.* ความหายนะ kwamhaiyana

hawk *n* เร่ขายของ rekaikong

hawker *n* คนเร่ขายของ konrekaikong

hawthorn *n.* กิ่งที่มีหนาม gingtiminam

hay *n.* ฟาง fang

hazard *n.* สิ่งที่เป็นอันตราย singtipen-
antarai

hazard *v.t* อันตราย antarai

haze *n.* หมอกควัน mokkwan

hazy *a.* พร่ามัว pramua

he *pron.* เขาผู้ชาย kaopuchai

head *n.* หัว hua

head *v.t* ควบคุม kuabkum

headache *n.* ปวดหัว puadhua

heading *n.* หัวเรื่อง huareuang

headlong *adv.* อย่างเร่งรีบ yangrengrib

headstrong *a.* หัวแข็ง huakaeng

heal *v.i.* รักษา raksa

health *n.* สุขภาพ sookapab

healthy *a.* สุขภาพดี sookapabdi

heap *n.* กอง gong

heap *v.t* กองไว้ gongwai

hear *v.t.* ได้ยิน daiyin

hearsay *n.* คำกล่าวอ้าง kamglao-ang

heart *n.* หัวใจ huajai

hearth *n.* เตาไฟ taofai

heartily *adv.* อย่างจริงใจ yangjingjai

heat *n.* ความร้อน kwamron

heat *v.t* ทำให้ร้อน tamhairon

heave *v.i.* ลาก lak

heaven *n.* สวรรค์ sawan

heavenly *a.* ที่วิเศษ tiwised

hedge *n.* แนวพุ่มไม้ naewpommai

hedge *v.t* ล้อม lom

heed *v.t.* เอาใจใส่ aowjaisai

heed *n* การเอาใจใส่ gan-aowjaisai

heel *n.* สันเท้า sontao

hefty *a.* แข็งแรง kaengraeng

height *n.* ความสูง kwamsoong

heighten *v.t.* ทำให้สูง tamhaisoong

heinous *a.* เลวร้าย lewrai

heir *n.* ผู้ได้รับมรดก pudairabmoradok

hell *n.* นรก narok

helm *n.* ตำแหน่งผู้นำ tamnaengpunam

helmet *n.* หมวกกันน็อค muakgannok

help *v.t.* ช่วย chuay

help *n* การช่วยเหลือ ganchuayleua

helpful *a.* เป็นประโยชน์ penprayod

helpless *a.* ไร้ประโยชน์ raiprayod

helpmate *n.* เพื่อน peuan

hemisphere *n.* ครึ่งโลก kreunglok

hemp *n.* กัญชา gancha

hen *n.* ไก่ gai

hence *adv.* ดังนั้น dangnan

henceforth *adv.* ต่อจากนี้ tawjakni

henceforward *adv.* ต่อจากนี้ tawjakni

henchman *n.* ลูกน้อง looknong

henpecked *a.* กลัวภรรยา gluapanraya

her *pron.* เขาผู้หญิง kaopuying

her *a* ของเขาผู้หญิง kongkaopuying

herald *n.* ผู้สื่อข่าว puseukao

herald *v.t* แจ้งข่าว jaengkao

herb *n.* สมุนไพร samoonprai

herculean *a.* ยากมาก yakmak

herd *n.* ฝูงสัตว์ foongsat

herdsman *n.* คนเลี้ยงสัตว์ konliangsat

here ที่นี่ tini

hereabouts *adv.* อยู่แถวนี้ yutaewni

hereafter *adv.* ต่อจากนี้ tawjakni

hereditary *n.* ทางกรรมพันธุ์
tanggammapan

heredity *n.* พันธุกรรม pantugam

heritable *a.* เป็นมรดกตกทอด
penmoradoktoktod

heritage *n.* มรดก moradok

hermit *n.* ฤษี reusi

hermitage *n.* อาศรม a-som

hernia *n.* ไส้เลื่อน saileuan

hero *n.* วีรบุรุษ wiraburud

heroic *a.* กล้าหาญ glahan

heroine *n.* วีรสตรี wirasatri

heroism *n.* วีรกรรม wiragam

herring *n.* ปลา pla

hesitant *a.* ไม่แน่ใจ mainaejai
hesitate *v.i.* ลังเล langlei
hesitation *n.* การลังเลใจ ganlangleijai
hew *v.t.* โค่น kon
heyday *n.* ช่วงรุ่งเรือง chuangroongreuang
hibernation *n.* การจำศีล ganjamsin
hiccup *n.* สะอึก samlak
hide *n.* หนังสัตว์ nangsat
hide *v.t* ซ่อน son
hideous *a.* น่ากลัว naglua
hierarchy *n.* ลำดับการบังคับบัญชา
lamdabganbangkabbancha
high *a.* สูง soong
highly *adv.* อย่างสูง yangsoong
Highness *n.* คำเรียกเจ้า kamriekjao
highway *n.* ทางหลวง tangluang
hilarious *a.* น่าขำ nakam
hilarity *n.* ความสนุกสนาน
kwamsanooksanan
hill *n.* ภูเขา pukao
hillock *n.* โคก kok
him *pron.* เขาผู้ชาย kaopuchai
hinder *v.t.* ขัดขวาง kadkwang
hindrance *n.* การขัดขวาง gankadkwang
hint *n.* คำใบ้ kambai
hint *v.i* บอกใบ้ bokbai
hip *n* สะโพก sapok
hire *n.* การจ้าง ganjang
hire *v.t* จ้าง jang
hireling *n.* คนรับจ้าง konrabjang
his *pron.* ของเขาผู้ชาย kongkaopuchai
hiss *n* เสียงขู่ siangku
hiss *v.i* ทำเสียงขู่ tamsiangku
historian *n.* นักประวัติศาสตร์
nakprawatsat
historic *a.* ที่เกิดขึ้นในประวัติศาสตร์
tigedkeunnaiprawatsat
historical *a.*
เกี่ยวกับการศึกษาประวัติศาสตร์
giawgabgansuksaprawatsat
history *n.* ประวัติศาสตร์ prawatsat
hit *v.t.* ตี ti

hit *n* การตี ganti
hitch *n.* สิ่งกีดขวาง singgidkwang
hither *adv.* ที่นี่ tini
hitherto *adv.* จนบัดนี้ jonbadni
hive *n.* รังผึ้ง rangpeung
hoarse *a.* เสียงแหบ sianghaeb
hoax *n.* การหลอกลวง ganlokluang
hoax *v.t* หลอกลวง lawkluang
hobby *n.* งานอดิเรก ngan-a-direk
hobby-horse *n.* ม้าโยก mayok
hockey *n.* ฮอกกี้ hocky
hoist *v.t.* ชักรอก chakrok
hold *n.* การควบคุม gankuabkum
hold *v.t* ถือ teu
hole *n* หลุม loom
hole *v.t* เป็นหลุม penloom
holiday *n.* วันหยุด wanyud
hollow *a.* เป็นโพรง penprong
hollow *n.* โพรง prong
hollow *v.t* ทำให้เป็นโพรง tamhaipenprong
holocaust *n.* การสังหารหมู่ gansanghanmu
holy *a.* ศักดิ์สิทธิ์ saksit
homage *n.* การคารวะ gankarawa
home *n.* บ้าน ban
homicide *n.* การฆาตกรรม gankatagam
homoeopath *n.* นักบำบัดแบบองค์รวม
nakbambadbaeb-ongruam
homeopathy *n.*
ศาสตร์การบำบัดแบบองค์รวม
satkanbambatbaeb-ongruam
homogeneous *a.* เหมือนกัน meuangan
honest *a.* ซื่อสัตย์ seusat
honesty *n.* ความซื่อสัตย์ kwamseusat
honey *n.* น้ำผึ้ง nampeung
honeycomb *n.* รังผึ้ง rangpeung
honeymoon *n.* การดื่มน้ำผึ้งพระจันทร์
gandeumnampeungprajan
honorarium *n.* เงินสมนาคุณ
ngeunsomanakun
honorary *a.* เป็นเกียรติ pengiad
honour *n.* เกียรติยศ giadtiyod
honour *v. t* ให้เกียรติ haigiad

honourable *a.* น่าเคารพ nakaorob

hood *n.* ฝากระโปรงรถ fagrapongrod

hoodwink *v.t.* ตบตา tobta

hoof *n.* กีบ gib

hook *n.* ตะขอ takaw

hooligan *n.* อันธพาล an-tapan

hoot *n.* เสียงโห่ siangho

hoot *v.i* โห่ ho

hop *v. i* กระโดด gradod

hop *n* การกระโดด gangradod

hope *v.t.* หวัง wang

hope *n* ความหวัง kwamwang

hopeful *a.* มีความหวัง mikwamwang

hopeless *a.* ไร้ความหวัง raikwamwang

horde *n.* โขลง klong

horizon *n.* ขอบฟ้า kobfa

horn *n.* เขา kao

hornet *n.* แตน taen

horrible *a.* น่ากลัว naglua

horrify *v.t.* ทำให้กลัว tamhaiglua

horror *n.* ความน่ากลัว kwamnaglua

horse *n.* ม้า ma

horticulture *n.* การปศุสัตว์ ganpasusat

hose *n.* สายยาง saiyang

hosiery *n.* ถุงเท้ายาว tungtaoyao

hospitable *a.* โอบอ้อมอารี ob-om-a-ri

hospital *n.* โรงพยาบาล rongpayaban

hospitality *n.* ความโอบอ้อมอารี kwam-
ob-om-a-ri

host *n.* เจ้าบ้าน jaoban

hostage *n.* ตัวประกัน tuapragan

hostel *n.* ที่พัก tipak

hostile *a.* เป็นศัตรู pensattru

hostility *n.* ความเป็นศัตรู kwampensattru

hot *a.* ร้อน ron

hotchpotch *n.* จับฉ่าย jabchai

hotel *n.* โรงแรม rongraem

hound *n.* สุนัขล่าเนื้อ sunaklaneua

hour *n.* ชั่วโมง chuamong

house *n* บ้าน ban

house *v.t* ให้ที่พัก haitipak

how *adv.* อย่างไร yangrai

however *adv.* อย่างไรก็ดี yangraigawdi

however *conj* อย่างไรก็ดี yangraigawdi

howl *v.t.* หอน hon

howl *n* การเห่าหอน ganhaohon

hub *n.* จุดศูนย์กลาง judsoonglang

hubbub *n.* เสียงอึกทึก siang-eukkateuk

huge *a.* ใหญ่ yai

hum *v. i* ฮัมเพลง humpleng

hum *n* เสียงฮัมเพลง sianghumpleng

human *a.* เกี่ยวกับมนุษย์ giawgabmanud

humane *a.* มีมนุษยธรรม mimanudsayatam

humanitarian *a* นักมนุษยธรรม
nakmanudsayatam

humanity *n.* มนุษยชาติ manudsayachat

humanize *v.t.* มีใจเมตตา mijaimetta

humble *a.* ถ่อมตัว tomtua

humdrum *a.* น่าเบื่อ nabeua

humid *a.* ชื้น cheun

humidity *n.* ความชื้น kwamcheun

humiliate *v.t.* ทำให้อาย tamhai-ai

humiliation *n.* ความอับอาย kwam-ab-ai

humility *n.* ความอ่อนน้อม kwam-onnom

humorist *n.* ผู้มีอารมณ์ขัน pumi-a-romkan

humorous *a.* มีอารมณ์ขัน mi-a-romkan

humour *n.* อารมณ์ขัน a-romkan

hunch *n.* ลางสังหรณ์ langsanghon

hundred *n.* ร้อย roy

hunger *n* ความหิว kwamhew

hungry *a.* หิว hew

hunt *v.t.* ล่า la

hunt *n* การล่า ganla

hunter *n.* ผู้ล่า pula

huntsman *n.* นายพราน naipran

hurdle1 *n.* เครื่องกีดขวาง
kreuanggidkwang

hurdle *v.t* กระโดดข้ามรั้ว gradodkamrua

hurl *v.t.* ขว้าง kwang

hurrah *interj.* คำอุทานแสดงความยินดี
kam-u-tansadaengkwamyindi

hurricane *n.* เฮอริเคน hurricane

hurry *v.t.* เร่งรีบ rengrib

hurry *n* การเร่งรีบ ganrengrib

hurt *v.t.* บาดเจ็บ badjeb
hurt *n* การบาดเจ็บ ganbadjeb
husband *n* สามี sami
husbandry *n.* การเพาะปลูก ganpawpluk
hush *n* ความเงียบ kwam-ngiab
hush *v.i* ทำให้เงียบ tamhai-ngiab
husk *n.* แกลบ glab
husky *a.* ที่มีเปลือก timipleuak
hut *n.* กระท่อม gratom
hyaena, hyena *n.* ไฮยีน่า hyaena
hybrid *a.* ลูกผสม lookpasom
hybrid *n* สิ่งที่เกิดจากการผสม
  singtigeudjakganpasom
hydrogen *n.* ไฮโดรเจน hydrogen
hygiene *n.* สุขลักษณะ sukkalaksana
hygienic *a.* ถูกสุขลักษณะ
  tooksukkalaksana
hymn *n.* เพลงสวด plengsuad
hyperbole *n.* การพูดเกินจริง
  ganpudgeunjing
hypnotism *n.* การสะกดจิต gansagodjit
hypnotize *v.t.* สะกดจิต sagodjit
hypocrisy *n.* การเสแสร้ง gansesaeng
hypocrite *n.* ผู้เสแสร้ง pusesaeng
hypocritical *a.* เสแสร้ง sesaeng
hypothesis *n.* ข้อสันนิษฐาน kawsannitan
hypothetical *a.* โดยสมมติ doeysommut
hysteria *n.* โรคประสาท rokprasat
hysterical *a.* ตีโพยตีพาย tipoytipai

I *pron.* สรรพนามบุรุษที่หนึ่ง
  sabpanamburudtineung
ice *n.* น้ำแข็ง namkaeng
iceberg *n.* ภูเขาน้ำแข็ง pukaonamkaeng
icicle *n.* แท่งน้ำแข็ง taengnamkaeng
icy *a.* เป็นน้ำแข็ง pennamkaeng
idea *n.* ความคิด kwamkid
ideal *a.* ดีเลิศ dileud
ideal *n* อุดมคติ u-domkati

idealism *n.* อุดมคตินิยม u-domkatiniyom
idealist *n.* นักอุดมคติ nak-u-domkati
idealistic *a.* ในอุดมคติ nai-u-domkati
idealize *v.t.* ทำตามอุดมคติ tamtam-u-
  domkati
identical *a.* เหมือนกัน meungan
indentification *n.* การแสดงตัว
  gansadaengtua
identify *v.t.* แสดงตัว sadaengtua
identity *n.* ลักษณะเฉพาะ laksanachapaw
idiocy *n.* คนโง่ kon-ngo
idiom *n.* สำนวน samnuan
idiomatic *a.* เป็นสำนวน pensamnuan
idiot *n.* คนโง่ kon-ngo
idiotic *a.* โง่ ngo
idle *a.* เกียจคร้าน giadkran
idleness *n.* ความเกียจคร้าน kwamgiadkran
idler *n.* คนเกียจคร้าน kongiadkran
idol *n.* คนที่ได้รับความชื่นชมอย่างมาก
  kontidairabkwamcheunchomyangmak
idolater *n.* ผู้เคารพรูปปั้น
  pukaorobroobpan
if *conj.* ถ้า tam
ignoble *a.* ชั่วช้า chuacha
ignorance *n.* การไม่ใส่ใจ ganmaisaijai
ignorant *a.* ไม่ใส่ใจ maisaijai
ignore *v.t.* ไม่ใส่ใจ maisaijai
ill *a.* ป่วย puay
ill *adv.* ไม่ดี maidi
ill *n* การป่วย ganpuay
illegal *a.* ผิดกฎหมาย pidgodmai
illegibility *n.* สภาพที่ผิดกฎหมาย
  sapabtipidgodmai
illegible *a.* อ่านยาก an-yak
illegitimate *a.* ไม่ชอบธรรม maichobtam
illicit *a.* ผิดกฎหมาย pidgodmai
illiteracy *n.* การไม่รู้หนังสือ
  ganmairunangseu
illiterate *a.* ไม่รู้หนังสือ mairunangseu
illness *n.* ความเจ็บป่วย kwamjebpuay
illogical *a.* ไร้เหตุผล raihedpon
illuminate *v.t.* ส่องสว่าง songsawang

illumination *n.* การส่องสว่าง
gansongsawang

illusion *n.* ภาพหลอน pablon

illustrate *v.t.* ขยายความ kayaikwam

illustration *n.* การขยายความ
gankayaikwam

image *n.* ภาพ pab

imagery *n.* จินตภาพ jintapab

imaginary *n.* มโนภาพ manopab

imagination *n.* การจินตนาการ
ganjintanagan

imaginative *a.* เฟื่อฝัน peufan

imagine *v.t.* นึกคิด neukkid

imitate *v.t.* เลียนแบบ lianbaeb

imitation *n.* การเลียนแบบ ganlianbaeb

imitator *n.* ผู้เลียนแบบ pulianbaeb

immaterial *a.* ไม่มีตัวตน maimituaton

immature *a.* ไม่สมบูรณ์ maisomboon

immaturity *n.* ความไม่สมบูรณ์
kwammaisomboon

immeasurable *a.* วัดไม่ได้ watmaidai

immediate *a* ทันที tanti

immemorial *a.* นมนาน nomnan

immense *a.* มโหฬาร mahoran

immensity *n.* ความมโหฬาร
kwammahoran

immerse *v.t.* หมกมุ่น mokmoon

immersion *n.* การหมกมุ่น ganmokmoon

immigrant *n.* ผู้อพยพ pu-obpayob

immigrate *v.i.* อพยพ monobpayob

immigration *n.* การอพยพ gan-obpayob

imminent *a.* ใกล้เข้ามา glailkaoma

immodest *a.* ไม่สุภาพ ̀maisupab

immodesty *n.* ความไม่สุภาพ
kwammaisupab

immoral *a.* ไม่มีศีลธรรม maimisinratam

immorality *n.* ความไม่มีศีลธรรม
kwammaimisinratam

immortal *a.* เป็นอมตะ pen-ammata

immortality *n.* ความเป็นอมตะ kwampen-
ammata

immortalize *v.t.* ทำให้เป็นอมตะ
tamhaipen-ammata

immovable *a.* เคลื่อนย้ายไม่ได้
keuanyaimaidai

immune *a.* มีภูมิคุ้มกัน mipumkumgan

immunity *n.* ภูมิคุ้มกัน pumkumgan

immunize *v.t.* สร้างภูมิคุ้มกัน
sangpumkumgan

impact *n.* ผลกระทบ pongratob

impart *v.t.* แจ้ง jaeng

impartial *a.* เป็นกลาง penglang

impartiality *n.* ความเป็นกลาง
kwanpenglang

impassable *a.* ห้ามผ่าน hampan

impasse *n.* ทางตัน tangton

impatience *n.* ความไม่อดทน kwammai-
odton

impatient *a.* ไม่อดทน mai-odton

impeach *v.t.* กล่าวโทษ glaotod

impeachment *n.* การกล่าวโทษ
ganglaotod

impede *v.t.* กีดขวาง gidkwang

impediment *n.* สิ่งกีดขวาง singgidkwang

impenetrable *a.* ผ่านเข้าไปไม่ได้
pankaomaidai

imperative *a.* จำเป็น jampen

imperfect *a.* ไม่สมบูรณ์ maisomboon

imperfection *n.* ความไม่สมบูรณ์
kwammaisomboon

imperial *a.* ยิ่งใหญ่ yingyai

imperialism *n.* ลัทธิจักรวรรดินิยม
lattijakgawatniyom

imperil *v.t.* ทำให้เกิดอันตราย
tamhaigeud-antarai

imperishable *a.* ยั่งยืน yangyeun

impersonal *a.* ไม่มีตัวตน maimituaton

impersonate *v.t.* เลียนแบบ lianbaeb

impersonation *n.* การปลอมตัว
ganpromtua

impertinence *n.* ความหยาบคาย
kwamyabkai

impertinent *a.* หยาบคาย yabkai

impetuosity *n.* ความใจเร็ว kwamjairew

impetuous *a.* ใจเร็ว jairew

implement *n.* เครื่องมือ kreungmeu

implement *v.t.* ทำให้มีผล tamhaimipon

implicate *v.t.* เกี่ยวพัน giawpan

implication *n.* ความเกี่ยวพัน kwamgiawpan

implicit *a.* เป็นนัย pennai

implore *v.t.* อ้อนวอน on-wawn

imply *v.t.* บอกเป็นนัย bokpennai

impolite *a.* ไม่สุภาพ maisupab

import *v.t.* นำเข้า namkao

import *n.* การนำเข้า gannamkao

importance *n.* ความสำคัญ kwamsamkan

important *a.* สำคัญ samkan

impose *v.t.* กำหนด gamnod

imposing *a.* สง่างาม sa-nga-ngam

imposition *n.* การวางข้อกำหนด ganwangkawgamnod

impossibility *n.* ความเป็นไปไม่ได้ kwampenpaimaidai

impossible *a.* เป็นไปไม่ได้ penpaimaidai

impostor *n.* คนหลอกลวง konlokluang

imposture *n.* การหลอกลวง ganlokluang

impotence *n.* ความไร้สมรรถภาพ kwamraisamadtapab

impotent *a.* ไร้สมรรถภาพ riasamadtapab

impoverish *v.t.* ทำให้ยากจน tamhaiyakjon

impracticability *n.* การไม่สามารถทำได้ ganmaisamadtamdai

impracticable *a.* ไม่สามารถทำได้ maisamadtamdai

impress *v.t.* ประทับใจ pratabjai

impression *n.* ความประทับใจ kwampratabjai

impressive *a.* น่าประทับใจ napratabjai

imprint *v.t.* ประทับ pratab

imprint *n.* รอยประทับ roypratab

imprison *v.t.* ติดคุก tidkook

improper *a.* ไม่เหมาะสม maimawsom

impropriety *n.* ความไม่เหมาะสม kwammaimawsom

improve *v.t.* ปรับปรุง prabprung

improvement *n.* การปรับปรุง ganprabprung

imprudence *n.* ความไม่รอบคอบ kwammairobkob

imprudent *a.* ไม่รอบคอบ mairobkob

impulse *n.* แรงกระตุ้น raenggratoon

impulsive *a.* หุนหัน hunhan

impunity *n.* การพ้นโทษ ganpontod

impure *a.* ไม่บริสุทธิ์ maiborisut

impurity *n.* ความไม่บริสุทธิ์ kwammaiborisut

impute *v.t.* ใส่ความ saikwam

in *prep.* ใน nai

inability *n.* การไร้ความสามารถ ganraikwamsamad

inaccurate *a.* ไม่ถูกต้อง maitooktong

inaction *n.* ความเฉื่อยชา kwamcheuaycha

inactive *a.* เฉื่อยชา cheuycha

inadmissible *a.* ยอมรับไม่ได้ yomrabmaidai

inanimate *a.* ไม่มีชีวิตชีวา maimichiwitchiwa

inapplicable *a.* ใช้ไม่ได้ chaimaidai

inattentive *a.* เพิกเฉย peukcheuy

inaudible *a.* ไม่ได้ยิน maidaiyin

inaugural *a.* เกี่ยวกับการรับตำแหน่ง giawgabganrabtamnaeng

inauguration *n.* พิธีเข้ารับตำแหน่ง pitikaorabtamnaeng

inauspicious *a.* อัปมงคล ab-pamongkon

inborn *a.* โดยกำเนิด doeygamneud

incalculable *a.* มากมาย makmai

incapable *a.* ไร้ความสามารถ raikwamsamad

incapacity *n.* การไร้ความสามารถ ganraikwamsamad

incarnate *a.* เกิดใหม่ geudmai

incarnate *v.t.* มาเกิดใหม่ maheudmai

incarnation *n.* การเกิดใหม่ gangeudmai

incense *v.t.* จุดธูป judtoob
incense *n.* ธูป toob
incentive *n.* สิ่งจูงใจ singjungjai
inception *n.* การเริ่มต้น ganreumton
inch *n.* หน่วยวัด neuywat
incident *n.* เหตุการณ์ hedgan
incidental *a.* บังเอิญ bang-eun
incite *v.t.* กระตุ้น gratoon
inclination *n.* การโน้มเอียง gannom-eing
incline *v.i.* โค้ง kong
include *v.t.* รวม ruam
inclusion *n.* การรวม ganruam
inclusive *a.* ครอบคลุม krobklum
incoherent *a.* ไม่ต่อเนื่อง maitawneuang
income *n.* รายได้ raidai
incomparable *a.* หาที่เปรียบไม่ได้
   hatipriabmidai
incompetent *a.* ไร้สมรรถภาพ
   raisamadtapab
incomplete *a.* ไม่สมบูรณ์ maisomboon
inconsiderate *a.* ไม่มีน้ำใจ maiminamjai
inconvenient *a.* ไม่สะดวก maisaduak
incorporate *v.t.* รวมกัน ruamgan
incorporate *a.* เป็นหนึ่งเดียว
   penneungdiaw
incorporation *n.* การรวมเข้าด้วยกัน
   ganruamkaoduaygan
incorrect *a.* ไม่ถูกต้อง maitooktong
incorrigible *a.* แก้ไขไม่ได้ gaekaimaidai
incorruptible *a.* ซื่อตรง seutrong
increase *v.t.* เพิ่ม peum
increase *n* การเพิ่มขึ้น ganpeumkeun
incredible *a.* เหลือเชื่อ leuacheua
increment *n.* การเพิ่มขึ้น ganpeumkeun
incriminate *v.t.* กล่าวโทษ glaotod
incubate *v.i.* ฟักไข่ fakkai
inculcate *v.t.* ตอกย้ำ tokyam
incumbent *n.* ผู้ดำรงตำแหน่ง
   pudamrongtamnaeng
incumbent *a* ที่อยู่ในตำแหน่ง
   tiyunaitamnaeng
incur *v.t.* ก่อให้เกิด gawhaigeud

incurable *a.* รักษาไม่หาย raksamaihai
indebted *a.* ติดหนี้ tidni
indecency *n.* ความหยาบคาย kwamyabkai
indecent *a.* หยาบคาย yabkai
indecision *n.* ความไม่แน่ใจ
   kwammainaejai
indeed *adv.* อย่างแท้จริง yangtaejing
indefensible *a.* ป้องกันไม่ได้
   pongganmaidai
indefinite *a.* ไม่จำกัด maijamgad
indemnity *n.* ค่าปรับ kaprab
independence *n.* ความเป็นอิสระ
   kwampen-issara
independent *a.* เป็นอิสระ pen-issara
indescribable *a.* เกินกว่าจะพรรณนา
   geungwajapannana
index *n.* ดัชนี dachani
Indian *a.* เกี่ยวกับอินเดีย giawgab-india
indicate *v.t.* บ่งชี้ bongchi
indication *n.* การบ่งชี้ ganbongchi
indicative *a.* ที่บ่งชี้ tibongchi
indicator *n.* ตัวบ่งชี้ tuabongchi
indict *v.t.* ฟ้องร้อง fongrong
indictment *n.* คำฟ้องร้อง kamfongrong
indifference *n.* ความไม่แตกต่าง
   kwammaitaektang
indifferent *a.* ไม่แตกต่าง maitaektang
indigenous *a.* พื้นเมือง peunmuang
indigestible *a.* ย่อยยาก yoiyak
indigestion *n.* อาการอาหารไม่ย่อย a-gan-
   a-hanmaiyoi
indignant *a.* โกรธ grot
indignation *n.* ความโกรธ kwamgrot
indigo *n.* สีคราม sikram
indirect *a.* อ้อม om
indiscipline *n.* การไม่มีวินัย
   gammaimiwinai
indiscreet *a.* ไม่รอบคอบ mairobkob
indiscretion *n.* ความไม่รอบคอบ
   kwammairobkob
indiscriminate *a.* ไม่เจาะจง maijawjong
indispensable *a.* ขาดไม่ได้ kadmaidai

indisposed *a.* ป่วย puay

indisputable *a.* โต้แย้งไม่ได้ toyaengmaidai

indistinct *a.* คลุมเครือ klumkreua

individual *a.* ส่วนตัว suantao

individualism *n.* ปัจเจกบุคคล padjekbukkon

individuality *n.* ความเป็นเอกเทศ kwampen-ekkated

indivisible *a.* แบ่งแยกไม่ได้ baengyaekmaidai

indolent *a.* ขี้เกียจ kigiad

indomitable *a.* ทรหด torahod

indoor *a.* ภายในอาคาร painai-a-kan

indoors *adv.* ในร่ม nairom

induce *v.t.* ชักชวน chakchuan

inducement *n.* เหตุจูงใจ hedjungjai

induct *v.t.* ชักนำ chaknam

induction *n.* การชักนำ ganchaknam

indulge *v.t.* ตามใจ tamjai

indulgence *n.* การผ่อนผัน ganponpan

indulgent *a.* ผ่อนผันให้ ponpanhai

industrial *a.* เกี่ยวกับอุตสาหกรรม giawgab-utsahagam

industrious *a.* อุตสาหะ utsaha

industry *n.* อุตสาหกรรม utsahagam

ineffective *a.* ขาดประสิทธิภาพ kadprasidtipab

inert *a.* เฉื่อยชา cheuaycha

inertia *n.* ความเฉื่อย kwamcheuay

inevitable *a.* เลี่ยงไม่ได้ liangmaidai

inexact *a.* คลาดเคลื่อน kladkleuan

inexorable *a.* ไม่ยอมแพ้ maiyompae

inexpensive *a.* ไม่แพง maipaeng

inexperience *n.* การไม่มีประสบการณ์ ganmaimiprasobgan

inexplicable *a.* อธิบายไม่ได้ a-tibaimaidai

infallible *a.* ไม่มีข้อผิดพลาด maimikawpidplad

infamous *a.* ไม่มีชื่อเสียง maimicheusiang

infamy *n.* การมีชื่อในทางลบ ganmicheunaitanglob

infancy *n.* วัยทารก waitarok

infant *n.* ทารก tarok

infanticide *n.* การฆ่าทารก gankatarok

infantile *a.* เหมือนทารก meuantarok

infantry *n.* ทหารราบ tahanrab

infatuate *v.t.* ทำให้หลงใหล tanhailonglai

infatuation *n.* ความหลงใหล kwamlonglai

infect *v.t.* ติดเชื้อ tidcheua

infection *n.* การติดเชื้อ gantidcheua

infectious *a.* ติดต่อกันได้ tidtawgandai

infer *v.t.* อนุมาน a-numan

inference *n.* การอนุมาน gan-a-numan

inferior *a.* ด้อยกว่า doykwa

inferiority *n.* ปมด้อย pomdoy

infernal *a.* เกี่ยวกับนรก giawgabnarok

infinite *a.* ไม่สิ้นสุด maisinsud

infinity *n.* ความไม่มีที่สิ้นสุด kwammaimitisinsud

infirm *a.* ไม่แข็งแรง maikaengraeng

infirmity *n.* ความไม่แข็งแรง kwammaikaengraeng

inflame *v.t.* ลุกเป็นไฟ lookpenfai

inflammable *a.* ไวไฟ waifai

inflammation *n.* การอักเสบ gan-akseb

inflammatory *a.* เกี่ยวกับการอักเสบ giawgabgan-akseb

inflation *n.* การขยายตัว gankayaitua

inflexible *a.* ยืดหยุ่น yeudyun

inflict *v.t.* ลงโทษ longtod

influence *n.* อิทธิพล ittpon

influence *v.t.* มีอิทธิพลต่อ mi-ittipontaw

influential *a.* มีอิทธิพลต่อ mi-ittipontaw

influenza *n.* ไข้หวัดใหญ่ kaiwatyai

influx *n.* การไหลทะลัก ganlaitalak

inform *v.t.* ให้ข้อมูล haikawmoon

informal *a.* ไม่เป็นทางการ maipentanggan

information *n.* ข้อมูล kawmoon

informative *a.* เป็นประโยชน์ penprayod

informer *n.* ผู้ให้ข้อมูล pukaikawmoon

infringe *v.t.* ฝ่าฝืน fafeun

infringement *n.* การฝ่าฝืน ganfafeun

infuriate *v.t.* ทำให้โกรธ tamhaigrot

infuse *v.t.* แช่ chae

infusion *n.* การแช่ ganchae

ingrained *a.* ติดแน่น tidnaen

ingratitude *n.* ความอกตัญญู kwam-a-gatanyu

ingredient *n.* ส่วนผสม suanpasom

inhabit *v.t.* อยู่อาศัย yu-a-sai

inhabitable *a.* อยู่ได้ yudai

inhabitant *n.* ผู้อยู่อาศัย puyu-a-sai

inhale *v.i.* หายใจเข้า haijaikao

inherent *a.* เป็นปกติวิสัย penpagatiwisai

inherit *v.t.* สืบต่อ seubtaw

inheritance *n.* การรับมรดก ganrabmoradok

inhibit *v.t.* ห้าม ham

inhibition *n.* การห้าม ganham

inhospitable *a.* ไม่เป็นมิตร maipenmid

inhuman *a.* โหดร้าย hodrai

inimical *a.* ไม่เป็นมิตร maipenmid

inimitable *a.* เลียนแบบไม่ได้ lianbaebmaidai

initial *a.* เบื้องต้น beungton

initial *n.* อักษรแรกของชื่อ aksonraekkongcheu

initial *v.t* ลงชื่อแรก longcheuraek

initiate *v.t.* ริเริ่ม rireum

initiative *n.* การริเริ่ม ganrireum

inject *v.t.* ฉีด chid

injection *n.* การฉีดยา ganchidya

injudicious *a.* ไม่ฉลาด maichalad

injunction *n.* คำสั่งห้าม kamsangham

injure *v.t.* บาดเจ็บ badjeb

injurious *a.* ได้รับบาดเจ็บ dairabpadjeb

injury *n.* การบาดเจ็บ ganbadjeb

injustice *n.* ความไม่ยุติธรรม kwammaiyutitam

ink *n.* หมึก meuk

inkling *n.* ความเฉลียวใจ kwamchaliawjai

inland *a.* บริเวณภายในประเทศ bariwenpainaipratet

inland *adv.* เข้าในประเทศ kaonaipratet

in-laws *n.* โดยการสมรส doygansomrod

inmate *n.* นักโทษ naktod

inmost *a.* สุดซึ้ง sudseung

inn *n.* โรงแรม rongraem

innate *a.* โดยกำเนิด doeygamneud

inner *a.* ข้างใน kangnai

innermost *a.* ส่วนในสุด suannaisud

innings *n.* แต้มเบสบอล taem-baseball

innocence *n.* ความไร้เดียงสา kwamraidiangsa

innocent *a.* ไร้เดียงสา raidiangsa

innovate *v.t.* สร้างนวัตกรรม sangnawattagam

innovation *n.* นวัตกรรม nawattagam

innovator *n.* ผู้สร้างนวัตกรรม pusaengnawattagam

innumerable *a.* นับไม่ถ้วน nabmaituan

inoculate *v.t.* ปลูกฝี plukfee

inoculation *n.* การปลูกฝี ganplukfee

inoperative *a.* ไม่ได้ผล maidaipon

inopportune *a.* ผิดกาละเทศะ pidgalatesa

input *n.* ข้อมูล kawmoon

inquest *n.* การสอบสวน gansobsuan

inquire *v.t.* สอบสวน sobsuan

inquiry *n.* การสอบสวน gansobsuan

inquisition *n.* การสอบสวน gansobsuan

inquisitive *a.* อยากรู้อยากเห็น yakruyakhen

insane *a.* ขาดสติ kadsati

insanity *n.* วิกลจริต wigonjarit

insatiable *a.* ไม่รู้จักพอ mairujakpaw

inscribe *v.t.* จารึก jareuk

inscription *n.* การจารึก ganjareuk

insect *n.* แมลง malaeng

insecticide *n.* ยาฆ่าแมลง yakamalaeng

insecure *a.* ไม่มั่นคง maimaikong

insecurity *n.* ความไม่มั่นคง kwammaimankong

insensibility *n.* การไร้ความรู้สึก ganraikwamruseuk

insensible *a.* ไร้ความรู้สึก raikwamruseuk

inseparable *a.* แยกไม่ได้ yaekmaidai

insert *v.t.* แทรก saek
insertion *n.* การแทรก gansaek
inside *n.* ส่วนใน suannai
inside *prep.* ภายใน painai
inside *a* ภายใน painai
inside *adv.* ภายใน painai
insight *n.* ความเข้าใจลึกซึ้ง
  kwamkaojaileukseung
insignificance *n.* ความไม่สำคัญ
  kwammaisamkan
insignificant *a.* ไม่สำคัญ maisamkan
insincere *a.* ไม่จริงใจ maijingjai
insincerity *n.* ความไม่จริงใจ
  kawmmaijingjai
insinuate *v.t.* สอดแทรก sodsaek
insinuation *n.* การสอดแทรก gansodsaek
insipid *a.* จืดชืด jeudcheud
insipidity *n.* ความจืดชืด kwamjeudcheud
insist *v.t.* ยืนยัน yeunyan
insistence *n.* การยืนยัน ganyeunyan
insistent *a.* ยืนกราน yeungran
insolence *n.* ความทะนง kwamtanong
insolent *a.* อวดดี uad-di
insoluble *n.* ไม่ละลาย mailalai
insolvency *n.* การล้มละลาย ganlomlalai
insolvent *a.* ล้มละลาย lomlalai
inspect *v.t.* ตรวจสอบ truadsob
inspection *n.* การตรวจสอบ gantruadsob
inspector *n.* ผู้ตรวจสอบ putruadsob
inspiration *n.* แรงบันดาลใจ
  raengbandanjai
inspire *v.t.* บันดาลใจ bandanjai
instability *n.* ความไม่มั่นคง
  kwammaimankong
install *v.t.* ติดตั้ง tidtang
installation *n.* การติดตั้ง gantidtang
instalment *n.* การผ่อนชำระเป็นงวด
  ganponchamrapen-nguad
instance *n.* ตัวอย่าง tuayang
instant *n.* ชั่วขณะ chuakana
instant *a.* ทันที tanti
instantaneous *a.* ทันที tanti

instantly *adv.* ในทันที naitanti
instigate *v.t.* กระตุ้น gratoon
instigation *n.* การกระตุ้น gangratoon
instill *v.t.* ปลูกฝัง plukfang
instinct *n.* สัญชาตญาณ sanchattayan
instinctive *a.* เกี่ยวกับสัญชาตญาณ
  giawgabsanchattayan
institute *n.* แต่งตั้งเป็นทางการ
  taengtangpentanggan
institution *n.* สถาบัน sataban
instruct *v.t.* สั่ง sang
instruction *n.* คำสั่ง kamsang
instructor *n.* ผู้สอน pusawn
instrument *n.* เครื่องดนตรี kreungdontri
instrumental *a.* เป็นอุปกรณ์ pen-oopagon
instrumentalist *n.* นักดนตรี nakdontri
insubordinate *a.* แข็งข้อ kaengkaw
insubordination *n.* การแข็งข้อ
  gankaengkaw
insufficient *a.* ไม่พอเพียง maipawpiang
insular *a.* มีทัศนคติแคบ mitasanakatikaeb
insularity *n.* การโดดเดี่ยว gandoddiaw
insulate *v.t.* หุ้มฉนวน humchanuan
insulation *n.* ฉนวน chanuan
insulator *n.* ฉนวน chanuan
insult *n.* การดูถูก gandutook
insult *v.t.* ดูถูก dutook
insupportable *a.* ทนไม่ได้ tonmaidai
insurance *n.* การประกัน ganpragan
insure *v.t.* รับรอง rabrong
insurgent *a.* ก่อกบฏ gawgabot
insurgent *n.* กบฏ gabot
insurmountable *a.* เอาชนะไม่ได้
  owlchanamaidai
insurrection *n.* การจลาจล ganjarajon
intact *a.* ไม่เสียหาย maisiahai
intangible *a.* จับต้องไม่ได้ jabtongmaidai
integral *a.* ครบถ้วน krobtuan
integrity *n.* ความซื่อสัตย์ kwamseusat
intellect *n.* ปัญญา panya
intellectual *a.* เกี่ยวกับปัญญา
  giawgabpanya

intellectual *n.* ผู้มีสติปัญญา pumisatipanya

intelligence *n.* ความฉลาด kwamchalad

intelligent *a.* ฉลาด chalad

intelligentsia *n.* กลุ่มปัญญาชน glompanyachon

intelligible *a.* เข้าใจได้ kaojaidai

intend *v.t.* ตั้งใจ tangjai

intense *a.* เครียด kriad

intensify *v.t.* ทำให้เครียด tamhaikriad

intensity *n.* ความเครียด kwamkriad

intensive *a.* เข้ม kem

intent *n.* ความตั้งใจ kwamtangjai

intent *a.* ตั้งใจ tangjai

intention *n.* ความตั้งใจ kwamtangjai

intentional *a.* ตั้งใจ tangjai

intercept *v.t.* สกัด sagad

interception *n.* การสกัดกั้น gansagadgan

interchange *n.* การแลกเปลี่ยน ganlaekplian

interchange *v.* แลกเปลี่ยน laekplian

intercourse *n.* การร่วมเพศ ganruamped

interdependence *n.* การพึ่งพากัน ganpeungpagan

interdependent *a.* พึ่งพากัน peungpagan

interest *n.* ความสนใจ kwamsonjai

interested *a.* รู้สึกสนใจ ruseuksonjai

interesting *a.* น่าสนใจ nasonjai

interfere *v.i.* แทรกแซง saeksaeng

interference *n.* การแทรกแซง gansaeksaeng

interim *n.* ช่วงระหว่างเวลา cheungrawangwela

interior *a.* ภายใน painai

interior *n.* การตกแต่งภายใน gantoktaengpainai

interjection *n.* การพูดแทรก ganpudsaek

interlock *v.t.* ประสานกัน prasangan

interlude *n.* การแสดงสลับฉาก gansadaengsalabchak

intermediary *n.* สื่อกลาง seuglang

intermediate *a.* ทันที tanti

interminable *a.* ไม่สิ้นสุด maisinsud

intermingle *v.t.* ผสม pasom

intern *v.t.* ฝึกหัด feukhad

internal *a.* ภายใน painai

international *a.* ระหว่างประเทศ rawangprated

interplay *n.* การมีปฏิสัมพันธ์ ganmipratisampan

interpret *v.t.* ตีความ tikwam

interpreter *n.* ล่าม lam

interrogate *v.t.* ซักถาม saktam

interrogation *n.* การซักถาม gansaktam

interrogative *a.* เกี่ยวกับการซักถาม giawgabgansaktam

interrogative *n* ประโยคคำถาม prayokkamtam

interrupt *v.t.* แทรก saek

interruption *n.* การแทรกแซง gansaeksang

intersect *v.t.* ตัดกัน tadgan

intersection *n.* สี่แยก siyaek

interval *n.* ช่วงเวลา chuangwela

intervene *v.i.* แทรกแซง saeksaeng

intervention *n.* การแทรกแซง gansaeksaeng

interview *n.* การสัมภาษณ์ gansampat

interview *v.t.* สัมภาษณ์ sampat

intestinal *a.* เกี่ยวกับลำไส้ giawgablamsai

intestine *n.* ลำไส้ lamsai

intimacy *n.* ความใกล้ชิด kwamglaichid

intimate *a.* ใกล้ชิด glaichid

intimate *v.t.* ทำให้ใกล้ชิด tamhaiglaichid

intimation *n.* การพูดเป็นนัย ganpudpennai

intimidate *v.t.* ขู่ ku

intimidation *n.* การขู่ ganku

into *prep.* เกี่ยวกับ giawgab

intolerable *a.* ทนไม่ได้ tonmaidai

intolerance *n.* การทนไม่ได้ gantonmaidai

intolerant *a.* ทนไม่ได้ tonmaidai

intoxicant *n.* ของมึนเมา kongmeunmao

intoxicate *v.t.* ทำให้มึนเมา tamhaimeunmao

intoxication *n.* การมึนเมา ganmeunmao

intransitive *a. (verb)* ไม่ถ่ายทอด maitaitod

intrepid *a.* กล้าหาญ glahan

intrepidity *n.* ความกล้าหาญ kwamglahan

intricate *a.* ซับซ้อน sabson

intrigue *v.t.* วางแผนร้าย wangpaenrai

intrigue *n* กลอุบาย gon-u-bai

intrinsic *a.* เนื้อแท้ neuatae

introduce *v.t.* แนะนำ naenam

introduction *n.* การแนะนำ gannaenam

introductory *a.* เป็นการแนะนำ penganaenam

introspect *v.i.* สำรวจความรู้สึกตัวเอง samruadkwamrusuktua-eng

introspection *n.* การทบทวนความรู้สึกตัวเอง gantobtuankwamrusuktua-eng

intrude *v.t.* บุกรุก bukruk

intrusion *n.* การบุกรุก ganbukruk

intuition *n.* สัญชาตญาณ sanchattayan

intuitive *a.* โดยสัญชาตญาณ doeysanchattayan

invade *v.t.* บุกรุก bukruk

invalid *a.* เป็นโมฆะ penmoka

invalid *a.* ทุพพลภาพ tubponrapab

invalid *n* คนไข้ konkai

invalidate *v.t.* หักล้าง haklang

invaluable *a.* หาค่ามิได้ hakamidai

invasion *n.* การรุกราน ganrukran

invective *n.* คำหยาบ kamyab

invent *v.t.* ประดิษฐ์ pradid

invention *n.* การประดิษฐ์ ganpradid

inventive *a.* สร้างสรรค์ sasangsan

inventor *n.* นักประดิษฐ์ nakpradid

invert *v.t.* กลับกัน glabgan

invest *v.t.* ลงทุน longtoon

investigate *v.t.* สอบสวน sobsuan

investigation *n.* การสอบสวน gansobsuan

investment *n.* การลงทุน ganlongtoon

invigilate *v.t.* เฝ้าดู faodu

invigilation *n.* การเฝ้าดู ganfaodu

invigilator *n.* ผู้เฝ้าดู pufaodu

invincible *a.* เอาชนะไม่ได้ awlchanamaidai

inviolable *a.* ละเมิดไม่ได้ lameudmaidai

invisible *a.* มองไม่เห็น mongmaihen

invitation *n.* การเชิญ gancheun

invite *v.t.* เชิญ cheun

invocation *n.* คำขอร้อง kamkawrong

invoice *n.* ใบเสร็จ baised

invoke *v.t.* กระตุ้น gratoon

involve *v.t.* เกี่ยวข้อง giawkong

inward *a.* ภายใน painai

inwards *adv.* เข้าข้างใน kaokangnai

irate *a.* โกรธ grot

ire *n.* ความโกรธ kwamgrot

Irish *a.* เกี่ยวกับประเทศไอร์แลนด์ giawgabprated-irland

Irish *n.* ชาวไอร์แลนด์ chao-irland

irksome *a.* น่ารำคาญ naramkan

iron *n.* เหล็ก lek

iron *v.t.* รีด rid

ironical *a.* เหน็บแนม nebnaem

irony *n.* การเหน็บแนม gannebnaem

irradiate *v.i.* ฉายรังสี chairangsi

irrational *a.* ไร้เหตุผล raihedpon

irreconcilable *a.* เข้ากันไม่ได้ kaoganmaidai

irrecoverable *a.* กู้คืนไม่ได้ gukeunmaidai

irrefutable *a.* แย้งไม่ได้ yaengmaidai

irregular *a.* ไม่ปกติ maipakati

irregularity *n.* ความผิดปกติ kwampidpagati

irrelevant *a.* ไม่เกี่ยวข้อง maigiawkong

irrespective *a.* ไม่คำนึงถึง maikamneungteung

irresponsible *a.* ไม่รับผิดชอบ mairabpidchob

irrigate *v.t.* ทดน้ำ todnam

irrigation *n.* การชลประทาน ganchonrapratan

irritable *a.* น่ารำคาญ naramkan

irritant *a.* ระคายเคือง rakaikeung

irritant *n.* สารที่ทำให้ระคายเคือง santitamhairakaikeuang

irritate *v.t.* รำคาญ ramkan

irritation *n.* ความรำคาญ kwamramkan

irruption *n.* การบุกรุก ganbukruk

island *n.* เกาะ gao

isle *n.* เกาะ gao

isobar *n.* เส้นบนแผนที่อากาศ senbonpaenti-a-gad

isolate *v.t.* แยก yaek

isolation *n.* โดดเดี่ยว doddiฟw

issue *v.i.* ออก awk

issue *n.* ประเด็น praden

it *pron.* มัน man

Italian *a.* เกี่ยวกับประเทศอิตาลี giawgabprated-italy

Italian *n.* คนอิตาเลียน kon-italian

italic *a.* เอน ein

italics *n.* ตัวเอน tua-ein

itch *n.* อาการคัน a-gankan

itch *v.i.* คัน kan

item *n.* รายการ raigan

ivory *n.* งาช้าง nga-chang

ivy *n* ไอวี่ ivy

jab *v.t.* ต่อย toy

jabber *v.t.* พูดรัว pudrua

jack *n.* แม่แรง maeraeng

jack *v.t.* บอกผ่าน bokpan

jackal *n.* คนไม่ซื่อตรง konmaiseutrong

jacket *n.* แจกเก็ต jacket

jade *n.* หยก yok

jail *n.* ตาราง tarang

jailer *n.* ผู้คุม pukum

jam *n.* การติดขัด gantidkad

jam *v.t.* ติด tid

jar *n.* ขวดโหล kwadlow

jargon *n.* ภาษาเฉพาะกลุ่ม pasachapawglum

jasmine, jessamine *n.* ดอกมะลิ dawkmali

jaundice *n.* โรคดีซ่าน rokdisan

jaundice *v.t.* เป็นโรคดีซ่าน penrokdisan

javelin *n.* แหลน laen

jaw *n.* ขากรรไกร kagangrai

jay *n.* นกชนิดหนึ่ง nokchanidneung

jealous *a.* อิจฉา id-cha

jealousy *n.* ความอิจฉา kwam-id-cha

jean *n.* กางเกงยีน kangkaengyin

jeer *v.i.* เย้ยหยัน yeiyan

jelly *n.* เยลลี่ jelly

jeopardize *v.t.* ทำให้บาดเจ็บ tamhaibadjeb

jeopardy *n.* การบาดเจ็บ ganbadjeb

jerk *n.* การกระตุก gangratook

jerkin *n.* เสื้อกล้าม seuaglam

jerky *a.* กระตุก gratook

jersey *n.* เสื้อยืด seuayeud

jest *n.* การพูดตลก ganpudtalok

jest *v.i.* พูดตลก pudtalok

jet *n.* เครื่องบินไอพ่น kreungbin-i-pon

Jew *n.* คนยิว kon-yew

jewel *n.* อัญมณี an-yamani

jewel *v.t.* เพชรพลอย pedploy

jeweller *n.* คนขายเพชรพลอย konkaipedploy

jewellery *n.* เครื่องเพชรพลอย kreungpedploy

jingle *n.* เสียงกริ่ง sianggring

jingle *v.i.* ส่งเสียงกรุ่งกริ่ง songsianggrunggring

job *n.* งาน ngan

jobber *n.* พ่อค้าขายส่ง pawkakaisong

jobbery *n.* การทุจริต gantujarit

jocular *a.* ตลก talok

jog *v.t.* วิ่ง wing

join *v.t.* ร่วม ruam

joiner *n.* ช่างไม้ changmai

joint *n.* ข้อต่อ kawtaw

jointly *adv.* พร้อมกัน promgan

joke *n.* เรื่องตลก reuangtalok

joke *v.i.* พูดตลก pudtalok

joker *n.* ตัวตลก tuatalok
jollity *n.* ความรื่นเริง kwamreunreung
jolly *a.* รื่นเริง reunreung
jolt *n.* การกระตุก gangratook
jolt *v.t.* กระตุก gratook
jostle *n.* การกระทบกระแทก gangratobgrataek
jostle *v.t.* กระแทก grataek
jot *n.* ข้อความสั้นๆ kawkwamsansan
jot *v.t.* จดย่อๆ jodyawyaw
journal *n.* นิตยสาร nittayasan
journalism *n.* วารสารศาสตร์ warasansat
journalist *n.* นักข่าว nakkao
journey *n.* การเดินทาง gandeontang
journey *v.i.* เดินทาง deontang
jovial *a.* รื่นเริง reunreung
joviality *n.* ความรื่นเริง kwamreunreung
joy *n.* ความสนุก kwamsanook
joyful, joyous *n.* สนุก sanook
jubilant *a.* ปลึ้มปีติ pleumpiti
jubilation *n.* ความปลึ้มปีติ kwampleumpiti
jubilee *n.* งานฉลอง ngan-chalong
judge *n.* ผู้พิพากษา pupipaksa
judge *v.i.* ตัดสิน tadsin
judgement *n.* คำตัดสิน kamtadsin
judicature *n.* องค์การฝ่ายตุลาการ ongganfaitulagan
judicial *a.* เกี่ยวกับการพิจารณาคดี giawgabganpijaranakadi
judiciary *n.* การพิจารณาคดี ganpijaranakadi
judicious *a.* สุขุม sukum
jug *n.* เหยือก yeuak
juggle *v.t.* ตบตา tobta
juggler *n.* นักเล่นกล naklengon
juice *n* น้ำผลไม้ nampolamai
juicy *a.* ฉ่ำ cham
jumble *n.* ความยุ่งเหยิง kwamyungyeung
jumble *v.t.* ยุ่งเหยิง yungyeung
jump *n.* การกระโดด gangradod
jump *v.i* กระโดด gradod

junction *n.* ชุมทาง chumtang
juncture *n.* จุดเชื่อม judchuam
jungle *n.* ป่า pa
junior *a.* อ่อนวัยกว่า on-waigwa
junior *n.* รุ่นน้อง roonnong
junk *n.* เศษขยะ sedkaya
jupiter *n.* ดาวจูปีเตอร์ daojupiter
jurisdiction *n.* เขตอำนาจศาล kedamnadsan
jurisprudence *n.* หลักกฎหมาย lakgodmai
jurist *n.* นักกฎหมาย nakgodmai
juror *n.* ลูกขุน lookkun
jury *n.* คณะลูกขุน kanalookkun
juryman *n.* คณะลูกขุนชาย kanalookkunchai
just *a.* ยุติธรรม yutitam
just *adv.* เพิ่ง peung
justice *n.* ความยุติธรรม kwamyutitam
justifiable *a.* สมเหตุสมผล somhedsompon
justification *n.* ความสมเหตุสมผล kwamsomhedsompon
justify *v.t.* ให้เหตุผล haihedpon
justly *adv.* อย่างยุติธรรม yangyutitam
jute *n.* ปอ paw
juvenile *a.* เยาว์ yao

keen *a.* ชำนาญ chamnan
keenness *n.* ความชำนาญ kwamchamnan
keep *v.t.* รักษา raksa
keeper *n.* ผู้รักษา puraksa
keepsake *n.* ของที่ระลึก kongtiraleuk
kennel *n.* บ้านสุนัข bansunak
kerchief *n.* ผ้าเช็ดหน้า pachedna
kernel *n.* แก่น gaen
kerosene *n.* น้ำมันก๊าด nammangad
ketchup *n.* ซอสมะเขือเทศ sodmakeuated
kettle *n.* กา ga

key *n.* กุญแจ goonjae

key *v.t* ไขกุญแจ kaigoonjae

kick *n.* การเตะ gante

kick *v.t.* เตะ tay

kid *n.* เด็ก dek

kidnap *v.t.* ลักพาตัว lakpatua

kidney *n.* ไต tai

kill *v.t.* ฆ่า ka

kill *n.* การฆ่า ganka

kiln *n.* กิเลน gilen

kin *n.* ญาติ yad

kind *n.* ชนิด chanid

kind *a* ใจดี jaidi

kindergarten ; *n.* อนุบาล a-nuban

kindle *v.t.* จุดไฟ judfai

kindly *adv.* เมตตา medta

king *n.* กษัตริย์ gasat

kingdom *n.* อาณาจักร a-najak

kinship *n.* ตระกูล tragoon

kiss *n.* การจูบ ganjoob

kiss *v.t.* จูบ joob

kit *n.* ชุดเครื่องมือ chudkreuangmeu

kitchen *n.* ครัว krua

kite *n.* ว่าว waw

kith *n.* เพื่อน peuan

kitten *n.* ลูกแมว lookmaew

knave *n.* คนโกง kongong

knavery *n.* ความไม่ซื่อสัตย์
  kwammaiseusat

knee *n.* หัวเข่า huakao

kneel *v.i.* คุกเข่า kukkao

knife *n.* มีด mid

knight *n.* อัศวิน asawin

knight *v.t.* แต่งตั้งอัศวิน taengtang-asawin

knit *v.t.* ถัก tak

knock *v.t.* เคาะ kaw

knot *n.* น็อต knot

knot *v.t.* ผูกเงื่อน puk-ngeuan

know *v.t.* รู้ ru

knowledge *n.* ความรู้ kwamru

L

label *n.* ป้าย pai

label *v.t.* ติดป้าย tidpai

labial *a.* เกี่ยวกับริมฝีปาก
  giawgabrimfeepak

laboratory *n.* ห้องทดลอง hongtodrong

laborious *a.* ลำบาก lambak

labour *n.* แรงงาน raeng-ngan

labour *v.i.* ใช้แรงงาน chairaeng-ngan

laboured *a.* เปลืองแรง pleuangraeng

labourer *n.* ผู้ใช้แรงงาน puchairaeng-
  gnan

labyrinth *n.* เขาวงกต kaowonggot

lac, lakh *n* จำนวนแสนรูปี
  jamnuansaenrupi

lace *n.* ลูกไม้ lookmai

lace *v.t.* ประดับด้วยลูกไม้
  pradabdoydawkmai

lacerate *v.t.* ฉีกขาด chikkad

lachrymose *a.* ขี้แย kiyae

lack *n.* ความขาดแคลน kwamkadklan

lack *v.t.* ขาด kad

lackey *n.* คนรับใช้ชาย konrabchaichai

lacklustre *a.* น่าเบื่อ nabeua

laconic *a.* สั้นกระชับ sangrachab

lactate *v.i.* ให้น้ำนม hainamnom

lactometer *n.* เครื่องมือวัดความข้นของนม
  kreungmeuwatkwamkonkongnom

lactose *n.* แลกโตส lactose

lacuna *n.* ช่องว่าง chongwang

lacy *a.* คล้ายลูกไม้ klailookmai

lad *n.* เด็กหนุ่ม deknum

ladder *n.* บันได bandai

lade *v.t.* เด็กหนุ่ม deknum

ladle *n.* ทัพพี tabpi

ladle *v.t.* ตักด้วยทัพพี takdoeytabpi

lady *n.* หญิงสาว yingsao

lag *v.i.* อ่อนแรง on-raeng

laggard *n.* คนล้าหลัง konlalang

lagoon *n.* ทะเลสาบ talaysab

lair *n.* ถ้ำ tam
lake *n.* ทะเลสาบ talaysab
lama *n.* พระธิเบต pratibet
lamb *n.* แกะ gae
lambaste *v.t.* โจมตี jomti
lame *a.* พิการ pigan
lame *v.t.* ทำให้พิการ tamhaipigan
lament *v.i.* เสียใจ siajai
lament *n.* ความเสียใจ kwamsiajai
lamentable *a.* น่าเสียใจ nasiajai
lamentation *n.* ความเสียใจ kwamsiajai
lambkin *n.* ลูกแกะ lookgae
laminate *v.t.* เคลือบ kleuab
lamp *n.* ตะเกียง tagiang
lampoon *n.* คำถางถาง kamtaktang
lampoon *v.t.* ถากถาง taktang
lance *n.* หอก hawk
lance *v.t.* ทิ่มด้วยหอก timduayhawk
lancer *n.* พลหอก ponhawk
lancet *n.* มีดหมอ midmaw
land *n.* ที่ดิน tidin
land *v.i.* ลงจอด longjod
landing *n.* การลงจอด ganlongjod
landscape *n.* ภูมิประเทศ pumiprated
lane *n.* ช่องทาง chongtang
language *n.* ภาษา pasa
languish *v.i.* อ่อนแรง on-raeng
lank *a.* ผอมสูง pomsoong
lantern *n.* ตะเกียง tagieng
lap *n.* ตัก tak
lapse *v.i.* ระงับ ra-ngab
lapse *n.* การหมดอายุ ganmod-a-yu
lard *n.* มันหมู manmu
large *a.* ใหญ่ yai
largesse *n.* การให้ ganhai
lark *n.* การเล่นสนุก ganlensanook
lascivious *a.* เสื่อมเสียทางเพศ
  seuamsiatangped
lash *a.* ตำหนิ tamni
lash *n.* คำตำหนิ kamtamni
lass *n.* เด็กสาว deksao
last *a.* สุดท้าย sudtai

last *adv.* ในที่สุด naitisud
last *v.i.* คงอยู่ kongyu
last *n.* สิ่งสุดท้าย singsudtai
lastly *adv.* สุดท้ายนี้ sudtaini
lasting *a.* ทนทาน tontan
latch *n.* กลอน glon
late *a.* ที่ผ่านมา tipanma
late *adv.* ล่าช้า lacha
lately เมื่อไม่นานมานี้ meumainanmani
latent *a.* ที่ซ่อนเร้น tisonren
lath *n.* ไม้ระแนง mairanaeng
lathe *n.* เครื่องกลึง kreunggreung
lathe กลึง grueng
lather *n.* ฟองสบู่ fongsabu
latitude *n.* เส้นรุ้ง senroong
latrine *n.* ห้องน้ำ hongnam
latter *a.* ต่อมา tawma
lattice *n.* โครงสร้างที่ขัดเป็นตาราง
  krongsangtikadpentarang
laud *v.t.* สรรเสริญ sanseun
laud *n.* การสรรเสริญ gansanseun
laudable *a.* สมควรยกย่อง
  somkuanyokyong
laugh *n.* เสียงหัวเราะ sianghuaraw
laugh *v.i* หัวเราะ huaraw
laughable *a.* หัวเราะได้ huarawdai
laughter *n.* การหัวเราะ ganhuaraw
launch *v.t.* เริ่ม reum
launch *n.* การเริ่ม ganreum
launder *v.t.* ซักรีด sakrid
laundress *n.* หญิงซักรีด yingsakrid
laundry *n.* การซักรีด gansakrid
laurel *n.* ความดีความชอบ
  kwamdikwamchob
laureate *a.* ได้รับเกียรติ dairabgiad
laureate *n.* ผู้ได้รับรางวัล pudairabrangwan
lava *n.* ลาวา lava
lavatory *n.* ห้องน้ำ hongnam
lavender *n.* ลาเวนเดอร์ lavender
lavish *a.* ฟุ่มเฟือย fumfeuay
lavish *v.t.* ใช้จ่ายฟุ่มเฟือย chaijaifumfeuay
law *n.* กฎหมาย godmai

lawful *a.* ถูกกฎหมาย tookgodmai
lawless *a.* ผิดกฎหมาย pidgodmai
lawn *n.* สนามหญ้า sanamya
lawyer *n.* ทนาย tanai
lax *a.* หลวม luam
laxative *n.* ยาถ่าย yatai
laxative *a* ผ่อนคลาย ponklai
laxity *n.* ความหย่อน kwamyon
lay *v.t.* วาง wang
lay *a.* เป็นฆราวาส penkarawat
lay *n* คู่นอน kunon
layer *n.* ชั้น chan
layman *n.* ฆราวาส karawat
laze *v.i.* เกียจคร้าน giadkran
laziness *n.* ความขี้เกียจ kwamkigiad
lazy *n.* ขี้เกียจ kigiad
lea *n.* ทุ่งหญ้า tungya
leach *v.t.* กรอง grong
lead *n.* ตะกั่ว tagua
lead *v.t.* นำ nam
lead *n.* การนำ gannam
leaden *a.* ทำด้วยตะกั่ว tamduaytagua
leader *n.* ผู้นำ punam
leadership *n.* ความเป็นผู้นำ
　kwampenpunam
leaf *n.* ใบไม้ baimai
leaflet *n.* ใบปลิว baiplew
leafy *a.* เต็มไปด้วยใบ tempaidauybai
league *n.* สหพันธ์ sahapan
leak *n.* การรั่วไหล ganrualai
leak *v.i.* รั่ว rua
leakage *n.* การรั่ว ganrua
lean *n.* การเอน gan-ein
lean *v.i.* เอน ein
leap *v.i.* กระโดด gradod
leap *n* การกระโดด gangradod
learn *v.i.* เรียน rian
learned *a.* คงแก่เรียน konggaerian
learner *n.* ผู้เรียน purian
learning *n.* การเรียนรู้ ganrianru
lease *n.* การเช่า ganchao
lease *v.t.* เช่า chao

least *a.* น้อยที่สุด noytisud
least *adv.* อย่างน้อยที่สุด yangnoitisud
leather *n.* หนัง nang
leave *n.* การจาก ganjak
leave *v.t.* จาก jak
lecture *n.* การบรรยาย ganbanyai
lecture *v* บรรยาย banyai
lecturer *n.* ผู้บรรยาย pubanyai
ledger *n.* แผ่นหินเหนือหลุมฝังศพ
　paenhinneualumfangsob
lee *n.* ที่บังลม tibanglom
leech *n.* ปลิง pling
leek *n.* ต้นหอม tonhom
left *a.* ซ้าย sai
left *n.* ด้านซ้าย dansai
leftist *n* ผู้นิยมฝ่ายซ้าย putiyomfaisai
leg *n.* ขา ka
legacy *n.* มรดก moradok
legal *a.* ถูกกฎหมาย tookgodmai
legality *n.* ความถูกต้องตามกฎหมาย
　kwamtooktongtamgodmai
legalize *v.t.* ทำให้ถูกกฎหมาย
　tamhaitookgodmai
legend *n.* ตำนาน tamnan
legendary *a.* เป็นตำนาน pentamnan
leghorn *n.* ไก่ gai
legible *a.* อ่านออกได้ an-awkdai
legibly *adv.* อ่านง่าย an-ngai
legion *n.* กองทหาร gongtahan
legionary *n.* เกี่ยวกับกองทหาร
　giawgabgongtahan
legislate *v.i.* ออกกฎหมาย awkgodmai
legislation *n.* การออกกฎหมาย gan-
　awkgodmai
legislative *a.* เกี่ยวกับการออกกฎหมาย
　giawgabgan-awkgodmai
legislator *n.* ผู้ออกกฎหมาย pu-
　awkgodmai
legislature *n.* สภานิติบัญญัติ
　sapanitibanyat
legitimacy *n.* ความชอบธรรม
　kwamchobtam

legitimate *a.* ชอบธรรม chobtam
leisure *n.* สันทนาการ santanagan
leisure *a* เพื่อความบันเทิง peuakwambanteung
leisurely *a.* ความสบาย kwamsabai
leisurely *adv.* อย่างไม่รีบร้อน yangmairibron
lemon *n.* มะนาว manao
lemonade *n.* น้ำมะนาว nammanao
lend *v.t.* ให้ยืม haiyeum
length *n.* ความยาว kwamyao
lengthen *v.t.* ทำให้ยาว tamhaiyao
lengthy *a.* ที่ยืดยาว tiyeudyao
lenience, leniency *n.* ความปรานี kwamprani
lenient *a.* ปรานี prani
lens *n.* เลนส์ lens
lentil *n.* ถั่วชนิดหนึ่ง tauchanidneung
Leo *n.* ราศีสิงห์ rasising
leonine *a* เกี่ยวกับสิงโต giawgabsingto
leopard *n.* เสือ seua
leper *n.* คนเป็นโรคเรื้อน konperokreuan
leprosy *n.* โรคเรื้อน rokreun
leprous *a.* เกี่ยวกับโรคเรื้อน giawgabrokreun
less *a.* น้อย noy
less *n* จำนวนที่น้อยกว่า jamnuantinoykwa
less *adv.* น้อย noy
less *prep.* หักออก hak-awk
lessee *n.* ผู้เช่า puchao
lessen *v.t* ทำให้ลดลง tamhailodlong
lesser *a.* น้อยกว่า noykwa
lesson *n.* บทเรียน bodrian
lest *conj.* ด้วยเกรงว่า dauykrengwa
let *v.t.* ปล่อย ploy
lethal *a.* อันตราย antarai
lethargic *a.* เฉื่อยชา cheuycha
lethargy *n.* ความเฉื่อยชา kwamcheuaycha
letter *n* จดหมาย jobmai
level *n.* ระดับ radab
level *a* เสมอกัน sameugan
level *v.t.* ทำให้เรียบ tamhairiab

lever *n.* ชะแลง chalaeng
lever *v.t.* งัด ngad
leverage *n.* การงัด gan-ngad
levity *n.* ความคะนอง kwamkanong
levy *v.t.* ยึดทรัพย์ yeudsab
levy *n.* การยึดทรัพย์ ganyeudsab
lewd *a.* ลามก lamok
lexicography *n.* การรวบรวมพจนานุกรม ganruabruampojjananugrom
lexicon *n.* พจนานุกรม pojjananugrom
liability *n.* ความรับผิด kwamrabpid
liable *a.* รับผิดชอบ rabpidchob
liaison *n.* ผู้ประสานงาน puprasan-ngan
liar *n.* คนโกหก kongohok
libel *n.* การหมิ่นประมาท ganminpramat
libel *v.t.* หมิ่นประมาท minpramat
liberal *a.* อิสระ isara
liberalism *n.* เสรีนิยม seriniyom
liberality *n.* ความโอบอ้อมอารี kwam-ob-aom-ari
liberate *v.t.* ปล่อยเป็นอิสระ ploypen-isara
liberation *n.* อิสรภาพ isarapab
liberator *n.* ผู้กู้อิสรภาพ pugu-isarapab
libertine *n.* คนไร้ศีลธรรม konraisinratam
liberty *n.* อิสรภาพ isarabab
librarian *n.* บรรณารักษ์ bannarak
library *n.* ห้องสมุด hongsamud
licence *n.* ใบอนุญาต bai-a-nuyad
license *v.t.* อนุญาต a-nuyad
licensee *n.* ผู้ได้รับอนุญาต pudairab-a-nuyad
licentious *a.* ไร้ศีลธรรม raisilatam
lick *v.t.* เลีย lia
lick *n* การเลีย ganlia
lid *n.* ฝา fa
lie *v.i.* วาง wang
lie *v.i* โกหก gohok
lie *n* การโกหก gangohok
lien *n.* ข้อผูกมัด kawpukmad
lieu *n.* การแทน gantaen
lieutenant *n.* ร้อยโท royto
life *n* ชีวิต chiwit

lifeless *a.* ไร้ชีวิตชีวา raichiwitchiwa
lifelong *a.* ตลอดชีวิต talawdchiwit
lift *n.* ลิฟต์ lift
lift *v.t.* ยก yok
light *n.* แสง saeng
light *a* สว่าง sawang
light *v.t.* จุดไฟ judfai
lighten *v.i.* ทำให้สว่าง tamhaisawang
lighter *n.* ไฟแช็ก faichak
lightly *adv.* เบา bao
lightening *n.* การทำให้เบาขึ้น gantamhaibaokeun
lignite *n.* ลิกไนต์ lignite
like *a.* เหมือนกัน meuangan
like *n.* สิ่งที่ชอบ sintichob
like *v.t.* ชอบ chob
like *prep* เป็นลักษณะเฉพาะ penlaksanachapaw
likelihood *n.* ความเป็นไปได้ kwampenpaidai
likely *a.* เป็นไปได้ penpaidai
liken *v.t.* เปรียบเสมือน priabsameuan
likeness *n.* ความชอบ kwamchob
likewise *adv.* เช่นเดียวกัน chaindiaogan
liking *n.* ความชอบ kwamchob
lilac *n.* ดอกไลแลค dawk-lilac
lily *n.* ดอกลิลี่ dawk-lily
limb *n.* กิ่ง ging
limber *v.t.* ทำให้งอได้ tamhai-ngawdai
limber *n* รถลากปืนใหญ่ rodlakpeunyai
lime *n.* มะนาว manao
lime *v.t* ทำให้เป็นคราบเหนียว tanhaipenkrabneow
lime *n.* ปูนขาว poonkao
limelight *n.* ไฟฉายบนเวที faichaibonweti
limit *n.* การจำกัด ganjamgad
limit *v.t.* จำกัด jamgad
limitation *n.* การจำกัด ganjamgad
limited *a.* ถูกจำกัด tookjamgad
limitless *a.* ไม่จำกัด maijamgad
line *n.* แถว taew
line *v.t.* เข้าแถว kaotaew

line *v.t.* ทำให้เป็นรอย tamhaipenroy
lineage *n.* เชื้อสาย cheuasai
linen *n.* ลินิน linin
linger *v.i.* อ้อยอิ่ง auy-ing
lingo *n.* ภาษาเฉพาะกลุ่ม pasachapawglum
lingua franca *n.* ภาษากลาง pasaglang
lingual *a.* เกี่ยวกับภาษา giawgabpasa
linguist *n.* ผู้เชี่ยวชาญด้านภาษา puchiawchandanpasa
linguistic *a.* เกี่ยวกับภาษา giawgabpasa
linguistics *n.* ภาษาศาสตร์ pasasat
lining *n* การบุรอง ganburong
link *n.* ความเชื่อมโยง kwamcheuamyong
link *v.t* เชื่อมโยง cheuamyong
linseed *n.* เมล็ดฝ้าย maledfai
lintel *n.* ทับหลัง tablang
lion *n* สิงโต singto
lioness *n.* สิงโตตัวเมีย singtotuamia
lip *n.* ริมฝีปาก rimfeepak
liquefy *v.t.* กลายเป็นของเหลว glaipenkonglew
liquid *a.* เป็นของเหลว penkonglew
liquid *n* ของเหลว konglew
liquidate *v.t.* ชำระหนี้ chamrani
liquidation *n.* การชำระหนี้ ganchamrani
liquor *n.* เหล้า lao
lisp *v.t.* พูดไม่ชัด pudmaichad
lisp *n* การพูดไม่ชัด ganpudmaichad
list *n.* รายการ raigan
list *v.t.* ทำรายการ tanraigan
listen *v.i.* ฟัง fung
listener *n.* ผู้ฟัง pufang
listless *a.* ไร้ชีวิตชีวา raichiwitchiwa
lists *n.* สนามกีฬา sanamgila
literacy *n.* การอ่านออกเขียนได้ gan-an-awkkiandai
literal *a.* ตามตัวอักษร tamtau-awkson
literary *a.* เกี่ยวกับการประพันธ์ giawgabganprapan
literate *a.* รู้หนังสือ runangseu
literature *n.* วรรณคดี wannakadi

litigant *n.* คู่กรณี kugorani
litigate *v.t.* ฟ้องร้อง fongrong
litigation *n.* การฟ้องร้อง ganfongrong
litre *n.* ลิตร litre
litter *n.* ขยะ kaya
litter *v.t.* ทิ้งเรี่ยราด tingriarad
litterateur *n.* นักวรรณคดี nakwannakadi
little *a.* เล็กน้อย leknoy
little *adv.* ไม่มาก maimak
little *n.* สิ่งเล็กน้อย singleknoy
littoral *a.* ชายฝั่ง chaifang
liturgical *a.* เกี่ยวกับพิธีสวด
  giawgabpitisuad
live *v.i.* มีชีวิต michiwit
live *a.* มีชีวิตชีวา michiwitchiwa
livelihood *n.* การดำรงชีพ
  gandamrongchib
lively *a.* สดชื่น sodcheun
liver *n.* ตับ tab
livery *n.* เครื่องแบบ kreungbaeb
living *a.* มีชีวิตอยู่ michiwityu
living *n* การดำรงชีพ gandamrongchib
lizard *n.* จิ้งจก jingjok
load *n.* ของบรรทุก kongbantook
load *v.t.* บรรจุ banju
loadstar *n.* ดาวนำทาง daonamtang
loadstone *n.* แร่แม่เหล็ก raemaelek
loaf *n.* ขนมปัง kanompang
loaf *v.i.* เดินทอดน่อง duentodnong
loafer *n.* คนขี้เกียจ konkigiad
loan *n.* การกู้ยืม ganguyeum
loan *v.t.* กู้ยืม guyeum
loath *a.* เกลียดชัง gliadchang
loathe *v.t.* ทำให้เกลียด tamhaigliad
loathsome *a.* น่ารังเกียจ naranggiad
lobby *n.* ล็อบบี้ lobby
lobe *n.* ติ่งหู tinghu
lobster *n.* ล็อบสเตอร์ lobster
local *a.* ท้องถิ่น tongtin
locale *n.* สถานที่เกิดเหตุ satantigeudhed
locality *n.* ท้องถิ่น tongtin
localize *v.t.* จำกัด jamgad

locate *v.t.* ตั้งอยู่ tangyu
location *n.* ทำเล tamlay
lock *n.* การติดขัด gantidkad
lock *v.t* ลงกลอน longglon
lock *n* แม่กุญแจ maegunjae
locker *n.* ล็อกเกอร์ locker
locket *n.* ล็อกเกต locket
locomotive *n.* หัวรถจักร huarodjak
locus *n.* สถานที่ satanti
locust *n.* ตั๊กแตน takgataen
locution *n.* สำนวน samnuan
lodge *n.* ที่พัก tipak
lodge *v.t.* พัก pak
lodging *n.* การเข้าพัก gankaopak
loft *n.* การตีลูกโด่ง gantilookdong
lofty *a.* ชั้นสูง chansoong
log *n.* การบันทึก ganbanteuk
logarithm *n.* ลอการิทึม logarithm
loggerhead *n.* คนโง่ kon-ngo
logic *n.* ตรรกะ takga
logical *a.* เกี่ยวกับตรรกะ giawgabtakga
logician *n.* ผู้เชี่ยวชาญในตรรกวิทยา
  puchiawchannaitakgawittaya
loin *n.* เอว eiw
loiter *v.i.* ทอดหุ่ย todhui
loll *v.i.* แกว่ง gwaeng
lollipop *n.* อมยิ้ม om-yim
lone *a.* โดดเดี่ยว doddiaw
loneliness *n.* ความเหงา kwam-ngao
lonely *a.* เหงา ngao
lonesome *a.* เหงา ngao
long *a.* ยาว yao
long *adv* ยาวนาน yaonan
long *v.i* ปรารถนา pratana
longevity *n.* การมีอายุยืน ganmi-a-yuyeun
longing *n.* ความปรารถนา kwampratana
longitude *n.* เส้นแวง senwaeng
look *v.i* ค้นหา konha
look *n* การค้นหา gankonha
loom *n* เครื่องทอผ้า kreuangtawpa
loom *v.i.* ทอผ้า tawpa
loop *n.* ห่วง huang

loop-hole *n.* ช่องโหว่ chongwo
loose *a.* หลวม luam
loose *v.t.* ปล่อย ploy
loosen *v.t.* ทำให้หลวม tamhailuam
loot *n.* การปล้น ganplon
loot *v.i.* ปล้น plon
lop *v.t.* ตัด tad
lop *n.* ส่วนที่ถูกตัดออก suantitooktad-awk
lord *n.* ลอร์ด lord
lordly *a.* สง่า sa-nga
lordship *n.* ตำแหน่งขุนนาง tamnaengkunnang
lore *n.* เรื่องเล่า reuanglao
lorry *n.* รถบรรทุก rodbantook
lose *v.t.* สูญเสีย soonsia
loss *n.* ความสูญเสีย kwamsoonsia
lot *n.* การจับสลาก gangabchalak
lot *n* ที่ดิน tidin
lotion *n.* โลชั่น lotion
lottery *n.* ล็อตเตอรี่ lottery
lotus *n.* ดอกบัว dawkbua
loud *a.* ดัง dang
lounge *v.i.* เดินทอดน่อง deuntawdnong
lounge *n.* ห้องพักรอ hongpakraw
louse *n.* หมัด mad
lovable *a.* เป็นที่รัก pentirak
love *n* ความรัก kwamrak
love *v.t.* รัก rak
lovely *a.* น่ารัก narak
lover *n.* คนรัก konrak
loving *a.* ชอบ chob
low *a.* ต่ำ tam
low *adv.* ต่ำ tam
low *v.i.* ร้องเสียงต่ำ rongsiangtam
low *n.* น้อย noy
lower *v.t.* ลดต่ำลง lodtamlong
lowliness *n.* ความต่ำต้อย kwamtamtoy
lowly *a.* ต่ำต้อย tamtoy
loyal *a.* ซื่อสัตย์ seusat
loyalist *n.* ผู้ซื่อสัตย์ puseusat
loyalty *n.* ความซื่อสัตย์ kwamseusat
lubricant *n.* สารหล่อลื่น sanlawleun

lubricate *v.t.* หล่อลื่น lawleun
lubrication *n.* การหล่อลื่น ganlawleun
lucent *a.* สว่าง sawang
Lucerne *n.* เมืองลูเซิร์น meuang-lucent
lucid *a.* สว่าง sawang
lucidity *n.* ความสว่าง kwamsawang
luck *n.* ความโชคดี kwamchokdi
luckily *adv.* โชคดี chokdi
luckless *a.* โชคร้าย chokrai
lucky *a.* โชคดี chokdi
lucrative *a.* มีกำไร migamrai
lucre *n.* ผลกำไร pongamrai
luggage *n.* สัมภาระ sampara
lukewarm *a.* อุ่น aun
lull *v.t.* กล่อม glom
lull *n.* ภาวะสงบนิ่ง pawasa-ngobning
lullaby *n.* เพลงกล่อมเด็ก plengglomdek
luminary *n.* สิ่งที่ให้แสงสว่าง singtihaisaengsawang
luminous *a.* เรืองแสง reuangsaeng
lump *n.* ก้อน gon
lump *v.t.* รวมเป็นก้อน ruampengon
lunacy *n.* ความวิกลจริต kwamwigonjarit
lunar *a.* เกี่ยวกับดวงจันทร์ giawgabduangjan
lunatic *n.* คนบ้า konba
lunatic *a.* บ้า ba
lunch *n.* อาหารกลางวัน a-hanglangwan
lunch *v.i.* เตรียมอาหารกลางวัน triam-a-hanglangwan
lung *n* ปอด pod
lunge *n.* การแทง gantaeng
lunge *v.i* แทง taeng
lurch *n.* การซวนเซ gansuansay
lurch *v.i.* ซวนเซ suanse
lure *n.* สิ่งล่อ singlaw
lure *v.t.* ล่อใจ lawjai
lurk *v.i.* หลบ lob
luscious *a.* หอมหวาน homwan
lush *a.* เขียวชอุ่ม kiawcha-um
lust *n.* ตัณหา tanha
lustful *a.* ตัณหาจัด tanhajad

lustre *n.* ชื่อเสียง cheusiang
lustrous *a.* รุ่งโรจน์ rungrod
lusty *a.* แข็งแรง kaengraeng
lute *n.* เกรียง griang
luxuriance *n.* ความอุดมสมบูรณ์ kwam-u-
domsomboon
luxuriant *a.* อุดมสมบูรณ์ udomsomboon
luxurious *a.* ฟุ่มเฟือย fumfeuay
luxury *n.* ความฟุ่มเฟือย kwamfumfeuay
lynch *v.t.* ลงประชาทัณฑ์ longprachatan
lyre *n.* พิณ pin
lyric *a.* เกี่ยวกับบทกวี giawgabbodgawi
lyric *n.* บทกวี bodgawi
lyrical *a.* เกี่ยวกับโคลง giawgabklong
lyricist *n.* ผู้แต่งเพลง putaengpleng

M

magical *a.* วิเศษ wised
magician *n.* นักเล่นกล naklengon
magisterial *a.* เชื่อถือได้ cheuateudai
magistracy *n.* ตำแหน่งพนักงานปกครอง
tamnaengpanak-nganpokkrong
magistrate *n.* เจ้าหน้าที่ฝ่ายปกครอง
jaonanifaipokkrong
magnanimity *n.* ความใจกว้าง
kwamjaigwang
magnanimous *a.* ใจบุญ jaiboon
magnate *n.* ผู้มีอิทธิพล pumi-ittipon
magnet *n.* แม่เหล็ก maelek
magnetic *a.* มีเสน่ห์ดึงดูด
misanaedeungdud
magnetism *n.* อำนาจแม่เหล็ก am-
nadmaelek
magnificent *a.* งดงาม ngod-ngam
magnify *v.t.* เพิ่มขนาด peumkanad
magnitude *n.* ขนาดใหญ่ kanadyai
magpie *n.* นกกางเขน nokgangken
mahogany *n.* ต้นมะฮอกกานี ton-
mahogany
mahout *n.* ควาญช้าง kwanchang

maid *n.* สาวใช้ saochai
maiden *n.* สาวโสด saosod
maiden *a.* เกี่ยวกับหญิงสาว
kiawgabyingsao
mail *n.* จดหมาย jodmai
mail *v.t.* ส่งจดหมาย songjodmai
mail *n* เกราะ graw
main *a* หลัก lak
main *n* ส่วนสำคัญ suansamkan
mainly *adv.* ส่วนใหญ่ suanyai
mainstay *n.* หัวเรี่ยวหัวแรง
huariawhuaraeng
maintain *v.t.* รักษา raksa
maintenance *n.* การดูแลรักษา
gandulaeraksa
maize *n.* ข้าวโพด kaopod
majestic *a.* ยิ่งใหญ่ yingyai
majesty *n.* ความมีอำนาจ kwammi-amnad
major *a.* ส่วนใหญ่ suanyai
major *n* พันตรี pantri
majority *n.* เสียงส่วนใหญ่ siangsuanyai
make *v.t.* ทำ tam
make *n* การกระทำ gangratam
maker *n.* ผู้ทำ putam
mal adjustment *n.* การปรับตัวได้ไม่ดี
ganprabtuadaimaidi
mal administration *n.* การบริหารที่มิชอบ
ganborihantimichob
malady *n.* การป่วย ganpuay
malaria *n.* มาลาเรีย malaria
maladroit *a.* ไม่ชำนาญ maichamnan
malafide *a.* โชคร้าย chokrai
malafide *adv* โชคร้าย chokrai
malaise *n.* อาการป่วย a-ganpuay
malcontent *a.* ไม่พอใจ maipawjai
malcontent *n* ความไม่พอใจ
kwammaipawjai
male *a.* เกี่ยวกับผู้ชาย giawgabpuchai
male *n* ผู้ชาย puchai
malediction *n.* การด่า ganda
malefactor *n.* ผู้กระทำผิด pugratampid
maleficent *a.* ชั่วร้าย chuarai

malice *n.* ความมุ่งร้าย kwammungrai

malicious *a.* ชั่วร้าย chuarai

malign *v.t.* ใส่ร้าย sairai

malign *a* ร้ายแรง rairaeng

malignancy *n.* โรคร้าย rokrai

malignant *a.* ร้ายแรง rairaeng

malignity *n.* การมุ่งร้าย ganmungrai

malleable *a.* ว่าง่าย wa-ngai

malmsey *n.* เหล้าองุ่น lao-a-ngun

malnutrition *n.* ภาวะขาดสารอาหาร pawakadsan-a-han

malpractice *n.* การกระทำผิด gangratampid

malt *n.* ข้าวมอลต์ kao-malt

mal-treatment *n.* การทารุณ gantaroon

mamma *n.* เต้านม taonom

mammal *n.* สัตว์เลี้ยงลูกด้วยนม satlianglookduaynom

mammary *a.* เกี่ยวกับเต้านม giawgabtaonom

mammon *n.* ทรัพย์สิน sabsin

mammoth *n.* ช้างแมมมอธ chang-mammoth

mammoth *a* มหีมา mahuma

man *n.* ผู้ชาย puchai

man *v.t.* จัดหาคน jadhakon

manag *v.t.* จัดการ jadgan

manageable *a.* จัดการได้ jadgandai

management *n.* การจัดการ ganjadgan

manager *n.* ผู้จัดการ pujadgan

managerial *a.* เกี่ยวกับการจัดการ giawgabganjadgan

mandate *n.* คำสั่ง kamsang

mandatory *a.* เกี่ยวกับคำสั่ง giawgabkamsang

mane *n.* แผงขนคอสัตว์ paengkonkosat

manes *n.* วิญญาณ winyan

manful *a.* กล้าหาญ glahan

manganese *n.* แมงกานีส mangganese

manger *n.* รางหญ้า rangya

mangle *v.t.* ทำลาย tamlai

mango *n* มะม่วง mamuang

manhandle *v.t.* กระทำโดยแรงมนุษย์ gratamdoeyraengmanud

manhole *n.* ปากทางเข้าท่อ paktangkaotaw

manhood *n.* ความเป็นชาย kwampenchai

mania *n* ความคลั่งใคล้ kwamklangklai

maniac *n.* คนบ้า konba

manicure *n.* การทำเล็บ gantamleb

manifest *a.* แจ่มแจ้ง jamjaeng

manifest *v.t.* ปรากฎ pragod

manifestation *n.* ความชัดเจน kwamchadjen

manifesto *n.* แถลงการณ์ talaenggan

manifold *a.* หลากหลาย laklai

manipulate *v.t.* ปลุกปั่น plukpan

manipulation *n.* การปลุกปั่น ganplukpan

mankind *n.* มนุษยชาติ manudsayachat

manlike *a.* คล้ายคน klaikon

manliness *n* ความเป็นชาย kwampenchai

manly *a.* อย่างลูกผู้ชาย yanglookpuchai

manna *n.* กระยาทิพย์ grayatib

mannequin *n.* หุ่นแสดงแบบ hoonsadaengbab

manner *n.* มารยาท marayad marayat

mannerism *n.* ธรรมเนียมปฏิบัติ tamniampatibad

mannerly *a.* สุภาพ supab

manoeuvre *n.* การซ้อมรบ gansawmrob

manoeuvre *v.i.* ซ้อมรบ somrob

manor *n.* คฤหาสน์ kareuhad

manorial *a.* เกี่ยวกับคฤหาสน์ giawgabkareuhad

mansion *n.* แมนชั่น mansion

mantel *n.* หิ้งที่อยู่เหนือเตาผิง hingtiyuneuataoping

mantle *n* เสื้อคลุม seuaklum

mantle *v.t* คลุม klum

manual *a.* ด้วยมือ duaymeu

manual *n* คู่มือ kumeu

manufacture *v.t.* ผลิต palit

manufacture *n* การผลิต ganpalid

manufacturer *n* ผู้ผลิต pupalid

manumission *n.* การปลดปล่อยทาส ganplodploytad

manumit *v.t.* ปลดปล่อยทาส plodploytad

manure *n.* ปุ๋ยคอก puikok

manure *v.t.* ใส่ปุ๋ย saipui

manuscript *n.* ต้นฉบับ tonchabab

many *a.* มากมาย makmai

map *n* แผนที่ paenti

map *v.t.* ทำแผนที่ tampaenti

mar *v.t.* ทำให้เสียหาย tamhaisiahai

marathon *n.* มาราธอน marathon

maraud *v.i.* ปล้น plon

marauder *n.* ผู้ปล้น puplon

marble *n.* หินอ่อน hin-on

march *n* มีนาคม minakom

march *n.* การเดินขบวน gandeunkabuan

march *v.i* เดินขบวน deunkabuan

mare *n.* ม้าตัวเมีย matuamia

margarine *n.* เนยเทียม neytiam

margin *n.* ขอบ kob

marginal *a.* เล็กน้อย leknoy

marigold *n.* ดอกดาวเรือง dawkdaoreuang

marine *a.* ทางทะเล tangtalay

mariner *n.* นาวิกโยธิน nawiggayotin

marionette *n.* หุ่นกระบอก hoongrabawk

marital *a.* เกี่ยวกับการแต่งงาน giawgabgantaeng-ngan

maritime *a.* ทางทะเล tantalay

mark *n.* รอย roy

mark *v.t* ทำเครื่องหมาย tamkreuangmai

marker *n.* สิ่งที่ใช้ทำเครื่องหมาย singtichaitamkruengmai

market *n* ตลาด talad

market *v.t* จ่ายตลาด jaitalad

marketable *a.* ซื้อขายได้ seukaidai

marksman *n.* นักแม่นปืน nakmaenpeun

marl *n.* ดินร่วน dinruan

marmalade *n.* แยม yam

maroon *n.* สีน้ำตาลแดง sinamtandeang

maroon *a* สีน้ำตาลแดง sinamtandeang

maroon *v.t* ปล่อยเกาะ ploygaw

marriage *n.* การแต่งงาน gantaeng-ngan

marriageable *a.* แต่งงานได้ taeng-ngandai

marry *v.t.* แต่งงาน taeng-ngan

Mars *n* ดาวอังคาร dao-angkan

marsh *n.* บึง beung

marshal *n* จอมพล jompon

marshal *v.t* รวมกำลัง ruamgamlang

marshy *a.* เป็นบึง penbuang

marsupial *n.* สัตว์จำพวกจิงโจ้ satjampuakjingjo

mart *n.* ศูนย์การค้า soonganka

marten *n.* พังพอน pangpon

martial *a.* เกี่ยวกับสงคราม giawgabsongkram

martinet *n.* ผู้เคร่งในระเบียบ pukrengnairabiab

martyr *n.* ผู้ทนทุกข์ putontook

martyrdom *n.* ความทุกข์ทรมาน kwamtooktoraman

marvel *n.* สิ่งมหัศจรรย์ singmahatsajan

marvel *v.i* ตกตะลึง toktaleung

marvellous *a.* มหัศจรรย์ mahadsajan

mascot *n.* สิ่งนำโชค singnamchok

masculine *a.* เกี่ยวกับเพศชาย giawgabpedchai

mash *n.* มันบด manbod

mash *v.t* บด bod

mask *n.* หน้ากาก nagak

mask *v.t.* ใส่หน้ากาก sainagak

mason *n.* ช่างก่ออิฐ changgaw-id

masonry *n.* อาชีพก่อสร้าง a-chibgawsang

masquerade *n.* งานแฟนซี nganfansi

mass *n.* ปริมาณมาก parimanmak

mass *v.i* รวมกันเป็นก้อน ruamganpengon

massacre *n.* การสังหารหมู่ gansanghanmu

massacre *v.t.* สังหารหมู่ sanghanmu

massage *n.* การนวด gannuad

massage *v.t.* นวด nuad

masseur *n.* คนนวด konnuad

massive *a.* มาก mak

massy *a.* มาก mak

mast *n.* เสากระโดงเรือ saogradongreua

master *n.* นาย nai

master *v.t.* ควบคุม kwabkum

masterly *a.* ชำนาญ chamnan

masterpiece *n.* งานชิ้นเอก nganchin-ek

mastery *n.* ความชำนาญ kwamchamnan

masticate *v.t.* เคี้ยว kiaw

masturbate *v.i.* สำเร็จความใคร่ด้วยตัวเอง samredkwamkraiduaytau-eng

mat *n.* พรม prom

matador *n .* นักสู้วัว naksuwua

match *n.* การแข่งขัน gankaengkan

match *v.i.* เข้ากัน kaogan

match *n* คู่เหมือน kumeuan

matchless *a.* ไม่คู่ควร maikukuan

mate *n.* เพื่อน peuan

mate *v.t.* จับคู่ jabku

mate *n* คู่ครอง kukrong

mate *v.t.* แต่งงาน taeng-ngan

material *a.* เกี่ยวข้องกับวัตถุ giawkonggabwattu

material *n* วัตถุ wattu

materialism *n.* วัตถุนิยม wattuniyom

materialize *v.t.* ทางวัตถุ tangwatti

maternal *a.* ทางแม่ tangmae

maternity *n.* ความเป็นแม่ kwampenmae

mathematical *a.* เกี่ยวกับคณิตศาสตร์ giawgabkanidsat

mathematician *n.* นักคณิตศาสตร์ nakkanidsat

mathematics *n* คณิตศาสตร์ kanidsat

matinee *n.* การแสดงในเวลากลางวัน sansadaengnaiwelaklangwan

matriarch *n.* ผู้นำหญิง punamying

matricidal *a.* เกี่ยวกับการฆ่าแม่ตัวเอง giawgabgankamaetua-eng

matricide *n.* การฆ่าแม่ตัวเอง gankamaetua-eng

matriculate *v.t.* สมัครเป็นนักศึกษา samakpennaksuksa

matriculation *n.* การสมัครเป็นนักศึกษา gansamakpennaksuksa

matrimonial *a.* เกี่ยวกับการแต่งงาน giawgabgantaeng-ngan

matrimony *n.* การแต่งงาน gantaeng-ngan

matrix *n* เมตริก matrix

matron *n.* หญิงที่มีสามีแล้ว yingtimisamilaew

matter *n.* เรื่อง reuang

matter *v.i.* เป็นเรื่องราว penreungrao

mattock *n.* พลั่ว plua

mattress *n.* ที่นอน tinon

mature *a.* เป็นผู้ใหญ่ penpuyai

mature *v.i* เติบโต teubto

maturity *n.* ความเป็นผู้ใหญ่ kwampenpuyai

maudlin *a* สะอึกสะอื้น sa-euk-sa-euan

maul *n.* ค้อน kawn

maul *v.t* ทุบตี tubti

maulstick *n.* ไม้ทาสี maitasi

maunder *v.t.* พูดไม่รู้เรื่อง pudmairureuang

mausoleum *n.* สุสาน susan

mawkish *a.* จืดชืด jeudcheud

maxilla *n.* ขากรรไกรบน kagangraibon

maxim *n.* หลักการ lakgan

maximize *v.t.* ทำให้สูงสุด tamhaisoongsud

maximum *a.* สูงสุด soongsud

maximum *n* จำนวนสูงสุด jamnuansoongsud

May *n.* พฤษภาคม prudsapakom

may *v* อาจจะ adja

mayor *n.* นายกเทศมนตรี nayoktedsamontri

maze *n.* ทางวกวน tangwokwon

me *pron.* ฉัน chan

mead *n.* ทุ่งหญ้า tungya

meadow *n.* ทุ่งหญ้า tungya

meagre *a.* ขาดแคลน kadklan

meal *n.* มื้ออาหาร mua-a-han

mealy *a.* เป็นผง penpong

mean *a.* ใจร้าย jairai

mean *n.* ค่าเฉลี่ย kachalia

mean *v.t* หมายถึง maiteung

meander *v.i.* คดเคี้ยว kodkiaw
meaning *n.* ความหมาย kwammai
meaningful *a.* มีความหมาย mikwammai
meaningless *a.* ไร้ความหมาย raikwammai
meanness *n.* ความเลว kwamlew
means *n* วิธี witi
meanwhile *adv.* ขณะที่ kanati
measles *n* หัด had
measurable *a.* วัดได้ waddai
measure *n.* การวัด ganwad
measure *v.t* วัด wad
measureless *a.* ไม่จำกัด maijamgad
measurement *n.* การวัด ganwad
meat *n.* เนื้อ neua
mechanic *n.* ช่างยนต์ changyon
mechanic *a* ทางกลไก tanggongai
mechanical *a.* เกี่ยวกับเครื่องจักร
    giawgabkreuangjak
mechanics *n.* กลศาสตร์ gonlasat
mechanism *n.* กลไก gongai
medal *n.* เหรียญตรา riantra
medallist *n.* ผู้ชนะเลิศ puchanaleud
meddle *v.i.* ก้าวก่าย gaogai
medieval *a.* ยุคกลาง yukglang
medieval *a.* ล้าสมัย lasamai
median *a.* ตรงกลาง trongglang
mediate *v.i.* ไกล่เกลี่ย glaiglia
mediation *n.* การไกล่เกลี่ย ganglaiglia
mediator *n.* ผู้ไกล่เกลี่ย puglaiglia
medical *a.* ทางการแพทย์ tanganpaet
medicament *n.* ยา ya
medicinal *a.* มีคุณสมบัติเป็นยา
    mikoonnasombatpenya
medicine *n.* ยา ya
medico *n.* หมอ maw
mediocre *a.* ธรรมดา tammada
mediocrity *n.* ความธรรมดา
    kwamtammada
meditate *v.t.* ทำสมาธิ tamsamati
mediation *n.* การอยู่ตรงกลาง
    ganyutrongglang

meditative *a.* อยู่ระหว่างกลาง
    yurawangglang
medium *n* สื่อกลาง seuglang
medium *a* ปานกลาง panglang
meek *a.* นอบน้อม nobnom
meet *n.* การพบปะ ganpobpa
meet *v.t.* พบปะ pobpa
meeting *n.* การประชุม ganprachum
megalith *n.* หินขนาดใหญ่ hinkanadyai
megalithic *a.* เกี่ยวกับหิน giawgabhin
megaphone *n.* โทรโข่ง torakong
melancholia *n.* ภาวะซึมเศร้า
    pawaseumsao
melancholic *a.* เศร้าโศก saosok
melancholy *n.* ความเศร้า kwamsao
melancholy *adj* เศร้า sao
melee *n.* การต่อสู้อย่างชุลมุน
    gantawsuyangchunlamoon
meliorate *v.t.* บรรเทา bantao
mellow *a.* เบิกบาน beukban
melodious *a.* ไพเราะ pairaw
melodrama *n.* เรื่องประโลมโลก
    reuangpraromlok
melodramatic *a.* เกี่ยวกับเรื่องประโลมโลก
    giawgabreuangpraromlok
melody *n.* ท่วงทำนอง tuangtamnong
melon *n.* เมลอน melon
melt *v.i.* ละลาย lalai
member *n.* สมาชิก samachik
membership *n.* การเป็นสมาชิก
    ganpensamachik
membrane *n.* เยื่อบุผิว yeuabupew
memento *n.* ของที่ระลึก kongtirareuk
memoir *n.* บันทึก banteuk
memorable *a.* น่าจดจำ najodjam
memorandum *n* บันทึกความจำ
    banteukkwamjam
memorial *n.* ที่ระลึก tirareuk
memorial *a* เป็นที่ระลึก pentirareuk
memory *n.* ความจำ kwamjam
menace *n* ภัยอันตราย pai-antarai
menace *v.t* คุกคาม kukkam

mend *v.t.* ซ่อมแซม somsaem

mendacious *a.* โกหก gohok

menial *a.* เหมือนคนใช้ meuankonchai

menial *n* คนรับใช้ konrabchai

meningitis *n.* เยื่อหุ้มสมองอักเสบ yeuahumsamong-akseb

menopause *n.* ภาวะหมดประจำเดือน pawamodprajamdeuan

menses *n.* ภาวะมีประจำเดือน pawamiprajamdeuan

menstrual *a.* เกี่ยวกับประจำเดือน giawgabprajamdeuan

menstruation *n.* การมีประจำเดือน ganmiprajamdeuan

mental *a.* ทางด้านจิตใจ tangdanjidjai

mentality *n.* ความสามารถทางจิตใจ kwamsamadtangjidjai

mention *n.* การอ้างถึง gan-angteung

mention *v.t.* อ้างถึง angteung

mentor *n.* ผู้ให้คำปรึกษา puhaikampreuksa

menu *n.* เมนู menu

mercantile *a.* เกี่ยวกับการค้าขาย giawgabgankakai

mercenary *a.* รับจ้าง rabjang

mercerise *v.t.* ทำให้ดีขึ้น tamhaidikeun

merchandise *n.* สินค้า sinka

merchant *n.* พ่อค้า pawka

merciful *a.* เมตตา metta

merciless *adj.* ไร้เมตตา raitetta

mercurial *a.* เกี่ยวกับปรอท giawgabparod

mercury *n.* ปรอท parod

mercy *n.* ความเมตตา kwammetti

mere *a.* เพียงเท่านั้น piangtaonan

merge *v.t.* รวมกัน ruamgan

merger *n.* การรวมกัน ganruamgan

meridian *a.* เกี่ยวกับเส้นเมอริเดียน giawgabsenmeridian

merit *n.* คุณธรรม kunnatam

merit *v.t* ควรได้รับ kwuandairab

meritorious *a.* มีความดีความชอบ mikwamdikwamchob

mermaid *n.* นางเงือก nang-ngeuk

merman *n.* เงือกชาย ngeukchai

merriment *n.* ความสนุกสนาน kwamsanooksanan

merry *a* สุขสันต์ sooksan

mesh *n.* ตาข่าย takai

mesh *v.t* ทำให้เข้ากัน tamhaikaogan

mesmerism *n.* การสะกดจิต gansagodjit

mesmerize *v.t.* สะกดจิต sagodjit

mess *n.* สภาพรกรุงรัง sapabrokroongrang

mess *v.i* ทำให้รก tamhairok

message *n.* สาร san

messenger *n.* คนส่งเอกสาร konsong-ekgasan

messiah *n.* พระเจ้า prachao

Messrs. *n.* คำนำหน้าชื่อ kamnamnacheu

metabolism *n.* การเผาผลาญอาหาร ganpaopan-a-han

metal *n.* โลหะ loha

metallic *a.* เกี่ยวกับโลหะ giawgabloha

metallurgy *n.* วิธีแยกโลหะออกจากแร่ witiyaekloha-awkjakrae

metamorphosis *n.* การเปลี่ยนรูปร่าง ganplianroobrang

metaphor *n.* การเปรียบเทียบ ganpriabtiab

metaphysical *a.* เกี่ยวกับอภิปรัชญา giawgab-apipradya

metaphysics *n.* อภิปรัชญา apipradya

mete *v.t* แจกจ่าย jaekjai

meteor *n.* ดาวตก daotok

meteoric *a.* เกี่ยวกับอุกกาบาต giawgab-u-gabat

meteorologist *n.* นักพยากรณ์อากาศ nakpayagon-a-gad

meteorology *n.* การพยากรณ์อากาศ ganpayagon-a-gad

meter *n.* เมตร meter

method *n.* วิธี witi

methodical *a.* มีแบบแผน mipaebpan

metre *n.* เมตร metre

metric *a.* เกี่ยวกับระบบการวัด giawgabrabobganwat

metrical *a.* เกี่ยวกับระบบการวัด
giawgabrabobganwat
metropolis *n.* เมืองใหญ่ meuangyai
metropolitan *a.* เกี่ยวกับเมืองใหญ่
giawgabmeungyai
metropolitan *n.* คนที่อยู่ในเมืองใหญ่
kontiyunaimeuangyai
mettle *n.* ความกล้าหาญ kwamglahan
mettlesome *a.* กล้าหาญ glahan
mew *v.i.* (แมว)ร้อง (maew)rong
mew *n.* เสียงแมวร้อง siangmaewrong
mezzanine *n.* ชั้นลอย chanroy
mica *n.* แร่ไมกา raemica
microfilm *n.* ไมโครฟิล์ม microfilm
micrology *n.* ความสนใจในสิ่งเล็กๆ
kwamsonjainaisingleklek
micrometer *n.* ไมโครเมตร micrometer
microphone *n.* ไมโครโฟน microphone
microscope *n.* กล้องจุลทรรศน์
glongjunratad
microscopic *a.* มีขนาดเล็กมาก
mikanadlek
microwave *n.* ไมโครเวฟ microwave
mid *a.* กลาง glang
midday *n.* กลางวัน glangwan
middle *a.* กลาง glang
middle *n* ทางสายกลาง tangsaiglang
middleman *n.* คนกลาง konglang
middling *a.* ปานกลาง panglang
midget *n.* คนแคระ konkrae
midland *n.* ตอนกลางของประเทศ
tonglangkongprated
midnight *n.* เที่ยงคืน tiangkeun
mid-off *n.* ตำแหน่งผู้เล่นคริกเกต
tamnaengpulencriket
mid-on *n.* ตำแหน่งผู้เล่นคริกเกต
tamnaengpulencriket
midriff *n.* กะบังลม gabanglom
midst ท่ามกลาง tamglang
midsummer *n.* ช่วงกลางฤดูร้อน
chuangglangreuduron
midwife *n.* คนทำคลอด kontamklod

might *n.* อำนาจ amnad
mighty *adj.* มีกำลัง migamlang
migraine *n.* ไมเกรน migraine
migrant *n.* ผู้อพยพ pu-oppyob
migrate *v.i.* อพยพ oppayob
migration *n.* การอพยพ gan-obpayob
milch *a.* ให้นม hainom
mild *a.* อ่อน on
mildew *n.* เชื้อรา cheuara
mile *n.* ไมล์ mile
mileage *n.* ระยะทางเป็นไมล์
rayatangpenmile
milestone *n.* เหตุการณ์สำคัญ
hedgansamkan
milieu *n.* สิ่งแวดล้อม singwaedlom
militant *a.* เกี่ยวกับการทำสงคราม
giabgabgantamsongkram
militant *n* ผู้ทำสงคราม putamsongkram
military *a.* ทางการทหาร tangantahan
military *n* กองทัพ gongtab
militate *v.i.* ต่อสู้ tawsu
militia *n.* ทหารกองหนุน tahangongnoon
milk *n.* นม nom
milk *v.t.* รีดนม ridnom
milky *a.* ขุ่น kun
mill *n.* โรงสี rongsi
mill *v.t.* สีข้าว sikao
millennium *n.* สหัสวรรษ sahasawat
miller *n.* เจ้าของโรงสี jaokongrongsi
millet *n.* ข้าวฟ่าง kaofang
milliner *n.* ช่างทำหมวก changtammuak
milliner *n.* หมวกสตรี muaksatri
millinery *n.* ร้านขายหมวกสตรี
rankaimuaksatri
million *n.* ล้าน lan
millionaire *n.* เศรษฐี sedti
millipede *n.* กิ้งกือ ginggeu
mime *n.* ละครใบ้ lakonbai
mime *v.i* แสดงละครใบ้ sadaenglakonbai
mimesis *n.* การทำสำเนา gantamsamnao
mimic *a.* ล้อเลียน lawlian
mimic *n* การล้อเลียน ganlawlian

mimic *v.t* ล้อเลียน lawlian

mimicry *n* การล้อเลียน ganlawlian

minaret *n.* หอคอยสุเหร่า hawkoisulao

mince *v.t.* สับ sab

mind *n.* จิตใจ jidjai

mind *v.t.* ระวัง rawang

mindful *a.* สนใจ sonjai

mindless *a.* ไม่สนใจ maisonjai

mine *pron.* ของฉัน kongchan

mine *n* เหมืองแร่ meuangrae

miner *n.* คนงานเหมือง kon-nganmeuang

mineral *n.* แร่ rae

mineral *a* ที่เป็นแร่ tipenrae

mineralogist *n.* ผู้ศึกษาเกี่ยวกับแร่ pusuksagiawgabrae

mineralogy *n.* การศึกษาเกี่ยวกับแร่ gansuksagiawgabrae

mingle *v.t.* ผสม pasom

miniature *n.* การจำลอง ganjamlong

miniature *a.* เล็กมาก lekmak

minim *n.* หน่วยวัดความจุของเหลวที่น้อยที่สุด nuaywatkwamjukonglewtinoytisud

minimal *a.* เล็กที่สุด lektisud

minimize *v.t.* ทำให้น้อย tamhainoy

minimum *n.* จำนวนต่ำสุด jamnuantamsud

minimum *a* อย่างต่ำ yangtam

minion *n.* คนรับใช้ konrabchai

minister *n.* พระ pra

minister *v.i.* ดูแล dulae

ministrant *a.* ช่วยเหลือได้ chuayleuadai

ministry *n.* กระทรวง grasuang

mink *n.* เสื้อขนมิงค์ seuakonmink

minor *a.* เล็กน้อย leknoy

minor *n* ผู้เยาว์ puyao

minority *n.* คนกลุ่มน้อย konglomnoy

minster *n.* โบสถ์ bod

mint *n.* มินท์ mint

mint *n* โรงกษาปณ์ ronggasab

mint *v.t.* ปั๊มเหรียญ pamrian

minus *prep.* ลบ lob

minus *a* ต่ำกว่าศูนย์ tamkwasoon

minus *n* จำนวนต่ำกว่าศูนย์ jamnuantamkwasoon

minuscule *a.* เล็กมาก lekmak

minute *a.* เล็กมาก lekmak

minute *n.* นาที nati

minutely *adv.* ทุกนาที tooknati

minx *n.* หญิงแพศยา yingpaedsaya

miracle *n.* สิ่งมหัศจรรย์ singmahadsajan

miraculous *a.* มหัศจรรย์ mahadsajan

mirage *n.* ภาพลวงตา pabluangta

mire *n.* หล่ม lom

mire *v.t.* ติดหล่ม tidlom

mirror *n* กระจก grajok

mirror *v.t.* ส่องกระจก songgrajok

mirth *n.* ความรื่นเริง kwamreunreung

mirthful *a.* รื่นเริง reunreung

misadventure *n.* ความโชคร้าย kwamchokrai

misalliance *n.* ความสัมพันธ์ที่ไม่เหมาะสม kwamsampantimaimawsom

misanthrope *n.* ผู้เกลียดชังคนอื่น pugliadchangkon-eun

misapplication *n.* การใช้ผิดวัตถุประสงค์ ganchaipidwattuprasong

misapprehend *v.t.* เข้าใจผิด kaojaipid

misapprehension *n* การเข้าใจผิด gankaojaipid

misappropriate *v.t.* ไม่เหมาะสม maimawsom

misappropriation *n.* ความไม่เหมาะสม kwammaimawsom

misbehave *v.i.* ประพฤติตัวไม่เหมาะสม prapeudtuamaimawsom

misbehaviour *n.* การประพฤติตัวไม่เหมาะสม ganpraprudtuamaimawsom

misbelief *n.* ความเชื่อที่ผิด kawmcheuatipid

miscalculate *v.t.* คำนวณผิด kawmnuanpid

miscalculation *n.* การคำนวณผิด gankamnuanpid

miscall *v.t.* เรียกชื่อผิด riakcheupid

miscarriage *n.* การแท้ง gantaeng

miscarry *v.i.* แท้ง taeng

miscellaneous *a.* เบ็ดเตล็ด bedtaled

miscellany *n.* เรื่องเบ็ดเตล็ด reuangbedtaled

mischance *n.* โชคร้าย chokrai

mischief *n* การก่อกวน gangawguan

mischievous *a.* เจ้าเล่ห์ chaore

misconceive *v.t.* เข้าใจผิด kaojaipid

misconception *n.* การเข้าใจผิด gankaojaipid

misconduct *n.* การประพฤติผิด ganpraprudpid

misconstrue *v.t.* แปลผิด plaepid

miscreant *n.* คนเลว konlew

misdeed *n.* การกระทำผิด gankratampid

misdemeanour *n.* การทำความผิดเล็กๆ น้อยๆ gantamkwampidlekleknoynoy

misdirect *v.t.* หลงทาง longtang

misdirection *n.* การหลงทาง ganlongtang

miser *n.* คนตระหนี่ kontrani

miserable *a.* ทุกข์ยาก tookyak

miserly *a.* ตระหนี่ trani

misery *n.* ความทุกข์ยาก kwamtookyak

misfire *v.i.* ยิงไม่ออก yingmai-awk

misfit *n.* เสื้อผ้าผิดขนาด seuapapidkanad

misfortune *n.* โชคร้าย chokrai

misgive *v.t.* ทำให้สงสัย tamhaisongsai

misgiving *n.* ความสงสัย kwamsongsai

misguide *v.t.* แนะนำผิด naenampid

mishap *n.* อุบัติเหตุ u-bathed

misjudge *v.t.* ตัดสินใจผิด tadsinjaipid

mislead *v.t.* ทำให้เข้าใจผิด tamhaikaojaipid

mismanagement *n.* การจัดการผิดพลาด ganjadganpidplad

mismatch *v.t.* จับคู่ผิด jabkupid

misnomer *n.* การเรียกชื่อผิด ganriakcheupid

misplace *v.t.* วางผิดที่ wangpidti

misprint *n.* การพิมพ์ผิด ganpimpid

misprint *v.t.* พิมพ์ผิด pimpid

misrepresent *v.t.* เป็นตัวอย่างที่ผิด pentuayangtipid

misrule *n.* การปกครองที่ไม่ดี ganpokkrongtimaidi

miss *n.* การพลาด ganplad

miss *v.t.* ทำพลาด tamplad

missile *n.* ขีปนาวุธ kipanawut

mission *n.* หน้าที่ nati

missionary *n.* หมอสอนศาสนา mawsonsasana

missis, missus *n..* คำเรียกผู้หญิง kamriakpuying

missive *n.* สาร san

mist *n.* หมอก mawk

mistake *n.* ความผิดพลาด kwampidplad

mistake *v.t.* ผิดพลาด pidplad

mister *n.* คำเรียกผู้ชาย kamriakpuchai

mistletoe *n.* ต้นกาฝาก tongafak

mistreat *d* ข่มเหง komkeng

mistress *n.* เมียน้อย mianoy

mistrust *n.* ความไม่ไว้ใจ kwammaiwaijai

mistrust *v.t.* ไม่ไว้ใจ miwaijai

misty *a.* ไม่ชัดเจน maichadjen

misunderstand *v.t.* เข้าใจผิด kaojaipid

misunderstanding *n.* ความเข้าใจผิด kwamkwaojaipid

misuse *n.* การใช้ในทางที่ผิด ganchainaitangtipid

misuse *v.t.* ใช้ในทางที่ผิด chainaitangtipid

mite *n.* ไร rai

mite *n* ของเล็กๆ kongleklek

mithridate *n.* ยาถอนพิษ yatawnpid

mitigate *v.t.* บรรเทา bantao

mitigation *n.* การบรรเทา ganbantao

mitre *n.* หมวกที่พระใส่ muaktiprasai

mitten *n.* ถุงมือ tungmeu

mix *v.i* ผสม pasom

mixture *n.* การผสม ganpasom

moan *v.i.* คราง krang

moan *n.* การครวญคราง gankruankrang

moat *n.* คูน้ำรอบเมือง kunamrobmuang

moat *v.t.* ล้อมรอบด้วยคูน้ำ lomrobduaykunam

mob *n.* ฝูงชน foongchon

mob *v.t.* ก่อความวุ่นวาย gawkwamwunwai

mobile *a.* เคลื่อนที่ได้ kleuantidai

mobility *n.* การเคลื่อนที่ได้ง่าย gankleuntidaiyai

mobilize *v.t.* เคลื่อนที่ได้ kleuandidai

mock *v.i.* ล้อเลียน lawlian

mock *adj* ล้อเลียน lawlian

mockery *n.* การล้อเลียน ganlawlian

modality *n.* แบบ baeb

mode *n.* วิธีการ witigan

model *n.* ต้นแบบ tonbaeb

model *v.t.* จำลองแบบ jamlongbaeb

moderate *a.* ปานกลาง panglang

moderate *v.t.* บรรเทา bantao

moderation *n.* ความพอประมาณ kwampawpraman

modern *a.* ทันสมัย tansamai

modernity *n.* ความทันสมัย kwamtansami

modernize *v.t.* ทำให้ทันสมัย tamhaitansamai

modest *a.* ถ่อมตัว tomtua

modesty *n* การถ่อมตัว gantomtua

modicum *n.* จำนวนเล็กน้อย jamnuanleknoy

modification *n.* การปรับเปลี่ยน ganprabplian

modify *v.t.* ปรับเปลี่ยน plabplian

modulate *v.t.* ปรับเปลี่ยน plabplian

moil *v.i.* ทำงานหนัก tam-ngannak

moist *a.* ชื้น cheun

moisten *v.t.* ทำให้ชื้น tamhaicheun

moisture *n.* ความชื้น kwamcheun

molar *n.* ฟันกราม fungram

molar *a* เกี่ยวกับฟันกราม giawgabfungram

molasses *n* กากน้ำตาล gaknamtan

mole *n.* ไฝ fai

molecular *a.* เกี่ยวกับโมเลกุล giawgabmolecule

molecule *n.* โมเลกุล molecule

molest *v.t.* ลวนลาม luanlam

molestation *n.* การลวนลาม ganluanlam

molten *a.* หลอมละลายได้ lawmlalaidai

moment *n.* ชั่วขณะ chuakana

momentary *a.* ชั่วขณะ chuakana

momentous *a.* ชั่วขณะ chuakana

momentum *n.* โมเมนตัม momentum

monarch *n.* กษัตริย์ gasat

monarchy *n.* การปกครองที่มีกษัตริย์เป็นประมุข ganpokkrongtimigasatpenpramuk

monastery *n.* วัด wat

monasticism *n* ความสันโดษ kwamsandod

Monday *n.* วันจันทร์ wanjan

monetary *a.* ทางการเงิน tanggan-ngeun

money *n.* เงิน ngeun

monger *n.* พ่อค้า pawka

mongoose *n.* พังพอน pangpon

mongrel *a* พันทาง pantang

monitor *n.* ผู้ดูแล pudulae

monitory *a.* เป็นเครื่องเตือน penkreuangtuan

monk *n.* พระ pra

monkey *n.* ลิง ling

monochromatic *a.* สีเดียว sidiaw

monocle *n.* แว่นตาข้างเดียว waentakangdiaw

monocular *a.* มีตาข้างเดียว mitakangdiaw

monody *n.* การคร่ำครวญ gankramkruan

monogamy *n.* การมีคู่ครองคนเดียว ganmikukrongkondiaw

monogram *n.* อักษรย่อ aksonyaw

monograph *n.* บทความ bodkwam

monogynous *a.* มีเกสรเพศเมียหนึ่งอัน migesonpetmianeung-an

monolatry *n.* การบูชาพระเจ้าองค์เดียว ganbuchaprajao-ongdiaw

monolith *n.* หินขนาดใหญ่ก้อนเดียว hinkanadyaigondiaw

monologue *n.* บทพูดเดี่ยว bodpuddiaw

monopolist *n.* ผู้ถือเอกสิทธิ์ puteu-akgasit

monopolize *v.t.* ผูกขาด pukkad
monopoly *n.* ระบบผูกขาด rabobpukkad
monosyllable *n.* คำพยางค์เดียว
kampayangdiaw
monosyllabic *a.* มีพยางค์เดียว
mipayangdiaw
monotheism *n.* เอกเทวนิยม aktewaniyom
monotheist *n.* ผู้เชื่อในลัทธิเอกเทวนิยม
pucheunailatti-aktewaniyom
monotonous *a.* ซ้ำซาก samsak
monotony *n* ความซ้ำซาก kwamsamsak
monsoon *n.* มรสุม morasum
monster *n.* ปีศาจ pisad
monstrous *a.* ชั่วร้าย chuarai
monstrous *n.* ความน่ากลัว kwamnaglua
month *n.* เดือน deuan
monthly *a.* ทุกเดือน tookdeuan
monthly *adv* ทุกเดือน tookdeuan
monthly *n* นิตยสารรายเดือน
nitayasanraideuan
monument *n.* อนุสาวรีย์ a-nusawari
monumental *a.* ยิ่งใหญ่ yingyai
moo *v.i* (วัว) ร้อง (wua)rong
mood *n.* อารมณ์ a-rom
moody *a.* หงุดหงิด ngud-ngid
moon *n.* พระจันทร์ prajan
moor *n.* ทุ่งโล่ง tunglong
moor *v.t* จอดเรือ jawdreua
moorings *n.* ท่าจอดเรือ tajawdreua
moot *n.* การโต้แย้ง gantoyaeng
mop *n.* ไม้ถูพื้น maitupeun
mop *v.t.* ถูพื้น tupeun
mope *v.i.* เศร้าโศก saosok
moral *a.* มีคุณธรรม mikunnatam
moral *n.* คุณธรรม kunnatam
morale *n.* กำลังใจ gamlangjai
moralist *n.* ผู้มีศีลธรรม pumisinlatam
morality *n.* ความดีงาม kwamdi-ngam
moralize *v.t.* สั่งสอนศีลธรรม
sangsonsinlatam
morbid *a.* ผิดปกติ pidpagati
morbidity *n* ความไม่สบาย kwammaisabai

more *a.* มากกว่า makkwa
more *adv* มากกว่า makkwa
moreover *adv.* ยิ่งกว่านั้น yingkwanan
morganatic *a.* เกี่ยวกับการแต่งงาน
giawgabgantaeng-ngan
morgue *n.* ที่เก็บศพ tigebsob
moribund *a.* ใกล้ตาย glaitai
morning *n.* เวลาเช้า welachao
moron *n.* คนปัญญาอ่อน konpanya-on
morose *a.* มีอารมณ์ขุ่นมัว mi-a-
romkunmua
morphia *n.* มอร์ฟีน maw-fin
morrow *n.* พรุ่งนี้ prungni
morsel *n.* จำนวนเล็กน้อย jamnaunleknoy
mortal *a.* ถึงตาย teungtai
mortal *n* การตาย gantai
mortality *n.* การตาย gantai
mortar *v.t.* โบกปูน bokpoon
mortgage *n.* การจำนอง ganjamnong
mortgage *v.t.* จำนอง jamnong
mortagagee *n.* ผู้รับจำนอง purabjamnong
mortgator *n.* ผู้จำนอง pujamnong
mortify *v.t.* ทำให้อับอาย tamhai-ab-ai
mortuary *n.* ห้องดับจิต hongdabjit
mosaic *n.* โมเสค mosaic
mosque *n.* สุเหร่า surao
mosquito *n.* ยุง yung
moss *n.* ตะไคร่น้ำ takrainam
most *a.* มากที่สุด maktisud
most *adv.* ที่สุด tisud
most *n* ส่วนใหญ่ suanyai
mote *n.* ขี้ผึ้ง kipeung
motel *n.* โมเต็ล motel
moth *n.* ชีปะขาว chipakao
mother *n* แม่ mae
mother *v.t.* เลี้ยงดู liangdu
motherhood *n.* ความเป็นแม่
kwampenmae
motherlike *a.* เหมือนแม่ meuanmae
motherly *a.* เกี่ยวกับแม่ giawgabmae
motif *n.* บรรทัดฐาน bantadtan
motion *n.* การเคลื่อนไหว kleuanwai

motion *v.i.* เคลื่อนไหว kleunwai

motionless *a.* ไม่เคลื่อนไหว maikleunwai

motivate *v* จูงใจ jungjai

motivation *n.* แรงจูงใจ raengjungjai

motive *n.* แรงจูงใจ raengjungjai

motley *a.* หลากสี laksi

motor *n.* รถยนต์ rodyon

motor *v.i.* ขับรถ kabrod

motorist *n.* คนขับรถยนต์ konkabrodyon

mottle *n.* จุดด่างดำ juddangdam

motto *n.* คติ kati

mould *n.* แม่พิมพ์ maepim

mould *v.t.* หล่อ law

mould *n* การฝึกฝน ganfeukfon

mould *n* เชื้อรา cheuara

mouldy *a.* ปกคลุมด้วยรา pokklumduayra

moult *v.i.* ลอกคราบ lawkkrab

mound *n.* เนิน neun

mount *n.* ม้า ma

mount *v.t.* ขึ้นม้า keunma

mount *n* ภูเขา pukao

mountain *n.* ภูเขา pukao

mountaineer *n.* นักปีนเขา nakpinkao

mountainous *a.* เต็มไปด้วยภูเขา
tempaiduaypukao

mourn *v.i.* เศร้าโศก saosok

mourner *n.* ผู้เศร้าโศก pusaosok

mournful *n.* เศร้าโศก saosok

mourning *n.* ความเศร้า kwamsao

mouse *n.* หนู nu

moustache *n.* หนวด nuad

mouth *n.* ปาก pak

mouth *v.t.* พูด pud

mouthful *n.* เต็มปาก tempak

movable *a.* เคลื่อนที่ได้ kleuantidai

movables *n.* สังหาริมทรัพย์
sangharimmasab

move *n.* การเคลื่อนไหว gankleuanwai

move *v.t.* เคลื่อนไหว kleuanwai

movement *n.* การเคลื่อนไหว
gankleuanwai

mover *n.* สิ่งที่เคลื่อนไหวได้
singtikleuanwaidai

movies *n.* ภาพยนตร์ pabpayon

mow *v.t.* ตัดหญ้า tadya

much *a* มาก mak

much *adv* อย่างมาก yangmak

mucilage *n.* เมือก meuak

muck *n.* ปุ๋ยคอก puikok

mucous *a.* เป็นเมือก penmeuak

mucus *n.* ขี้มูก kimook

mud *n.* โคลน klon

muddle *n.* ความวุ่นวาย kwamwunwai

muddle *v.t.* ทำให้วุ่นวาย tamhaiwunwai

muffle *v.t.* หุ้ม hoom

muffler *n.* ท่อไอเสีย taw-ai-sia

mug *n.* เหยือก yeuak

muggy *a.* เปียกชื้น piakcheun

mulatto *n.* ลูกครึ่งผิวขาวกับผิวดำ
lookkreungpewkaogabpewdam

mulberry *n.* ผลมัลเบอรี่ pon-mulberry

mule *n.* ล่อ law

mulish *a.* ดื้อ deu

mull *n.* ผ้าฝ้าย pafai

mull *v.t.* ครุ่นคิด krunkid

mullah *n.* ผู้สอนศาสนาอิสลาม
pusonsasana-islam

mullion *n.* หิน hin

multifarious *a.* หลากหลาย laklai

multiform *n.* หลากหลายรูปทรง
laklairoobsong

multilateral *a.* พหุภาคี pahupaki

multiparous *a.* ตั้งครรภ์หลายครั้ง
tangkanlaikrang

multiple *a.* หลาย lai

multiple *n* ผลคูณ ponkun

multiped *n.* มีเท้าจำนวนมาก
mitaojamnuanmak

multiplex *a.* หลายด้าน laidan

multiplicand *n.* ตัวตั้งคูณ tuatangkun

multiplication *n.* การคูณ gankun

multiplicity *n.* ความหลากหลาย
kwamlaklai

multiply *v.t.* คูณ kun

multitude *n.* ความหลากหลาย kwamlaklai

mum *a.* นิ่งเงียบ ning-ngiab

mum *n* แม่ mae

mumble *v.i.* พูดเสียงอู้อี้ pudsiang-u-i

mummer *n.* นักแสดงละครใบ้ naksadaenglakonbai

mummy *n.* แม่ mae

mummy *n* มัมมี่ mummy

mumps *n.* คางทูม kangtum

munch *v.t.* เคี้ยว kiaw

mundane *a.* ทางโลก tanglok

municipal *a.* ส่วนท้องถิ่น suantongtin

municipality *n.* เทศบาล tedsaban

munificent *a.* ใจกว้าง jaigwang

muniment *n.* หนังสือแสดงกรรมสิทธิ์ที่ดิน nangseusadaenggammasittidin

munitions *n.* อาวุธ a-wut

mural *a.* เกี่ยวกับผนัง giawgabpanang

mural *n.* จิตรกรรมฝาผนัง jittagamfapanang

murder *n.* ฆาตกรรม kattagam

murder *v.t.* ฆ่า ka

murderer *n.* ฆาตกร kattagon

murderous *a.* เกี่ยวกับการฆาตกรรม giawgabgankattagam

murmur *n.* บ่นพึมพำ bonpeumpum

murmur *v.t.* เสียงพึมพำ siangpuempum

muscle *n.* กล้ามเนื้อ glamneua

muscovite *n.* ประชาชนในกรุงมอสโก prachachonnaigrungmosco

muscular *a.* เกี่ยวกับกล้ามเนื้อ giawgabglamneua

muse *v.i.* ครุ่นคิด krunkid

muse *n* โพรงไม้ prongmai

museum *n.* พิพิธภัณฑ์ pipitapan

mush *n.* อาหารบด a-hanbod

mushroom *n.* เห็ด hed

music *n.* ดนตรี dontri

musical *a.* เกี่ยวกับดนตรี giawgabdontri

musician *n.* นักดนตรี nakdontri

musk *n.* ขี้ชะมด kichamod

musket *n.* ปืนคาบศิลา peunkabsila

musketeer *n.* ทหารปืนคาบศิลา tahanpeunkabsila

muslin *n.* ผ้าฝ้าย pafai

must *v.* ต้อง tong

must *n.* สิ่งจำเป็น singjampen

must *n* เหล้าไวน์ใหม่ laowaimai

mustache *n.* หนวด nuad

mustang *n.* ม้าป่า mapa

mustard *n.* มัสตาร์ด mustard

muster *v.t.* รวบรวม ruabruam

muster *n* การรวบรวม ganruabruam

musty *a.* เหม็นอับ men-ab

mutation *n.* การกลายพันธุ์ ganglaipan

mutative *a.* กลายพันธุ์ได้ glaipandai

mute *a.* ใบ้ bai

mute *n.* คนใบ้ konbai

mutilate *v.t.* ตัดส่วนสำคัญออก tansuansamkan-awk

mutilation *n.* การตัดส่วนสำคัญออก gantadsuansamkan-awk

mutinous *a.* ขัดขืน kadkeun

mutiny *n.* การขัดขืนคำสั่ง gankadkeunkamsang

mutiny *v. i* ขัดขืนคำสั่ง kadkeunkamsang

mutter *v.i.* บ่น bon

mutton *n.* เนื้อแกะ neuagae

mutual *a.* ร่วมกัน ruamgan

muzzle *n.* ตะกร้อครอบปากสุนัข tagrawkrobpaksunak

muzzle *v.t* สวมตะกร้อครอบปากสุนัข suamtagrawkrobpaksunak

my *a.* ของฉัน kongchan

myalgia *n.* อาการปวดกล้ามเนื้อ a-ganpuadglamneua

myopia *n.* ภาวะสายตาสั้น pawasaitasan

myopic *a.* สายตาสั้น saitasan

myosis *n.* รูม่านตาหด rumantahod

myriad *n.* จำนวนมหาศาล jamnuanmahasan

myriad *a* มหาศาล mahasan

myrrh *n.* ยางไม้หอม yangmaihom

myrtle *n.* ดอกเมอเทิล dawk-myrtle

myself *pron.* ตัวของฉัน tuakongchan

mysterious *a.* ลึกลับ leuklab

mystery *n.* ความลึกลับ kwamleuklab

mystic *a.* ลึกลับ leuklab

mystic *n* ผู้มีเวทมนตร์ pumiwetmon

mysticism *n.* การร่ายเวทมนตร์ ganraiwetmon

mystify *v.t.* ทำให้ลึกลับ tamhaileuklab

myth *n.* ตำนาน tamnan

mythical *a.* เกี่ยวกับตำนาน giawgabtamnan

mythological *a.* เกี่ยวกับตำนาน giawgabtamnan

mythology *n.* ตำนาน tamnan

nab *v.t.* จับ jab

nabob *n.* คนร่ำรวย konramruay

nadir *n.* จุดต่ำสุด judtamsud

nag *n.* การรบกวน ganrobguan

nag *v.t.* จู้จี้ juji

nail *n.* ตะปู tapu

nail *v.t.* ดอกตะปู tawktapu

naive *a.* ไร้เดียงสา raidiangsa

naivete *n.* ความไร้เดียงสา kwamraidiangsa

naivety *n.* ความซื่อตรง kwamseutrong

naked *a.* เปลือย pleuay

name *n.* ชื่อ cheu

name *v.t.* ตั้งชื่อ tangcheu

namely *adv.* กล่าวคือ glaokeu

namesake *n.* ผู้ที่มีชื่อซ้ำกับคนอื่น pumicheusamgabkon-eun

nap *v.i.* งีบ ngib

nap *n.* การงีบ gan-ngib

nap *n* ขนอ่อนของพืช kon-onkongpeud

nape *n.* ต้นคอ tonkaw

napkin *n.* ผ้าเช็ดปาก pachedpak

narcissism *n.* การหลงตัวเอง ganlongtua-eng

narcissus *n* ต้นนาซีซัส ton-narcissus

narcosis *n.* การง่วงนอน gan-nguangnon

narcotic *n.* สารเสพติด sansebtid

narrate *v.t.* บรรยาย banyai

narration *n.* การเล่าเรื่อง ganlaoreuang

narrative *n.* เรื่องเล่า reuanglao

narrative *a.* เกี่ยวกับเรื่องเล่า giawgabreuanglao

narrator *n.* ผู้บรรยาย pubanyai

narrow *a.* แคบ kaeb

narrow *v.t.* ทำให้แคบ tamhaikaeb

nasal *a.* ทางนาสิก tangnasik

nasal *n* พยัญชนะเสียงนาสิก payanchanasiangnasik

nascent *a.* เริ่มใหม่ reummai

nasty *a.* น่ารังเกียจ naranggiad

natal *a.* เกี่ยวกับการเกิด giawgabgangeud

natant *a.* ลอยน้ำได้ loynamdai

nation *n.* ชาติ chat

national *a.* แห่งชาติ haengchat

nationalism *n.* ชาตินิยม chatniyom

nationalist *n.* ผู้รักชาติ purakchat

nationality *n.* สัญชาติ sanchat

nationalization *n.* การทำให้เป็นชาติ gantamhaibenchat

nationalize *v.t.* ทำให้เป็นของรัฐ tamhaipenkongrat

native *a.* พื้นเมือง peunmeuang

native *n* ชาวพื้นเมือง chaopeunmeuang

nativity *n.* การกำเนิด gangamneud

natural *a.* ตามธรรมชาติ tamtammachat

naturalist *n.* นักธรรมชาตินิยม namtammachatniyom

naturalize *v.t.* ทำให้เป็นธรรมชาติ tamhaipentammachat

naturally *adv.* ตามธรรมชาติ tamtammachat

nature *n.* ธรรมชาติ tammachat

naughty *a.* ซน son

nausea *n.* อาการคลื่นไส้ a-gankleunsai

nautic(al) *a.* ทางทะเล tangtalay
naval *a.* เกี่ยวกับเรือ giawgabreua
nave *n.* ทางเดินยาว tangdeunyao
navigable *a.* ผ่านไปได้ panpaidai
navigate *v.i.* หาเส้นทาง hasentang
navigation *n.* การเดินเรือ gandeunreua
navigator *n.* ต้นหนเรือ tonhonreua
navy *n.* กองทัพเรือ gongtabreua
nay *adv.* ไม่ mai
neap *a.* กระแสน้ำที่ลดลง
  grasaenamtilodlong
near *a.* ใกล้ glai
near *prep.* ใกล้ glai
near *adv.* ใกล้ glai
near *v.i.* เข้าใกล้ kaoglai
nearly *adv.* เกือบ geuab
neat *a.* เรียบร้อย riabroy
nebula *n.* กลุ่มก๊าซ glomgas
necessary *n.* ความจำเป็น kwamjampen
necessary *a* จำเป็น jampen
necessitate *v.t.* จำเป็น jampen
necessity *n.* ความจำเป็น kwamjampen
neck *n.* คอ kaw
necklace *n.* สร้อยคอ soikaw
necklet *n.* สร้อยคอ soikaw
necromancer *n.* หมอผี mawpi
necropolis *n.* สุสาน susan
nectar *n.* น้ำหวาน namwan
need *n.* ความจำเป็น kwamjampen
need *v.t.* จำเป็น jampen
needful *a.* จำเป็น jampen
needle *n.* เข็ม kem
needless *a.* ไม่จำเป็น maijampen
needs *adv.* จำเป็น jampen
needy *a.* จำเป็น jampen
nefandous *a.* พูดไม่ได้ pudmaidai
nefarious *a.* ชั่วร้าย chuarai
negation *n.* คำปฏิเสธ kampatised
negative *a.* เชิงปฏิเสธ cheuangpatised
negative *n.* คำปฏิเสธ kampatised
negative *v.t.* คัดค้าน kadkan
neglect *v.t.* ละเลย laleuy

neglect *n.* การละเลย ganlaleuy
negligence *n.* การละเลย ganlaleuy
negligent *a.* ไม่สนใจ maisonjai
negligible *a.* ไม่สำคัญ maisamkan
negotiable *a.* เจรจาได้ jerajadai
negotiate *v.t.* เจรจา jeraja
nagotiation *n.* การเจรจา ganjeraja
negotiator *n.* ผู้เจรจา pujeraja
negress *n.* หญิงนิโกร yingnegro
negro *n.* นิโกร negro
neigh *v.i.* (ม้า)ร้อง (ma)rong
neigh *n.* เสียงร้องของม้า
  siangrongkongma
neighbour *n.* เพื่อนบ้าน peuanpan
neighbourhood *n.* บริเวณข้างเคียง
  boriwenkangkiang
neighbourly *a.* เป็นเพื่อน penpeuan
neither *conj.* ไม่ทั้งสองอย่าง
  maitangsongyang
nemesis *n.* กรรมตามสนอง gamtamsanong
neolithic *a.* ยุคหินใหม่ yukhinmai
neon *n.* ก๊าซเฉื่อย gascheuay
nephew *n.* หลานชาย lanchai
nepotism *n.* การเล่นพรรคเล่นพวก
  ganlenpaklenpuak
Neptune *n.* ดาวเนปจูน daoneptune
nerve *n.* เส้นประสาท senprasat
nerveless *a.* ไม่มีกำลัง maimigamlang
nervous *a.* ตื่นเต้น tuenten
nescience *n.* ความไม่รู้ kwammairu
nest *n.* รัง rang
nest *v.t.* ทำรัง tamrang
nether *a.* ต่ำกว่า tamkwa
nestle *v.i.* ซบ sob
nestling *n.* ลูกอ่อน look-on
net *n.* ตาข่าย takai
net *v.t.* ดักด้วยตาข่าย dakduaytakai
net *a* สุทธิ sutti
net *v.t.* ได้กำไร daigamrai
nettle *n.* พืชชนิดหนึ่ง peudchanidneung
nettle *v.t.* ทำให้ขุ่นเคือง tamhaikunkeuang
network *n.* เครือข่าย kreuakai

neurologist *n.* นักประสาทวิทยา nakprasatwitaya

neurology *n.* ประสาทวิทยา prasatwitaya

neurosis *n.* โรคประสาท rokprasat

neuter *a.* ไร้เพศ raiped

neuter *n* ผู้เป็นกลาง pupenglang

neutral *a.* เป็นกลาง penglang

neutralize *v.t.* ทำให้เป็นกลาง tamhaipenglang

neutron *n.* นิวตรอน neutron

never *adv.* ไม่เคย maikeuy

nevertheless *conj.* อย่างไรก็ดี yangraigawdi

new *a.* ใหม่ mai

news *n.* ข่าว kao

next *a.* ต่อไป tawpai

next *adv.* ถัดไป tadpai

nib *n.* ปลาย plai

nibble *v.t.* เล็ม lem

nibble *n* การเล็ม ganlem

nice *a.* ดี di

nicety *n.* ความประณีต kwampranit

niche *n.* ช่อง chong

nick *n.* รอยบาก roybak

nickel *n.* นิกเกิล nickel

nickname *n.* ชื่อเล่น cheulen

nickname *v.t.* ตั้งชื่อเล่น tangcheulen

nicotine *n.* นิโคติน nicotine

niece *n.* หลานสาว lansao

niggard *n.* คนขี้เหนียว konkiniaw

niggardly *a.* ขี้เหนียว kiniaw

nigger *n.* คนผิวดำ konpewdam

nigh *adv.* ใกล้เข้ามา glaikaoma

nigh *prep.* ใกล้ klai

night *n.* กลางคืน glangkeun

nightingale *n.* นกไนติงเกล nok-nightingale

nightly *adv.* ทุกคืน tookkeun

nightmare *n.* ฝันร้าย funrai

nightie *n.* ชุดนอน chudnon

nihilism *n.* การทำลายล้าง gantamlailang

nil *n.* จำนวนศูนย์ chamnuansoon

nimble *a.* ว่องไว wongwai

nimbus *n.* เมฆฝน mekfon

nine *n.* เก้า gao

nineteen *n.* สิบเก้า sibgao

nineteenth *a.* ที่สิบเก้า tisibgao

ninetieth *a.* ที่เก้าสิบ tigaosib

ninth *a.* ที่เก้า tigao

ninety *n.* เก้าสิบ gaosib

nip *v.t* ขลิบ klib

nipple *n.* หัวนม huanom

nitrogen *n.* ไนโตรเจน nitrogen

no *a.* ไม่ mai

no *adv.* ไม่ mai

no *n* คำปฏิเสธ kampatised

nobility *n.* ความสูงส่ง kwamsoongsong

noble *a.* ชั้นสูง chansoong

noble *n.* คนชั้นสูง konchansoong

nobleman *n.* ผู้ดี pudi

nobody *pron.* ไม่มีใคร maimikrai

nocturnal *a.* กลางคืน glangkeun

nod *v.i.* พยักหน้า payakna

node *n.* ต่อม tom

noise *n.* เสียง siang

noisy *a.* เสียงดัง siangdang

nomad *n.* ผู้เร่ร่อน pureron

nomadic *a.* เร่ร่อน reron

nomenclature *n.* การตั้งชื่อ gantangcheu

nominal *a.* เกี่ยวกับชื่อ giabgabcheu

nominate *v.t.* เสนอชื่อ saneucheu

nomination *n.* การเสนอชื่อ gansaneucheu

nominee *n* ผู้ได้รับการเสนอชื่อ pudairabgansaneucheu

non-alignment *n.* การไม่ฝักใฝ่ฝ่ายใด ganmaifakfaifaidai

nonchalance *n.* ความเมินเฉย kwammeuncheuy

nonchalant *a.* เมินเฉย meuncheuy

none *pron.* ไม่มีเลย maimileuy

none *adv.* ไม่เลย maileuy

nonentity *n.* สิ่งที่ไม่สำคัญ singtimaisamkan

nonetheless *adv.* อย่างไรก็ดี yangraigawdi

nonpareil *a.* ไม่มีที่เปรียบ maimitipriab

nonpareil *n.* สิ่งที่ไม่มีใครเทียบได้ singtimaimikraitiabdai

nonplus *v.t.* ทำให้ประหลาดใจ tamhaipraladjai

nonsense *n.* เรื่องไร้สาระ reuangraisara

nonsensical *a.* ไม่มีความหมาย maimikwammai

nook *n.* มุม moom

noon *n.* เที่ยงวัน tiangwan

noose *n.* ห่วง huang

noose *v.t.* ทำห่วง tamhuang

nor *conj* ไม่ mai

norm *n.* บรรทัดฐาน bantadtan

norm *n.* ค่าปกติ kapagati

normal *a.* ปกติ pagati

normalcy *n.* ภาวะปกติ pawapagati

normalize *v.t.* ทำให้ปกติ tamhaipagati

north *n.* ทิศเหนือ tidneua

north *a* เหนือ neua

north *adv.* ทางเหนือ tangneua

northerly *a.* ทางเหนือ tangneua

northerly *adv.* ทางเหนือ tangneua

northern *a.* ทางทิศเหนือ tangtidneua

nose *n.* จมูก jamook

nose *v.t* สูดกลิ่น sudglin

nosegay *n.* ดอกไม้ช่อเล็ก dawkmaichawlek

nosey *a.* สอดรู้สอดเห็น sawdrusawdhen

nosy *a.* สอดรู้สอดเห็น sawdrusawdhen

nostalgia *n.* การคิดถึงความหลัง gankidteungkwamlang

nostril *n.* รูจมูก rujamook

nostrum *n.* ยาสามัญประจำบ้าน yasamanprajamban

not *adv.* ไม่เคย maikeuy

notability *n.* ความมีชื่อเสียง kwammicheusiang

notable *a.* มีชื่อเสียง micheusiang

notary *n.* เจ้าหน้าที่รับรองเอกสาร jaonatirabrong-ekgasan

notation *n.* หมายเหตุ maihed

notch *n.* รอยบาก roybak

note *n.* ข้อความ kawkwam

note *v.t.* จด jod

noteworthy *a.* น่าสังเกต nasangged

nothing *n.* การไม่มีอะไร ganmaimi-a-rai

nothing *adv.* ไม่มีอะไร maimi-a-rai

notice *n.* ข้อสังเกต kawsangged

notice *v.t.* สังเกต sangged

notification *n.* การแจ้ง ganjaeng

notify *v.t.* แจ้ง jaeng

notion *n.* ความคิด kwamkid

notional *a.* ที่ประมาณการไว้ tipramanganwai

notoriety *n.* ชื่อเสียงในทางไม่ดี cheusiangnaitangmaidi

notorious *a.* มีชื่อเสียงในทางไม่ดี micheusiangnaitangmaidi

notwithstanding *prep.* อย่างไรก็ดี yangraigawdi

notwithstanding *adv.* อย่างไรก็ดี yangraigawdi

notwithstanding *conj.* อย่างไรก็ดี yangraigawdi

nought *n.* ศูนย์ soon

noun *n.* คำนาม kamnam

nourish *v.t.* เลี้ยงดู liangdu

nourishment *n.* อาหารบำรุงร่างกาย a-hanbamrunggranggai

novel *a.* ใหม่ mai

novel *n* นวนิยาย nawaniyai

novelette *n.* เรื่องสั้น reuangsan

novelist *n.* นักแต่งนวนิยาย naktaengnawaniyai

novelty *n.* ความใหม่ kwammai

november *n.* พฤศจิกายน prusajigayon

novice *n.* ผู้บวชใหม่ pubuadmai

now *adv.* ขณะนี้ kanani

now *conj.* เนื่องจาก neuangjak

nowhere *adv.* ขณะนี้ kanani

noxious *a.* เป็นอันตราย pen-antarai

nozzle *n.* หัวฉีด huachid

nuance *n.* ความแตกต่างเล็กน้อย kwamtaektangleknoy

nubile *a.* พร้อมที่จะแต่งงาน promtijataeng-ngan

nuclear *a.* เกี่ยวกับนิวเคลียร์ giawgabnuclear

nucleus *n.* ใจกลาง jaiglang

nude *a.* เปลือยกาย pleuaygai

nude` *n* คนเปลือย konpleuay

nudity *n.* การเปลือยกาย ganpleuaygai

nudge *v.t.* กระทุ้ง gatung

nugget *n.* ก้อน gon

nuisance *n.* การรบกวน ganrobguan

null *a.* ไม่มีค่า maimika

nullification *n.* ความไร้ค่า kwamraika

nullify *v.t.* ทำให้ไร้ค่า tamhairaika

numb *a.* ชา cha

number *n.* ตัวเลข tualek

number *v.t.* ใส่ตัวเลข saitualek

numberless *a.* นับไม่ถ้วน nabmaituan

numeral *a.* เกี่ยวกับตัวเลข giawgabtualek

numerator *n.* ตัวเศษ tuased

numerical *a.* เกี่ยวกับตัวเลข giawgabtualek

numerous *a.* มาก mak

nun *n.* ชี chi

nunnery *n.* สำนักชี samnakchi

nuptial *a.* เกี่ยวกับการแต่งงาน giabgabgantaeng-ngan

nuptials *n.* การแต่งงาน gantaeng-ngan

nurse *n.* พยาบาล payaban

nurse *v.t* พยาบาล payaban

nursery *n.* สถานรับเลี้ยงเด็ก satanrabliangdek

nurture *n.* การเลี้ยงดู ganliangdu

nurture *v.t.* เลี้ยงดู liangdu

nut *n* ถั่ว tua

nutrition *n.* โภชนาการ pochanagan

nutritious *a.* มีคุณค่าทางโภชนาการ mikunkatangpochanagan

nutritive *a.* มีคุณค่าทางโภชนาการ mikunkatangpochanagan

nuzzle *v.* ดุนด้วยจมูก dunduayjamook

nylon *n.* ไนลอน nylon

nymph *n.* นางไม้ nangmai

O

oak *n.* ต้นโอ๊ค ton-oak

oar *n.* ไม้พาย maipai

oarsman *n.* คนพายเรือ konpaireua

oasis *n.* โอเอซิส oasis

oat *n.* ข้าวโอ๊ต kao-oat

oath *n.* สาบานตน sabanton

obduracy *n.* ความดื้อดึง kwamdeuran

obdurate *a.* ดื้อ deu

obedience *n.* ความเชื่อฟัง kwamcheuafang

obedient *a.* เชื่อฟัง cheuafang

obeisance *n.* การคำนับ gankamnab

obesity *n.* ความอ้วน kwam-uan

obey *v.t.* เชื่อฟัง cheuafang

obituary *a.* ไว้อาลัย wai-a-lai

object *n.* วัตถุ wattu

object *v.t.* คัดค้าน kadkan

objection *n.* การคัดค้าน gankadkan

objectionable *a.* ค้านได้ kandai

objective *n.* เป้าหมาย paomai

objective *a.* ไม่ลำเอียง mailam-iang

oblation *n.* การบวงสรวง ganbuangsuang

obligation *n.* ข้อผูกมัด kawpukmad

obligatory *a.* เป็นพันธะ penpanta

oblige *v.t.* บังคับ bangkab

oblique *a.* อ้อม om

obliterate *v.t.* ขจัดร่องรอย kajadrongroy

obliteration *n.* การขจัดร่องรอย gankajadrongroy

oblivion *n.* การหลงลืม ganlongleum

oblivious *a.* ไม่นึกถึง maineukteung

oblong *a.* ที่เป็นรูปสี่เหลี่ยมผืนผ้า tipenroobsiliampeunpa

oblong *n.* รูปสี่เหลี่ยมผืนผ้า roobsiliampeunpa

obnoxious *a.* น่ารังเกียจ naranggiad

obscene *a.* ลามก lamok

obscenity *n.* ความลามก kamlamok

obscure *a.* คลุมเครือ klumkreua

obscure *v.t.* ปิดบัง pidbang

obscurity *n.* ความคลุมเครือ kwamklumkreua

observance *n.* การสังเกต gansangget

observant *a.* ช่างสังเกต changsangket

observation *n.* การสังเกตการณ์ gansanggetgan

observatory *n.* หอสังเกตการณ์ hawsangketgan

observe *v.t.* สังเกต sangket

obsess *v.t.* ครอบงำ krob-ngam

obsession *n.* การครอบงำ gankrob-ngam

obsolete *a.* ล้าสมัย lasamai

obstacle *n.* อุปสรรค u-pasak

obstinacy *n.* ความดื้อดึง kwamdeudeung

obstinate *a.* ดื้อดึง deudeung

obstruct *v.t.* ขัดขวาง kadkwang

obstruction *n.* การขัดขวาง gankadkwang

obstructive *a.* กีดขวาง gidkwang

obtain *v.t.* ได้รับ dairab

obtainable *a.* หามาได้ hamadai

obtuse *a.* ทื่อ teum

obvious *a.* ชัดเจน chadjen

occasion *n.* โอกาส o-gad

occasion *v.t* เป็นเหตุให้ penhedhai

occasional *a.* เป็นครั้งคราว penkrangkrao

occasionally *adv.* บางครั้ง bangkrang

occident *n.* ภาคตะวันตก paktawan-awk

occidental *a.* ทางตะวันตก tangtawantok

occult *a.* ลึกลับ leuklab

occupancy *n.* การครอบครอง gankrobkrong

occupant *n.* ผู้ครอบครอง pukrobkrong

occupation *n.* อาชีพ a-chib

occupier *n.* ผู้ครอบครอง pukrobkrong

occupy *v.t.* จอง jong

occur *v.i.* เกิดขึ้น geudkeun

occurrence *n.* สิ่งที่เกิดขึ้น singtigeudkeun

ocean *n.* มหาสมุทร mahasamud

oceanic *a.* แห่งมหาสมุทร haengmahasamud

octagon *n.* รูปแปดเหลี่ยม roobpaedliam

octangular *a.* มีแปดมุม mipaedmoom

octave *n.* เสียงแปดคู่ siangpaedku

October *n.* ตุลาคม tulakom

octogenarian *a.* มีอายุระหว่าง 80 - 89 ปี mi-a-yurawangpaedsibteungpaedsibgaopi

octogenarian *n.* คนที่มีอายุระหว่าง 80 - 89 ปี kontimi-a-yurawangpaedsibtuangpaedsibgaopi

octroi *n.* ภาษีผ่านด่าน pasipandan

ocular *a.* เกี่ยวกับสายตา giawgabsaita

oculist *n.* จักษุแพทย์ jaksupaed

odd *a.* แปลก plaek

oddity *n.* คนประหลาด konpralad

odds *n.* โอกาสที่เป็นไปได้ o-gadtipenpaidai

ode *n.* บทกวี bodgawi

odious *a.* น่ารังเกียจ naranggiad

odium *n.* ความเกลียดชัง kwamgliadchang

odorous *a.* ที่มีกลิ่นหอม timiglinhom

odour *n.* กลิ่น glin

offence *n.* การทำให้ขุ่นเคือง gantamhaikunkeuang

offend *v.t.* ทำให้โกรธ tamhaigrot

offender *n.* ผู้กระทำผิด pugratampid

offensive *a.* ก้าวร้าว gaorao

offensive *n* การรุก ganruk

offer *v.t.* เสนอ saneu

offer *n* การเสนอ gansaneu

offering *n.* ของถวาย kongtawai

office *n.* สำนักงาน samnak-ngan

officer *n.* เจ้าหน้าที่ jaonati

official *a.* ทางการ tanggan

official *n* เจ้าหน้าที่ jaonati

officially *adv.* เป็นทางการ pentanggan

officiate *v.i.* ทำหน้าที่ tamnati

officious *a.* เจ้ากี้เจ้าการ jaogijaogan

offing *n.* ตำแหน่งที่อยู่ไกล
tamtaengtiyuglai

offset *v.t.* ชดเชย chodcheuy

offset *n* สิ่งชดเชย singchodcheuy

offshoot *n.* กิ่งก้าน ginggan

offspring *n.* ลูกหลาน looklan

oft *adv.* บ่อย boy

often *adv.* บ่อย boy

ogle *v.t.* ทำตาหวาน tamtawan

ogle *n* การยักคิ้วหลิ่วตา ganyakkewlewta

oil *n.* น้ำมัน namman

oil *v.t* หยอดน้ำมัน yodnamman

oily *a.* มัน man

ointment *n.* ขี้ผึ้ง kipeung

old *a.* แก่ gae

oligarchy *n.* คณาธิปไตย kanatipatai

olive *n.* มะกอก magok

olympiad *n.* การแข่งขันระหว่างประเทศ
gankaengkanrawaengpratet

omega *n.* ตอนจบ tawnjob

omelette *n.* ไข่เจียว kaijiaw

omen *n.* โชคลาง choklang

ominous *a.* ที่เป็นลาง tipenlang

omission *n.* การละเลย ganlaleuy

omit *v.t.* ละทิ้ง lating

omnipotence *n.* การมีอำนาจไม่สิ้นสุด
ganmi-amnardmaisinsud

omnipotent *a.* มีอำนาจทุกอย่าง mi-
amnardtookyang

omnipresence *n.* การพบเห็นในทุกที่
ganpobhennaitookti

omnipresent *a.* พบเห็นในทุกที่
pobhennaitookti

omniscience *n.* ความรอบรู้ kwamrobru

omniscient *a.* ที่รอบรู้ tirobru

on *prep.* บน bon

on *adv.* ต่อเนื่อง tawneuang

once *adv.* ครั้งหนึ่ง krangneung

one *a.* หนึ่ง neung

one *pron.* คนหนึ่ง konneung

oneness *n.* ความเป็นหนึ่งเดียว
kwampenneungdiaw

onerous *a.* ยาก yak

onion *n.* หัวหอม huahom

on-looker *n.* ผู้สังเกตการณ์ pusanggedgan

only *a.* เท่านั้น taonan

only *adv.* เท่านั้น taonan

only *conj.* แต่ tae

onomatopoeia *n.* การเลียนเสียงธรรมชาติ
ganliansiangtammachat

onrush *n.* การไหลบ่า ganlaiba

onset *n.* การโจมตี ganjomti

onslaught *n.* การโจมตี ganjomti

onus *n.* หน้าที่ nati

onward *a.* ไปข้างหน้า paikangna

onwards *adv.* ไปข้างหน้า paikangna

ooze *n.* การไหลซึม ganlaiseum

ooze *v.i.* ไหลซึม laiseum

opacity *n.* ความคลุมเครือ
kwamklumkreua

opal *n.* โอปอล opal

opaque *a.* ขุ่น kun

open *a.* เปิด peud

open *v.t.* เปิด peud

opening *n.* การเปิด ganpeud

openly *adv.* อย่างเปิดเผย yangpeudpeuy

opera *n.* โอเปร่า opera

operate *v.t.* ดำเนินการ damneuangan

operation *n.* การดำเนินการ
gandamneungan

operative *a.* พร้อมใช้งาน promchai-ngan

operator *n.* ผู้ดำเนินการ pudamneungan

opine *v.t.* แสดงความเห็น
sadaengkwamhen

opinion *n.* ความเห็น kwamhen

opium *n.* ฝิ่น fin

opponent *n.* คู่แข่งขัน kukaengkan

opportune *a.* เหมาะสม mawsom

opportunism *n.* การฉวยโอกาส ganchuay-
o-gad

opportunity *n.* โอกาส o-gad

oppose *v.t.* ต่อต้าน tawtan

opposite *a.* ตรงข้าม trongkam

opposition *n.* ฝ่ายตรงข้าม faitrongkam

oppress *v.t.* กดขี่ godki
oppression *n.* การกดขี่ gangodki
oppressive *a.* ที่กดขี่ tigodki
oppressor *n.* ผู้กดขี่ pugodki
opt *v.i.* เลือก leuak
optic *a.* เกี่ยวกับตา giawgabta
optician *n.* คนขายแว่นตา konkaiwaenta
optimism *n.* การมองโลกในแง่ดี
  ganmongloknai-ngaedi
optimist *n.* ผู้มองโลกในแง่ดี
  pumongloknai-ngaedi
optimistic *a.* มองโลกในแง่ดี mongloknai-
  ngaedi
optimum *n.* ภาวะที่ดีที่สุด pawatiditisud
optimum *a* เหมาะที่สุด mawtisud
option *n.* ทางเลือก tangleuak
optional *a.* เป็นทางเลือก pentangleuak
opulence *n.* ความมั่งคั่ง kwammangkang
opulent *a.* มั่งคั่ง mangkang
oracle *n.* คำทำนาย kamtamnai
oracular *a.* เป็นการทำนาย pengantamnai
oral *a.* เกี่ยวกับปาก giawgabpak
orally *adv.* โดยปากเปล่า doeypakplao
orange *n.* ส้ม som
orange *a* สีส้ม sisom
oration *n.* การปราศรัย ganprasai
orator *n.* ผู้กล่าวคำปราศรัย
  puglaokamprasai
oratorical *a.* เกี่ยวกับศิลปะในการพูด
  giawgabsinlapanaiganpud
oratory *n.* ห้องสวด hongsuad
orb *n.* วัตถุทรงกลม wattusongglom
orbit *n.* วงโคจร wongkojon
orchard *n.* สวนผลไม้ suanponlamai
orchestra *n.* ออร์เคสตร้า orchestra
orchestral *a.* เกี่ยวกับออร์เคสตร้า
  giawgab-orchestra
ordeal *n.* ความเจ็บปวด kwamjebpuad
order *n.* คำสั่ง kamsang
order *v.t* สั่ง sang
orderly *a.* อย่างมีระเบียบ yangmirabiab

orderly *n.* เจ้าหน้าที่โรงพยาบาล
  jaonatirongpayaban
ordinance *n.* กฎหมาย godmai
ordinarily *adv.* โดยปกติ doeypakati
ordinary *a.* ปกติ pakati
ordnance *n.* สรรพาวุธ sanpawit
ore *n.* แร่ rae
organ *n.* อวัยวะ a-waiyawa
organic *a.* เกี่ยวกับอวัยวะ giawgab-a-
  waiyawa
organism *n.* สิ่งมีชีวิต singmichiwit
organization *n.* องค์กร ong-gon
organize *v.t.* จัดการ jadgan
orient *n.* ประเทศแถบตะวันออก
  pratedtaebtawan-awk
orient *v.t.* กำหนดตำแหน่ง
  gamnodtamnaeng
oriental *a.* เกี่ยวกับประเทศทางตะวันออก
  giawgabpratedtawan-awk
  giawgabpratedtangtawan-awk
oriental *n* ชาวตะวันออก chaotawan-awk
orientate *v.t.* หันหน้าไปทางทิศตะวันออก
  hannapaitangtidtawan-awk
origin *n.* ต้นกำเนิด tongamneud
original *a.* แรกเริ่ม raekreum
original *n* ต้นฉบับ tonchabab
originality *n.* ความคิดริเริ่ม
  kwamkidrireum
originate *v.t.* เริ่มต้น reumton
originator *n.* ผู้เริ่มต้น pureumton
ornament *n.* เครื่องประดับ kreuangpradab
ornament *v.t.* ประดับ pradab
ornamental *a.* ที่ใช้ประดับ tichaipradab
ornamentation *n.* การประดับ ganpradab
orphan *n.* เด็กกำพร้า dekgampra
orphan *v.t* ทำให้เป็นเด็กกำพร้า
  tamhaipendekgampra
orphanage *n.* สถานเลี้ยงเด็กกำพร้า
  satanliangdekgampra
orthodox *a.* ดั้งเดิม dangdeum
orthodoxy *n.* หลักความเชื่อ
  lakkwamcheua

oscillate *v.i.* แกว่ง gwaeng
oscillation *n.* การแกว่ง gangwaeng
ossify *v.t.* ทำให้แข็ง tamhaikaeng
ostracize *v.t.* ขับไล่ kablai
ostrich *n.* นกกระจอกเทศ nokgrajokted
other *a.* อื่นๆ eun-eun
other *pron.* คนอื่น kon-eun
otherwise *adv.* ไม่เช่นนั้น maichennan
otherwise *conj.* ไม่เช่นนั้น maichennan
otter *n.* นาก nak
ottoman *n.* ชาวตุรกี chaoturagi
ounce *n.* ออนซ์ ounce
our *pron.* ของเรา kongrao
oust *v.t.* ขับไล่ kablai
out *adv.* ออกไป awkpai
out-balance *v.t.* มีน้ำหนักกว่า
    minamnakmakkwa
outbid *v.t.* เสนอราคาสูงกว่า
    saneurakasungkwa
outbreak *n.* การกระจาย gangrajai
outburst *n.* การระเบิด ganrabeud
outcast *n.* คนนอกคอก konnawkkok
outcast *a* นอกคอก nokkok
outcome *n.* ผลลัพธ์ ponlab
outcry *a.* โวยวาย woiwai
outdated *a.* ล้าสมัย lasamai
outdo *v.t.* เอาชนะ aow-chana
outdoor *a.* กลางแจ้ง glangjaeng
outer *a.* รอบนอก robnok
outfit *n.* เครื่องมือ kreuangmeu
outfit *v.t* ติดตั้งเครื่องมือ
    tidtangkreuangmeu
outgrow *v.t.* โตเร็วกว่า torewkwa
outhouse *n.* เรือนหลังเล็ก reuanlanglek
outing *n.* การออกนอกบ้าน gan-
    awknawkban
outlandish *a.* แปลกประหลาด plaekpralad
outlaw *n.* คนทำผิดกฎหมาย
    kontampidgodmai
outlaw *v.t* ทำผิดกฎหมาย tampidgodmai
outline *n.* แผนการคร่าวๆ
    paengankraokrao

outline *v.t.* ร่าง rang
outlive *v.i.* มีอายุยืนกว่า mi-a-yu-yeunkwa
outlook *n.* ทัศนคติ tasanakati
outmoded *a.* ล้าสมัย lasamai
outnumber *v.t.* มีจำนวนมากกว่า
    mijamnuanmakkwa
outpatient *n.* คนไข้นอก konkainok
outpost *n.* ด่านหน้า danna
output *n.* ผลผลิต ponpalid
outrage *n.* ความโกรธ kwamgrot
outrage *v.t.* ทำให้โกรธ tamhaigrot
outright *adv.* โดยสมบูรณ์ doeysomboon
outright *a* โดยสมบูรณ์ doeysomboon
outrun *v.t.* วิ่งเร็วกว่า wingrewkwa
outset *n.* การเริ่มต้น ganreumton
outshine *v.t.* บดบังรัศมี bodbangrasami
outside *a.* ที่อยู่ด้านนอก tiyudannawk
outside *n* ข้างนอก kangnawk
outside *adv* ภายนอก painok
outside *prep* นอกจาก nawkjak
outsider *n.* คนนอก konnawk
outsize *a.* มีขนาดใหญ่เป็นพิเศษ
    mikanadyaipenpised
outskirts *n.pl.* ชานเมือง chanmeuang
outspoken *a.* พูดจาเปิดเผย
    pudjapeudpeuy
outstanding *a.* โดดเด่น dodden
outward *a.* ที่มองเห็นได้ timonghendai
outward *adv* ที่มุ่งไปด้านนอก
    timungpaidannok
outwards *adv* มุ่งไปด้านนอก
    mungpaidannok
outwardly *adv.* ไปทางด้านนอก
    paitangdannok
outweigh *v.t.* มีน้ำหนักเกิน minamnakgeun
outwit *v.t.* ฉลาดกว่า chaladkwa
oval *a.* วงรี wongri
oval *n* รูปวงรี roobwongri
ovary *n.* รังไข่ของสตรี rangkaikongsatri
ovation *n.* การปรบมือต้อนรับ
    ganprobmeutawnrab
oven *n.* เตาอบ tao-ob

over *prep.* เหนือ neua
over *adv* เหนือ neua
over *n* ปริมาณเกิน parimangeun
overact *v.t.* กระทำเกินเลย gratamgeunleuy
overall *n.* ภาพรวม pabruam
overall *a* โดยรวม doeyruam
overawe *v.t.* ขู่ ku
overboard *adv.* นอกลำเรือ nokramreua
overburden *v.t.* รับภาระหนักเกินไป rabparanakguenpai
overcast *a.* มีเมฆมาก mimekmak
overcharge *v.t.* คิดเงินแพงเกินไป kidngeunpaenggeunpai
overcharge *n* ค่าธรรมเนียมแพงเกินไป katamniampaenggeunpai
overcoat *n.* เสื้อคลุม seuaklum
overcome *v.t.* เอาชนะ aow-chana
overdo *v.t.* ทำมากเกินไป tammakgeunpai
overdose *n.* การกินยาเกินขนาด ganginyageunkanad
overdose *v.t.* กินยาเกินขนาด ginyageunkanad
overdraft *n.* การเบิกเงินเกินบัญชี ganbeuk-ngeun-geunbanchi
overdraw *v.t.* ถอนเงินเกิน tawn-ngeun-geun
overdue *a.* พ้นกำหนด pongamnod
overhaul *v.t.* ยกเครื่อง yokkreuang
overhaul *n.* การยกเครื่อง ganyokkreung
overhear *v.t.* ได้ยินโดยไม่ตั้งใจ daiyindoeymaitangjai
overjoyed *a* ดีใจเหลือเกิน dijaileuageun
overlap *v.t.* ทับกัน tabgan
overlap *n* ส่วนที่ทับกัน suantitabgan
overleaf *adv.* กลับด้าน glabdan
overload *v.t.* บรรทุกเกินพิกัด bantookgeunpigad
overload *n* การบรรทุกเกินพิกัด ganbantookgeunpigad
overlook *v.t.* พลาดไป pladpai
overnight *adv.* ตลอดคืน talodkeun

overnight *a* ในช่วงกลางคืน naichuangglangkeun
overpower *v.t.* เอาชนะ aow-chana
overrate *v.t.* ตีค่าสูงเกินไป tikasoonggeunpai
overrule *v.t.* ปฏิเสธ patised
overrun *v.t* บุกรุก bukruk
oversee *v.t.* ตรวจสอบ truadsob
overseer *n.* ผู้ตรวจสอบ putraudsob
overshadow *v.t.* ข่ม kom
oversight *n.* การมองข้ามไป ganmongkampai
overt *a.* ชัดเจน chadjen
overtake *v.t.* ตามทัน tamtan
overthrow *v.t.* ล้มล้าง lomlang
overthrow *n* การล้มล้าง ganlomlang
overtime *adv.* นอกเวลาปกติ nokwelapakati
overtime *n*
เงินพิเศษจากการทำงานนอกเวลา ngeunpisetjakgantam-ngannokwela
overture *n.* การทาบทาม gantabtam
overwhelm *v.t.* รู้สึกท่วมท้น ruseuktuamton
overwork *v.i.* ทำงานมากไป tam-ngan-makgpai
overwork *n.* การทำงานมากไป gantam-ngan-makpai
owe *v.t* เป็นหนี้ penni
owl *n.* นกเค้าแมว nokkaomaew
own *a.* ที่เป็นเจ้าของ tipenjaokong
own *v.t.* เป็นเจ้าของ penjaokong
owner *n.* เจ้าของ jaokong
ownership *n.* ความเป็นเจ้าของ kwampenjaokong
ox *n.* วัว wua
oxygen *n.* ออกซิเจน oxygen
oyster *n.* หอยนางรม hoynangrom

P

pace *n* ฝีเท้า feetao

pace *v.i.* ก้าวเท้า gaotao

pacific *a.* สงบ sa-ngob

pacify *v.t.* ทำให้สงบ tamhaisa-ngob

pack *n.* ห่อของ hawkong

pack *v.t.* บรรจุ banju

package *n.* หีบห่อ hibhaw

packet *n.* ห่อของขนาดเล็ก
hawkongkanadlek

packing *n.* การห่อของ ganhawkong

pact *n.* ข้อตกลง kawtoklong

pad *n.* เบาะ baw

pad *v.t.* บุ bu

padding *n.* เบาะรอง bawlong

paddle *v.i.* พาย pai

paddle *n* ไม้พาย maipai

paddy *n.* นาข้าว nakao

page *n.* หน้ากระดาษ nagradad

page *v.t.* เรียก riak

pageant *n.* การประกวด ganpraguad

pageantry *n.* ขบวนแห่ kabuanhae

pagoda *n.* เจดีย์ jedi

pail *n.* ถัง tang

pain *n.* ความเจ็บปวด kwamjebpuad

pain *v.t.* ทำให้เจ็บปวด tamhaijebpuad

painful *a.* เจ็บปวด jebpuad

painstaking *a.* อุตสาหะ udsaha

paint *n.* สี si

paint *v.t.* ทาสี tasi

painter *n.* ช่างทาสี changtasi

painting *n.* การทาสี gantasi

pair *n.* คู่ ku

pair *v.t.* จับคู่ jabku

pal *n.* เพื่อน peuan

palace *n.* วัง wang

palanquin *n.* แคร่ krae

palatable *a.* อร่อย a-roy

palatal *a.* เกี่ยวกับเพดานปาก
giawgabpedanpak

palate *n.* เพดานปาก pedanpak

palatial *a.* ใหญ่โต yaito

pale *n.* ไม้รั้ว mairua

pale *a* ไม่มีสี maimisi

pale *v.i.* ซีด sid

palette *n.* จานผสมสี janpasomsi

palm *n.* ต้นปาล์ม ton-palm

palm *v.t.* เอามือลูบ owlmeuloob

palm *n.* ฝ่ามือ fameu

palmist *n.* หมอดูลายมือ maudulaimeu

palmistry *n.* วิชาดูลายมือ wichadulaimeu

palpable *a.* ชัดเจน chadjen

palpitate *v.i.* เต้นรัว tenrua

palpitation *n.* อาการใจสั่น a-ganjaisan

palsy *n.* อัมพาต ammapat

paltry *a.* ไม่สำคัญ maisamkan

pamper *v.t.* ตามใจ tamjai

pamphlet *n.* แผ่นพับ paenpab

pamphleteer *n.* คนเขียนแผ่นพับ
konkianpaenpab

panacea *n.* ยาครอบจักรวาล
yakrobjakkawan

pandemonium *n.* ความโกลาหล
kwamkolahon

pane *n.* บานกระจก banjrajok

panegyric *n.* คำสรรเสริญ kamsanseun

panel *n.* แผง paeng

panel *v.t.* ตกแต่ง toktaeng

pang *n.* อาการเจ็บปลาบ a-ganjebplab

panic *n.* ความตื่นตระหนก
kwamteuntranok

panorama *n.* ทัศนียภาพเชิงกว้าง
tasaniyababcheunggwang

pant *v.i.* หายใจหอบ haijaihob

pant *n.* อาการหอบ a-ganhob

pantaloon *n.* ตัวตลก tuatalok

pantheism *n.* ลัทธิพระเจ้าคือจักรวาล
lattiprajaokeujakkawan

pantheist *n.* ผู้เชื่อลัทธิพระเจ้าคือจักรวาล
pucheulattiprajaokeujakkawan

panther *n.* เสือดำ seuadam

pantomime *n.* ละครใบ้ lakonbai

pantry *n.* ห้องเก็บอาหาร honggeb-a-han

papacy *n.* ตำแหน่งสันตปาปา
tamnaengsantapapa

papal *a.* เกี่ยวกับสันตปาปา
giawgabsantapapa

paper *n.* กระดาษ gradad

par *n.* การเท่ากัน gantaogan

parable *n.* นิทานสอนใจ nitansonjai

parachute *n.* ร่มชูชีพ romchuchib

parachutist *n.* นักกระโดดร่ม
tangradodrom

parade *n.* พาเหรด pared

parade *v.t.* เดินพาเหรด deunpared

paradise *n.* สวรรค์ sawan

paradox *n.* สิ่งผิดปกติ singpidpagati

paradoxical *a.* ขัดแย้ง kadyaeng

paraffin *n.* พาราฟิน paraffin

paragon *n.* ตัวอย่างที่ดีเลิศ
tuayangtidileud

paragraph *n.* ย่อหน้า yawna

parallel *a.* ขนาน kanan

parallel *v.t.* ทำให้ขนานกัน tamhaikanan

parallelism *n.* ความเท่าเทียม
kwamtaotiam

parallelogram *n.* สี่เหลี่ยมรูปขนาน
siliamroobkanan

paralyse *v.t.* อ่อนเปลี้ย on-plia

paralysis *n.* อัมพาต ammapat

paralytic *a.* เป็นอัมพาต pen-ammapat

paramount *n.* ผู้ปกครองชั้นสูงสุด
pupokkrongchansoongsud

paramour *n.* ชู้รัก churak

paraphernalia *n. pl* ของใช้ส่วนตัว
kongchaisuantua

paraphrase *n.* การเขียนประโยคใหม่
gankianprayokmai

paraphrase *v.t.* เขียนประโยคใหม่
kianprayokmai

parasite *n.* ปาราสิต parasite

parcel *n.* ห่อของ hawkong

parcel *v.t.* ห่อ haw

parch *v.t.* ทำให้แห้ง tamhaihaeng

pardon *v.t.* ยกโทษ yoktod

pardon *n.* การอภัยโทษ gan-a-paiyatod

pardonable *a.* ให้อภัยได้ hai-a-paidai

parent *n.* ผู้ปกครอง pupokkrong

parentage *n.* วงศ์ตระกูล wongtragoon

parental *a.* เกี่ยวกับพ่อแม่
giawgabpawmae

parenthesis *n.* วงเล็บ wongleb

parish *n.* เขตทางศาสนา kedsasana

parity *n.* ความเท่าเทียม kwamtaotiam

park *n.* สวนสาธารณะ suansatarana

park *v.t.* จอดรถ jawdrod

parlance *n.* คำพูด kampud

parley *n.* การเจรจา ganjeraja

parley *v.i* เจรจา jeraja

parliament *n.* รัฐสภา rattasapa

parliamentarian *n.* สมาชิกรัฐสภา
samachikratasapa

parliamentary *a.* เกี่ยวกับรัฐสภา
giawgabrattasapa

parlour *n.* ห้องรับแขก hongrabkaek

parody *n.* การล้อเลียน ganlawlian

parody *v.t.* ล้อเลียน lawlian

parole *n.* ทัณฑ์บน tanbon

parole *v.t.* ทำทัณฑ์บน tamtanbon

parricide *n.* การฆ่าพ่อแม่ gankapawmae

parrot *n.* นกแก้ว nokgaew

parry *v.t.* ปัดป้อง padpong

parry *n.* การปัดป้อง ganpadpong

parson *n.* บาทหลวง badluang

part *n.* ส่วน suan

part *v.t.* แยก yaek

partake *v.i.* เข้าร่วม kaoruam

partial *a.* ลำเอียง lam-iang

partiality *n.* ความลำเอียง kwamlam-iang

participate *v.i.* เข้าร่วม kaoruam

participant *n.* ผู้เข้าร่วม pukaoruam

participation *n.* การเข้าร่วม gankaoruam

particle *a.* อนุภาค a-nupak

particular *a.* เฉพาะ chapaw

particular *n.* รายละเอียด raira-iad

partisan *n.* ผู้แบ่งพรรคแบ่งพวก pubaengpakbaengpuak

partisan *a.* ซึ่งแบ่งพวก seungbaengpuak

partition *n.* ฉาก chak

partition *v.t.* แบ่ง baeng

partner *n.* หุ้นส่วน hunsuan

partnership *n.* ความเป็นหุ้นส่วน kwampenhunsuan

party *n.* งานเลี้ยง nganliang

pass *v.i.* ผ่าน pan

pass *n* บัตรผ่าน badpan

passage *n.* ทางผ่าน tangpan

passenger *n.* ผู้โดยสาร pudoeysan

passion *n.* ความหลงใหล kwamlonglai

passionate *a.* หลงใหล longlai

passive *a.* อยู่เฉย yucheuy

passport *n.* หนังสือเดินทาง nangseudeuntang

past *a.* ที่ผ่านไปแล้ว tipanpailaew

past *n.* อดีต a-did

past *prep.* เลยผ่าน leuypan

paste *n.* ของเหนียว kongniaw

paste *v.t.* แปะ pae

pastel *n.* ดินสอสี dinsawsi

pastime *n.* งานอดิเรก ngan-a-direk

pastoral *a.* เกี่ยวกับทุ่งหญ้า giawgabtungya

pasture *n.* ทุ่งหญ้าเลี้ยงสัตว์ tungyaliangsat

pasture *v.t.* ปล่อยให้สัตว์เล็มหญ้า ployhaisatlemya

pat *v.t.* ลูบ loob

pat *n* การลูบ ganloob

pat *adv* คล่อง klong

patch *v.t.* ปะ pa

patch *n* แผ่นปะ paenpa

patent *a.* ได้รับการคุ้มครองจากสิทธิบัตร dairabgankumklongjaksitibat

patent *n* สิทธิบัตร sitibat

patent *v.t.* จดสิทธิบัตร jodsitibat

paternal *a.* ฝ่ายบิดา faibida

path *n.* ทางเดิน tangdeun

pathetic *a.* น่าเวทนา nawetana

pathos *n.* ความสงสาร kwamsongsan

patience *n.* ความอดทน kwam-odton

patient *a.* อดทน odton

patient *n* คนป่วย konpuay

patricide *n.* การฆ่าบิดา gankabida

patrimony *n.* มรดกของบิดา moradokkongbida

patriot *n.* ผู้รักชาติ purakchat

patriotic *a.* ด้วยความรักชาติ duaykwamrakchat

partiotism *n.* ความรักชาติ kwamrakchat

patrol *v.i.* ลาดตระเวน ladtrawen

patrol *n* การลาดตระเวน ganladtrawen

patron *n.* ผู้อุปถัมภ์ pu-ooppatam

patronage *n.* การอุปถัมภ์ gan-u-patam

patronize *v.t.* อุปถัมภ์ oppatam

pattern *n.* แบบแผน baebpaen

paucity *n.* ควมขัดสน kwamkadson

pauper *n.* ยาจก yajok

pause *n.* การหยุดชั่วคราว ganyudchuakrao

pause *v.i.* หยุดชั่วคราว yudchuakrao

pave *v.t.* ปูทาง putang

pavement *n.* ทางเดิน tangdeun

pavilion *n.* ปะรำ param

paw *n.* อุ้งเท้า ungtao

paw *v.t.* ตะปบ tapob

pay *v.t.* จ่าย jai

pay *n* การจ่าย ganjai

payable *a.* สามารถชำระหนี้ได้ samadchamranidai

payee *n.* ผู้รับเงิน purab-ngeun

payment *n.* การจ่ายเงิน ganjai-ngeun

pea *n.* ถั่ว tua

peace *n.* สันติภาพ santipab

peaceable *a.* สงบสุข sa-ngobsook

peaceful *a.* สงบสุข sa-ngobsook

peach *n.* ลูกพีช look-peach

peacock *n.* นกยูง nokyung

peahen *n.* นกยูงตัวเมีย nokyungtuamia

peak *n.* จุดสูงสุด judsoongsud

pear *n.* ลูกแพร์ lookpear

pearl *n.* ไข่มุก kaimook
peasant *n.* ชาวไร่ชาวนา chaoraichaona
peasantry *n.* ชาวไร่ชาวนา chaoraichaona
pebble *n.* กรวด gruad
peck *n.* การจิก ganjik
peck *v.i.* จิก jik
peculiar *a.* ประหลาด pralad
peculiarity *n.* คุณสมบัติเฉพาะ
kunnasombatchapaw
pecuniary *a.* เกี่ยวกับเงิน giawgab-ngeun
pedagogue *n.* ครู kru
pedagogy *n.* ครุศาสตร์ karusat
pedal *n.* คันเร่ง kanreng
pedal *v.t.* เหยียบคันเร่ง yiabkanreng
pedant *n.* คนอวดรู้ kon-uad-ru
pedantic *a.* อวดรู้ uad-ru
pedantry *n.* การอวดรู้ gan-uad-ru
pedestal *n.* แท่น taen
pedestrian *n.* คนเดินถนน kondeuntanon
pedigree *n.* ตระกูล tragoon
peel *v.t.* ปอกเปลือก pokpleuak
peel *n.* เปลือก pleuak
peep *v.i.* แอบดู ab-du
peep *n* การแอบดู gan-ab-du
peer *n.* เพื่อน peuan
peerless *a.* ดีเลิศ dileud
peg *n.* หมุด mud
peg *v.t.* ตอกหมุด tokmud
pelf *n.* ทรัพย์สมบัติ sabsombat
pell-mell *adv.* ยุ่งเหยิง yungyeung
pen *n.* คอก kok
pen *v.t.* ใส่คอก saikok
penal *a.* ทางอาญา tang-a-ya
penalize *v.t.* ลงโทษ longtod
penalty *n.* การลงโทษ ganlongtod
pencil *n.* ดินสอ dinsaw
pencil *v.t.* เขียนด้วยดินสอ
kiandeuydinsaw
pending *prep.* อยู่ระหว่าง yurawang
pending *a* ค้างอยู่ kangyu
pendulum *n.* ลูกตุ้ม looktum
penetrate *v.t.* แทรกแซง saeksaeng

penetration *n.* การแทรกแซง
gansaeksaeng
penis *n.* อวัยวะเพศชาย awaiyawapedchai
penniless *a.* หมดตัว modtua
penny *n.* เงินเพนนี ngeunpenny
pension *n.* บำนาญ bamnan
pension *v.t.* รับบำนาญ rabbamnan
pensioner *n.* ผู้รับบำนาญ purabbamnan
pensive *a.* ครุ่นคิด krunkid
pentagon *n.* รูปห้าเหลี่ยม roobhaliam
peon *n.* คนงาน kon-ngan
people *n.* ประชาชน prachachon
people *v.t.* อาศัย a-sai
pepper *n.* พริกไทย priktai
pepper *v.t.* ใส่พริกไทย saipriktai
per *prep.* ต่อ taw
perambulator *n.* รถเข็นเด็กทารก
rodkendektarok
perceive *v.t.* รับรู้ rabru
perceptible *adj* เข้าใจได้ kaojaidai
per cent *adv.* ร้อยละ royla
percentage *n.* อัตราร้อยละ attaroyla
perception *n.* การรับรู้ ganrabru
perceptive *a.* รับรู้ได้ rabrudai
perch *n.* คอน kawn
perch *v.i.* เกาะคอน gaokon
perennial *a.* ตลอดปี talodpi
perennial *n.* ไม้ยืนต้น maiyeunton
perfect *a.* สมบูรณ์ somboon
perfect *v.t.* ทำให้สมบูรณ์ tamhaisomboon
perfection *n.* ความสมบูรณ์
kwamsomboon
perfidy *n.* การทรยศ gantorayod
perforate *v.t.* ทำให้เป็นรู tamhaipenru
perforce *adv.* ด้วยความจำเป็น
deuykwamjampen
perform *v.t.* แสดง sadaeng
performance *n.* การแสดง gansadaeng
performer *n.* นักแสดง naksadaeng
perfume *n.* น้ำหอม namhom
perfume *v.t.* ใส่น้ำหอม sainamhom
perhaps *adv.* บางที bangti

peril *n.* ภัยอันตราย pai-antarai

peril *v.t.* ตกอยู่ในอันตราย tokyunai-antarai

perilous *a.* เต็มไปด้วยอันตราย tempaiduay-antarai

period *n.* ระยะเวลา rayawela

periodical *n.* วารสารที่ออกตามกำหนด warasanti-awktamgamnod

periodical *a.* เป็นช่วงๆ penchuangchuang

periphery *n.* ขอบนอก kobnok

perish *v.i.* ตาย tai

perishable *a.* ซึ่งตายได้ seungtaidai

perjure *v.i.* ให้การเท็จ haiganted

perjury *n.* การให้การเท็จ ganhaiganted

permanence *n.* ความถาวร kwamtawon

permanent *a.* ถาวร tavon

permissible *a.* ยอมได้ yomdai

permission *n.* การอนุญาต gan-a-nuyad

permit *v.t.* อนุญาต a-nuyad

permit *n.* ใบอนุญาต bai-a-nuyad

permutation *n.* การเปลี่ยนลำดับ ganplianramdab

pernicious *a.* เป็นอันตราย pen-antarai

perpendicular *a.* ตั้งฉาก tangchak

perpendicular *n.* เส้นตั้งฉาก sentangchak

perpetual *a.* ตลอดไป tarodpai

perpetuate *v.t.* ทำให้ถาวร tamhaitaworn

perplex *v.t.* สับสน sabson

perplexity *n.* ความสับสน kwamsabson

persecute *v.t.* ข่มเหง komheng

persecution *n.* การข่มเหง gankomheng

perseverance *n.* ความพยายาม kwampayayam

persevere *v.i.* พยายาม payayam

persist *v.i.* ยืนกราน yeungran

persistence *n.* การยืนกราน ganyeungran

persistent *a.* ดื้อ deu

person *n.* บุคคล bukkon

personage *n.* บุคคลสำคัญ bukkonsamkan

personal *a.* ส่วนตัว suantua

personality *n.* บุคลิกลักษณะ bukkaliklaksana

personification *n.* แบบอย่าง baebyang

personify *v.t.* แสดงบทบาท sadaengbodbat

personnel *n.* ฝ่ายบุคคล faibukkon

perspective *n.* ทัศนคติ tasanakati

perspiration *n.* เหงื่อ ngeua

perspire *v.i.* เหงื่อออก ngeua-awk

persuade *v.t.* ชักชวน chakchuan

persuasion *n.* การชักชวน ganchakchuan

pertain *v.i.* เกี่ยวกับ giawgab

pertinent *a.* ตรงประเด็น trongpraden

perturb *v.t.* ก่อกวน gawguan

perusal *n.* การอ่าน gan-an

peruse *v.t.* อ่าน an

pervade *v.t.* แผ่กระจาย paegrajai

perverse *a.* แปลก plaek

perversion *n.* ความวิปริต kwamwiparit

perversity *n.* ความวิปริต kwamwiparit

pervert *v.t.* หลงผิด longpid

pessimism *n.* การมองโลกในแง่ร้าย ganmongloknai-ngaerai

pessimist *n.* ผู้มองโลกในแง่ร้าย pumongloknai-ngaerai

pessimistic *a.* มองโลกในแง่ร้าย mongloknai-ngaerai

pest *n.* สัตว์ที่รบกวน sattirobguan

pesticide *n.* ยาฆ่าแมลง yakamalaeng

pestilence *n.* โรคติดต่อร้ายแรง roktidtawrairaeng

pet *n.* สัตว์เลี้ยง satliang

pet *v.t.* สัมผัส sampat

petal *n.* กลีบดอกไม้ glibdawkmai

petition *n.* การร้องเรียน ganrongrian

petition *v.t.* ร้องเรียน rongrian

petitioner *n.* ผู้ร้องเรียน purongrian

petrol *n.* น้ำมันเบนซิน nammanbensin

petroleum *n.* น้ำมันปิโตรเลียม nammanpetroleum

petticoat *n.* กระโปรงชั้นใน graprongchannai

petty *a.* เล็กน้อย leknoy

petulance *n.* ความน้อยใจ kwamnoyjai

petulant *a.* น้อยใจ noyjai
phantom *n.* ผี fee
pharmacy *n.* ร้านขายยา rankaiya
phase *n.* ช่วง chuang
phenomenal *a.* มหัศจรรย์ mahadsajan
phenomenon *n.* ปรากฏการณ์ pragodgan
phial *n.* ขวดแก้ว kuadgaew
philanthropic *a.* ใจบุญ jaiboon
philanthropist *n.* ผู้ใจบุญ pujaiboon
philanthropy *n.* ความใจบุญ
　kwamjaiboon
philological *a.* เกี่ยวกับนิรุกติศาสตร์
　giawgabniroktisat
philologist *n.* นักนิรุกติศาสตร์
　nakniruktisat
philology *n.* นิรุกติศาสตร์ niruktisat
philosopher *n.* นักปรัชญา nakpratya
philosophical *a.* ทางปรัชญา tangpratya
philosophy *n.* ปรัชญา pratya
phone *n.* โทรศัพท์ torasab
phonetic *a.* เกี่ยวกับการออกเสียง
　giawgabgan-awksiang
phonetics *n.* สัทศาสตร์ sattasat
phosphate *n.* ฟอสเฟต phosphate
phosphorus *n.* ฟอสฟอรัส phosphorus
photo *n* ภาพ pab
photograph *v.t.* ถ่ายภาพ taipab
photograph *n* ภาพถ่าย pabtai
photographer *n.* ผู้ถ่ายภาพ putaipab
photographic *a.* เกี่ยวกับภาพถ่าย
　giawgabpabtai
photography *n.* การถ่ายภาพ gantaipab
phrase *n.* ถ้อยคำ toykam
phrase *v.t.* ถ่ายทอดด้วยคำพูด
　taitoddueykampud
phraseology *n.* การใช้สำนวนโวหาร
　ganchaisamnuanwohan
physic *n.* ยาถ่าย yatai
physic *v.t.* ใช้ยารักษา chaiyaraksa
physical *a.* เกี่ยวกับร่างกาย
　giawgabranggai
physician *n.* หมอ maw

physicist *n.* นักฟิสิกส์ nakphysic
physics *n.* ฟิสิกส์ physics
physiognomy *n.* สีหน้า sina
physique *n.* เรือนร่าง reuanrang
pianist *n.* นักเปียโน nakpiano
piano *n.* เปียโน piano
pick *v.t.* เลือก leuak
pick *n.* การเลือก ganleuak
picket *n.* รั้ว rua
picket *v.t.* ล้อมรั้ว lomrua
pickle *n.* ของดอง kongdong
pickle *v.t* ดอง dong
picnic *n.* ปิกนิก picnic
picnic *v.i.* ไปปิกนิก paipicnic
pictorial *a.* เกี่ยวกับภาพ giawgabpab
picture *n.* ภาพ pab
picture *v.t.* วาดภาพ wadpab
picturesque *a.* สวย suay
piece *n.* ชิ้นส่วน chinsuan
piece *v.t.* รวบรวม ruabruam
pierce *v.t.* เจาะ jaw
piety *n.* ความเคร่งศาสนา
　kwamkrengsanana
pig *n.* หมู mu
pigeon *n.* นกพิราบ nokpirab
pigmy *n.* คนแคระ konkrae
pile *n.* กอง gong
pile *v.t.* กอง gong
piles *n.* โรคริดสีดวงทวาร
　rokritsiduangtawan
pilfer *v.t.* วิ่งราว wingrao
pilgrim *n.* ผู้แสวงบุญ pusawaengboon
pilgrimage *n.* การจาริกแสวงบุญ
　ganjariksawaengboon
pill *n.* ยา ya
pillar *n.* เสา sao
pillow *n* หมอน mon
pillow *v.t.* หนุนหมอน nunmon
pilot *n.* นักบิน nakbin
pilot *v.t.* ขับเครื่องบิน kabkreuangbin
pimple *n.* สิว sew
pin *n.* หมุด mud

pin *v.t.* ปักหมุด pakmud

pinch *v.t.* ขัดขวาง katkwang

pinch *v.* หยิก yik

pine *n.* ต้นสน tonson

pine *v.i.* อ่อนแรง on-raeng

pineapple *n.* สับปะรด sabparod

pink *n.* สีชมพู sichompu

pink *a* สีชมพู sichompu

pinkish *a.* เป็นสีชมพู pensichompu

pinnacle *n.* จุดสุดยอด judsudyod

pioneer *n.* ผู้บุกเบิก pubukbeuk

pioneer *v.t.* บุกเบิก bukbeuk

pious *a.* เคร่งศาสนา krengsasana

pipe *n.* ท่อ taw

pipe *v.i* ส่งผ่านท่อ songpantaw

piquant *a.* รสจัด rodjad

piracy *n.* การโจรกรรม ganjoragam

pirate *n.* โจรสลัด jonsalad

pirate *v.t* ปล้น plon

pistol *n.* ปืนพก peunpok

piston *n.* ลูกสูบ looksoob

pit *n.* หลุม loom

pit *v.t.* กลายเป็นหลุม glaipenloom

pitch *n.* การขว้าง gankwang

pitch *v.t.* ขว้าง kwang

pitcher *n.* ผู้ขว้าง pukwang

piteous *a.* น่าสงสาร nasongsan

pitfall *n.* หลุมพราง loomprang

pitiable *a.* น่าสงสาร nasongsan

pitiful *a.* น่าสงสาร nasongsan

pitiless *a.* โหดร้าย hodrai

pitman *n.* คนขุดหลุม konkudloom

pittance *n.* เงินเล็กน้อย ngeunleknoy

pity *n.* ความสงสาร kwamsongsan

pity *v.t.* สงสาร songsan

pivot *n.* แกนหมุน gaenmoon

pivot *v.t.* หมุน moon

placard *n.* ป้ายประกาศ paipragad

place *n.* สถานที่ satanti

place *v.t.* วาง wang

placid *a.* สงบนิ่ง sa-ngobning

plague *n.* โรคระบาด rokrabad

plague *v.t.* ทำให้เกิดโรคระบาด tamhaigeudrokrabad

plain *a.* ธรรมดา tammada

plain *n.* ที่ราบ tirab

plaintiff *n.* โจทก์ jod

plan *n.* แผนการ paengan

plan *v.t.* วางแผน wangpaen

plane *n.* เครื่องบิน kreuangbin

plane *v.t.* บิน bin

plane *a.* ระนาบ ranab

plane *n* ระดับ radab

planet *n.* โลก lok

planetary *a.* เกี่ยวกับโลก giawgablok

plank *n.* ไม้กระดาน maigradan

plank *v.t.* ปูกระดาน pugradan

plant *n.* พืช peud

plant *v.t.* ปลูก pluk

plantain *n.* พืชชนิดหนึ่ง peudchanidneung

plantation *n.* สวน suan

plaster *n.* ปูนปลาสเตอร์ poonplaster

plaster *v.t.* ฉาบ chab

plate *n.* แม่พิมพ์ maepim

plate *v.t.* ชุบ chub

plateau *n.* ที่ราบสูง tirabsoong

platform *n.* ชานชาลา chanchala

platonic *a.* ฉันท์เพื่อน chanpeuan

platoon *n.* หมวด muad

play *n.* ละคร lakon

play *v.i.* เล่นละคร lenlakon

player *n.* ผู้เล่น pulen

plea *n.* คำร้อง kamrong

plead *v.i.* ให้การ haigan

pleader *n.* ผู้ยื่นคำร้อง puyeunkamrong

pleasant *a.* น่ายินดี nayindi

pleasantry *n.* การหยอกล้อ ganyoklaw

please *v.t.* ยินดี yindi

pleasure *n.* ความยินดี kwamyindi

plebiscite *n.* การลงประชามติ ganlongprachamati

pledge *n.* ข้อผูกมัด kawpukmad

pledge *v.t.* วางมัดจำ wangmadjam

plenty *n.* จำนวนมาก jamnuanmak

plight *n.* คำมั่น kamman
plod *v.i.* ย่ำเท้า yamtao
plot *n.* อุบาย u-bai
plot *v.t.* วางแผน wangpaen
plough *n.* คันไถ kantai
plough *v.i* ไถ tai
ploughman *n.* คนไถดิน kontaidin
pluck *v.t.* ถอน tawn
pluck *n* การถอน gantawn
plug *n.* ปลั๊กไฟ plugfai
plug *v.t.* อุดรู ud-ru
plum *n.* ต้นพลัม tonplum
plumber *n.* ช่างประปา changprapa
plunder *v.t.* ปล้น plon
plunder *n* การปล้น ganplon
plunge *v.t.* จุ่ม joom
plunge *n* การจุ่ม ganjoom
plural *a.* รูปพหูพจน์ roobpahupod
plurality *n.* ความเป็นพหูพจน์
   kwampenpahupod
plus *a.* เพิ่ม peum
plus *n* จำนวนที่เพิ่มขึ้น
   jamnuantipeumkeun
ply *v.t.* ใช้สอย chaisoy
ply *n* รอยพับ roypab
pneumonia โรคปอดบวม rokpodbuam
pocket *n.* กระเป๋า grapao
pocket *v.t.* ใส่กระเป๋า saigrapao
pod *n.* ฝักถั่ว faktua
poem *n.* กลอน glon
poesy *n.* กวีนิพนธ์ gawinipon
poet *n.* นักกวี nakgawi
poetaster *n.* นักกวีชั้นเลว nakgawichanlew
poetess *n.* นักกวีหญิง nakgawiying
poetic *a.* เกี่ยวกับบทกวี giawgabbodgawi
poetics *n.* งานกวีนิพนธ์ ngangawinipon
poetry *n.* บทกวี botgawi
poignacy *n.* ความเจ็บปวด kwamjebpuad
poignant *a.* เจ็บปวด jebpuad
point *n.* ประเด็น praden
point *v.t.* ชี้ประเด็น chipraden
poise *v.t.* ทรงตัว songtua

poise *n* ความสมดุล kwamsomdun
poison *n.* ยาพิษ yapid
poison *v.t.* วางยาพิษ wangyapid
poisonous *a.* เป็นพิษ penpid
poke *v.t.* แหย่ yae
poke *n.* การทิ่ม gantim
polar *n.* ขั้ว kua
pole *n.* เสา sao
police *n.* ตำรวจ tamruad
policeman *n.* ตำรวจ tamruad
policy *n.* นโยบาย nayobai
polish *v.t.* ขัด kad
polish *n* การขัด gankad
polite *a.* สุภาพ supab
pliteness *n.* ความสุภาพ kwamsupab
politic *a.* ฉลาด chalad
political *a.* ทางการเมือง tangganmeuang
politician *n.* นักการเมือง nakganmeuang
politics *n.* การเมือง ganmeuang
polity *n.* ระบบการปกครอง
   rabobganpokkrong
poll *n.* การสำรวจความเห็น
   gansamruadkwamhen
poll *v.t.* สุ่มตัวอย่าง sumtuayang
pollen *n.* ละอองเกสรดอกไม้ la-
   onggesondawkmai
pollute *v.t.* ทำให้เป็นพิษ tamhaipenpid
pollution *n.* มลพิษ monlapid
polo *n.* กีฬาโปโล gilapolo
polygamous *a.* ที่มีคู่ครองหลายคน
   timikukronglaikon
polygamy *n.* การมีคู่ครองหลายคน
   ganmikukronglaikon
polyglot *n.* ผู้รู้หลายภาษา purulaipasa
polyglot *a.* รู้หลายภาษา rulaipasa
polytechnic *a.* เกี่ยวกับโปลีเทคนิค
   giawgabpolytechnic
polytechnic *n.* โรงเรียนโปลีเทคนิค
   rongrianpolyrtechnic
polytheism *n.* พุทเทวนิยม
   payutewaniyom

polytheist *n.* ผู้นับถือลัทธิพหุเทวนิยม punabteulattipahutewaniyom

polytheistic *a.* เกี่ยวกับพหุเทวนิยม giawgabpahutewaniyom

pomp *n.* พิธีเอิกเกริก piti-eukgareuk

pomposity *n.* การวางมาด ganwangmad

pompous *a.* วางมาด wangmad

pond *n.* บ่อน้ำ bawnam

ponder *v.t.* ครุ่นคิด krunkid

pony *n.* ม้า ma

poor *a.* ยากจน yakjon

pop *v.i.* ทำให้เกิดเสียง tamhaigeudsiang

pop *n* เสียงดัง siangdang

pope *n.* โป๊ป pope

poplar *n.* ต้นไม้ tonmai

poplin *n.* ผ้าฝ้าย pafai

populace *n.* ประชากร prachakon

popular *a.* ได้รับความนิยม dairabkwamniyom

popularity *n.* ความนิยม kwamniyom

popularize *v.t.* ทำให้ได้รับความนิยม tamhaidairabkwamniyom

populate *v.t.* อาศัยอยู่ a-saiyu

population *n.* ประชากร prachakon

populous *a.* มีพลเมืองหนาแน่น miponlameungnanaen

porcelain *n.* เครื่องถ้วยชาม kreuangtuaycham

porch *n.* ระเบียง rabiang

pore *n.* รูขุมขน rukumkon

pork *n.* หมู mu

porridge *n.* ข้าวต้ม kaotom

port *n.* ท่าเรือ tareua

portable *a.* หิ้วได้ hewdai

portage *n.* การขนย้าย gankonyai

portal *n.* ประตู pratu

portend *v.t.* เป็นลาง penlang

porter *n.* คนเฝ้าประตู konfaopratu

portfolio *n.* แฟ้มประวัติ faemprawat

portico *n.* หน้ามุข namook

portion *n* สัดส่วน sadsuan

portion *v.t.* แบ่ง baeng

portrait *n.* รูปคน roobkon

portraiture *n.* ศิลปะการวาดภาพคน silapaganwadpabkon

portray *v.t.* วาดภาพ wadpab

portrayal *n.* การวาดภาพคน ganwadpabkon

pose *v.i.* วางท่า wangta

pose *n.* ท่าทาง tatang

position *n.* ตำแหน่ง tamnaeng

position *v.t.* จัดวาง jadwang

positive *a.* เชิงบวก cheungbuak

possess *v.t.* ครอบครอง krobkrong

possession *n.* การครอบครอง gankrobkrong

possibility *n.* ความเป็นไปได้ kwampenpaidai

possible *a.* เป็นไปได้ penpaidai

post *n.* ที่มั่น timan

post *v.t.* จัดกำลัง jadgamlang

post *n* ตำแหน่ง tamnaeng

post *v.t.* ประกาศ pragad

post *adv.* ด้านหลัง danlang

postage *n.* ค่าส่งของทางไปรษณีย์ kasongkongtangpraisani

postal *a.* เกี่ยวกับไปรษณีย์ giawgabpraisani

post-date *v.t.* ลงวันที่ช้ากว่าวันจริง longwantichakwawanjing

poster *n.* โปสเตอร์ poster

posterity *n.* คนรุ่นหลัง konroonlang

posthumous *a.* หลังมรณกรรม langmoranagam

postman *n.* บุรุษไปรษณีย์ burudpraisani

postmaster *n.* นายไปรษณีย์ naipraisani

post-mortem *a.* เกิดขึ้นหลังการตาย geudkeunlanggantai

post-mortem *n.* การชันสูตรศพ ganchannasudsob

post-office *n.* ที่ทำการไปรษณีย์ titamganpraisani

postpone *v.t.* เลื่อน leuan

postponement *n.* การเลื่อน ganleuan

postscript *n.* คำลงท้าย kamlongtai
posture *n.* ท่าทาง tatang
pot *n.* กระถาง gratang
pot *v.t.* ปลูกลงกระถาง pluklonggratang
potash *n.* ด่าง dang
potassium *n.* โปแตสเซียม potassium
potato *n.* มันฝรั่ง manfarang
potency *n.* ศักยภาพ sagayapab
potent *a.* มีอำนาจ mi-ammad
potential *a.* มีศักยภาพ misakgayapab
potential *n.* ศักยภาพ sakgayapab
pontentiality *n.* ศักยภาพ sakgayapab
potter *n.* ช่างปั้นหม้อ changpanmaw
pottery *n.* เครื่องปั้นดินเผา
    kreuangpandinpao
pouch *n.* ถุง tung
poultry *n.* สัตว์ปีก satpik
pounce *v.i.* กระโจน grajon
pounce *n* การกระโจน gangrajon
pound *n.* เงินปอนด์ ngeunpound
pound *v.t.* บด bod
pour *v.i.* ริน rin
poverty *n.* ความยากจน kwamyamjon
powder *n.* ผง pong
powder *v.t.* บดเป็นผง bodpenpong
power *n.* อำนาจ ammad
powerful *a.* มีอำนาจ mi-ammad
practicability *n.* การปฏิบัติได้
    ganpatibaddai
practicable *a.* ปฏิบัติได้ patibaddai
practical *a.* ใช้ได้จริง chaidaijing
practice *n.* การปฏิบัติ ganpatibat
practise *v.t.* ปฏิบัติ patibat
practitioner *n.* ผู้ปฏิบัติ pupatibat
pragmatic *a.* เน้นการปฏิบัติ nenganpatibat
pragmatism *n.* ปฏิบัตินิยม patibatniyom
praise *n.* การยกย่อง ganyokyong
praise *v.t.* ยกย่อง yokyong
praiseworthy *a.* ควรแก่การยกย่อง
    kuangaeganyokyong
prank *n.* การล้อเล่น ganlawlen
prattle *v.i.* พูดไร้สาระ pudraisara

prattle *n.* การพูดไร้สาระ ganpudraisara
pray *v.i.* สวด suad
prayer *n.* การสวดมนต์ gansuadmon
preach *v.i.* เทศนา tesana
preacher *n.* นักเทศน์ nakted
preamble *n.* คำนำ kamnam
precaution *n.* ความระมัดระวัง
    kwamramadrawang
precautionary *a.* ระมัดระวัง ramadrawang
precede *v.* อยู่ข้างหน้า yukangna
precedence *n.* การอยู่หน้า ganyuna
precedent *n.* ตัวอย่างที่มีมาก่อน
    tuayangtimimagon
precept *n.* คำสอน kamson
preceptor *n.* ครู kru
precious *a.* มีค่า mika
precis *n.* บทคัดย่อ bodkadyaw
precise *n.* ย่อความ yawkwam
precision *n.* ความแม่นยำ kwammaenyam
precursor *n.* สารตั้งต้น santangton
predecessor *n.* บรรพบุรุษ banpaburud
predestination *n.* พรหมลิขิต promlikit
predetermine *v.t.* กำหนดไว้ล่วงหน้า
    gamnodwailuangna
predicament *n.*
    สภาพกลืนไม่เข้าคายไม่ออก
    sapabkleunmaikaokaimai-awk
predicate *n.* ภาคแสดง paksadaeng
predict *v.t.* ทำนาย tamnai
prediction *n.* การทำนาย gantamnai
predominance *n.* การมีอำนาจเหนือกว่า
    ganmi-amnadneuakwa
predominant *a.* ที่เหนือกว่า tineaukwa
predominate *v.i.* เหนือกว่า neaukwa
pre-eminence *n.* ความเหนือกว่า
    kwamneuakwa
pre-eminent *a.* เหนือกว่า neuakwa
preface *n.* คำนำ kamnam
preface *v.t.* เขียนคำนำ kiankamnam
prefect *n.* ความสมบูรณ์ kwamsomboon
prefer *v.t.* ชอบ chob
preference *n.* ความชอบ kwamchob

preferential *a.* พึงพอใจ peungpawjai
prefix *n.* คำนำหน้า kamnamna
prefix *v.t.* ใส่คำนำหน้า saikamnamna
pregnancy *n.* การตั้งครรภ์ gantangkan
pregnant *a.* ท้อง tong
prehistoric *a.* ก่อนประวัติศาสตร์
  gonprawatsat
prejudice *n.* ความลำเอียง kwamlam-iang
prelate *n.* พระราชาคณะ prarachakana
preliminary *a.* ในชั้นต้น naichanton
preliminary *n* ชั้นต้น chanton
prelude *n.* การบรรเลงนำ ganbanlengnam
prelude *v.t.* บรรเลงนำ banlengnam
premarital *a.* ก่อนสมรส gonsomrod
premature *a.* ก่อนกำหนด gongamnod
premeditate *v.t.* ไตร่ตรองล่วงหน้า
  traitrongluangna
premeditation *n.* การไตร่ตรองล่วงหน้า
  gantraitrongluangna
premier *a.* ครั้งแรก krangraek
premier *n* นายกรัฐมนตรี nayokrattamontri
premiere *n.* การแสดงรอบปฐมทัศน์
  gansadaengrobpratommatat
premium *n.* คุณภาพดี kunnapabdi
premonition *n.* การเตือนล่วงหน้า
  ganteuanluangna
preoccupation *n.* การเข้าครอบครองก่อน
  gankaokrobkronggon
preoccupy *v.t.* เข้าครอบครองก่อน
  kaokrobkronggon
preparation *n.* การเตรียมการ
  gantriamgan
preparatory *a.* เป็นการเตรียมพร้อม
  pengantriamprom
prepare *v.t.* เตรียม triam
preponderance *n.* การมีอำนาจสูงสุด
  ganmi-amnadsoongsud
preponderate *v.i.* เหนือกว่า neuakwa
preposition *n.* คำบุพบท kambupabot
prerequisite *a.* ต้องมีก่อน tongmigon
prerequisite *n* สิ่งที่ต้องมีก่อน
  singtitongmigon

prerogative *n.* อำนาจพิเศษ amnadpised
prescience *n.* การรู้ล่วงหน้า ganruluangna
prescribe *v.t.* จ่ายยา jaiya
prescription *n.* การจ่ายยา ganjaiya
presence *n.* การปรากฏตัว ganpragottua
present *a.* ขณะปัจจุบัน kanapatjuban
present *n.* ของขวัญ kongkwan
present *v.t.* เสนอ saneu
presentation *n.* การนำเสนอ gannamsaneu
presently *adv.* ในช่วงเวลานี้
  naichuangwelani
preservation *n.* การเก็บรักษา
  gangebraksa
preservative *n.* สารกันเสีย sangansia
preservative *a.* ที่รักษาไว้ tiraksawai
preserve *v.t.* ถนอมอาหาร gantanom-a-
  han
preserve *n.* ผลไม้แช่อิ่ม ponlamaichae-im
preside *v.i.* เป็นประธาน penpratan
president *n.* ประธานาธิบดี pratanatibodi
presidential *a.* เกี่ยวกับประธานาธิบดี
  giawgabpratanatibodi
press *v.t.* กด god
press *n* การกด gangod
pressure *n.* ความกดดัน kwamgoddan
pressurize *v.t.* เพิ่มความกดดัน
  peumkwamgoddan
prestige *n.* ชื่อเสียง cheusiang
prestigious *a.* มีชื่อเสียง misheusiang
presume *v.t.* สันนิษฐาน sannitan
presumption *n.* การสันนิษฐาน
  gansannitan
presuppose *v.t.* สันนิษฐาน sannitan
presupposition *n.* การสันนิษฐาน
  gansannitan
pretence *n.* การเสแสร้ง gansesaeng
pretend *v.t.* เสแสร้ง sesaeng
pretension *n.* การเรียกร้อง ganriakrong
pretentious *a.* โอ้อวด o-uad
pretext *n* ข้ออ้าง kaw-ang
prettiness *n.* ความน่ารัก kwamnarak
pretty *a* น่ารัก narak

pretty *adv.* น่ารัก narak
prevail *v.i.* ชนะ chana
prevalence *n.* ความชุก kwamchuk
prevalent *a.* แพร่หลาย praelai
prevent *v.t.* ป้องกัน ponggan
prevention *n.* การป้องกัน ganponggan
preventive *a.* เชิงป้องกัน cheungponggan
previous *a.* ก่อนหน้า gonna
prey *n.* เหยื่อ yeua
prey *v.i.* เป็นเหยื่อ penyeua
price *n.* ราคา raka
price *v.t.* กำหนดราคา gamnodraka
prick *n.* รอยแทง roytaeng
prick *v.t.* แทง taeng
pride *n.* ความภูมิใจ kwampumjai
pride *v.t.* รู้สึกภูมิใจ ruseukpumjai
priest *n.* พระ pra
priestess *n.* พระผู้หญิง prapuyai
priesthood *n.* การบวชเป็นพระ
　ganbuadpenpra
prima facie *adv.* เบื้องต้น beuangton
primarily *adv.* ในเบื้องต้น naibeungton
primary *a.* เบื้องต้น beungton
prime *a.* สำคัญ samkan
prime *n.* ขั้นแรก kanraek
primer *n.* สารที่ใช้เคลือบเนื้อไม้
　santichaikreubneuamai
primeval *a.* ครั้งแรกเริ่ม krangraekkreum
primitive *a.* ดั้งเดิม dangdeum
prince *n.* เจ้าชาย jaochai
princely *a.* แบบเจ้าชาย baebjaochai
princess *n.* เจ้าหญิง jaoying
principal *n.* ครูใหญ่ kruyai
principal *a* สำคัญ samkan
principle *n.* หลักการ lakgan
print *v.t.* พิมพ์ pim
print *n* การพิมพ์ ganpim
printer *n.* เครื่องพิมพ์ kreuangpim
prior *a.* ก่อนหน้า gonna
prior *n* รองอธิการวัด rong-atiganwat
prioress *n.* หัวหน้าแม่ชี huanamaechi

priority *n.* ลำดับความสำคัญ
　lamdabkwamsamkan
prison *n.* คุก kuk
prisoner *n.* นักโทษ naktod
privacy *n.* ความเป็นส่วนตัว
　kwampensuantua
private *a.* ส่วนตัว suantua
privation *n.* การถอดถอน gantodton
privilege *n.* สิทธิพิเศษ sitipiset
prize *n.* รางวัล rangwan
prize *v.t.* ให้รางวัล hairangwan
probability *n.* ความน่าจะเป็น
　kwamnajapen
probable *a.* เป็นไปได้ penpaidai
probably *adv.* บางที bangti
probation *n.* การภาคทัณฑ์ ganpaktan
probationer *n.* ผู้ทำภาคทัณฑ์
　putampaktan
probe *v.t.* สืบสวน seubsuan
probe *n* การสืบสวน ganseubsuan
problem *n.* ปัญหา panha
problematic *a.* ที่เป็นปัญหา tipenpanha
procedure *n.* ขั้นตอน kanton
proceed *v.i.* พิจารณาคดี pijaranakadi
proceeding *n.* การพิจารณาคดี
　ganpijaranakadi
proceeds *n.* รายได้ raidai
process *n.* แนวทางปฏิบัติ naewtangpatibat
procession *n.* การดำเนินการ
　gandamneungan
proclaim *v.t.* ประกาศ pragad
proclamation *n.* การประกาศ ganpragad
proclivity *n.* แนวโน้ม naewnom
procrastinate *v.i.* ผัดวันประกันพรุ่ง
　patwanpraganprung
procrastination *n.* การผัดวันประกันพรุ่ง
　ganpatwanpraganprung
proctor *n.* ตัวแทน tuataen
procure *v.t.* จัดหา jadha
procurement *n.* การจัดการ ganjadgan
prodigal *a.* ฟุ่มเฟือย fumfeuay

prodigality *n.* ความฟุ่มเฟือย
  kwamfumfeuay
produce *v.t.* ผลิต palit
produce *n.* พืชผัก peudpak
product *n.* ผลิตภัณฑ์ palittapan
production *n.* การผลิต ganpalid
productive *a.* ได้ผล daipon
productivity *n.* การเพิ่มผลผลิต
  ganpeumponpalit
profane *a.* หยาบคาย yabkai
profane *v.t.* พูดคำหยาบ pudkamyab
profess *v.t.* แสดงตัว sadaengtua
profession *n.* อาชีพ a-chip
professional *a.* มีอาชีพ meu-a-chip
professor *n.* อาจารย์ a-jan
proficiency *n.* ความมีประสิทธิภาพ
  kwammiprasitipab
proficient *a.* ประสิทธิภาพ prasitipad
profile *n.* ประวัติย่อ prawatyaw
profile *v.t.* วาดโครงร่าง wadkrongrang
profit *n.* กำไร gamrai
profit *v.t.* ได้กำไร daigamrai
profitable *a.* มีผลกำไร mipongamrai
profiteer *n.* พ่อค้าหน้าเลือด pawkanaleud
profiteer *v.i.* ค้ากำไรเกินควร
  kagamraigeunkuan
profligacy *n.* ความฟุ่มเฟือย
  kwamfumfeuay
profligate *a.* ฟุ่มเฟือย fumfeuay
profound *a.* ลึก leuk
profundity *n.* ความลึก kwamleuk
profuse *a.* ฟุ่มเฟือย fumfeuay
profusion *n.* ความฟุ่มเฟือย
  kwamfumfeuay
progeny *n.* ลูกหลาน looklan
programme *n.* โปรแกรม program
programme *v.t.* เขียนโปรแกรม
  kianprogram
progress *n.* ความก้าวหน้า kwamgaona
progress *v.i.* ก้าวหน้า gaona
progressive *a.* ก้าวหน้า gaona
prohibit *v.t.* ห้าม ham

prohibition *n.* การห้าม ganham
prohibitive *a.* ห้าม ham
prohibitory *a.* ห้าม ham
project *n.* แผนงาน paen-ngan
project *v.t.* เสนอ saneu
projectile *n.* ขีปนาวุธ kipanawut
projectile *a* พุ่งออกไปได้ pung-awkpaidai
projection *n.* การฉายภาพ ganchaipab
projector *n.* เครื่องฉายภาพ
  kreuangchaipab
proliferate *v.i.* แพร่พันธุ์ praepan
proliferation *n.* การแพร่พันธุ์ ganpraepan
prolific *a.* ลูกดก lookdok
prologue *n.* อารัมบท a-rumpabod
prolong *v.t.* ยืดเวลา yeudwela
prolongation *n.* การยืดเวลา
  ganeyeudwela
prominence *n.* ความเด่นชัด
  kwamdenchad
prominent *a.* เด่นชัด denchad
promise *n* คำสัญญา kamsanya
promise *v.t* ให้สัญญา haisanya
promising *a.* ที่มีความหวัง
  timikwamwang
promissory *a.* เกี่ยวกับสัญญา
  giabgabsanya
promote *v.t.* ส่งเสริม songseum
promotion *n.* การส่งเสริม gansongseum
prompt *a.* พร้อม prom
prompt *v.t.* กระตุ้น gratoon
prompter *n.* คนบอกบท konbokbod
prone *a.* นอนคว่ำ nonkwam
pronoun *n.* สรรพนาม sapanam
pronounce *v.t.* ออกเสียง awksiang
pronunciation *n.* การออกเสียง gan-
  awksiang
proof *n.* การพิสูจน์ ganpisud
proof *a* ที่ผ่านการทดสอบ tipangantodsob
prop *n.* ไม้ค้ำยัน maikamyan
prop *v.t.* ค้ำ kam
propaganda *n.* การโฆษณาชวนเชื่อ
  gankodsanachuancheua

propagandist *n.* นักโฆษณา nakkodsana
propagate *v.t.* เผยแพร่ peuyprae
propagation *n.* การเผยแพร่ ganpeuyprae
propel *v.t.* ขับเคลื่อน kabkreuan
proper *a.* เหมาะสม mawsom
property *n.* ทรัพย์สิน sabsin
prophecy *n.* การทำนาย gantamnai
prophesy *v.t.* ทำนาย tamnai
prophet *n.* ศาสดา sasada
prophetic *a.* เกี่ยวกับการทำนาย
   giabgabgantamnai
proportion *n.* สัดส่วน sadsuan
proportion *v.t.* ทำให้ได้สัดส่วน
   tamhaidaisadsuan
proportional *a.* ได้สัดส่วน daisadsuan
proportionate *a.* ได้สัดส่วน daisadsuan
proposal *n.* ข้อเสนอ kawsaneu
propose *v.t.* เสนอ saneu
proposition *n.* ข้อเสนอ kawsaneu
propound *v.t.* เสนอ saneu
proprietary *a.* ซึ่งเป็นเจ้าของ
   seungpenjaokong
proprietor *n.* เจ้าของ jaokong
propriety *n.* ความเหมาะสม
   kwammawsom
prorogue *v.t.* ปิดประชุม pidprachum
prosaic *a.* ธรรมดา tammada
prose *n.* ร้อยแก้ว roykaew
prosecute *v.t.* ฟ้องร้อง fongrong
prosecution *n.* การฟ้องร้อง ganfongrong
prosecutor *n.* อัยการ ai-yagan
prosody *n.* ฉันทลักษณ์ chantalak
prospect *n.* การคาดการณ์ gankadgan
prospective *a.* ที่คาดหวังไว้ tikadwangwai
prospsectus *n.* หนังสือชี้ชวน
   nangseuchichuan
prosper *v.i.* เจริญก้าวหน้า jareungaona
prosperity *n.* ความก้าวหน้า kwamgaona
prosperous *a.* ก้าวหน้า gaona
prostitute *n.* โสเภณี sopeni
prostitute *v.t.* ขายตัว kaitua

prostitution *n.* การค้าประเวณี
   gankapraweni
prostrate *a.* หมดกำลัง modgamlang
prostrate *v.t.* ทำให้หมดกำลัง
   tamhaimodgamlang
prostration *n.* การหมดกำลัง
   ganmodgamlang
protagonist *n.* ตัวเอก tua-ek
protect *v.t.* ปกป้อง pokpong
protection *n.* การปกป้อง ganpokpong
protective *a.* ปกป้อง pokpong
protector *n.* ผู้ปกป้อง pupokpong
protein *n.* โปรตีน protein
protest *n.* การประท้วง ganpratuang
protest *v.i.* ประท้วง pratuang
protestation *n.* การประท้วง ganpratuang
prototype *n.* ต้นแบบ tonbaeb
proud *a.* ภูมิใจ pumjai
prove *v.t.* พิสูจน์ pisud
proverb *n.* ภาษิต pasit
proverbial *a.* ที่เกี่ยวกับสุภาษิต
   tigiawgabsupasit
provide *v.i.* ให้ hai
providence *n.* ความสามารถในการจัดการ
   kwamsamadnaiganjadgan
provident *a.* ที่เตรียมไว้สำหรับอนาคต
   titriamwaisamrab-a-nakot
providential *a.* โชคดี chokdi
province *n.* จังหวัด jangwat
provincial *a.* เขตจังหวัด kedjangwat
provincialism *n.* ลัทธิท้องถิ่น lattitongtin
provision *n.* การจัดหา ganjadha
provisional *a.* ชั่วคราว chuakrao
proviso *n.* เงื่อนไข ngeunkai
provocation *n.* การยั่วยุ ganyuayu
provocative *a.* กวนโทสะ guantosa
provoke *v.t.* ยั่วยุ yuayu
prowess *n.* ความกล้าหาญ kwamglahan
proximate *a.* ใกล้ glai
proximity *n.* ความใกล้ชิด kwamglaichid
proxy *n.* ตัวแทน tuataen
prude *n.* คนเคร่งครัด konkrengkrad

prudence *n.* ความรอบคอบ kwamrobkob
prudent *a.* ประหยัด prayad
prudential *a.* รอบคอบ robkob
prune *v.t.* ตัดออก tad-awk
pry *v.i.* สอดรู้สอดเห็น sodrusodhen
psalm *n.* เพลงสวด plengsuad
pseudonym *n.* นามปากกา nampakga
psyche *n.* จิตวิญญาณ jidwinyan
psychiatrist *n.* จิตแพทย์ jittapaet
psychiatry *n.* จิตเวช jittawet
psychic *a.* ทางจิต tangjit
psychological *a.* ทางจิตวิทยา
　tangjitwittaya
psychologist *n.* นักจิตวิทยา nakjitwittaya
psychology *n.* จิตวิทยา jitwittaya
psychopath *n.* คนโรคจิต konrokjit
psychosis *n.* โรคจิต rokjit
psychotherapy *n.* การบำบัดโรคจิต
　ganbambatrokjit
puberty *n.* วัยแรกรุ่น wairaekroon
public *a.* สาธารณะ satarana
public *n.* มหาชน mahachon
publication *n.* การประชาสัมพันธ์
　ganprachasampan
publicity *n.* การเผยแพร่ ganpeuyprae
publicize *v.t.* เผยแพร่ peuyprae
publish *v.t.* พิมพ์ pim
publisher *n.* ผู้โฆษณา pukodsana
pudding *n.* พุดดิ้ง pudding
puddle *n.* แอ่งน้ำ aeng-nam
puddle *v.t.* ทำให้เป็นแอ่ง tamhaipen-aeng
puerile *a.* เกี่ยวกับเด็ก giawgabdek
puff *n.* ลมหายใจ lomhaijai
puff *v.i.* หอบ hob
pull *v.t.* ดึง deung
pull *n.* การดึง gandeung
pulley *n.* รอก rawk
pullover *n.* การจอดข้างทาง
　ganjodkangtang
pulp *n.* เนื้อผลไม้ neuaponlamai
pulp *v.t.* แยกเนื้อผลไม้ yaekneuaponlamai

pulpit *a.* เกี่ยวกับธรรมมาสน์
　giawgabtammat
pulpy *a.* เป็นเนื้อเยื่อ penneauyeua
pulsate *v.i.* เต้นเป็นจังหวะ tenpenjangwa
pulsation *n.* การเต้นเป็นจังหวะ
　gantenpenjangwa
pulse *n.* ชีพจร chippajon
pulse *v.i.* เต้นเป็นจังหวะ tenpenjangwa
pulse *n* เมล็ดพืชที่กินได้
　maledpeudtigindai
pump *n.* การสูบ gansoob
pump *v.t.* สูบ soob
pumpkin *n.* ฟักทอง faktong
pun *n.* การเล่นคำ ganlenkam
pun *v.i.* เล่นคำ lenkam
punch *n.* การชก ganchok
punch *v.t.* ชก chok
punctual *a.* ตรงเวลา tronglewa
punctuality *n.* การตรงต่อเวลา
　gantrongtawwela
punctuate *v.t.* ขัดจังหวะ kadjangwa
punctuation *n.* การขัดจังหวะ
　gankadjangwa
puncture *n.* รู ru
puncture *v.t.* เจาะ jaw
pungency *n.* ความฉุน kwamchun
pungent *a.* ฉุน chun
punish *v.t.* ทำโทษ tamtod
punishment *n.* การทำโทษ gantamtod
punitive *a.* เกี่ยวกับการทำโทษ
　giawgabgantamtod
puny *a.* เล็ก lek
pupil *n.* นักเรียน nakrian
puppet *n.* หุ่นกระบอก hungrabawk
puppy *n.* ลูกสุนัข looksunak
purblind *a.* กึ่งบอด geungbod
purchase *n.* การซื้อ ganseu
purchase *v.t.* ซื้อ seu
pure *a* บริสุทธิ์ borisud
purgation *n.* การล้างบาป ganlangbab
purgative *n.* ยาถ่าย yatai
purgative *a* ที่ระบายท้อง tirabaitong

purgatory *n.* นรก narok
purge *v.t.* กำจัด gamjad
purification *n.* การชำระล้างบาป ganchamralangbab
purify *v.t.* ทำให้บริสุทธิ์ tamhaiborisut
purist *n.* ความเจ้าระเบียบ kwamjaorabiab
puritan *n.* ผู้เคร่งศาสนา pukrengsasana
puritanical *a.* เคร่งศาสนา krengsasana
purity *n.* ความบริสุทธิ์ kwamborisut
purple *adj./n.* สีม่วง simuang
purport *n.* ความหมาย kwammai
purport *v.t.* อ้างว่า angwa
purpose *n.* ความตั้งใจ kwamtangjai
purpose *v.t.* ตั้งใจ tangjai
purposely *adv.* อย่างตั้งใจ yangtangjai
purr *n.* พูดพึมพำ pudpeumpam
purr *v.i.* พึมพำ peumpam
purse *n.* กระเป๋า grapao
purse *v.t.* ทำปากย่น tampakyon
pursuance *n.* การติดตาม gantidtam
pursue *v.t.* ติดตาม tidtam
pursuit *n.* การติดตาม gantidtam
purview *n.* บทกฎหมาย bodgodmai
pus *n.* น้ำหนอง namnong
push *v.t.* ดัน dan
push *n.* การดัน gandan
put *v.t.* ใส่ sai
puzzle *n.* คำปริศนา kamprisana
puzzle *v.t.* ทำให้งง tamhai-ngong
pygmy *n.* คนแคระ konkrae
pyorrhoea *n.* เหงือกเป็นหนอง ngeuakpennong
pyramid *n.* รูปทรงปิรามิด roobsongpyramid
pyre *n.* กองฟืน gongfeun
python *n.* งูหลาม ngu-lam

quack *v.i.* (เป็ด) ร้อง (ped)rong
quack *n* เสียงเป็ดร้อง siangpedrong
quackery *n.* การหลอกลวง ganlokluang
quadrangle *n.* รูปสี่เหลี่ยมจัตุรัส roobsiliamjaturat
quadrangular *a.* เป็นรูปสี่เหลี่ยมจัตุรัส penroobsiliamjaturat
quadrilateral *a. & n.* รูปสี่เหลี่ยม roobsiliam
quadruped *n.* สัตว์สี่เท้า satsitao
quadruple *a.* สี่เท่า sitao
quadruple *v.t.* ทำให้เป็นสี่เท่า tamhaipensitao
quail *n.* นกกระทา nokgrata
quaint *a.* มหัศจรรย์ mahadsajan
quake *v.i.* สั่น san
quake *n* การสั่น gansan
qualification *n.* คุณสมบัติ kunnasombat
qualify *v.i.* มีคุณสมบัติ mikunnasombat
qualitative *a.* มีคุณสมบัติ mikunnasombat
quality *n.* คุณภาพ kunnapab
quandary *n.* ความไม่แน่ใจ kwammainaejai
quantitative *a.* เกี่ยวกับปริมาณ giawgabpariman
quantity *n.* ปริมาณ pariman
quantum *n.* ควอนตัม quantum
quarrel *n.* การทะเลาะ gantalaw
quarrel *v.i.* ทะเลาะ talaw
quarrelsome *a.* ชอบทะเลาะวิวาท chobtalawwiwat
quarry *n.* เหมือง meuang
quarry *v.i.* ทำเมืองหิน tammeuangrae
quarter *n.* ไตรมาส trimat
quarter *v.t.* จัดหาที่พัก jadhatipak
quarterly *a.* ทุกสามเดือน tooksamdeaun
queen *n.* ราชินี rachini
queer *a.* แปลก plaek
quell *v.t.* ระงับ ra-ngub
quench *v.t.* ระงับ ra-ngub
query *n.* คำถาม kamtam
query *v.t* ถาม tam
quest *n.* การค้นหา gankonha

quest *v.t.* ค้นหา konha
question *n.* คำถาม kamtam
question *v.t.* ตั้งคำถาม tangkamtam
questionable *a.* น่าสงสัย nasongsai
questionnaire *n.* แบบสอบถาม baebsobtam
queue *n.* การเข้าแถว gankaotaew
quibble *n.* การพูดคลุมเครือ ganpudklumkreua
quibble *v.i.* พูดคลุมเครือ pudklumkreu
quick *a.* เร็ว rew
quick *n* หนังใต้เล็บ nangtaileb
quicksand *n.* ทรายดูด saidud
quicksilver *n.* ปรอท parod
quiet *a.* เงียบ ngiab
quiet *n.* ความเงียบ kwam-ngiab
quiet *v.t.* ทำให้เงียบ tamhai-ngiab
quilt *n.* ผ้านวม panuam
quinine *n.* ยาควินิน yaquinine
quintessence *n.* แก่นสาร gaensan
quit *v.t.* เลิก leuk
quite *adv.* ค่อนข้าง konkang
quiver *n.* เสียงสั่น siangsan
quiver *v.i.* สั่น san
quixotic *a.* เพ้อฝัน peufan
quiz *n.* คำถาม kamtam
quiz *v.t.* ตั้งคำถาม tangkamtam
quorum *n.* องค์ประกอบ ong-pragob
quota *n.* โควต้า quota
quotation *n.* การอ้างถึง gan-angteung
quote *v.t.* อ้างถึง angteung
quotient *n.* ผลหาร ponhan

R

rabbit *n.* กระต่าย gratai
rabies *n.* โรคพิษสุนัขบ้า rokpitsunakba
race *n.* ชาติพันธุ์ chatpan
race *v.i* แข่งขัน kaengkan
racial *a.* เกี่ยวกับเชื้อชาติ giawgabcheuchat

racialism *n.* การเหยียดสีผิว ganyiadsipew
rack *v.t.* ขูด kud
rack *n.* ชั้น chan
racket *n.* ไม้แร็กเก็ต mairacket
radiance *n.* ความสว่าง kwamsawang
radiant *a.* สว่างไสว sawangsawai
radiate *v.t.* ฉายแสง chaisaeng
radiation *n.* การฉายแสง ganchaisaeng
radical *a.* รุนแรง roonraeng
radio *n.* วิทยุ wittayu
radio *v.t.* ติดต่อทางวิทยุ tidtawtangwittayu
radish *n.* หัวไชเท้า huachaitao
radium *n.* ธาตุเรเดียม tadredium
radius *n.* รัศมี rasami
rag *n.* ผ้าขี้ริ้ว pakirew
rag *v.t.* ดุด่า duda
rage *n.* ความโกรธ kwamgrot
rage *v.i.* โกรธ grot
raid *n.* การจู่โจม ganjujom
raid *v.t.* จู่โจม jujom
rail *n.* ราว rao
rail *v.t.* ใส่ราว sairao
raling *n.* ราวลูกกรง raolookgrong
raillery *n.* การหยอกล้อ ganyoklaw
railway *n.* รางรถไฟ rangrodfai
rain *v.i.* ฝนตก fontok
rain *n* ฝน fon
rainy *a.* มีฝนตก mifontok
raise *v.t.* ยก yok
raisin *n.* ลูกเกด lookged
rally *v.t.* การชุมนุม ganchumnum
rally *n* ชุมนุม chumnum
ram *n.* แกะตัวผู้ gaetuapu
ram *v.t.* ตอก tok
ramble *v.t.* เดินเล่น deunlen
ramble *n* การเดินเล่น gandeunlen
rampage *v.i.* โมโห moho
rampage *n.* การโมโห ganmoho
rampant *a.* รุนแรง roonraeng
rampart *n.* เขื่อนดิน keuan
rancour *n.* ความขมขื่น kwamkomkeun

random *a.* สุ่มตัวอย่าง sumtuayang
range *v.t.* ตั้งระยะ tangraya
range *n.* ระยะ raya
ranger *n.* ผู้ท่องเที่ยว putongtiaw
rank *n.* ตำแหน่ง tamnaeng
rank *v.t.* จัดตำแหน่ง jadtamnaeng
rank *a* หนาแน่น nanaen
ransack *v.t.* ปล้น plon
ransom *n.* การเรียกค่าไถ่ ganriakkatai
ransom *v.t.* เรียกค่าไถ่ riakkatai
rape *n.* การข่มขืน gankomkeun
rape *v.t.* ข่มขืน komkeun
rapid *a.* เร็ว rew
rapidity *n.* ความเร็ว kwamrew
rapier *n.* กระบี่ grabi
rapport *n.* ความเป็นมิตร kwampenmit
rapt *a.* ปลาบปลื้ม plabpleum
rapture *n.* ความปลาบปลื้ม
  kwamplabpleum
rare *a.* หายาก hayak
rascal *n.* คนพาล konpan
rash *a.* เป็นผื่นคัน penpeunkan
rat *n.* หนู nu
rate *v.t.* ตีราคา tiraka
rate *n.* ราคา raka
rather *adv.* ค่อนข้าง konkang
ratify *v.t.* ยืนยัน yeunyan
ratio *n.* สัดส่วน sadsuan
ration *n.* การปันส่วน ganpanpon
rational *a.* มีเหตุมีผล mihedmipon
rationale *n.* เหตุผล hedpon
rationality *n.* ความมีเหตุมีผล
  kwammihedmipon
rationalize *v.t.* ให้เหตุผล haihedpon
rattle *v.i.* ส่งเสียงรัว songsiangrua
rattle *n* เสียงรัว siangrua
ravage *n.* การทำลายล้าง gantamlairang
ravage *v.t.* ทำลายล้าง tamlailang
rave *v.i.* พูดเพ้อเจ้อ pudpeujeu
raven *n.* นกสีดำ noksidam
ravine *n.* เหว hew
raw *a.* ดิบ dib

ray *n.* รังสี rangsi
raze *v.t.* รื้อถอน reutawn
razor *n.* มีดโกน midgon
reach *v.t.* เอื้อม euam
react *v.i.* ตอบสนอง tobsanong
reaction *n.* การตอบสนอง gantobsanong
reactinary *a.* ตรงข้าม trongkam
read *v.t.* อ่าน an
reader *n.* ผู้อ่าน pu-an
readily *adv.* พร้อม prom
readiness *n.* ความพร้อม kwamprom
ready *a.* พร้อม prom
real *a.* จริง jing
realism *n.* สัจนิยม sajjaniyom
realist *n.* ผู้ยอมรับความจริง
  puyomrabkwamjing
realistic *a.* ปฏิบัติได้จริง patibatdaijing
reality *n.* ความเป็นจริง kwampenjing
realization *n.* ความเข้าใจ kwamkaojai
realize *v.t.* เข้าใจ kaojai
really *adv.* จริง jing
realm *n.* อาณาจักร a-najak
ream *n.* รีม ream
reap *v.t.* กระโดด gradod
reaper *n.* เครื่องเกี่ยวข้าว kreuanggiawkao
rear *n.* ด้านหลัง danlang
rear *v.t.* เพาะปลูก pawpluk
reason *n.* เหตุผล hedpon
reason *v.i.* ให้เหตุผล haihedpon
reasonable *a.* มีเหตุมีผล mihedmipon
reassure *v.t.* ยืนยัน yeunyan
rabate *n.* ส่วนลด suanlod
rebel *v.i.* ก่อจลาจล gawjarajon
rebel *n.* ผู้ก่อจลาจล pugawjarajon
rebellion *n.* การจลาจล ganjarajon
rebellious *a.* เกี่ยวกับการจลาจล
  giawgabganjarajon
rebirth *n.* การเกิดใหม่ gangeudmai
rebound *v.i.* สะท้อนกลับ saton
rebound *n.* การสะท้อนกลับ gansatonglab
rebuff *n.* การบอกปัด ganbawkpad
rebuff *v.t.* บอกปัด bawkpad

rebuke *v.t.* ดุด่า duda
rebuke *n.* การดุด่า ganduda
recall *v.t.* ระลึก rareuk
recall *n.* การระลึกได้ ganrareukdai
recede *v.i.* ถอยหลัง toylang
receipt *n.* ใบเสร็จ baised
receive *v.t.* รับ rab
receiver *n.* ผู้รับ purab
recent *a.* ไม่นานมานี้ mainanmani
recently *adv.* ไม่นานมานี้ mainanmani
reception *n.* การต้อนรับ gantawnrab
receptive *a.* เกี่ยวกับการรับ
  giawgabgantawnrab
recess *n.* การหยุดพัก ganyudpak
recession *n.* การตกต่ำทางเศรษฐกิจ
  gantoktamtangsedtagid
recipe *n.* สูตร sut
recipient *n.* ผู้รับ purab
reciprocal *a.* ต่างตอบแทนกัน
  tangtobtangan
reciprocate *v.t.* ต่างตอบแทนกัน
  tangtobtanga
recital *n.* การท่องจำ gantongjam
recitation *n.* การท่องจำ gantongjam
recite *v.t.* ท่องจำ tongjam
reckless *a.* ประมาท pramat
reckon *v.t.* คิด kid
reclaim *v.t.* เรียกร้องคืน riakrongkeun
reclamation *n* การฟื้นฟู ganfeunfu
recluse *n.* ผู้สันโดษ pusandod
recognition *n.* การรับรอง ganrabrong
recognize *v.t.* รับรอง rabrong
recoil *v.i.* ถอยหลัง toylang
recoil *n.* การถอยหลัง gantoylang
recollect *v.t.* ระลึก raleuk
recollection *n.* ความทรงจำ kwamsongjam
recommend *v.t.* แนะนำ naenam
recommendation *n.* คำแนะนำ
  kamnaenam
recompense *v.t.* ตอบแทน tobtaen
recompense *n.* ค่าชดเชย kachodcheuy
reconcile *v.t.* คืนดี keundi

reconciliation *n.* การคืนดี gankeundi
record *v.t.* บันทึก banteuk
record *n.* การบันทึก ganbanteuk
recorder *n.* เครื่องบันทึกเสียง
  keuangbanteuksiang
recount *v.t.* นับใหม่ nabmai
recoup *v.t.* เอาคืน aowkeun
recourse *n.* การขอความช่วยเหลือ
  gankawkwamchuayleua
recover *v.t.* ฟื้นตัว feuntua
recovery *n.* การฟื้นตัว ganfeuntua
recreation *n.* การพักผ่อน ganpakpon
recruit *n.* สมาชิกใหม่ samachikmai
recruit *v.t.* รับคนใหม่ rabkonmai
rectangle *n.* สี่เหลี่ยมผืนผ้า siliampeunpa
rectangular *a.* เป็นรูปสี่เหลี่ยมผืนผ้า
  penroobsiliampeunpa
rectification *n.* การทำให้ถูกต้อง
  gantamhaitooktong
rectify *v.i.* ทำให้ถูกต้อง tamhaitooktong
rectum *n.* ช่องทวารหนัก chongtawannak
recur *v.i.* เกิดซ้ำ geudsam
recurrence *n.* การเกิดซ้ำ gangeudsam
recurrent *a.* ซึ่งเกิดซ้ำ seunggeudsam
red *a.* สีแดง sidaeng
red *n.* สีแดง sidaeng
redden *v.t.* ทำให้แดง tamhaidaeng
reddish *a.* ค่อนข้างแดง konkangdaeng
redeem *v.t.* ชดใช้ chodchai
redemption *n.* การชดใช้ ganchodchai
redouble *v.t.* เพิ่มเป็นทวีคูณ
  peumpentawikun
redress *v.t.* แก้ไข gaekai
redress *n* การชดเชย ganchodcheuy
reduce *v.t.* ลดลง lodlong
reduction *n.* การลดลง ganlodlong
redundance *n.* ความซ้ำซาก kwamsamsak
redundant *a.* ซ้ำซาก samsak
reel *n.* หลอดด้าย loddai
reel *v.i.* ม้วน muan
refer *v.t.* อ้างถึง ang-teung
referee *n.* ผู้ตัดสิน putadsin

reference *n.* การอ้างถึง gan-angteung

referendum *n.* ประชามติ prachamati

refine *v.t.* กลั่น glan

refinement *n.* ความปราณีต kwampranit

refinery *n.* โรงกลั่น rongglan

reflect *v.t.* สะท้อนกลับ satonglab

reflection *n.* การสะท้อนกลับ gansatonglab

reflective *a.* ที่สะท้อนกลับ tisantonglab

reflector *n.* แผ่นสะท้อนกลับ
paensatonglab

reflex *n.* ภาพสะท้อน pabsaton

reflex *a* มีปฏิกิริยาตอบกลับโดยทันที
mipatigiriyatobgladdoeytanti

reflexive *a* ที่สะท้อนกลับ tisantonglab

reform *v.t.* ปฏิรูป patiroob

reform *n.* การปฏิรูป ganpatiroob

reformation *n.* การปฏิรูป ganpatiroob

reformatory *n.*
สถานปรับปรุงความประพฤติ
satantiprabprungkwampraprud

reformatory *a* ปฏิรูป patiroob

reformer *n.* ผู้ปฏิรูป pupratiroob

refrain *v.i.* ระงับ ra-ngab

refrain *n* ลูกคู่ lookku

refresh *v.t.* ทำให้สดชื่น tamhaisodcheun

refreshment *n.* เครื่องดื่ม kreuangdeum

refrigerate *v.t.* แช่เย็น chaeyen

refrigeration *n.* การแช่เย็น ganchaeyen

refrigerator *n.* ตู้เย็น tuyen

refuge *n.* ที่หลบภัย tilobpai

refugee *n.* ผู้ลี้ภัย pulipai

refulgence *n.* ความสว่าง kwamsawang

refulgent *a.* เจิดจ้า jeudja

refund *v.t.* ใช้คืน chaikeun

refund *n.* การคืนเงิน gankeun-nguen

refusal *n.* การปฏิเสธ ganpatised

refuse *v.t.* ปฏิเสธ patised

refuse *n.* ขยะ kaya

refutation *n.* การลบล้าง ganloblang

refute *v.t.* ปฏิเสธ patised

regal *a.* เกี่ยวกับเจ้า giawgabjao

regard *v.t.* เอาใจใส่ aow-jaisai

regard *n.* ความเอาใจใส่ kwam-aowjaisai

regenerate *v.t.* เกิดใหม่ geudmai

regeneration *n.* การปฏิรูป ganpatiroob

regicide *n.* ผู้ปลงพระชนม์
puplongprachon

regime *n.* ระบอบการปกครอง
rabobganpokkrong

regiment *n.* กรมทหาร gromtahan

regiment *v.t.* จัดเป็นกรมกอง
janpengromgong

region *n.* ภูมิภาค pumipak

regional *a.* เกี่ยวกับภูมิภาค
giawgabpumipak

register *n.* สมุดลงทะเบียน
samudlongtabian

register *v.t.* จดทะเบียน jodtabian

registrar *n.* นายทะเบียน naitabian

registration *n.* การจดทะเบียน
ganjobtabian

registry *n.* สำนักทะเบียน samnaktabian

regret *v.i.* เสียใจ siajai

regret *n* ความเสียใจ kwamsiajai

regular *a.* ปกติ pagati

regularity *n.* ความสม่ำเสมอ
kwamsamamsameu

regulate *v.t.* วางระเบียบ wangrabiab

regulation *n.* กฎระเบียบ godrabiab

regulator *n.* ผู้ออกกฎระเบียบ pu-
awkgodrabiab

rehabilitate *v.t.* ฟื้นฟูสุขภาพ
feunfusukkapab

rehabilitation *n.* การฟื้นฟูสุขภาพ
ganfeunfusukkapab

rehearsal *n.* การซ้อม gansom

rehearse *v.t.* ซ้อม som

reign *v.i.* ครองราชย์ krongrat

reign *n* รัชกาล rachagan

reimburse *v.t.* ชดใช้ chodchai

rein *n.* วิธีควบคุม witikuabkum

rein *v.t.* ควบคุม kuabkum

reinforce *v.t.* เสริม seum

reinforcement *n.* การเสริมกำลัง ganseumgamlang

reinstate *v.t.* ให้กลับมารับตำแหน่งเดิม haiglabmarabtamnaengdeum

reinstatement *n.* การกลับเข้ารับตำแหน่งเดิม ganglabkaorabtamnaengdeum

reiterate *v.t.* พูดซ้ำ pudsam

reiteration *n.* การกล่าวซ้ำ ganglaosam

reject *v.t.* ปฏิเสธ patised

rejection *n.* การปฏิเสธ ganpatised

rejoice *v.i.* ยินดี yindi

rejoin *v.t.* กลับเข้าร่วม glabkaoruam

rejoinder *n.* คำตอบ kamtob

rejuvenate *v.t.* ทำให้อ่อนเยาว์ tamhai-on-yao

rejuvenation *n.* การทำให้อ่อนเยาว์ gantamhai-on-yao

relapse *v.i.* ทรุด sud

relapse *n.* การกำเริบของโรค gangamreubkongrok

relate *v.t.* เกี่ยวข้อง giawkong

relation *n.* ความเกี่ยวข้อง kwamgiawkong

relative *a.* ที่เกี่ยวข้องกัน tigiawkonggan

relative *n.* ญาติ yad

relax *v.t.* ผ่อนคลาย ponklai

relaxation *n.* การผ่อนคลาย ganponklai

relay *n.* การถ่ายทอด gantaitod

relay *v.t.* ถ่ายทอด taitod

release *v.t.* ปล่อย ploy

release *n* การปล่อย ganploy

relent *v.i.* ผ่อนปรน ponpron

relentless *a.* ไม่ผ่อนผัน maiponpan

relevance *n.* ความสัมพันธ์ kwamsampan

relevant *a.* เกี่ยวเนื่อง giawneung

reliable *a.* ไว้ใจได้ waijaidai

reliance *n.* ความไว้วางใจ kwamwaiwangjai

relic *n.* สิ่งตกทอด siangtoktod

relief *n.* การผ่อนคลาย ganponklai

relieve *v.t.* ผ่อนคลาย ponklai

religion *n.* ศาสนา sasana

religious *a.* เคร่งศาสนา krengsasana

relinquish *v.t.* สละ sala

relish *v.t.* เพลิดเพลิน pleudpleun

relish *n* ความเพลิดเพลิน kwampleudpleun

reluctance *n.* ความลังเลใจ kwamlanlayjai

reluctant *a.* ลังเลใจ langlayjai

rely *v.i.* ไว้ใจ waijai

remain *v.i.* คงอยู่ kongyu

remainder *n.* ส่วนที่เหลืออยู่ suantileuayu

remains *n.* ซากศพ saksob

remand *v.t.* ส่งกลับ songglab

remand *n* การส่งตัวผู้ต้องหากลับ gansongtuaputonghaglab

remark *n.* ความเห็น kwamhen

remark *v.t.* ให้ความเห็น haikwamhen

remarkable *a.* น่าทึ่ง nateung

remedial *a.* รักษาได้ raksadai

remedy *n.* การรักษา ganraksa

remedy *v.t* รักษา raksa

remember *v.t.* จำได้ jamdai

remembrance *n.* ความทรงจำ kwamsongjam

remind *v.t.* เตือน teuan

reminder *n.* เครื่องเตือนความใจ kreuangteuankwamjam

reminiscence *n.* ความทรงจำ kwamsongjam

reminiscent *a.* ชวนให้นึกถึง chuanhaineuktuang

remission *n.* การผ่อนคลาย ganponklai

remit *v.t.* ผ่อนคลาย ponklai

remittance *n.* การส่งเงิน gansong-ngeun

remorse *n.* การสำนึกผิด gansamneukpid

remote *a.* ไกล glai

removable *a.* เคลื่อนที่ได้ kleuantidai

removal *n.* การย้าย ganyai

remove *v.t.* ย้าย yai

remunerate *v.t.* จ่ายค่าชดเชย jaikachodcheuy

remuneration *n.* การจ่ายค่าชดเชย ganjaikachodcheuy

remunerative *a.* เป็นค่าตอบแทน penkatobtaen

renaissance *n.* การฟื้นฟูใหม่ ganfeunfumai

render *v.t.* ยอม yom

rendezvous *n.* การนัดหมาย gannadmai

renew *v.t.* ทำใหม่ tammai

renewal *n.* การต่ออายุ gantaw-a-yu

renounce *v.t.* สละ sala

renovate *v.t.* ปรับปรุงใหม่ prabprungmai

renovation *n.* การปรับปรุงใหม่ ganprabprungmai

renown *n.* ชื่อเสียง cheusiang

renowned *a.* มีชื่อเสียง micheusiang

rent *n.* ค่าเช่า kachao

rent *v.t.* เช่า chao

renunciation *n.* การสละ gansala

repair *v.t.* ซ่อม som

repair *n.* การซ่อม gansom

raparable *a.* ซ่อมได้ somdai

repartee *n.* คำตอบที่เฉียบแหลม kamtobtichiablaem

repatriate *v.t.* ส่งกลับประเทศ songglabprated

repatriate *n* คนที่ถูกส่งกลับประเทศ kontitooksongglabprated

repatriation *n.* การส่งกลับประเทศ gansongglabprated

repay *v.t.* จ่ายคืน jaikeun

repayment *n.* การชำระคืน ganchamrakeun

repeal *v.t.* ยกเลิก yokleuk

repeal *n* การยกเลิก ganyokleuk

repeat *v.t.* พูดซ้ำ pudsam

repel *v.t.* ขับไล่ kablai

repellent *a.* ต้านทานไว้ tantanwai

repellent *n* ยากันยุง yaganyung

repent *v.i.* รู้สึกผิด ruseukpid

repentance *n.* การสำนึกผิด gansamneukpid

repentant *a.* สำนึกผิด samneukpid

repercussion *n.* ผลของการกระทำ ponkonggangratam

repetition *n.* การพูดซ้ำ ganpudsam

replace *v.t.* แทนที่ taenti

replacement *n.* การแทนที่ gantaenti

replenish *v.t.* เติม teum

replete *a.* สมบูรณ์ somboon

replica *n.* สำเนา samnao

reply *v.i.* ตอบ tob

reply *n* คำตอบ kamtob

report *v.t.* รายงาน rai-ngan

report *n.* รายงาน rai-ngan

reporter *n.* ผู้รายงาน purai-ngan

repose *n.* การพักผ่อน ganpakpon

repose *v.i.* นอนพัก nonpak

repository *n.* โกดัง godang

represent *v.t.* ทำหน้าที่แทน tamnatitaen

representation *n.* การเป็นตัวแทน ganpentuataen

representative *n.* ตัวแทน tuataen

representative *a.* เป็นตัวแทน pentuataen

repress *v.t.* อดกลั้น od-glan

repression *n.* ความอดกลั้น kwan-od-glan

reprimand *n.* การตำหนิ gantamni

reprimand *v.t.* ตำหนิ tamni

reprint *v.t.* พิมพ์ซ้ำ pimsam

reprint *n.* การพิมพ์ซ้ำ ganpimsam

reproach *v.t.* ตำหนิ tamni

reproach *n.* การตำหนิ gantamni

reproduce *v.t.* สืบพันธุ์ seubpan

reproduction *n* การสืบพันธุ์ ganseubpan

reproductive *a.* เกี่ยวกับการสืบพันธุ์ giawgabganseubpan

reproof *n.* การตำหนิ gantamni

reptile *n.* สัตว์เลื้อยคลาน satleuayklan

republic *n.* สาธารณรัฐ sataranarat

republican *a.* เกี่ยวกับสาธารณรัฐ giawgabsataranarat

republican *n* สมาชิกพรรคริพับริกัน samachikpakripublican

repudiate *v.t.* ปฏิเสธ patised

repudiation *n.* การปฏิเสธ ganpatised

repugnance *n.* การต่อต้าน gantawtan

repugnant *a.* ต่อต้าน tawtan

repulse *v.t.* ขับไล่ kablai

repulse *n.* การขับไล่ gankablai

repulsion *n.* การผลัก ganplak

repulsive *a.* น่ารังเกียจ naranggiad

reputation *n.* ชื่อเสียง cheusiang

repute *v.t.* ยกย่อง yokyong

repute *n.* ชื่อเสียง cheusiang

request *v.t.* ขอร้อง kawrong

request *n* การขอร้อง gankawrong

requiem *n.* การสวดมนต์ส่งวิญญาณผู้ตาย gansuadmonsongwinyanputai

require *v.t.* ต้องการ tonggan

requirement *n.* ความต้องการ kwamtonggan

requisite *a.* จำเป็น jampen

requiste *n* สิ่งจำเป็น singjampen

requisition *n.* คำร้อง kamrong

requisition *v.t.* เรียกร้อง riakrong

requite *v.t.* ตอบสนอง tobsanong

rescue *v.t.* ช่วยเหลือ cheuayleau

rescue *n* ความช่วยเหลือ kwamcheuayleau

research *v.i.* วิจัย wijai

research *n* การวิจัย ganwijai

resemblance *n.* ความคล้ายคลึง kwamklaikleung

resemble *v.t.* คล้าย klai

resent *v.t.* ไม่พอใจ maipawjai

resentment *n.* ความไม่พอใจ kwammaipawjai

reservation *n.* ข้อจำกัด kawjamgad

reserve *v.t.* จอง jong

rservoir *n.* อ่างเก็บน้ำ ang-gebnam

reside *v.i.* อาศัย a-sai

residence *n.* ที่พักอาศัย tipak-a-sai

resident *a.* เกี่ยวกับที่พักอาศัย giawgabtipak-a-sai

resident *n* ผู้พักอาศัย pupak-a-sai

residual *a.* ที่เหลืออยู่ tileauyu

residue *n.* สิ่งที่เหลืออยู่ singtileuayu

resign *v.t.* ลาออก la-awk

resignation *n.* การลาออก ganla-awk

resist *v.t.* ต่อต้าน tawtan

resistance *n.* การต่อต้าน gantawtan

resistant *a.* ต่อต้าน tawtan

resolute *a.* แน่วแน่ naewnae

resolution *n.* การแก้ปัญหา gangaepanha

resolve *v.t.* แก้ปัญหา gaepanha

resonance *n.* เสียงก้อง sianggong

resonant *a.* ก้อง gong

resort *v.i.* อาศัย a-sai

resort *n* ที่พักตากอากาศ tipaktak-a-gad

resound *v.i.* ดังก้อง danggong

resource *n.* แหล่งที่มา laengtima

resourceful *a.* อุดมสมบูรณ์ u-domsomboon

respect *v.t.* เคารพ kaorob

respect *n.* ความเคารพ kwamkaorob

respectful *a.* น่าเคารพ nakaorob

respective *a.* ตามลำดับ tamlamdab

respiration *n.* การหายใจ ganhaijai

respire *v.i.* หายใจ haijai

resplendent *a.* สุกสว่าง suksawang

respond *v.i.* ตอบ tob

respondent *n.* จำเลย jamleuy

response *n.* คำตอบ kamtob

responsibility *n.* ความรับผิดชอบ kwamrabpidchob

responsible *a.* รับผิดชอบ rabpidchob

rest *v.i.* พัก pak

rest *n* การพักผ่อน ganpakpon

restaurant *n.* ร้านอาหาร ran-a-han

restive *a.* ดื้อรั้น deuran

restoration *n.* การฟื้นฟู ganfeunfu

restore *v.t.* ฟื้นฟู feunfu

restrain *v.t.* ยับยั้ง yabyang

restrict *v.t.* จำกัด jamgad

restriction *n.* การจำกัด ganjamgad

restrictive *a.* จำกัด jamgad

result *v.i.* เป็นผล penpon

result *n.* ผลลัพธ์ ponlab

resume *v.t.* ดำเนินต่อ damneuantaw

resume *n.* ประวัติย่อ prawatyaw

resumption *n.* การเริ่มต้นใหม่ ganreumtonmai

resurgence *n.* การฟื้นคืน ganfeunkeun
resurgent *a.* ฟื้นคืน feunkeun
retail *v.t.* ขายปลีก kaiplik
retail *n.* การขายปลีก gankaiplik
retail *adv.* เกี่ยวกับการขายปลีก
 giawgabgankaiplik
retail *a* ในราคาขายปลีก nairakakaiplik
retailer *n.* ผู้ค้าปลีก pukaplik
retain *v.t.* เก็บไว้ gebwai
retaliate *v.i.* แก้แค้น gaekaen
retaliation *n.* การแก้แค้น gangaekaen
retard *v.t.* ทำให้ช้า tamhaicha
retardation *n.* ความปัญญาอ่อน
 kwampanya-on
retention *n.* การเก็บรักษา gangebraksa
retentive *a.* ที่รักษาไว้ tiraksawai
reticence *n.* ความเงียบ kwam-ngiab
reticent *a.* พูดน้อย pudnoy
retina *n.* จอประสาทตา jawprasatta
retinue *n.* กลุ่มผู้ติดตาม glumputidtam
retire *v.i.* เกษียณ gasian
retirement *n.* การเกษียณอายุ gangasian-
 a-yu
retort *v.t.* โต้ตอบ totob
retort *n.* การพูดย้อน ganpudyawn
retouch *v.t.* ตกแต่ง toktaeng
retrace *v.t.* ย้อนรอยเดิม yawnroydeum
retread *v.t.* หล่อดอกยาง lawdawkyang
retread *n.* ยางรถที่หล่อดอกใหม่
 yangrodtilawdawkmai
retreat *v.i.* ล่าถอย latoy
retrench *v.t.* ประหยัด prayad
retrenchment *n.* ความประหยัด
 kwamprayad
retrieve *v.t.* กู้ gu
retrospect *n.* การรำลึกถึงอดีต
 ganramleukteung-a-dit
retrospection *n.* การรำลึกถึงอดีต
 ganramleukteung-a-dit
retrospective *a.* รำลึกถึงอดีต
 ramleuktuang-a-dit
return *v.i.* ย้อนกลับ yawnglab

return *n.* การย้อนกลับ ganyawnglab
revel *v.i.* สนุกสนาน sanooksanan
revel *n.* งานรื่นเริง ngan-reunreung
revelation *n.* การเปิดเผย ganpeudpeuy
reveller *n.* ผู้ร่วมงานรื่นเริง
 puruamnganreunreung
revelry *n.* ความสนุกสนาน
 kwamsanooksanan
revenge *v.t.* แก้แค้น gaekaen
revenge *n.* การแก้แค้น gangaekaen
revengeful *a.* ผูกพยาบาท pukpayabat
revenue *n.* รายได้ raidai
revere *v.t.* เคารพ kaorob
reverence *n.* ความเคารพ kwamkaorob
reverend *a.* น่าเคารพ nakaorob
reverent *a.* น่าเคารพ nakaorob
reverential *a.* ด้วยความเคารพ
 duaykwamkaorob
reverie *n.* การฝันกลางวัน ganfanglangwan
reversal *n.* การพลิกกลับ ganplikglab
reverse *a.* ตรงกันข้าม tronggankam
reverse *n* การถอยหลัง gantoylang
reverse *v.t.* ถอยหลัง toylang
reversible *a.* พลิกกลับได้ plikglabdai
revert *v.i.* กลับสู่สภาพเดิม
 glabsusapabdeum
review *v.t.* ทบทวน tobtuan
review *n* การทบทวน gantobtuan
revise *v.t.* แก้ไข gaekai
revision *n.* การแก้ไข gangaekai
revival *n.* การฟื้นฟู ganfeunfu
revive *v.i.* ฟื้นคืนสติ feunkeunsati
revocable *a.* เพิกถอนได้ peuktawndai
revocation *n.* การเพิกถอน ganpeuktawn
revoke *v.t.* เพิกถอน peuktawn
revolt *v.i.* ปฏิวัติ patiwat
revolt *n.* การปฏิวัติ ganpatiwat
revolution *n.* การปฏิวัติ ganpatiwat
revolutionary *a.* เกี่ยวกับการปฏิวัติ
 giawgabganpatiwat
revolutionary *n* การปฏิวัติ ganpatiwat
revolve *v.i.* หมุนรอบ moonrob

revolver *n.* ปืนพก peunpok

reward *n.* รางวัล rangwan

reward *v.t.* รับรางวัล rabrangwan

rhetoric *n.* การใช้ถ้อยคำโน้มน้าว
ganchaitoykamnomnao

rhetorical *a.* เชิงสำนวนโวหาร
cheungsamnuanwohan

rheumatic *a.* เกี่ยวกับโรคไขข้อ
giawgabrokkaikaw

rheumatism *n.* โรคไขข้ออักเสบ
rokkaikaw-akseb

rhinoceros *n.* แรด raed

rhyme *n.* เสียงสัมผัสในบทกวี
siangsampadnaibodgawi

rhyme *v.i.* ใช้เสียงสัมผัส chaisiangsampad

rhymester *n.* กวีที่สร้างงานไม่มีคุณภาพ
gawitisang-nganmaimikunnapab

rhythm *b.* จังหวะ jangwa

rhythmic *a.* เป็นจังหวะ penjangwa

rib *n.* ซี่โครง sikrong

ribbon *n.* โบว์ bo

rice *n.* ข้าว kao

rich *a.* รวย ruay

riches *n.* ความร่ำรวย kwamramruay

richness *a.* ความร่ำรวย kwamramruay

rick *n.* กองฟาง gongfang

rickets *n.* โรคกระดูกอ่อน rokgraduk-on

rickety *a.* อ่อนแอ on-ae

rickshaw *n.* รถลาก rodlak

rid *v.t.* กำจัด gamjad

riddle *n.* เกมปริศนา gaimprisana

riddle *v.i.* ตอบปริศนา tobprisana

ride *v.t.* ขี่ ki

ride *n* การขี่ ganki

rider *n.* ผู้ขี่ puki

ridge *n.* สัน san

ridicule *v.t.* เยาะเย้ย yawyei

ridicule *n.* การเยาะเย้ย ganyawyei

ridiculous *a.* น่าขำ nakam

rifle *v.t.* ค้น kon

rifle *n* ปืนยาว peunyao

rift *n.* ความแตกร้าว kwamtaekrao

right *a.* ถูกต้อง tooktong

right *adv* เหมาะสม mawsom

right *n* ความถูกต้อง kwamtooktong

right *v.t.* ทำให้ถูกต้อง tamhaitooktong

righteous *a.* ชอบธรรม chobtam

rigid *a.* แข็ง kaeng

rigorous *a.* เข้มงวด kem-nguad

rigour *n.* ความรุนแรง kwamroonraeng

rim *n.* ขอบ kob

ring *n.* แหวน waen

ring *v.t.* สั่นกระดิ่ง sangrading

ringlet *n.* ปอยผม poypom

ringworm *n.* ขี้กลาก kiglak

rinse *v.t.* ล้าง lang

riot *n.* การจลาจล ganjalajon

riot *v.t.* ก่อจลาจล gawjalajon

rip *v.t.* ฉีก chik

ripe *a* สุก sook

ripen *v.i.* ทำให้สุก tamhaisook

ripple *n.* คลื่น kleun

ripple *v.t.* ทำให้กระเพื่อม
tamhaigrapeuam

rise *v.* ขึ้น keun

rise *n.* การเพิ่มขึ้น ganpeumkeun

risk *v.t.* เสี่ยง siang

risk *n.* การเสี่ยง gansiang

risky *a.* เป็นอันตราย pen-antarai

rite *n.* พิธีกรรม pitigam

ritual *n.* พิธีกรรม pitigam

ritual *a.* เกี่ยวกับพิธีกรรม giawgabpitigam

rival *n.* คู่แข่ง kukaeng

rival *v.t.* แข่งขัน kaengkan

rivalry *n.* การแข่งขัน gankaengkan

river *n.* แม่น้ำ maenam

rivet *n.* หมุด mud

rivet *v.t.* ตอกหมุด tokmud

rivulet *n.* ลำธาร lamtan

road *n.* ถนน tanon

roam *v.i.* ท่องเที่ยวไป tongtiawpai

roar *n.* การคำราม gankamram

roar *v.i.* คำราม kamram

roast *v.t.* ย่าง yang

roast *a* คั่ว kua
roast *n* เนื้อย่าง neauyang
rob *v.t.* ปล้น plon
robber *n.* โจร jon
robbery *n.* การปล้น ganplon
robe *n.* เสื้อคลุม seuaklum
robe *v.t.* สวมเสื้อคลุม suamseuaklum
robot *n.* หุ่นยนต์ hunyon
robust *a.* แข็งแรง kaengraeng
rock *v.t.* โยก yok
rock *n.* หิน hin
rocket *n.* จรวด jaruad
rod *n.* คันเบ็ด kanbeid
rodent *n.* หนู nu
roe *n.* ไข่ปลา kaipla
rogue *n.* อันธพาล antapan
roguery *n.* ความมีเล่ห์เหลี่ยม
    kwammilayliam
roguish *a.* ขี้โกง kigong
role *n.* บทบาท bodbat
roll *n.* ม้วน muan
roll *v.i.* ม้วน muan
roll-call *n.* การขานชื่อ gankancheu
roller *n.* ลูกกลิ้ง lookgling
romance *n.* เรื่องรักใคร่ reuangrakkrai
romantic *a.* เกี่ยวกับเรื่องรักใคร่
    giawgabreungrakkrai
romp *v.i.* วิ่งเล่น winglen
romp *n.* การวิ่งเล่น ganwinglen
rood *n.* ไม้กางเขน maigangkaen
roof *n.* หลังคา langka
roof *v.t.* มุงหลังคา munglangka
rook *n.* นกชนิดหนึ่ง nokchanidneung
rook *v.t.* โกง gong
room *n.* ห้อง hong
roomy *a.* กว้าง gwang
roost *n.* คอน kon
roost *v.i.* เกาะคอน gaokon
root *n.* ราก rak
root *v.i.* หยั่งราก yangrak
rope *n.* เชือก cheuak
rope *v.t.* ผูกเชือก pukcheuak

rosary *n.* สายลูกประคำ sailookprakam
rose *n.* ดอกกุหลาบ dawkgulab
roseate *a.* มองโลกในแง่ดี mongloknai-
    ngaedi
rostrum *n.* แท่น taen
rosy *a.* ร่าเริง rareung
rot *n.* เรื่องไร้สาระ reuangraisara
rot *v.i.* เน่า nao
rotary *a.* หมุนรอบ moonrob
rotate *v.i.* หมุนเวียน moonwian
rotation *n.* การหมุนเวียน ganmoonwian
rote *n.* ทางเดิน tangdeun
rouble *n.* เงินรูเบิล ngeunrouble
rough *a.* ขรุขระ klukla
round *a.* กลม glom
round *adv.* กลม glom
round *n.* ทรงกลม songglom
round *v.t.* ทำให้กลม tamhaiklom
rouse *v.i.* ปลุก pluk
rout *v.t.* ตีพ่าย tipai
rout *n* ความชุลมุน kwamchunlamun
route *n.* เส้นทาง sentang
routine *n.* กิจวัตรประจำ
    giggawatprajamwan
routine *a* เป็นประจำ penprajam
rove *v.i.* เดินไปมา deunpaideunma
rover *n.* คนเร่ร่อน konreron
row *n.* แถว taew
row *v.t.* พาย pai
row *n* การทะเลาะวิวาท gantalawwiwat
row *n.* เสียงโวยวาย siangwoywai
rowdy *a.* เกเร gayray
royal *a.* เกี่ยวกับราชวงศ์
    giawgabrachawong
royalist *n.* ผู้จงรักภักดีต่อกษัตริย์
    pujongrakpakditawgasat
royalty *n.* ความจงรักภักดี
    kwamjongrakpakdi
rub *v.t.* ขัด kad
rub *n* การขัด gankad
rubber *n.* ยางลบ yangrob
rubbish *n.* ขยะ kaya

rubble *n.* เศษหิน sedhin
ruby *n.* ทับทิม tabtim
rude *a.* หยาบคาย yabkai
rudiment *n.* มูลฐาน muntan
rudimentary *a.* เป็นพื้นฐาน penpeuntan
rue *v.t.* รู้สึกเสียใจ rusuksiajai
rueful *a.* เสียใจ siajai
ruffian *n.* นักเลง nakleng
ruffle *v.t.* กระเพื่อม grapeum
rug *n.* พรม prom
rugged *a.* ขรุขระ krukra
ruin *n.* ซากปรักหักพัง sakparakhakpang
ruin *v.t.* ทำลาย tamrai
rule *n.* การปกครอง ganpokkrong
rule *v.t.* ปกครอง pokkrong
ruler *n.* ผู้ปกครอง pupokkrong
ruling *n.* คำวินิจฉัย kamwinitchai
rum *n.* เหล้ารัม laorum
rum *a* ทำจากเหล้ารัม tamjaklaorum
rumble *v.i.* ส่งเสียงดัง songsiangdang
rumble *n.* เสียงดัง siangdang
ruminant *a.* เกี่ยวกับสัตว์เคี้ยวเอื้อง
  giawgabsadkiaw-euang
ruminant *n.* สัตว์เคี้ยวเอื้อง satkiaw-eung
ruminate *v.i.* เคี้ยวเอื้อง kiaw-eung
rumination *n.* การสำรอก gansamrok
rummage *v.i.* ค้น kon
rummage *n* การค้น gankon
rummy *n.* ไพ่รัมมี่ pairummy
rumour *n.* ข่าวลือ kaoreu
rumour *v.t.* กระจายข่าว gangrajaikao
run *v.i.* วิ่ง wing
run *n.* การวิ่ง ganwing
rung *n.* ซี่ล้อ silaw
runner *n.* นักวิ่ง nakwing
rupee *n.* เงินรูปี ngeunrupi
rupture *n.* การแตกออก gantaek-awk
rupture *v.t.* แตกออก taek-awk
rural *a.* ท้องถิ่น tongtin
ruse *n.* อุบาย u-bai
rush *n.* การรีบเร่ง ganribreing
rush *v.t.* รีบเร่ง ribreng

rush *n* การจู่โจม ganjujom
rust *n.* สนิม sanim
rust *v.i* ขึ้นสนิม keunsanim
rustic *a.* เรียบง่าย riab-ngai
rustic *n* ชาวชนบท chaochonnabot
rusticate *v.t.* ไปอยู่ชนบท paiyuchonnabot
rustication *n.* การไปอยู่ชนบท
  ganpaiyuchonnabot
rusticity *n.* ความเป็นคนบ้านนอก
  kwampenkonbannok
rusty *a.* เป็นสนิม pensanim
rut *n.* ร่องทาง rongtang
ruthless *a.* ไร้ความปรานี raikwamprani
rye *n.* ข้าวไรย์ kaorye

S

sabbath *n.* วันประกอบพิธีทางศาสนาคริสต์
  wanpragobpititangsasanakrit
sabotage *n.* การทำลายล้าง gantamlairang
sabotage *v.t.* ทำลายล้าง tamlailang
sabre *n.* กระบี่ grabi
sabre *v.t.* ฟันด้วยกระบี่ fanduaygrabi
saccharin *n.* ขันฑสกร kantosagon
saccharine *a.* หวานเกินไป wangeunpai
sack *n.* กระสอบ grasob
sack *v.t.* ไล่ lai
sacrament *n.*
  พิธีรับเข้าเป็นคริสต์ศาสนิกชน
  pitirabkaopenchisasanigachon
sacred *a.* ศักดิ์สิทธิ์ saksit
sacrifice *n.* การเสียสละ gansiasara
sacrifice *v.t.* เสียสละ siasara
sacrificial *a.* เกี่ยวกับการเสียสละ
  giawgabgansiasara
sacrilege *n.* การลบหลู่ศาสนา
  ganrobrusasana
sacrilegious *a.* มีความผิดฐานล่วงเกิน
  mikwampidtanluanggeun
sacrosanct *a.* ศักดิ์สิทธิ์ saksit
sad *a.* เศร้า sao

sadden *v.t.* ทำให้เศร้า tamhaisao
saddle *n.* อานม้า anma
saddle *v.t.* ใส่อาน sai-an
sadism *n.* การกระทำทารุณทางเพศ gangratamtaruntangped
sadist *n.* คนที่ชอบความรุนแรง kontichobkwamrunraeng
safe *a.* ปลอดภัย plodpai
safe *n.* ความปลอดภัย kwamplodpai
safeguard *n.* สิ่งป้องกัน singponggan
safety *n.* ความปลอดภัย kwamplodpai
saffron *n.* หญ้าฝรั่น yafaran
saffron *a* สีเหลืองอมส้ม sileuang-omsom
sagacious *a.* เฉียบแหลม chiablaem
sagacity *n.* ความฉลาด kwamchalad
sage *n.* คนฉลาด konchalad
sage *a.* ฉลาด chalad
sail *n.* การเดินเรือ gandeunreua
sail *v.i.* เดินเรือ deunreua
sailor *n.* ทหารเรือ tahanreua
saint *n.* นักบุญ nakboon
saintly *a.* คล้ายนักบุญ klainakbun
sake *n.* ผลประโยชน์ ponprayod
salable *a.* เหมาะกับการขาย mawsomgabgankai
salad *n.* สลัด salad
salary *n.* รายได้ raidai
sale *n.* การขาย gankai
salesman *n.* เซลส์แมน salesman
salient *a.* โดดเด่น dodden
saline *a.* ประกอบด้วยเกลือ pragobduaygleua
salinity *n.* สารละลายเกลือ sanlalaigleua
saliva *n.* น้ำลาย namlai
sally *n.* การโจมตี ganjomti
sally *v.i.* ตีฝ่าวงล้อม tifawonglom
saloon *n.* รถเก๋ง rodgeng
salt *n.* เกลือ gleua
salt *v.t* ใส่เกลือ saigleua
salty *a.* เค็ม kem
salutary *a.* ที่เป็นประโยชน์ tipenprayod

salutation *n.* การแสดงความเคารพ gansadaengkwamkaorob
salute *v.t.* คำนับ kamnab
salute *n* การคำนับ gankamnab
salvage *n.* การกอบกู้ gangobgu
salvage *v.t.* กอบกู้ gobgu
salvation *n.* กอบกู้ gobgu
same *a.* การไถ่บาป gantaibab
sample *n.* ตัวอย่าง tuayang
sample *v.t.* ให้ตัวอย่าง haituayang
sanatorium *n.* สถานพยาบาล satanpayaban
sanctification *n.* การล้างบาป ganlangbab
sanctify *v.t.* ล้างบาป langbab
sanction *n.* การลงโทษ ganlongtod
sanction *v.t.* ลงโทษ longttod
sanctity *n.* สิ่งศักดิ์สิทธิ์ singsaksit
sanctuary *n.* ที่หลบภัย tilobpai
sand *n.* ทราย sai
sandal *n.* รองเท้าแตะ rongtaotae
sandalwood *n.* ไม้จันทน์ maijan
sandwich *n.* แซนด์วิช sandwich
sandwich *v.t.* ประกบ pragob
sandy *a.* ประกอบด้วยทราย pragobduaysai
sane *a.* มีสติ misati
sanguine *a.* ร่าเริง rareung
sanitary *a.* ถูกสุขลักษณะ tooksuklaksana
sanity *n.* การมีสุขภาพจิตดี ganmisukkapabjidti
sap *n.* น้ำหล่อเลี้ยง namlawliang
sap *v.t.* ดูดออก dud-awk
sapling *n.* ต้นไม้อ่อน tonmai-on
sapphire *n.* พลอยสีน้ำเงิน ploysinam-ngeun
sarcasm *n.* การเสียดสี gansiadsi
sarcastic *a.* ช่างเสียดสี changsiadsi
sardonic *a.* เยาะเย้ย yawyei
satan *n.* ซาตาน satan
satchel *n.* ย่าม yam
satellite *n.* ดาวเทียม daotiam
satiable *a.* น่าพอใจ napawjai
satiate *v.t.* ทำให้พอใจ tamhaipawjai

satiety *n.* ความเต็มอิ่ม kwamtem-im

satire *n.* การเสียดสี gansiadsi

satirical *a.* ชอบถากถาง chobtaktang

satirist *n.* ผู้ชอบถากถาง puchobtaktang

satirize *v.t.* ถากถาง taktang

satisfaction *n.* ความพอใจ kwampawjai

satisfactory *a.* น่าพอใจ napawjai

satisfy *v.t.* พอใจ pawjai

saturate *v.t.* ทำให้ชุ่ม tamhaichum

saturation *n.* การทำให้อิ่มตัว gantamhai-imtua

Saturday *n.* วันเสาร์ wansao

sauce *n.* น้ำปรุงรส namprungrod

saucer *n.* จานรอง janrong

saunter *v.t.* เดินทอดน่อง deuantodnong

savage *a.* โหดร้าย hodrai

savage *n* คนป่าเถื่อน konpateuan

savagery *n.* ความป่าเถื่อน kwampateuan

save *v.t.* ป้องกัน ponggan

save *prep* ปลอดภัย plodpai

saviour *n.* ผู้ช่วยชีวิต puchuaychiwit

savour *n.* รสชาติ rotchat

savour *v.t.* มีรสชาติ mirotchat

saw *n.* เลื่อย leuy

saw *v.t.* เลื่อย leuy

say *v.t.* พูด pud

say *n.* การพูด ganpud

scabbard *n.* ปลอกมีด plokmid

scabies *n.* โรคหิด rokhid

scaffold *n.* นั่งร้าน nangran

scale *n.* เครื่องชั่ง kreuangchang

scale *v.t.* วัด wat

scalp *n* หนังศีรษะ nangsisa

scamper *v.i* วิ่งเล่น winglen

scamper *n* การวิ่งเล่น ganwinglen

scan *v.t.* ตรวจสอบ truadsob

scandal *n* เรื่องอื้อฉาว reuang-eu-chao

scandalize *v.t.* ทำให้เสียชื่อเสียง tamhaisiacheusiang

scant *a.* ขาดแคลน kadklan

scanty *a.* ขาดแคลน kadklan

scapegoat *n.* แพะรับบาป paerabbab

scar *n* รอยแผลเป็น royplaepen

scar *v.t.* ทำให้เกิดแผลเป็น tamhaipenplaepen

scarce *a.* ขาดแคลน kadklan

scarcely *adv.* อย่างขาดแคลน yangkadklan

scarcity *n.* ความขาดแคลน kwamkadklan

scare *n.* ความกลัว kwamglua

scare *v.t.* ตกใจ tokjai

scarf *n.* ผ้าพันคอ papankaw

scatter *v.t.* กระจาย grajai

scavenger *n.* คนเก็บขยะ kongebkaya

scene *n.* เหตุการณ์ hedgan

scenery *n.* ภาพเหตุการณ์ pabhedgan

scenic *a.* เกี่ยวกับภาพภูมิประเทศ giawgabpabpumiprated

scent *n.* กลิ่น glin

scent *v.t.* ได้กลิ่น daiglin

sceptic *n.* ผู้สงสัย pusongsai

sceptical *a.* น่าสงสัย nasongsai

scepticism *n.* ความสงสัย kwamsongsai

sceptre *n.* คทา kata

schedule *n.* กำหนดการ gamnodgan

schedule *v.t.* ทำกำหนดการ tamgamnodgan

scheme *n.* แผนการ paengan

scheme *v.i.* วางแผนการ wangpaengan

schism *n.* ความแตกแยก kwamtaekyaek

scholar *n.* นักวิชาการ nakwichagan

scholarly *a.* คงแก่เรียน konggaerian

scholarship *n.* ทุนการศึกษา toongansuksa

scholastic *a.* เกี่ยวกับการศึกษา giawgabgansuksa

school *n.* โรงเรียน rongrian

science *n.* วิทยาศาสตร์ witayasat

scientific *a.* เกี่ยวกับวิทยาศาสตร์ giawgabwitayasat

scientist *n.* นักวิทยาศาสตร์ nakwitayasat

scintillate *v.i.* เป็นประกาย penpragai

scintillation *n.* การเกิดประกายไฟ gandgeudpragaifai

scissors *n.* กรรไกร gangai

scoff *n.* การพูดเยาะเย้ย ganpudyawyei

scoff *v.i.* พูดเยาะเย้ย pudyawyei

scold *v.t.* ดุด่า duda

scooter *n.* รถมอเตอร์ไซด์ขนาดเล็ก rodmotersaikanadlek

scope *n.* ขอบเขต kobked

scorch *v.t.* ย่างเกรียม yanggriam

score *n.* คะแนน kanaen

score *v.t.* ทำคะแนน tamkanaen

scorer *n.* ผู้ให้คะแนน puhaikanaen

scorn *n.* การดูหมิ่น gandumin

scorn *v.t.* ดูหมิ่น dumin

scorpion *n.* แมงป่อง mangpong

Scot *n.* คนสก็อต konscot

scotch *a.* เกี่ยวกับสก๊อตแลนด์ giawgabscottland

scotch *n.* รอยบาก roybak

scot-free *a.* ไม่ได้รับการลงโทษ maidairabganlongtod

scoundrel *n.* คนชั่ว konchua

scourge *n.* ความหายนะ kwamhaiyana

scourge *v.t.* หวด huad

scout *n* ลูกเสือ lookseua

scout *v.i* สอดแนม sodnam

scowl *v.i.* ทำหน้าบึ้ง tamnabeung

scowl *n.* การทำหน้าบึ้ง gantamnabeung

scramble *v.i.* กวน guan

scramble *n* การแย่งชิง ganyaengching

scrap *n.* เศษเล็กๆ sedleklek

scratch *n.* รอยข่วน roykuan

scratch *v.t.* ข่วน kuan

scrawl *v.t.* เขียนหวัดๆ kianwatwat

scrawl *n* การเขียนหวัดๆ gankianwatwat

scream *v.i.* กรีดร้อง gridrong

scream *n* การกรีดร้อง gangridrong

screen *n.* การกลั่นกรอง ganglangrong

screen *v.t.* กลั่นกรอง glangrong

screw *n.* ตะปูเกลียว tapugliaw

screw *v.t.* ขันสกรู kansagru

scribble *v.t.* เขียนหวัดๆ kianwatwat

scribble *n.* ลายมือหวัด laimeuwat

script *n.* ลายมือ laimeu

scripture *n.* คัมภีร์ไบเบิ้ล kampibible

scroll *n.* ม้วนกระดาษ muangradat

scrutinize *v.t.* พินิจพิเคราะห์ pinitpikraw

scrutiny *n.* การพินิจพิเคราะห์ ganpinitpikraw

scuffle *n.* การต่อสู้กันอุตลุด gantawsugan-udtalud

scuffle *v.i.* ต่อสู้กันอุตลุด tawsugan-udtalud

sculptor *n.* ช่างแกะสลัก changgaesalak

sculptural *a.* เกี่ยวกับการแกะสลัก giawgabgangaesalak

sculpture *n.* การแกะสลัก gangaesalak

scythe *n.* เคียว kiaw

scythe *v.t.* เกี่ยวด้วยเคียว giawduaykiaw

sea *n.* ทะเล talay

seal *n.* แมวน้ำ maewnam

seal *n.* ตราประทับ trapratab

seal *v.t.* ประทับตรา pratabtra

seam *n.* ตะเข็บ takeb

seam *v.t.* เย็บตะเข็บ yebtakeb

seamy *a.* ที่ราบรื่น tirabreun

search *n.* การค้นหา gankonha

search *v.t.* ค้นหา konha

season *n.* ฤดูกาล rudugan

season *v.t.* เพิ่มรสชาติ peumrodchat

seasonable *a.* เหมาะกับฤดูกาล mawgabreudugan

seasonal *a.* ตามฤดูกาล tamreudugan

seat *n.* ที่นั่ง tinang

seat *v.t.* นั่ง nang

secede *v.i.* แยกตัวออก yaektua-awk

secession *n.* การแยกตัวออก ganyaektua-awk

secessionist *n.* ผู้สนับสนุนการแบ่งแยกดินแดน pusanabsanoonganbaengyaekdindaen

seclude *v.t.* แยกตัว yaektua

secluded *a.* เป็นส่วนตัว pensuantua

seclusion *n.* การเก็บตัว gangebtua

second *a.* ที่สอง tisong

second *n* วินาที winati

second *v.t.* สนับสนุน sanabsanoon
secondary *a.* ลำดับที่สอง lamdabtisong
seconder *n.* ผู้ช่วย puchuay
secrecy *n.* ความลับ kwamlab
secret *a.* ลับ lab
secret *n.* ความลับ kwamlab
secretariat (e) *n.* กองเลขาธิการ
　gonglekatigan
secretary *n.* เลขานุการ lekanugan
secrete *v.t.* หลั่ง lang
secretion *n.* การหลั่ง ganlang
secretive *a.* อย่างเป็นความลับ
　yangpenkwamlab
sect *n.* นิกาย nigai
sectarian *a.* สมาชิกของนิกาย
　samachikkongnigai
section *n.* กลุ่ม glum
sector *n.* ส่วน suan
secure *a.* ปลอดภัย plodpai
secure *v.t.* ทำให้ปลอดภัย tamhaiplodpai
security *n.* ความปลอดภัย kwamplodpai
sedan *n.* รถเก๋ง rodgeng
sedate *a.* เงียบ ngiab
sedate *v.t.* ทำให้เงียบ tamhai-ngiab
sedative *a.* สงบ sa-ngob
sedative *n* ยาระงับประสาท yara-
　ngabprasat
sedentary *a.* ไม่เคลื่อนไหว maikleuanwai
sediment *n.* ตะกอน tagon
sedition *n.* การปลุกระดม ganplukradom
seditious *a.* ก่อความไม่สงบ
　gawkwammaisa-ngob
seduce *n.* ยั่วยวน yuayuan
seduction *n.* การยั่วยวน ganyuayuan
seductive *a* ซึ่งยั่วยวน seungyuayuan
see *v.t.* เห็น hen
seed *n.* เมล็ด maled
seed *v.t.* หว่านเมล็ด wanmaled
seek *v.t.* หา ha
seem *v.i.* ดูเหมือน dumeuan
seemly *a.* เหมาะสม mawsom
seep *v.i.* รั่วซึม ruaseum

seer *n.* ผู้ทำนายเหตุการณ์ในอนาคต
　putannaihedgannai-anakot
seethe *v.i.* โกรธ grot
segment *n.* กลุ่ม glum
segment *v.t.* แยกกลุ่ม yaekglum
segregate *v.t.* แยกออก yaek-awk
segregation *n.* การแบ่งแยก ganbaengyaek
seismic *a.* ไหวสะเทือน waisateuan
seize *v.t.* จับ jab
seizure *n.* การจับกุม ganjabgoom
seldom *adv.* แทบจะไม่ taebjamai
select *v.t.* เลือก leuak
select *a* ดีเลิศ dileud
selection *n.* การคัดเลือก gankadleuak
selective *a.* อย่างเลือกเฟ้น yangleuakfen
self *n.* ตัวเอง tua-eng
selfish *a.* เห็นแก่ตัว hengaetua
selfless *a.* ไม่เห็นแก่ตัว maihengaetua
sell *v.t.* ขาย kai
seller *n.* คนขาย konkai
semblance *n.* ความคล้ายกัน kwamklaigan
semen *n.* น้ำอสุจิ nam-a-suji
semester *n.* ภาคการศึกษา pakganseuksa
seminal *a.* เกี่ยวกับน้ำอสุจิ giawgabnam-a-
　suji
seminar *n.* การสัมมนา gansamana
senate *n.* วุฒิสภา wutisapa
senator *n.* วุฒิสมาชิก wutisamachik
senatorial *a.* เกี่ยวกับสภาสูง
　giawgabsapasoong
send *v.t.* ส่ง song
senile *a.* แก่ gae
senility *n.* คนแก่ kongae
senior *a.* อาวุโส a-wuso
senior *n.* ผู้อาวุโส pu-a-wuso
seniority *n.* ความมีอาวุโส kwammi-a-
　wuso
sensation *n.* ความรู้สึกต่อการสัมผัส
　kwamruseuktawgansampat
sensational *a.* เกี่ยวกับความรู้สึก
　giawgabkwamruseuk
sense *n.* ประสาทสัมผัส prasatsampat

sense *v.t.* สัมผัส sampat

senseless *a.* ไม่มีความรู้สึก maimikwamruseuk

sensibility *n.* การตอบสนองต่อสิ่งกระตุ้น gantobsanongtawsinggratun

sensible *a.* อ่อนไหว on-wai

sensitive *a.* ไวต่อความรู้สึก waitawkwamruseuk

sensual *a.* หมกมุ่นทางเพศ mokmuntangpet

sensualist *n.* ผู้หมกมุ่นทางเพศ pumokmuntangpet

sensuality *n.* การหมกมุ่นทางเพศ ganmokmuntangpet

sensuous *a.* เกี่ยวกับความรู้สึก giawgabkwamruseuk

sentence *n.* ประโยค prayok

sentence *v.t.* แต่งประโยค taengprayok

sentience *n.* ความรู้สึก kwamruseuk

sentient *a.* ซึ่งมีความรู้สึก seungmikwamruseuk

sentiment *n.* อารมณ์ a-rom

sentimental *a.* อารมณ์อ่อนไหว a-rom-on-wai

sentinel *n.* ยาม yam

sentry *n.* ยาม yam

separable *a.* แยกออกจากกันได้ yaek-awkjakgandai

separate *v.t.* แยกกันได้ yaekgandai

separate *a.* แยกออกจากกันได้ yaek-awkjakgandai

separation *n.* การแยกออกจากกัน ganyaek-awkjakgan

sepsis *n.* การติดเชื้อ gantidcheua

September *n.* กันยายน ganyayon

septic *a.* ติดเชื้อ tidcheua

sepulchre *n.* สุสาน susan

sepulture *n.* การฝังศพ ganfangsob

sequel *n.* เรื่องราวต่อมา reuangraotawma

sequence *n.* เหตุการณ์ที่เกิดขึ้นเป็นลำดับ hedgantigeudkeunpenlamdab

sequester *v.t.* โดดเดี่ยว doddiaw

serene *a.* สงบ sa-ngob

serenity *n.* ความสงบ kwamsa-ngob

serf *n.* ทาส tad

serge *n.* กุ้งฝอย gungfoy

sergeant *n.* จ่า ja

serial *a.* ต่อเนื่องกัน tawneuanggan

serial *n.* สิ่งที่ต่อเนื่องกัน singtitawneuanggan

series *n.* อนุกรม a-nugrom

serious *a* เครียด kriad

sermon *n.* การเทศนา gantesana

sermonize *v.i.* เทศนา tesana

serpent *n.* งู ngu

serpentine *n.* แร่สีเขียว raesikiaw

servant *n.* คนรับใช้ konrabchai

serve *v.t.* รับใช้ rabchai

serve *n.* การรับใช้ ganrabchai

service *n.* การบริการ ganborigan

service *v.t* ให้บริการ haiborigan

serviceable *a.* ให้บริการได้ haiborigangdai

servile *a.* ยอมรับใช้ yomrabdai

servility *n.* การยอมรับใช้ ganyomrabchai

session *n.* การประชุม ganprachum

set *v.t* วาง wang

set *a* แน่วแน่ naewnae

set *n* ชุด chud

settle *v.i.* ตกลง toklong

settlement *n.* การตกลง gantoklong

settler *n.* ผู้จัดการ pujadgan

seven *n.* เจ็ด jed

seven *a* เจ็ด jed

seventeen *n., a* สิบเจ็ด sibjed

seventeenth *a.* ที่สิบเจ็ด tisibjed

seventh *a.* ที่เจ็ด tijed

seventieth *a.* ที่เจ็ดสิบ tisibjed

seventy *n., a* เจ็ดสิบ jedsib

sever *v.t.* ค่าชดเชย kachodcheuy

several *a* แทนกัน taengan

severance *n.* เงินชดเชยเมื่อเลิกจ้าง ngeunchodcheuymeuleujang

severe *a.* รุนแรง roonraeng

severity *n.* ความรุนแรง kwamrunraeng

sew *v.t.* เย็บ yeb

sewage *n.* สิ่งปฏิกูล singpatigoon

sewer *n* ท่อน้ำเสีย tawnamsia

sewerage *n.* การระบายน้ำทิ้ง
ganrabainamting

sex *n.* เพศ ped

sexual *a.* เกี่ยวกับเพศ giawgabped

sexuality *n.* เรื่องทางเพศ reuangtangped

sexy *a.* ที่ดึงดูดทางเพศ
tideungdudtangped

shabby *a.* ชำรุดมาก chamrudmak

shackle *n.* กุญแจมือ goonjaemeu

shackle *v.t.* ใส่กุญแจมือ saigoonjaemeu

shade *n.* ร่ม rom

shade *v.t.* ทำให้เกิดร่มเงา
tamhaigeudrom-ngao

shadow *n.* เงา ngao

shadow *v.t* ทอดเงา tod-ngao

shadowy *a.* มีร่มเงา mirom-ngao

shaft *n.* ด้าม dam

shake *v.i.* ถ่อ taw

shake *n* การสั่น gansan

shaky *a.* สั่น san

shallow *a.* ตื้น teun

sham *v.i.* ปลอมแปลง plomplang

sham *n* การปลอมแปลง ganplomplaeng

sham *a* ปลอมแปลงได้ plomplangdai

shame *n.* การละอายใจ ganla-ai-jai

shame *v.t.* รู้สึกละลายใจ ruseukla-ai-jai

shameful *a.* น่าละอายใจ nala-ai-jai

shameless *a.* ไม่ละอายใจ maila-ai-jai

shampoo *n.* ยาสระผม yasapom

shampoo *v.t.* สระผม sapom

shanty *a.* ร่าเริง rareung

shape *n.* รูปร่าง roobrang

shape *v.t* ทำให้เป็นรูปร่าง
tamhaipenroobrang

shapely *a.* มีรูปร่างดี miroobrangdi

share *n.* การแบ่งปัน gambaengpan

share *v.t.* แบ่งปัน baengpan

share *n* หุ้น hun

shark *n.* ฉลาม chalam

sharp *a.* แหลม laem

sharp *adv.* ตรงเวลา trongwela

sharpen *v.t.* ทำให้แหลม tamhailaem

sharpener *n.* กบเหลาดินสอ goblaodinsaw

sharper *n.* คนมีเล่ห์เหลี่ยม konmilayliam

shatter *v.t.* แตกละเอียด taekla-iad

shave *v.t.* โกน goan

shave *n* มีดโกน midgon

shawl *n.* ผ้าคลุมไหล่ paklumlai

she *pron.* เขาผู้หญิง kaopuying

sheaf *n.* ฟ่อน fon

shear *v.t.* ตัด tad

shears *n. pl.* กรรไกร gangrai

shed *v.t.* ทิ้ง ting

shed *n* เพิง peung

sheep *n.* แกะ gae

sheepish *a.* ขี้อาย ki-ai

sheer *a.* เต็มที่ temti

sheet *n.* ผ้าปูที่นอน paputinon

sheet *v.t.* คลี่ออก kli-awk

shelf *n.* ชั้น chan

shell *n.* เปลือก pleuak

shell *v.t.* ปอกเปลือก pokpleuak

shelter *n.* ที่กำบัง tigambang

shelter *v.t.* หลบ lob

shelve *v.t.* วางบนชั้น wangbonchan

shepherd *n.* คนเลี้ยงแกะ konlianggae

shield *n.* โล่ lo

shield *v.t.* ป้องกัน ponggan

shift *v.t.* เคลื่อนย้าย gankleuanyai

shift *n* การเคลื่อนย้าย gangkeuanyai

shifty *a.* มีเล่ห์เหลี่ยม milayliam

shilling *n.* เหรียญชิลลิ่ง rianshilling

shilly-shally *v.i.* ไม่แน่ใจ mainaejai

shilly-shally *n.* ความไม่แน่ใจ
kwammainaejai

sbin *n.* หน้าแข้ง nakaeng

shine *v.i.* ส่องแสง songsaeng

shine *n* แสงสว่าง saengsawang

shiny *a.* เป็นมันเงา penman-ngao

ship *n.* เรือ reua

ship *v.t.* เดินทางโดยเรือ deuntangdoeyreua

shipment *n.* การขนส่งสินค้าทางเรือ gankonsongsinkatangreua

shire *n.* แขวงปกครองในอังกฤษ kwangpokkrongnai-anglid

shirk *v.t.* หลีกเลี่ยง leakliang

shirker *n.* ผู้หลีกเลี่ยง puleakliang

shirt *n.* เสื้อผ้า seuapa

shiver *v.i.* สั่น san

shoal *n.* ฝูง foong

shoal *n* หาดตื้น hadteun

shock *n.* การตกใจ gantokjai

shock *v.t.* ตกใจ tokjai

shoe *n.* รองเท้า rongtao

shoe *v.t.* สวมรองเท้า suamrongtao

shoot *v.t.* ยิง ying

shoot *n* การยิงปืน ganyingpeun

shop *n.* ร้าน ran

shop *v.i.* ซื้อของ seukong

shore *n.* ชายฝั่ง chaifang

short *a.* สั้น san

short *adv.* สั้น san

shortage *n.* การขาดแคลน gankadklaen

shortcoming *n.* จุดอ่อน jud-on

shorten *v.t.* ทำให้สั้น tamhaisan

shortly *adv.* อย่างรวบรัด yangruabrad

shorts *n. pl.* กางเกงขาสั้น ganggengkasan

shot *n.* การฉีดยา ganchidya

shoulder *n.* ไหล่ lai

shoulder *v.t.* รับภาระ rabpara

shout *n.* การตะโกน gantagoan

shout *v.i.* ตะโกน tagon

shove *v.t.* ผลัก plak

shove *n.* การผลัก ganplak

shovel *n.* พลั่ว plua

shovel *v.t.* ขุด kud

show *v.t.* แสดง sadaeng

show *n.* การแสดง gansadaeng

shower *n.* การอาบน้ำ gan-ab-nam

shower *v.t.* อาบน้ำ ab-nam

shrew *n.* หญิงอารมณ์ร้าย ying-a-romrai

shrewd *a.* หลักแหลม laklaem

shriek *n.* การกรีดร้อง gangridrong

shriek *v.i.* กรีดร้อง gridrong

shrill *a.* อย่างโหยหวน yanghoeyhuan

shrine *n.* แท่นบูชา taebucha

shrink *v.i* หด hod

shrinkage *n.* การหด ganhod

shroud *n.* ผ้าห่อศพ pahawsob

shroud *v.t.* คลุม klum

shrub *n.* ต้นไม้เตี้ย tonmaitia

shrug *v.t.* ยักไหล่ yaklai

shrug *n* การยักไหล่ ganyaklai

shudder *v.i.* สั่นกลัว sanglua

shudder *n* อาการสั่นกลัว a-gansanglua

shuffle *v.i.* สับเปลี่ยน sabplian

shuffle *n.* การสับเปลี่ยน gansabplian

shun *v.t.* กรีดร้อง gridrong

shunt *v.t.* หลบเลี่ยง lobliang

shut *v.t.* ปิด pid

shutter *n.* บานเกล็ด bangled

shuttle *n.* กระสวย grasuay

shuttle *v.t.* เคลื่อนที่ไปมา kleuantipaima

shuttlecock *n.* ลูกขนไก่ lookkongai

shy *n.* ความอาย keuan-ai

shy *v.i.* เขินอาย keun-ai

sick *a.* ป่วย puay

sickle *n.* เคียว kiaw

sickly *a.* เจ็บป่วยบ่อย jebpuayboy

sickness *n.* ความเจ็บป่วย kwamjebpuay

side *n.* ด้านข้าง dankang

side *v.i.* เข้าข้าง kaokang

siege *n.* โจมตี jomti

siesta *n.* การงีบหลับตอนเที่ยง gan-ngiblabtontiang

sieve *n.* ตะแกรง tagraeng

sieve *v.t.* กรอง grong

sift *v.t.* กรอง grong

sigh *n.* การถอนหายใจ gantawnhaijai

sigh *v.i.* ถอนหายใจ tawnhaijai

sight *n.* การเห็น ganhen

sight *v.t.* เห็น hen

sightly *a.* น่ามอง namong

sign *n.* ป้าย pai
sign *v.t.* ทำเครื่องหมาย tamkreuangmai
signal *n.* สัญญาณ sanyan
signal *a.* เป็นสัญญาณ pensanyan
signal *v.t.* ให้สัญญาณ haisanyan
signatory *n.* ผู้ลงนามในสัญญา
  pulongnamnaisanya
signature *n.* การลงนาม ganlongnam
significance *n.* ความสำคัญ kwamsamkan
significant *a.* สำคัญ samkan
signification *n.* ความสำคัญ kwamsamkan
signify *v.t.* มีความหมาย mikwammai
silence *n.* ความเงียบ kwam-ngiab
silence *v.t.* ทำให้เงียบ tamhai-ngiab
silencer *n.* ผู้ทำให้เงียบ putamhai-ngiab
silent *a.* เงียบ ngiab
silhouette *n.* ภาพเงา pam-ngao
silk *n.* ไหม mai
silken *a.* คล้ายไหม klaimai
silky *a.* นุ่มเหมือนไหม noommeunmai
silly *a.* โง่ ngo
silt *n.* โคลน klon
silt *v.t.* เต็มไปด้วยโคลน tempaiduayklon
silver *n.* เครื่องเงิน kreuang-ngeun
silver *a* สีเงิน si-ngeun
silver *v.t.* เคลือบเงิน kleub-ngeun
similar *a.* คล้าย klai
similarity *n.* ความคล้ายกัน kwamklaigan
simile *n.* การเปรียบเทียบ ganpriabtiab
similitude *n.* ความคล้ายกัน kwamklaigan
simmer *v.i.* เคี่ยว kiaw
simple *a.* ง่าย ngai
simpleton *n.* คนโง่ kon-ngo
simplicity *n.* ความเรียบง่าย kwamriab-
  ngai
simplification *n.* การทำให้เรียบง่าย
  gantamhairiab-ngai
simplify *v.t.* ทำให้ง่าย tamhai-ngai
simultaneous *a.* ขณะเดียวกัน
  kanadiawgan
sin *n.* บาป bab
sin *v.i.* ทำบาป tambab

since *prep.* ตั้งแต่ tangtae
since *conj.* เนื่องจาก neuangjak
since *adv.* ตั้งแต่นั้นมา tangtaenanma
sincere *a.* จริงใจ jingjai
sincerity *n.* ความจริงใจ kwamjingjai
sinful *a.* เป็นบาป penbab
sing *v.i.* ร้องเพลง rongpleng
singe *v.t.* ทำให้ไหม้ tamhaimai
singe *n* การทำให้ไหม้ gantamhaimai
singer *n.* นักร้อง nakrong
single *a.* โสด sod
single *n.* เดี่ยว diaw
single *v.t.* คัดเลือก kadleuak
singular *a.* พิเศษ pised
singularity *n.* ลักษณะเฉพาะ
  laksanachapaw
singularly *adv.* อย่างพิเศษ yangpised
sinister *a.* เป็นลางร้าย penlangrai
sink *v.i.* จม jom
sink *n* อ่าง ang
sinner *n.* คนบาป konbab
sinuous *a.* คดเคี้ยว kodkiaw
sip *v.t.* จิบ jib
sip *n.* การจิบ ganjib
sir *n.* ท่าน tan
siren *n.* ไซเรน siren
sister *n.* พี่หรือน้องสาว pireunongsao
sisterhood *n.* ความเป็นพี่น้อง
  kwampenpinong
sisterly *a.* เหมือนพี่น้อง meuanpinong
sit *v.i.* นั่ง nang
site *n.* สถานที่ตั้ง satantitang
situation *n.* สถานการณ์ satanagan
six *n., a* หก hok
sixteen *n., a.* สิบหก sibsok
sixteenth *a.* ที่สิบหก tisibhok
sixth *a.* ที่หก tihok
sixtieth *a.* ที่หกสิบ tihoksib
sixty *n., a.* หกสิบ hoksib
sizable *a.* มีขนาดใหญ่ mikanadyai
size *n.* ขนาด kanad
size *v.t.* วัดขนาด watkanad

sizzle *v.i.* ส่งเสียงแฉ songsiangchae
sizzle *n.* เสียงดังแฉ siangdangchae
skate *n.* รองเท้าสเก็ต rongtaosaget
skate *v.t.* เล่นสเก็ต lensaget
skein *n.* กลุ่มด้าย glumdai
skeleton *n.* โครงกระดูก kronggradook
sketch *n.* ภาพร่าง pabrang
sketch *v.t.* ร่าง rang
sketchy *a.* คร่าวๆ kraokrao
skid *v.i.* ลื่น leun
skid *n* การลื่น ganleun
skilful *a.* มีทักษะ mitaksa
skill *n.* ทักษะ taksa
skin *n.* ผิว pew
skin *v.t* ถลอกหนัง taloknang
skip *v.i.* กระโดด gradod
skip *n* การกระโดด gangradod
skipper *n.* ผู้นำทีม punamteam
skirmish *n.* การโต้เถียงกันเล็กน้อย gantotiangganleknoy
skirmish *v.t.* โต้เถียงกันเล็กน้อย totiangganleknoy
skirt *n.* กระโปรง graprong
skirt *v.t.* อยู่ริม yurim
skit *n.* เรื่องล้อเลียน reuanglawlian
skull *n.* กระโหลก gralok
sky *n.* ท้องฟ้า tongfa
sky *v.t.* โยนให้สูง yonhaisoong
slab *n.* แผ่นหิน paenhin
slack *a.* หย่อน yawn
slacken *v.t.* ทำให้หย่อน tamhaiyawn
slacks *n.* กางเกงทรงหลวม gangengsongluam
slake *v.t.* บรรเทา bantao
slam *v.t.* กระแทก grataek
slam *n* การกระแทก gangrataek
slander *n.* คำพูดให้ร้าย kampudhairai
slander *v.t.* พูดให้ร้าย pudhairai
slanderous *a.* หมิ่นประมาท minpramat
slang *n.* คำแสลง kamsalaeng
slant *v.t.* เอน en
slant *n* การลาดเอียง ganlad-iang

slap *n.* การตบ gantob
slap *v.t.* ตบ tob
slash *v.t.* ฟัน fun
slash *n* รอยฟัน royfun
slate *n.* หินชนวน hinchanuan
slattern *n.* โสเภณี sopeni
slatternly *a.* เหมือนโสเภณี meuansopeni
slaughter *n.* การฆ่าสัตว์ gankasat
slaughter *v.t.* ฆ่า ka
slave *n.* ทาส tad
slave *v.i.* ทำงานหนัก tam-ngannak
slavery *n.* ความเป็นทาส kwampentad
slavish *a.* อย่างทาส yangtad
slay *v.t.* ฆ่า ka
sleek *a.* ลื่น leun
sleep *v.i.* หลับ lab
sleep *n.* การหลับ ganlab
sleeper *n.* คนนอนหลับ konnonlab
sleepy *a.* ขี้เซา kisao
sleeve *n* แขนเสื้อ kaenseu
sleight *n.* กลอุบาย gon-u-bai
slender *n.* รูปร่างผอมบาง roobrangpombang
slice *n.* การเฉือน gancheuan
slice *v.t.* เฉือน cheuan
slick *a* ลื่นเป็นมัน leunpenman
slide *v.i.* ลื่น leun
slide *n* การลื่นไถล ganleuntalai
slight *a.* เล็กน้อย leknoy
slight *n.* สิ่งเล็กน้อย singleknoy
slight *v.t.* มองข้าม mongkam
slim *a.* ผอม pom
slim *v.i.* ทำให้ผอม tamhaipom
slime *n.* เลน lain
slimy *a.* บอบบาง bobbang
sling *n.* ห่วงเชือก huangcheuak
slip *v.i.* ลื่น leun
slip *n.* การลื่นไถล ganleuntalai
slipper *n.* รองเท้าแตะ rongtaotae
slippery *a.* ลื่น leun
slipshod *a.* สะเพร่า saprao
slit *n.* รอยกรีดยาว roygridyao

slit *v.t.* กรีดตามยาว gridtamyao

slogan *n.* สโลแกน slogan

slope *n.* พื้นที่ลาดเอียง peuntilad-iang

slope *v.i.* ลาดเอียง lad-iang

sloth *n.* ความขี้เกียจ kwamkigiad

slothful *n.* ขี้เกียจ kigiad

slough *n.* โคลนตม klontom

slough *n.* คราบ krab

slough *v.t.* ลอกคราบ lawkkrab

slovenly *a.* อย่างประมาท yangpramat

slow *a* ช้า cha

slow *v.i.* ทำให้ช้า tamhaicha

slowly *adv.* อย่างช้าๆ yangchacha

slowness *n.* ความช้า kwamcha

sluggard *n.* คนขี้เกียจ konkigiad

sluggish *a.* ขี้เกียจ kigiad

sluice *n.* ช่องระบายน้ำ chongrabainam

slum *n.* สลัม slum

slumber *v.i.* งีบหลับ ngiblab

slumber *n.* การงีบหลับ gan-ngiblab

slump *n.* การตกต่ำ gantoktam

slump *v.i.* ทรุดตัว sudtua

slur *n.* การพูดไม่ชัด ganpudmaichad

slush *n.* โคลน klon

slushy *a.* เฉอะแฉะ cheuchae

slut *n.* โสเภณี sopeni

sly *a.* มีเล่ห์เหลี่ยม milayliam

smack *n.* การตี ganti

smack *v.i.* ตี ti

smack *n* รสชาติ rodchat

smack *n.* เรือหาปลา reuahapla

smack *v.t.* จูบเสียงดัง joobsiangdang

small *a.* เล็ก lek

small *adv.* น้อย noy

smallness *n.* ความน้อย kwamnoy

smallpox *n.* ฝีดาษ fidad

smart *a.* ฉลาด chalad

smart *v.i* ทำให้ฉลาด tamhaichalad

smart *n* ความฉลาด kwamchalad

smash *v.t.* ต่อย toy

smash *n* การต่อย gantoy

smear *v.t.* ทาทำให้เปื้อน tamhaipeuan

smear *n.* รอยเปื้อน roypeuan

smell *n.* กลิ่น glin

smell *v.t.* ได้กลิ่น daiglin

smelt *v.t.* หลอม lom

smile *n.* รอยยิ้ม royyim

smile *v.i.* ยิ้ม yim

smith *n.* ช่างเหล็ก changlek

smock *n.* เสื้อสตรี seuasatri

smog *n.* หมอกควัน mokkwan

smoke *n.* ควัน kwan

smoke *v.i.* รมควัน romkwan

smoky *a.* เต็มไปด้วยควัน tempaiduaykwan

smooth *a.* เรียบ riab

smooth *v.t.* ทำให้เรียบ tamhairiab

smother *v.t.* ทำให้หอบ tamhaihob

smoulder *v.i.* คุกรุ่น kugrun

smug *a.* สบายใจ sabaijai

smuggle *v.t.* ลักลอบนำเข้า laklobnamkao

smuggler *n.* ผู้ลักลอบนำเข้า pulaklobnamkao

snack *n.* อาหารว่าง a-hanwang

snag *n.* ตอ taw

snail *n.* ทาก tak

snake *n.* งู ngu

snake *v.i.* เลื้อย leuy

snap *v.t.* ฉวย chuay

snap *n* การหยิบฉวย ganyibchuay

snap *a* หุนหัน hunhan

snare *n.* กับดัก gabdak

snare *v.t.* วางกับดัก wanggabdak

snarl *n.* เสียงขู่ siangku

snarl *v.i.* ดุด่า duda

snatch *v.t.* คว้า kwa

snatch *n.* การฉกฉวย ganchokchuay

sneak *v.i.* แอบ ab

sneak *n* คนไม่น่าไว้ใจ konmainawaijai

sneer *v.i* ยิ้มเยาะ yimyaw

sneer *n* คำพูดเยาะเย้ย kampudyawyei

sneeze *v.i.* จาม jam

sneeze *n* การจาม ganjam

sniff *v.i.* สูด sud

sniff *n* เสียงสูดจมูก siangsudjamuk

snob *n.* คนหัวสูง konhuasoong

snobbery *n.* พฤติกรรมของคนหัวสูง prutigam:kongkonhuasoong

snobbish *a.* วางมาด wangmad

snore *v.i.* กรน gron

snore *n* การกรน gangron

snort *v.i.* หายใจแรง haijairaeng

snort *n.* การหายใจแรง ganhaijairaeng

snout *n.* จมูก jamook

snow *n.* หิมะ hima

snow *v.i.* หิมะตก himatok

snowy *a.* ปกคลุมไปด้วยหิมะ pokklumpaiduayhima

snub *v.t.* ดูแคลน duklaen

snub *n.* การดูแคลน ganduklaen

snuff *n.* ยานัตถุ์ yanat

snug *a.* อบอุ่น ob-aun

so *adv.* มาก mak

so *conj.* ดังนั้น dangnan

soak *v.t.* จุ่ม jum

soak *n.* การแช่ ganchae

soap *n.* สบู่ sabu

soap *v.t.* ฟอกสบู่ foksabu

soapy *a.* เต็มไปด้วยฟองสบู่ tempaiduayfongsabu

soar *v.i.* บิน bin

sob *v.i.* สะอื้น sa-eun

sob *n* การสะอื้น gansa-eun

sober *a.* สร่างเมา sangmao

sobriety *n.* ความมีสติ kwammisati

sociability *n.* ความสามารถในการเข้าสังคม kwamsamadnaigankaosangkom

sociable *a.* เข้ากับคนง่าย kaogabkon-ngai

social *n.* ทางสังคม tangsangkom

socialism *n* สังคมนิยม sangkomniyom

socialist *n,a* นักสังคมนิยม naksangkomniyom

society *n.* สังคม sangkom

sociology *n.* สังคมศาสตร์ sangkomsat

sock *n.* ถุงเท้า tungtao

socket *n.* เต้าเสียบ taosiab

sod *n.* หญ้า ya

sodomite *n.* ผู้ร่วมเพศทางทวารหนัก puruampedtangtawannak

sodomy *n.* การร่วมเพศทางทวารหนัก ganruampedtangtawannak

sofa *n.* โซฟา sofa

soft *n.* ความนุ่ม kwamnum

soften *v.t.* ทำให้นุ่ม tamhainoom

soil *n.* ดิน din

soil *v.t.* ทำให้เปื้อน tamhaipeuan

sojourn *v.i.* พักแรม pakraem

sojourn *n* การพักแรม ganpakraem

solace *v.t.* ปลอบใจ plobjai

solace *n.* การปลอมใจ ganplobjai

solar *a.* เกี่ยวกับดวงอาทิตย์ giawgabduang-a-tit

solder *n.* เหล็กผสม lekpasom

solder *v.t.* เชื่อมโลหะ cheumloha

soldier *n.* ทหาร tahan

soldier *v.i.* เป็นทหาร pentahan

sole *n.* ฝ่าเท้า fatao

sole *v.t* ทำพื้นรองเท้า tampeunrongtao

sole *a* ลำพัง lampang

solemn *a.* เคร่งขรึม krengkreum

solemnity *n.* ความเคร่งขรึม kwamkreungkreum

solemnize *v.t.* ทำให้เคร่งขรึม tamhaikreungkreum

solicit *v.t.* เรียกร้อง riakrong

solicitation *n.* การเรียกร้อง ganriakrong

solicitor *n.* ผู้เรียกร้อง puriakrong

solicitious *a.* เป็นกังวล pengangwon

solicitude *n.* ความกังวล kwamgangwon

solid *a.* แข็ง kaeng

solid *n* ของแข็ง kongkaeng

solidarity *n.* ความสามัคคี kwamsamakki

soliloquy *n.* การพูดกับตัวเอง ganpudgabtua-eng

solitary *a.* โดดเดี่ยว doddiaw

solitude *n.* การอยู่โดดเดี่ยว ganyudoddiaw

solo *n* การแสดงเดี่ยว gansadaengdiaw

solo *a.* เพียงลำพัง pianglampang

solo *adv.* โดยลำพัง dueylampang

soloist *n.* คนเล่นดนตรีขึ้นเดียว konlendontrichindiaw

solubility *n.* ความสามารถในการแก้ปัญหา kwamsamadnaigangaepanha

soluble *a.* แก้ปัญหาได้ gaepanya

solution *n.* การแก้ปัญหา gangaepanha

solve *v.t.* แก้ปัญหา gaepanya

solvency *n.* ความสามารถในการชำระหนี้ kwamsamadnaiganchamrani

solvent *a.* ซึ่งชำระหนี้ได้ seungchamranidai

solvent *n* ตัวทำละลาย tuatamlalai

sombre *a.* สลัว salao

some *a.* เล็กน้อย leknoy

some *pron.* บางส่วน bangsuan

somebody *pron.* บางคน bangkon

somebody *n.* บางคน bangkon

somehow *adv.* อย่างไรก็ดี yangraigawdi

someone *pron.* บางคน bangkon

somersault *n.* การตีลังกา gantilanga

somersault *v.i.* ตีลังกา tilangga

something *pron.* บางสิ่ง bangsing

something *adv.* บางอย่าง bangyang

sometime *adv.* บางเวลา banglewa

sometimes *adv.* บางครั้ง bangkrang

somewhat *adv.* ค่อนข้าง konkang

somewhere *adv.* บางแห่ง banghaeng

somnambulism *n.* การเดินละเมอ gandeuanlameu

somnambulist *n.* คนเดินละเมอ kondeuanlameu

somnolence *n.* ความง่วงนอน kwam-nguangnon

somnolent *n.* ง่วงนอน nguangnon

son *n.* ลูกชาย lookchai

song *n.* เพลง pleng

songster *n.* นักร้อง nakrong

sonic *a.* เกี่ยวกับเสียง giawgabsiang

sonnet *n.* โคลง klong

sonority *n.* ความกังวาล kwamgangwan

soon *adv.* ในไม่ช้า naimaicha

soot *n.* เขม่า kamao

soot *v.t.* ทำให้เปื้อนเขม่า tamhaipeuan

soothe *v.t.* บรรเทา bantao

sophism *n.* การให้เหตุผลอย่างชาญฉลาด ganhaihedponyangchanchalad

sophist *n.* นักปราชญ์ nakprad

sophisticate *v.t.* รอบรู้ robru

sophisticated *a.* ซับซ้อน sabsawn

sophistication *n.* ความซับซ้อน kwamsabsawn

sorcerer *n.* พ่อมด pawmod

sorcery *n.* เวทมนตร์ wedmon

sordid *a.* เลวทราม lewsam

sore *a.* เจ็บปวด jebpuad

sore *n* ความเจ็บปวด kwamjebpuad

sorrow *n.* ความเสียใจ kwamsiajai

sorrow *v.i.* เสียใจ siajai

sorry *a.* เสียใจ siajai

sort *n.* การแยกประเภท ganyaekpraped

sort *v.t* แยกประเภท yaekpraped

soul *n.* วิญญาณ winyan

sound *a.* สมบูรณ์ somboon

sound *v.i.* ทำให้เกิดเสียง tamhaigeudsiang

sound *n* เสียง siang

soup *n.* ซุป soup

sour *a.* เปรี้ยว priaw

sour *v.t.* ทำให้เปรี้ยว tamhaipriaw

source *n.* ที่มา tima

south *n.* ทิศใต้ tidtai

south *a.* ทิศใต้ tidtai

south *adv* ทางใต้ tangtai

southerly *a.* ทางทิศใต้ tangtidtai

southern *a.* ทางทิศใต้ tangtidtai

souvenir *n.* ของที่ระลึก kongtiraleuk

sovereign *n.* ผู้มีอำนาจสูงสุด pumi-amnadsoongsud

sovereign *a* เกี่ยวกับอำนาจสูงสุด giawgab-amnadsoongsud

sovereignty *n.* อำนาจสูงสุดในการปกครอง amnadsoongsudnaiganpokkrong

sow *v.t.* หว่าน wan

sow *n.* การหว่าน ganwan
space *n.* ที่ว่าง tiwang
space *v.t.* เว้นระยะ wenraya
spacious *a.* กว้าง gwang
spade *n.* พลั่ว plua
spade *v.t.* ขุดดิน kuddin
span *n.* ช่วงเวลา chuangwela
span *v.t.* ขยาย kayai
Spaniard *n.* คนสเปน konspain
spaniel *n.* สุนัขพันธุ์หนึ่ง sunakpanneung
Spanish *a.* เกี่ยวกับสเปน giawgabspain
Spanish *n.* คนสเปน konspain
spanner *n.* กุญแจเลื่อน goongaeleun
spare *v.t.* เก็บไว้ gebwai
spare *a* ว่าง wang
spare *n.* อะไหล่ a-rai
spark *n.* ประกายไฟ pragaifai
spark *v.i.* เกิดประกายไฟ geudpragaifai
spark *n.* ความมีชีวิตชีวา
  kwammichiwitchiwa
sparkle *v.i.* เกิดประกายไฟ geudpragaifai
sparkle *n.* แสงวาบ saengwab
sparrow *n.* นกกระจอก nokgrajawk
sparse *a.* บางตา bangta
spasm *n.* การชักกระตุก ganchakgratuk
spasmodic *a.* หดเกร็ง hodgreng
spate *n.* น้ำท่วม namtuam
spatial *a.* เกี่ยวกับอวกาศ giawgab-a-wa-
  gad
spawn *n.* กลุ่มไข่ปลา glumkaipla
spawn *v.i.* วางไข่ wangkai
speak *v.i.* พูด pud
speaker *n.* ผู้พูด pupud
spear *n.* หลาว lao
spear *v.t.* พุ่งหลาว gongna
spearhead *n.* กองหน้า punglao
spearhead *v.t.* เป็นกองหน้า pengongna
special *a.* พิเศษ pised
specialist *n.* ผู้เชี่ยวชาญ puchiawchan
speciality *n.* ความพิเศษ kwampised
specialization *n.* ความชำนาญพิเศษ
  kwamchamnanpised

specialize *v.i.* ชำนาญ chamnan
species *n.* ชนิด chanid
specific *a.* เฉพาะ chapaw
specification *n.* รายละเอียด raira-iad
specify *v.t.* ให้รายละเอียด hairaira-iad
specimen *n.* ตัวอย่าง tuayang
speck *n.* จุดด่าง juddang
spectacle *n.* ปรากฏการณ์ pragodgan
spectacular *a.* น่าตื่นเต้น nateunten
spectator *n.* ผู้ชม puchom
spectre *n.* ปีศาจ pisad
speculate *v.i.* คาดเดา kaddao
speculation *n.* การคาดเดา gankaddao
speech *n.* คำพูด kampud
speed *n.* ความเร็ว kwamrew
speed *v.i.* เร่งความเร็ว rengkwamreiw
speedily *adv.* อย่างรวดเร็ว yangruadrew
speedy *a.* รวดเร็ว ruadreiw
spell *n.* คำสาป kamsab
spell *v.t.* สะกดคำ sagodkam
spell *n* ระยะเวลา rayawela
spend *v.t.* ใช้ chai
spendthrift *n.* คนฟุ่มเฟือย konfumfeuay
sperm *n.* ตัวอสุจิ tua-a-suji
sphere *n.* รูปทรงกลม roobsongglom
spherical *a.* กลม glom
spice *n.* เครื่องเทศ kreuangted
spice *v.t.* ใส่เครื่องเทศ saikeuangtet
spicy *a.* เผ็ดร้อน pedron
spider *n.* แมงมุม maengmoom
spike *n.* เหล็กแหลม leklaem
spike *v.t.* แทงด้วยเหล็กแหลม
  tangduayleklaem
spill *v.i.* ทำหก tamhok
spill *n* การทำหก gantamhok
spin *v.i.* หมุน moon
spin *n.* การหมุน ganmoon
spinach *n.* ผักขม pakkom
spinal *a.* เกี่ยวกับกระดูกสันหลัง
  giawgabgradooksanlang
spindle *n.* แกนหมุน gaenmoon
spine *n.* กระดูกสันหลัง gradooksanlang

spinner *n.* เครื่องปั่นด้าย kreuangpandai

spinster *n.* หญิงโสด yingsod

spiral *n.* วงก้นหอย wonggonhoy

spiral *a.* เป็นเกลียว pengliaw

spirit *n.* วิญญาณ winyan

spirited *a.* กล้าหาญ glahan

spiritual *a.* เกี่ยวกับจิตใจ giawgabjitjai

spiritualism *n.* ลัทธิเกี่ยวกับจิตวิญญาณ lattigiawgabjitwinyan

spiritualist *n.* ผู้เชื่อเรื่องจิตวิญญาณ pucheuareuangjitwinyan

spirituality *n.* ความเชื่อเรื่องจิตวิญญาณ kwamcheuareuangjitwinyan

spit *v.i.* ถ่มน้ำลาย tomnamlai

spit *n* การถ่มน้ำลาย gantomnamlai

spite *n.* เจตนาร้าย jettanarai

spittle *n* น้ำลาย namlai

spittoon *n.* กระโถน gratoan

splash *v.i.* สาด sad

splash *n* การสาด gansad

spleen *n.* ม้าม mam

splendid *a.* วิเศษ wised

splendour *n.* ความงดงาม kwam-ngod-ngam

splinter *n.* เศษเล็กๆ sedleklek

splinter *v.t.* ทำให้แตก tamhaitaek

split *v.i.* แตก taek

split *n* การแตก gantaek

spoil *v.t.* เน่าเสีย naosia

spoil *n* ของเสีย kongsia

spoke *n.* ซี่ล้อรถ silawrod

spokesman *n.* โฆษก kosok

sponge *n.* ฟองน้ำ fongnam

sponge *v.t.* ดูดซับด้วยฟองน้ำ dudsabduayfongnam

sponsor *n.* ผู้สนับสนุน pusanabsanoon

sponsor *v.t.* สนับสนุน sanabsanoon

spontaneity *n.* ความเป็นธรรมชาติ kwampentammachat

spontaneous *a.* เกิดขึ้นเอง geudkeuan-eng

spoon *n.* ช้อน chon

spoon *v.t.* ตักด้วยช้อน takduaychon

spoonful *n.* เต็มช้อน temchon

sporadic *a.* กระจัดกระจาย grajadgrajai

sport *n.* กีฬา gila

sport *v.i.* เล่นกีฬา lengila

sportive *a.* ร่าเริง rareung

sportsman *n.* นักกีฬา nakgila

spot *n.* จุด jud

spot *v.t.* ทำให้เป็นจุดด่าง tamhaipenjuddang

spotless *a.* ไม่มีรอยด่าง maimiroydang

spousal *n.* งานแต่งงาน ngantaeng-ngan

spouse *n.* คู่สมรส kusomrod

spout *n.* รางน้ำ rangnam

spout *v.i.* พ่น pon

sprain *n.* อาการเคล็ด a-gankled

sprain *v.t.* ทำให้เคล็ด tamhaikled

spray *n.* สเปรย์ spray

spray *n* ละอองน้ำ la-ongnam

spray *v.t.* ฉีดสเปรย์ chidspray

spread *v.i.* กระจาย grajai

spread *n.* การกระจาย gangrajai

spree *n.* การเล่นสนุกสนาน ganlensanook

sprig *n.* กิ่งไม้เล็กๆ gingmaileklek

sprightly *a.* มีชีวิตชีวา michiwitchiwa

spring *v.i.* ดีดตัว didtua

spring *n* สปริง spring

sprinkle *v. t.* โปรย proy

sprint *v.i.* วิ่งเต็มฝีเท้า wingtemfeetao

sprint *n* การวิ่งในระยะสั้น ganwingnairayasan

sprout *v.i.* แตกหน่อ taeknaw

sprout *n* ต้นอ่อน ton-on

spur *n.* สิ่งกระตุ้น singgratoon

spur *v.t.* กระตุ้น gratoon

spurious *a.* ปลอม plom

spurn *v.t.* ปัด pad

spurt *v.i.* พ่น pon

spurt *n* การพ่น ganpon

sputnik *n.* ดาวเทียมดวงแรกของโลก daotiamduangraek

sputum *n.* เสมหะ semha

spy *n.* นักสืบ nakseub

spy *v.i.* สืบ seub

squad *n.* กลุ่มคน glumkon

squadron *n.* กองเรือรบ gongreuarob

squalid *a.* สกปรก sokgaprok

squalor *n.* ความสกปรก kwamsokgaqprok

squander *v.t.* ใช้จ่ายสุรุ่ยสุร่าย chaijaisuruisurai

square *n.* สี่เหลี่ยม siliam

square *a* เป็นสี่เหลี่ยม pensiliam

square *v.t.* ทำให้เป็นสี่เหลี่ยม tamhaipensiliam

squash *v.t.* บด bod

squash *n* การบด ganbod

squat *v.i.* นั่งยองๆ nangyongyong

squeak *v.i.* ร้องเสียงแหลม rongsianglaem

squeak *n* เสียงลั่นเอี๊ยดๆ sianglan-iad-iad

squeeze *v.t.* บีบ beeb

squint *v.i.* หรี่ตา rita

squint *n* การชำเลืองมอง ganchamleuangmong

squire *n.* ผู้ดีบ้านนอก pudibannawk

squirrel *n.* กระรอก grarawk

stab *v.t.* แทง taeng

stab *n.* การแทง gantaeng

stability *n.* ความมั่นคง kwammankong

stabilization *n.* การทำให้มั่นคง gantamhaimankong

stabilize *v.t.* ทำให้มั่นคง tamhaimankong

stable *a.* มั่นคง mankong

stable *n* คอกม้า kokma

stable *v.t.* นำเข้าคอก namkaokok

stadium *n.* สเตเดียม stadium

staff *n.* พนักงาน panak-ngan

staff *v.t.* จ้างงาน jang-ngan

stag *n.* กวางตัวผู้ gwangtuapu

stage *n.* เวที weti

stage *v.t.* ขึ้นเวที keunweti

stagger *v.i.* เซ say

stagger *n.* การเซ ganse

stagnant *a.* นิ่ง ning

stagnate *v.i.* ซบเซา sobsao

stagnation *n.* ความซบเซา kwamsobsao

staid *a.* เงียบขรึม ngiabkreum

stain *n.* คราบ krab

stain *v.t.* เป็นคราบ penkrab

stainless *a.* ไร้คราบ raikrab

stair *n.* บันได bandai

stake *n* เงินเดิมพัน ngeundeumpan

stake *v.t.* วางเดิมพัน wangdeumpan

stale *a.* อับ ab

stale *v.t.* เก่า gao

stalemate *n.* การคุมเชิงกัน gankumcheunggan

stalk *n.* การย่องเข้าใกล้ ganyongkaoglai

stalk *v.i.* ย่องเข้าใกล้ yongkaoglai

stalk *n* ลำต้น lamton

stall *n.* คอก kok

stall *v.t.* เข้าคอก kaokok

stallion *n.* ม้าตัวผู้ matuapu

stalwart *a.* ซื่อสัตย์ seusat

stalwart *n* คนซื่อสัตย์ konseusat

stamina *n.* ความแข็งแรง kwamkaengraeng

stammer *v.i.* พูดติดอ่าง pudtid-ang

stammer *n* การพูดติดอ่าง ganpudtid-ang

stamp *n.* สแตมป์ sataem

stamp *v.i.* ติดสแตมป์ tidsataem

stampede *n.* ความแตกตื่น kwamtaekteun

stampede *v.i* แตกตื่น taekteun

stand *v.i.* ยืน yeun

stand *n.* จุดยืน judyeun

standard *n.* มาตรฐาน matratan

standard *a* ได้มาตรฐาน daimatratan

standardization *n.* การมีมาตรฐาน ganmimattratan

standardize *v.t.* ทำให้เป็นมาตรฐาน tamhaipenmatratan

standing *n.* ตำแหน่ง tamnaeng

standpoint *n.* จุดยืน judyeun

standstill *n.* การหยุดนิ่ง ganyudning

stanza *n.* ฉันท์ chan

staple *n.* อาหารหลัก a-hanlak

staple *a* สำคัญ samkan

star *n.* ดวงดาว duangdao

star *v.t.* แสดงนำ sadaengnam
starch *n.* แป้ง paeng
starch *v.t.* ลงแป้ง longpaeng
stare *v.i.* จ้อง jong
stare *n.* การจ้อง ganjong
stark *a.* ว่างเปล่า wangplao
stark *adv.* สิ้นเชิง sincheung
starry *a.* เต็มไปด้วยดวงดาว tempaiduayduangdao
start *v.t.* เริ่ม reum
start *n* การเริ่ม ganreum
startle *v.t.* สะดุ้ง sadung
starvation *n.* การอดอยาก gan-audyak
starve *v.i.* อดอาหาร aud-a-han
state *n.* สภาพ sapab
state *v.t* เน้นย้ำ nenyam
stateliness *n.* ความยิ่งใหญ่ kwamyingyai
stately *a.* ใหญ่โต yaito
statement *n.* คำแถลงการณ์ kamtalaenggan
statesman *n.* รัฐบุรุษ rataburut
static *n.* คงที่ kongti
statics *n.* วิชาการช่างแขนงหนึ่ง wichaganchangkanaengneung
station *n.* สถานี satani
station *v.t.* เข้าประจำที่ kaoprajamti
stationary *a.* ประจำที่ prajamti
stationer *n.* คนขายเครื่องเขียน konkaikreungkian
stationery *n.* เครื่องเขียน kreungkian
statistical *a.* ทางสถิติ tangsatiti
statistician *n.* นักสถิติ naksatiti
statistics *n.* สถิติศาสตร์ satitisat
statue *n.* รูปปั้น roobpan
stature *n.* ความสูง kwamsoong
status *n.* สถานะ satana
statute *n.* ข้อบังคับ kwabangkab
statutory *a.* ตามกฎหมาย tamgodmai
staunch *a.* ซื่อสัตย์ seusat
stay *v.i.* อยู่ yu
stay *n* การอยู่ ganyu
steadfast *a.* แน่นอน naenon

steadiness *n.* ความแน่นอนkwamnaenon
steady *a.* มั่นคง mankong
steady *v.t.* ทำให้มั่นคง tamhaimankong
steal *v.i.* ขโมย kamoey
stealthily *adv.* อย่างลับๆ yanglablab
steam *n* ไอน้ำ ai-nam
steam *v.i.* ปล่อยไอน้ำ ploy-ai-nam
steamer *n.* หม้อไอน้ำ maw-ai-nam
steed *n.* ม้า ma
steel *n.* เหล็ก lek
steep *a.* ชัน chan
steep *v.t.* ชัน chan
steeple *n.* ยอดหลังคา yodlangka
steer *v.t.* นำทาง namtang
stellar *a.* เหมือนดาว meundao
stem *n.* ลำต้น geudjak
stem *v.i.* เกิดจาก keudjak
stench *n.* กลิ่นเหม็น glinmen
stencil *n.* ลายฉลุ laichalu
stencil *v.i.* คัดลอกลาย kadlawklai
stenographer *n.* ผู้จดชวเลข pujodchawalek
stenography *n.* การเขียนชวเลข gankianchawalek
step *n.* ก้าว gao
step *v.i.* ก้าว gao
steppe *n.* ที่ราบกว้างใหญ่ tirabgwangyai
stereotype *n.* แบบแผนตายตัว baebpaentaitua
stereotype *v.t.* ทำโลหะแม่พิมพ์ tamlohamaepim
stereotyped *a.* ธรรมดา tamada
sterile *a.* ปราศจากเชื้อ prasajakcheua
sterility *n.* การเป็นหมัน ganpenman
sterilization *n.* การทำให้ปราศจากเชื้อ gantamhaiprasajakcheua
sterilize *v.t.* ทำให้ปราศจากเชื้อ tamhaiprasajakcheua
sterling *a.* เกี่ยวกับเงินสเทอร์ลิง giawgab-ngeunsterling
sterling *n.* เงินสเทอร์ลิง ngeunsterling
stern *a.* เข้มงวด kem-nguad

stern *n.* ท้ายเรือ taireua

stethoscope *n.* หูฟัง hufang

stew *n.* สตูว์ stew

stew *v.t.* เคี่ยว kiaw

steward *n.* พนักงานต้อนรับบนเครื่องบิน panak-ngantonrabbonkreuangbin

stick *n.* ไม้เท้า maitao

stick *v.t.* แทง taeng

sticker *n.* สติ๊กเกอร์ sticker

stickler *n.* ความยุ่งยาก kwamyungyak

sticky *a.* เหนียว niaw

stiff *a.* แข็ง kaeng

stiffen *v.t.* ทำให้แข็ง tamhaikaeng

stifle *v.t.* ทำให้หายใจไม่ออก tamhaihaijaimai-awk

stigma *n.* รอยด่าง roydang

still *a.* นิ่ง ning

still *adv.* ยังคง yangkong

still *v.t.* ทำให้นิ่ง tamhaining

still *n.* ความเงียบสงบ kwam-ngiabsa-ngob

stillness *n.* ความนิ่ง kwamning

stilt *n.* ไม้ต่อขา maitawka

stimulant *n.* สิ่งกระตุ้น singgratoon

stimulate *v.t.* กระตุ้น gratoon

stimulus *n.* ตัวกระตุ้น tuagratoon

sting *v.t.* ต่อย toy

sting *n.* ความเจ็บปวด kwamjebpuad

stingy *a.* ขี้เหนียว kiniaw

stink *v.i.* ส่งกลิ่นเหม็น songglinmen

stink *n* กลิ่นเหม็น glinmen

stipend *n.* เงินเดือน ngeundeuan

stipulate *v.t.* กำหนดเงื่อนไข gamnod-ngeuankai

stipulation *n.* การกำหนดเงื่อนไข gangamnod-ngeuankai

stir *v.i.* กวน guan

stirrup *n.* โกลน glon

stitch *n.* รอยเย็บ royyeb

stitch *v.t.* เย็บ yeb

stock *n.* คลังสินค้า klangsinka

stock *v.t.* สะสมไว้ sasomwai

stock *a.* ที่สะสมไว้ tisasomwai

stocking *n.* ถุงน่อง tungnong

stoic *n.* คนปลงตก konplongtok

stoke *v.t.* เติมเชื้อเพลิง teumcheuapleung

stoker *n.* คนควบคุมเตาไฟ konkwabkumtaofai

stomach *n.* ท้อง tong

stomach *v.t.* อดทน audton

stone *n.* หิน hin

stone *v.t.* ปา pa

stony *a.* เต็มไปด้วยหิน tempaiduayhin

stool *n.* อุจจาระ udjara

stoop *v.i.* ก้มตัว gomtua

stoop *n* การก้มตัว gangomtua

stop *v.t.* หยุด yud

stop *n* การหยุด ganyud

stoppage *n* การหยุด ganyud

storage *n.* คลังสินค้า klangsinka

store *n.* ร้าน ran

store *v.t.* กักตุน gaktoon

storey *n.* ชั้น chan

stork *n.* นกกระสา nokgrasa

storm *n.* พายุ payu

storm *v.i.* จู่โจม jujom

stormy *a.* ราวกับพายุ raogabpayu

story *n.* เรื่องราว reuangrao

stout *a.* ล่ำ lam

stove *n.* เตา tao

stow *v.t.* จัดเก็บ jatgeb

straggle *v.i.* หลงทาง longtang

straggler *n.* คนที่หลงทาง kontilongtang

straight *a.* ตรง trong

straight *adv.* ทันที tanti

straighten *v.t.* ทำให้ตรง tamhaitrong

straightforward *a.* ตรงไปตรงมา trongpaitrongma

straightway *adv.* โดยตรง doeytrong

strain *v.t.* ทำให้ดึง tamhaiteung

strain *n* การทำให้ดึง gantamhaiteung

strait *n.* ช่องแคบ chongkaeb

straiten *v.t.* ทำให้ลำบาก tamhailambak

strand *v.i.* เกยตื้น geuyteun

strand *n* ชายฝั่ง chaifang

strange *a.* แปลก plaek

stranger *n.* คนแปลกหน้า konplaekna

strangle *v.t.* บีบคอ beebkaw

strangulation *n.* การบีบคอ ganbeebkaw

strap *n.* สายรัด sairad

strap *v.t.* รัดด้วยสายหนัง radduaysainang

stratagem *n.* กลอุบาย gon-u-bai

strategic *a.* เกี่ยวกับกลยุทธ์ giawgabgonrayud

strategist *n.* นักยุทธศาสตร์ nakyudtasat

strategy *n.* ยุทธวิธี yudtawiti

stratum *n.* ชั้นบรรยากาศ chanbanyagad

straw *n.* ฟาง fang

strawberry *n.* สตรอเบอรี่ strawberry

stray *v.i.* พลัดหลง pladlong

stray *a* ซึ่งพลัดหลง seungpladlong

stray *n* คนที่หลงทาง kontilongtang

stream *n.* ลำธาร lamtan

stream *v.i.* ไหล lai

streamer *n.* ธง tong

streamlet *n.* ห้วย huay

street *n.* ถนน tanon

strength *n.* ความเข้มแข็ง kwamkemkaeng

strengthen *v.t.* ทำให้เข้มแข็ง tamhaikemkaeng

strenuous *a.* ขยัน kayan

stress *n.* ความเครียด kwamkriad

stress *v.t* เครียด kriad

stretch *v.t.* ขยายออก kayai-awk

stretch *n* การขยายออก gankayai-awk

stretcher *n.* เปลหาม playham

strew *v.t.* โปรย proy

strict *a.* เข้มงวด kem-nguad

stricture *n.* การจำกัด ganjamgad

stride *v.i.* ก้าวเดิน gaodeuan

stride *n* ความก้าวหน้า kwamgaona

strident *a.* แข็งกร้าว kaenggrao

strife *n.* ความพยายาม kwampayayam

strike *v.t.* หยุดงานประท้วง gannadyudngan

strike *n* การนัดหยุดงาน gannadyudnganpratuang

striker *n.* คนที่หยุดงานประท้วง kontiyudnganpratuang

string *n.* เชือก cheuak

string *v.t.* ผูกเชือก pukcheuak

stringency *n.* ความเข้มงวด kwamkemnguad

stringent *a.* เข้มงวด kem-nguad

strip *n.* ทางยาว tangyao

strip *v.t.* แก้ผ้า gaepa

stripe *n.* ริ้ว riew

stripe *v.t.* ทำให้เป็นริ้ว tamhaipenriew

strive *v.i.* ต่อสู้ tawsu

stroke *n.* ท่าว่ายน้ำ tawainam

stroke *v.t.* ตีกรรเชียง tiganchiang

stroke *n* การอุดตันของเส้นเลือดที่ไปเลี้ยงสมอง gan-udtankongsenleudtipailiangsamong

stroll *v.i.* เดินเล่น deunlen

stroll *n* การเดินเล่น gandeunlen

strong *a.* แข็งแรง kaengraeng

stronghold *n.* ที่มั่น timan

structural *a.* ทางโครงสร้าง tankrongsang

structure *n.* โครงสร้าง krongsang

struggle *v.i.* ต่อสู้ tawsu

struggle *n* การต่อสู้ gantawsu

strumpet *n.* โสเภณี sopeni

strut *v.i.* เดินวางท่า deunwangta

strut *n* ไม้ค้ำ maikam

stub *n.* โคน kon

stubble *n.* ตอ taw

stubborn *a.* ดื้อ deu

stud *n.* ตะปุ tapu

stud *v.t.* ทำให้เป็นปุ่ม tamhaipenpum

student *n.* นักเรียน nakrian

studio *n.* สตูดิโอ studio

studious *a.* ขยันเรียน kayanrian

study *v.i.* เรียน rian

study *n.* การศึกษา gansuksa

stuff *n.* สิ่งของ singkong

stuff *v.t.* ยัดไส้ yadsai

stuffy *a.* คัดจมูก kadjamook

stumble *v.i.* สะดุด sadud

stumble *n.* การสะดุด gansadud
stump *n.* ตอไม้ tawmai
stump *v.t* เดินกระแทกเท้า deungrataektao
stun *v.t.* ทำให้งง tamhai-ngong
stunt *v.t.* แสดงโลดโผน sadaenglodpon
stunt *n* การแสดงโลดโผน
  gansadaengloadpoan
stupefy *v.t.* ทำให้มึนงง tamhaimun-ngong
stupendous *a.* ใหญ่โต yaito
stupid *a* โง่ ngo
stupidity *n.* ความโง่ kwam-ngo
sturdy *a.* แข็งแกร่ง kaenggrang
sty *n.* คอกหมู kokmu
stye *n.* โรคกุ้งยิง rokgungying
style *n.* สไตล์ style
subdue *v.t.* ปราบ prab
subject *n.* หัวข้อ huakaw
subject *a* มีแนวโน้ม minaewnom
subject *v.t.* ขึ้นอยู่กับ keunyugab
subjection *n.* การอยู่ใต้อำนาจ ganyutai-
  amnad
subjective *a.* ส่วนตัว suantua
subjudice *a.* ต่อหน้าศาล tawnasan
subjugate *v.t.* ปราบปราม prabpram
subjugation *n.* การปราบปราม
  ganprabpram
sublet *v.t.* ให้เช่าช่วง haichaochuang
sublimate *v.t.* ทำให้บริสุทธิ์ tamhaiborisut
sublime *a.* สูงส่ง soonsong
sublime *n* สิ่งที่สูงส่ง singtisoongsong
sublimity *n.* ความสูงส่ง kwamsoongsong
submarine *n.* เรือดำน้ำ reuadamnam
submarine *a* ซึ่งอยู่ใต้น้ำ seungyutainam
submerge *v.i.* จุ่มน้ำ jumnam
submission *n.* การยอมจำนน
  ganyomjamnon
submissive *a.* อ่อนน้อม on-nom
submit *v.t.* ยอม yom
subordinate *a.* อยู่ใต้บังคับบัญชา
  yutaibangkabbancha
subordinate *n* ผู้อยู่ใต้บังคับบัญชา
  puyutaibangkabbancha

subordinate *v.t.* ทำให้อยู่ใต้บังคับบัญชา
  tamhaiyutaibangkabbancha
subordination *n.* การอยู่ใต้บังคับบัญชา
  ganyutaibangkabbancha
subscribe *v.t.* สมัครเป็นสมาชิก
  samakpensamachik
subscription *n.* การสมัครเป็นสมาชิก
  gansamakpensamachik
subsequent *a.* ที่ตามมา titamma
subservience *n.* การอ่อนน้อม gan-on-nom
subservient *a.* ยอมรับใช้ yomrabchai
subside *v.i.* ลดลง lodlong
subsidiary *a.* เสริม seum
subsidize *v.t.* ให้เงินอุดหนุน hai-ngeun-
  udnoon
subsidy *n.* การให้เงินอุดหนุน ganhai-
  ngeun-udnoon
subsist *v.i.* รอดชีวิต rodchiwit
subsistence *n.* การดำรงชีพ
  gandamrongchib
substance *n.* สสาร sasan
substantial *a.* มากมาย makmai
substantially *adv.* อย่างมาก yangmak
substantiate *v.t.* พิสูจน์ pisud
substantiation *n.* การพิสูจน์ ganpisud
substitute *n.* ผู้แทนที่ putaenti
substitute *v.t.* แทนที่ taenti
substitution *n.* การแทนที่ gantaenti
subterranean *a.* อยู่ใต้ดิน yutaidin
subtle *a.* บาง bang
subtlety *n.* ความบอบบาง kwambobbang
subtract *v.t.* หักออก hak-awk
subtraction *n.* การหักออก ganhak-awk
suburb *n.* ชานเมือง chanmeuang
suburban *a.* นอกเมือง nokmeuang
subversion *n.* การบ่อนทำลาย
  ganbontamlai
subversive *a.* ซึ่งล้มล้าง seunglomlang
subvert *v.t.* ล้มล้าง lomlang
succeed *v.i.* สำเร็จ samred
success *n.* ความสำเร็จ kwamsamred
successful *a* มีผลสำเร็จ miponsamreid

succession *n.* การสืบตำแหน่ง ganseubtamnaeng

successive *a.* ต่อเนื่องกัน tawneuanggan

successor *n.* ผู้สืบตำแหน่ง puseubtamnaeng

succour *n.* การช่วยเหลือ ganchuayleua

succour *v.t.* ช่วยเหลือ chuayreua

succumb *v.i.* ยอมจำนน yomjamnon

such *a.* เช่นนี้ chenni

such *pron.* บุคคลเช่นนี้ bukkonchenni

suck *v.t.* ดูด dud

suck *n.* การดูด gandud

suckle *v.t.* ให้ดูดนม haidudnom

sudden *n.* สิ่งที่เกิดในทันที singtigeudkeunnaitanti

suddenly *adv.* ในทันที naitanti

sue *v.t.* ฟ้องร้อง fongrong

suffer *v.t.* ทนทุกข์ tontook

suffice *v.i.* เพียงพอ piangpaw

sufficiency *n.* ความพอเพียง kwampawpiang

sufficient *a.* พอเพียง pawpiang

suffix *n.* คำเสริมท้าย kamseumtai

suffix *v.t.* ต่อท้าย tawtai

suffocate *v.t* หายใจไม่ออก haijaimai-awk

suffocation *n.* การขาดอากาศหายใจ gankad-a-gadhaijai

suffrage *n.* สิทธิในการเลือกตั้ง sittinaiganleuaktang

sugar *n.* น้ำตาล namtan

sugar *v.t.* ใส่น้ำตาล sainamtan

suggest *v.t.* แนะนำ naenam

suggestion *n.* คำแนะนำ kamnaenam

suggestive *a.* แนะนำได้ naenamdai

suicidal *a.* อยากฆ่าตัวตาย yakkatuatai

suicide *n.* การฆ่าตัวตาย gankatuatai

suit *n.* คำร้อง kamrong

suit *v.t.* ทำให้เหมาะสม tamhaimawsom

suitability *n.* ความเหมาะสม kwammawsom

suitable *a.* เหมาะสม mawsom

suite *n.* ห้องชุด pufongrong

suitor *n.* ผู้ฟ้องร้อง pufongrong

sullen *a.* บึ้งตึง beungteung

sulphur *n.* กำมะถัน gammatan

sulphuric *a.* เกี่ยวกับกำมะถัน giawgabgammatan

sultry *a.* ร้อนอบอ้าว ron-ob-aow

sum *n.* จำนวนรวม jamnuamruam

sum *v.t.* รวมยอด ruamyod

summarily *adv.* โดยสรุป dueysaroob

summarize *v.t.* สรุป saroob

summary *n.* การสรุป gansaroob

summary *a* โดยย่อ doeyyaw

summer *n.* ฤดูร้อน reuduron

summit *n.* การประชุม ganprachum

summon *v.t.* เรียกตัว riaktua

summons *n.* หมายเรียก mairiak

sumptuous *a.* หรูหรา rura

sun *n.* ดวงอาทิตย์ duang-a-tit

sun *v.t.* อาบแดด ab-dad

Sunday *n.* วันอาทิตย์ wan-a-tit

sunder *v.t.* แบ่ง baeng

sundry *a.* หลายหลาย laklai

sunny *a.* มีแดด midad

sup *v.i.* ทานอาหารค่ำ tan-a-hankam

superabundance *n.* ความอุดมสมบูรณ์ kwam-u-domsomboon

superabundant *a.* อุดมสมบูรณ์ u-domsomboon

superb *a.* ดีเลิศ dileud

superficial *a.* ผิวเผิน pewpeun

superficiality *n.* ความฉาบฉวย kwamchabchuay

superfine *a.* ดีเยี่ยม diyiam

superfluity *n.* สิ่งฟุ่มเฟือย singfumfeuay

superfluous *a.* ฟุ่มเฟือย fumfeuay

superhuman *a.* เหนือมนุษย์ neuamanud

superintend *v.t.* ควบคุม kuabkum

superintendence *n.* การควบคุม gankuabkum

superintendent *n.* ผู้ดูแล pudulae

superior *a.* เหนือกว่า neuakwa

superiority *n.* ความเหนือกว่า kwamneuakwa

superlative *a.* ซึ่งอยู่ในขั้นสูงสุด seungyunaikansungsud

superlative *n.* ขั้นสูงสุด kansoongsud

superman *n.* ยอดมนุษย์ yodmanud

supernatural *a.* เหนือธรรมชาติ neuatammachad

supersede *v.t.* เข้าแทนที่ kaotaenti

supersonic *a.* เร็วกว่าเสียง rewgwasiang

superstition *n.* ความเชื่อโชคลาง kwamcheuchoklang

superstitious *a.* เกี่ยวกับโชคลาง giawgabchoklang

supertax *n.* ภาษีที่เก็บเพิ่มเติม pasitigebpeum

supervise *v.t.* ควบคุม kuabkum

supervision *n.* การควบคุม gankuabkum

supervisor *n.* ผู้ควบคุม pukuabkum

supper *n.* อาหารเย็น a-hanyen

supple *a.* ยอมตาม yomtam

supplement *n.* ส่วนเสริม suanseum

supplement *v.t.* เสริม seum

supplementary *a.* เพิ่มเติม peumteum

supplier *n.* ผู้จัดหาให้ pujadhahai

supply *v.t.* จัดหาให้ jadhahai

supply *n* อุปทาน u-patan

support *v.t.* สนับสนุน sanabsanoon

support *n.* การสนับสนุน gansanabsanoon

suppose *v.t.* สมมุติ sommud

supposition *n.* ข้อสมมุติ kawsommud

suppress *v.t.* ปราบ prab

suppression *n.* การปราบปราม ganprabpram

supremacy *n.* ความยิ่งใหญ่ kwamyingyai

supreme *a.* ที่สุด tisud

surcharge *n.* การเก็บเงินเพิ่ม gangeb-ngeunpeum

surcharge *v.t.* เก็บเงินเพิ่ม geb-ngeunpeum

sure *a.* แน่นอน naenon

surely *adv.* อย่างแน่นอน yangnaenon

surety *n.* ความแน่นอน kwamnaenon

surf *n.* คลื่น kleun

surface *n.* ผิวหน้า pewna

surface *v.i* โผล่ขึ้นมาที่ผิวหน้า plokeunmatipewna

surfeit *n.* สิ่งที่มากเกินไป singtimakgeunpai

surge *n.* การเพิ่มขึ้นอย่างรวดเร็ว ganpeumkeunyangruadrew

surge *v.i.* เพิ่มขึ้นอย่างรวดเร็ว peumkeunyangruadrew

surgeon *n.* หมอผ่าตัด mawpatad

surgery *n.* การผ่าตัด ganpatad

surmise *n.* การสันนิษฐาน gansannitan

surmise *v.t.* สันนิษฐาน sannitan

surmount *v.t.* ผ่านพ้น panpon

surname *n.* นามสกุล namsakun

surpass *v.t.* เกินกว่า geungwa

surplus *n.* ส่วนเกิน suangeun

surprise *n.* แปลกใจ plaekjai

surprise *v.t.* ทำให้แปลกใจ tamhaiplaekjai

surrender *v.t.* ยอมแพ้ yompae

surrender *n* การยอมแพ้ ganyompae

surround *v.t.* ล้อมรอบ lomrob

surroundings *n.* สิ่งแวดล้อม siangwaedlom

surtax *n.* ภาษีส่วนเพิ่ม pasiseunpeum

surveillance *n.* การตรวจตรา gantruadtra

survey *n.* การสำรวจ gansamruad

survey *v.t.* สำรวจ samruad

survival *n.* การรอดชีวิต ganrodchiwit

survive *v.i.* รอดชีวิต rodchiwit

suspect *v.t.* สงสัย songsai

suspect *a.* น่าสงสัย nasongsai

suspect *n* ผู้ต้องสงสัย putongsongsai

suspend *v.t.* ระงับชั่วคราว ra-ngabchuakrao

suspense *n.* ความวิตกกังวล kwamwitokgangwon

suspension *n.* การระงับชั่วคราว ganra-ngabchuakrao

suspicion *n.* ความน่าสงสัย kwamnasongsai

suspicious *a.* น่าสงสัย nasongsai

sustain *v.t.* ยั่งยืน yangyeun

sustenance *n.* การยังชีพ ganyangchib

swagger *v.i.* เดินกร่าง deungrang

swagger *n* การวางโต ganwangto

swallow *v.t.* กลืน gleun

swallow *n.* การกลืน gangleun

swallow *n.* นกนางแอ่น noknang-an

swamp *n.* หนองน้ำ nongnam

swamp *v.t.* ทำให้ท่วม tamhaituam

swan *n.* หงส์ hong

swarm *n.* ฝูง fung

swarm *v.i.* อพยพไปเป็นกลุ่ม obpayobpaipenglum

swarthy *a.* ดำคล้ำ damklam

sway *v.i.* แกว่ง gwaeng

sway *n* การแกว่ง gangwang

swear *v.t.* สาบาน saban

sweat *n.* เหงื่อ ngeua

sweat *v.i.* เหงื่อออก ngeu-awk

sweater *n.* สเวตเตอร์ sweater

sweep *v.i.* กวาด gwad

sweep *n.* การกวาด gangwad

sweeper *n.* เครื่องปัดกวาด kreuangpadgwad

sweet *a.* หวาน wan

sweet *n* ขนมหวาน kanonwan

sweeten *v.t.* ทำให้หวาน tamhaiwan

sweetmeat *n.* ลูกกวาด lookgwad

sweetness *n.* ความหวาน kwamwan

swell *v.i.* บวม buam

swell *n* คลื่นขนาดใหญ่ kleunkanadyai

swift *a.* เร็วกว่าเสียง rewgwasiang

swim *v.i.* ว่ายน้ำ wainam

swim *n* การว่ายน้ำ ganwainam

swimmer *n.* นักว่ายน้ำ nakwainam

swindle *v.t.* โกง gong

swindle *n.* การหลอกลวง ganlokluang

swindler *n.* คนหลอกลวง konlokluang

swine *n.* หมู mu

swing *v.i.* แกว่ง gwaeng

swing *n* ชิงช้า chingcha

swiss *n.* คนสวิส konswiss

swiss *a* เกี่ยวกับประเทศสวิสเซอร์แลนด์ giawgabpratedswitzerland

switch *n.* สวิตช์ switch

switch *v.t.* เปลี่ยน plian

swoon *n.* การเป็นลม ganpenlom

swoon *v.i* เป็นลม penlom

swoop *v.i.* โฉบ chob

swoop *n* การโฉบ ganchob

sword *n.* ดาบ dab

sycamore *n.* ต้นมะเดื่อ tonmadeua

sycophancy *n.* การประจบประแจง ganprajobprajaeng

sycophant *n.* คนประจบประแจง konprajobprajaeng

syllabic *n.* การออกเสียงทีละพยางค์ gan-awksiangtilapayang

syllable *n.* พยางค์ payang

syllabus *n.* หลักสูตร laksut

sylph *n.* หญิงรูปร่างแบบบาง yingroobrangbaebbang

sylvan *a.* ร่มรื่น romreun

symbol *n.* สัญลักษณ์ sanyalak

symbolic *a.* เกี่ยวกับสัญลักษณ์ giawgabsanyalak

symbolism *n.* สัญลักษณ์นิยม sanyalakniyom

symbolize *v.t.* เป็นสัญลักษณ์ pensanyalak

symmetrical *a.* สมมาตรกัน sommatgan

symmetry *n.* ความสมมาตร kwamsommat

sympathetic *a.* น่าสงสาร nasongsan

sympathize *v.i.* เห็นใจ henjai

sympathy *n.* ความเห็นใจ kwamhenjai

symphony *n.* วงซิมโฟนี wongsymphony

symposium *n.* การประชุมสัมนา ganprachumsamana

symptom *n.* อาการ a-gan

symptomatic *a.* เกี่ยวกับอาการ giawgab-a-gan

synonym *n.* คำที่มีความหมายเหมือนกัน
  kamtimikwammaimeuangan
synonymous *a.* มีความหมายเหมือนกัน
  mikwammaimeuangan
synopsis *n.* สาระสำคัญ sarasamkan
syntax *n.* การสร้างประโยค gansangprayok
synthesis *n.* การสังเคราะห์ gansangkraw
synthetic *a.* เกี่ยวกับการสังเคราะห์
  giawgabgansangkraw
synthetic *n* สารสังเคราะห์ sansangkraw
syringe *n.* หลอดฉีดยา lawdchidya
syringe *v.t.* ฉีดยา chidya
syrup *n.* น้ำเชื่อม namcheuam
system *n.* ระบบ rabob
systematic *a.* เป็นระบบ penlabob
systematize *v.t.* ทำให้เป็นระบบ
  tamhaipenrabob

T

table *n.* โต๊ะ to
table *v.t.* วางบนโต๊ะ wangbonto
tablet *n.* ยาเม็ด yamed
taboo *n.* สิ่งต้องห้าม singtongham
taboo *a* ต้องห้าม tongham
taboo *v.t.* ห้าม ham
tabular *a.* เป็นตาราง pentarang
tabulate *v.t.* จัดเป็นตาราง jatpentarang
tabulation *n.* การทำเป็นตาราง
  gantampentarang
tabulator *n.* ผู้ทำตาราง putamtarang
tacit *a.* เป็นนัย pennai
taciturn *a.* เงียบขรึม ngiabkreum
tackle *n.* รอก rok
tackle *v.t.* จัดการ jadgan
tact *n.* ยุทธวิธี yuttawiti
tactful *a.* มีชั้นเชิง michancheung
tactician *n.* นักกลยุทธ์ nakgonrayut
tactics *n.* กลยุทธ์ gonrayut
tactile *a.* รับรู้ได้ด้วยการสัมผัส
  rabrudaiduaygansampad

tag *n.* แถบป้าย taebpai
tag *v.t.* ติดป้าย tidpai
tail *n.* หาง hang
tailor *n.* ช่างตัดเสื้อ chantadseua
tailor *v.t.* ตัดเสื้อ tadseua
taint *n.* รอยเปื้อน roypeuan
taint *v.t.* มีรอยเปื้อน miroypeuan
take *v.t* เอา aow
tale *n.* นิยาย niyai
talent *n.* พรสวรรค์ ponsawan
talisman *n.* เครื่องราง kreuangrang
talk *v.i.* พูด pud
talk *n* การพูด ganpud
talkative *a.* ช่างพูด changpud
tall *a.* สูง soong
tallow *n.* มันแข็ง mankaeng
tally *n.* บันทึก banteuk
tally *v.t.* นับคะแนน nabkanaen
tamarind *n.* มะขาม makam
tame *a.* เชื่อง cheuang
tame *v.t.* ทำให้เชื่อง tamhaicheuang
tamper *v.i.* ยุ่ง yung
tan *v.i.* ทำให้สีผิวเข้มขึ้น
  tamhaisipewkemkeun
tan *n., a.* สีแทน sitaen
tangent *n.* เส้นสัมผัส sensampad
tangible *a.* รูปธรรม roobpatam
tangle *n.* ความยุ่งเหยิง kwamyungyeung
tangle *v.t.* ทำให้ยุ่งเหยิง
  tamhaiyungyeung
tank *n.* ถังขนาดใหญ่ tangkanadyai
tanker *n.* เรือบรรทุก reuabantook
tanner *n.* คนฟอกหนัง konfoknang
tannery *n.* โรงฟอกหนัง rongfoknang
tantalize *v.t.* ยั่วเย้า yuayao
tantamount *a.* เท่ากัน taogan
tap *n.* ก๊อกน้ำ gognam
tap *v.t.* เคาะ kaw
tape *n.* สายวัด saiwad
tape *v.t* บันทึกเสียง banteuksiang
taper *v.i.* ทำให้ลดลง tamhailodlong
taper *n* เทียนขนาดเล็ก tiankanadlek

tapestry *n.* พรม prom

tar *n.* น้ำมันดิบ nammandib

tar *v.t.* ลาดยาง ladyang

target *n.* เป้าหมาย paomai

tariff *n.* ค่าธรรมเนียม katamniam

tarnish *v.t.* ทำให้เสื่อมเสีย tamhaiseumsia

task *n.* งาน ngan

task *v.t.* ทำงาน tam-ngan

taste *n.* รสชาติ rodchat

taste *v.t.* ชิม chim

tasteful *a.* มีรสชาติ mirodchat

tasty *a.* รสดี roddi

tatter *n.* ผ้าขี้ริ้ว pakirew

tatter *v.t* ฉีกขาด chikkad

tattoo *n.* รอยสัก roysak

tattoo *v.i.* สักลาย saklai

taunt *v.t.* เหน็บแนม nebnaem

taunt *n* การเหน็บแนม gannebnaem

tavern *n.* ร้านขายเหล้า rankailao

tax *n.* ภาษี pasi

tax *v.t.* เก็บภาษี gebpasi

taxable *a.* ต้องเสียภาษี tongsiapasi

taxation *n.* ระบบการจัดเก็บภาษี
rabobganjadgebpasi

taxi *n.* แท็กซี่ taxi

taxi *v.i.* โดยสารแท็กซี่ doeysantaxi

tea *n* ชา cha

teach *v.t.* สอน son

teacher *n.* ครู kru

teak *n.* ไม้สัก maisak

team *n.* ทีม team

tear *v.t.* ฉีกออก chik-awk

tear *n.* การฉีก gan-chik

tear *n.* น้ำตา namta

tearful *a.* น้ำตานอง namtanong

tease *v.t.* ยั่วเย้า yuayao

teat *n.* หัวนม huanom

technical *n.* ทางการช่าง tanganchang

technicality *n.* ลักษณะทางเทคนิค
laksanatangteknik

technician *n.* ช่าง chang

technique *n.* เทคนิค technique

technological *a.* ทางเทคโนโลยี
tangtechnology

technologist *n.* ผู้เชี่ยวชาญทางเทคโนโลยี
puchiawchantangtechnology

technology *n.* เทคโนโลยี technology

tedious *a.* น่าเบื่อ nabeua

tedium *n.* ความน่าเบื่อ kwamnabeua

teem *v.i.* มีอยู่เต็ม miyutem

teenager *n.* วัยรุ่น wairoon

teens *n. pl.* ช่วงวัยรุ่น chuangwairoon

teethe *v.i.* ฟันขึ้น funkeun

teetotal *a.* เกี่ยวกับการเลิกเหล้า
giawgabganleuklao

teetotaller *n.* ผู้ถูกห้ามไม่ให้ดื่มเหล้า
putookhammaihaideumlao

telecast *n.* การออกอากาศ gan-awk-a-gad

telecast *v.t.* ออกอากาศ awk-a-gad

telecommunications *n.* โทรคมนาคม
torakamanakom

telegram *n.* โทรเลข toralek

telegraph *n.* ระบบการส่งโทรเลข
rabobgansongtoralek

telegraph *v.t.* การส่งโทรเลข
gansongtoralek

telegraphic *a.* เกี่ยวกับการส่งโทรเลข
giawgabgansongtoralek

telegraphist *n.* ผู้ส่งโทรเลข pusongtoralek

telegraphy *n.* เทคนิคการส่งโทรเลข
teknikgansongtoralek

telepathic *a.* เกี่ยวกับการส่งโทรจิต
giawgabgansongtorajit

telepathist *n.* ผู้มีพลังจิต pumipalangjit

telepathy *n.* โทรจิต torajit

telephone *n.* โทรศัพท์ torasab

telephone *v.t.* พูดโทรศัพท์ pudtorasab

telescope *n.* กล้องส่องทางไกล
glongsongtangglai

telescopic *a.* เกี่ยวกับกล้องส่องทางไกล
giawgabklongsongtangglai

televise *v.t.* ถ่ายทอดโทรทัศน์ taitodtoratat

television *n.* โทรทัศน์ toratat

tell *v.t.* บอก bawk

teller *n.* พนักงานรับฝากเงิน panak-nganrabfak-ngeun

temper *n.* อารมณ์ a-rom

temper *v.t.* ทำให้บรรเทา tamhaibantao

temperament *n.* อารมณ์ปรวนแปร a-rompruanprae

temperamental *a.* ที่มีอารมณ์ปรวนแปร timi-a-rompruanprae

temperance *n.* การควบคุมอารมณ์ gankuabkum-a-rom

temperate *a.* ควบคุมอารมณ์ได้ดี kuabkum-a-romdaidi

temperature *n.* อุณหภูมิ aunhapum

tempest *n.* พายุ payu

tempestuous *a.* มีพายุแรง mipayulaeng

temple *n.* วัด wat

temple *n* ขมับ kamab

temporal *a.* เกี่ยวกับขมับ giawgabkamab

temporary *a.* ชั่วคราว chuakrao

tempt *v.t.* ล่อลวง lawkluang

temptation *n.* การล่อใจ ganlawjai

tempter *n.* ผู้ยั่วยวน puyuayuan

ten *n., a* สิบ sib

tenable *a.* ที่สมเหตุสมผล tisomhedsompon

tenacious *a.* เหนียว niaw

tenacity *n.* ความดื้อรั้น kwamdeuran

tenancy *n.* การเช่า ganchao

tenant *n.* ผู้เช่า puchao

tend *v.i.* โน้มเอียง nom-iang

tendency *n.* แนวโน้ม naewnom

tender *n* การยื่นประมูล ganyeunpramoon

tender *v.t.* ยื่นประมูล yeunpramoon

tender *n* ผู้ดูแล pudulae

tender *a* อ่อนโยน on-yon

tenet *n.* ข้อคิดเห็น kawkidhen

tennis *n.* เทนนิส tennis

tense *n.* กาล gan

tense *a.* ตึงเครียด teungkriad

tension *n.* ความเครียด kwamkriad

tent *n.* เต้นท์ tent

tentative *a.* แนวโน้ม naewnom

tenure *n.* ช่วงเวลาที่ดำรงตำแหน่ง chuangwelatidamrongtamnaeng

term *n.* วาระ wara

term *v.t.* กำหนดเวลา gamnodwela

terminable *a.* สิ้นสุดลงได้ sinsudlongdai

terminal *a.* ปลาย plai

terminal *n* สถานีปลายทาง sataniplaitang

terminate *v.t.* สิ้นสุด sinsud

termination *n.* การสิ้นสุด gansinsud

terminological *a.* เกี่ยวกับคำศัพท์เฉพาะ giawgabkamsabchapaw

terminology *n.* คำศัพท์เฉพาะทาง kamsabchapawtang

terminus *n.* ปลายทาง plaitang

terrace *n.* ระเบียง rabiang

terrible *a.* แย่ yae

terrier *n.* สุนัขพันธุ์หนึ่ง sunakpanneung

terrific *a.* เยี่ยม yiam

terrify *v.t.* ทำให้กลัว tamhaiglua

territorial *a.* เกี่ยวกับอาณาเขต giawgab-a-naket

territory *n.* อาณาเขต a-naket

terror *n.* ความหวาดกลัว kwamwadglua

terrorism *n.* ลัทธิการก่อการร้าย lattigangawganrai

terrorist *n.* ผู้ก่อการร้าย pugawganrai

terrorize *v.t.* ทำให้กลัว tamhaiglua

terse *a.* กะทัดรัด gatadrad

test *v.t.* ทดสอบ todsob

test *n* การทดสอบ gantodsob

testament *n.* พินัยกรรม pinaigam

testicle *n.* ลูกอัณฑะ look-anta

testify *v.i.* พิจารณาคดี pijaranakadi

testimonial *n.* หนังสือรับรอง nangseurabrong

testimony *n.* หลักฐาน laktan

tete-a-tete *n.* การสนทนาสองต่อสอง gansontanasongtawsong

tether *n.* เชือกล่าม cheuaklam

tether *v.t.* ล่ามด้วยเชือก lamduaycheuak

text *n.* เนื้อหา neuaha

textile *a.* เกี่ยวกับสิ่งทอ giawgabsingtaw

textile *n* สิ่งทอ singtaw

textual *n.* เกี่ยวกับต้นฉบับ giawgabtonchabab

texture *n.* เนื้อผ้า neuapa

thank *v.t.* ขอบคุณ kobkun

thanks *n.* การขอบคุณ gankobkun

thankful *a.* รู้สึกขอบคุณ ruseukkobkun

thankless *a.* ไม่รู้สึกขอบคุณ mairuseukkobkun

that *a.* นั้น nan

that *dem. pron.* สิ่งนั้น singnan

that *rel. pron.* โน่น noen

that *adv.* เช่นนั้น chennan

that *conj.* ว่า wa

thatch *n.* หลังคามุงจาก lankamungjak

thatch *v.t.* มุมหลังคาด้วยจาก munglangkaduayjak

thaw *v.i* ละลาย lalai

thaw *n* การละลาย ganlalai

theatre *n.* โรงละคร ronglakon

theatrical *a.* เกี่ยวกับละคร giawgablakon

theft *n.* ขโมย kamoey

their *a.* ของเขาเหล่านั้น kongkaolaonan

theirs *pron.* สิ่งที่เป็นของเขาทั้งหลาย singtipenkongkaotanglai

theism *n.* เทวนิยม tewaniyom

theist *n.* ผู้นับถือพระเจ้า punabteuprajao

them *pron.* พวกเขา puakkao

thematic *a.* เกี่ยวกับใจความสำคัญ giawgabjaikwamsamkan

theme *n.* หัวข้อหลัก huakawlak

then *adv.* หลังจากนั้น langjaknan

then *a* ดังนั้น dangnan

thence *adv.* จากนั้น jaknan

theocracy *n.* เทวาธิปไตย tewatipatai

theologian *n.* นักเทววิทยา naktewaniyom

theological *a.* ทางเทววิทยา tangtewaniyom

theology *n.* เทววิทยา tewaniyom

theorem *n.* ข้อพิสูจน์ทางคณิตศาสตร์ kawpisudtangkanitsat

theoretical *a.* เกี่ยวกับทฤษฎี giawgabtridsadi

theorist *n.* นักทฤษฎี naktridsadi

theorize *v.i.* สร้างทฤษฎี sangtridsadi

theory *n.* ทฤษฎี tridsadi

therapy *n.* การบำบัด ganbambat

there *adv.* ที่นั่น tinan

thereabouts *adv.* ในบริเวณนั้น naiboriwennan

thereafter *adv.* หลังจากนั้น lanjaknan

thereby *adv.* ดังนั้น dangnan

therefore *adv.* ดังนั้น dangnan

thermal *a.* เกี่ยวกับความร้อน giawgabkwamron

thermometer *n.* เครื่องวัดอุณหภูมิ kreuangwat-aun-hapum

thermos (flask) *n.* กระติกน้ำร้อน gratiknamron

thesis *n.* วิทยานิพนธ์ witayanipon

thick *a.* หนา na

thick *n.* ส่วนที่หนา suantina

thick *adv.* อย่างหนา yangna

thicken *v.i.* ทำให้หนา tamhaina

thicket *n.* พุ่มไม้หนา pummaina

thief *n.* โจร jon

thigh *n.* ต้นขา tonka

thimble *n.* ปลอกนิ้ว ploknew

thin *a.* ผอม pom

thin *v.t.* ทำให้บาง tamhaibang

thing *n.* สิ่งของ singkong

think *v.t.* คิด kid

thinker *n.* นักคิด nakkid

third *a.* ที่สาม tisam

third *n.* ลำดับที่สาม lamdabtisam

thirdly *adv.* ในลำดับสาม nailamdabsam

thirst *n.* ความกระหาย kwamgrahai

thirst *v.i.* กระหายน้ำ grahainam

thirsty *a.* กระหายน้ำ grahainam

thirteen *n.* สิบสาม sibsam

thirteen *a* สิบสาม sibsam

thirteenth *a.* ที่สิบสาม tisibsam

thirtieth *a.* ที่สามสิบ tisamsib

thirtieth *n* ลำดับที่สามสิบ lamdabtisamsib
thirty *n.* สามสิบ samsib
thirty *a* สามสิบ samsib
thistle *n.* พืชมีหนาม peudminam
thither *adv.* ไกลออกไป glai-awkpai
thorn *n.* หนาม nam
thorny *a.* มีหนามมาก minammak
thorough *a* ละเอียดที่ถ้วน la-iadtituan
thoroughfare *n.* ทางสัญจร tangsanjon
though *conj.* ถึงแม้ว่า teungmaewa
though *adv.* อย่างไรก็ดี yangraigawdi
thought *n* ความคิด kwamkid
thoughtful *a.* ครุ่นคิด krunkid
thousand *n.* หนึ่งพัน neungpan
thousand *a* หนึ่งพัน neungpan
thrall *n.* ทาส tad
thralldom *n.* ความเป็นทาส kwampentad
thrash *v.t.* เฆี่ยน kian
thread *n.* ด้าย dai
thread *v.t* ร้อยด้าย roydai
threadbare *a.* เก่ามาก gaomak
threat *n.* การคุกคาม gankukkam
threaten *v.t.* ทำให้กลัว tamhaiglua
three *n.* สาม sam
three *a* สาม sam
thresh *v.t.* นวดข้าว nuadkao
thresher *n.* เครื่องนวดข้าว kreuangnuadkao
threshold *n.* ธรณีประตู toranipratu
thrice *adv.* สามครั้ง samkrang
thrift *n.* ความประหยัด kwamprayad
thrifty *a.* ประหยัด prayad
thrill *n.* ความตื่นเต้น kwamteunten
thrill *v.t.* ทำให้ตื่นเต้น tamhaiteunten
thrive *v.i.* เจริญเติบโต jareunteubto
throat *n.* คอ kaw
throaty *a.* เสียงแหบ sianghaeb
throb *v.i.* เต้นเป็นจังหวะ tenpenjangwa
throb *n.* การเต้นเป็นจังหวะ gantenpenjangwa
throe *n.* อาการปวดเกร็ง a-ganpuadgreng
throne *n.* บัลลังก์ banlang

throne *v.t.* ขึ้นครองราชย์ keunkrongrat
throng *n.* ฝูงชน foongchon
throng *v.t.* ทำให้เนืองแน่น tamhaineuangnaen
throttle *n.* หัวเปิดปิดน้ำ huapeudpidnam
throttle *v.t.* อุด ud
through *prep.* ผ่านไป panpai
through *adv.* โดยตลอด doeytalod
through *a* ตลอด talod
throughout *adv.* โดยตลอด doeytalod
throughout *prep.* โดยตลอด doeytalod
throw *v.t.* ขว้าง kwang
throw *n.* การขว้าง gankwang
thrust *v.t.* ผลัก plak
thrust *n* การผลัก ganplak
thud *n.* เสียงดังตุบ siangdangtub
thud *v.i.* ทำให้เกิดเสียงดังตุบ tamhaigeudsiangdangtub
thug *n.* นักเลง nakleng
thumb *n.* นิ้วโป้ง newpong
thumb *v.t.* ยกนิ้ว yoknew
thump *n.* การทุบ gantub
thump *v.t.* ทุบ tub
thunder *n.* เสียงฟ้าร้อง siangfarong
thunder *v.i.* ฟ้าร้อง farong
thunderous *a.* ราวกับเสียงฟ้าร้อง raogawsiangfarong
Thursday *n.* วันพฤหัสบดี wanparuhasabori
thus *adv.* ดังนั้น dangnan
thwart *v.t.* ขัดขวาง kadkwang
tiara *n.* มงกุฎ monggut
tick *n.* หมัด mad
tick *v.i.* ทำเครื่องหมาย tamkreuangmai
ticket *n.* ตั๋ว tua
tickle *v.t.* ทำให้คัน tamhaikan
ticklish *a.* จั๊กจี้ jakgaji
tidal *a.* เกี่ยวกับน้ำขึ้นน้ำลง giawgabnamkeunnamlong
tide *n.* คลื่นทะเล kleuntalay
tidings *n. pl.* ข่าว kao

tidiness *n.* ความเป็นระเบียบ
  kwampenrabiab
tidy *a.* เรียบร้อย riabroy
tidy *v.t.* ทำให้เรียบร้อย tamhairiabroy
tie *v.t.* ผูก puk
tie *n* การผูก ganpuk
tier *n.* แถวที่นั่ง taewtinang
tiger *n.* เสือ seua
tight *a.* แน่น naen
tighten *v.t.* ทำให้แน่น tamhainaen
tigress *n.* เสือตัวเมีย seuatuamia
tile *n.* กระเบื้อง grabeuang
tile *v.t.* ปูกระเบื้อง pugrabeuang
till *prep.* จนกระทั่ง jongratang
till *n. conj.* จนกระทั่ง jongratang
till *v.t.* เตรียมที่เพาะปลูก triamtipawpluk
tilt *v.i.* ทำให้เอียง tamhai-iang
tilt *n.* การเอียงลาด ganlad-iang
timber *n.* ไม้ซุง maisung
time *n.* เวลา wela
time *v.t.* จับเวลา jabwela
timely *a.* ถูกเวลา tookwela
timid *a.* ขี้ขลาด kiklad
timidity *n.* ความขี้ขลาด kwamkiklad
timorous *a.* ขี้กลัว kiglua
tin *n.* กระป๋อง grapong
tin *v.t.* บรรจุกระป๋อง panjugrapong
tincture *n.* ยาทิงเจอร์ yatinger
tincture *v.t.* แต้มสี taemsi
tinge *n.* สีจางๆ sijangjang
tinge *v.t.* แต้มสีจางๆ taemsijangjang
tinker *n.* ช่างบัดกรี changbadgri
tinsel *n.* สิ่งประดับแวววาว
  singpradagwaewwow
tint *n.* สีอ่อน si-on
tint *v.t.* แต้มสีจางๆ taemsijangjang
tiny *a.* เล็กน้อย leknoy
tip *n.* เงินทิป ngeuntib
tip *v.t.* ให้ทิป haitib
tip *n.* ปลาย plai
tip *v.t.* กระดก gradok
tip *n.* คำแนะนำ kamnaenam

tip *v.t.* เซ say
tipsy *a.* เมา mao
tirade *n.* คำด่า kamda
tire *v.t.* ทำให้เบื่อ tamhaibeua
tiresome *a.* น่าเบื่อหน่าย nabeuanai
tissue *n.* เนื้อเยื่อ neuayeua
titanic *a.* ใหญ่โต yaito
tithe *n.* ภาษีย่อย pasiyoi
title *n.* หัวเรื่อง huareuang
titular *a.* มีตำแหน่ง mitamnaeng
toad *n.* คางคก kangkok
toast *n.* ขนมปังปิ้ง kanonpangping
toast *v.t.* ปิ้ง ping
tobacco *n.* ยาสูบ yasoob
today *adv.* ในวันนี้ naiwanni
today *n.* วันนี้ wanni
toe *n.* นิ้วเท้า newtao
toe *v.t.* ยืนด้วยปลายเท้า yeunduayplaitao
toffee *n.* ลูกอม look-om
toga *n.* เสื้อคลุม seuaklum
together *adv.* รวมกัน ruamgan
toil *n.* งานหนัก ngannak
toil *v.i.* ทำงานหนัก tam-ngannak
toilet *n.* ห้องสุขา hongsuka
toils *n. pl.* การทำงานหนัก gantam-
  ngannak
token *n.* ของที่ระลึก kongtiraleuk
tolerable *a.* ทนได้ tondai
tolerance *n.* ความอดทน kwam-odton
tolerant *a.* อดทน odton
tolerate *v.t.* อดทน odton
toleration *n.* ความอดทน kwam-odton
toll *n.* ค่าธรรมเนียมการใช้ถนน
  katamniamganchaitanon
toll *n* การตีระฆัง gantirakang
toll *v.t.* ตีระฆัง tirakang
tomato *n.* มะเขือเทศ makeuatet
tomb *n.* หลุมฝังศพ lumfangsob
tomboy *n.* ทอมบอย tomboy
tomcat *n.* เสือผู้หญิง seuapuying
tome *n.* หนังสือเล่มหนา nangseulemna
tomorrow *n.* พรุ่งนี้ prungni

tomorrow *adv.* พรุ่งนี้ prungni
ton *n.* ตัน ton
tone *n.* เฉดสี chedsi
tone *v.t.* ปรับสีให้กลมกลืน
  prabsihaiglomgleun
tongs *n. pl.* คีม kim
tongue *n.* ลิ้น lin
tonic *a.* เกี่ยวกับการบำรุงสุขภาพ
  giawgabganbamroongsukgapab
tonic *n.* ยาบำรุง yabamroong
to-night *n.* คืนนี้ keunni
tonight *adv.* คืนนี้ keunni
tonne *n.* ตัน ton
tonsil *n.* ทอลซิล tonsil
tonsure *n.* การโกนผม gangonpom
too *adv.* มากเกินไป makgeunpai
tool *n.* เครื่องมือ kreuangmeu
tooth *n.* ฟัน fun
toothache *n.* ปวดฟัน puadfan
toothsome *a.* มีรสอร่อย mirod-a-roy
top *n.* จุดสูงสุด judsoongsud
top *v.t.* ต่อยอด tawyod
top *n.* ด้านบน danbon
topaz *n.* บุษราคัม busarakam
topic *n.* หัวข้อ huakaw
topical *a.* เฉพาะที่ chapawti
topographer *n.* ผู้ชำนาญการทำแผนที่
  puchamnangantampaenti
topographical *a.* เกี่ยวกับการทำแผนที่
  giawgabgantampaenti
topography *n.* การทำแผนที่ gantampaenti
topple *v.i.* โค่น kon
topsy turvy *a.* ยุ่งเหยิง yungyeung
topsy turvy *adv* อย่างยุ่งเหยิง
  yangyungyeung
torch *n.* คบไฟ kobfai
torment *n.* ทำให้ทรมาน tamhaitawraman
torment *v.t.* ความทรมาน kwamtawraman
tornado *n.* พายุหมุน payumoon
torpedo *n.* ตอร์ปิโด torpedo
torpedo *v.t.* ทำลาย tamlai
torrent *n.* กระแสน้ำเชี่ยว grasanamchiaw

torrential *a.* ไหลเชี่ยว laichiaw
torrid *a.* ร้อนจัด ronjad
tortoise *n.* เต่า tao
tortuous *a.* บิดงอ bid-ngaw
torture *n.* การทรมาน gantawraman
torture *v.t.* ทรมาน tawraman
toss *v.t.* โยน yoan
toss *n* การโยน ganyoen
total *a.* ทั้งหมด tangmod
total *n.* ผลรวม ponruam
total *v.t.* รวมยอด ruamyod
totality *n.* จำนวนทั้งหมด
  jamnuantangmod
touch *v.t.* สัมผัส sampad
touch *n* การสัมผัส gansampad
touchy *a.* ขี้โมโห kimoho
tough *a.* แข็งแรง kaengraeng
toughen *v.t.* ทำให้แข็งแรง
  tamhaikaengraeng
tour *n.* การท่องเที่ยว gantongtiaw
tour *v.i.* ท่องเที่ยว tongtiaw
tourism *n.* ธุรกิจการท่องเที่ยว
  turagidtongtiaw
tourist *n.* นักท่องเที่ยว naktongtiaw
tournament *n.* การแข่งขัน gankaengkan
towards *prep.* เกี่ยวกับ giawgab
towel *n.* ผ้าขนหนู pakonnu
towel *v.t.* เช็ดให้แห้ง chedhaihaeng
tower *n.* หอคอย hawkoy
tower *v.i.* ตระหง่าน tra-ngan
town *n.* เมือง meuang
township *a.* เขตชุมชน ketchumchon
toy *n.* ของเล่น konglen
toy *v.i.* เล่น len
trace *n.* ร่อยรอย rongroy
trace *v.t.* ติดตาม tidtam
traceable *a.* ติดตามได้ tidtamdai
track *n.* การสะกดรอย gansagodroy
track *v.t.* สะกดรอย sagodroy
tract *n.* พื้นที่ peunti
tract *n* ระบบ rabob
traction *n.* การลาก ganlak

tractor *n.* แทรกเตอร์ tractor
trade *n.* การค้า ganka
trade *v.i* ค้าขาย kakai
trader *n.* ผู้ค้า puka
tradesman *n.* พ่อค้า pawka
tradition *n.* ประเพณี prapeni
traditional *a.* เป็นประเพณี penprapeni
traffic *n.* การลักลอบค้าขาย
ganlaklobkakai
traffic *v.i.* ลักลอบค้าขาย laklobkakai
tragedian *n.* ผู้แสดงโศกนาฏกรรม
pusadaengsoganatagam
tragedy *n.* โศกนาฏกรรม soganatgam
tragic *a.* น่าเศร้า nasao
trail *n.* ทางเดิน tangdeun
trail *v.t.* ตามรอย tamroy
trailer *n.* รถพ่วง rodpuang
train *n.* รถไฟ rodfai
train *v.t.* อบรม ob-rom
trainee *n.* ผู้อบรม pu-ob-rom
training *n.* การอบรม gan-ob-rom
trait *n.* คุณสมบัติ kunnasombat
traitor *n.* ผู้ทรยศ putawrayod
tram *n.* รถราง rodrang
trample *v.t.* กระทืบ krateub
trance *n.* การอยู่ในภวังค์ ganyunaipawang
tranquil *a.* สงบ sa-ngob
tranquility *n.* ความสงบ kwamsa-ngob
tranquillize *v.t.* ทำให้สงบ tamhaisa-ngob
transact *v.t.* เจรจา jeraja
transaction *n.* การติดต่อทางธุรกิจ
gantidtawtangturagid
transcend *v.t.* เอาชนะ aow-chana
transcendent *a.* ดีกว่า dikwa
transcribe *v.t.* คัดลอก kadlok
transcription *n.* การคัดลอก gankadlok
transfer *n.* การขนย้าย gankonyai
transfer *v.t.* ขนย้าย konyai
transferable *a.* ขนย้ายได้ konyaidai
transfiguration *n.* การเปลี่ยนรูป
ganplianroob
transfigure *v.t.* เปลี่ยนรูป plianroob

transform *v.* เปลี่ยนแปลง plianplang
transformation *n.* การเปลี่ยนแปลง
ganplianplaeng
transgress *v.t.* กระทำผิด gratampid
transgression *n.* การกระทำผิด
gangratampid
transit *n.* การเดินทางผ่าน
gandeuntangpan
transition *n.* การเปลี่ยน ganplian
transitive *n.* เกี่ยวกับการส่งผ่าน
giawgabgansongpan
transitory *n.* ชั่วคราว chuakrao
translate *v.t.* แปล plae
translation *n.* การแปล ganplae
transmigration *n.* การย้ายถิ่นฐาน
ganyaitintan
transmission *n.* การส่งผ่าน gansongpan
transmit *v.t.* ส่งผ่าน songpan
transmitter *n.* เครื่องส่ง kreuangsong
transparent *a.* โปร่งใส prongsai
transplant *v.t.* ปลูกถ่าย pluktai
transport *v.t.* ขนย้าย konyai
transport *n.* การขนส่ง gankonsong
transportation *n.* การขนส่ง gankonsong
trap *n.* กับดัก gabdak
trap *v.t.* วางกับดัก wanggabdak
trash *n.* ขยะ kaya
travel *v.i.* เดินทาง deuntang
travel *n* การเดินทาง gandeuntang
traveller *n.* นักเดินทาง nakduantang
tray *n.* ถาด tad
treacherous *a.* ทรยศ tawrayod
treachery *n.* การทรยศ gantawrayod
tread *v.t.* ย่ำ yam
tread *n* การก้าวย่าง gangaoyang
treason *n.* การทรยศ gantawrayod
treasure *n.* สมบัติ sombat
treasure *v.t.* ตีค่า tika
treasurer *n.* เหรัญญิก heiranyik
treasury *n.* กระทรวงการคลัง
grasuangganklang
treat *v.t.* รักษา raksa

treat *n* อาหารที่น่าทาน a-hantinatan
treatise *n.* บทความ bodkwam
treatment *n.* การบำบัด ganbambat
treaty *n.* สัญญา sanya
tree *n.* ต้นไม้ tonmai
trek *v.i.* เดินช้าๆ deunchacha
trek *n.* การเดินทาง gandeuntang
tremble *v.i.* สั่น san
tremendous *a.* ใหญ่โต yaito
tremor *n.* การสั่นไหว gansanwai
trench *n.* คู ku
trench *v.t.* ขุดคู kudku
trend *n.* แนวโน้ม naewnom
trespass *v.i.* ล่วงล้ำ luanglam
trespass *n.* การล่วงล้ำ ganluanglam
trial *n.* การทดลอง gantodlong
triangle *n.* สามเหลี่ยม samliam
triangular *a.* เป็นรูปสามเหลี่ยม penroobsamliam
tribal *a.* เกี่ยวกับชนเผ่า giawgabchonpao
tribe *n.* ชนเผ่า chonpao
tribulation *n.* ความยากลำบาก kwamyaklambak
tribunal *n.* ศาล san
tributary *n.* แควน้ำ kwaenam
tributary *a.* ที่เป็นสายย่อยของแม่น้ำ tipensaiyoikongmaenam
trick *n* มายากล mayagon
trick *v.t.* ใช้เล่ห์เลี่ยม chailayliam
trickery *n.* การใช้กลอุบาย ganchaigon-u-bai
trickle *v.i.* หยด yod
trickster *n.* คนโกง kongong
tricky *a.* มีเล่ห์เหลี่ยม milayliam
tricolour *a.* สามสี samsi
tricolour *n* ธงสามสี tongsamsi
tricycle *n.* จักรยานสามล้อ jakgayansamlaw
trifle *n.* เรื่องไร้สาระ reuangraisara
trifle *v.i* พูดเล่น pudlen
trigger *n.* ไกปืน gaipeun
trim *a.* ผอมบาง pombang

trim *n* การตัด gantad
trim *v.t.* ตัดแต่ง tadtaeng
trinity *n.* กลุ่มที่มีสามคน glumtimisamkon
trio *n.* กลุ่มที่มีสามคน glumtimisamkon
trip *v.t.* เดินทาง deuntang
trip *n.* การเดินทาง gandeuntang
tripartite *a.* ไตรภาคี tripaki
triple *a.* มีสามส่วน misamsuan
triple *v.t.,* ทำให้เป็นสาม tamhaipensam
triplicate *a.* เป็นสามเท่า pensamtao
triplicate *n* เอกสารสามฉบับ ekgasansamchabab
triplicate *v.t.* เพิ่มขึ้นสามเท่า peumkeunsamtao
triplication *n.* การทำให้เป็นสามเท่า gantamhaipensamtao
tripod *n.* โต๊ะสามขา tosamka
triumph *n.* ชัยชนะ chaichana
triumph *v.i.* ได้รับชัยชนะ dairabchaichana
triumphal *a.* ยินดี yindi
triumphant *a.* ภาคภูมิใจจากชัยชนะ pakpumjaijakchaichana
trivial *a.* เล็กน้อย leknoy
troop *n.* กองทหาร gongtahan
troop *v.i* เดินขบวน deunkabuan
trooper *n.* ทหารม้า tahanma
trophy *n.* รางวัล rangwan
tropic *n.* เขตร้อน kedron
tropical *a.* เกี่ยวกับเขตร้อน giawgabkedron
trot *v.i.* วิ่งเยาะๆ wingyawyaw
trot *n* การวิ่งเยาะๆ ganwingyawyaw
trouble *n.* ปัญหา panha
trouble *v.t.* รบกวน robguan
troublesome *a.* เป็นปัญหา penpanha
troupe *n.* คณะผู้แสดง kanapusadaeng
trousers *n. pl* กางเกงขายาว gangengkayao
trowel *n.* เกรียง griang
truce *n.* การพักรบ ganpakrob
truck *n.* รถบรรทุก rodbantook
true *a.* จริง jing

trump *n.* แตร trae
trump *v.t.* เป่าแตร paotrae
trumpet *n.* แตร trae
trumpet *v.i.* เป่าแตร paotrae
trunk *n.* ลำต้น lamton
trust *n.* ความไว้วางใจ kwamwaiwangjai
trust *v.t* ไว้ใจ waijai
trustee *n.* ผู้ดูแลทรัพย์สิน pudulaesabsin
trustful *a.* ไว้ใจได้ waijaidai
trustworthy *a.* น่าไว้ใจ nawaijai
trusty *n.* น่าไว้วางใจ nawaiwangjai
truth *n.* ความจริง kwamjing
truthful *a.* ซื่อสัตย์ seusat
try *v.i.* พยายาม payayam
try *n* ความพยายาม kwampayayam
trying *a.* ที่ยากลำบาก tiyaklambak
tryst *n.* การนัดพบ gannadpob
tub *n.* ถังน้ำ tangnam
tube *n.* หลอด lod
tuberculosis *n.* วัณโรค wanarok
tubular *a.* เป็นหลอด penlod
tug *v.t.* ดึง deung
tuition *n.* ค่าเล่าเรียน kalaorian
tumble *v.i.* ล้ม lom
tumble *n.* การล้ม ganlom
tumbler *n.* นักกายกรรม nakgaiyagam
tumour *n.* เนื้องอก neua-ngwak
tumult *n.* ความอลเวง kwam-onlaweng
tumultuous *a.* โกลาหล golahon
tune *n.* ทำนอง tamnong
tune *v.t.* ตั้งเสียง tangsiang
tunnel *n.* อุโมงค์ u-mong
tunnel *v.i.* ขุดอุโมงค์ kud-u-mong
turban *n.* ผ้าโพกศีรษะ papoksisa
turbine *n.* กังหัน ganhan
turbulence *n.* ความวุ่นวาย kwamwunwai
turbulent *a.* วุ่นวาย wunwai
turf *n.* สนามหญ้า sanamya
turkey *n.* ไก่งวง gai-nguang
turmeric *n.* ขมิ้น kamin
turmoil *n.* ความวุ่นวาย kwamwunwai
turn *v.i.* เลี้ยว liaw

turn *n* การหัน ganhan
turner *n.* เครื่องหมุน kruangmoon
turnip *n.* หัวผักกาด huapakgad
turpentine *n.* น้ำมันสน nammanson
turtle *n.* เต่า tao
tusk *n.* งาช้าง nga-chang
tussle *n.* การดิ้นรน gandinron
tussle *v.i.* ดิ้นรน dinron
tutor *n.* ครูพิเศษ krupised
tutorial *a.* เกี่ยวกับการสอน giawgabganson
tutorial *n.* การเรียนพิเศษ ganrianpised
twelfth *a.* ที่สิบสอง tisibsong
twelfth *n.* ลำดับที่สิบสอง lamdabtisibsong
twelve *n.* สิบสอง sibsong
twelve *n* สิบสอง sibsong
twentieth *a.* ที่ยี่สิบ tiyisib
twentieth *n* ลำดับที่ยี่สิบ lamdabtiyisib
twenty *a.* ยี่สิบ yisib
twenty *n* ยี่สิบ yisib
twice *adv.* สองครั้ง songkrang
twig *n.* กิ่งไม้ gingmai
twilight *n* แสงสลัว sangsalua
twin *n.* แฝด faed
twin *a* เป็นฝาแฝด penfafaed
twinkle *v.i.* ส่องแสงระยิบ songsaengrayib
twinkle *n.* แสงระยิบระยับ saengrayibrayab
twist *v.t.* บิด bid
twist *n.* การบิด ganbid
twitter *n.* ความตื่นเต้น kwamteunten
twitter *v.i.* ร้องเสียงแหลม rongsianglaem
two *n.* สอง song
two *a.* สอง song
twofold *a.* สองเท่า songtao
type *n.* ชนิด chanid
type *v.t.* พิมพ์ pim
typhoid *n.* ไทฟอยด์ typhoid
typhoon *n.* พายุไต้ฝุ่น payutyphoon
typhus *n.* ไข้รากสาดใหญ่ kairaksadyai
typical *a.* แบบอย่าง baedyang
typify *v.t.* เป็นตัวอย่าง pentuayang
typist *n.* ผู้พิมพ์ pupim

tyranny *n.* ระบบทรราชย์ rabobtorarat
tyrant *n.* ผู้กดขี่ pugodki
tyre *n.* ยางรถ yanrod

U

udder *n.* เต้านม taonom
uglify *v.t.* ทำให้น่าเกลียด tamhainagliad
ugliness *n.* ความน่าเกลียด kwamnagliad
ugly *a.* น่าเกลียด nagliad
ulcer *n.* แผลเปื่อย plaepeuy
ulcerous *a.* เกี่ยวกับแผลเปื่อย
  giawgabplaepeuy
ulterior *a.* อย่างลี้ลับ yanglilab
ultimate *a.* สูงสุด soongsud
ultimately *adv.* อย่างสูงสุด yangsoongsud
ultimatum *n.* คำขาด kamkad
umbrella *n.* ร่ม rom
umpire *n.* กรรมการตัดสิน
  gammagantadsin
umpire *v.t.,* เป็นกรรมการ pengammagan
unable *a.* ไม่สามารถ maisamad
unanimity *n.* การยอมรับเป็นเอกฉันท์
  ganyomrabpen-ekgachan
unanimous *a.* เป็นเอกฉันท์ pen-ekgachan
unaware *a.* ไม่รู้ตัว mairutua
unawares *adv.* อย่างไม่ตั้งใจ
  yangmaitangjai
unburden *v.t.* ปลดภาระ plodpara
uncanny *a.* แปลก plaek
uncertain *a.* ไม่แน่ใจ mainaejai
uncle *n.* ลุง loong
uncouth *a.* งุ่มง่าม ngum-ngam
under *prep.* ใต้ tai
under *adv* ใต้ tai
under *a* ข้างล่าง kanglang
undercurrent *n.* กระแสใต้น้ำ
  grasaetainam
underdog *n* ไก่รองบ่อน gairongbon
undergo *v.t.* ประสบ prasob

undergraduate *n.*
  นักศึกษาระดับปริญญาตรี
  naksuksaradabparinyatri
underhand *a.* ไม่เปิดเผย maipeudpei
underline *v.t.* ขีดเส้นใต้ kidsentai
undermine *v.t.* บ่อนทำลาย bontamrai
underneath *adv.* ข้างใต้ kangtai
underneath *prep.* ข้างใต้ kangtai
understand *v.t.* เข้าใจ kaojai
undertake *v.t.* รับภาระ rabpara
undertone *n.* เสียงเบา siangbao
underwear *n.* ชุดชั้นใน chudchannai
underworld *n.* โลกมิจฉาชีพ
  lokmitchachib
undo *v.t.* ยกเลิก yokleuk
undue *a.* ไม่เหมาะสม mailawsom
undulate *v.i.* กระเพื่อม grapeum
undulation *n.* การกระเพื่อม gangrapeum
unearth *v.t.* ขุด kud
uneasy *a.* ไม่ง่าย mai-ngai
unfair *a* ไม่ยุติธรรม maiyutitam
unfold *v.t.* คลี่ kli
unfortunate *a.* โชคไม่ดี chokmaidi
ungainly *a.* ไม่สง่างาม maisa-nga-ngam
unhappy *a.* ไม่มีความสุข
  maimikwamsook
unification *n.* การรวมตัวกัน
  ganruamtuagan
union *n.* สหภาพ sahapab
unionist *n.* สมาชิกสหภาพ
  samachiksahabab
unique *a.* เป็นอันหนึ่งอันเดียวกัน pen-
  anneung-andiawgan
unison *n.* ความพร้อมเพรียง
  kwamprompriang
unit *n.* หน่วย nuay
unite *v.t.* รวมตัว ruamtua
unity *n.* ความเป็นอันหนึ่งอันเดียว
  kwampen-anneung-andiawgan
universal *a.* สากล sagon
universality *n.* ความเป็นสากล
  kwampensagon

universe *n.* จักรวาล jakgawan

university *n.* มหาวิทยาลัย mahawitayalai

unjust *a.* ไม่ยุติธรรม maiyutitam

unless *conj.* ยกเว้น yokwen

unlike *a* ไม่เหมือน maimeuan

unlike *prep* แตกต่างจาก taektangjak

unlikely *a.* ที่ไม่น่าจะเกิดขึ้น
timainajageudkeun

unmanned *a.* ไม่มีคนอยู่ maimikonyu

unmannerly *a* ไม่สุภาพ maisupab

unprincipled *a.* ขาดคุณธรรม kadkunatam

unreliable *a.* ไว้ใจไม่ได้ waijaimaidai

unrest *n* ความไม่สงบสุข kwammaisa-
ngobsuk

unruly *a.* ไม่มีวินัย maimiwinai

unsettle *v.t.* ทำให้รู้สึกไม่มั่นคง
tamhairusukmaimankong

unsheathe *v.t.* ชักออกจากฝัก chak-
awkjakfak

until *prep.* จนกระทั่ง jongratang

until *conj* ก่อนที่จะ gontija

untoward *a.* ดื้อรั้น deuran

unwell *a.* ไม่สบาย maisabai

unwittingly *adv.* โดยไม่รู้ doeymairu

up *adv.* ตั้งตรง tangtrong

up *prep.* ข้างบน kangbon

upbraid *v.t* ดุด่า duda

upheaval *n.* ความวุ่นวาย kwamwunwai

uphold *v.t* สนับสนุน sanabsanoon

upkeep *n* การบำรุงรักษา
ganbamroongraksa

uplift *v.t.* ยกขึ้น yokkeun

uplift *n* การยกขึ้นสูง ganyokkeunsoong

upon *prep* บน bon

upper *a.* เหนือ neua

upright *a.* ที่ตั้งขึ้น titangkeun

uprising *n.* การปฏิวัติ ganpatiwat

uproar *n.* ความบ้าคลั่ง kwampaklang

uproarious *a.* เอะอะ ae-a

uproot *v.t.* ถอนต้นไม้ tawntonmai

upset *v.t.* ไม่พอใจ maipawjai

upshot *n.* ผลสุดท้าย ponsudtai

upstart *n.* ผู้ร่ำรวยอย่างรวดเร็ว
puramruayyangruadrew

up-to-date *a.* ทันสมัย tansamai

upward *a.* ขึ้นไป keunpai

upwards *adv.* เหนือขึ้นไป neuakeunpai

urban *a.* เกี่ยวกับเมือง giawgabmeuang

urbane *a.* เป็นผู้ดี penpudi

urbanity *n.* คุณสมบัติของชาวเมือง
kunsombatkongchaomeuang

urchin *n.* เด็กซน dekson

urge *v.t* เร่ง reng

urge *n* การเร่ง ganreng

urgency *n.* ความรีบเร่ง kwamribreng

urgent *a.* ด่วน duan

urinal *n.* โถปัสสาวะ topasawa

urinary *a.* เกี่ยวกับปัสสาวะ
giawgabpasawa

urinate *v.i.* ถ่ายปัสสาวะ taipasawa

urination *n.* การถ่ายปัสสาวะ
gantaipasawa

urine *n.* ปัสสาวะ pasawa

urn *n* โกศ goat

usage *n.* การใช้ ganchai

use *n.* วิธีใช้ witichai

use *v.t.* ใช้ chai

useful *a.* เป็นประโยชน์ penprayod

usher *n.* เจ้าหน้าที่ต้อนรับ jaonatitonrab

usher *v.t.* นำทาง namtang

usual *a.* ปกติ pagati

usually *adv.* เสมอ sameu

usurer *n.* เจ้าหนี้ jaoni

usurp *v.t.* ช่วงชิง chuangching

usurpation *n.* การแย่งชิงอำนาจ
ganyaengching-amnad

usury *n.* การเรียกดอกเบี้ยเกินอัตรา
ganriakdawkbiageun-atta

utensil *n.* เครื่องใช้ kreuangchai

uterus *n.* มดลูก modlook

utilitarian *a.* ถือประโยชน์เป็นสำคัญ
teuprayodpensamkan

utility *n.* สาธารณูปโภค sataranupapok

utilization n. การใช้ให้เป็นประโยชน์ ganchaihaipenprayod
utilize v.t. ใช้ประโยชน์ chaiprayod
utmost a. อย่างมาก yangmak
utmost n ระดับสูงสุด radabsoongsud
utopia n . ดินแดนในอุดมคติ dindaennai-udomkati
utopian a. เกี่ยวกับดินแดนในอุดมคติ giawgabdindaennai-udomkati
utter v.t. พูด pud
utter a ทั้งหมด tangmod
utterance n. ระดับสูงสุด radabsoongsud
utterly adv. อย่างที่สุด yangtisud

vacancy n. ตำแหน่งว่าง tamnaengwang
vacant a. ว่าง wang
vacate v.t. ปล่อยให้ว่าง ployhaiwang
vacation n. ช่วงลาพักผ่อน chuanglapakpon
vaccinate v.t. ฉีดวัคซีน chidwaksin
vaccination n. การให้วัคซีน kanhaiwaksin
vaccinator n. ผู้ฉีดวัคซีน puchidwaksin
vaccine n. วัคซีน waksin
vacillate v.i. เปลี่ยนใจง่าย plianjai-ngai
vacuum n. สูญญากาศ soonyagad
vagabond n. คนร่อนเร่ konronray
vagabond a ร่อนเร่ ronray
vagary n. ความไม่แน่นอน kwammainaenon
vagina n. ช่องคลอด chongklod
vague a. คลุมเครือ klumkreua
vagueness n. ความคลุมเครือ kwamklumkreua
vain a. ไร้ประโยชน์ raiprayod
vainglorious a. หยิ่ง ying
vainglory n. ความทะนงตัว kwamtanongtua
vainly adv. อย่างไร้ประโยชน์ yangraiprayod

vale n. หุบเขา hubkao
valiant a. กล้าหาญ glahan
valid a. มีเหตุผล mihedpon
validate v.t. ทำให้สมบูรณ์ tamhaisomboon
validity n. ความมีเหตุผล kwammihedpon
valley n. หุบเขา hubkao
valour n. ความกล้าหาญ kwamglahan
valuable a. มีค่า mika
valuation n. การประเมินราคา ganprameunraka
value n. คุณค่า kunka
value v.t. มีคุณค่า mikunka
valve n. ลิ้นปิดเปิด linpidpeud
van n. รถตู้ rodtu
vanish v.i. หายไป haipai
vanity n. ความหยิ่ง kwamying
vanquish v.t. ปราบปราม prabpram
vaporize v.t. ทำให้ระเหย tamhairaheuy
vaporous a. เต็มไปด้วยไอ tempaiduay-ai
vapour n. ไอน้ำ ainam
variable a. เปลี่ยนแปลงได้ plianplangdai
variance n. การเปลี่ยนแปลง ganplianplaneg
variation n. การเปลี่ยนแปลง ganplianplaneg
varied a. หลากหลาย laklai
variety n. ความหลากหลาย kwamlaklai
various a. แตกต่าง taektang
varnish n. น้ำมันเคลือบเงา nammankleuab-ngao
varnish v.t. เคลือบเงา kleuab-ngao
vary v.t. เปลี่ยนแปลง plianplang
vasectomy n. การทำหมันชาย gantammanchai
vaseline n. วาสลีน vaseline
vast a. ใหญ่ yai
vault n. หลังคาโค้ง lankakong
vault n. ห้องใต้ดิน hongtaidin
vault v.i. กระโดดข้ามสิ่งกีดขวาง gradodkamsinggidkwang
vegetable n. ผัก pak

vegetable *a.* เกี่ยวกับผัก giawgabpak

vegetarian *n.* คนที่กินแต่ผัก kontigintaepak

vegetarian *a* ที่ไม่กินเนื้อสัตว์ timaiginneuasat

vegetation *n.* พืชผัก peudpak

vehemence *n.* ความเร่งร้อน kwamrengron

vehement *a.* เร่าร้อน raoron

vehicle *n.* ยานพาหนะ yanpahana

vehicular *a.* เกี่ยวกับยานพาหนะ giawgabyanpahana

veil *n.* ผ้าคลุมหน้า paklumna

veil *v.t.* คลุมหน้า klumna

vein *n.* เส้นเลือดดำ senleuaddam

velocity *n.* ความเร็ว kwamrew

velvet *n.* กำมะหยี่ gammayi

velvety *a.* นุ่มเหมือนกำมะหยี่ noommeungammayi

venal *a.* ติดสินบนได้ tidsinbondai

venality *n.* การรับสินบน ganrabsinbon

vendor *n.* ผู้ค้า puka

venerable *a.* น่านับถือ nanabteu

venerate *v.t.* เคารพ kaorob

veneration *n.* ความเคารพ kwamkaorob

vengeance *n.* การแก้แค้น gangaekaen

venial *a.* ยกโทษให้ได้ yoktodhaidai

venom *n.* พิษสัตว์ pidsat

venomous *a.* ซึ่งมีพิษ seungmipid

vent *n.* ช่องลม chonglom

ventilate *v.t.* ระบายลม rabailom

ventilation *n.* การระบายลม ganrabailom

ventilator *n.* เครื่องระบายอากศ kruangrabai-a-gad

venture *n.* การเสี่ยงภัย gansiangpai

venture *v.t.* เสี่ยงภัย siangpai

venturesome *a.* อันตราย antarai

venturous *a.* อันตราย antarai

venue *n.* สถานที่ satanti

veracity *n.* ความสัตย์จริง kwamsatjing

verendah *n.* แกลเลอรี่หลังคาเปิด gallerylangkapeud

verb *n.* คำกริยา kamgariya

verbal *a.* ทางวาจา tangwaja

verbally *adv.* ทางวาจา tangwaja

verbatim *a.* คำต่อคำ kamtawkam

verbatim *adv.* อย่างคำต่อคำ yangkamtawkam

verbose *a.* ใช้คำฟุ่มเฟือย chaikamfumfeuay

verbosity *n.* การใช้คำฟุ่มเฟือย ganchaikamfumfeuay

verdant *a.* เขียวขจี kiawkaji

verdict *n.* คำตัดสิน kamtadsin

verge *n.* ริม rim

verification *n.* การพิสูจน์ ganpisud

verify *v.t.* พิสูจน์ pisud

verisimilitude *n.* ความคล้ายกัน kwamklaigan

veritable *a.* จริง jing

vermillion *n.* สีแดงสด sidaengsod

vermillion *a.* สีแดงสด sidaengsod

vernacular *n.* ภาษาที่ใช้ประจำวัน pasatichaiprajamwan

vernacular *a.* เกี่ยวกับภาษาพื้นเมือง giawgabpasapeunmeuang

vernal *a.* เกี่ยวกับฤดูใบไม้ผลิ giawgabreudubaimaipli

versatile *a.* เก่งหลายอย่าง gengraiyang

versatility *n.* ความสามารถรอบตัว kwamsamadrobtua

verse *n.* โคลง klong

versed *a.* เชี่ยวชาญ chiawchan

versification *n.* การแต่งบทกลอน gantaengbodglon

versify *v.t.* ทำให้เป็นบทกวี tamhaipenbodgawi

version *n.* ฉบับ chabab

versus *prep.* ต่อสู้กับ tawsugab

vertical *a.* แนวตั้ง naewtang

verve *n.* ความมีชีวิตชีวา kwammichiwitchiwa

very *a.* มาก mak

vessel *n.* หลอดเลือด lawdleud

vest *n.* เสื้อกล้าม seuaglam

vest *v.t.* สวมเสื้อ suamseua

vestige *n.* ร่องรอย rongroy

vestment *n.* เสื้อคลุมของพระ seuaklumkongpra

veteran *n.* ทหารผ่านศึก tahanpanseuk

veteran *a.* มีประสบการณ์ miprasobgan

veterinary *a.* เกี่ยวกับสัตวแพทย์ giawbgabsatawapaed

veto *n.* การยับยั้ง ganyabyang

veto *v.t.* ยับยั้ง yabyang

vex *v.t.* ก่อกวน gawguan

vexation *n* ความหงุดหงิด kwam-ngud-ngid

via *prep.* โดยทาง doeytaeng

viable *a.* มีชีวิตอยู่ได้ michiwityudai

vial *n.* ขวดเล็ก kuadlek

vibrate *v.i.* สั่น san

vibration *n.* การสั่น gansan

vicar *n.* พระ pra

vicarious *a.* เป็นตัวแทน pentuataen

vice *n.* รอง rong

viceroy *n.* อุปราช u-parad

vice-versa *adv.* ในทางกลับกัน naitangglabgan

vicinity *n.* บริเวณใกล้เคียง boriwenglaikiang

vicious *a.* ชั่วร้าย chuarai

vicissitude *n.* การเปลี่ยนแปลง ganpliangplaeng

victim *n.* เหยื่อ yeua

victimize *v.t.* ทำให้เป็นเหยื่อ tamhaipenyeua

victor *n.* ผู้ชนะ puchana

victorious *a.* มีชัยชนะ michaichana

victory *n.* ชัยชนะ chaichana

victuals *n. pl* เสบียงอาหาร sabiang-a-han

vie *v.i.* แข่งขัน kaengkan

view *n.* ความเห็น kwamhen

view *v.t.* พิจารณา pijarana

vigil *n.* การเฝ้าระวัง ganfaorawang

vigilance *n.* การระแวดระวัง ganrawaedrawang

vigilant *a.* ระแวดระวัง rawaedwawang

vigorous *a.* แข็งแรง kaengraeng

vile *a.* เลวทราม lewsam

vilify *v.t.* ใส่ความ saikwam

villa *n.* บ้านพักตากอากาศ banpaktak-a-gad

village *n.* หมู่บ้าน muban

villager *n.* ชาวบ้าน chaoban

villain *n.* ตัวร้าย tuarai

vindicate *v.t.* แก้ต่าง gaitang

vindication *n.* การแก้ตัว gangaetua

vine *n.* ต้นองุ่น ton-a-ngun

vinegar *n.* น้ำส้มสายชู namsomsaichu

vintage *n.* เหล้าองุ่น lao-a-ngun

violate *v.t.* ฝ่าฝืน fafeun

violation *n.* การฝ่าฝืน ganfafeun

violence *n.* ความรุนแรง kwamrunraeng

violent *a.* รุนแรง roonraeng

violet *n.* สีม่วง simuang

violin *n.* ไวโอลิน violin

violinist *n.* นักไวโอลิน nakviolin

virgin *n.* พรหมจรรย์ promajan

virgin *n* หญิงพรหมจารี yingprommajari

virginity *n.* ความบริสุทธิ์ kwamborisut

virile *a.* มีลักษณะของเพศชาย milaksanakongpedchai

virility *n.* ความเป็นชาย kwampenchai

virtual *a* เสมือน sameuan

virtue *n.* คุณธรรม kunatam

virtuous *a.* เที่ยงธรรม tiangtam

virulence *n.* ความเป็นพิษ kwampenpit

virulent *a.* ร้ายแรง rairaeng

virus *n.* ไวรัส virus

visage *n.* ใบหน้า baina

visibility *n.* ความสามารถในการมองเห็น kwamsamadnaiganmonghen

visible *a.* มองเห็นได้ monghendai

vision *n.* การมองเห็น ganmonghen

visionary *a.* เพ้อฝัน peufan

visionary *n.* จินตนาการ jintanagan

visit *n.* การเยี่ยมเยียน ganyiamyian

visit *v.t.* เยี่ยม yiam

visitor *n.* นักท่องเที่ยว naktongtiaw
vista *n.* ความเห็น kwamhen
visual *a.* เกี่ยวกับสายตา giawgabsaita
visualize *v.t.* นึกภาพในใจ neukpabnaijai
vital *a.* สำคัญ samkan
vitality *n.* กำลังวังชา gamlangwangcha
vitalize *v.t.* ทำให้มีชีวิตชีวา
    tamhaimichiwitchiwa
vitamin *n.* วิตามิน vitamin
vitiate *v.t.* ทำให้เสีย tamhaisia
vivacious *a.* มีชีวิตชีวา michiwitchiwa
vivacity *n.* ความมีชีวิตชีวา
    kwammichiwitchiwa
viva-voce *adv.* โดยวาจา doeywaja
viva-voce *a* โดยวาจา doeywaja
viva-voce *n* การลงมติด้วยวิธีเปล่งเสียง
ganlongmatiduaywitiplengsiang
vivid *a.* ชัด chad
vixen *n.* หมาจิ้งจอกตัวเมีย
    majingjoktuamia
vocabulary *n.* คำศัพท์ kamsab
vocal *a.* เกี่ยวกับเสียง giawgadsiang
vocalist *n.* นักร้อง nakrong
vocation *n.* อาชีพ a-chib
vogue *n.* สมัยนิยม samainiyom
voice *n.* เสียง siang
voice *v.t.* ให้เสียง haisiang
void *a.* ที่เป็นโมฆะ tipenmoka
void *v.t.* ทำให้เป็นโมฆะ tamhaipenmoka
void *n.* ความว่างเปล่า kwamwangplao
volcanic *a.* เกี่ยวกับภูเขาไฟ
    giawgabpukaofai
volcano *n.* ภูเขาไฟ pukaofai
volition *n.* ความปรารถนา kwampratana
volley *n.* การระดมยิง ganradomying
volley *v.t* ระดมยิง radomying
volt *n.* โวลต์ volt
voltage *n.* แรงดันไฟฟ้า raengdanfaifa
volume *n.* ปริมาณ pariman
voluminous *a.* มากมาย makmai
voluntarily *adv.* โดยสมัครใจ
    doeysamakjai

voluntary *a.* โดยสมัครใจ doeysamakjai
volunteer *n.* การอาสาสมัคร gan-a-
    sasamak
volunteer *v.t.* อาสาสมัคร a-sasamak
voluptuary *n.* ผู้มีกิเลส pumigiled
voluptuous *a.* มีกิเลส migiled
vomit *v.t.* อาเจียน a-jian
vomit *n* การอาเจียน gan-a-jian
voracious *a.* ตะกละ tagla
votary *n.* ผู้อุทิศตัว pu-u-tidtua
vote *n.* การลงคะแนน ganlongkanaen
vote *v.i.* ลงคะแนน longkanaen
voter *n.* ผู้ลงคะแนน pulongkanaen
vouch *v.i.* รับรองคุณภาพ
    rabrongkunnapab
voucher *n.* ใบสำคัญจ่าย baisamkanjai
vouchsafe *v.t.* ยินยอม yinyom
vow *n.* คำสัญญา kamsanya
vow *v.t.* ให้คำสัญญา haikamsanya
vowel *n.* เสียงสระ siangsara
voyage *n.* การเดินทาง gandeuntang
voyage *v.i.* เดินทาง deuntang
voyager *n.* ผู้เดินทาง pudeuntang
vulgar *a.* หยาบคาย yabkai
vulgarity *n.* ความหยาบคาย kwamyabkai
vulnerable *a.* อ่อนแอ on-ae
vulture *n.* นกแร้ง nokraeng

W

wade *v.i.* เดินลุยน้ำ deunluinam
waddle *v.i.* เดินเตาะแตะ deuntawtae
waft *v.t.* ล่องลอย longloy
waft *n* ลมพัดเบาๆ lompadbaobao
wag *v.i.* แกว่ง gwaeng
wag *n* การแกว่ง gangwaeng
wage *v.t.* ว่าจ้าง wajang
wage *n.* ค่าจ้าง kajang
wager *n.* การพนัน ganpanan
wager *v.i.* พนัน panan
wagon *n.* ตู้สินค้ารถไฟ tusinkarodfai

wail *v.i.* ร้องไห้คร่ำครวญ ronghaikramkruan

wail *n* การร้องไห้คร่ำครวญ ganronghaikramkruan

wain *n.* การบุด้วยแผ่นไม้ ganbuduaypaenmai

waist *n.* เอว aew

waistband *n.* ผ้าคาดเอว pakad-aew

waistcoat *n.* เสื้อโค้ทสั้น seuakotsan

wait *v.i.* คอย koy

wait *n.* การรอคอย ganrawkoy

waiter *n.* พนักงานเสิร์ฟชาย panak-nganseubchai

waitress *n.* สาวเสิร์ฟ saoseub

waive *v.t.* สละสิทธิ์ salasit

wake *v.t.* ตื่นตัว teuntua

wake *n* การเฝ้าศพก่อนทำพิธีฝัง ganfaosobgontampitifang

wake *n* การตื่น ganteun

wakeful *a.* ที่ตื่นตัว titeuntua

walk *v.i.* เดิน deun

walk *n* การเดิน gandeun

wall *n.* กำแพง gampaeng

wall *v.t.* ก่อกำแพง gawgampaeng

wallet *n.* กระเป๋าสตางค์ grapaosatang

wallop *v.t.* เฆี่ยน kian

wallow *v.i.* เกลือกกลิ้ง gleuakgling

walnut *n.* วอลนัท walnut

walrus *n.* สิงโตทะเล singtotalay

wan *a.* ซีด sid

wand *n.* ไม้กายสิทธิ์ maigayasit

wander *v.i.* เดินเล่น deunlen

wane *v.i.* ลดลง lodlong

wane *n* การลดลง ganlodlong

want *v.t.* ต้องการ tonggan

want *n* ความต้องการ kwamtonggan

wanton *a.* ขาดความยับยั้ง kadkwamyabyang

war *n.* สงคราม songkram

war *v.i.* ทำสงคราม tamsongkram

warble *v.i.* ร้อง rong

warble *n* เสียงสั่นรัว siangsanrua

warbler *n.* นกกระจิบ nokgrajib

ward *n.* หอผู้ป่วย hawpupuay

ward *v.t.* ป้องกัน ponggan

warden *n.* พัศดี pasadi

warder *n.* ผู้คุม pukum

wardrobe *n.* เสื้อคลุม seuaklum

wardship *n.* การคุ้มกัน gankumgan

ware *n.* เครื่องปั้นดินเผา kreuangpandinpao

warehouse *v.t* โกดังสินค้า godangsinka

warfare *n.* การทำสงคราม gantamsongkram

warlike *a.* ชอบสงคราม chobsongkram

warm1 *a.* อบอุ่น ob-aun

warm *v.t.* ทำให้อบอุ่น tamhai-ob-aun

warmth *n.* ความอบอุ่น kwam-ob-aun

warn *v.t.* เตือน teuan

warning *n.* การเตือน ganteuan

warrant *n.* การประกัน ganpragan

warrant *v.t.* ประกัน pragan

warrantee *n.* ผู้ถูกรับรอง putookrabrong

warrantor *n.* ผู้รับรอง purabrong

warranty *n.* การรับรอง ganrabrong

warren *n.* โพรงกระต่าย pronggratai

warrior *n.* นักรบ nakrob

wart *n.* หูด hud

wary *a.* ระมัดระวัง ramadrawang

wash *v.t.* ซักล้าง saklang

wash *n* การซักล้าง gansaklang

washable *a.* ซักได้ sakdai

washer *n.* เครื่องซักผ้า kreuangsakpa

wasp *n.* ตัวต่อ tuataw

waspish *a.* เจ้าอารมณ์ jao-a-rom

wassail *n.* การดื่มอวยพร gandeum-auypon

wastage *n.* การสูญเสีย gansoonsia

waste *a.* ไร้ประโยชน์ raiprayod

waste *n.* ของเสีย kongsia

waste *v.t.* ทำลาย tamlai

wasteful *a.* ฟุ่มเฟือย fumfeuay

watch *v.t.* เฝ้าดู faodu

watch *n.* การเฝ้าดู ganfaodu

watchful *a.* เฝ้าระวัง faorawang

watchword *n.* รหัส rahad

water *n.* น้ำ nam

water *v.t.* รดน้ำ rodnam

waterfall *n.* น้ำตก namtok

water-melon *n.* แดงโม taengmo

waterproof *a.* กันน้ำได้ gannamdai

waterproof *n* การกันน้ำ gangannam

waterproof *v.t.* ทำให้กันน้ำ
tamhaigannam

watertight *a.* กันน้ำ gannam

watery *a.* เกี่ยวกับน้ำ giawgabnam

watt *n.* วัตต์ watt

wave *n.* คลื่น kleun

wave *v.t.* โบก bok

waver *v.i.* แกว่ง gwaeng

wax *n.* ขี้ผึ้ง kipeung

wax *v.t.* เคลือบด้วยขี้ผึ้ง
kleuabduaykipeung

way *n.* ทาง tang

wayfarer *n.* ผู้เดินทาง pudeuntang

waylay *v.t.* ดักโจมตี dakjomti

wayward *a.* เอาแต่ใจ aowtaejai

weak *a.* อ่อนแอ on-ae

weaken *v.t. & i* ทำให้อ่อนแอ tamhai-on-
ae

weakling *n.* ผู้ที่อ่อนแอ puti-on-ae

weakness *n.* ความอ่อนแอ kwam-on-ae

weal *n.* รอยเฆี่ยน roykian

wealth *n.* ความร่ำรวย kwamramruay

wealthy *a.* ร่ำรวย ramruay

wean *v.t.* หย่านม yanom

weapon *n.* อาวุธ a-wud

wear *v.t.* สวมใส่ suamsai

weary *a.* เมื่อยล้า meuayla

weary *v.t. & i* ทำให้เบื่อหน่าย
tamhaibeunai

weary *a.* อ่อนล้า onla

weary *v.t.* เบื่อหน่าย beuanai

weather *n* อากาศ a-gad

weather *v.t.* ทนต่อการเปลี่ยนแปลง
tontawganplianplang

weave *v.t.* ทอ taw

weaver *n.* ผู้ทอ putaw

web *n.* ใยแมงมุม yaimaengmoom

webby *a.* เป็นเส้นใย pensenyai

wed *v.t.* แต่งงาน taeng-ngan

wedding *n.* การแต่งงาน gantaeng-ngan

wedge *n.* ลิ่ม lim

wedge *v.t.* ตอกด้วยลิ่ม tokduaylim

wedlock *n.* การสมรส gansomrod

Wednesday *n.* วันพุธ wanput

weed *n.* วัชพืช wachapeud

weed *v.t.* กำจัดวัชพืช gamjadwachapeud

week *n.* สัปดาห์ sabda

weekly *a.* รายสัปดาห์ raisabda

weekly *adv.* รายสัปดาห์ raisabda

weekly *n.* นิตยสารรายสัปดาห์
nitayasanraisabda

weep *v.i.* ร้องไห้ ronghai

weevil *n.* ตัวด้วง tuaduang

weigh *v.t.* ชั่งน้ำหนัก changnamnak

weight *n.* น้ำหนัก namnak

weightage *n.* น้ำหนักตามอายุ namnaktam-
a-yu

weighty *a.* มีน้ำหนักมาก minamnakmak

weir *n.* ทำนบ tamnob

weird *a.* แปลก plaek

welcome *a.* เป็นที่ยอมรับ pentiyomrab

welcome *n* การต้อนรับ gantonrab

welcome *v.t* ยินดีต้อนรับ yinditonrab

weld *v.t.* เชื่อม cheuam

weld *n* การเชื่อม gancheuam

welfare *n.* สวัสดิการ sawatdigan

well *a.* ดี di

well *adv.* ดี di

well *n.* บ่อน้ำ bawnam

well *v.i.* ท่วมท้น tuamtoan

wellington *n.* เมืองเวลลิงตัน
meuangwellington

well-known *a.* เป็นที่รู้จักดี pentirujakdi

well-read *a.* อ่านหนังสือมาก an-
nangseumak

well-timed *a.* เหมาะกับเวลา mawgabwela

well-to-do *a.* ร่ำรวย ramruay

welt *n.* ตะเข็บ takeb

welter *n.* ความสับสน kwamsabson

wen *n.* เนื้องอกบนผิวหนัง neua-
ngokbonpewnang

wench *n.* โสเภณี sopeni

west *n.* ทิศตะวันตก tidtawantok

west *a.* ทางทิศตะวันตก tangtidtawantok

west *adv.* ทางทิศตะวันตก tangtidtawantok

westerly *a.* ตั้งอยู่ทางตะวันตก
tangyutangtawantok

westerly *adv.* เกี่ยวกับทิศตะวันตก
giawgabtidtawantok

western *a.* ทางทิศตะวันตก
tangtidtawantok

wet *a.* เปียก piak

wet *v.t.* ทำให้เปียก tamhaipiak

wetness *n.* ความเปียก kwampiak

whack *v.t.* ตีอย่างแรง tiyangraeng

whale *n.* ปลาวาฬ plawan

wharfage *n.* ค่าธรรมเนียมในการใช้ท่าเรือ
katamniamnaiganchaitareua

what *a.* อะไร a-rai

what *pron.* อะไร a-rai

what *interj.* อะไรนะ a-raina

whatever *pron.* อะไรก็ตาม a-raigawtam

wheat *n.* ข้าวสาลี kaosali

wheedle *v.t.* โน้มน้าว nomnow

wheel *n.* ล้อ law

wheel *v.t.* หมุน moon

whelm *v.t.* ท่วมท้น tuamtoan

whelp *n.* ลูกสัตว์ looksat

when *adv.* เมื่อ meua

when *conj.* ขณะที่ kanati

whence *adv.* จากที่ไหน jaktinai

whenever *adv. conj* เมื่อไรก็ตาม
meuraigawtam

where *adv.* ที่ไหน tinai

where *conj.* ในที่ซึ่ง naitiseung

whereabout *adv.* ที่ไหน tinai

whereas *conj.* ขณะที่ kanati

whereat *conj.* ที่ซึ่ง tisuang

wherein *adv.* ในที่นั้น naitinan

whereupon *conj.* ในทุกๆ ที่ naitooktookti

wherever *adv.* ไม่ว่าที่ไหนก็ตาม
maiwatinaigawtam

whet *v.t.* ลับให้คม labhaikom

whether *conj.* ไม่ว่าจะ maiwaja

which *pron.* สิ่งที่ singti

which *a* อันไหน an-nai

whichever *pron* ไม่ว่าอันไหนก็ตาม
maiwa-annaigawtam

whiff *n.* ร่อยรอย rongroy

while *n.* ชั่วขณะ chuakana

while *conj.* ขณะที่ kanati

while *v.t.* ทำให้เวลาผ่านไป
tamhaiwelapanpai

whim *n.* ความคิดเพ้อฝัน kwamkidpeufan

whimper *v.i.* ร้องคร่ำครวญ
rongkramkruan

whimsical *a.* แปลก plaek

whine *v.i.* ครวญคราง kruankrang

whine *n* การครวญคราง gankruankrang

whip *v.t.* หวด huad

whip *n.* แส้ sae

whipcord *n.* เชือกฟั่นcheuakfan

whir *n.* เสียงดังกระหึ่ม siangdanggraheum

whirl *n.i.* หมุน moon

whirl *n* การหมุนเวียน ganmoonwian

whirligig *n.* ม้าหมุน mamoon

whirlpool *n.* น้ำวน namwoan

whirlwind *n.* ลมหมุน lommoon

whisk *v.t.* ปัด pad

whisk *n* ไม้ขนไก่ maikongai

whisker *n.* หนวดเครา nuadkrao

whisky *n.* วิสกี้ whisky

whisper *v.t.* กระซิบ grasib

whisper *n* การกระซิบ gangrasib

whistle *v.i.* ผิวปาก pewpak

whistle *n* เสียงผิวปาก siangpewpak

white *a.* สีขาว sikao

white *n* สีขาว sikao

whiten *v.t.* ทำให้ขาว tamhaikao

whitewash *n.* การปิดบังข้อเท็จจริง
ganpidbangkawtedjing

whitewash *v.t.* ปิดบังข้อเท็จจริง
  pidbangkawtedjing

whither *adv.* ทางไหน tangnai

whitish *a.* ค่อนข้างขาว konkangkao

whittle *v.t.* เหลา lao

whiz *v.i.* ทำเสียงดัง tamsiangdang

who *pron.* ใคร krai

whoever *pron.* ใครก็ตาม kraigawtam

whole *a.* ทั้งหมด tangmod

whole *n* ทั้งหมด tangmod

whole-hearted *a.* เต็มใจ temjai

wholesale *n.* การขายส่ง gankaisong

wholesale *a* แบบขายส่ง baebkaisong

wholesale *adv.* โดยขายส่ง doeykaisong

wholesaler *n.* คนขายส่ง konkaisong

wholesome *a.* เป็นประโยชน์ penprayod

wholly *adv.* ทั้งหมด tangmod

whom *pron.* ใคร krai

whore *n.* โสเภณี sopeni

whose *pron.* ของใคร kongkrai

why *adv.* ทำไม tammai

wick *n.* ไส้ตะเกียง saitagiang

wicked *a.* ชั่วร้าย chuarai

wicker *n.* เครื่องจักรสาน kreuangjaksan

wicket *n.* ประตูเล็ก pratulek

wide *a.* กว้าง gwang

wide *adv.* กว้าง gwang

widen *v.t.* ทำให้กว้าง tamhaigwang

widespread *a.* แพร่หลาย praelai

widow *n.* แม่หม้าย maemai

widow *v.t.* เป็นหม้าย penmai

widower *n.* พ่อหม้าย pawmai

width *n.* ความกว้าง kwamgwang

wield *v.t.* จัดการ jadgan

wife *n.* ภรรยา panraya

wig *n.* ผมปลอม pomplom

wight *n.* สิ่งมีชีวิต singmichiwit

wigwam *n.* กระท่อมอินเดียนแดง
  gratomindiandaeng

wild *a.* ดุร้าย durai

wilderness *n.* ที่รกร้าง tirokrang

wile *n.* อุบาย u-bai

will *n.* ความตั้งใจ kwamtangjai

will *v.t.* ต้องการ tonggan

willing *a.* เต็มใจ temjai

willingness *n.* ความเต็มใจ kwamtemjai

willow *n.* ต้นหลิว tonlew

wily *a.* เจ้าเล่ห์ jaolay

wimble *n.* สว่าน sawan

wimple *n.* ผ้าโพกศีรษะสตรี papoksisasatri

win *v.t.* ชนะ chana

win *n* ชัยชนะ chaichana

wince *v.i.* สะดุ้ง sadung

winch *n.* เครื่องกว้าน kreuanggwan

wind *n.* ลม lom

wind *v.t.* ได้กลิ่น daiglin

wind *v.t.* คดเคี้ยว kodkiaw

windbag *n.* คนคุยโว konkuiwo

winder *n.* เครื่องม้วนด้าย kreuangmuandai

windlass *v.t.* เดินอ้อม deuan-om

windmill *n.* กังหันลม ganghanlom

window *n.* หน้าต่าง natang

windy *a.* ลมแรง lomraeng

wine *n.* ไวน์ wine

wing *n.* ปีก peek

wink *v.i.* ขยิบตา kayibta

wink *n* การขยิบตา gankayibta

winner *n.* ผู้ชนะ puchana

winnow *v.t.* เป่าออก pao-awk

winsome *a.* อย่างมีเสน่ห์ yangmisanay

winter *n.* ฤดูหนาว reudunao

winter *v.i* เก็บรักษาไว้ในช่วงฤดูหนาว
  gebraksawainaichuangreudunao

wintry *a.* เกี่ยวกับฤดูหนาว
  giawgabreudunao

wipe *v.t.* เช็ด ched

wipe *n.* การเช็ด ganched

wire *n.* สายไฟ saifai

wire *v.t.* ต่อสายไฟ tawsaifai

wireless *a.* ไร้สาย raisai

wireless *n* ระบบไร้สาย rabobraisai

wiring *n.* ระบบสายไฟ rabobsaifai

wisdom *n.* ปัญญา panya

wisdom-tooth *n.* ฟันกรามซี่สุดท้าย fungramsisudtai

wise *a.* ฉลาด chalad

wish *n.* ความปรารถนา kwampratana

wish *v.t.* ปรารถนา pratana

wishful *a.* ด้วยความปรารถนา duaykwampratana

wisp *n.* หนึ่งกำมือ neunggammeu

wistful *a.* ด้วยความโหยหา duaykwamhoyha

wit *n.* ปัญญา panya

witch *n.* แม่มด maemod

witchcraft *n.* เวทมนต์คาถา wedmonkata

witchery *n.* การใช้เวทมนต์คาถา ganchaiwedmonkata

with *prep.* ด้วย duay

withal *adv.* นอกจากนี้ nokjakni

withdraw *v.t.* ถอน tawn

withdrawal *n.* การถอน gantawn

withe *n.* กิ่งหวาย gingwai

wither *v.i.* เหี่ยวแห้ง heiwhaeng

withhold *v.t.* ระงับ ra-ngab

within *prep.* ภายใน painai

within *adv.* ภายใน painai

within *n.* ภายใน painai

without *prep.* โดยปราศจาก doeyprasajak

without *adv.* ปราศจาก prasajak

without *n* ปราศจาก prasajak

withstand *v.t.* ทนต่อ tontaw

witless *a.* โง่ ngo

witness *n.* พยาน payan

witness *v.i.* เป็นพยาน penpayan

witticism *n.* คำคม kamkom

witty *a.* ฉลาด chalad

wizard *n.* พ่อมด pawmod

wobble *v.i* โยก yok

woe *n.* ความเศร้า kwamsao

woebegone *a.* เต็มไปด้วยความเศร้า tempaiduaykwamsao

woeful *n.* เลวร้าย lewrai

wolf *n.* หมาป่า mapa

woman *n.* ผู้หญิง puying

womanhood *n.* ความเป็นผู้หญิง kwampenpuying

womanish *a.* เหมือนผู้หญิง meuanpuying

womanise *v.t.* ทำให้เป็นผู้หญิง tamhaipenpuying

womb *n.* มดลูก modlook

wonder *n* ความแปลกใจ kwamplaekjai

wonder *v.i.* แปลกใจ plaekjai

wonderful *a.* มหัศจรรย์ mahadsajan

wondrous *a.* มหัศจรรย์ mahadsajan

wont *a.* เคยชิน keuychin

wont *n* ความเคยชิน kwamkeuychin

wonted *a.* ปกติ pakati

woo *v.t.* แสวงหา saweangha

wood *n.* ไม้ mai

woods *n.* ป่าไม้ pamai

wooden *a.* ทำด้วยไม้ tamduaymai

woodland *n.* ป่าไม้ pamai

woof *n.* เนื้อผ้า neuapa

wool *n.* ขนสัตว์ konsat

woollen *a.* ทำด้วยขนสัตว์ tamduaykonsat

woollen *n* ผ้าขนสัตว์ pakonsat

word *n.* คำพูด kampud

word *v.t* พูด pud

wordy *a.* ใช้คำฟุ่มเฟือย chaikamfumfeuay

work *n.* งาน ngan

work *v.t.* ทำงาน tam-ngan

workable *a.* ทำงานได้ tam-ngandai

workaday *a.* ปกติ pagati

worker *n.* คนงาน kon-ngan

workman *n.* ช่างฝีมือ changfeemeu

workmanship *n.* ทักษะการทำงาน taksagantam-ngan

workshop *n.* โรงฝึกงาน rongfeuk-ngan

world *n.* โลก lok

worldling *n.* มนุษย์ปุถุชน manudputuchon

worldly *a.* เจนโลก jenlok

worm *n.* หนอน non

wormwood *n.* ไม้พุ่ม maipum

worn *a.* หมดแรง monraeng

worry *n.* ความกังวล kwamgangwon

worry *v.i.* กังวล gangwon

worsen *v.t.* ทำให้แย่ tamhaiyae

worship *n.* การสักการะ gansakgara

worship *v.t.* สักการะ sakgara

worshipper *n.* ผู้นับถือ punabteu

worst *n.* สิ่งที่แย่ที่สุด singtiyaetisud

worst *a* แย่ที่สุด yaetisud

worst *v.t.* ชนะ chana

worsted *n.* ด้ายขนสัตว์ duaykonsat

worth *n.* มูลค่า moonka

worth *a* มีค่า mika

worthless *a.* ไม่คู่ควร maikukuan

worthy *a.* คู่ควร kukuan

would-be *a.* อยากจะเป็น yakgapen

wound *n.* อาการบาดเจ็บ a-ganbadjeb

wound *v.t.* บาดเจ็บ badjeb

wrack *n.* ความหายนะ kwamhaiyana

wraith *n.* ผี pi

wrangle *v.i.* ทะเลาะ talaw

wrangle *n.* การทะเลาะ gantalaw

wrap *v.t.* ห่อ haw

wrap *n* การห่อ ganhaw

wrapper *n.* หีบห่อ hibhaw

wrath *n.* ความโกรธเคือง kwamgrodkreuang

wreath *n.* พวงหรีด puangrid

wreathe *v.t.* คล้องพวงมาลัย klongpuangmalai

wreck *n.* ซากเรือแตก sakreuataek

wreck *v.t.* ทำให้อับปาง tamhai-abpang

wreckage *n.* ซากปรักหักพัง sakparakhakpang

wrecker *n.* ผู้ทำลาย putamlai

wren *n.* นกชนิดหนึ่ง nokchanidneung

wrench *n.* ประแจ prajae

wrench *v.t.* บิด bid

wrest *v.t.* แย่งชิง yaengching

wrestle *v.i.* ปล้ำ plam

wrestler *n.* นักมวยปล้ำ nakmuayplam

wretch *n.* ผู้เคราะห์ร้าย pukrawrai

wretched *a.* เคราะห์ร้าย krawrai

wrick *n* การเคล็ดขัดยอก gankledkadyok

wriggle *v.i.* บิดตัว bidtua

wriggle *n* การบิดตัว ganbidtua

wring *v.t* บีบ bib

wrinkle *n.* รอยย่น royyon

wrinkle *v.t.* ทำให้ย่น tamhaiyon

wrist *n.* ข้อมือ kawmeu

writ *n.* หมายศาล maisan

write *v.t.* เขียน kian

writer *n.* นักเขียน nakkian

writhe *v.i.* บิด bid

wrong *a.* ผิด pid

wrong *adv.* ผิด pid

wrong *v.t.* ทำผิด tampid

wrongful *a.* ไม่ถูกต้อง maitooktong

wry *a.* เบี้ยว biaw

xerox *n.* การถ่ายสำเนา gantaisamnao

xerox *v.t.* ถ่ายสำเนา taisamnao

Xmas *n.* คริสต์มาส krisamat

x-ray *n.* การถ่ายภาพด้วยรังสีเอ็กซ์ gantaipabduayrangsi-x

x-ray *a.* เกี่ยวกับการเอ็กซ์เรย์ giawgabgan-x-ray

x-ray *v.t.* ถ่ายภาพด้วยรังสีเอ็กซ์ taipabduayrangsi-x

xylophagous *a.* กินเนื้อไม้ ginneuamai

xylophilous *a.* เติบโตในเนื้อไม้ teubtonaineuamai

xylophone *n.* ระนาด ranad

yacht *n.* เรือใบ reuabai

yacht *v.i* แล่นเรือใบ laenreuabai

yak *n.* วัวป่า wuapa
yap *v.i.* เห่า hao
yap *n* การเห่า ganhao
yard *n.* หลา la
yarn *n.* เส้นด้าย sendai
yawn *v.i.* หาว hao
yawn *n.* การหาว ganhao
year *n.* ปีละครั้ง pilakrang
yearly *a.* รายปี raipi
yearly *adv.* ปีละครั้ง pirakrang
yearn *v.i.* ปรารถนา pratana
yearning *n.* ความปรารถนา kwampratana
yeast *n.* ยีสต์ yeast
yell *v.i.* ตะโกน tagoan
yell *n* การตะโกน gantagoan
yellow *a.* สีเหลือง sileuang
yellow *n* สีเหลือง sileuang
yellow *v.t.* ระบายสีเหลือง rabaisileaung
yellowish *a.* ค่อนข้างเหลือง
    konkangleuang
Yen *n.* เงินเยน ngeun-yen
yeoman *n.* ชาวนาเจ้าของที่ดิน
    chaonajaokongtidin
yes *adv.* ใช่ chai
yesterday *n.* เมื่อวานนี้ meuwanni
yesterday *adv.* เมื่อวานนี้ meuwanni
yet *adv.* ยังคง yangkong
yet *conj.* แม้กระนั้น maegranan
yield *v.t.* ยอม yom
yield *n* การยินยอม ganyinyom
yoke *n.* แอก aek
yoke *v.t.* ใส่แอก sai-aek
yolk *n.* ไข่แดง kaideang
yonder *a.* ทางโน้น tangnoan
yonder *adv.* ทางโน้น tangnoan
young *a.* อ่อนวัย on-wai
young *n* คนหนุ่มสาว konnumsao
youngster *n.* คนหนุ่มสาว konnumsao
youth *n.* เยาวชน yaowachon
youthful *a.* หนุ่มสาว noomsao

Z

zany *a.* ตลกโง่ๆ talok-ngo-ngo
zeal *n.* ความกระตือรือร้น
    kwamgrateureuron
zealot *n.* ผู้กระตือรือร้น pugrateureuron
zealous *a.* กระตือรือร้น grateureuron
zebra *n.* ม้าลาย malai
zenith *n.* จุดสูงสุด judsoongsud
zephyr *n.* ลมตะวันตก lomtawantok
zero *n.* ศูนย์ soon
zest *n.* ความสนุกสนาน kwamsanooksanan
zigzag *n.* รูปฟันปลา roobfanpla
zigzag *a.* เป็นรูปฟันปลา penroobfanpla
zigzag *v.i.* เคลื่อนที่เป็นรูปฟันปลา
    kleuantipenroobfanpla
zinc *n.* สังกะสี sanggasi
zip *n.* ซิป zip
zip *v.t.* รูดซิป rudzip
zodiac *n* จักรราศี jakrasi
zonal *a.* เกี่ยวกับเขต giawgabket
zone *n.* เขต ket
zoo *n.* สวนสัตว์ suansat
zoological *a.* เกี่ยวกับสัตว์ giawgabsat
zoologist *n.* นักสัตววิทยา
    naksattawawitaya
zoology *n.* สัตววิทยา sattawawitaya
zoom *n.* การขยายภาพ gankayaipab
zoom *v.i.* ขยายภาพ kayaipab

THAI-ENGLISH

A

ab *v.i.* แอบ sneak
ab *a.* อับ stale
abdad *v.i.* อาบแดด bask
ab-dad *v.t.* อาบแดด sun
ab-du *v.i.* แอบดู peep
abnam *v. t* อาบน้ำ bathe
ab-nam *v.t.* อาบน้ำ shower
ab-pamongkon *a.* อัปมงคล inauspicious
a-chib *n.* อาชีพ career
a-chib *n.* อาชีพ occupation
a-chib *n.* อาชีพ vocation
a-chibgawsang *n.* อาชีพก่อสร้าง masonry
a-chip *n.* อาชีพ profession
acre *n.* เอเคอร์ acre
ad-a-gadkao *v.t.* อัดอากาศเข้า aerify
ad-fai *v. t* อัดไฟ electrify
adja *v* อาจจะ may
a-did *n.* อดีต past
ae-a *a.* เอะอะ uproarious
aek *n.* แอก yoke
aeng-nam *n.* แอ่งน้ำ puddle
aew *n.* เอว waist
a-gad *n* อากาศ air
a-gad *n* อากาศ weather
a-gan *n.* อาการ symptom
a-gan-a-hanmaiyoi *n.*
อาการอาหารไม่ย่อย indigestion
a-gan-ai *n.* อาการไอ cough
a-ganbadjeb *n.* อาการบาดเจ็บ wound
a-ganjaisan *n.* อาการใจสั่น palpitation
a-ganjebplab *n.* อาการเจ็บปลาบ pang
a-gankan *n.* อาการคัน itch
a-gankled *n.* อาการเคล็ด sprain
a-gankleunsai *n.* อาการคลื่นไส้ nausea
a-gan-na-daeng *n* อาการหน้าแดง blush
a-ganpae *n.* อาการแพ้ allergy
a-ganpuad *n.* อาการปวด ache
a-ganpuadbuam *n* อาการปวดบวม blain

a-ganpuadglamneua *n.*
อาการปวดกล้ามเนื้อ myalgia
a-ganpuadgreng *n.* อาการปวดเกร็ง throe
a-ganpuay *n.* อาการป่วย ailment
a-ganpuay *n.* อาการป่วย malaise
a-ganranam *n.* อาการนาม gerund
a-gansalob *n* อาการสลบ anaesthesia
a-gansan *n* อาการสั่น ague
a-gansanglua *n* อาการสั่นกลัว shudder
a-gansaohodhu *n* อาการเศร้าหดหู่
depression
a-gantongruang *n* อาการท้องร่วง
diarrhoea
a-han *n.* อาหาร aliment
a-han *n.* อาหาร cuisine
a-han *n* อาหาร feed
a-han *n* อาหาร food
a-hanbamrungranggai *n.*
อาหารบำรุงร่างกาย nourishment
a-hanbod *n.* อาหารบด mush
a-hanchao *n* อาหารเช้า breakfast
a-hanlangwan *n.* อาหารกลางวัน lunch
a-hanlaekreuangdeum *n*
อาหารและเครื่องดื่ม batch
a-hanlak *n.* อาหารหลัก staple
a-hanleudrod *n.* อาหารเลิศรส dainty
a-hanriaknamyoi *n* อาหารเรียกน้ำย่อย
appetizer
a-han-sat *n* อาหารสัตว์ fodder
a-hantinatan *n* อาหารที่น่าทาน treat
a-hanwang *n.* อาหารว่าง snack
a-hanyen *n* อาหารเย็น dinner
a-hanyen *n.* อาหารเย็น supper
a-hiwa *n.* อหิวาต์ cholera
ai *v. i.* ไอ cough
ainam *n.* ไอน้ำ vapour
ai-nam *n* ไอน้ำ steam
ai-yagan *n.* อัยการ prosecutor
a-jan *n.* อาจารย์ professor
a-ganhob *n.* อาการหอบ pant
a-jian *v.t.* อาเจียน vomit
a-kan *n* อาคาร building

a-kan *n* อาคาร edifice
a-kati *n* อคติ bias
aksonbraille *n* อักษรเบรล braille
aksonraekkongcheu *n.* อักษรแรกของชื่อ initial
aksonyaw *n.* อักษรย่อ monogram
aktewaniyom *n.* เอกเทวนิยม monotheism
album *n.* อัลบั้ม album
alcohol *n* อัลกอฮอล์ alcohol
almond *n.* อัลมอนด์ almond
aluminium *n.* อัลลูมิเนียม aluminium
amen *interj.* อาเมน amen
ammad *n.* อำนาจ power
ammapat *n.* อัมพาต palsy
ammapat *n.* อัมพาต paralysis
amnad *n.* อำนาจ might
am-nadmaelek *n.* อำนาจแม่เหล็ก magnetism
amnadpised *n.* อำนาจพิเศษ prerogative
amnadsoongsudnaiganpokkrong *n.* อำนาจสูงสุดในการปกครอง sovereignty
amp *n* แอมป์ ampere
an *v.t.* อ่าน peruse
an *v.t.* อ่าน read
a-najak *n* อาณาจักร empire
a-najak *n.* อาณาจักร kingdom
a-najak *n.* อาณาจักร realm
a-naket *n* อาณาเขต domain
a-naket *n.* อาณาเขต territory
a-nakod *n* อนาคต future
a-nanikom *n* อาณานิคม colony
anatipatai *n* อนาธิปไตย anarchy
an-awkdai *a.* อ่านออกได้ legible
ang *n.* อ่าง basin
ang *n* อ่าง sink
ang-gebnam *n.* อ่างเก็บน้ำ rservoir
ang-glid *n* อังกฤษ albion
ang-ing *v.t.* อ้างอิง adduce
ang-ingteung *a.* อ้างอิงถึง allusive
angteung *v. t* อ้างถึง cite
angteung *v.t.* อ้างถึง mention
angteung *v.t.* อ้างถึง quote

ang-teung *v.t.* อ้างถึง refer
a-ngun *n.* องุ่น grape
a-ngunhaeng *n.* องุ่นแห้ง currant
angwa *v.t.* อ้างว่า purport
a-nidja *interj.* อนิจจา alas
anma *n.* อานม้า saddle
an-nai *a* อันไหน which
an-nangseumak *a.* อ่านหนังสือมาก well-read
an-ngai *adv.* อ่านง่าย legibly
an-raek *pron* อันแรก former
antapan *n.* อันธพาล rogue
an-tapan *n* อันธพาล bully
an-tapan *n.* อันธพาล hooligan
antarai *a* อันตราย fatal
antarai *v.t* อันตราย hazard
antarai *a.* อันตราย lethal
antarai *a.* อันตราย venturesome
antarai *a.* อันตราย venturous
an-tarai *a* อันตราย dangerous
a-nuban *n.* อนุบาล kindergarten ;
a-nugrom *n.* อนุกรม series
a-numad *v.t.* อนุมัติ approve
a-numan *v.t.* อนุมาน infer
a-nupak *a.* อนุภาค particle
a-nusan *n* อนุสาร booklet
a-nuyad *v.t.* อนุญาต allow
a-nuyad *v.t.* อนุญาต license
a-nuyad *v.t.* อนุญาต permit
a-nuyatotulagan *n.* อนุญาโตตุลาการ arbitration
an-yak *a.* อ่านยาก illegible
an-yamani *n* อัญมณี gem
an-yamani *n.* อัญมณี jewel
aob *v.t.* อบ bake
ao-chana *v. t.* เอาชนะ defeat
aow *n.* อ่าว gulf
aow *v.t* เอา take
aow-chana *v.t.* เอาชนะ outdo
aow-chana *v.t.* เอาชนะ overcome
aow-chana *v.t.* เอาชนะ overpower
aow-chana *v.t.* เอาชนะ transcend

aowjaisai *v.t.* เอาใจใส่ heed
aow-jaisai *v.t.* เอาใจใส่ regard
aowkeun *v.t.* เอาคืน recoup
aowtaejai *a.* เอาแต่ใจ wayward
a-pakkang *adv.,* อ้าปากค้าง agape
a-pakkang *v.i.* อ้าปากค้าง gape
a-pak-kang *v.i* อ้าปากค้าง gasp
apartment *n.* อพาร์ตเมนต์ apartment
apipradya *n.* อภิปรัชญา metaphysics
a-pitansab *n.* อภิธานศัพท์ glossary
apple *n.* แอปเปิ้ล apple
apricot *n.* แอปริคอต apricot
a-rai *n.* อะไหล่ spare
a-rai *a.* อะไร what
a-rai *pron.* อะไร what
a-raigawtam *pron.* อะไรก็ตาม whatever
a-raina *interj.* อะไรนะ what
a-lawad *adv.* อาละวาด amuck
a-rayatam *n.* อารยธรรม civilization
a-roi *a.* อร่อย dainty
a-rom *n* อารมณ์ emotion
a-rom *n.* อารมณ์ mood
a-rom *n.* อารมณ์ sentiment
a-rom *n.* อารมณ์ temper
a-romkan *n.* อารมณ์ขัน humour
a-rom-on-wai *a.* อารมณ์อ่อนไหว
 sentimental
a-rompruanprae *n.* อารมณ์ปรวนแปร
 temperament
a-roy *a* อร่อย delicious
a-roy *a.* อร่อย palatable
a-rumpabod *n.* อารัมบท prologue
a-sai *v. i* อาศัย dwell
a-sai *v.t.* อาศัย people
a-sai *v.i.* อาศัย reside
a-sai *v.i.* อาศัย resort
a-saiyu *v.t.* อาศัยอยู่ populate
asajan *n* อัฒจรรย์ amphitheatre
a-sasamak *v.t.* อาสาสมัคร volunteer
asawin *n.* อัศวิน knight
a-som *n.* อาศรม hermitage
a-tewaniyom *n* อเทวนิยม atheism

a-tibai *v. t.* อธิบาย explain
a-tibaimaidai *a.* อธิบายไม่ได้
 inexplicable
a-tibaipeumteum *v. t* อธิบายเพิ่มเติม
 elaborate
atichoke *n.* อาติโช๊ค artichoke
a-tom *n.* อะตอม atom
atta *n* อัตตา ego
attachiwaprawat *n.* อัตชีวประวัติ
 autobiography
attachiwaprawat *v.t* อัติชีวประวัติ
 biography
attanomat *a.* อัตโนมัติ automatic
attaroyla *n.* อัตราร้อยละ percentage
atta-tipatai *n* อัตาธิปไตย autocracy
auan *a* อ้วน fat
aud-a-han *v.i.* อดอาหาร starve
audton *v.t.* อดทน stomach
auk *n* อก bosom
auk-siang *v.t* ออกเสียง accent
aun *a.* อุ่น lukewarm
aunhapum *n.* อุณหภูมิ temperature
auy-ing *v.i.* อ้อยอิ่ง linger
a-waiyawa *n.* อวัยวะ organ
awaiyawapedchai *n.* อวัยวะเพศชาย penis
awk *v.i.* ออก issue
awk-a-gad *v.t.* ออกอากาศ telecast
awkbaeb *v. t.* ออกแบบ design
awk-dawk *v.i* ออกดอก blossom
awk-gamlanggai *v. t* ออกกำลัง exercise
awkgodmai *v. t* ออกกฎหมาย enact
awkgodmai *v.i.* ออกกฎหมาย legislate
awkpai *adv.* ออกไป out
awksiang *v.t.* ออกเสียง pronounce
awksiangpayanraeksam *v.*
 ออกเสียงพยางค์แรกซ้ำ alliterate
awksiangtamraifan *v.*
 ออกเสียงตามไรฟัน assibilate
awl-chanamaidai *a.* เอาชนะไม่ได้
 invincible
a-wud *n.* อาวุธ weapon
a-wuso *a.* อาวุโส senior

a-wut *n.* อาวุธ arm
a-wut *n.* อาวุธ munitions
a-yu *n.* อายุ age
a-nusawari *n.* อนุสาวรีย์ monument

B

ba *a.* บ้า lunatic
bab *n.* บาป sin
backhand *n.* แบกแฮนด์ backhand
bacon *n.* เบคอน bacon
bacteria *n.* แบคทีเรีย bacteria
badger *n.* แบดเจอร์ badger
badjeb *v.t.* บาดเจ็บ hurt
badjeb *v.t.* บาดเจ็บ injure
badjeb *v.t.* บาดเจ็บ wound
badluang *n.* บาทหลวง parson
badminton *n.* แบดมินตัน badminton
badpan *n* บัตรผ่าน pass
baeb *n.* แบบ modality
baebjaochai *a.* แบบเจ้าชาย princely
baebkaisong *a* แบบขายส่ง wholesale
baebpaen *n.* แบบแผน pattern
baebpaentaitua *n.* แบบแผนตายตัว
    stereotype
baebsobtam *n.* แบบสอบถาม
    questionnaire
baebyang *n.* แบบอย่าง personification
baedyang *a.* แบบอย่าง typical
baeng *v. t* แบ่ง divide
baeng *v.t.* แบ่ง partition
baeng *v.t.* แบ่ง portion
baeng *v.t.* แบ่ง sunder
baengkreung *v. t* แบ่งครึ่ง bisect
baengkreung *v.t.* แบ่งครึ่ง halve
baengpan *v.t.* แบ่งปัน share
baengradab *v.t* แบ่งระดับ grade
baengsan *v.t.* แบ่งสรร allot
baengyaek *v. t.* แบ่งแยก discriminate
baengyaekmaidai *a.* แบ่งแยกไม่ได้
    indivisible

bai *a.* ใบ้ mute
bai-a-nuyad *n.* ใบอนุญาต licence
bai-a-nuyad *n.* ใบอนุญาต permit
baigraprao *n.* ใบกระเพรา basil
baimai *n* ใบไม้ foliage
baimai *n.* ใบไม้ leaf
baimid *n.* ใบมีด blade
baina *n.* ใบหน้า visage
baiplew *n.* ใบปลิว handbill
baiplew *n.* ใบปลิว leaflet
baiplu *n* ใบพลู betel
baisamkanjai *n.* ใบสำคัญจ่าย voucher
baised *n.* ใบเสร็จ invoice
baised *n.* ใบเสร็จ receipt
bai-sed *n.* ใบเสร็จ chit
ball *n.* บอล ball
ballet *sn.* บัลเลต์ ballet
ballon *n.* บอลลูน balloon
bamnan *n.* บ่านาญ pension
ban *n.* บ้าน home
ban *n* บ้าน house
banchi *n.* บัญชี account
bandai *n.* บันได ladder
bandai *n.* บันได stair
bandanjai *v.t.* บันดาลใจ inspire
bang *adv.* บ้าง any
bang *a* บาง flimsy
bang *a.* บาง subtle
bangalow *n* บังกาโล bungalow
bang-eun *a.* บังเอิญ incidental
banghaeng *adv.* บางแห่ง somewhere
banghian *n* บังเหียน bridle
banghian *n.* บังเหียน harness
bangkab *v. t* บังคับ compel
bangkab *v.t* บังคับ force
bangkab *v.t.* บังคับ oblige
bangkon *pron.* บางคน somebody
bangkon *n.* บางคน somebody
bangkon *pron.* บางคน someone
bangkrang *adv.* บางครั้ง occasionally
bangkrang *adv.* บางครั้ง sometimes
bangled *n.* บานเกล็ด shutter

banglewa *adv.* บางเวลา sometime
bangsing *pron.* บางสิ่ง something
bangsuan *pron.* บางส่วน some
bangta *a.* บางตา sparse
bangti *adv.* บางที perhaps
bangti *adv.* บางที probably
bangyang *adv.* บางอย่าง something
banjo *n.* แบนโจ banjo
banjrajok *n.* บานกระจก pane
banju *v.t.* บรรจุ contain
banju *v.t.* บรรจุ load
banju *v.t.* บรรจุ pack
banjuheephaw *v.t.* บรรจุหีบห่อ bale
banjukrapong *v. t.* บรรจุกระป๋อง can
banjupan *n.* บรรจุภัณฑ์ bale
banlang *n.* บัลลังก์ throne
banlengnam *v.t.* บรรเลงนำ prelude
banlupon *v.t.* บรรลุผล attain
bannanugrom *n* บรรณานุกรม bibliography
bannarak *n.* บรรณารักษ์ librarian
bannarak *n* บรรณารักษ์ bibliographer
bannatigan *n* บรรณาธิการ editor
banpaburud *n.* บรรพบุรุษ ancestor
banpaburud *n* บรรพบุรุษ forefather
banpaburud *n.* บรรพบุรุษ predecessor
banpaktak-a-gad *n.* บ้านพักตากอากาศ villa
bansunak *n.* บ้านสุนัข kennel
bantadtan *n.* บรรทัดฐาน motif
bantadtan *n.* บรรทัดฐาน norm
bantao *v.t.* บรรเทา abate
bantao *v.t.* บรรเทา allay
bantao *v.t.* บรรเทา alleviate
bantao *v.t.* บรรเทา mitigate
bantao *v.t.* บรรเทา moderate
bantao *v.t.* บรรเทา slake
bantao *v.t.* บรรเทา soothe
bantao *v.t.* บรรเทา meliorate
banteuk *n.* บันทึก memoir
banteuk *v.t.* บันทึก record
banteuk *n.* บันทึก tally

banteukkwamjam *n* บันทึกความจำ memorandum
banteuksiang *v.t* บันทึกเสียง tape
bantook *v. t.* บรรทุก carry
bantookgeunpigad *v.t.* บรรทุกเกินพิกัด overload
banyagad *n.* บรรยากาศ atmosphere
banyagad *n.* บรรยากาศ climate
banyai *v. t* บรรยาย describe
banyai *v* บรรยาย lecture
banyai *v.t.* บรรยาย narrate
bao *adv.* เบา lightly
bariwenpainaipratet *a.* บริเวณภายในประเทศ inland
barloynam *n.* บาร์ลอยน้ำ coper
barometer *n* บาโรมิเตอร์ barometer
batlongkanan *n* บัตรลงคะแนน ballot
baw *n* เบาะ cushion
baw *n.* เบาะ pad
bawk *v.t.* บอก tell
bawkpad *v.t.* บอกปัด rebuff
bawnam *n.* บ่อน้ำ pond
bawnam *n.* บ่อน้ำ well
bawpaknamsia *n.* บ่อพักน้ำเสีย cesspool
bawsae *n* เบาะแส clue
beaver *n* บีเวอร์ beaver
bedtaled *a.* เบ็ดเตล็ด miscellaneous
beeb *v.t.* บีบ squeeze
beeb-ad *v. t.* บีบอัด compress
beebkaw *v.t.* บีบคอ strangle
beer *n* เบียร์ beer
benkwamsonjai *v.t. & i.* เบนความสนใจ deflect
bensaita *v.t.* เบนสายตา avert
bengban *v.i.* เบ่งบาน bloom
beua *v. t* เบื่อ bore
beuanai *v.t.* เบื่อหน่าย weary
beuangton *a* เบื้องต้น elementary
beuangton *adv.* เบื้องต้น prima facie
beukban *a.* เบิกบาน mellow
beung *n.* บึง marsh
beungteung *a.* บึ้งตึง sullen

beungton *a.* เบื้องต้น initial
beungton *a.* เบื้องต้น primary
biangbein *v. i* เบี่ยงเบน deviate
biaw *a.* เบี้ยว wry
bib *v.t* บีบ wring
bib-ad *v. t* บีบอัด crush
bible *n* ไบเบิ้ล bible
bid *v.t.* บิด twist
bid *v.t.* บิด wrench
bid *v.i.* บิด writhe
bidbeuan *v. t* บิดเบือน distort
bid-ngaw *a.* บิดงอ tortuous
bidtua *v.i.* บิดตัว wriggle
biengben *v. t* เบี่ยงเบน divert
bill *n* บิล bill
bin *v.i* บิน fly
bin *v.t.* บิน plane
bin *v.i.* บิน soar
binsung *adj* บินสูง altivalent
biscuit *n* บิสกิต biscuit
bishop *n* บิชอป bishop
bo *n.* โบว์ ribbon
bobbang *a.* บอบบาง slimy
bod *n.* โบสถ์ cathedral
bod *n.* บท chapter
bod *n.* โบสถ์ church
bod *v.i.* บด grind
bod *v.t* บด mash
bod *n.* โบสถ์ minster
bod *v.t.* บด pound
bod *v.t.* บด squash
bodbangrasami *v.t.* บดบังรัศมี outshine
bodbannatigan *n* บทบรรณาธิการ editorial
bodbat *n.* บทบาท role
bodgawi *n.* บทกวี lyric
bodgawi *n.* บทกวี ode
bodgawiwai-a-lai *n* บทกวีไว้อาลัย elegy
bodgodmai *n.* บทกฎหมาย purview
bodkadyaw *n* บทคัดย่อ abstract
bodkadyaw *n.* บทคัดย่อ precis
bodkwam *n.* บทความ monograph

bodkwam *n.* บทความ treatise
bodpenpong *v.t.* บดเป็นผง powder
bodpuddiaw *n.* บทพูดเดี่ยว monologue
bodrian *n.* บทเรียน lesson
bodsontana *n* บทสนทนา dialogue
boey *v. t.* โบย cane
boey *v.t* โบย flog
bok *v.t.* โบก wave
bokbai *v.i* บอกใบ้ hint
bokpan *v.t.* บอกผ่าน jack
bokpennai *v.t.* บอกเป็นนัย imply
bokpoon *v.t.* โบกปูน mortar
bon *v. i* บ่น bleat
bon *v.i.* บ่น grumble
bon *v.i.* บ่น mutter
bon *prep.* บน on
bon *prep* บน upon
bon-a-gad *a.* บนอากาศ airy
bongchi *v. i* บ่งชี้ denote
bongchi *v.t.* บ่งชี้ indicate
bonpeumpum *n.* บ่นพึมพำ murmur
bontamrai *v.t.* บ่อนทำลาย undermine
bontiang *adv.* บนเตียง abed
bonus *n* โบนัส bonus
bonyanpahana *n* บนยานพาหนะ abode
boran *a.* โบราณ ancient
boran *a.* โบราณ archaic
boribod *n* บริบท context
borihan *v.t.* บริหาร administer
borijak *v. t* บริจาค contribute
borijak *v. t* บริจาค donate
borijak *v. t* บริจาค endow
boripok *v. t* บริโภค consume
borisat *n.* บริษัท company
borisat *n* บริษัท corporation
borisat *n* บริษัท firm
borisud *a.* บริสุทธิ์ chaste
borisud *a* บริสุทธิ์ pure
boriwenglaikiang *n.* บริเวณใกล้เคียง vicinity
boriwenkangkiang *n.* บริเวณข้างเคียง neighbourhood

botgawi *n.* บทกวี poetry
bot-kwam *n* บทความ article
botsongtai *n* บทส่งท้าย epilogue
boy *adv.* บ่อย oft
boy *adv.* บ่อย often
brandy *n* บรั่นดี brandy
broccoli *n.* บร็อคโคลี่ broccoli
bu *v.t.* บุ pad
buab *n.* บวบ gourd
buam *v.i.* บวม swell
bucha *v. t* บูชา enshrine
bukbeuk *v.t.* บุกเบิก pioneer
bukkaliklaksana *n.* บุคลิกลักษณะ
  character
bukkaliklaksana *n.* บุคลิกลักษณะ
  personality
bukkon *n.* บุคคล person
bukkonchenni *pron.* บุคคลเช่นนี้ such
bukkonsamkan *n.* บุคคลสำคัญ
  personage
bukkontammada *n* บุคคลธรรมดา carl
bukruk *v.t.* บุกรุก intrude
bukruk *v.t.* บุกรุก invade
bukruk *v.t* บุกรุก overrun
buntao *v.t.* บรรเทา assuage
buri *n* บุหรี่ cheroot
buri *n.* บุหรี่ cigarette
burudpraisani *n.* บุรุษไปรษณีย์ postman
busarakam *n.* บุษราคัม topaz
bypass *n* บายพาส bypass

cabaret *n.* คาบาเร่ย์ cabaret
cadmium *n* แคดเมียม cadmium
cake *n.* เค้ก cake
calcium *n* แคลเซียม calcium
calorie *n.* แคลอรี่ calorie
camp *n.* แคมป์ camp
carbon *n.* คาร์บอน carbon
card *n.* การ์ด card

carrot *n.* แครอท carrot
cartoon *n.* การ์ตูน cartoon
cashier *n.* แคชเชียร์ cashier
castrol *adj* คาสตรอล castrol
catalogue *n.* แคตาล็อก catalogue
catholic *a.* แคธอลิก catholic
cent *n* เซนต์ cent
cha *adv* ช้า behind
cha *a.* ชา numb
cha *a* ช้า slow
cha *n* ชา tea
chab *v. t.* ฉาบ cement
chab *v.t.* ฉาบ plaster
chabab *n.* ฉบับ version
chababpim *n* ฉบับพิมพ์ edition
chababyaw *n.* ฉบับย่อ digest
chabdeuytong *a.* ฉาบด้วยทอง gilt
chad *n* ชาด cinnabar
chad *a.* ชัด vivid
chadjaeng *a* ชัดแจ้ง flagrant
chadjen *a* ชัดเจน clear
chadjen *a.* ชัดเจน conspicuous
chadjen *a.* ชัดเจน evident
chadjen *a.* ชัดเจน explicit
chadjen *a.* ชัดเจน obvious
chadjen *a.* ชัดเจน overt
chadjen *a.* ชัดเจน palpable
chad-jen *a.* ชัดเจน articulate
chae *v.t.* แช่ infuse
chaeng *v. t* แช่ง curse
chaeyen *v.t.* แช่เย็น refrigerate
chai *v.t.* ใช้ spend
chai *v.t.* ใช้ use
chai *adv.* ใช่ yes
chai-ak-son-songtua *adj* ใช้อักษรสองตัว
  biliteral
chaichana *n* ชัยชนะ conquest
chaichana *n.* ชัยชนะ triumph
chaichana *n.* ชัยชนะ victory
chaichana *n* ชัยชนะ win
chaidaen *n.* ชายแดน frontier
chaidaijing *a.* ใช้ได้จริง practical

chaifang *n* ชายฝั่ง coast
chaifang *a.* ชายฝั่ง littoral
chaifang *n.* ชายฝั่ง shore
chaifang *n* ชายฝั่ง strand
chaihad *n* ชายหาด beach
chaijaifumfeuay *v.t.* ใช้จ่ายฟุ่มเฟือย lavish
chaijaisuruisurai *v.t.* ใช้จ่ายสุรุ่ยสุร่าย squander
chaikamfumfeuay *a.* ใช้คำฟุ่มเฟือย verbose
chaikamfumfeuay *a.* ใช้คำฟุ่มเฟือย wordy
chaikeun *v.t.* ใช้คืน refund
chailayliam *v.t.* ใช้เล่ห์เหลี่ยม trick
chaimaidai *a.* ใช้ไม่ได้ inapplicable
chainaitangtipid *v.t.* ใช้ในทางที่ผิด misuse
chaingan *adv.* เช่นกัน either
chaipeuakwam-ngam *a.* ใช้เพื่อความงาม cosmetic
chaiprayod *v.t.* ใช้ประโยชน์ avail
chaiprayod *v.t.* ใช้ประโยชน์ utilize
chaiprayoddai *a* ใช้ประโยชน์ได้ available
chairaeng-ngan *v.i.* ใช้แรงงาน labour
chairangsi *v.i.* ฉายรังสี irradiate
chaisaeng *v.t.* ฉายแสง radiate
chaisiangsampad *v.i.* ใช้เสียงสัมผัส rhyme
chaisoy *v.t.* ใช้สอย ply
chaitimikamprapreudmaidi *n* ชายที่มีความประพฤติไม่ดี cad
chaiyaraksa *v.t.* ใช้ยารักษา physic
chak *n.* ฉาก partition
chak-awkjakfak *v.t.* ชักออกจากฝัก unsheathe
chakcha *v.i.* ชักช้า dawdle
chakchuan *v. t* ชักชวน convince
chakchuan *v.t.* ชักชวน induce
chakchuan *v.t.* ชักชวน persuade
chakjung *v. t* ชักจูง commove
chaknam *v.t.* ชักนำ induct

chakrok *v.t.* ชักรอก hoist
chalad *n.* ฉลาด acumen
chalad *a.* ฉลาด artful
chalad *a.* ฉลาด clever
chalad *a.* ฉลาด intelligent
chalad *a.* ฉลาด politic
chalad *a.* ฉลาด sage
chalad *a.* ฉลาด smart
chalad *a.* ฉลาด wise
chalad *a.* ฉลาด witty
chaladkwa *v.t.* ฉลาดกว่า outwit
chalaeng *n.* ชะแลง lever
chalam *n.* ฉลาม shark
chaliawchalad *a.* เฉลียวฉลาด apt
chalong *v. t. & i.* ฉลอง celebrate
cham *n* ชาม bowl
cham *a.* ฉ่ำ juicy
chamlae *v. t* ชำแหละ dissect
chamleuang *v.i.* ชำเลือง glance
chamnan *a.* ชำนาญ adept
chamnan *a.* ชำนาญ keen
chamnan *a.* ชำนาญ masterly
chamnan *v.i.* ชำนาญ specialize
chamnuansoon *n.* จำนวนศูนย์ nil
chamrani *v.t.* ชำระหนี้ liquidate
chamrudmak *a.* ชำรุดมาก shabby
chan *n.* ชั้น layer
chan *pron.* ฉัน me
chan *n.* ชั้น rack
chan *n.* ชั้น shelf
chan *n.* ฉันท์ stanza
chan *a.* ชัน steep
chan *v.t.* ชัน steep
chan *n.* ชั้น storey
chana *v. t* ชนะ conquer
chana *v.i.* ชนะ prevail
chana *v.t.* ชนะ win
chana *v.t.* ชนะ worst
chanaleud *v. t.* ชนะเลิศ champion
chanbanyagad *n.* ชั้นบรรยากาศ stratum
chanchala *n.* ชานชาลา platform
chang *n* ช้าง elephant

chang *n.* ช่าง technician
changbadgri *n.* ช่างบัดกรี tinker
changfeemeu *n.* ช่างฝีมือ artisan
changfeemeu *n.* ช่างฝีมือ workman
changfit *n* ช่างฟิต fitter
changgaesalak *n.* ช่างแกะสลัก sculptor
changgaw-id *n.* ช่างก่ออิฐ mason
changgrajok *n.* ช่างกระจก glazier
changlang *n* ชั้นกลาง alto
changlek *n.* ช่างเหล็ก smith
changmai *n.* ช่างไม้ carpenter
changmai *n.* ช่างไม้ joiner
chang-mammoth *n.* ช้างแมมมอธ mammoth
changnamnak *v.t.* ชั่งน้ำหนัก weigh
changpanmaw *n.* ช่างปั้นหม้อ potter
changprapa *n.* ช่างประปา plumber
changpud *v. t.* ช่างพูด chatter
changpud *a.* ช่างพูด talkative
changsangket *a.* ช่างสังเกต observant
changsiadsi *a.* ช่างเสียดสี sarcastic
changsomrongtaw *n* ช่างซ่อมรองเท้า cobbler
changtadpom *n.* ช่างตัดผม barber
changtammuak *n.* ช่างทำหมวก milliner
changtasi *n.* ช่างทาสี painter
changtilek *n* ช่างตีเหล็ก blacksmith
changtong *n.* ช่างทอง goldsmith
changyebpa *n.* ช่างเย็บผ้า cosier
changyon *n.* ช่างยนต์ mechanic
chani *n.* ชะนี gibbon
chanid *n.* ชนิด kind
chanid *n.* ชนิด species
chanid *n.* ชนิด type
chanmeuang *n.pl.* ชานเมือง outskirts
chanmeuang *n.* ชานเมือง suburb
chanpeuan *a.* ฉันท์เพื่อน platonic
chanroy *n.* ชั้นลอย mezzanine
chansoong *a.* ชั้นสูง noble
chansoong *a.* ชั้นสูง lofty
chantadseua *n.* ช่างตัดเสื้อ tailor
chantaidin *n.* ชั้นใต้ดิน basement

chantalak *n.* ฉันทลักษณ์ prosody
chanton *n* ชั้นต้น preliminary
chanuan *n.* ฉนวน insulation
chanuan *n.* ฉนวน insulator
chao *a* เช้า early
chao *v.t.* เช่า lease
chao *v.t.* เช่า rent
chaoban *n.* ชาวบ้าน villager
jaobao *n.* เจ้าบ่าว bridegroom
chaochonnabot *n* ชาวชนบท rustic
chao-irland *n.* ชาวไอร์แลนด์ Irish
chaona *n* ชาวนา farmer
chaonajaokongtidin *n.* ชาวนาเจ้าของที่ดิน yeoman
chaopeunmeuang *n. pl* ชาวพื้นเมือง aborigines
chaopeunmeuang *n* ชาวพื้นเมือง native
chaopramong *n* ชาวประมง fisherman
chaoraichaona *n.* ชาวไร่ชาวนา peasant
chaoraichaona *n.* ชาวไร่ชาวนา peasantry
chaore *a.* เจ้าเล่ห์ mischievous
jaosao *n* เจ้าสาว bride
chaotangchat *n* ชาวต่างชาติ foreigner
chaotawan-awk *n* ชาวตะวันออก oriental
chaoturagi *n.* ชาวตุรกี ottoman
chapaw *a* เฉพาะ exclusive
chapaw *a.* เฉพาะ particular
chapaw *a.* เฉพาะ specific
chapawjud *a* เฉพาะจุด focal
chapawti *a.* เฉพาะที่ topical
chat *n.* ชาติ nation
chatjen *a.* ชัดเจน apparent
chatniyom *n.* ชาตินิยม nationalism
chatpan *n.* ชาติพันธุ์ race
chaw *n* ช่อ bunch
chawdawkmai *n* ช่อดอกไม้ bouquet
chawgong *a.* ฉ้อโกง fraudulent
chaya *n.* ฉายา alias
ched *v.t.* เช็ด wipe
chedhaihaeng *v.t.* เช็ดให้แห้ง towel
chedsi *n.* เฉดสี tone
cheese *n.* ชีส cheese

chaindiaogan *adv* เช่นเดียวกัน alike
chaindiaogan *adv.* เช่นเดียวกัน likewise
chennan *adv.* เช่นนั้น that
chenni *a.* เช่นนี้ such
cheque *n.* เช็ค cheque
cheu *n.* ชื่อ name
cheua *v. t* เชื่อ believe
cheuafang *a.* เชื่อฟัง obedient
cheuafang *v.t.* เชื่อฟัง obey
cheuak *n* เชือก cord
cheuak *n.* เชือก rope
cheuak *n.* เชือก string
cheuakfan *n.* เชือกฟั่น whipcord
cheuaklam *n.* เชือกล่าม tether
cheuam *v. t.* เชื่อม candy
cheuam *v.t.* เชื่อม weld
cheuamak *n* เชื้อหมัก ferment
cheuamtaw *adj.* เชื่อมต่อ annectant
cheuamtaw *v.t.* เชื่อมต่อ append
cheuamtaw *v. t* เชื่อมต่อ couple
cheuamtaw *v.t.* เชื่อมต่อ fuse
cheuamyong *v. t.* เชื่อมโยง connect
cheuamyong *v.t* เชื่อมโยง link
cheuan *v.t.* เฉือน slice
cheuang *a* เชื่อง docile
cheuang *a.* เชื่อง tame
cheuangpatised *a.* เชิงปฏิเสธ negative
cheuangpriabtiab *a* เชิงเปรียบเทียบ
  comparative
cheuapleung *n.* เชื้อเพลิง fuel
cheuara *n.* เชื้อรา fungus
cheuara *n.* เชื้อรา mildew
cheuara *n* เชื้อรา mould
cheuarok *n.* เชื้อโรค germ
cheuasai *n.* เชื้อสาย lineage
cheuateudai *a.* เชื่อถือได้ magisterial
cheuaycha *a.* เฉื่อยชา inert
cheuayleau *v.t.* ช่วยเหลือ rescue
cheuchae *a.* เฉอะแฉะ slushy
cheulen *n.* ชื่อเล่น nickname
cheumeuangnaigreece *n.* ชื่อเมืองในกรีซ
  Corinth

cheumloha *v.t.* เชื่อมโลหะ solder
cheun *a* ชื้น damp
cheun *a.* ชื้น humid
cheun *v.t.* เชิญ invite
cheun *a.* ชื้น moist
cheunchom *v.t* ชื่นชม acclaim
cheunchom *a.* ชื่นชม adorable
cheunchom *v.t.* ชื่นชม appreciate
cheunchom *v. t.* ชื่นชม cherish
cheung-a-nurakniyom *a* เชิงอนุรักษ์นิยม
  conservative
cheungbuak *a.* เชิงบวก positive
cheungponggan *a.* เชิงป้องกัน preventive
cheungpriabtiab *a.* เชิงเปรียบเทียบ
  allegorical
cheungrawangwela *n.* ช่วงระหว่างเวลา
  interim
cheungsamnuanwohan *a.*
  เชิงสำนวนโวหาร rhetorical
cheungwikraw *a* เชิงวิเคราะห์ analytical
cheusiang *n* ชื่อเสียง fame
cheusiang *n.* ชื่อเสียง lustre
cheusiang *n.* ชื่อเสียง prestige
cheusiang *n.* ชื่อเสียง renown
cheusiang *n.* ชื่อเสียง reputation
cheusiang *n.* ชื่อเสียง repute
cheusiangnaitangmaidi *n.*
  ชื่อเสียงในทางไม่ดี notoriety
cheuycha *a.* เฉื่อยชา inactive
cheuycha *a.* เฉื่อยชา lethargic
chi *n.* ชี nun
chiablaem *a.* เฉียบแหลม sagacious
chiabplan *a.* เฉียบพลัน acute
chiawchan *a* เชี่ยวชาญ expert
chiawchan *a.* เชี่ยวชาญ versed
chibhai *v. t.* ฉิบหาย damn
chid *v.t.* ฉีด inject
chidspray *v.t.* ฉีดสเปรย์ spray
chidwaksin *v.t.* ฉีดวัคซีน vaccinate
chidya *v.t.* ฉีดยา syringe
chijang *v. t* ชี้แจง elucidate
chijang *v. t* ชี้แจง clarify

chik v.t. ฉีก rip

chik-awk v.t. ฉีกออก tear

chikkad v.t. ฉีกขาด lacerate

chikkad v.t ฉีกขาด tatter

chim v.t. ชิม delibate

chim v.t. ชิม taste

chingabsapab-a-gad v.t
ชินกับสภาพอากาศ acclimatise

chingcha n ชิงช้า swing

chingchang v. t ชิงชัง despise

chingchang v.t. ชิงชัง hate

chinsuan n. ชิ้นส่วน piece

chinsuanleklek n ชิ้นส่วนเล็กๆ bit

chipakao n. ชีปะขาว moth

chippajon n. ชีพจร pulse

chipraden v.t. ชี้ประเด็น point

chitang v. t ชี้ทาง direct

chiwawittaya n ชีววิทยา biology

chiwit n ชีวิต life

chlorine n คลอรีน chlorine

chob v.t. ชอบ like

chob a. ชอบ loving

chob v.t. ชอบ prefer

chob v.i. โฉบ swoop

chobsangsan adj. ชอบสังสรรค์ convivial

chobsangson a ชอบสั่งสอน didactic

chobsongkram a. ชอบสงคราม warlike

chobtaktang a. ชอบถากถาง satirical

chobtalawwiwat a. ชอบทะเลาะวิวาท
quarrelsome

chobtam a. ชอบธรรม legitimate

chobtam a. ชอบธรรม righteous

chobtawsu a. ชอบต่อสู้ combatant

chocolate n ช็อกโกแลต chocolate

chodchai v.t. ชดใช้ redeem

chodchai v.t. ชดใช้ reimburse

chodcheuy v.t ชดเชย compensate

chodcheuy v.t. ชดเชย offset

chodchuang adv. โชติช่วง ablaze

chok n. โชค fortune

chok v.t. ชก punch

chokchata n โชคชะตา destiny

chokchata n โชคชะตา fate

chokdi a. โชคดี fortunate

chokdi adv. โชคดี luckily

chokdi a. โชคดี lucky

chokdi a. โชคดี providential

choklang n. โชคลาง omen

chokmaidi a. โชคไม่ดี unfortunate

chokrai a. โชคร้าย luckless

chokrai a. โชคร้าย malafide

chokrai adv โชคร้าย malafide

chokrai n. โชคร้าย mischance

chokrai n. โชคร้าย misfortune

chom v. t ชม compliment

chon v. t. ชน clash

chon v. i ชน crash

chon n. ช้อน spoon

chonchan n ชนชั้น caste

chonchan n ชนชั้น class

chonchansoong n. ชนชั้นสูง aristocracy

chong n. ช่อง aperture

chong n. ช่อง niche

chongkaeb n. ช่องแคบ defile

chongkaeb n. ช่องแคบ strait

chongklod n. ช่องคลอด vagina

chonglom n. ช่องลม vent

chongrabainam n. ช่องระบายน้ำ sluice

chongtang n ช่องทาง channel

chongtang n. ช่องทาง lane

chongtawannak n. ช่องทวารหนัก rectum

chongtong n ช่องท้อง anticardium

chongwang n ช่องว่าง blank

chongwang n ช่องว่าง gap

chongwang n. ช่องว่าง lacuna

chongwo n. ช่องโหว่ loop-hole

chonlom v.i ชนล้ม bowl

chonpao n. ชนเผ่า tribe

chuacha a. ชั่วช้า ignoble

chuakana n. ชั่วขณะ instant

chuakana n. ชั่วขณะ moment

chuakana a. ชั่วขณะ momentary

chuakana a. ชั่วขณะ momentous

chuakana n. ชั่วขณะ while

chuakrao *a.* ชั่วคราว provisional
chuakrao *a.* ชั่วคราว temporary
chuakrao *n.* ชั่วคราว transitory
chuakru *adv.* ชั่วครู่ awhile
chuamong *n.* ชั่วโมง hour
chuang *n.* ช่วง phase
chuangching *v.t.* ช่วงชิง usurp
chuangchiwitkongsat *n* ช่วงชีวิตของสัตว์
  fauna
chuangglangreuduron *n.*
  ช่วงกลางฤดูร้อน midsummer
chuanglapakpon *n.* ช่วงลาพักผ่อน
  vacation
chuangpak *n* ช่วงพัก break
chuangroongreuang *n.* ช่วงรุ่งเรือง
  heyday
chuangwairoon *a.* ช่วงวัยรุ่น adolescent
chuangwairoon *n. pl.* ช่วงวัยรุ่น teens
chuangwela *n.* ช่วงเวลา interval
chuangwela *n.* ช่วงเวลา span
chuangwelasamkannai-a-did *n*
  ช่วงเวลาสำคัญในอดีต epoch
chuangwelatidamrongtamnaeng *n.*
  ช่วงเวลาที่ดำรงตำแหน่ง tenure
chuanhaineuktuang *a.* ชวนให้นึกถึง
  reminiscent
chuarai *a* ชั่วร้าย evil
chuarai *a.* ชั่วร้าย maleficent
chuarai *a.* ชั่วร้าย malicious
chuarai *a.* ชั่วร้าย monstrous
chuarai *a.* ชั่วร้าย nefarious
chuarai *a.* ชั่วร้าย vicious
chuarai *a.* ชั่วร้าย wicked
chuay *v.t.* ช่วย help
chuay *v.t.* ฉวย snap
chuayleua *v.t* ช่วยเหลือ aid
chuayleua *v.t.* ช่วยเหลือ assist
chuayleua *v.t* ช่วยเหลือ favour
chuayleuadai *a.* ช่วยเหลือได้ ministrant
chuayreua *v.t.* ช่วยเหลือ succour
chub *v.t.* ชุบ plate
chubloha *v.t.* ชุบโลหะ galvanize

chud *n* ชุด set
chudchad *a.* ฉูดฉาด gaudy
chudchannai *n.* ชุดชั้นใน underwear
chudkreuangmeu *n.* ชุดเครื่องมือ kit
chudnon *n.* ชุดนอน nightie
chuk *v.i.* ชุก abound
chumnum *n* ชุมนุม rally
chumtang *n.* ชุมทาง junction
chun *a.* ฉุน pungent
churak *n.* ชู้รัก paramour
cigar *n.* ซิการ์ cigar
cinnamon *n.* ซินนามอน cinnamon
clinic *n.* คลินิก clinic
clone *n.* โคลน daub
clutch *n* คลัตช์ clutch
coach *n* โค้ช coach
cobalt *n* โคบอลต์ cobalt
cocaine *n* โคเคน cocaine
coma *n.* โคม่า coma
concert *n.* คอนเสิร์ต concert
concrete *n* คอนกรีต concrete
counter *n.* เคาน์เตอร์ counter
cream *n* ครีม cream
credit *n* เครดิต credit
cricket *n* คริกเก็ต cricket
crystal *n* คริสตัล crystal
cupid *n* คิวปิด Cupid
curfew *n* เคอร์ฟิว curfew
custard *n* คัสตาร์ด custard

D

dab *n.* ดาบ sword
dabfai *v.t.* ดับไฟ extinguish
dabplaipeun *n* ดาบปลายปืน bayonet
dachani *n.* ดัชนี index
dadfareua *n* ดาดฟ้าเรือ deck
dai *n.* ด้าย thread
daidai *a.* ใดๆ any
daigamrai *v.t.* ได้กำไร net
daigamrai *v.t.* ได้กำไร profit

daiglin *v.t.* ได้กลิ่น scent

daiglin *v.t.* ได้กลิ่น smell

daiglin *v.t.* ได้กลิ่น wind

daima *v.t.* ได้มา acquire

daimajak *v. t.* ได้มาจาก derive

daimatratan *a* ได้มาตรฐาน standard

daipon *a.* ได้ผล productive

daiprayod *v. t.* ได้ประโยชน์ benefit

daipriab *v.t.* ได้เปรียบ advantage

dairab *v. t* ได้รับ earn

dairab *v.t.* ได้รับ gain

dairab *v.t.* ได้รับ get

dairab *v.t.* ได้รับ obtain

dairabchaichana *v.i.* ได้รับชัยชนะ triumph

dairabgankumklongjaksitibat *a.* ได้รับการคุ้มครองจากสิทธิบัตร patent

dairabganyokwen *a* ได้รับการยกเว้น exempt

dairabgiad *a.* ได้รับเกียรติ laureate

dairabkwamniyom *a.* ได้รับความนิยม popular

dairabpadjeb *a.* ได้รับบาดเจ็บ injurious

daisadsuan *a.* ได้สัดส่วน proportional

daisadsuan *a.* ได้สัดส่วน proportionate

daiyin *a* ได้ยิน audible

daiyin *v.t.* ได้ยิน hear

daiyindoeymaitangjai *v.t.* ได้ยินโดยไม่ตั้งใจ overhear

dakduaytakai *v.t.* ดักด้วยตาข่าย net

dakjomti *v.t.* ดักโจมตี waylay

dam *a* ดำ black

dam *n.* ด้าม shaft

damneuantaw *v.t.* ดำเนินต่อ resume

damneuangan *v.t.* ดำเนินการ operate

damklam *a.* ดำคล้ำ swarthy

damnam *v. i* ดำน้ำ dive

damnam *v.i.* ดำน้ำ duck

damneunpai *adv.* ดำเนินไป afoot

dan *n.* ด่าน barricade

dan *v.t.* ดัน push

dan-awkma *v. t.* ดันออกมา eject

danbon *n.* ด้านบน top

dang *n* ด่าง alkali

dang *adv.* ดัง aloud

dang *a.* ดัง loud

dang *n.* ด่าง potash

dangdeum *a.* ดั้งเดิม orthodox

dangdeum *a.* ดั้งเดิม primitive

dangela *a.* ด้านกีฬา athletic

danggong *v.i.* ดังก้อง resound

dangnan *adv.* ดังนั้น hence

dangnan *conj.* ดังนั้น so

dangnan *a* ดังนั้น then

dangnan *adv.* ดังนั้น thereby

dangnan *adv.* ดังนั้น therefore

dangnan *adv.* ดังนั้น thus

dankang *n.* ด้านข้าง side

danlang *adv.* ด้านหลัง post

danlang *n.* ด้านหลัง rear

danna *n.* ด้านหน้า front

danna *n.* ด่านหน้า outpost

danna-a-kan *n* ด้านหน้าอาคาร facade

dansai *n.* ด้านซ้าย left

danwichagan *a* ด้านวิชาการ academic

dao *v.i* เดา guess

dao-angkan *n* ดาวอังคาร Mars

daohang *n* ดาวหาง comet

daojupiter *n.* ดาวจูปีเตอร์ jupiter

daonamtang *n.* ดาวนำทาง loadstar

daoneptune *n.* ดาวเนปจูน Neptune

daotiam *n.* ดาวเทียม satellite

daotiamduangraek *n.* ดาวเทียมดวงแรกของโลก sputnik

daotok *n.* ดาวตก meteor

darasat *n.* ดาราศาสตร์ astronomy

dauykrengwa *conj.* ด้วยเกรงว่า lest

dawkbua *n.* ดอกบัว lotus

dawkdaffodil *n.* ดอกแดฟโฟดิล daffodil

dawkdaisy *n* ดอกเดซี่ daisy

dawkdaoreuang *n.* ดอกดาวเรือง marigold

dawkgralam *n.* ดอกกระหล่ำ cauliflower

dawkgulab *n.* ดอกกุหลาบ rose

dawk-lilac *n.* ดอกไลแลค lilac
dawk-lily *n.* ดอกลิลลี่ lily
dawkmai *n* ดอกไม้ blossom
dawkmai *n* ดอกไม้ flower
dawkmaichawlek *n.* ดอกไม้ช่อเล็ก
   nosegay
dawkmali *n.* ดอกมะลิ jasmine, jessamine
dawk-myrtle *n.* ดอกเมอเทิล myrtle
deddiaw *a* เด็ดเดี่ยว decisive
didtua *v.i.* ติดตัว spring
dek *n* เด็ก child
dek *n.* เด็ก kid
dekchai *n* เด็กชาย boy
dekgampra *n.* เด็กกำพร้า orphan
deknum *n.* เด็กหนุ่ม lad
deknum *v.t.* เด็กหนุ่ม lade
deksao *n.* เด็กสาว girl
deksao *n.* เด็กสาว lass
dekson *n.* เด็กซน urchin
den *a* เด่น dominant
denchad *a.* เด่นชัด prominent
deontang *v.i.* เดินทาง journey
deu *a.* ดื้อ mulish
deu *a.* ดื้อ obdurate
deu *a.* ดื้อ persistent
deu *a.* ดื้อ stubborn
deuan *n.* เดือน month
deuan-om *v.t.* เดินอ้อม windlass
deuantodnong *v.t.* เดินทอดน่อง saunter
deudeung *a.* ดื้อดึง obstinate
deum *v. t* ดื่ม drink
deumlao *v. i* ดื่มเหล้า booze
deun *v.t* เดิน ambulate
deun *v.i.* เดิน walk
deunchacha *v.i.* เดินช้าๆ trek
deung *v.t.* ดึง pull
deung *v.t.* ดึง tug
deungdud *v.t.* ดึงดูด attract
deungrang *v.i.* เดินกร่าง swagger
deungrataektao *v.t* เดินกระแทกเท้า
   stump
deunkabuan *v.i* เดินขบวน march

deunkabuan *v.i* เดินขบวน troop
deunlen *v.t.* เดินเล่น ramble
deunlen *v.i.* เดินเล่น stroll
deunlen *v.i.* เดินเล่น wander
deunluinam *v.i.* เดินลุยน้ำ wade
deunpaideunma *v.i.* เดินไปมา rove
deunpared *v.t.* เดินพาเหรด parade
deunreua *v.i* เดินเรือ boat
deunreua *v.i.* เดินเรือ sail
deuntang *v.i.* เดินทาง travel
deuntang *v.t.* เดินทาง trip
deuntang *v.i.* เดินทาง voyage
deuntangdoeyreua *v.t.* เดินทางโดยเรือ
   ship
deuntangpaima *v. t* เดินทางไปมา
   commute
deuntawdnong *v.i.* เดินทอดน่อง lounge
deuntawtae *v.i.* เดินเตาะแตะ waddle
deunwangta *v.i.* เดินวางท่า strut
deuran *a.* ดื้อรั้น restive
deuran *a.* ดื้อรั้น untoward
deuykwamjampen *adv.* ด้วยความจำเป็น
   perforce
di *a* ดี fine
di *a.* ดี good
di *a.* ดี nice
di *a.* ดี well
di *adv.* ดี well
diary *n* ไดอารี่ diary
diaw *n.* เดี่ยว single
dib *a.* ดิบ raw
didnew *n.* ดีดนิ้ว click
dijai *a.* ดีใจ glad
dijaileuageun *a* ดีใจเหลือเกิน overjoyed
dikeun *v.t.* ดีขึ้น ameliorate
dikeun *adv.* ดีขึ้น better
dikwa *a* ดีกว่า better
dikwa *a.* ดีกว่า transcendent
dileud *a.* ดีเลิศ ideal
dileud *a.* ดีเลิศ peerless
dileud *a* ดีเลิศ select
dileud *a.* ดีเลิศ superb

din *n* ดิน clay

din *n.* ดิน clod

din *n.* ดิน soil

dindaennai-udomkati *n* .
ดินแดนในอุดมคติ utopia

dindonsamliam *n* ดินดอนสามเหลี่ยม
delta

dinpeun *n.* ดินปืน amberite

dinron *v.i.* ดิ้นรน tussle

dinruan *n.* ดินร่วน marl

dinsaw *n.* ดินสอ pencil

dinsawsi *n.* ดินสอสี pastel

dip *a* ดิบ crude

disc *n.* ดิสก์ disc

diyiam *a.* ดีเยี่ยม superfine

dodden *a* โดดเด่น eminent

dodden *a.* โดดเด่น outstanding

dodden *a.* โดดเด่น salient

doddiaw *a.* โดดเดี่ยว lone

doddiaw *v.t.* โดดเดี่ยว sequester

doddiaw *a.* โดดเดี่ยว solitary

doddiฝw *n.* โดดเดี่ยว isolation

doey *prep* โดย by

doeybang-eun *a* โดยบังเอิญ accidental

doeybang-eun *a.* โดยบังเอิญ haphazard

doeychalia *a.* โดยเฉลี่ย average

doeyfaidiaw *a* โดยฝ่ายเดียว ex-parte

doeyfaidiaw *adv* โดยฝ่ายเดียว ex-parte

doeygamneud *a.* โดยกำเนิด inborn

doeygamneud *a.* โดยกำเนิด innate

doeyganbangkab *a* โดยการบังคับ
forcible

doeykaisong *adv.* โดยขายส่ง wholesale

doeymairu *adv.* โดยไม่รู้ unwittingly

doeypakati *adv.* โดยปกติ ordinarily

doeypakplao *adv.* โดยปากเปล่า orally

doeyparagan *a.* โดยพลการ arbitrary

doeyprasajak *prep.* โดยปราศจาก without

doeyrob *adj.* โดยรอบ ambient

doeyruam *a* โดยรวม overall

doeysamakjai *adv.* โดยสมัครใจ
voluntarily

doeysamakjai *a.* โดยสมัครใจ voluntary

doeysanchattayan *a.* โดยสัญชาตญาณ
intuitive

doeysantaxi *v.i.* โดยสารแท็กซี่ taxi

doeysincheuang *adv* โดยสิ้นเชิง
downright

doeysincheung *adv.* โดยสิ้นเชิง entirely

doeysomboon *adv.* โดยสมบูรณ์ outright

doeysomboon *a* โดยสมบูรณ์ outright

doeysommut *a.* โดยสมมติ hypothetical

doeytaeng *prep.* โดยทาง via

doeytalod *adv.* โดยตลอด through

doeytalod *adv.* โดยตลอด throughout

doeytalod *prep.* โดยตลอด throughout

doeytrong *adv* โดยตรง due

doeytrong *adv.* โดยตรง straightway

doeytuapai *adv.* โดยทั่วไป generally

doeywaja *adv.* โดยวาจา viva-voce

doeywaja *a* โดยวาจา viva-voce

doeyyaw *a* โดยย่อ summary

dollar *n* ดอลลาร์ dollar

dong *v.t.* ดอง condite

dong *v.t* ดอง pickle

dongsob *v. t* ดองศพ embalm

dontri *n.* ดนตรี music

doygansomrod *n.* โดยการสมรส in-laws

doykwa *a.* ด้อยกว่า inferior

du *v. t.* ดุ chide

duan *a* ด่วน express

duan *a.* ด่วน urgent

duang-a-tit *n.* ดวงอาทิตย์ sun

duangdao *n.* ดวงดาว star

duay *adv.* ด้วย along

duay *adv.* ด้วย also

duay *prep.* ด้วย with

duaygan *adv.* ด้วยกัน altogether

duaykonsat *n.* ต้ายขนสัตว์ worsted

duaykwamhoyha *a.* ด้วยความโหยหา
wistful

duaykwamkaorob *a.* ด้วยความเคารพ
reverential

duaykwamlob *adv* ด้วยความโลภ avidly

duaykwampratana *a.* ด้วยความปรารถนา wishful

duaykwamrak *a.* ด้วยความรัก amorous

duaykwamrakchat *a.* ด้วยความรักชาติ patriotic

duaykwamrakkrai *a* ด้วยความรักใคร่ fond

duaymeu *a.* ด้วยมือ manual

dud *v.t.* ดูด suck

duda *v.t.* ดุด่า rag

duda *v.t.* ดุด่า rebuke

duda *v.t.* ดุด่า scold

duda *v.i.* ดุด่า snarl

duda *v.t* ดุด่า upbraid

dud-awk *v.t.* ดูดออก sap

dudgleun *v.t* ดูดกลืน absorb

dudkaohagan *v.i.* ดูดเข้าหากัน gravitate

dudsabduayfongnam *v.t.* ดูดซับด้วยฟองน้ำ sponge

duentodnong *v.i.* เดินทอดน่อง loaf

dueylampang *adv.* โดยลำพัง solo

dueysaroob *adv.* โดยสรุป summarily

duke *n* ดยุค duke

duklaen *v.t.* ดูแคลน snub

dulae *v. i.* ดูแล care

dulae *v.t.* ดูแล foster

dulae *v.i.* ดูแล minister

dumeuan *v.i.* ดูเหมือน seem

dumin *v.t.* ดูหมิ่น scorn

dunduayjamook *v.* ดุนด้วยจมูก nuzzle

dunpinid *n* ดุลยพินิจ discretion

durai *a* ดุร้าย ferocious

durai *a* ดุร้าย fierce

durai *a.* ดุร้าย wild

dutook *v.t.* ดูถูก affront

dutook *v. t.* ดูถูก disdain

dutook *v.t.* ดูถูก insult

dynamo *n* ไดนาโม dynamo

E

eid *n.* อิฐ adobe

eid *n* อิฐ brick

eik-krang *adv.* อีกครั้ง again

eik-krang *adv.* อีกครั้ง anew

ein *a.* เอน italic

ein *v.i.* เอน lean

eiw *n.* เอว loin

ek-gasan *n* เอกสาร document

ekgasansamchabab *n* เอกสารสามฉบับ triplicate

elf *n* เอลฟ์ elf

en *v.t.* เอน slant

ether *n* อีเธอร์ ether

euam *v.t.* เอื้อม reach

eun *a* อื่น else

eun-eun อื่นๆ etcetera

eun-eun *a.* อื่นๆ other

fa *n.* ฝา lid

fad *v.t.* ฟาด bang

faed *n.* แฝด twin

faedtang *a.* แฝดต่าง fraternal

faem-ekkasan *n* แฟ้มเอกสาร file

faemprawat *n.* แฟ้มประวัติ portfolio

fafeun *v.t.* ฝ่าฝืน infringe

fafeun *v.t.* ฝ่าฝืน violate

fagrapongrod *n.* ฝากระโปรงรถ hood

fagraprongrod *n* ฝากระโปรงเครื่อง bonnet

fai *n.* ฝ้าย cotton

fai *n* ไฟ fire

fai *n.* ไฝ mole

faibida *a.* ฝ่ายบิดา paternal

faibukkon *n.* ฝ่ายบุคคล personnel

faichaibonweti *n.* ไฟฉายบนเวที limelight

faichak *n.* ไฟแช็ก lighter

faifa *n* ไฟฟ้า electricity

faitrongkam *n.* ฝ่ายตรงข้าม opposition

fakkai *v.i.* ฟักไข่ incubate

fak-ngeun *v.t.* ฝากเงิน bank

fak-nguen *v. t* ฝากเงิน deposit

fakrob *n.* ฝาครอบ cap

faktong *n.* ฟักทอง pumpkin

faktua *n.* ฝักถั่ว pod

falang *n.* ฝรั่ง guava

fameu *n.* ฝ่ามือ palm

fun *v.t.* ฟัน slash

fun *n.* ฟัน tooth

fanduaygrabi *v.t.* ฟันด้วยกระบี่ sabre

fang *v. t.* ฝัง bury

fang *n.* ฟาง hay

fung *v.i.* ฟัง listen

fang *n.* ฟาง straw

fungram *n.* ฟันกราม molar

fungramsisudtai *n.* ฟันกรามซี่สุดท้าย wisdom-tooth

funkeun *v.i.* ฟันขึ้น teethe

funrai *n.* ฝันร้าย nightmare

faodu *v.t.* เฝ้าดู invigilate

faodu *v.t.* เฝ้าดู watch

faorawang *a.* เฝ้าระวัง watchful

farm *n.* ฟาร์ม barton

farm *n* ฟาร์ม farm

farong *v.i.* ฟ้าร้อง thunder

fashion *n* แฟชั่น fad

fashion *n* แฟชั่น fashion

fatao *n.* ฝ่าเท้า sole

fee *n* ฝี abscess

fee *n.* ผี phantom

feekannasut *n* ฝีคัณฑสูตร fistula

feetao *n* ฝีเท้า pace

feuak *n.* เฝือก cast

feukfon *v. t.* ฝึกฝน drill

feukhad *v.t.* ฝึกหัด intern

feunfu *v.t.* ฟื้นฟู restore

feunfusukkapab *v.t.* ฟื้นฟูสุขภาพ rehabilitate

feunkeun *a.* ฟื้นคืน resurgent

feunkeunsati *v.i.* ฟื้นคืนสติ revive

feuntua *v.t.* ฟื้นตัว recover

fidad *n.* ฝีดาษ smallpox

fin *n.* ฝิ่น opium

fokcham *v.t.* ฟกช้ำ contuse

foksabu *v.t.* ฟอกสบู่ soap

foksi *v. t* ฟอกสี bleach

fon *n* ฝน rain

fon *n.* ฟอน sheaf

fong *n* ฟอง bubble

fong *n* ฟอง foam

fongnam *n.* ฟองน้ำ sponge

fongrong *v.t.* ฟ้องร้อง indict

fongrong *v.t.* ฟ้องร้อง litigate

fongrong *v.t.* ฟ้องร้อง prosecute

fongrong *v.t.* ฟ้องร้อง sue

fongsabu *n.* ฟองสบู่ lather

fontok *v.i.* ฝนตก rain

fontoknak *n* ฝนตกหนัก downpour

fontokployploy *n* ฝนตกปรอยๆ drizzle

foon *n* ฝุ่น dust

foong *n.* ฝูง shoal

foongchon *n* ฝูงชน crowd

foongchon *n* ฝูงชน flock

foongsat *n.* ฝูงสัตว์ herd

fossil *n.* ฟอสซิล fossil

franchise *n.* แฟรนไชส์ frachise

fumfeuay *a* ฟุ่มเฟือย extravagant

fumfeuay *a.* ฟุ่มเฟือย lavish

fumfeuay *a.* ฟุ่มเฟือย luxurious

fumfeuay *a.* ฟุ่มเฟือย prodigal

fumfeuay *a.* ฟุ่มเฟือย profligate

fumfeuay *a.* ฟุ่มเฟือย profuse

fumfeuay *a.* ฟุ่มเฟือย superfluous

fumfeuay *a.* ฟุ่มเฟือย wasteful

fun *v. i.* ฝัน slash

fung *n.* ฝูง listen

foongchon *n* ฝูงชน confluence

foongchon *n.* ฝูงชน mob

foongchon *n.* ฝูงชน throng
furniture *n.* เฟอร์นิเจอร์ furniture
fuse *n* ฟิวส์ fuse

ga *n* กา crow
ga *n.* กา kettle
gabanglom *n.* กะบังลม midriff
gabdak *n.* กับดัก snare
gabdak *n.* กับดัก trap
gabot *n.* กบฏ insurgent
gabtan *n.* กัปตัน captain
gad *v. t.* กัด bite
gadgron *a.* กัดกร่อน caustic
gadgron *adj.* กัดกร่อน corrosive
gae *n* แกะ agnus
gae *v.t.* แก้ alter
gae *n.* แกะ lamb
gae *a.* แก่ old
gae *a.* แก่ senile
gae *n.* แกะ sheep
gaegwa *a* แก่กว่า elder
gaekaen *v.t.* แก้แค้น avenge
gaekaen *v.i.* แก้แค้น retaliate
gaekaen *v.t.* แก้แค้น revenge
gaekai *v.t.* แก้ไข amend
gaekai *v. t* แก้ไข edit
gaekai *v.t* แก้ไข fix
gaekai *v.t.* แก้ไข redress
gaekai *v.t.* แก้ไข revise
gaekaimaidai *a.* แก้ไขไม่ได้ incorrigible
gaem *n* แก้ม cheek
gaen *n.* แกน axle
gaen *n.* แกน core
gaen *n.* แก่น kernel
gaenku *adj* แกนคู่ biaxial
gaenmoon *n.* แกนหมุน pivot
gaenmoon *n.* แกนหมุน spindle
gaensan *n.* แก่นสาร quintessence
gaepa *v.t.* แก้ผ้า strip

gaepanha *v.t.* แก้ปัญหา resolve
gaepanya *a.* แก้ปัญหาได้ soluble
gaepanya *v.t.* แก้ปัญหา solve
gaesalak *v. t.* แกะสลัก carve
gaetua *v.t* แก้ตัว excuse
gaetuamia *n* แกะตัวเมีย ewe
gaetuapu *n.* แกะตัวผู้ ram
gaew *n.* แก้ว glass
gaewlao *n.* แก้วเหล้า goblet
gaewtichainaihongtodlong *n*
แก้วที่ใช้ในห้องทดลอง beaker
gafae *n* กาแฟ coffee
gai *n.* ไก่ chicken
gai *n* ไก่ cock
gai *n.* ไก่ hen
gai *n.* ไก่ leghorn
gaijae *n.* ไก่แจ้ bantam
gaimprisana *n.* เกมปริศนา riddle
gain *n* เกณฑ์ criterion
gai-nguang *n.* ไก่งวง turkey
gaipeun *n.* ไกปืน trigger
gairongbon *n* ไก่รองบ่อน underdog
gaitang *v.t.* แก้ต่าง vindicate
gaiwipak *n.* กายวิภาค anatomy
gakkang *v. t* กักขัง detain
gaknamtan *n* กากน้ำตาล molasses
gaktoon *v.t.* กักตุน store
galaxy *n.* กาแล็กซี่ galaxy
gallery *n.* แกลเลอรี่ gallery
gallerylangkapeud *n.*
แกลเลอรี่หลังคาเปิด verendah
gallon *n.* แกลลอน gallon
gambaengpan *n.* การแบ่งปัน share
gamguam *a.* กำกวม ambiguous
gamguam *a* กำกวม equivocal
gamjad *v. t* กำจัด dispose
gamjad *v. t* กำจัด eliminate
gamjad *v. t* กำจัด eradicate
gamjad *v.t.* กำจัด purge
gamjad *v.t.* กำจัด rid
gamjadwachapeud *v.t.* กำจัดวัชพืช weed
gamlai *n.* กำไล bangle

gamlaitao *n* กำไลเท้า anklet
gamlang *n* กำลัง force
gamlangjai *n.* กำลังใจ morale
gamlangtahan *n.* กำลังทหาร armament
gamlangwangcha *n.* กำลังวังชา vitality
gammagantadsin *n.* กรรมการตัดสิน
umpire
gammaimiwinai *n.* การไม่มีวินัย
indiscipline
gammatan *n.* กำมะถัน sulphur
gammayi *n.* กำมะหยี่ velvet
gamnod *v.t* กำหนด formulate
gamnod *v.t.* กำหนด impose
gamnodgan *n.* กำหนดการ schedule
gamnod-ngeuankai *v.t.* กำหนดเงื่อนไข
stipulate
gamnodraka *v.t.* กำหนดราคา price
gamnodtamnaeng *v.t.* กำหนดตำแหน่ง
orient
gamnodwailuangna *v.t.*
กำหนดไว้ล่วงหน้า predetermine
gamnodwela *v.t.* กำหนดเวลา term
jamnuantangmod *n.* จำนวนทั้งหมด
totality
gampaeng *n.* กำแพง wall
gampan *n* กำปั้น fist
gampangsoong *n.* กำแพงสูง bawn
gamrai *n.* กำไร profit
kamsangham *n.* คำสั่งห้าม injunction
gamtamsanong *n.* กรรมตามสนอง
nemesis
gan *n.* กาล tense
gan-ab-du *n* การแอบดู peep
gan-ab-nam *n* การอาบน้ำ bath
gan-ab-nam *n.* การอาบน้ำ shower
gan-a-jian *n.* การอาเจียน vomit
gan-akseb *n.* การอักเสบ inflammation
gan-an *n.* การอ่าน perusal
gan-an-awkkiandai *n.*
การอ่านออกเขียนได้ literacy
gan-angteung *n* การอ้างถึง allusion
gan-angteung *n.* การอ้างถึง mention

gan-angteung *n.* การอ้างถึง quotation
gan-angteung *n.* การอ้างถึง reference
gan-an-kraokrao *n* การอ่านคร่าวๆ browse
gan-a-numad *n.* การอนุมัติ approval
gan-a-numan *n.* การอนุมาน inference
gan-a-nuyad *n.* การอนุญาต admittance
gan-a-nuyad *n.* การอนุญาต allowance
gan-a-nuyad *n.* การอนุญาต permission
gan-aowjaisai *n* การเอาใจใส่ heed
gan-a-paiyatod *n.* การอภัยโทษ pardon
gan-a-pakkang *n.* การอ้าปากค้าง gasp
gan-a-piprai *n.* การอภิปราย debate
gan-a-sasamak *n.* การอาสาสมัคร
volunteer
gan-a-tibai *n* การอธิบาย explanation
gan-audyak *n.* การอดอยาก starvation
gan-awkbaeb *n.* การออกแบบ architecture
gan-awk-a-gad *n.* การออกอากาศ telecast
gan-awkbaeb *n.* การออกแบบ design
gan-awkdawk *n* การออกดอก bloom
gan-awkgamlanggai *n.* การออกกำลัง
exercise
gan-awkgodmai *n.* การออกกฎหมาย
legislation
gan-awknawkban *n.* การออกนอกบ้าน
outing
gan-awksiang *n.* การออกเสียง
pronunciation
ganawksiangpayangraeksam *n.*
การออกเสียงซ้ำของพยางค์แรก
alliteration
gan-awksiangtilapayang *n.*
การออกเสียงทีละพยางค์ syllabic
gan-a-yadsab *n.* การอายัดทรัพย์
attachment
ganbadjeb *n* การบาดเจ็บ hurt
ganbadjeb *n.* การบาดเจ็บ injury
ganbadjeb *n.* การบาดเจ็บ jeopardy
ganbaeng *n.* การแบ่ง compartment
ganbaengket *n.* การแบ่งเขต demarcation
ganbaengsan *n.* การแบ่งสรร allotment

ganbaengyaek *n* การแบ่งแยก discrimination

ganbaengyaek *n.* การแบ่งแยก segregation

ganbambat *n.* การบำบัด treatment

ganbambat *n.* การบำบัด therapy

ganbambatrokjit *n.* การบำบัดโรคจิต psychotherapy

ganbamroongraksa *n* การบำรุงรักษา upkeep

ganbanchi *n.* การบัญชี accountancy

ganbangkab *n* การบังคับ compulsion

ganbanlengnam *n.* การบรรเลงนำ prelude

ganbanlupon *n.* การบรรลุผล attainment

ganbantao *n.* การบรรเทา abatement

ganbantao *n.* การบรรเทา alleviation

ganbantao *n.* การบรรเทา mitigation

ganbanteuk *n.* การบันทึก log

ganbanteuk *n.* การบันทึก record

ganbantookgeunpigad *n* การบรรทุกเกินพิกัด overload

ganbanyai *n.* การบรรยาย lecture

ganbawkpad *n.* การบอกปัด rebuff

ganbeebkaw *n.* การบีบคอ strangulation

ganbeuk-ngeun-geunbanchi *n.* การเบิกเงินเกินบัญชี overdraft

ganbiangbein *n* การเบี่ยงเบน deviation

ganbiangbein-akpawapagati *n.* การเบี่ยงเบนจากภาวะปกติ aberrance

ganbid *n.* การบิด twist

ganbidtua *n* การบิดตัว wriggle

ganbin *n.* การบิน aviation

ganbod *n* การบด squash

ganbon *n.* การบ่น croak

ganbongchi *n.* การบ่งชี้ indication

ganbontamlai *n.* การบ่อนทำลาย subversion

ganborigan *n.* การบริการ service

ganborihan *n.* การบริหาร administration

ganborihantimichob *n.* การบริหารที่มิชอบ mal administration

ganborijak *n* การบริจาค contribution

ganborijak *n.* การบริจาค donation

ganboripok *n* การบริโภค consumption

ganbuadpenpra *n.* การบวชเป็นพระ priesthood

ganbuangsuang *n.* การบวงสรวง oblation

ganbuchaprajao-ongdiaw *n.* การบูชาพระเจ้าองค์เดียว monolatry

ganbuduaypaenmai *n.* การบุด้วยแผ่นไม้ wain

ganbukruk *n.* การบุกรุก intrusion

ganbukruk *n.* การบุกรุก irruption

ganburong *n* การบุรอง lining

gancha *n.* กัญชา hemp

ganchae *n.* การแช่ infusion

ganchae *n.* การแช่ soak

ganchaeng *n.* การแช่ง damnation

ganchaeyen *n.* การแช่เย็น refrigeration

ganchai *n.* การใช้ usage

ganchaigon-u-bai *n.* การใช้กลอุบาย trickery

ganchaihaipenprayod *n.* การใช้ให้เป็นประโยชน์ utilization

ganchaikamfumfeuay *n.* การใช้คำฟุ่มเฟือย verbosity

ganchainaitangtipid *n.* การใช้ในทางที่ผิด misuse

ganchaipab *n.* การฉายภาพ projection

ganchaipidwattuprasong *n.* การใช้ผิดวัตถุประสงค์ misapplication

ganchaisaeng *n.* การฉายแสง radiation

ganchaisamnuanwohan *n.* การใช้สำนวนโวหาร phraseology

ganchaitoykamnomnao *n.* การใช้ถ้อยคำโน้มน้าว rhetoric

ganchaiwedmonkata *n.* การใช้เวทมนต์คาถา witchery

ganchakchuan *n.* การชักชวน persuasion

ganchakgratuk *n.* การชักกระตุก spasm

ganchaknam *n.* การชักนำ induction

ganchaleumchalong *n* การเฉลิมฉลอง festivity

ganchalong *n.* การฉลอง celebration

ganchalongkrobrobpi *n.*
การฉลองครบรอบปี anniversary

ganchamlae *n* การชำแหละ dissection

gan-chamleuang *n.* การชำเลือง glance

ganchamleuangmong *n* การชำเลืองมอง
squint

ganchamrakeun *n.* การชำระคืน
repayment

ganchamralang *n* การชำระล้าง ablution

ganchamralangbab *n.* การชำระล้างบาป
purification

ganchamrani *n.* การชำระหนี้ liquidation

ganchamreuang *n.* การชำเลือง glimpse

ganchannasudsob *n.* การชันสูตรศพ post-
mortem

ganchao *n.* การเช่า lease

ganchao *n.* การเช่า tenancy

ganchawgong *n.* การฉ้อโกง fraud

ganched *n.* การเช็ด wipe

gancheekkad *n.* การฉีกขาด avulsion

gancheuafang *n* การเชื่อฟัง deference

gancheuam *n* การเชื่อม weld

gancheuan *n.* การเฉือน slice

gancheudchu *n.* การเชิดชู glorification

gancheun *n.* การเชิญ invitation

gancheunchom *n* การชื่นชม acclaim

gancheunchom *n.* การชื่นชม admiration

ganchidya *n.* การฉีดยา injection

ganchidya *n.* การฉีดยา shot

ganchijang *n* การชี้แจง clarification

gan-chik *n.* การฉีก tear

ganchob *n* การโฉบ swoop

ganchodchai *n.* การชดใช้ redemption

ganchodcheuy *n* การชดเชย redress

ganchok *n.* การชก punch

ganchokchuay *n.* การฉกฉวย snatch

ganchokmuay *n* การชกมวย boxing

ganchon *n.* การชน clash

ganchongan *n* การชนกัน crash

ganchonrapratan *n.* การชลประทาน
irrigation

ganchuay-o-gad *n.* การฉวยโอกาส
opportunism

ganchuayleua *n* การช่วยเหลือ help

ganchuayleua *n.* การช่วยเหลือ succour

ganchumnum *v.t.* การชุมนุม rally

ganda *n.* การด่า malediction

gandaima *n.* การได้มา acquirement

gandamneungan *n.* การดำเนินการ
operation

gandamneungan *n.* การดำเนินการ
procession

gandamnam *n* การดำน้ำ dive

gandamrongchib *n.* การดำรงชีพ
livelihood

gandamrongchib *n* การดำรงชีพ living

gandamrongchib *n.* การดำรงชีพ
subsistence

gandan *n.* การดัน push

gandeontang *n.* การเดินทาง journey

gandeuanlameu *n.* การเดินละเมอ
somnambulism

gandeum-auypon *n.* การดื่มอวยพร
wassail

gandeumnampeungprajan *n.*
การดื่มน้ำผึ้งพระจันทร์ honeymoon

gandeun *n* การเดิน walk

gandeung *n.* การดึง pull

gandeungdud *n.* การดึงดูด attraction

gandeunkabuan *n.* การเดินขบวน march

gandeunlen *n* การเดินเล่น ramble

gandeunlen *n* การเดินเล่น stroll

gandeunreua *n.* การเดินเรือ navigation

gandeunreua *n.* การเดินเรือ sail

gandeuntang *n* การเดินทาง travel

gandeuntang *n.* การเดินทาง trek

gandeuntang *n.* การเดินทาง trip

gandeuntang *n.* การเดินทาง voyage

gandeuntang *n.* การเดินทาง excursion

gandeuntangpan *n.* การเดินทางผ่าน
transit

gandgeudpragaifai *n.* การเกิดประกายไฟ
scintillation

gandikeun *n* การดีขึ้น betterment
gandinron *n.* การดิ้นรน tussle
gandoddiaw *n.* การโดดเดี่ยว insularity
gandud *n.* การดูด suck
ganduda *n.* การดูด่า rebuke
ganduklaen *n.* การดูแคลน snub
gandulae *n.* การดูแล care
gandulaeraksa *n.* การดูแลรักษา maintenance
gandumin *n* การดูหมิ่น contempt
gandumin *n.* การดูหมิ่น scorn
gandutook *n* การดูถูก affront
gandutook *n* การดูถูก disdain
gandutook *n.* การดูถูก insult
gan-ein *n.* การเอน lean
ganeyeudwela *n.* การยืดเวลา prolongation
ganfafeun *n.* การฝ่าฝืน infringement
ganfafeun *n.* การฝ่าฝืน violation
ganfak-ngeun *n.* การฝากเงิน deposit
ganfanglangwan *n.* การฝันกลางวัน reverie
ganfangsob *n* การฝังศพ burial
ganfangsob *n.* การฝังศพ sepulture
ganfaodu *n.* การเฝ้าดู invigilation
ganfaodu *n.* การเฝ้าดู watch
ganfaorawang *n.* การเฝ้าระวัง vigil
ganfaosobgontampitifang *n* การเฝ้าศพก่อนทำพิธีฝัง wake
ganfeukfon *n* การฝึกฝน drill
ganfeukfon *n* การฝึกฝน mould
ganfeunfu *n* การฟื้นฟู reclamation
ganfeunfu *n.* การฟื้นฟู restoration
ganfeunfu *n.* การฟื้นฟู revival
ganfeunfumai *n.* การฟื้นฟูใหม่ renaissance
ganfeunfusukkapab *n.* การฟื้นฟูสุขภาพ rehabilitation
ganfeunkeun *n.* การฟื้นคืน resurgence
ganfongrong *n.* การฟ้องร้อง litigation
ganfongrong *n.* การฟ้องร้อง prosecution

ganfongyaeng *n.* การฟ้องแย้ง countercharge
ganfeuntua *n.* การฟื้นตัว recovery
gang *n.* แก๊ง gang
gangabchalak *n.* การจับสลาก lot
gangadgron *n* การกัดกร่อน erosion
gangaekaen *n.* การแก้แค้น retaliation
gangaekaen *n.* การแก้แค้น revenge
gangaekaen *n.* การแก้แค้น vengeance
gangaekai *n* การแก้ไข alteration
gangaekai *n.* การแก้ไข amendment
gangaekai *n.pl.* การแก้ไข amends
gangaekai *n* การแก้ไข fix
gangaekai *n.* การแก้ไข revision
gangaepanha *n.* การแก้ปัญหา resolution
gangaepanha *n.* การแก้ปัญหา solution
gangaesalak *n.* การแกะสลัก sculpture
gangaetua *n.* การแก้ตัว vindication
gangai *n.* กรรไกร scissors
gangamjad *n* การกำจัด clearance
gangamjad *n* การกำจัด disposal
gangamjad *n* การกำจัด elimination
gangamneud *n.* การกำเนิด nativity
gangamnod-ngeuankai *n.* การกำหนดเงื่อนไข stipulation
gangamreubkongrok *n.* การกำเริบของโรค relapse
gangannam *n* การกันน้ำ waterproof
gangaoyang *n* การก้าวย่าง tread
gangawguan *n* การก่อกวน mischief
gangawsang *n* การก่อสร้าง construction
gangawtang *n* การก่อตั้ง establishment
gangawtang *n.* การก่อตั้ง foundation
gangebgiaw *n.* การเก็บเกี่ยว harvest
gangeb-ngeunpeum *n.* การเก็บเงินเพิ่ม surcharge
gangebraksa *n.* การเก็บรักษา preservation
gangebraksa *n.* การเก็บรักษา retention
gangebtua *n.* การเก็บตัว seclusion
gangengkayao *n. pl* กางเกงขายาว trousers

gangengsongluam *n.* กางเกงทรงหลวม slacks

gangeud *n.* การเกิด birth

gangeudkeunnaitanti *n* การเกิดขึ้นในทันที abruption

gangeudmai *n.* การเกิดใหม่ incarnation

gangeudmai *n.* การเกิดใหม่ rebirth

gangeudruamgan *n.* การเกิดร่วมกัน concrescence

gangeudsam *n.* การเกิดซ้ำ recurrence

ganggengkasan *n. pl.* กางเกงขาสั้น shorts

ganggengkima *n.* กางเกงขี่ม้า breeches

ganghanlom *n.* กังหันลม windmill

gangila *n.* การกีฬา athletics

gangin-im-geunpai *n* การกินอิ่มเกินไป glut

ganginyageunkanad *n.* การกินยาเกินขนาด overdose

gankleuanyai *n* การเคลื่อนย้าย shift

ganglabkaorabtamnaengdeum *n.* การกลับเข้ารับตำแหน่งเดิม reinstatement

ganglaiglia *n.* การไกล่เกลี่ย mediation

ganglaipan *n.* การกลายพันธุ์ mutation

ganglangrong *n.* การกลั่นกรอง screen

ganglaoha *n* การกล่าวหา accusation

ganglaosam *n.* การกล่าวซ้ำ reiteration

ganglaotod *n.* การกล่าวโทษ impeachment

gangleun *n.* การกลืน gulp

gangleun *n.* การกลืน swallow

gangobgu *n.* การกอบกู้ salvage

gangod *n* การกด press

gangodki *n.* การกดขี่ oppression

gangohok *n* การโกหก lie

gangomtua *n* การก้มตัว stoop

gangong *n.* การโกง cheat

gangonpom *n.* การโกนผม tonsure

gangplon *n.* แก๊งค์ปล้น dacoity

gangradod *n* การกระโดด hop

gangradod *n.* การกระโดด jump

gangradod *n* การกระโดด leap

gangradod *n* การกระโดด skip

gangrai *n. pl.* กรรไกร shears

gangrajai *n.* การกระจาย outbreak

gangrajaikao *v.t.* กระจายข่าว rumour

gangrajai *n.* การกระจาย spread

gangrajaisiang *n* การกระจายเสียง broadcast

gangrajon *n* การกระโจน pounce

gangrapeum *n.* การกระเพื่อม undulation

gangrasib *n* การกระซิบ whisper

gangrataek *n* การกระแทก dash

gangrataek *n* การกระแทก slam

gangratam *n.* การกระทำ action

gangratam *n* การกระทำ deed

gangratam *n* การกระทำ make

gangratampid *n.* การกระทำผิด malpractice

gangratampid *n.* การกระทำผิด transgression

gangratamtaruntangped *n.* การกระทำทารุณทางเพศ sadism

gangratobgrataek *n.* การกระทบกระแทก jostle

gangratook *n.* การกระตุก jerk

gangratook *n.* การกระตุก jolt

gangratoon *n.* การกระตุ้น instigation

gangridrong *n* การกรีดร้อง scream

gangridrong *n.* การกรีดร้อง shriek

gangron *n* การกรน snore

ganguson *n* การกุศล benevolence

ganguson *n.* การกุศล charity

gangwad *n.* การกวาด sweep

gangwaeng *n.* การแกว่ง oscillation

gangwaeng *n* การแกว่ง wag

gangwang *n* การแกว่ง sway

gangwon *a.* กังวล anxious

gangwon *v. t* กังวล concern

gangwon *v.i.* กังวล worry

ganhai *n.* การให้ largesse

ganhai-a-pai *n.* การให้อภัย condonation

ganhaiganted *n.* การให้การเท็จ perjury

ganhaihedponyangchanchalad *n.*
การให้เหตุผลอย่างชาญฉลาด sophism
ganhaijai *n.* การหายใจ respiration
ganhaijairaeng *n.* การหายใจแรง snort
ganhai-ngeun-udnoon *n.*
การให้เงินอุดหนุน subsidy
ganhaipai *n* การหายไป disappearance
ganham *n.* การห้าม inhibition
ganham *n.* การห้าม prohibition
ganhamadai *n.* การหามาได้ acquisition
ganhan *n.* กังหัน turbine
ganhan *n* การหัน turn
ganhao *n* การเห่า yap
ganhao *n.* การหาว yawn
ganhaohon *n* การเห่าหอน howl
ganhareu *n* การหารือ consultation
ganhaw *n* การห่อ wrap
ganhawkong *n.* การห่อของ packing
ganhen *n.* การเห็น sight
ganhod *n.* การหด shrinkage
ganhorongcheunchom *n* การโห่ร้องชื่นชม
acclamation
ganhuaraw *n.* การหัวเราะ laughter
ganjoob *n.* การจูบ basial
ganjab *n.* การจับ catch
ganjab *n* การจับ grasp
ganjabgoom *n.* การจับกุม arrest
ganjabgoom *n.* การจับกุม seizure
ganjabpenchaleoy *n.* การจับเป็นเชลย
capture
ganjabyeud *n* การจับยึด grip
ganjadgan *n.* การจัดการ arrangement
ganjadgan *n.* การจัดการ management
ganjadgan *n.* การจัดการ procurement
ganjadganpidplad *n.* การจัดการผิดพลาด
mismanagement
ganjadha *n.* การจัดหา provision
ganjadpraped *n* การจัดประเภท
classification
ganjadsadaeng *n.* การจัดแสดง exhibition
ganjadsan *n.* การจัดสรร allocation
ganjadsan *n.* การจัดสรร appropriation

ganjaekjai *n* การแจกจ่าย distribution
ganjaeng *n.* การแจ้ง notification
ganjai *n* การจ่าย pay
ganjaikachodcheuy *n.* การจ่ายค่าชดเชย
remuneration
ganjai-ngeun *n.* การจ่ายเงิน payment
ganjaiya *n.* การจ่ายยา prescription
ganjak *n* การจาก departure
ganjak *n.* การจาก leave
ganjakla *n.* การจากลา adieu
ganjalajon *n.* การจลาจล riot
ganjam *n* การจาม sneeze
ganjamgad *n.* การจำกัด confinement
ganjamgad *n.* การจำกัด limit
ganjamgad *n.* การจำกัด limitation
ganjamgad *n.* การจำกัด restriction
ganjamgad *n.* การจำกัด stricture
ganjamlong *n.* การจำลอง miniature
ganjamnong *n.* การจำนอง mortgage
ganjamsin *n.* การจำศีล hibernation
ganjang *n.* การจ้าง hire
ganjang-ngan *n* การจ้างงาน employment
ganjarajon *n.* การจลาจล insurrection
ganjarajon *n.* การจลาจล rebellion
ganjareuk *n.* การจารึก inscription
ganjariksawaengboon *n.*
การจาริกแสวงบุญ pilgrimage
ganjatwang-ongpragob *n*
การจัดวางองค์ประกอบ composition
ganjeeb *n.* การจีบ courtship
ganjeraja *n.* การเจรจา nagotiation
ganjeraja *n.* การเจรจา parley
ganjeuajang *n* การเจือจาง arefaction
ganjeuapon *n.* การเจือปน adulteration
ganjib *n* การจีบ flirt
ganjib *n.* การจิบ sip
ganjik *n.* การจิก peck
ganjintanagan *n.* การจินตนาการ
imagination
ganjob *n.* การจบ closure
ganjobtabian *n.* การจดทะเบียน
registration

ganjodkangtang *n.* การจอดข้างทาง pullover

ganjomti *n.* การโจมตี ambush

ganjomti *n.* การโจมตี barrage

ganjomti *n* การโจมตี battery

ganjomti *n.* การโจมตี onset

ganjomti *n.* การโจมตี onslaught

ganjomti *n.* การโจมตี sally

ganjomtiduayrabeud *n* การโจมตีด้วยระเบิด bombardment

ganjong *n.* การจ้อง stare

ganjoob *n.* การจูบ kiss

ganjoom *n.* การจุ่ม dip

ganjoom *n* การจุ่ม plunge

ganjoragam *n.* การโจรกรรม piracy

ganjujom *n.* การจู่โจม attack

ganjujom *n.* การจู่โจม raid

ganjujom *n* การจู่โจม rush

ganjungjai *n* การจูงใจ allurement

ganka *n* การค้า commerce

ganka *n.* การฆ่า kill

ganka *n.* การค้า trade

gankabida *n.* การฆ่าบิดา patricide

gankablai *n* การขับไล่ eviction

gankablai *n.* การขับไล่ expulsion

gankablai *n.* การขับไล่ repulse

gankabrodma *n.* การขับรถม้า cartage

gankabrongsalabgan *n.* การขับร้องสลับกัน antiphony

gankad *n* การขัด polish

gankad *n* การขัด rub

gankad-a-gadhaijai *n.* การขาดอากาศหายใจ suffocation

gankaddao *n.* การคาดเดา conjecture

gankaddao *n.* การคาดเดา guess

gankaddao *n.* การคาดเดา speculation

gankaddun *n* การขาดดุล deficit

gankadgan *n.* การคาดการณ์ anticipation

gankadgan *n* การคาดการณ์ estimation

gankadgan *n.* การคาดการณ์ prospect

gankadjangwa *n.* การขัดจังหวะ punctuation

gankadkan *n* การคัดค้าน demur

gankadkan *n.* การคัดค้าน objection

gankadkeunkamsang *n.* การขัดขืนคำสั่ง mutiny

gankadklaen *n.* การขาดแคลน shortage

gankadkunasombat *n* การขาดคุณสมบัติ disqualification

gankadkwang *n* การขัดขวาง defiance

gankadkwang *n.* การขัดขวาง hindrance

gankadkwang *n.* การขัดขวาง obstruction

gankadleuak *n.* การคัดเลือก selection

gankadleuaknaksadaeng *n* การคัดเลือกนักแสดง casting

gankadlok *n.* การคัดลอก transcription

gankaengkan *n.* การแข่งขัน competition

gankaengkan *n* การแข่งขัน contention

gankaengkan *n.* การแข่งขัน contest

gankaengkan *n.* การแข่งขัน game

gankaengkan *n.* การแข่งขัน match

gankaengkan *n.* การแข่งขัน rivalry

gankaengkan *n.* การแข่งขัน tournament

gankaengkanrawaengpratet *n.* การแข่งขันระหว่างประเทศ olympiad

gankaengkanrawaengsongkon *n* การแข่งขันระหว่างสองคน duel

gankaengkaw *n.* การแข่งข้อ insubordination

gankai *n.* การขาย sale

gankaiplik *n.* การขายปลีก retail

gankaisong *n.* การขายส่ง wholesale

gankajadrongroy *n.* การขจัดร่องรอย obliteration

ganhak-awk *n.* การหักออก subtraction

gankam *n* การข้าม cross

gankamaetua-eng *n.* การฆ่าแม่ตัวเอง matricide

gankamnab *n* การคำนับ bow

gankamnab *n.* การคำนับ obeisance

gankamnab *n* การคำนับ salute

gankamnuan *n.* การคำนวณ calculation

gankamnuan *n.* การคำนวณ computation

gankamnuanpid *n.* การคำนวณผิด miscalculation

gankamram *n.* การคำราม roar

gankancheu *n.* การขานชื่อ roll-call

gankaoglai *n.* การเข้าใกล้ approach

gankaojaipid *n* การเข้าใจผิด misapprehension

gankaojaipid *n.* การเข้าใจผิด misconception

gankaokrobkronggon *n.* การเข้าครอบครองก่อน preoccupation

gankaopak *n.* การเข้าพัก lodging

gankaorahadlab *n.* การเข้ารหัสลับ cryptography

gankaoruam *n.* การเข้าร่วม attendance

gankaoruam *n.* การเข้าร่วม participation

gankaotaew *n.* การเข้าแถว queue

gankaoteung *n* การเข้าถึง accession

gankapawmae *n.* การฆ่าพ่อแม่ parricide

gankapinong *n.* การฆ่าพี่น้อง fratricide

gankapraweni *n.* การค้าประเวณี prostitution

gankarawa *n.* การคารวะ homage

gankasat *n.* การฆ่าสัตว์ slaughter

gankatagam *n.* การฆาตกรรม homicide

gankatarok *n.* การฆ่าทารก infanticide

gankatuatai *n.* การฆ่าตัวตาย suicide

gankawkwamchuayleua *n.* การขอความช่วยเหลือ recourse

gankawrong *n* การขอร้อง request

gankayai *n.* การขยาย expansion

gankayai-awk *n* การขยายออก stretch

gankayaikwam *n* การขยายความ amplification

gankayaikwam *n.* การขยายความ illustration

gankayaipab *n.* การขยายภาพ zoom

gankayaitua *n.* การขยายตัว inflation

gankayibta *n* การขยิบตา wink

gankeundi *n.* การคืนดี reconciliation

gankeun-nguen *n.* การคืนเงิน refund

ganki *n* การขี่ ride

gankianchawalek *n.* การเขียนชวเลข stenography

gankianprayokmai *n.* การเขียนประโยคใหม่ paraphrase

gankianwatwat *n* การเขียนหวัดๆ scrawl

gankidluangna *n* การคิดล่วงหน้า forethought

gankidteungkwamlang *n.* การคิดถึงความหลัง nostalgia

ganklan *n* การคลาน crawl

ganglaeng *n* การแกล้ง bluff

ganglaoha *n* การกล่าวหา blame

gankledkadyok *n* การเคล็ดขัดยอก wrick

gankleuab *n* การเคลือบ coating

gankleuab *n* การเคลือบ glaze

gankleuanwai *n.* การเคลื่อนไหว move

gankleuanwai *n.* การเคลื่อนไหว movement

gankleuntidaiyai *n.* การเคลื่อนที่ได้ง่าย mobility

gankleunwai *n.* การเคลื่อนไหว motion

gankobchu *n.* การคบชู้ adultery

gankobkun *n.* การขอบคุณ thanks

gankodsana *n* การโฆษณา advertisement

gankodsanachuancheua *n.* การโฆษณาชวนเชื่อ propaganda

gankomheng *n.* การข่มเหง persecution

gankomheng *n* การข่มเหง abuse

gankomkeun *n.* การข่มขืน rape

gankomku *n.* การข่มขู่ harassment

gankon *n* การค้น rummage

gankongyu *n* การคงอยู่ existence

gankonha *n* การค้นหา look

gankonha *n.* การค้นหา quest

gankonha *n.* การค้นหา search

gankonpob *n.* การค้นพบ discovery

gankonsong *n* การขนส่ง conveyance

gankonsong *n.* การขนส่ง transport

gankonsong *n.* การขนส่ง transportation

gankonsongsinkatangreua *n.* การขนส่งสินค้าทางเรือ shipment

gankonyai *n.* การขนย้าย portage

gankonyai *n.* การขนย้าย transfer

gankoomgan *n* การคุ้มกัน escort

gankramkruan *n.* การคร่ำครวญ monody

gankratampid *n.* การกระทำผิด misdeed

gankrobkrong *n.* การครอบครอง occupancy

gankrobkrong *n.* การครอบครอง possession

gankrob-ngam *n* การครอบงำ domination

gankrob-ngam *n.* การครอบงำ obsession

gankrobrobneungroypi *n.* การครบรอบหนึ่งร้อยปี centenary

gankruankrang *n.* การครวญคราง moan

gankruankrang *n* การครวญคราง whine

ganku *n.* การขู่ intimidation

gankuabkum *n* การควบคุม control

gankuabkum *n* การควบคุม dictation

gankuabkum *n.* การควบคุม hold

gankuabkum *n.* การควบคุม superintendence

gankuabkum *n.* การควบคุม supervision

gankuabkum-a-rom *n.* การควบคุมอารมณ์ temperance

gankuabma *n.* การควบม้า gallop

gankuabruam *n* การควบรวม amalgamation

gankud *n* การขุด dig

gankud *n* การขุด graze

gankudkon *n.* การขุดค้น excavation

gankuimo *n* การคุยโม้ boast

gankukkam *n.* การคุกคาม threat

gankumcheunggan *n.* การคุมเชิงกัน stalemate

gankumgan *n.* การคุ้มกัน wardship

gankumkrong *v* การคุ้มครอง custody

gankun *n.* การคูณ multiplication

gankupeidpong *n* การขู่เปิดโปง blackmail

ganguyeum *n.* การกู้ยืม loan

gankwambat *n* การคว่ำบาตร boycott

gankwang *n.* การขว้าง pitch

gankwang *n.* การขว้าง throw

gankwuabkum-a-han *n* การควบคุมอาหาร diet

ganla *n* การล่า hunt

ganla-ai-jai *n.* การละอายใจ shame

ganla-awk *n.* การลาออก resignation

ganlab *n.* การหลับ sleep

ganlad-iang *n* การลาดเอียง slant

ganlad-iang *n.* การเอียงลาด tilt

ganladtrawen *n* การลาดตระเวน patrol

ganlaekplian *n* การแลกเปลี่ยน exchange

ganlaekplian *n.* การแลกเปลี่ยน interchange

ganlai *n* การไหล flow

ganlai-awk *n* การไล่ออก dismissal

ganlaiba *n.* การไหลบ่า onrush

ganlaiseum *n.* การไหลซึม ooze

ganlaitalak *n.* การไหลทะลัก influx

ganlaitam *n.* การไล่ตาม chase2

ganlak *n* การลาก drag

ganlak *n.* การลาก traction

ganlaklobkakai *n.* การลักลอบค้าขาย traffic

ganlakpatua *n* การลักพาตัว abduction

ganlakpliansinka *n.* การแลกเปลี่ยนสินค้า barter2

ganlaktonpasusat *n* การลักต้อนปศุสัตว์ abaction

ganlalai *n* การละลาย thaw

ganlaleuy *n* การละเลย neglect

ganlaleuy *n.* การละเลย negligence

ganlaleuy *n.* การละเลย omission

ganlang *n.* การหลั่ง secretion

ganlangbab *n.* การล้างบาป purgation

ganlangleijai *n.* การลังเลใจ hesitation

ganlangbab *n.* การล้างบาป sanctification

ganlaoreuang *n.* การเล่าเรื่อง narration

ganlating *n* การละทิ้ง abnegation

ganlawenjakganruamped *n.* การละเว้นจากการร่วมเพศ celibacy

ganlawjai *n.* การล่อใจ temptation

ganlawklaichalu *n* การลอกลายฉลุ cyclostyle

ganlawkluang *n* การหลอกลวง duplicity
ganlawlen *n.* การล้อเล่น prank
ganlawleun *n.* การหล่อลื่น lubrication
ganlawlian *n* การล้อเลียน mimic
ganlawlian *n* การล้อเลียน mimicry
ganlawlian *n.* การล้อเลียน mockery
ganlawlian *n.* การล้อเลียน parody
ganlawluanghaitampid *n*
การล่อลวงให้ทำผิด debauch
ganleekliang *n.* การหลีกเลี่ยง avoidance
ganlem *n* การเล็ม nibble
ganlenkam *n.* การเล่นคำ pun
ganlenpaklenpuak *n.*
การเล่นพรรคเล่นพวก nepotism
ganlensanook *n.* การเล่นสนุก lark
ganlensanook *n.* การเล่นสนุกสนาน spree
ganlentalok *n* การเล่นตลก antic
ganleuak *n.* การเลือก pick
ganleuaktang *n* การเลือกตั้ง election
ganleuan *n.* การเลื่อน adjournment
ganleuan *n.* การเลื่อน postponement
ganleuklom *v* การเลิกล้ม abolition
ganleun *n* การลื่น skid
ganleuntalai *n* การลื่นไถล slide
ganleuntalai *n.* การลื่นไถล slip
ganlia *n* การเลีย lick
ganlianbaeb *n.* การเลียนแบบ imitation
ganliangdu *n.* การเลี้ยงดู nurture
ganliangpeung *n.* การเลี้ยงผึ้ง apiculture
ganliang-umla *n* การเลี้ยงอำลา farewell
ganliansiangtammachat *n.*
การเลียนเสียงธรรมชาติ onomatopoeia
ganlikliang *n* การหลีกเลี่ยง evasion
ganloblang *n.* การลบล้าง refutation
ganloblik *n* การหลบหลีก elusion
ganlobni *n* การหลบ dodge
ganlobni *n* การหลบหนี escape
ganlobsanghan *n* การลอบสังหาร
assassination
ganlodlong *n* การลดลง decrease
ganlodlong *n.* การลดลง decrement
ganlodlong *n* การลดลง ebb

ganlodlong *n.* การลดลง reduction
ganlodlong *n* การลดลง wane
ganlodraka *n* การลดราคา discount
ganlokluang *n* การหลอกลวง deceit
ganlokluang *n* การหลอกลวง deception
ganlokluang *n.* การหลอกลวง hoax
ganlokluang *n.* การหลอกลวง imposture
ganlokluang *n.* การหลอกลวง quackery
ganlokluang *n.* การหลอกลวง swindle
ganlom *n* การล้ม fall
ganlom *n.* การล้ม tumble
ganlomkawhak *n* การล้มคอหัก breakneck
ganlomlalai *n.* การล้มละลาย bankruptcy
ganlomlalai *n.* การหลอมละลาย fusion
ganlomlalai *n.* การล้มละลาย insolvency
ganlomlang *n* การล้มล้าง overthrow
ganlomrob *n.* การล้อมรอบ enclosure
ganlongjod *n.* การลงจอด landing
ganlongkanaen *n.* การลงคะแนน vote
ganlongmatiduaywitiplengsiang *n*
การลงมติด้วยวิธีเปล่งเสียง viva-voce
ganlongnam *n.* การลงนาม signature
ganlongprachamati *n.* การลงประชามติ
plebiscite
ganlongtang *n.* การหลงทาง misdirection
ganlongtod *n.* การลงโทษ penalty
ganlongtod *n.* การลงโทษ sanction
ganlongtoon *n.* การลงทุน investment
ganlongtua-eng *n.* การหลงตัวเอง
narcissism
ganloob *n* การลูบ pat
ganloy *n* การลอย buoyancy
ganluanglam *n.* การล่วงล้ำ trespass
ganluanlam *n.* การลวนลาม molestation
ganmaifakfaifaidai *n.* การไม่ฝักใฝ่ฝ่ายใด
non-alignment
ganmaikaoruam *n.* การไม่เข้าร่วม absence
ganmaimi-a-rai *n.* การไม่มีอะไร nothing
ganmaimiprasobgan *n.*
การไม่มีประสบการณ์ inexperience
ganmairunangseu *n.* การไม่รู้หนังสือ
illiteracy

ganmaisaijai *n.* การไม่ใส่ใจ ignorance

ganmaisamadtamdai *n.*
การไม่สามารถทำได้ impracticability

ganmak *n* การหมัก fermentation

ganmanmai *n.* การหมั้นหมาย betrothal

ganmateung *n.* การมาถึง arrival

ganmateungkongsingsamkan *n.*
การมาถึงของสิ่งสำคัญ advent

ganmeuang *n.* การเมือง politics

ganmi-amnadneuakwa *n.*
การมีอำนาจเหนือกว่า predominance

ganmi-amnadsoongsud *n.*
การมีอำนาจสูงสุด preponderance

ganmi-amnardmaisinsud *n.*
การมีอำนาจไม่สิ้นสุด omnipotence

ganmi-a-yuyeun *n.* การมีอายุยืน
longevity

ganmicheunaitanglob *n.*
การมีชื่อในทางลบ infamy

ganmikukrongkondiaw *n.*
การมีคู่ครองคนเดียว monogamy

ganmikukronglaikon *n.*
การมีคู่ครองหลายคน polygamy

ganmikukrongpromgansongkon *n*
การมีคู่ครองพร้อมกันสองคน bigamy

ganmimattratan *n.* การมีมาตรฐาน
standardization

ganminpramat *n.* การหมิ่นประมาท libel

ganmiprajamdeuan *n.* การมีประจำเดือน
menstruation

ganmipratisampan *n.* การมีปฏิสัมพันธ์
interplay

ganmisukkapabjidti *n.* การมีสุขภาพจิตดี
sanity

ganmod-a-yu *n* การหมดอายุ lapse

ganmodgamlang *n.* การหมดกำลัง
prostration

ganmoho *n.* การโมโห rampage

ganmokmoon *n.* การหมกมุ่น immersion

ganmokmuntangpet *n.*
การหมกมุ่นทางเพศ sensuality

ganmonghen *n.* การมองเห็น vision

ganmongkampai *n.* การมองข้ามไป
oversight

ganmongloknai-ngaedi *n.*
การมองโลกในแง่ดี optimism

ganmongloknai-ngaerai *n.*
การมองโลกในแง่ร้าย pessimism

ganmoon *n.* การหมุน spin

ganmoonwian *n* การหมุนเวียน circulation

ganmoonwian *n.* การหมุนเวียน rotation

ganmoonwian *n* การหมุนเวียน whirl

ganman *n.* การหมั้น engagement

ganmeunmao *n.* การมึนเมา intoxication

ganmungrai *n.* การมุ่งร้าย malignity

gannab *n.* การนับ count

gannabteuhaipenprajao *n.*
การนับถือให้เป็นพระเจ้า apotheosis

gannadmai *n.* การนัดหมาย appointment

gannadmai *n.* การนัดหมาย rendezvous

gannadpob *n.* การนัดพบ tryst

gannadyud-ngan *n* การนัดหยุดงาน strike

gannaenam *n.* การแนะนำ introduction

gannam *n.* การนำ lead

gannam *a.* กันน้ำ watertight

gannamdai *a.* กันน้ำได้ waterproof

gannamkao *n.* การนำเข้า import

gannamsaneu *n.* การนำเสนอ presentation

gannamsong *n* การนำส่ง delivery

gannebnaem *n.* การเหน็บแนม irony

gannebnaem *n* การเหน็บแนบ taunt

gannen *n* การเน้น emphasis

gannerated *n.* การเนรเทศ banishment

gannerated *n.* การเนรเทศ exile

gan-ngad *n.* การงัด leverage

gan-ngeun *n* การเงิน finance

gan-ngib *n.* การงีบ nap

gan-ngiblab *n.* การงีบหลับ slumber

gan-ngiblabtontiang *n.*
การงีบหลับตอนเที่ยง siesta

gan-nguangnon *n.* การง่วงนอน narcosis

ganninta *n.* การนินทา gossip

ganniratodsagam *n.* การนิรโทษกรรม
amnesty

gannom-eing *n.* การโน้มเอียง inclination
gannongleuad *n* การนองเลือด bloodshed
gannuad *n.* การนวด massage
gan-obgod *n* การโอบกอด embrace
gan-obpayob *n* การอพยพ evacuation
gan-obpayob *n.* การอพยพ immigration
gan-ob-rom *n.* การอบรม training
gan-od-a-han *n* การอดอาหาร fast
gan-on-nom *n.* การอ่อนน้อม subservience
gan-obpayob *n.* การอพยพ migration
gan-o-uad *n* การโอ้อวด brag
ganpacheunna *n.* การเผชิญหน้า confrontation
ganpacheunna *n.* การเผชิญหน้า encounter
ganpadpong *n.* การปัดป้อง parry
ganpaiyuchonnabot *n.* การไปอยู่ชนบท rustication
ganpajonpai *n* การผจญภัย adventure
ganpakpon *n.* การพักผ่อน recreation
ganpakpon *n.* การพักผ่อน repose
ganpakpon *n* การพักผ่อน rest
ganpakraem *n.* การพักแรม sojourn
ganpakrob *n.* การพักรบ armistice
ganpakrob *n.* การพักรบ truce
ganpaktan *n.* การภาคทัณฑ์ probation
ganpalid *n* การผลิต manufacture
ganpalidrian *n* การผลิตเหรียญ coinage
ganpalid *n.* การผลิต production
ganpanan *n* การพนัน bet
ganpanan *v.i.* พนัน gamble
ganpanan *n* การพนัน gamble
ganpanan *n.* การพนัน wager
ganpansuan *n* การปันส่วน ration
ganpanuak *n* การผนวก annexation
ganpaomai *n* การเผาไหม้ burn
ganpaopan-a-han *n.* การเผาผลาญอาหาร metabolism
ganpaosob *n* การเผาศพ cremation
ganpasom *n* การผสม blend
ganpasom *n.* การผสม mixture
ganpasompan *n* การผสมพันธุ์ breed

ganpasompasan *n* การผสมผสาน compost
ganpasusat *n.* การปศุสัตว์ horticulture
ganpatad *n.* การผ่าตัด surgery
ganpatagan *n* การปะทะกัน collision
ganpatana *n.* การพัฒนา advancement
ganpatibaddai *n.* การปฏิบัติได้ practicability
ganpatibat *n.* การปฏิบัติ practice
ganpatiroob *n.* การปฏิรูป reform
ganpatiroob *n.* การปฏิรูป reformation
ganpatiroob *n.* การปฏิรูป regeneration
ganpatised *n* การปฏิเสธ decline
ganpatised *n* การปฏิเสธ denial
ganpatised *n.* การปฏิเสธ refusal
ganpatised *n.* การปฏิเสธ repudiation
ganpatised *n.* การปฏิเสธ rejection
ganpatiwat *n.* การปฏิวัติ revolt
ganpatiwat *n.* การปฏิวัติ revolution
ganpatiwat *n* การปฏิวัติ revolutionary
ganpatiwat *n.* การปฏิวัติ uprising
ganpattana *n.* การพัฒนา development
ganpatu *n* การปะทุ eruption
ganpatwanpraganprung *n.* การผัดวันประกันพรุ่ง procrastination
ganpawpluk *n.* การเพาะปลูก husbandry
ganpayagon-a-gad *n.* การพยากรณ์อากาศ meteorology
ganpayakon *n* การพยากรณ์ forecast
ganpengmong *n* การเพ่งมอง gaze
ganpenkai *n* การเป็นไข้ fever
ganpenlom *n.* การเป็นลม swoon
ganpenman *n.* การเป็นหมัน sterility
ganpenpatipak *n* การเป็นปฏิปักษ์ antagonism
ganpensamachik *n.* การเป็นสมาชิก membership
ganpensod *n.* การเป็นโสด celibacy
ganpentuataen *n.* การเป็นตัวแทน representation
ganpeud *n.* การเปิด opening
ganpeudpeuy *n.* การเปิดเผย candour

ganpeudpeuy *n.* การเปิดเผย revelation

ganpeuktawn *n.* การเพิกถอน revocation

ganpeum *n.* การเพิ่ม addition

ganpeumkeun *n.* การเพิ่มขึ้น augmentation

ganpeumkeun *n* การเพิ่มขึ้น increase

ganpeumkeun *n.* การเพิ่มขึ้น increment

ganpeumkeun *n.* การเพิ่มขึ้น rise

ganpeumkeunyangruadrew *n.* การเพิ่มขึ้นอย่างรวดเร็ว surge

ganpeumponpalit *n.* การเพิ่มผลผลิต productivity

ganpeungpa *n* การพึ่งพา dependence

ganpeungpagan *n.* การพึ่งพากัน interdependence

ganpeungpapu-eun *n* การพึ่งพาผู้อื่น anaclisis

ganpeuyprae *n.* การเผยแพร่ propagation

ganpeuyprae *n.* การเผยแพร่ publicity

ganpidbangcheu *n.* การปิดบังชื่อ anonymity

ganpidbangkawtedjing *n.* การปิดบังข้อเท็จจริง whitewash

ganpidlom *n* การปิดล้อม blockade

ganpidsamai *n* การผิดสมัย anachronism

ganpidsanya *n* การผิดสัญญา breach

ganpidsanya *n.* การผิดสัญญา default

ganpijaranakadi *n.* การพิจารณาคดี proceeding

ganpijarana *n* การพิจารณา consideration

ganpijarana *n* การพิจารณา contemplation

ganpijaranakadi *n.* การพิจารณาคดี judiciary

ganpim *n* การพิมพ์ print

ganpimpid *n.* การพิมพ์ผิด misprint

ganpimsam *n.* การพิมพ์ซ้ำ reprint

ganpin *n.* การปีน climb1

ganpinitpikraw *n.* การพินิจพิเคราะห์ scrutiny

ganpinkeun *n.* การปีนขึ้น ascent

ganpipaksa-longtod *n* การพิพากษาลงโทษ conviction

ganpisud *n.* การพิสูจน์ proof

ganpisud *n.* การพิสูจน์ substantiation

ganpisud *n.* การพิสูจน์ verification

ganplad *n.* การพลาด miss

ganplae *n.* การแปล translation

ganplak *n.* การผลัก repulsion

ganplak *n.* การผลัก shove

ganplak *n* การผลัก thrust

ganpleuaygai *n.* การเปลือยกาย nudity

ganplian *n.* การเปลี่ยน transition

ganpliangplaeng *n.* การเปลี่ยนแปลง vicissitude

ganplianjaigatanhan *n.* การเปลี่ยนใจกะทันหัน caprice

ganplianplaeng *n.* การเปลี่ยนแปลง change

ganplianplaeng *n* การเปลี่ยนแปลง conversion

ganplianplaeng *n.* การเปลี่ยนแปลง transformation

ganplianplaeng *n.* การเปลี่ยนแปลง variance

ganplianplaeng *n.* การเปลี่ยนแปลง variation

ganplianplaengchacha *n.* การเปลี่ยนแปลงช้าๆ gradation

ganplianramdab *n.* การเปลี่ยนลำดับ permutation

ganplianroob *n.* การเปลี่ยนรูป transfiguration

ganplianroobrang *n.* การเปลี่ยนรูปร่าง metamorphosis

ganpliansasana *n* การเปลี่ยนศาสนา convert

ganplikglab *n.* การพลิกกลับ reversal

ganplobjai *n* การปลอบใจ consolation

ganplobjai *n.* การปลอมใจ solace

ganplod-a-wut *n.* การปลดอาวุธ disarmament

ganplodployhaipen-issara n. การปลดปล่อยให้เป็นอิสระ emancipation

ganplodploytad n. การปลดปล่อยทาส manumission

ganplomplaeng n การปลอมแปลง forgery

ganplomplaeng n การปลอมแปลง sham

ganplomtua n การปลอมตัว disguise

ganplon n. การปล้น loot

ganplon n การปล้น plunder

ganplon n. การปล้น robbery

ganploy n การปล่อย release

ganploytua n. การปล่อยตัว acquittal

ganplu n กานพลู clove

ganplukfee n. การปลูกฝี inoculation

ganplukpan n การปลุกปั่น agitation

ganplukpan n. การปลุกปั่น manipulation

ganplukradom n. การปลุกระดม sedition

ganpluktai-a-waiyawa n. การปลูกถ่ายอวัยวะ graft

ganpobhennaitookti n. การพบเห็นในทุกที่ omnipresence

ganpobpa n. การพบปะ meet

ganpokkrong n. การปกครอง governance

ganpokkrong n. การปกครอง rule

ganpokkrongtimaidi n. การปกครองที่ไม่ดี misrule

ganpokkrongtimigasatpenpramuk n. การปกครองที่มีกษัตริย์เป็นประมุข monarchy

ganpokpid n. การปกปิด cover

ganpokpong n. การปกป้อง protection

ganpon n การพ่น spurt

ganponchamrapen-nguad n. การผ่อนชำระเป็นงวด instalment

ganponggan n การป้องกัน defence

ganponggan n. การป้องกัน prevention

ganponjaktamnaeng n. การพ้นจากตำแหน่ง discharge

ganponklai n. การผ่อนคลาย relaxation

ganponklai n. การผ่อนคลาย relief

ganponklai n. การผ่อนคลาย remission

ganponpan n. การผ่อนผัน indulgence

ganpontod n. การพ้นโทษ impunity

ganprabgae n. การปรับแก้ adjustment

ganprabplian n. การปรับเปลี่ยน modification

ganprabpram n. การปราบปราม subjugation

ganprabpram n. การปราบปราม suppression

ganprabprung n. การปรับปรุง improvement

ganprabprungmai n. การปรับปรุงใหม่ renovation

ganprabtua n. การปรับตัว adaptation

ganprabtuadaimaidi n. การปรับตัวได้ไม่ดี mal adjustment

ganprachasampan n. การประชาสัมพันธ์ publication

ganprachum n. การประชุม assembly

ganprachum n การประชุม conference

ganprachum n การประชุม convention

ganprachum n การประชุม meeting

ganprachum n. การประชุม session

ganprachum n. การประชุม summit

ganprachumsamana n. การประชุมสัมมนา symposium

ganpradab n. การประดับ ornamentation

ganpradid n. การประดิษฐ์ invention

ganpraepan n. การแพร่พันธุ์ proliferation

ganpraetat n. การแปรธาตุ alchemy

ganpragad n. การประกาศ proclamation

ganpragan n. การประกัน insurance

ganpragan n. การประกัน warrant

ganpragantua n. การประกันตัว bail

ganpragob n. การประกอบ concoction

ganpragottua n การปรากฏตัว appearance

ganpragottua n. การปรากฏตัว presence

ganpraguad n. การประกวด pageant

ganprajan n. การประจาน denunciation

ganprajobprajaeng n. การประจบประแจง sycophancy

ganpralongfeemeu *n* การประลองฝีมือ bout

ganprameun *n.* การประเมิน assessment

ganprameunraka *n.* การประเมินราคา valuation

ganpramoon *n* การประมูล auction

ganpramoon *n* การประมูล bid

ganpranam *n* การประณาม condemnation

ganpraprudpid *n.* การประพฤติผิด misconduct

ganpraprudtuamaimawsom *n.* การประพฤติตัวไม่เหมาะสม misbehaviour

ganprasai *n.* การปราศรัย oration

ganprasan-ngan *n* การประสานงาน co-ordination

ganpratuang *n.* การประท้วง demonstration

ganpratuang *n.* การประท้วง protest

ganpratuang *n.* การประท้วง protestation

ganpriabtiab *n* การเปรียบเทียบ comparison

ganpriabtiab *n.* การเปรียบเทียบ metaphor

ganpriabtiab *n.* การเปรียบเทียบ simile

ganprobmeu *n.* การปรบมือ applause

ganprobmeu *n* การปรบมือ clap

ganprobmeutawnrab *n.* การปรบมือต้อนรับ ovation

ganpromtua *n.* การปลอมตัว impersonation

ganpuay *n* การป่วย ill

ganpuay *n.* การป่วย malady

ganpud *n.* การพูด say

ganpud *n* การพูด talk

ganpudgabtua-eng *n.* การพูดกับตัวเอง soliloquy

ganpudgeunjing *n.* การพูดเกินจริง exaggeration

ganpudgeunjing *n.* การพูดเกินจริง hyperbole

ganpudklumkreua *n.* การพูดคลุมเครือ quibble

ganpudkui *n.* การพูดคุย chat

ganpudmaichad *n* การพูดไม่ชัด lisp

ganpudmaichad *n.* การพูดไม่ชัด slur

ganpudpennai *n.* การพูดเป็นนัย intimation

ganpudplam *n.* การพูดพล่าม babble

ganpudraisara *n.* การพูดไร้สาระ prattle

ganpudsaek *n.* การพูดแทรก interjection

ganpudsam *n.* การพูดซ้ำ repetition

ganpudtalok *n.* การพูดตลก jest

ganpudtid-ang *n* การพูดติดอ่าง stammer

ganpudyangmiwatasin *n* การพูดอย่างมีวาทศิลป์ eloquence

ganpudyawn *n.* การพูดย้อน retort

ganpudyawyei *n.* การพูดเยาะเย้ย scoff

ganpuk *n* การผูก tie

ganrab *n.* การรับ admission

ganra-bad *n* การระบาด epidemic

ganrabailom *n.* การระบายลม ventilation

ganrabainam *n* การระบายน้ำ drainage

ganrabainamting *n.* การระบายน้ำทิ้ง sewerage

ganrabchai *n.* การรับใช้ serve

ganrabeud *n* การระเบิด burst

ganrabeud *n.* การระเบิด explosion

ganrabeud *n.* การระเบิด outburst

ganrabeud *n* การระเบิด blast

ganrabbudboontam *n* การรับบุตรบุญธรรม adoption

ganrabmoradok *n.* การรับมรดก inheritance

ganrabrong *n.* การรับรอง assurance

ganrabrong *n.* การรับรอง guarantee

ganrabrong *n.* การรับรอง recognition

ganrabrong *n.* การรับรอง warranty

ganrabru *n* การรับรู้ cognizance

ganrabru *n* การรับรู้ conception

ganrabsinbon *n.* การรับสินบน venality

ganradomying *n.* การระดมยิง volley

ganradomyingpeunyai *n. v. & t*
การระดมยิงปืนใหญ่ cannonade

ganra-gnabchuakrao *n.* การระงับชั่วคราว
abeyance

ganraikwamruseuk *n.* การไร้ความรู้สึก
insensibility

ganraikwamsamad *n.*
การไร้ความสามารถ inability

ganraikwamsamad *n.*
การไร้ความสามารถ incapacity

ganraiprayod *n.* การไร้ประโยชน์ futility

ganraiwetmon *n.* การร่ายเวทมนตร์
mysticism

ganraksa *n* การรักษา cure

ganraksa *n.* การรักษา remedy

ganraksakwamsa-ad *n*
การรักษาความสะอาด cleanliness

ganraksapromajan *n.* การรักษาพรมจรรย์
chastity

ganramleukteung-a-dit *n.*
การรำลึกถึงอดีต retrospect

ganramleukteung-a-dit *n.*
การรำลึกถึงอดีต retrospection

ganra-ngabchuakrao *n.* การระงับชั่วคราว
suspension

ganranggiad *n.* การรังเกียจ aversion

ganrangta *n* การล้างตา eyewash

ganrareukdai *n.* การระลึกได้ recall

ganrareukteung *n.* การระลึกถึง
commemoration

ganrawaedrawang *n.* การระแวดระวัง
vigilance

ganrawkoy *n.* การรอคอย wait

ganreum *n* การเริ่ม start

ganreingkwamrew *n* การเร่งความเร็ว
acceleration

ganreng *n* การเร่ง urge

ganrengrib *n* การเร่งรีบ hurry

ganreu *n* การเรอ belch

ganreum *n* การเริ่ม commencement

ganreum *n.* การเริ่ม launch

ganreumton *n.* การเริ่มต้น inception

ganreumton *n.* การเริ่มต้น outset

ganreumtonmai *n.* การเริ่มต้นใหม่
resumption

ganriak *n.* การเรียก call

ganriakcheupid *n.* การเรียกชื่อผิด
misnomer

ganriakdawkbiageun-atta *n.*
การเรียกดอกเบี้ยเกินอัตรา usury

ganriakkatai *n.* การเรียกค่าไถ่ ransom

ganriakrong *n.* การเรียกร้อง calling

ganriakrong *n* การเรียกร้อง claim

ganriakrong *n* การเรียกร้อง demand

ganriakrong *n.* การเรียกร้อง pretension

ganriakrong *n.* การเรียกร้อง solicitation

ganrianpised *n.* การเรียนพิเศษ tutorial

ganrianru *n.* การเรียนรู้ learning

ganribreing *n.* การรีบเร่ง rush

ganriekprachum *n.* การเรียกประชุม
convocation

ganrireum *n.* การริเริ่ม initiative

ganrobguan *n* การรบกวน botheration

ganrobguan *n.* การรบกวน nag

ganrobguan *n.* การรบกวน nuisance

ganrobrusasana *n.* การลบหลู่ศาสนา
sacrilege

ganrodchiwit *n.* การรอดชีวิต survival

ganlomrob *n.* การล้อมรอบ circumfluence

ganronghai *n* การร้องไห้ cry

ganronghaikramkruan *n*
การร้องไห้คร่ำครวญ wail

ganrongkaw *n* การร้องขอ adjuration

ganrongkaw *n.* การร้องขอ entreaty

ganlongleum *n.* การหลงลืม oblivion

ganrongpleing *n* การร้องเพลง chant

ganrong-prasan-siang *n.*
การร้องประสานเสียง chorus

ganrongrian *n.* การร้องเรียน petition

ganronnarong *n.* การรณรงค์ campaign

ganrookjontam *n* การรุกจนแต้ม
checkmate

ganrabru *n.* การรับรู้ perception

ganrua *n.* การรั่ว leakage

ganruabruambodprapan *n.*
การรวบรวมบทประพันธ์ anthology
ganruabruampojjananugrom *n.*
การรวบรวมพจนานุกรม lexicography
ganrualai *n.* การรั่วไหล leak
ganruam *n.* การรวม inclusion
ganruamgan *n* การรวมกัน combination
ganruamgan *n.* การรวมกัน conjuncture
ganruamgan *n.* การรวมกัน merger
ganruamglum *n* การรวมกลุ่ม
consolidation
ganruamkaoduaygan *n.*
การรวมเข้าด้วยกัน incorporation
ganruammeu *n* การร่วมมือ co-operation
ganruamped *n.* การร่วมเพศ intercourse
ganruampedtangtawannak *n.*
การร่วมเพศทางทวารหนัก sodomy
ganruabruam *n* การรวบรวม muster
ganruamtua *n* การรวมตัว embodiment
ganruamtuagan *n.* การรวมตัวกัน
unification
ganruhenpenjai *n.* การรู้เห็นเป็นใจ
connivance
ganruk *n* การรุก offensive
ganrukran *n* การรุกราน aggression
ganrukran *n.* การรุกราน invasion
ganruluangna *n.* การรู้ล่วงหน้า
foreknowledge
ganruluangna *n* การรู้ล่วงหน้า foresight
ganruluangna *n.* การรู้ล่วงหน้า prescience
gansabplian *n.* การสับเปลี่ยน shuffle
gansad *n* การสาด splash
gansadaeng *n* การแสดง display
gansadaeng *n.* การแสดง performance
gansadaeng *n.* การแสดง show
gansadaengdiaw *n.* การแสดงเดี่ยว solo
gansadaengkwamkaorob *n.*
การแสดงความเคารพ salutation
gansadaengkwamsiajai *n*
การแสดงความเสียใจ condolence
gansadaengkwamyindi *n*
การแสดงความยินดี congratulation

gansadaengrobpratommatat *n.*
การแสดงรอบปฐมทัศน์ premiere
gansadaengsalabchak *n.*
การแสดงสลับฉาก interlude
gansadaengtua *n.* การแสดงตัว
indentification
gansadaengloadpoan *n*
การแสดงโลดโผน stunt
gansadeang *n.* การแสดง acting
gansadud *n.* การสะดุด stumble
gansaek *n.* การแทรก insertion
gansaeksaeng *n.* การแทรกแซง
interference
gansaeksaeng *n.* การแทรกแซง
intervention
gansaeksaeng *n.* การแทรกเซง
penetration
gansaeksang *n.* การแทรกแซง
interruption
gansa-eun *n* การสะอื้น sob
gansagadgan *n.* การสกัดกั้น interception
gansagodjit *n.* การสะกดจิต hypnotism
gansagodjit *n.* การสะกดจิต mesmerism
gansagodroy *n.* การสะกดรอย track
gansairai *n* การใส่ร้าย defamation
gansakgara *n.* การสักการะ worship
gansaklang *n* การซักล้าง wash
gansakrid *n.* การซักรีด laundry
gansaktam *n.* การซักถาม interrogation
gansala *n.* การสละ renunciation
gansalaitua *n.* การสลายตัว
decomposition
gansala-umnad *n* การสละอำนาจ
abdication
gansaroob *n* การสรุป brevity
gansamak *n.* การสมัคร application
gansamakpennaksuksa *n.*
การสมัครเป็นนักศึกษา matriculation
gansamakpensamachik *n.*
การสมัครเป็นสมาชิก subscription
gansamana *n.* การสัมนา seminar
gansamneukpid *n.* การสำนึกผิด remorse

gansamneukpid *n.* การสำนึกผิด
repentance
gansampad *n* การสัมผัส touch
gansampat *n.* การสัมภาษณ์ interview
gansamrok *n.* การสำรอก rumination
gansamruad *n.* การสำรวจ conspectus
gansamruad *n* การสำรวจ exploration
gansamruad *n.* การสำรวจ survey
gansamruadkwamhen *n.*
การสำรวจความเห็น poll
gansamruadprachagon *n.*
การสำรวจประชากร census
gansan *n* การสั่น quake
gansan *n* การสั่น shake
gansan *n.* การสั่น vibration
gansanabsanoon *n.* การสนับสนุน
advocacy
gansanabsanoon *n.* การสนับสนุน support
gansaneu *n* การเสนอ offer
gansaneucheu *n.* การเสนอชื่อ nomination
gansang *n* การสร้าง creation
gansangbaeb *n* การสร้างแบบ formation
gansanghan *n* การสังหาร carnage
gansanghanmu *n.* การสังหารหมู่
holocaust
gansanghanmu *n.* การสังหารหมู่ massacre
gansangget *n.* การสังเกต observance
gansanggetgan *n.* การสังเกตการณ์
observation
gansangkraw *n.* การสังเคราะห์ synthesis
gansangpabkleuanwai *n*
การสร้างภาพเคลื่อนไหว animation
gansangprayok *n.* การสร้างประโยค
syntax
gansannitan *n.* การสันนิษฐาน
presumption
gansannitan *n.* การสันนิษฐาน
presupposition
gansannitan *n.* การสันนิษฐาน surmise
gansanseun *n* การสรรเสริญ laud
gansanwai *n.* การสั่นไหว tremor
gansappa-ngok *n.* การสัปหงก doze

gansarapab *n* การสารภาพ confession
gansaroob *n.* การสรุป summary
gangasian-a-yu *n.* การเกษียณอายุ
retirement
gansasom *n* การสะสม accumulation
gansasom *n* การสะสม collection
gansatapana *n* การสถาปนา coronation
gansatonglab *n.* การสะท้อนกลับ rebound
gansatonglab *n.* การสะท้อนกลับ
reflection
gansawmrob *n.* การซ้อมรบ manoeuvre
ganse *n.* การเซ stagger
gansesaeng *n* การเสแสร้ง affectation
gansesaeng *n.* การเสแสร้ง hypocrisy
gansesaeng *n.* การเสแสร้ง pretence
ganseu *n.* การซื้อ purchase
ganseubpan *n* การสืบพันธุ์ reproduction
ganseubsagoon *n.* การสืบสกุล descent
ganseubsuan *n* การสืบสวน probe
ganseubtamnaeng *n.* การสืบตำแหน่ง
succession
ganseukai *n* การซื้อขาย deal
ganseumgamlang *n.* การเสริมกำลัง
reinforcement
ganseusan *n.* การสื่อสาร communication
gansia *n* การเสีย breakdown
gansiacheusiang *n* การเสียชื่อเสียง
disrepute
gansiadsi *n.* การเสียดสี sarcasm
gansiadsi *n.* การเสียดสี satire
gansiang *n.* การเสี่ยง risk
gansiangpai *n.* การเสี่ยงภัย venture
gansiaprayod *n* การเสียประโยชน์
disadvantage
gansiasara *n.* การเสียสละ sacrifice
gansinsud *n.* การสิ้นสุด end
gansinsud *n.* การสิ้นสุด termination
gansobsuan *n.* การสอบสวน inquest
gansobsuan *n.* การสอบสวน inquiry
gansobsuan *n.* การสอบสวน inquisition
gansobsuan *n.* การสอบสวน investigation
gansodsaek *n.* การสอดแทรก insinuation

gansom n. การซ้อม rehearsal

gansom n. การซ่อม repair

gansommudpriabtiab n. การสมมติเปรียบเทียบ allegory

gansomrod n. การสมรส wedlock

gansomruruamkid n การสมรู้ร่วมคิด collusion

gansomruruamkid n. การสมรู้ร่วมคิด conspiracy

gansong-awk n การส่งออก export

gansongglabprated n. การส่งกลับประเทศ repatriation

gansong-ngeun n. การส่งเงิน remittance

gansongpan n. การส่งผ่าน transmission

gansongsawang n. การส่องสว่าง illumination

gansongseum n การส่งเสริม boost

gansongseum n. การส่งเสริม promotion

gansongtoralek v.t. การส่งโทรเลข telegraph

gansongtuaputonghaglab n การส่งตัวผู้ต้องหากลับ remand

gansontana n การสนทนา conversation

gansontanasongtawsong n. การสนทนาสองต่อสอง tete-a-tete

gansoob n. การสูบ pump

gansoonsia n. การสูญเสีย wastage

gansoonsia n การสูญเสีย bereavement

gansuadmon n. การสวดมนต์ prayer

gansuadmonsongwinyanputai n. การสวดมนต์ส่งวิญญาณผู้ตาย requiem

gansuansay n. การชวนเซ lurch

gansuksa n การศึกษา education

gansuksa n. การศึกษา study

gansuksagiawgabrae n. การศึกษาเกี่ยวกับแร่ mineralogy

gantabtam n. การทาบทาม overture

gantad n การตัด cut

gantad n การตัด trim

gantadsinjai n การตัดสินใจ decision

gantadsinjai n. การตัดสินใจ determination

gantadsuansamkan-awk n. การตัดส่วนสำคัญออก mutilation

gantadton n การตัดทอน abridgement

gantadton n การตัดตอน extract

gantaek n การแตก split

gantaek-awk n. การแตกออก rupture

gantaeknaw n. การแตกหน่อ germination

gantaektuakongsell n การแตกตัวของเซล accrementition

gantaekyaek n การแตกแยก division

gantaen n. การแทน lieu

gantaeng n. การแทง lunge

gantaeng n. การแท้ง miscarriage

gantaeng n. การแทง stab

gantaengbodglon n. การแต่งบทกลอน versification

gantaeng-ngan n. การแต่งงาน marriage

gantaeng-ngan n. การแต่งงาน matrimony

gantaeng-ngan n. การแต่งงาน nuptials

gantaeng-ngan n. การแต่งงาน wedding

gantaengreuang n การแต่งเรื่อง fabrication

gantaengtangputaen n การแต่งตั้งผู้แทน deputation

gantaengtua n การแต่งตัว dress

gantaenti n. การแทนที่ replacement

gantaenti n. การแทนที่ substitution

gantagoan n การตะโกน yell

gantagoan n. การตะโกน shout

gantai n การตาย mortal

gantai n. การตาย mortality

gantaibab a. การไถ่บาป same

gantaikamsampad n. การทายคำสัมผัส crambo

gantaipab n. การถ่ายภาพ photography

gantaipabduayrangsi-x n. การถ่ายภาพด้วยรังสีเอ็กซ์ x-ray

gantaipasawa n. การถ่ายปัสสาวะ urination

gantaisamnao n. การถ่ายสำเนา xerox

gantaitoad n. การไถ่โทษ atonement

gantaitod n. การถ่ายทอด relay

gantagoan *n.i.* การตะโกน bawl

gantakteuan *n.* การตักเตือน admonition

gantakteuan *n.* การตักเตือน caution

gantaktuang *n* การตักตวง exploit

gantalaw *n.* การทะเลาะ quarrel

gantalaw *n.* การทะเลาะ wrangle

gantalawwiwat *n* การทะเลาะวิวาท fray

gantalawwiwat *n* การทะเลาะวิวาท row

gantamhaidikeun *n.* การทำให้ดีขึ้น amelioration

gantamhai-imtua *n.* การทำให้อิ่มตัว saturation

gantamhaibaokeun การทำให้เบาขึ้น lightening

gantamhaikrobtuan *n* การทำให้ครบถ้วน completion

gantamhaikunkeuang *n.* การทำให้ขุ่นเคือง offence

gantamhaimai *n* การทำให้ไหม้ singe

gantamhaimankong *n.* การทำให้มั่นคง stabilization

gantamhai-on-yao *n.* การทำให้อ่อนเยาว์ rejuvenation

gantamhaipawjai *n.* การทำให้พอใจ complaisance

gantamhaipenlon *n* การทำให้เป็นลอน crimp

gantamhaipensamtao *n.* การทำให้เป็นสามเท่า triplication

gantamhaipentirak *n.* การทำให้เป็นที่รัก endearment

gantamhaiprasajakcheua *n.* การทำให้ปราศจากเชื้อ sterilization

gantamhairiab-ngai *n.* การทำให้เรียบง่าย simplification

gantamhairoonraeng *n.* การทำให้รุนแรง aggravation

gantamhaiteung *n* การทำให้ตึง strain

gantamhaitooktong *n.* การทำให้ถูกต้อง rectification

gantamhok *n* การทำหก spill

gantamkwamdi *n.* การทำความดี benefaction

gantamlai *n* การทำลาย destruction

gantamlailang *n* การทำลายล้าง annihilation

gantamlailang *n.* การทำลายล้าง nihilism

gantamleb *n.* การทำเล็บ manicure

gantammanchai *n.* การทำหมันชาย vasectomy

gantamnabeung *n.* การทำหน้าบึ้ง frown

gantamnabeung *n.* การทำหน้าบึ้ง scowl

gantamnai *n.* การทำนาย prediction

gantamnai *n.* การทำนาย prophecy

gantam-ngan-makpai *n.* การทำงานมากไป overwork

gantam-ngannak *n. pl.* การทำงานหนัก toils

gantamni *n.* การตำหนิ censure

gantamni *n.* การตำหนิ reprimand

gantamni *n.* การตำหนิ reproach

gantamni *n.* การตำหนิ reproof

gantampaenti *n.* การทำแผนที่ topography

gantampentarang *n.* การทำเป็นตาราง tabulation

gantamkwampidlekleknoynoy *n.* การทำความผิดเล็กๆ น้อยๆ misdemeanour

gantamrai *n.* การทำร้าย assault

gantamlairang *n.* การทำลายล้าง ravage

gantamlairang *n.* การทำลายล้าง sabotage

gantamsam *n* การทำซ้ำ duplicate

gantamsamnao *n.* การทำสำเนา mimesis

gantamtaeng *n* การทำแท้ง abortion

gantamtod *n.* การทำโทษ punishment

gantamhaibenchat *n.* การทำให้เป็นชาติ nationalization

gantangchan *n* การตั้งชัน erection

gantangcheu *n.* การตั้งชื่อ nomenclature

gantangkan *n.* การตั้งครรภ์ pregnancy

gantanom-a-han *v.t.* ถนอมอาหาร preserve

gantansongkram *n.* การทำสงคราม warfare

gantaogan *n.* การเท่ากัน par

gantaroon *n.* การทารุณ mal-treatment

gantasi *n.* การทาสี painting

gantaw-a-yu *n.* การต่ออายุ renewal

gantawn *n* การถอน pluck

gantawn *n.* การถอน withdrawal

gantawnhaijai *n.* การถอนหายใจ sigh

gantawnrab *n.* การต้อนรับ reception

gantawraman *n.* การทรมาน torture

gantawrayod *n.* การทรยศ treachery

gantawrayod *n.* การทรยศ treason

gantawrong *n.* การต่อรอง bargain

gantawsu *n* การต่อสู้ combat1

gantawsu *n* การต่อสู้ fight

gantawsu *n* การต่อสู้ flight

gantawsu *n* การต่อสู้ struggle

gantawsugan-udtalud *n.* การต่อสู้กันอุตลุด scuffle

gantawsuyangchunlamoon *n.* การต่อสู้อย่างชุลมุน melee

gantawtan *n.* การต่อต้าน repugnance

gantawtan *n.* การต่อต้าน resistance

gante *n.* การเตะ kick

gantenpenjangwa *n.* การเต้นเป็นจังหวะ pulsation

gantenpenjangwa *n.* การเต้นเป็นจังหวะ throb

gantenram *n* การเต้นรำ dance

gantenruakonghuajai *n* การเต้นรัวของหัวใจ flutter

gantesana *n.* การเทศนา sermon

ganteuan *n.* การเตือน warning

ganteuanluangna *n.* การเตือนล่วงหน้า premonition

ganteubto *n.* การเติบโต growth

ganteun *n* การตื่น wake

ganti *n* การตี hit

ganti *n.* การตี smack

gantidcheua *n.* การติดเชื้อ infection

gantidcheua *n.* การติดเชื้อ sepsis

gantidkad *n.* การติดขัด jam

gantidkad *n.* การติดขัด lock

gantidnaen *n.* การติดแน่น adhesion

gantidtam *n.* การติดตาม pursuance

gantidtam *n.* การติดตาม pursuit

gantidtang *n.* การติดตั้ง installation

gantidtaw *n.* การติดต่อ contact

gantidtaw *n.* การติดต่อ dealing

gantidtawtangturagid *n.* การติดต่อทางธุรกิจ transaction

gantidya *n.* การติดยา addiction

gantilanga *n.* การตีลังกา somersault

gantilookdong *n.* การตีลูกโด่ง loft

gantim *n.* การทิ่ม poke

ganting *n* การทิ้ง drop

gantiraka *n.* การตีราคา estimate

gantirakang *n* การตีระฆัง toll

gantob *n.* การตบ slap

gantobsanong *n.* การตอบสนอง reaction

gantobsanongtawsinggratun *n.* การตอบสนองต่อสิ่งกระตุ้น sensibility

gantobtuan *n* การทบทวน review

gantobtuankwamrusuktua-eng *n.* การทบทวนความรู้สึกตัวเอง introspection

gantodlong *n* การทดลอง experiment

gantodlong *n.* การทดลอง trial

gantodsob *n.* การทดสอบ examination

gantodsob *n* การทดสอบ test

gantodton *n.* การถอดถอน privation

gantokjai *n.* การตกใจ shock

gantoklong *n.* การตกลง settlement

gantoktaeng *n* การตกแต่ง decoration

gantoktaengpainai *n.* การตกแต่งภายใน interior

gantoktam *n.* การตกต่ำ slump

gantoktamtangsedtagid *n.* การตกต่ำทางเศรษฐกิจ recession

gantom *n* การต้ม boil

gantomnamlai *n* การถ่มน้ำลาย spit

gantomtua *n* การถ่อมตัว abasement
gantomtua *n* การถ่อมตัว modesty
gantongjam *n.* การท่องจำ recital
gantongjam *n.* การท่องจำ recitation
gantongtiaw. *n.* การท่องเที่ยว tour
gantonmaidai *n.* การทนไม่ได้ intolerance
gantonrab *n* การต้อนรับ welcome
gantookgakkang *n.* การถูกกักขัง captivity
gantookprab *n* การถูกปรับ forfeit
gantorayod *n* การทรยศ betrayal
gantorayod *n.* การทรยศ perfidy
gantotiangganleknoy *n.*
    การโต้เถียงกันเล็กน้อย skirmish
gantotob *n.* การโต้ตอบ correspondence
gantoy *n* การต่อย smash
gantoyaeng *n.* การโต้แย้ง moot
gantoylang *n.* การถอยหลัง recoil
gantoylang *n* การถอยหลัง reverse
gantraitrongluangna *n.*
    การไตร่ตรองล่วงหน้า premeditation
gantriamgan *n.* การเตรียมการ preparation
gantriamprom *n* การเตรียมพร้อม
    expedition
gantrongtawwela *n.* การตรงต่อเวลา
    punctuality
gantruadsob *n.* การตรวจสอบ censorship
gantruadsob *n.* การตรวจสอบ inspection
gantruadsob *n* การตรวจสอบ check
gantruadsobbanchi *n.* การตรวจสอบบัญชี
    audit
gantruadtra *n.* การตรวจตรา surveillance
gantub *n.* การทุบ thump
gantujarit *n.* การทุจริต corruption
gantujarit *n.* การทุจริต jobbery
gantut *n* การทูต diplomacy
gan-uad-ru *n.* การอวดรู้ pedantry
gan-udtankongsenleudtipailiangsamong
    n
    การอุดตันของเส้นเลือดที่ไปเลี้ยงสมอง
    stroke
gan-umla *n.* การอำลา conge
gan-u-patam *n.* การอุปถัมภ์ patronage

gan-u-tidtua *n* การอุทิศตัว dedication
gan-u-tidtua *n* การอุทิศตัว devotion
ganwad *n* การวาด draw
ganwad *n.* การวัด measure
ganwad *n.* การวัด measurement
ganwadpabkon *n.* การวาดภาพคน
    portrayal
ganwadroob *n* การวาดรูป drawing
ganwai *v.t.* กันไว้ appropriate
ganwainam *n* การว่ายน้ำ swim
ganwan *n.* การหว่าน sow
ganwangkawgamnod *n.*
    การวางข้อกำหนด imposition
ganwangmad *n.* การวางมาด pomposity
ganwangnaew *n.* การวางแนว alignment
ganwangpleung *n* การวางเพลิง arson
ganwangto *n* การวางโต swagger
ganwijai *n* การวิจัย research
ganwijan *n* การวิจารณ์ criticism
ganwikraw *n.* การวิเคราะห์ analysis
ganwing *n* การวิ่ง canter
ganwing *n.* การวิ่ง run
ganwinglen *n.* การวิ่งเล่น romp
ganwinglen *n* การวิ่งเล่น scamper
ganwingnairayasan *n* การวิ่งในระยะสั้น
    sprint
ganwingyawyaw *n* การวิ่งเยาะๆ trot
ganwinichairok *n.* การวินิจฉัยโรค
    diagnosis
ganwiwad *n.* การวิวาท altercation
ganwiwad *v. i. & n* การวิวาท brawl
ganya *n* การหย่า divorce
ganyabyang *n.* การยับยั้ง veto
ganyaek-awk *n* การแยกออก detachment
ganyaek-awkjakgan *n.*
    การแยกออกจากกัน separation
ganyaekpraped *n.* การแยกประเภท sort
ganyaektua-awk *n.* การแยกตัวออก
    secession
ganyaengching *n* การแย่งชิง scramble
ganyaengching-amnad *n.*
    การแย่งชิงอำนาจ usurpation

ganyai *n.* การย้าย removal

ganyaitintan *n.* การย้ายถิ่นฐาน transmigration

ganyakkewlewta *n* การยักคิ้วหลิ่วตา ogle

ganyaklai *n* การยักไหล่ shrug

ganyangchib *n.* การยังชีพ sustenance

ganyanom *n* การหย่านม ablactation

ganyawnglab *n.* การย้อนกลับ return

ganyawyei *n.* การเยาะเย้ย ridicule

ganyayon *n.* กันยายน September

ganyebpaktakroy *n* การเย็บปักถักร้อย embroidery

ganyeudman *n.* การยึดมั่น adherence

ganyeudsab *n* การยึดทรัพย์ confiscation

ganyeudsab *n* การยึดทรัพย์ forfeiture

ganyeudsab *n.* การยึดทรัพย์ levy

ganyeud-um-nard *n.* การยึดอำนาจ coup

ganyeungran *n.* การยืนกราน persistence

ganyeunpramoon *n* การยื่นประมูล tender

ganyeunyan *n* การยืนยัน affirmation

ganyeunyan *n* การยืนยัน confirmation

ganyeunyan *n.* การยืนยัน insistence

ganyiadsipew *n.* การเหยียดสีผิว racialism

ganyiamyian *n.* การเยี่ยมเยียน visit

ganyibchuay *n* การหยิบฉวย snap

ganyingpeun *n.* การยิงปืน shoot

ganyinyom *n.* การยินยอม approbation

ganyinyom *n* การยินยอม yield

gan-yinyom *n.* การยินยอม consent

ganyoen *n* การโยน toss

ganyoi *n* การย่อย digestion

ganyoisalai *n* การย่อยสลาย decay

ganyokhaisoongkeun *n* การยกให้สูงขึ้น elevation

ganyokkeunsoong *n* การยกขึ้นสูง uplift

ganyokkreung *n.* การยกเครื่อง overhaul

ganyoklaw *n.* การหยอกล้อ pleasantry

ganyoklaw *n.* การหยอกล้อ raillery

ganyokleuk *n* การยกเลิก cancellation

ganyokleuk *n* การยกเลิก repeal

ganyokyaw *n* การยกยอ adulation

ganyokyong *n.* การยกย่อง praise

ganyomjamnon *n.* การยอมจำนน submission

ganyompae *n* การยอมแพ้ surrender

ganyomrab *n* การยอมรับ acceptance

ganyomrab *n.* การยอมรับ acknowledgement

ganyomrab *n.* การยอมรับ assent

ganyomrabchai *n.* การยอมรับใช้ servility

ganyomrabpen-ekgachan *n.* การยอมรับเป็นเอกฉันท์ unanimity

ganyomtam *n.* การยอมตาม acquiescence

ganyomtamtam *n.* การยอมทำตาม compliance

ganyongbao *n* การย่องเบา burglary

ganyongkaoglai *n.* การย่องเข้าใกล้ stalk

ganyu *n* การอยู่ stay

ganyuayu *n.* การยั่วยุ provocation

ganyuayuan *n.* การยั่วยวน seduction

ganyud *n* การหยุด stop

ganyud *n* การหยุด stoppage

ganyudchuakrao *n* การหยุดชั่วคราว halt

ganyudchuakrao *n.* การหยุดชั่วคราว pause

ganyudhaijaichuakrao *n* การหยุดหายใจชั่วคราว apnoea

ganyudning *n.* การหยุดนิ่ง standstill

ganyudoddiaw *n.* การอยู่โดดเดี่ยว solitude

ganyudpak *n.* การหยุดพัก recess

ganyuna *n.* การอยู่หน้า precedence

ganyunaipawang *n.* การอยู่ในภวังค์ trance

ganyuruamgan *n* การอยู่ร่วมกัน co-existence

ganyuruamgandoeymaitaeng-ngan *v. t* การอยู่ร่วมกันโดยไม่แต่งงาน cohabit

ganyuruamgandoeymaitaeng-ngan *n.* การอยู่ร่วมกันโดยไม่แต่งงาน concubinage

ganyutai-amnad *n.* การอยู่ใต้อำนาจ subjection

ganyutaibangkabbancha *n.*
การอยู่ใต้บังคับบัญชา subordination
ganyuti *n.* การยุติ close
ganyutrongglang *n.* การอยู่ตรงกลาง
mediation
ganyuyonghaitampid *n.* การยุยงให้ทำผิด
abetment
gao *n.* กาว adhesive
gao *n.* กาว glue
gao *n.* เกาะ island
gao *n.* เกาะ isle
gao *n.* เก้า nine
gao *v.t.* เก่า stale
gao *n.* ก้าว step
gao *v.i.* ก้าว step
gaodaknok *n* กาวดักนก birdlime
gaodeuan *v.i.* ก้าวเดิน stride
gaogae *a.* เก่าแก่ antiquated
gaogai *v.i.* ก้าวก่าย meddle
gao-ii *n.* เก้าอี้ chair
gao-ii-yao *n.* เก้าอี้ยาว couch
gaokon *v.i.* เกาะคอน perch
gaokon *v.i.* เกาะคอน roost
gaolad *n.* เกาลัด chestnut
gaomak *a.* เก่ามาก threadbare
gaona *v.t.* ก้าวหน้า advance
gaona *adv* ก้าวหน้า forward
gaona *v.i.* ก้าวหน้า progress
gaona *a.* ก้าวหน้า progressive
gaona *a.* ก้าวหน้า prosperous
gaorao *a.* ก้าวร้าว aggressive
gaorao *a.* ก้าวร้าว offensive
gaosib *n.* เก้าสิบ ninety
gaotao *v.i.* ก้าวเท้า pace
garaboon *n.* การบูร camphor
gariyachuay *n.* กริยาช่วย auxiliary
gas *n.* แก๊ส gas
gasat *n.* กษัตริย์ king
gasat *n.* กษัตริย์ monarch
gascheuay *n.* ก๊าซเฉื่อย neon
gasedtagam *n* เกษตรกรรม agriculture
gasedtagon *n.* เกษตรกร agriculturist

gasian *v.i.* เกษียณ retire
gatadrad *a.* กะทัดรัด terse
gatung *v.t.* กระทุ้ง nudge
gawgabot *a.* ก่อกบฏ insurgent
gawgamneud *v.t.* ก่อกำเนิด generate
gawgampaeng *v.t.* ก่อกำแพง wall
gawguan *v.t.* ก่อกวน perturb
gawguan *v.t.* ก่อกวน vex
gawhaigeud *v. t* ก่อให้เกิด beget
gawhaigeud *v.t.* ก่อให้เกิด incur
gawi *n.* กวี bard
gawinipon *n.* กวีนิพนธ์ poesy
gawitisang-nganmaimikunnapab *n.*
กวีที่สร้างงานไม่มีคุณภาพ rhymester
gawjalajon *v.t.* ก่อจลาจล riot
gawjarajon *v.i.* ก่อจลาจล rebel
gawkwammaisa-ngob *a.* ก่อความไม่สงบ
seditious
gawkwamwunwai *v.t.* ก่อความวุ่นวาย
mob
gawsang *v. t.* ก่อสร้าง construct
gawtigeudjakhinpagarang *n.*
เกาะที่เกิดจากหินปะการัง atoll
gawtuakeun-eik-krang *adj*
ก่อตัวขึ้นอีกครั้ง anamorphous
gay *a.* เกย์ gay
gayray *a.* เกเร rowdy
gear *n.* เกียร์ gear
geb-ngeunpeum *v.t.* เก็บเงินเพิ่ม
surcharge
gebpasi *v.t.* เก็บภาษี tax
jebpuayboy *a.* เจ็บป่วยบ่อย sickly
gebraksawainaichuangreudunao *v.i*
เก็บรักษาไว้ในช่วงฤดูหนาว winter
gebwai *v.t.* เก็บไว้ retain
gebwai *v.t.* เก็บไว้ spare
geuyteun *v.i.* เกยตื้น strand
geng *v.i* เก่ง excel
gengraiyang *a.* เก่งหลายอย่าง versatile
geuab *adv.* เกือบ nearly
geud *v.* เกิด born
geudgon *v.t.* เกิดก่อน antecede

geudkeuan-eng *a.* เกิดขึ้นเอง
spontaneous

geudkeun *v.i.* เกิดขึ้น arise

geudkeun *v. t* เกิดขึ้น befall

geudkeun *v.t.* เกิดขึ้น happen

geudkeun *v.i.* เกิดขึ้น occur

geudkeunlanggantai *a.*
เกิดขึ้นหลังการตาย post-mortem

geudkeunpromgan *v. i* เกิดขึ้นพร้อมกัน
coincide

geudkeuntooksongpi *adj* เกิดขึ้นทุกสองปี
biennial

geudmai *a.* เกิดใหม่ incarnate

geudmai *v.t.* เกิดใหม่ regenerate

geudpragaifai *v.i.* เกิดประกายไฟ spark

geudpragaifai *v.i.* เกิดประกายไฟ sparkle

geudsam *v.i.* เกิดซ้ำ recur

geun *v.t* เกิน exceed

geungbod *a.* กึ่งบอด purblind

geungwa *v.t.* เกินกว่า surpass

geungwajapannana *a.*
เกินกว่าจะพรรณนา indescribable

giabgabcheu *a.* เกี่ยวกับชื่อ nominal

giabgabgantaeng-ngan *a.*
เกี่ยวกับการแต่งงาน nuptial

giabgabgantamnai *a.* เกี่ยวกับการทำนาย
prophetic

giabgabgantamsongkram *a.*
เกี่ยวกับการทำสงคราม militant

giawgabpak *a.* เกี่ยวกับปาก oral

giawgabpak *a.* เกี่ยวกับผัก vegetable

giawgabreuanglao *a.* เกี่ยวกับเรื่องเล่า
narrative

giawgabsanya *a.* เกี่ยวกับสัญญา
promissory

giawgabsatawapaed *a.*
เกี่ยวกับสัตวแพทย์ veterinary

giawgabtamnan *a.* เกี่ยวกับตำนาน
mythical

giawgabtamnan *a.* เกี่ยวกับตำนาน
mythological

giawdkran *a.* เกียจคร้าน idle

giadkran *v.i.* เกียจคร้าน laze

giadtiyod *n.* เกียรติยศ honour

giawdong *a.* เกี่ยวดอง akin

giawduaykiaw *v.t.* เกี่ยวด้วยเคียว scythe

giawgab *prep* เกี่ยวกับ about

giawgab *prep.* เกี่ยวกับ considering

giawgab *prep.* เกี่ยวกับ into

giawgab *v.i.* เกี่ยวกับ pertain

giawgab *prep.* เกี่ยวกับ towards

giawgab-a-gad *a.* เกี่ยวกับอากาศ aerial

giawgab-a-wa-gad *a.* เกี่ยวกับอวกาศ
spatial

giawgab-a-gan *a.* เกี่ยวกับอาการ
symptomatic

giawgab-amnadsoongsud *a*
เกี่ยวกับอำนาจสูงสุด sovereign

giawgab-a-naket *a.* เกี่ยวกับอาณาเขต
territorial

giawgab-apipradya *a.* เกี่ยวกับอภิปรัชญา
metaphysical

giawgab-a-tom *a.* เกี่ยวกับอะตอม atomic

giawgab-a-waiyawa *a.* เกี่ยวกับอวัยวะ
organic

giawgabbaina *a* เกี่ยวกับใบหน้า facial

giawgabban *a* เกี่ยวกับบ้าน domestic

giawgabbodgawi *a.* เกี่ยวกับบทกวี lyric

giawgabbodgawi *a.* เกี่ยวกับบทกวี poetic

giawgabboranwattu *a.*
เกี่ยวกับโบราณวัตถุ antiquarian

giawgabborisat *adj.* เกี่ยวกับบริษัท
corporate

giawgabcheuchat *a.* เกี่ยวกับเชื้อชาติ
racial

giawgabchoklang *a.* เกี่ยวกับโชคลาง
superstitious

giawgabchonpao *a.* เกี่ยวกับชนเผ่า tribal

giawgabdek *a.* เกี่ยวกับเด็ก puerile

giawgabdindaennai-udomkati *a.*
เกี่ยวกับดินแดนในอุดมคติ utopian

giawgabdontri *a.* เกี่ยวกับดนตรี musical

giawgabduang-a-tit *a.*
เกี่ยวกับดวงอาทิตย์ solar

giawgabduangjan *a.* เกี่ยวกับดวงจันทร์ lunar

giawgabfaifa *a* เกี่ยวกับไฟฟ้า electric

giawgabfungram *a* เกี่ยวกับฟันกราม molar

giawgabfarangsed *a.* เกี่ยวกับฝรั่งเศส French

giawgabgammatan *a.* เกี่ยวกับกำมะถัน sulphuric

giawgabgan-akseb *a.* เกี่ยวกับการอักเสบ inflammatory

giawgabgan-awkgodmai *a.* เกี่ยวกับการออกกฎหมาย legislative

giawgabgan-awksiang *a.* เกี่ยวกับการออกเสียง phonetic

giawgabganbamroongsukgapab *a.* เกี่ยวกับการบำรุงสุขภาพ tonic

giawgabganborihan *a.* เกี่ยวกับการบริหาร administrative

giawgabganchalong *a* เกี่ยวกับการฉลอง festive

giawgabgandaiyin *adj.* เกี่ยวกับการได้ยิน auditive

giawgabgangaekai *a* เกี่ยวกับการแก้ไข editorial

giawgabgangaesalak *a.* เกี่ยวกับการแกะสลัก sculptural

giawgabgangeud *a.* เกี่ยวกับการเกิด natal

giawgabganjadgan *a.* เกี่ยวกับการจัดการ managerial

giawgabganjarajon *a.* เกี่ยวกับการจลาจล rebellious

giawgabgankaiplik *adv.* เกี่ยวกับการขายปลีก retail

giawgabgankakai *a.* เกี่ยวกับการค้าขาย mercantile

giawgabgankamaetua-eng *a* เกี่ยวกับการฆ่าแม่ตัวเอง matricidal

giawgabgankattagam *a.* เกี่ยวกับการฆาตกรรม murderous

giawgabsadkiaw-euang *a.* เกี่ยวกับสัตว์เคี้ยวเอื้อง ruminant

giawgabganleuklao *a.* เกี่ยวกับการเลิกเหล้า teetotal

giawgabganpatiwat *a.* เกี่ยวกับการปฏิวัติ revolutionary

giawgabganpijaranakadi *a.* เกี่ยวกับการพิจารณาคดี judicial

giawgabganprapan *a.* เกี่ยวกับการประพันธ์ literary

giawgabganrabtamnaeng *a.* เกี่ยวกับการรับตำแหน่ง inaugural

giawgabgansaktam *a.* เกี่ยวกับการซักถาม interrogative

giawgabgansangkraw *a.* เกี่ยวกับการสังเคราะห์ synthetic

giawgabganseub *a* เกี่ยวกับการสืบ detective

giawgabganseubpan *a.* เกี่ยวกับการสืบพันธุ์ reproductive

giawgabgansomrod *a* เกี่ยวกับการสมรส conjugal

giawgabganson *a.* เกี่ยวกับการสอน tutorial

giawgabgansongpan *n.* เกี่ยวกับการส่งผ่าน transitive

giawgabgansongtorajit *a.* เกี่ยวกับการส่งโทรจิต telepathic

giawgabgansongtoralek *a.* เกี่ยวกับการส่งโทรเลข telegraphic

giawgabgansuksa *a.* เกี่ยวกับการศึกษา scholastic

giawgabgansuksaprawatsat *a.* เกี่ยวกับการศึกษาประวัติศาสตร์ historical

giawgabgantaeng-ngan *a.* เกี่ยวกับการแต่งงาน marital

giawgabgantaeng-ngan *a.* เกี่ยวกับการแต่งงาน matrimonial

giawgabgantaeng-ngan *a.* เกี่ยวกับการแต่งงาน morganatic

giawgabgantampaenti *a.* เกี่ยวกับการทำแผนที่ topographical

giawgabgantamtod *a.*
เกี่ยวกับการทำโทษ punitive

giawgabgantawnrab *a.* เกี่ยวกับการรับ
receptive

giawgabgan-x-ray *a.*
เกี่ยวกับการเอ็กซ์เรย์ x-ray

giawgabglamneua *a.* เกี่ยวกับกล้ามเนื้อ
muscular

giawgabgongtahan *n.* เกี่ยวกับกองทหาร
legionary

giawgabgonrayud *a.* เกี่ยวกับกลยุทธ์
strategic

giawgabgradookkawmeu *adj*
เกี่ยวกับกระดูกข้อมือ carpal

giawgabgradooksanlang *a.*
เกี่ยวกับกระดูกสันหลัง spinal

giawgabgrapaw-a-han *a.*
เกี่ยวกับกระเพาะอาหาร gastric

giawgabgreek *a* เกี่ยวกับกรีก Greek

giawgabgymnastic *a.* เกี่ยวกับยิมนาสติก
gymnastic

giawgabhin *a.* เกี่ยวกับหิน megalithic

giawgabhuajai *adj* เกี่ยวกับหัวใจ cardiac

giawgab-india *a.* เกี่ยวกับอินเดีย Indian

giawgabjaikwamsamkan *a.*
เกี่ยวกับใจความสำคัญ thematic

giawgabjao *a.* เกี่ยวกับเจ้า regal

giawgabjitjai *a.* เกี่ยวกับจิตใจ spiritual

giawgabkamab *a.* เกี่ยวกับขมับ temporal

giawgabkamsabchapaw *a.*
เกี่ยวกับคำศัพท์เฉพาะ terminological

giawgabkamsang *a.* เกี่ยวกับคำสั่ง
mandatory

giawgabkamwised *a.* เกี่ยวกับคำวิเศษณ์
adverbial

giawgabkanidsat *a.* เกี่ยวกับคณิตศาสตร์
mathematical

giawgabkanitsat *a.* เกี่ยวกับคณิตศาสตร์
arithmetical

giawgabkareuhad *a.* เกี่ยวกับคฤหาสน์
manorial

giawgabkedron *a.* เกี่ยวกับเขตร้อน
tropical

giawgabket *a.* เกี่ยวกับเขต zonal

giawgabklong *a.* เกี่ยวกับโคลง lyrical

giawgabklongsongtangglai *a.*
เกี่ยวกับความรู้สึก telescopic

giawgabkreuangjak *a.* เกี่ยวกับเครื่องจักร
mechanical

giawgabkwamron *a.* เกี่ยวกับความร้อน
thermal

giawgabkwamruseuk *a.*
เกี่ยวกับความรู้สึก sensational

giawgabkwamruseuk *a.*
เกี่ยวกับความรู้สึก sensuous

giawgablakon *a* เกี่ยวกับละคร dramatic

giawgablakon *a.* เกี่ยวกับละคร theatrical

giawgablamsai *a.* เกี่ยวกับลำไส้ intestinal

giawgabloha *a.* เกี่ยวกับโลหะ metallic

giawgablok *a.* เกี่ยวกับโลก planetary

giawgablokmanud *a* เกี่ยวกับโลกมนุษย์
earthly

giawgabmae *a.* เกี่ยวกับแม่ motherly

giawgabmanud *a.* เกี่ยวกับมนุษย์ human

giawgabmeuang *a.* เกี่ยวกับเมือง urban

giawgabmeungyai *a.* เกี่ยวกับเมืองใหญ่
metropolitan

giawgabmolecule *a.* เกี่ยวกับโมเลกุล
molecular

giawgabmoom *a.* เกี่ยวกับมุม angular

giawgabnam *a.* เกี่ยวกับน้ำ watery

giawgabnam-a-suji *a.* เกี่ยวกับน้ำอสุจิ
seminal

giawgabnamkeunnamlong *a.*
เกี่ยวกับน้ำขึ้นน้ำลง tidal

giawgab-ngansasana *a*
เกี่ยวกับงานศาสนา clerical

giawgab-ngeun *a.* เกี่ยวกับเงิน pecuniary

giawgab-ngeunsterling *a.*
เกี่ยวกับเงินสเตอร์ลิง sterling

giawgabniroktisat *a.* เกี่ยวกับนิรุกติศาสตร์
philological

giawgabnuclear *a.* เกี่ยวกับนิวเคลียร์ nuclear

giawgab-orchestra *a.* เกี่ยวกับออร์เคสตร้า orchestral

giawgabpab *a.* เกี่ยวกับภาพ graphic

giawgabpab *a.* เกี่ยวกับภาพ pictorial

giawgabpabpumiprated *a.* เกี่ยวกับภาพภูมิประเทศ scenic

giawgabpabtai *a.* เกี่ยวกับภาพถ่าย photographic

giawgabpaendinyai *a* เกี่ยวกับแผ่นดินใหญ่ continental

giawgabpahutewaniyom *a.* เกี่ยวกับพหุเทวนิยม polytheistic

giawgabpanang *a.* เกี่ยวกับผนัง mural

giawgabpanya *a.* เกี่ยวกับปัญญา intellectual

giawgabpariman *a.* เกี่ยวกับปริมาณ quantitative

giawgabparod *a.* เกี่ยวกับปรอท mercurial

giawgabpasa *a.* เกี่ยวกับภาษา linguistic

giawgabpasa *a.* เกี่ยวกับภาษา lingual

giawgabpasapeunmeuang *a.* เกี่ยวกับภาษาพื้นเมือง vernacular

giawgabpasawa *a.* เกี่ยวกับปัสสาวะ urinary

giawgabpawmae *a.* เกี่ยวกับพ่อแม่ parental

giawgabped *a.* เกี่ยวกับเพศ sexual

giawgabpedanpak *a.* เกี่ยวกับเพดานปาก palatal

giawgabpedchai *a.* เกี่ยวกับเพศชาย masculine

giawgabpitigam *a.* เกี่ยวกับพิธีกรรม ritual

giawgabpitisuad *a.* เกี่ยวกับพิธีสวด liturgical

giawgabplaepeuy *a.* เกี่ยวกับแผลเปื่อย ulcerous

giawgabpolytechnic *a.* เกี่ยวกับโปลีเทคนิค polytechnic

giawgabponlameuang *a* เกี่ยวกับพลเมือง civic

giawgabponlameuang *a* เกี่ยวกับพลเมือง civil

giawgabpraisani *a.* เกี่ยวกับไปรษณีย์ postal

giawgabprajamdeuan *a.* เกี่ยวกับประจำเดือน menstrual

giawgabpratanatibodi *a.* เกี่ยวกับประธานาธิบดี presidential

giawgabprated-irland *a.* เกี่ยวกับประเทศไอร์แลนด์ Irish

giawgabprated-italy *a.* เกี่ยวกับประเทศอิตาลี Italian

giawgabpratedswitzerland *a* เกี่ยวกับประเทศสวิสเซอร์แลนด์ swiss

giawgabpratedtangtawan-awk *a.* เกี่ยวกับประเทศทางตะวันออก oriental

giawgabpuchai *a.* เกี่ยวกับผู้ชาย male

giawgabpukaofai *a.* เกี่ยวกับภูเขาไฟ volcanic

giawgabpumipak *a.* เกี่ยวกับภูมิภาค regional

giawgabpumisad *a.* เกี่ยวกับภูมิศาสตร์ geographical

giawgabrabobganwat *a.* เกี่ยวกับระบบการวัด metric

giawgabrabobganwat *a.* เกี่ยวกับระบบการวัด metrical

giawgabrabobsakdina *a* เกี่ยวกับระบบศักดินา feudal

giawgabrachawong *a.* เกี่ยวกับราชวงศ์ royal

giawgabranggai *a.* เกี่ยวกับร่างกาย physical

giawgabranggai *a* เกี่ยวกับร่างกาย corporal

giawgabrattasapa *a.* เกี่ยวกับรัฐสภา parliamentary

giawgabreua *a.* เกี่ยวกับเรือ naval

giawgabreuangpralomlok *a.* เกี่ยวกับเรื่องประโลมโลก melodramatic

giawgabreudubaimaipli *a.* เกี่ยวกับฤดูใบไม้ผลิ vernal

giawgabreudunao *a.* เกี่ยวกับฤดูหนาว wintry

giawgabreungrakkrai *a.* เกี่ยวกับเรื่องรักใคร่ romantic

giawgabrimfeepak *a.* เกี่ยวกับริมฝีปาก labial

giawgabrokkaikaw *a.* เกี่ยวกับโรคไขข้อ rheumatic

giawgabrokreun *a.* เกี่ยวกับโรคเรื้อน leprous

giawgabsaita *a.* เกี่ยวกับสายตา ocular

giawgabsaita *a.* เกี่ยวกับสายตา visual

giawgabsamong *adj* เกี่ยวกับสมอง cerebral

giawgabsanchattayan *a.* เกี่ยวกับสัญชาตญาณ instinctive

giawgabgansiasara *a.* เกี่ยวกับการเสียสละ sacrificial

giawgabsantapapa *a.* เกี่ยวกับสันตปาปา papal

giawgabsanyalak *a.* เกี่ยวกับสัญลักษณ์ symbolic

giawgabsapasoong *a.* เกี่ยวกับสภาสูง senatorial

giawgabsasanakrit *a.* เกี่ยวกับศาสนาคริสต์ Christian

giawgabsat *a.* เกี่ยวกับสัตว์ zoological

giawgabsataranarat *a.* เกี่ยวกับสาธารณรัฐ republican

giawgabsatri *a* เกี่ยวกับสตรี female

giawgabsatri *a* เกี่ยวกับสตรี feminine

giawgabsawan *adj* เกี่ยวกับสวรรค์ celestial

giawgabsawan *a* เกี่ยวกับสวรรค์ divine

giawgabscottland *a.* เกี่ยวกับสก๊อตแลนด์ scotch

giawgabsell *adj* เกี่ยวกับเซล cellular

giawgabsenmeridian *a.* เกี่ยวกับเส้นเมอริเดียน meridian

giawgabsiang *a* เกี่ยวกับเสียง acoustic

giawgabsiang *a.* เกี่ยวกับเสียง sonic

giawgabsikrong *adj.* เกี่ยวกับซี่โครง costal

giawgabsilapaclassic *a* เกี่ยวกับศิลปะคลาสสิก classical

giawgabsingtaw *a.* เกี่ยวกับสิ่งทอ textile

giawgabsingto *a* เกี่ยวกับสิงโต leonine

giawgabsinlapanaiganpud *a.* เกี่ยวกับศิลปะในการพูด oratorical

giawgabsongkram *a.* เกี่ยวกับสงคราม martial

giawgabspain *a.* เกี่ยวกับสเปน Spanish

giawgabta *a.* เกี่ยวกับตา optic

giawgabtakga *a.* เกี่ยวกับตรรกะ logical

giawgabtammat *a.* เกี่ยวกับธรรมมาสน์ pulpit

giawgabtanyahan *a* เกี่ยวกับธัญญาหาร cereal

giawgabtaonom *a.* เกี่ยวกับเต้านม mammary

giawgabnarok *a.* เกี่ยวกับนรก infernal

giawgabtidtawantok *adv.* เกี่ยวกับทิศตะวันตก westerly

giawgabtipak-a-sai *a.* เกี่ยวกับที่พักอาศัย resident

giawgabtonchabab *n.* เกี่ยวกับต้นฉบับ textual

giawgabtong *adj.* เกี่ยวกับท้อง alvine

giawgabtridsadi *a.* เกี่ยวกับทฤษฎี theoretical

giawgabtualek *a.* เกี่ยวกับตัวเลข numeral

giawgabtualek *a.* เกี่ยวกับตัวเลข numerical

giawgabtunghoom *adj* เกี่ยวกับถุงหุ้ม capsular

giawgabtungya *a.* เกี่ยวกับทุ่งหญ้า pastoral

giawgab-u-gabat *a.* เกี่ยวกับอุกกาบาต meteoric

giawgab-utsahagam *a.* เกี่ยวกับอุตสาหกรรม industrial

giawgabwitayasat *a.* เกี่ยวกับวิทยาศาสตร์ scientific

giawgabwongkojon *a* เกี่ยวกับวงโคจร cyclic

giawgabyanpahana *a.* เกี่ยวกับยานพาหนะ vehicular

giawgadsiang *a.* เกี่ยวกับเสียง vocal

giawkong *a.* เกี่ยวข้อง apposite

giawkong *v.t* เกี่ยวข้อง evolve

giawkong *v.t.* เกี่ยวข้อง involve

giawkong *v.t.* เกี่ยวข้อง relate

giawkonggabnakkawitalok *adj* เกี่ยวข้องกับนักกวีตลก aristophanic

giawkonggabwattu *a.* เกี่ยวข้องกับวัตถุ material

giawneung *a.* เกี่ยวเนื่อง relevant

giawpan *v.t.* เกี่ยวพัน implicate

gib *n.* กีบ hoof

gidjagan *n.* กิจการ activity

gidkwang *v.t* กีดขวาง block

gidkwang *v. t.* กีดขวาง encumber

gidkwang *v.t.* กีดขวาง impede

gidkwang *a.* กีดขวาง obstructive

gitjawatprajamwan *n.* กิจวัตรประจำ routine

gila *n.* กีฬา sport

gilapolo *n.* กีฬาโปโล polo

gilen *n.* กิเลน kiln

gin *v. t* กิน eat

gindai *a* กินได้ eatable

gindai *a* กินได้ edible

ging *n.* กิ่ง limb

ginggan *n.* กิ่งก้าน offshoot

ginggeu *n.* กิ่งกือ millipede

gingmai *n* กิ่งไม้ bough

gingmai *n.* กิ่งไม้ twig

gingmaileklek *n.* กิ่งไม้เล็กๆ sprig

gingtiminam *n.* กิ่งที่มีหนาม hawthorn

gingwai *n.* กิ่งหวาย withe

gin-imgeunpai *v.t.* กินอิ่มเกินไป glut

ginneuamai *a.* กินเนื้อไม้ xylophagous

ginyageunkanad *v.t.* กินยาเกินขนาด overdose

ginyangtagla *v. t* กินอย่างตะกละ cram

ginyangtakla *v. t* กินอย่างตะกละ devour

giraffe *n.* ยีราฟ giraffe

gla *a.* กล้า bold

gla *a* กล้า brave

glab *n.* แกลบ husk

glabgan *v.t.* กลับกัน invert

glabdan *adv.* กลับด้าน overleaf

glabkaoruam *v.t.* กลับเข้าร่วม rejoin

glabsusapabdeum *v.i.* กลับสู่สภาพเดิม revert

glaeng *v. t* แกล้ง bluff

glahan *a.* กล้าหาญ courageous

glahan *a* กล้าหาญ daring

glahan *a.* กล้าหาญ gallant

glahan *a.* กล้าหาญ heroic

glahan *a.* กล้าหาญ intrepid

glahan *a.* กล้าหาญ manful

glahan *a.* กล้าหาญ mettlesome

glahan *a.* กล้าหาญ spirited

glahan *a.* กล้าหาญ valiant

glahan *a.* กล้าหาญ chivalrous

glai *adv.* ใกล้ anigh

glai *a* ไกล far

glai *a.* ใกล้ near

glai *prep.* ใกล้ near

glai *adv.* ใกล้ near

glai *a.* ใกล้ proximate

glai *a.* ไกล remote

glai-awkpai *adv.* ไกลออกไป thither

glaichid *a.* ใกล้ชิด close

glaichid *a.* ใกล้ชิด intimate

glaigabkualokneua *n* ใกล้กับขั้วโลกเหนือ Arctic

glaigabkualoktai *a.* ใกล้กับขั้วโลกใต้ antarctic

glaiglai *adv* ใกล้ๆ around

glaiglia *v.i.* ไกล่เกลี่ย mediate

glaikaoma *adv.* ใกล้เข้ามา nigh

glailkaoma *a.* ใกล้เข้ามา imminent

glaipandai *a.* กลายพันธุ์ได้ mutative

glaipen *v. i* กลายเป็น become

glaipenkonglew v.t. กลายเป็นของเหลว liquefy

glaipenloom v.t. กลายเป็นหลุม pit

glaitai a. ใกล้ตาย moribund

glamneua n. กล้ามเนื้อ muscle

glamneuakaen n กล้ามเนื้อแขน biceps

glan v. t. กลั่น brew

glan v. t กลั่น distil

glan v.t. กลั่น refine

glang a. กลาง central

glang a. กลาง mid

glang a. กลาง middle

glangjaeng a. กลางแจ้ง outdoor

glangkeun n. กลางคืน night

glangkeun a. กลางคืน nocturnal

glangrong v.t. กลั่นกรอง screen

glangwan n. กลางวัน midday

glaoha v.t. กล่าวหา accuse

glaoha v. กล่าวหา arraign

glaokeu adv. กล่าวคือ namely

glaotod v.t. กล่าวโทษ impeach

glaotod v.t. กล่าวโทษ incriminate

gleua n. เกลือ salt

gleuakgling v.i. เกลือกกลิ้ง wallow

gleun v.t. กลืน swallow

gliad v.t. เกลียด abhor

gliad v.t. เกลียด grudge

gliadchang a. เกลียดชัง loath

gliaglom v. t เกลี้ยกล่อม coax

gliaw n. เกลียว curl

glin n. กลิ่น odour

glin n. กลิ่น scent

glin n. กลิ่น smell

glinmen n. กลิ่นเหม็น stench

glinmen n กลิ่นเหม็น stink

glum n กลุ่ม cluster

glom v.t. กล่อม lull

glom a. กลม round

glom adv. กลม round

glom a. กลม spherical

glumgas n. กลุ่มก๊าซ nebula

glumpanyachon n. กลุ่มปัญญาชน intelligentsia

glon n. กลอน latch

glon n. กลอน poem

glon n. โกลน stirrup

glong n กล่อง box

glong n. กล้อง camera

glong n กล่อง carton

glong n กล่อง cist

glong n กลอง drum

glongjunlatad n กล้องจุลทรรศน์ bioscope

glongjunratad n. กล้องจุลทรรศน์ microscope

glongsongtangglai n. กล้องส่องทางไกล binocular

glua a. กลัว afraid

glua v.t กลัว dread

glua v.i กลัว fear

gluakaw v.i. กลั้วคอ gargle

gluapanraya a. กลัวภรรยา henpecked

gluay n. กล้วย banana

glucose n. กลูโคส glucose

glum n. กลุ่ม constellation

glum n. กลุ่ม group

glum n. กลุ่ม section

glum n. กลุ่ม segment

glumdai n. กลุ่มด้าย clew

glumdai n. กลุ่มด้าย skein

glumkaipla n. กลุ่มไข่ปลา spawn

glumkon n. กลุ่มคน squad

glumputidtam n. กลุ่มผู้ติดตาม retinue

glumtimisamkon n. กลุ่มที่มีสามคน trinity

glumtimisamkon n. กลุ่มที่มีสามคน trio

glycerine n. กลีเซอไลน์ glycerine

goat n โกศ urn

gob n. กบ frog

gobgu v.t. กอบกู้ salvage

gobgu n. กอบกู้ salvation

goblaodinsaw n. กบเหลาดินสอ sharpener

god v.t. กด press

godang n. โกดัง godown

godang n. โกดัง repository

godangsinka *v.t* โกดังสินค้า warehouse
godki *v.t.* กดขี่ enslave
godki *v.t.* กดขี่ oppress
godmai *n.* กฎหมาย act
godmai *n.* กฎหมาย law
godmai *n.* กฎหมาย ordinance
godmaitongtin *n* กฎหมายท้องถิ่น bylaw, bye-law
godnaen *v.t.* กดแน่น constrict
godrabiab *n.* กฎระเบียบ regulation
gohok *v.i* โกหก lie
gohok *a.* โกหก mendacious
golahon *a.* โกลาหล tumultuous
golf *n.* กอล์ฟ golf
gomsisa *v. i.* ก้มศีรษะ crouch
gomtua *v.i.* ก้มตัว stoop
gon *prep.* ก่อน afore
gon *n.* กัน ass
gon *conj* ก่อน before
gon *n* ก้น bottom
gon *n* ก้อน cube
gon *a* ก่อน former
gon *n.* ก้อน lump
gon *n.* ก้อน nugget
goan *v.t.* โกน shave
gong *v. t.* โกง bilk
gong *v. t.* โกง cheat
gong *n.* กอง heap
gong *n.* กอง pile
gong *v.t.* กอง pile
gong *a.* ก้อง resonant
gong *v.t.* โกง rook
gong *v.t.* โกง swindle
gongai *n.* กลไก mechanism
gongamnod *a.* ก่อนกำหนด premature
gongeud *adj.* ก่อนเกิด antenatal
gongfai *n* กองไฟ bonfire
gongfang *n.* กองฟาง rick
gongfeun *n.* กองฟืน pyre
gonggamrangtahan *n* กองกำลังทหาร corps
gongkarawan *n.* กองคาราวาน caravan

gonglekatigan *n.* กองเลขาธิการ secretariat (e)
gongna *n* กองหน้า foreword
gongna *v.t.* พุ่งหลาว spear
punglao *n.* กองหน้า spearhead
gongponnoy *n.* กองพลน้อย brigade
gongreuarob *n* กองเรือรบ fleet
gongreuarob *n.* กองเรือรบ squadron
gongreuarob *n.* กองเรือรบ armada
gongtab *n.* กองทัพ army
gongtab *n* กองทัพ military
gongtahan *n* กองทหาร battalion
gongtahan *n.* กองทหาร legion
gongtahan *n.* กองทหาร troop
gongwai *v.t* กองไว้ heap
gonlasat *n.* กลศาสตร์ mechanics
gonna *adv.* ก่อนหน้า beforehand
gonna *a.* ก่อนหน้า previous
gonna *a.* ก่อนหน้า prior
gonnani *adv.* ก่อนหน้านี้ before
gonprawatsat *a.* ก่อนประวัติศาสตร์ prehistoric
gonrayut *n.* กลยุทธ์ tactics
gonsomrod *a.* ก่อนสมรส premarital
gongtabreua *n.* กองทัพเรือ navy
gontaeng-gnan *adj.* ก่อนแต่งงาน antenuptial
gontija *conj* ก่อนที่จะ until
gon-u-bai *n* กลอุบาย intrigue
gon-u-bai *n.* กลอุบาย sleight
gon-u-bai *n.* กลอุบาย stratagem
gonwelatigamnod *adv* ก่อนเวลาที่กำหนด by
goongaeleun *n.* กุญแจเลื่อน spanner
goonjae *n.* กุญแจ key
goonjaemeu *n* กุญแจมือ cuff
goonjaemeu *n.* กุญแจมือ handcuff
goonjaemeu *n.* กุญแจมือ shackle
gotbad *n* กฎบัตร charter
grabeuang *n.* กระเบื้อง tile
grabi *n.* กระบี่ rapier
grabi *n.* กระบี่ sabre

graboksoob *n.* กระบอกสูบ barrel

graboksub *n* กระบอกสูบ cylinder

grabong *n* กระบอง bat

grabong *n* กระบอง cub

grachab *a* กระชับ concise

gradad *n* กระดาษ foolscap

gradad *n.* กระดาษ paper

gradadkaeng *n.* กระดาษแข็ง cardboard

gradan *n* กระดาน board

gradang *a.* กระด้าง harsh

grading *n* กระดิ่ง bell

gradod *v. i* กระโดด hop

gradod *v.i* กระโดด jump

gradod *v.i.* กระโดด leap

gradod *v.t.* กระโดด reap

gradod *v.i.* กระโดด skip

gradodkamrua *v.t* กระโดดข้ามรั้ว hurdle

gradodkamsinggidkwang *v.i.* กระโดดข้ามสิ่งกีดขวาง vault

gradok *v.t.* กระดก tip

gradook *n.* กระดูก bone

gradooksanlang *n.* กระดูกสันหลัง backbone

gradooksanlang *n.* กระดูกสันหลัง spine

gradoom *n* กระดุม button

graen *v.t.* แกร็น depauperate

grajadgrajai *a.* กระจัดกระจาย sporadic

grahainam *adj.* กระหายน้ำ athirst

grahainam *v.i.* กระหายน้ำ thirst

grahainam *a.* กระหายน้ำ thirsty

grajai *v. t* กระจาย disperse

grajai *v.t.* กระจาย scatter

grajai *v.i.* กระจาย spread

grajaisiang *v. t* กระจายเสียง broadcast

grajok *n* กระจก mirror

grajokta *n* กระจกตา cornea

grajon *v.i.* กระโจน pounce

gralampli *n.* กระหล่ำปลี cabbage

gralok *n.* กะโหลก skull

gram *n.* กรัม gramme

grapao *n.* กระเป๋า pocket

grapao *n.* กระเป๋า purse

grapaodeuntang *n.* กระเป๋าเดินทาง baggage

grapaosatang *n.* กระเป๋าสตางค์ wallet

grapawpatsawa *n* กระเพาะปัสสาวะ bladder

grapeum *v.t.* กระเพื่อม ruffle

grapeum *v.i.* กระเพื่อม undulate

graph *n.* กราฟ graph

graprongchannai *n.* กระโปรงชั้นใน petticoat

grapong *n.* กระป๋อง can

grapong *n.* กระป๋อง canister

graprong *n.* กระโปรง skirt

grapong *n.* กระป๋อง tin

grapraw-a-hankongsat *n.* กระเพาะอาหารของสัตว์ craw

grapribta *v. i* กระพริบตา bat

grapribta *v. t. & i* กระพริบตา blink

grarawk *n.* กระรอก squirrel

grasaenamtilodlong *a.* กระแสน้ำที่ลดลง neap

grasae-ngeun *n* กระแสเงิน current

grasaetainam *n.* กระแสใต้น้ำ undercurrent

grasanamchiaw *n.* กระแสน้ำเชี่ยว torrent

grasib *v.t.* กระซิบ whisper

grasob *n.* กระสอบ sack

grasoon *n* กระสุน bullet

grasuang *n.* กระทรวง ministry

grasuangganklang *n.* กระทรวงการคลัง treasury

grasuay *n.* กระสวย shuttle

grataek *v. i.* กระแทก dash

grataek *v.t.* กระแทก jostle

grataek *v.t.* กระแทก slam

gratai *n.* กระต่าย rabbit

grataipa *n.* กระต่ายป่า hare

gratam *v.i.* กระทำ act

gratamdoeyraengmanud *v.t.* กระทำโดยแรงมนุษย์ manhandle

gratamgeunleuy *v.t.* กระทำเกินเลย overact

gratampid *v.t.* กระทำผิด transgress

gratang *n.* กระถาง pot
gratangtoob *n* กระถางธูป censer
grateureuron *adj* กระตือรือร้น alacrious
grateureuron *a.* กระตือรือร้น ardent
grateureuron *a* กระตือรือร้น eager
grateureuron *a* กระตือรือร้น energetic
grateureuron *a* กระตือรือร้น enthusiastic
grateureuron *a.* กระตือรือร้น zealous
gratiam *n.* กระเทียม garlic
gratiknamron *n.* กระติกน้ำร้อน thermos
(flask)
grating *n* กระทิง bison
gratoan *n.* กระโถน spittoon
gratob *v. t* กระทบ effect
gratom *n.* กระท่อม hut
gra-tom *n* กระท่อม cottage
gratomindiandaeng *n.*
กระท่อมอินเดียนแดง wigwam
gratommai *n.* กระท่อมไม้ cabin
gratook *a.* กระตุก jerky
gratook *v.t.* กระตุก jolt
gratoon *v.t.* กระตุ้น activate
gratoon *v.t* กระตุ้น goad
gratoon *v.t.* กระตุ้น incite
gratoon *v.t.* กระตุ้น instigate
gratoon *v.t.* กระตุ้น invoke
gratoon *v.t.* กระตุ้น prompt
gratoon *v.t.* กระตุ้น spur
gratoon *v.t.* กระตุ้น stimulate
gratoonkwamruseuktangped *a*
กระตุ้นความรู้สึกทางเพศ erotic
gratoon *v.t.* กระตุ้น arouse
graw *n.* เกราะ armature
graw *n* เกราะ mail
grawan *n.* กระวาน cardamom
grayatib *n.* กระยาทิพย์ manna
gred *n.* เกร็ด anecdote
griang *n.* เกรียง lute
griang *n.* เกรียง trowel
grid *n.* กริช dagger
gridrong *v.i.* กรีดร้อง scream
gridrong *v.i.* กรีดร้อง shriek

gridrong *v.t.* กรีดร้อง shun
gridtamyao *v.t.* กรีดตามยาว slit
grisadiga *n* กฤษฎีกา decree
grob *n.* กรอบ casing
grob *a* กรอบ crisp
grod *n* กรด acid
gromgong *n* กรมกอง department
gromtahan *n.* กรมทหาร regiment
gron *v. t* กร่อน erode
gron *v.i.* กรน snore
grong *n.* กรง cage
grong *v.t* กรอง filter
grong *v.t.* กรอง leach
grong *v.t.* กรอง sieve
grong *v.t.* กรอง sift
grongleb *n* กรงเล็บ claw
grongnokkanadyai *n.* กรงนกขนาดใหญ่
aviary
grot *a.* โกรธ angry
grot *a.* โกรธ furious
grot *a.* โกรธ indignant
grot *a.* โกรธ irate
grot *v.i.* โกรธ rage
grot *v.i.* โกรธ seethe
gruad *n.* กรวด pebble
gruay *n.* กรวย cone
grueng กลึง lathe
guan *v.i.* กวน scramble
guan *v.i.* กวน stir
guantosa *a.* กวนโทสะ provocative
guide *n.* ไกด์ guide
guitar *n.* กีตาร์ guitar
gukeunmaidai *a.* กู้คืนไม่ได้ irrecoverable
goompapan *n* กุมภาพันธ์ February
gunchon *n.* กันชน bumper
gwad *v.i.* กวาด sweep
gwaeng *v.i.* แกว่ง loll
gwaeng *v.i.* แกว่ง oscillate
gwaeng *v.i.* แกว่ง wag
gwaeng *v.i.* แกว่ง waver
gwang *n* กวาง deer
gwang *a.* กว้าง spacious

gwaeng *v.i.* แกว่ง sway
gwaeng *v.i.* แกว่ง swing
gwang *a.* กว้าง wide •
gwang *adv.* กว้าง wide
gwangtuapu *n.* กวางตัวผู้ stag
gymnastic *n.* ยิมนาสติก gymnastics

ha *n* ห้า five
ha *v.t.* หา seek
had *n* หัด measles
hadteun *n* หาดตื้น shoal
haebhaeng *a.* แหบแห้ง guttural
haeng *a* แห้ง dry
haengchat *a.* แห่งชาติ national
haenglaeng *adj.* แห้งแล้ง arid
haenglaeng *n* แห้งแล้ง barren
haengmahasamud *a.* แห่งมหาสมุทร oceanic
haengreuduron *adj* แห่งฤดูร้อน aestival
hai *v.t.* ให้ give
hai *v.t.* ให้ grant
hai *v.i.* ให้ provide
hai-a-han *v.t* ให้อาหาร feed
hai-a-pai *v.t* ให้อภัย absolve
hai-a-pai *v.t* ให้อภัย forgive
hai-a-paidai *a.* ให้อภัยได้ pardonable
haiborigan *v.t* ให้บริการ service
haiborigangdai *a.* ให้บริการได้ serviceable
haichaochuang *v.t.* ให้เช่าช่วง sublet
haidudnom *v.t.* ให้ดูดนม suckle
haigamlangjai *v. t* ให้กำลังใจ encourage
haigan *v.i.* ให้การ plead
haigansuksa *v. t* ให้การศึกษา educate
haiganted *v.t.* ให้การเท็จ forswear
haiganted *v.i.* ให้การเท็จ perjure
haigiad *v. t* ให้เกียรติ honour
haiglabmarabtamnaengdeum *v.t.*
   ให้กลับมารับตำแหน่งเดิม reinstate

haihedpon *v.t.* ให้เหตุผล justify
haihedpon *v.t.* ให้เหตุผล rationalize
haihedpon *v.i.* ให้เหตุผล reason
haijai *v. i.* หายใจ breathe
haijai *v.i.* หายใจ respire
haijaihob *v.i.* หายใจหอบ pant
haijaikao *v.i.* หายใจเข้า inhale
haijaimai-awk *v.t* หายใจไม่ออก suffocate
haijairaeng *v.i.* หายใจแรง snort
haikamman *v. t.* ให้คำมั่น commit
haikampreuksa *v. t.* ให้คำปรึกษา counsel
haikamsanya *v.t.* ให้คำสัญญา vow
haikawmoon *v.t.* ให้ข้อมูล inform
haikeunkrongrad *v. t* ให้ขึ้นครองราชย์ enthrone
haikwambanteung *v. t* ให้ความบันเทิง entertain
haikwamhen *v. i* ให้ความเห็น comment
haikwamhen *v.t.* ให้ความเห็น remark
hainamnom *v.i.* ให้น้ำนม lactate
hai-ngeun-udnoon *v.t.* ให้เงินอุดหนุน subsidize
hainom *a.* ให้นม milch
haipai *a* หายไป absent
haipai *v. i* หายไป disappear
haipai *v.i.* หายไป vanish
haiplao *adv.* ให้เปล่า gratis
haipragantuadai *a.* ให้ประกันตัวได้ bailable
hairaila-iad *v. t* ให้รายละเอียด detail
hairaira-iad *v.t.* ให้รายละเอียด specify
hairangwan *v.t.* ให้รางวัล prize
haisanya *v.t* ให้สัญญา promise
haisanyan *v.t.* ให้สัญญาณ signal
haisiang *v.t.* ให้เสียง voice
haisinbon *v. t.* ให้สินบน bribe
haisinbon *v. t.* ให้สินบน corrupt
haisitleuaktang *v.t.* ให้สิทธิ์เลือกตั้ง enfranchise
haitib *v.t.* ให้ทิป tip
haitipak *v.t* ให้ที่พัก house

haituayang *v.t.* ให้ตัวอย่าง sample
hai-umnad *v. t* ให้อำนาจ empower
hai-umnad *v.t.* ให้อำนาจ authorize
haiyana *a* หายนะ disastrous
haiyeum *v.t.* ให้ยืม lend
hakachalia *v.t.* หาค่าเฉลี่ย average
hakamidai *a.* หาค่ามิได้ invaluable
hak-awk *v.t.* หักออก deduct
hak-awk *prep.* หักออก less
hak-awk *v.t.* หักออก subtract
hakbanchi *v. t* หักบัญชี debit
haklang *v.t.* หักล้าง invalidate
ham *v.* ห้าม ban
ham *v.t* ห้าม bar
ham *v.t* ห้าม forbid
ham *v.t.* ห้าม inhibit
ham *v.t.* ห้าม prohibit
ham *a.* ห้าม prohibitive
ham *a.* ห้าม prohibitory
ham *v.t.* ห้าม taboo
hamadai *a.* หามาได้ obtainable
hamlaw *v. t* ห้ามล้อ brake
hampan *a.* ห้ามผ่าน impassable
hampram *v. t* ห้ามปราม dissuade
ham-pram *v.i.* ห้ามปราม dehort
han *n.* ห่าน goose
hang *n.* หาง tail
hangglai *adv.* ห่างไกล aloof
hangglai *a* ห่างไกล distant
hangglai *adv.* ห่างไกล far
hangklai *adv.* ห่างไกล afar
hannapaitangtidtawan-awk *v.t.*
　หันหน้าไปทางทิศตะวันออก orientate
hantuapu *n.* ห่านตัวผู้ gander
hao *v.t.* เห่า bark
hao *v.i.* เห่า yap
hao *v.i.* หาว yawn
hareu *v. t* หารือ consult
hareu *v. t.* หารือ discuss
harp *n.* ฮาร์พ harp
hasentang *v.i.* หาเส้นทาง navigate
hasib *n.* ห้าสิบ fifty

hatipriabmidai *a.* หาที่เปรียบไม่ได้
　incomparable
haunapao *n.* หัวหน้าเผ่า chieftain
haw *v. t* ห่อ envelop
haw *v.t.* ห่อ parcel
haw *v.t.* ห่อ wrap
hawhoom *v. t* ห่อหุ้ม encase
hawk *n.* หอก lance
hawkoisulao *n.* หอคอยสุเหร่า minaret
hawkong *n.* ห่อของ pack
hawkong *n.* ห่อของ parcel
hawkongkanadlek *n.* ห่อของขนาดเล็ก
　packet
hawkoy *n.* หอคอย tower
hawprachum *n.* หอประชุม auditorium
hawpupuay *n.* หอผู้ป่วย ward
hawsangketgan *n.* หอสังเกตการณ์
　observatory
haw-tasana *n* หอทัศนา belvedere
hayak *a.* หายาก rare
hed *n.* เห็ด mushroom
hedgan *n* เหตุการณ์ event
hedgan *n.* เหตุการณ์ happening
hedgan *n.* เหตุการณ์ incident
hedgan *n.* เหตุการณ์ scene
hedgannai-a-did *n.* เหตุการณ์ในอดีต
　chronicle
hedgansamkan *n.* เหตุการณ์สำคัญ
　milestone
hedgantigeudkeunpenlamdab *n.*
　เหตุการณ์ที่เกิดขึ้นเป็นลำดับ sequence
hedjungjai *n.* เหตุจูงใจ inducement
hedlaepon *n* เหตุและผล causality
hedpon *n.* เหตุผล rationale
hedpon *n.* เหตุผล reason
hedrai *n.* เหตุร้าย calamity
heiranyik *n.* เหรัญญิก treasurer
heiwhaeng *v.i.* เหี่ยวแห้ง wither
hen *v.t.* เห็น see
hen *v.t.* เห็น sight
henduay *a.* เห็นด้วย agreeable
henduay *v.t* เห็นด้วย approbate

henduay *v.i.* เห็นด้วย assent
henduay *v. i* เห็นด้วย consent
henduay *a* เห็นด้วย favourable
hengaetua *a.* เห็นแก่ตัว selfish
henjai *v.i.* เห็นใจ sympathize
hew *a.* หิว hungry
hew *n.* เหว ravine
hewdai *a.* หิ้วได้ portable
hewleuk *n* เหวลึก abyss
hibhaw *n.* หีบห่อ package
hibhaw *n.* หีบห่อ wrapper
hibsob *n* หีบศพ casket
hima *n.* หิมะ snow
himatok *v.i.* หิมะตก snow
hin *n.* หิน mullion
hin *n.* หิน rock
hin *n.* หิน stone
hinchanuan *n.* หินชนวน slate
hingtiyuneuataoping *n.*
 หิ้งที่อยู่เหนือเตาผิง mantel
hinkaeng *n.* หินแข็ง adamant
hinkanadyai *n* หินขนาดใหญ่ boulder
hinkanadyai *n.* หินขนาดใหญ่ megalith
hinkanadyaigondiaw *n.*
 หินขนาดใหญ่ก้อนเดียว monolith
hin-on *n.* หินอ่อน marble
ho *v.i* โห่ hoot
hob *v.i.* หอบ puff
hocky *n.* ฮอกกี้ hockey
hod *v. i* หด cockle
hod *v.i* หด shrink
hodgreng *a.* หดเกร็ง spasmodic
hodrai *a.* โหดร้าย atrocious
hodrai *a* โหดร้าย cruel
hodrai *a.* โหดร้าย inhuman
hodrai *a.* โหดร้าย pitiless
hodrai *a.* โหดร้าย savage
hoynangrom *n.* หอยนางรม oyster
hok *n., a* หก six
hoksib *n., a.* หกสิบ sixty
hom *a.* หอม fragrant
homwan *a.* หอมหวาน luscious

hon *v.t.* หอน howl
hong *n.* ห้อง chamber
hong *n.* ห้อง room
hong *n.* หงส์ swan
hongdabjit *n.* ห้องดับจิต mortuary
honggeb-a-han *n.* ห้องเก็บอาหาร pantry
hongkonkab *n.* ห้องคนขับ cock-pit
honglek *n.* ห้องเล็ก closet
hongnam *n.* ห้องน้ำ latrine
hongnam *n.* ห้องน้ำ lavatory
hongpakraw *n.* ห้องพักรอ lounge
hongrabkaek *n.* ห้องรับแขก parlour
hongsamud *n.* ห้องสมุด library
hongsuad *n.* ห้องสวด oratory
hongsuadmon *n.* ห้องสวดมนต์ chapel
hongsuka *n.* ห้องสุขา toilet
hongtaidin *n* ห้องใต้ดิน cellar
hongtaidin *n.* ห้องใต้ดิน vault
hongtodrong *n.* ห้องทดลอง laboratory
hongtong *n.* ห้องโถง hall
hongwadroob *n* ห้องวาดรูป drawing-room
hoobkao *n* หุบเขา dale
hoom *v.t.* หุ้ม muffle
hoongrabawk *n.* หุ่นกระบอก marionette
hoonjamlong *n* หุ่นจำลอง effigy
hoonsadaengbab *n.* หุ่นแสดงแบบ
 mannequin
horasat *n.* โหราศาสตร์ astrology
horong *n* โห่ร้อง clamour
horongyindi *v. t.* โห่ร้องยินดี cheer
hoy *v. t* ห้อย dangle
hu *n* หู ear
hua *n.* หัว head
huabeet *n* หัวบีท beet
huachaitao *n.* หัวไชเท้า radish
huachid *n.* หัวฉีด nozzle
huad *v.t.* หวด scourge
huad *v.t.* หวด whip
huadeu *a* หัวดื้อ dogmatic
huahom *n.* หัวหอม onion
huajai *n.* หัวใจ heart
huakaeng *a.* หัวแข็ง headstrong

huakaw *n.* หัวข้อ topic
huakao *n.* หัวเข่า knee
huakaw *n.* หัวข้อ subject
huakawlak *n.* หัวข้อหลัก theme
huakemkat *n* หัวเข็มขัด buckle
hualan *a.* หัวล้าน bald
huanabatluang *n.* หัวหน้าบาทหลวง archbishop
huanakon-ngan *n* หัวหน้าคนงาน foreman
huanamaechi *n.* หัวหน้าแม่ชี prioress
huanatudsawan *n* หัวหน้าทูตสวรรค์ archangel
huang *n.* ห่วง loop
huang *n.* ห่วง noose
huangcheuak *n.* ห่วงเชือก sling
huanom *n.* หัวนม nipple
huanom *n.* หัวนม teat
huapakgad *n.* หัวผักกาด turnip
huapeudpidnam *n.* หัวเปิดปิดน้ำ throttle
huaraw *v. i* หัวเราะ cackle
huaraw *v. i* หัวเราะ chuckle
huaraw *v.i.* หัวเราะ giggle
huaraw *v.i* หัวเราะ laugh
huarawdai *a.* หัวเราะได้ laughable
huareuang *n.* หัวเรื่อง heading
huareuang *n.* หัวเรื่อง title
huariawhuaraeng *n.* หัวเรี่ยวหัวแรง mainstay
huarodjak *n.* หัวรถจักร locomotive
huay *n* ห้วย bog
huay *n.* ห้วย brook
huay *n.* ห้วย streamlet
hubao *adj.* หูเบา credulity
hubkao *n.* หุบเขา vale
hubkao *n.* หุบเขา valley
hud *n.* หูด wart
hufang *n.* หูฟัง stethoscope
humchanuan *v.t.* หุ้มฉนวน insulate
humpleng *v. i* ฮัมเพลง hum
hun *n* หุ้น share
hungrabawk *n.* หุ่นกระบอก puppet
hunhan *a.* หุนหัน impulsive

hunhan *a* หุนหัน snap
hunsuan *n.* หุ้นส่วน partner
hunuak *a* หูหนวก deaf
hunyon *n.* หุ่นยนต์ robot
hurricane *n.* เฮอร์ริเคน hurricane
hyaena *n.* ไฮยีน่า hyaena, hyena
hydrogen *n.* ไฮโดรเจน hydrogen

id-cha *a* อิจฉา envious
id-cha *v. t* อิจฉา envy
id-cha *a.* อิจฉา jealous
isala *a.* อิสระ free
isara *a.* อิสระ liberal
isarabab *n.* อิสรภาพ liberty
isarapab *n.* อิสรภาพ liberation
ittpon *n.* อิทธิพล influence
ivy *n* ไอวี่ ivy

ja *n.* จ่า sergeant
jab *v. t.* จับ catch
jab *v.i.* จับ grapple
jab *v.t.* จับ grasp
jab *v.t.* จับ grip
jab *v.t.* จับ nab
jab *v.t.* จับ seize
jabchai *n.* จับฉ่าย hotchpotch
jabglum *v.t.* จับกลุ่ม group
jabgoom *v.t.* จับกุม arrest
jabgoom *v. t.* จับกุม capture
jabku *v.t. & i.* จับคู่ conjugate
jabku *v.t.* จับคู่ mate
jabku *v.t.* จับคู่ pair
jabkupid *v.t.* จับคู่ผิด mismatch
jabnaen *n* จับแน่น clasp
jabtongmaidai *a.* จับต้องไม่ได้ intangible

jabtuapenlim *v. t* จับตัวเป็นลิ่ม clot

jabwela *v.t.* จับเวลา time

jacket *n.* แจกเก็ต jacket

jadfaem *v.t* จัดแฟ้ม file

jadgamlang *v.t.* จัดกำลัง post

jadgan *v.t.* จัดการ arrange

jadgan *v. i* จัดการ cope

jadgan *v. i* จัดการ deal

jadgan *v.t* จัดการ handle

jadgan *v.t.* จัดการ manage

jadgan *v.t.* จัดการ organize

jadgan *v.t.* จัดการ tackle

jadgandai *a.* จัดการได้ manageable

jadha *v. i* จัดหา cater

jadha *v.t.* จัดหา procure

jadhahai *v. t* จัดหาให้ equip

jadhahai *v.t.* จัดหาให้ supply

jadhakon *v.t.* จัดหาคน man

jadha-ngeuntun *v.t* จัดหาเงินทุน finance

jadhatipak *v.t.* จัดหาที่พัก quarter

jadhatiyu *v.t* จัดหาที่อยู่ accommodate

jadnaew *v.t.* จัดแนว align

jad-ngan *v.i* จัดงาน feast

jadsadaeng *v. t* จัดแสดง exhibit

jadsan *v.t.* จัดสรร allocate

jadtamnaeng *v.t.* จัดตำแหน่ง rank

jadtriam *v.t* จัดเตรียม forearm

jadwang *v.t.* จัดวาง position

jaekjaeng *v. t* แจกแจง enumerate

jaekjai *v.t.* แจกจ่าย apportion

jaekjai *v. t* แจกจ่าย distribute

jaekjai *v.t* แจกจ่าย mete

jaeng *v.t.* แจ้ง apprise

jaeng *v.t.* แจ้ง impart

jaeng *v.t.* แจ้ง notify

jaengkao *v.t* แจ้งข่าว herald

jai *v. t* จ่าย expend

jai *v.t.* จ่าย pay

jaiboon *a* ใจบุญ benevolent

jaiboon *a* ใจบุญ bountiful

jaiboon *a.* ใจบุญ charitable

jaiboon *a.* ใจบุญ magnanimous

jaiboon *a.* ใจบุญ philanthropic

jaidam *a.* ใจดำ callous

jaidi *a.* ใจดี generous

jaidi *a* ใจดี kind

jaiglang *n.* ใจกลาง nucleus

jaiglangpao *n* ใจกลางเป้า bull's eye

jaigwang *a.* ใจกว้าง munificent

jaikachodcheuy *v.t.* จ่ายค่าชดเชย remunerate

jaikeun *v.t.* จ่ายคืน repay

jaikwamsamkan *n.* ใจความสำคัญ gist

jairai *a.* ใจร้าย mean

jairew *a.* ใจเร็ว impetuous

jaitalad *v.t* จ่ายตลาด market

jaiya *v.t.* จ่ายยา prescribe

jaiyen *a* ใจเย็น cool

jak *v. i.* จาก depart

jak *prep.* จาก from

jak *v.t.* จาก leave

jakgaji *a.* จั๊กจี้ ticklish

jakgapad *n* จักรพรรดิ์ emperor

jakgapaddini *n* จักรพรรดินี empress

jakgawan *n.* จักรวาล universe

jakgayan *n.* จักรยาน bicycle

jakgayansamlaw *n.* จักรยานสามล้อ tricycle

jaknan *adv.* จากนั้น thence

jakrasi *n* จักรราศี zodiac

jaksupaed *n.* จักษุแพทย์ oculist

jaktinai *adv.* จากที่ไหน whence

jam *v.i.* จาม sneeze

jamdai *v.t.* จำได้ remember

jamgad *v. t* จำกัด confine

jamgad *v.t.* จำกัด limit

jamgad *v.t.* จำกัด localize

jamgad *v.t.* จำกัด restrict

jamgad *a.* จำกัด restrictive

jamjaeng *a.* แจ่มแจ้ง manifest

jamleuy *n* จำเลย defendant

jamleuy *n.* จำเลย respondent

jamlongbaeb *v.t.* จำลองแบบ model

jamnaunleknoy *n.* จำนวนเล็กน้อย morsel

jamnong *v.t.* จำนอง mortgage

jamnuamruam *n.* จำนวนรวม sum

jamnuamsinkatisong *n.* จำนวนสินค้าที่ส่ง consignment

jamnuansontao *n* จำนวนสองเท่า double

jamnuansoongsud *n* จำนวนสูงสุด maximum

jamnuantamkwasoon *n* จำนวนต่ำกว่าศูนย์ minus

jamnuanleknoy *n.* จำนวนเล็กน้อย modicum

jamnuanmak *n.* จำนวนมาก plenty

jamnuanmahasan *n.* จำนวนมหาศาล myriad

jamnuanmakgeunpai *n* จำนวนมากเกินไป excess

jamnuanmahasan *n.* จำนวนนับมหาศาล decillion

jamnuanruam *n* จำนวนรวม amount

jamnuantamsud *n.* จำนวนต่ำสุด minimum

jamnuantangmod *n* จำนวนทั้งหมด all

jamnuantinoykwa *n* จำนวนที่น้อยกว่า less

jamook *n.* จมูก nose

jampen *a.* จำเป็น imperative

jampen *a* จำเป็น necessary

jampen *v.t.* จำเป็น necessitate

jampen *v.t.* จำเป็น need

jampen *a.* จำเป็น needful

jampen *adv.* จำเป็น needs

jampen *a.* จำเป็น needy

jampen *a.* จำเป็น requisite

jamook *n.* จมูก snout

jan *n* จาน dish

jang *v. t* จ้าง employ

jang *v.t* จ้าง hire

jadgan *v.t.* จัดการ wield

jang-hai *v.i* จางหาย fade

jang-ngan *v.t.* จ้างงาน staff

ja-ngoypak *n.* จงอยปาก beck

ja-ngoypaknok *n* จงอยปากนก beak

jangwa *n* จังหวะ beat

jangwa *b.* จังหวะ rhythm

jangwat *n.* จังหวัด province

jamnuansaenrupi *n* จำนวนแสนรูปี lac, lakh

jamnuantipeumkeun *n* จำนวนที่เพิ่มขึ้น plus

janpasomsi *n.* จานผสมสี palette

janpengromgong *v.t.* จัดเป็นกรมกอง regiment

janrong *n.* จานรอง saucer

jao-a-rom *a.* เจ้าอารมณ์ waspish

jaoban *n.* เจ้าบ้าน host

jaobao *n.* เจ้าบ่าว groom

jaochai *n.* เจ้าชาย prince

jaogijaogan *a.* เจ้ากี้เจ้าการ officious

jaokong *n.* เจ้าของ owner

jaokong *n.* เจ้าของ proprietor

jaokongrongsi *n.* เจ้าของโรงสี miller

jaolay *a* เจ้าเล่ห์ cunning

jaolay *a.* เจ้าเล่ห์ wily

jaonai *n* เจ้านาย boss

jaonanifaipokkrong *n.* เจ้าหน้าที่ฝ่ายปกครอง magistrate

jaonati *n.* เจ้าหน้าที่ functionary

jaonati *n.* เจ้าหน้าที่ officer

jaonati *n* เจ้าหน้าที่ official

jaonatirabrong-ekgasan *n.* เจ้าหน้าที่รับรองเอกสาร notary

jaonatirongpayaban *n.* เจ้าหน้าที่โรงพยาบาล orderly

jaonatitonrab *n.* เจ้าหน้าที่ต้อนรับ usher

jaoni *n* เจ้าหนี้ creditor

jaoni *n* เจ้าหนี้ debtor

jaoni *n.* เจ้าหนี้ usurer

jaopanak-ngansan *n.* เจ้าพนักงานศาล bailiff

jaoying *n.* เจ้าหญิง princess

jarake *n* จระเข้ alligator

jarake *n* จระเข้ crocodile

jareuk *v.t.* จารึก inscribe

jareungaona *v.i.* เจริญก้าวหน้า prosper

jareunteubto *v.i.* เจริญเติบโต thrive

jariyatam *n.* จริยธรรม ethics

jaruad *n.* จรวด rocket

jatgeb *v.t.* จัดเก็บ stow

jatpentarang *v.t.* จัดเป็นตาราง tabulate

jaw *v.t.* เจาะ pierce

jaw *v.t.* เจาะ puncture

jawdreua *v.t* จอดเรือ harbour

jawdreua *v.t* จอดเรือ moor

jawdrod *v.t.* จอดรถ park

jawprasatta *n.* จอประสาทตา retina

jebpuad *v.t.* เจ็บปวด agonize

jebpuad *a.* เจ็บปวด painful

jebpuad *a.* เจ็บปวด poignant

jebpuad *a.* เจ็บปวด sore

jed *n.* เจ็ด seven

jed *a* เจ็ด seven

jedi *n.* เจดีย์ pagoda

jedsib *n., a* เจ็บสิบ seventy

jib *v. t.* จีบ court

jelly *n.* เยลลี่ jelly

jenlok *a.* เจนโลก worldly

jeraja *v.t.* เจรจา negotiate

jeraja *v.i* เจรจา parley

jeraja *v.t.* เจรจา transact

jerajadai *a.* เจรจาได้ negotiable

jettanarai *n.* เจตนาร้าย spite

jeuapon *v.t.* เจือปน adulterate

jeudcheud *a.* จืดชืด insipid

jeudcheud *a.* จืดชืด mawkish

jeudja *a.* เจิดจ้า refulgent

jib *v.i* จีบ flirt

jib *v.t.* จิบ sip

jidjai *n.* จิตใจ mind

jidwinyan *n.* จิตวิญญาณ psyche

jik *v.i.* จิก peck

jing *a.* จริง actual

jing *a.* จริง real

jing *adv.* จริง really

jing *a.* จริง true

jing *a.* จริง veritable

jingjai *adv* จริงใจ bonafide

jingjai *a.* จริงใจ frank

jingjai *a.* จริงใจ sincere

jingjang *a* จริงจัง downright

jingjang *a* จริงจัง earnest

jingjok *n.* จิ้งจก lizard

jintanagan *n* จินตนาการ fancy

jintanagan *v.t* จินตนาการ fancy

jintanagan *v.t* จินตนาการ figure

jintanagan *n.* จินตนาการ visionary

jittagamfapanang *n.* จิตกรรมฝาผนัง mural

jittapaet *n.* จิตแพทย์ psychiatrist

jittawet *n.* จิตเวช psychiatry

jitwittaya *n.* จิตวิทยา psychology

job *v.t* จบ finish

jobmai *n* จดหมาย letter

jodyawyaw *v.t.* จดย่อๆ jot

jod *v.t.* จด note

jod *n.* โจทก์ plaintiff

jodmai *n.* จดหมาย mail

jodmaihed *n.pl.* จดหมายเหตุ annals

jodmaihed *n.pl.* จดหมายเหตุ archives

jodsitibat *v.t.* จดสิทธิบัตร patent

jodtabian *v.t.* จดทะเบียน register

pojjananugrom *n.* พจนานุกรม lexicon

jom *v.i.* จม sink

jomnam *v.i* จมน้ำ drown

jompon *n* จอมพล marshal

jomti *v.t.* โจมตี lambaste

jomti *n.* โจมตี siege

jomti-duay-ra-beud *v. t* โจมตีด้วยระเบิด bombard

jon *n.* โจร bandit

jon *n.* โจร dacoit

jon *n.* โจร robber

jon *n.* โจร thief

jonbadni *adv.* จนบัดนี้ hitherto

jong *v. t.* จอง book

jong *v.t.* จอง occupy

jong *v.t.* จอง reserve

jong *v.i.* จ้อง stare

jongkameng *adv* จ้องเขม็ง agaze
jongmong *v. t* จ้องมอง behold
jongratang *prep.* จนกระทั่ง till
jongratang *n. conj.* จนกระทั่ง till
jongratang *prep.* จนกระทั่ง until
jonsalad *n.* โจรสลัด pirate
joob *v.t.* จูบ kiss
jookmaikok *n.* จุกไม้ก๊อก cork
joom *v. t* จุ่ม dip
joom *v.t.* จุ่ม plunge
joobsiangdang *v.t.* จูบเสียงดัง smack
jud *n* จุด dot
jud *n.* จุด spot
judchuam *n.* จุดเชื่อม juncture
juddang *n.* จุดด่าง speck
juddangdam *n.* จุดด่างดำ mottle
judfai *v.t* จุดไฟ fire
judfai *v.t.* จุดไฟ kindle
judfai *v.t.* จุดไฟ light
judkaeng *n.* จุดแข็ง forte
judmai *n* จุดหมาย destination
jud-on *n.* จุดอ่อน shortcoming
judreum *n* จุดเริ่ม alpha
judsonjai *n* จุดสนใจ focus
judsoonglang *n.* จุดศูนย์กลาง hub
judsudyod *n.* จุดสุดยอด pinnacle
judsudyod *n.* จุดสุดยอด climax
judsoongsud *n.* จุดสูงสุด peak
judsoongsud *n.* จุดสูงสุด top
judsoongsud *n.* จุดสูงสุด zenith
judtadgan *n.* จุดตัดกัน crossing
judtamsud *n.* จุดต่ำสุด nadir
judtoob *v. t* จุดธูป cense
judtoob *v.t.* จุดธูป incense
judyeun *n.* จุดยืน stand
judyeun *n.* จุดยืน standpoint
juji *v.t.* จู้จี้ nag
jujom *v.* จู่โจม assail
jujom *v.t.* จู่โจม attack
jujom *v.t.* จู่โจม raid
jujom *v.i.* จู่โจม storm
jum *v.t.* จุ่ม soak

jumnam *v.i.* จุ่มน้ำ submerge
jungjai *v.t.* จูงใจ allure
jungjai *v* จูงใจ motivate
judreum *n.* จุดเริ่ม beginning

ka *v.t.* ฆ่า kill
ka *n.* ขา leg
ka *v.t.* ฆ่า murder
ka *v.t.* ฆ่า slaughter
ka *v.t.* ฆ่า slay
kab *v. t* ขับ drive
kabkleuan *v.t.* ขับเคลื่อน propel
kabkreuangbin *v.t.* ขับเครื่องบิน pilot
kablai *v. t* ขับไล่ evict
kablai *v. t.* ขับไล่ expel
kablai *v.t.* ขับไล่ ostracize
kablai *v.t.* ขับไล่ oust
kablai *v.t.* ขับไล่ repel
kablai *v.t.* ขับไล่ repulse
kablai *v. t* ขับไล่ displace
kabrod *v.i.* ขับรถ motor
kabuanhae *n.* ขบวนแห่ pageantry
kachaijai *n* ค่าใช้จ่าย expenditure
kachaijai *n.* ค่าใช้จ่าย expense
kachalia *n.* ค่าเฉลี่ย average
kachalia *n.* ค่าเฉลี่ย mean
kachao *n* ค่าเช่า cain
kachao *n.* ค่าเช่า rent
kachodcheuy *n* ค่าชดเชย compensation
kachodcheuy *n.* ค่าชดเชย recompense
kachodcheuy *v.t.* ค่าชดเชย sever
kad *v.t.* ขาด lack
kad *v.t.* ขัด polish
kad *v.t.* ขัด rub
kaddao *v. t* คาดเดา conjecture
kaddao *v.i.* คาดเดา speculate
kadgan *v.t.* คาดการณ์ anticipate
kadi *n.* คดี case
kadi-a-ya *n* คดีอาญา crime

kadjamook *a.* คัดจมูก stuffy
kadjangwa *v.t.* ขัดจังหวะ punctuate
kadkan *v. t* คัดค้าน demur
kadkan *v.t.* คัดค้าน negative
kadkan *v.t.* คัดค้าน object
kadkeun *a.* ขัดขืน mutinous
kadkeunkamsang *v. i* ขัดขืนคำสั่ง mutiny
kadklaenmak *a* ขาดแคลนมาก devoid
kadklan *adj.* ขาดแคลน deficient
kadklan *a.* ขาดแคลน meagre
kadklan *a.* ขาดแคลน scant
kadklan *a.* ขาดแคลน scanty
kadklan *a.* ขาดแคลน scarce
kadkunatam *a.* ขาดคุณธรรม unprincipled
kadkwamyabyang *a.* ขาดความยับยั้ง wanton
kadkwang *v.t* ขัดขวาง foil
kadkwang *v.t.* ขัดขวาง hinder
kadkwang *v.t.* ขัดขวาง obstruct
kadkwang *v.t.* ขัดขวาง thwart
kadlawklai *v.i.* คัดลอกลาย stencil
kadleuak *v.t.* คัดเลือก single
kadlok *v.t.* คัดลอก transcribe
kadmaidai *a.* ขาดไม่ได้ indispensable
kadoeysan *n* ค่าโดยสาร fare
kadprasidtipab *a.* ขาดประสิทธิภาพ ineffective
kadsati *a.* ขาดสติ insane
kadwang *v. t* คาดหวัง expect
kadyaeng *v. i* ขัดแย้ง conflict
kadyaeng *v. t* ขัดแย้ง contradict
kadyaeng *v. i* ขัดแย้ง dispute
kadyaeng *a.* ขัดแย้ง paradoxical
kaeb *a.* แคบ narrow
kaek *n.* แขก guest
kaeng *a* แข็ง firm
kaeng *a.* แข็ง frigid
kaeng *a.* แข็ง hard
kaeng *a.* แข็ง rigid
kaeng *a.* แข็ง solid
kaeng *a.* แข็ง stiff

kaenggrang *a.* แข็งแกร่ง sturdy
kaenggrao *a.* แข็งกร้าว strident
kaengkan *v.i* แข่งขัน race
kaengkan *v.t.* แข่งขัน rival
kaengkan *v.i.* แข่งขัน vie
kaengkangandai *a* แข่งขันกันได้ competitive
kaengkanrawangsongkon *v. i* แข่งขันระหว่างสองคน duel
kaengkaw *a.* แข็งข้อ insubordinate
kaengraeng *a.* แข็งแรง hefty
kaengraeng *a.* แข็งแรง lusty
kaengraeng *a.* แข็งแรง robust
kaengraeng *a.* แข็งแรง strong
kaengraeng *a.* แข็งแรง tough
kaengraeng *a.* แข็งแรง vigorous
kaenseu *n* แขนเสื้อ sleeve
kaentonlang *n* แขนท่อนล่าง forearm
kagamraigeunkuan *v.i.* ค้ากำไรเกินควร profiteer
kagangraibon *n.* ขากรรไกรบน maxilla
kagangrai *n.* ขากรรไกร jaw
kai *n* ไข่ egg
kai *v.t.* ขาย sell
kaideang *n.* ไข่แดง yolk
kaigoonjae *v.t* ไขกุญแจ key
kaijiaw *n.* ไข่เจียว omelette
kaikao *n* ไข่ขาว albumen
kaileuad-awk *n.* ไข้เลือดออก dengue
kaiman *n* ไขมัน fat
kaimook *n.* ไข่มุก pearl
kaipla *n.* ไข่ปลา roe
kaiplik *v.t.* ขายปลีก retail
kairaksadyai *n.* ไข้รากสาดใหญ่ typhus
kaitahan *n.* ค่ายทหาร barrack
kaitahan *n.* ค่ายทหาร cantonment
kaitua *v.t.* ขายตัว prostitute
kaiwad *n* ไข้หวัด cold
kaiwatyai *n.* ไข้หวัดใหญ่ influenza
kajadrongroy *v.t.* ขจัดร่องรอย obliterate
kajang *n.* ค่าจ้าง wage
kakai *v.i* ค้าขาย trade

kalaorian *n.* ค่าเล่าเรียน tuition
kaliangdu *n.* ค่าเลี้ยงดู alimony
kam *prep.* ข้าม across
kam *v. t* ข้าม cross
kam *v.t.* ค้ำ prop
kamab *n* ขมับ temple
kamao *n.* เขม่า soot
kambai *n.* คำใบ้ hint
kambanyai *n* คำบรรยาย description
kambanyaitaipab *n.* คำบรรยายใต้ภาพ caption
kambupabot *n.* คำบุพบท preposition
kamchaeng *n* คำแช่ง curse
kamcheuam *n.* คำเชื่อม conjunctive
kwamcheuatipid *n.* ความเชื่อที่ผิด misbelief
kamchom *n* คำชม complement
kamchom *n.* คำชม compliment
kamda *n.* คำด่า tirade
kamfongrong *n.* คำฟ้องร้อง indictment
kamgariya *n.* คำกริยา verb
kamglao-ang *n.* คำกล่าวอ้าง hearsay
kamin *n.* ขมิ้น curcuma
kamin *n.* ขมิ้น turmeric
kamjareukbonloomfangsob *n* คำจารึกบนหลุมฝังศพ epitaph
kamkad *n.* คำขาด ultimatum
kamkawrong *n.* คำขอร้อง invocation
kamkawtod *n.* คำขอโทษ apology
kamkom *n* คำคม byword
kamkom *n* คำคม epigram
kamkom *n.* คำคม witticism
kamkunnasab *n.* คำคุณศัพท์ adjective
kamlamok *n.* ความลามก obscenity
kamlongtai *n.* คำลงท้าย postscript
kamman *n.* คำมั่น plight
kamnab *v. t* คำนับ bow
kamnab *v.t.* คำนับ salute
kamnaenam *n* คำแนะนำ advice
kamnaenam *n* คำแนะนำ commendation
kamnaenam *n.* คำแนะนำ guidance

kamnaenam *n.* คำแนะนำ recommendation
kamnaenam *n.* คำแนะนำ suggestion
kamnaenam *n.* คำแนะนำ tip
kamnam *n.* คำนาม noun
kamnam *n.* คำนำ preamble
kamnam *n.* คำนำ preface
kamnamna *n.* คำนำหน้า prefix
kamnamnacheu *n.* คำนำหน้าชื่อ Messrs
kamniyam *n* คำนิยาม definition
kamnuan *v. t.* คำนวณ calculate
kamnuan *v.t.* คำนวณ compute
kamnuanpid *v.t.* คำนวณผิด miscalculate
kamoey *v.i.* ขโมย steal
kamoey *n.* ขโมย theft
kampangpei *n* คำพังเพย aphorism
kampatised *n.* คำปฏิเสธ negation
kampatised *n.* คำปฏิเสธ negative
kampatised *n* คำปฏิเสธ no
kampayangdiaw *n.* คำพยางค์เดียว monosyllable
kampibible *n.* คัมภีร์ไบเบิ้ล scripture
kampragad *n.* คำประกาศ announcement
kampragad *n* คำประกาศ declaration
kamprasom *n* คำประสม compound
kamprisana *n.* คำปริศนา puzzle
kampud *n.* คำพูด parlance
kampud *n.* คำพูด speech
kampud *n.* คำพูด word
kampudhairai *n.* คำพูดให้ร้าย slander
kampudyawyei *n* คำพูดเยาะเย้ย sneer
kamram *v.i.* คำราม growl
kamram *v.i.* คำราม grunt
kamram *v.i.* คำราม roar
kwamreunreung *n.* ความรื่นเริง jollity
kamriakpuchai *n.* คำเรียกผู้ชาย mister
kamriakpuying *n..* คำเรียกผู้หญิง missis, missus
kamriekjao *n.* คำเรียกเจ้า Highness
kamrong *n.* คำร้อง plea
kamrong *n.* คำร้อง requisition
kamrong *n.* คำร้อง suit

kamrongtook *n* คำร้องทุกข์ complaint

kamsab *n.* คำสาป spell

kamsab *n.* คำศัพท์ vocabulary

kamsabchapawtang *n.* คำศัพท์เฉพาะทาง terminology

kamsalaeng *n.* คำแสลง slang

kamsang *n* คำสั่ง command

kamsang *n.* คำสั่ง instruction

kamsang *n.* คำสั่ง mandate

kamsang *n.* คำสั่ง order

kamsangham *n* คำสั่งห้าม ban

kamsanseun *n.* คำสรรเสริญ panegyric

kamsanya *n* คำสัญญา promise

kamsanya *n.* คำสัญญา vow

kamseumtai *n.* คำเสริมท้าย suffix

kamson *n.* คำสอน precept

kamsonkongprayesu *n.* คำสอนของพระเยซู gospel

kamtadsin *n.* คำตัดสิน judgement

kamtadsin *n.* คำตัดสิน verdict

kamtaktang *n.* คำถากถาง lampoon

kamtalaenggan *n.* คำแถลงการณ์ communiqué

kamtam *n.* คำถาม query

kamtam *n.* คำถาม question

kamtam *n.* คำถาม quiz

kamtamnai *n.* คำทำนาย oracle

kamtamni *n* คำตำหนิ lash

kamtawkam *a.* คำต่อคำ verbatim

kamtimikwammaimeuangan *n.* คำที่มีความหมายเหมือนกัน synonym

kamtimikwammaitrongkam *n.* คำที่มีความหมายตรงข้าม antonym

kamtob *n* คำตอบ answer

kamtob *n.* คำตอบ rejoinder

kamtob *n* คำตอบ reply

kamtob *n.* คำตอบ response

kamtobtichiablaem *n.* คำตอบที่เฉียบแหลม repartee

kam-uaypon *n* คำอวยพร benison

kam-u-tan *n* คำอุทาน exclamation

kam-u-tansadaengkwammaipawjai *interj* คำอุทานแสดงความไม่พอใจ fie

kam-u-tansadaengkwamyindi *interj.* คำอุทานแสดงความยินดี hurrah

kam-u-ton *n.* คำอุทธรณ์ appeal

kamwijan *n* คำวิจารณ์ commentary

kamwinitchai *n.* คำวินิจฉัย ruling

kamwised *n.* คำวิเศษณ์ adverb

kamyab *n.* คำหยาบ invective

kamyaw *n* คำย่อ abbreviation

kamyawyei *n* คำเยาะเย้ย gibe

kamyokyaw *n* คำยกยอ flattery

kan *v. i* ขัน coo

kan *v. i* ขัน crow

kan *v.i.* คัน itch

kana *n* คณะ faculty

kana *n* ขาหน้า foreleg

kanabodi *n.* คณบดี dean

kanad *n.* ขนาด size

kanadiawgan *a.* ขณะเดียวกัน simultaneous

kanadyai *n.* ขนาดใหญ่ magnitude

kanaen *n.* คะแนน score

kanagammagan *n.* คณะกรรมการ commission

kanagammagan *n* คณะกรรมการ committee

kanalookkun *n.* คณะลูกขุน jury

kanalookkunchai *n.* คณะลูกขุนชาย juryman

kanan *a.* ขนาน parallel

kanangan *a.* ขนานกัน co-ordinate

kananganpai *prep.* ขนานกันไป along

kanani *adv.* ขณะนี้ now

kanani *adv.* ขณะนี้ nowhere

kanapatjuban *a.* ขณะปัจจุบัน present

kanapusadaeng *n.* คณะผู้แสดง troupe

kanati *conj.* ขณะที่ as

kanati *adv.* ขณะที่ meanwhile

kanati *conj.* ขณะที่ when

kanati *conj.* ขณะที่ whereas

kanati *conj.* ขณะที่ while

kanatipatai *n.* คณาธิปไตย oligarchy
kanbeid *n.* คันเบ็ด rod
kandai *a.* ค้านได้ objectionable
kang *n.* คาง chin
kangbon *prep.* ข้างบน above
kangbon *prep.* ข้างบน up
kangkaengyin *n.* กางเกงยีน jean
kangkang *adv.* ข้างๆ aside
kangkang *prep.* ข้างๆ beside
kangkao *n* ค้างคาว bat
kangkok *n.* คางคก toad
kanglang *adv.* ข้างหลัง back
kanglang *prep* ข้างหลัง behind
kanglang *adv* ข้างล่าง below
kanglang *adv* ข้างล่าง down
kanglang *a* ข้างล่าง under
kangna *a.* ข้างหน้า forward
kangna *a* ข้างหน้า front
kangnai *a.* ข้างใน inner
kangnawk *n* ข้างนอก outside
kangtai *adv* ข้างใต้ beneath
kangtai *adv.* ข้างใต้ underneath
kangtai *prep.* ข้างใต้ underneath
kangtum *n.* คางทูม mumps
kangyu *a* ค้างอยู่ pending
kanhaiwaksin *n.* การให้วัคซีน vaccination
kanidsat *n* คณิตศาสตร์ mathematics
kanitsat *n.* คณิตศาสตร์ arithmetic
kanom *n.* ขนม comfit
kanompang *n* ขนมปัง bread
kanompang *n* ขนมปังกรอบ cracker
kanompang *n.* ขนมปัง loaf
kanompangpon *n.* ขนมปังป่น crust
kanonpangping *n.* ขนมปังปิ้ง toast
kanonwan *n* ขนมหวาน sweet
kanrab *n.* คานรับ corbel
kanraek *n.* ขั้นแรก prime
kanreng *n.* คันเร่ง pedal
kansagru *v.t.* ขันสกรู screw
kansoongsud *n.* ขั้นสูงสุด superlative
kantai *n.* คันไถ plough
kantanu *n* คันธนู bow

kantarawwiwat *n* การทะเลาะวิวาท affray
kanti *n* ขันที eunuch
kanton *n.* ขั้นตอน procedure
kantosagon *n.* ขัณฑสกร saccharin
kao *v. t* เข้า enter
kao *n.* เขา horn
kao *n.* ข่าว news
kao *n.* ข้าว rice
kao *n. pl.* ข่าว tidings
kaobarley *n.* ข้าวบาร์เลย์ barley
kaofang *n.* ข้าวฟ่าง millet
kaofeuak *v. t.* เข้าเฝือก cast
kaogabkon-ngai *a.* เข้ากับคนง่าย sociable
kaogan *v.i.* เข้ากัน match
kaoganmaidai *a.* เข้ากันไม่ได้ irreconcilable
kaoglai *v.t.* เข้าใกล้ approach
kaoglai *v.i.* เข้าใกล้ near
kaoglum *v.t.* เข้ากลุ่ม ally
kaogwang *n.* เขากวาง antler
kaojai *v.t.* เข้าใจ apprehend
kaojai *n* เข้าใจ compass
kaojai *v. t* เข้าใจ comprehend
kaojai *v.t.* เข้าใจ realize
kaojai *v.t.* เข้าใจ understand
kaojaidai *a.* เข้าใจได้ apprehensive
kaojaidai *a.* เข้าใจได้ intelligible
kaojaidai *adj* เข้าใจได้ perceptible
kaojaipid *v.t.* เข้าใจผิด misapprehend
kaojaipid *v.t.* เข้าใจผิด misconceive
kaojaipid *v.t.* เข้าใจผิด misunderstand
kaokang *v.i.* เข้าข้าง side
kaokangnai *adv.* เข้าข้างใน inwards
kaokok *v.t.* เข้าคอก stall
kaokrobkronggon *v.t.* เข้าครอบครองก่อน preoccupy
kao-lek-lek *n.* เขาเล็กๆ cornicle
kaoleu *n* ข่าวลือ bruit
kao-malt *n.* ข้าวมอลต์ malt
kaonaipratet *adv.* เข้าในประเทศ inland
kao-oat *n.* ข้าวโอ๊ต oat
kaopod *n* ข้าวโพด corn

kaopod *n.* ข้าวโพด maize
kaoprajamti *v.t.* เข้าประจำที่ station
kaopuchai *pron.* เขาผู้ชาย he
kaopuchai *pron.* เขาผู้ชาย him
kaopuying *pron.* เขาผู้หญิง her
kaopuying *pron.* เขาผู้หญิง she
kaoreu *n.* ข่าวลือ rumour
kaorob *v. t* เคารพ esteem
kaorob *v.t.* เคารพ respect
kaorob *v.t.* เคารพ revere
kaorob *v.t.* เคารพ venerate
kaoruam *v.t.* เข้าร่วม attend
kaoruam *v.i.* เข้าร่วม partake
kaoruam *v.i.* เข้าร่วม participate
kaorye *n.* ข้าวไรย์ rye
kaosali *n.* ข้าวสาลี wheat
kaotaenti *v.t.* เข้าแทนที่ supersede
kaotaew *v.t.* เข้าแถว line
kaoteung *n* เข้าถึง access
kaotom *n.* ข้าวต้ม porridge
kaowonggot *n.* เขาวงกต labyrinth
kapagati *n.* ค่าปกติ norm
kaprab *n* ค่าปรับ fine
kaprab *n.* ค่าปรับ indemnity
karachagan *n* ข้าราชการ bureaucrat
karawat *n.* ฆราวาส layman
kareuhad *n.* คฤหาสน์ manor
karusat *n.* ครุศาสตร์ pedagogy
kasatkai *v. t* ฆ่าสัตว์ขาย butcher
kasiawela *n.* ค่าเสียเวลา demurrage
kasongkongtangpraisani *n.*
ค่าส่งของทางไปรษณีย์ postage
kata *n.* คทา sceptre
katamniam *n* ค่าธรรมเนียม fee
katamniam *n.* ค่าธรรมเนียม tariff
katamniamganchaitanon *n.*
ค่าธรรมเนียมการใช้ถนน toll
katamniamnaiganchaitareua *n.*
ค่าธรรมเนียมในการใช้ท่าเรือ wharfage
katamniampaenggeunpai *n*
ค่าธรรมเนียมแพงเกินไป overcharge
kati *n.* คติ motto

katkwang *v.t.* ขัดขวาง pinch
kattagam *n.* ฆาตกรรม murder
kattagon *n.* ฆาตกร murderer
kaw *v. t.* ขอ beg
kaw *v. i* ขอ cadge
kaw *v.t.* เคาะ knock
kaw *n.* คอ neck
kaw *v.t.* เคาะ tap
kaw *n.* คอ throat
kaw-ang *n* ข้ออ้าง pretext
kawbokprong *n* ข้อบกพร่อง demerit
kawgaetua *n* ข้อแก้ตัว excuse
kawgamnod *n* ข้อกำหนด clause
kawjamgad *n.* ข้อจำกัด reservation
kawkaetua *n.* ข้อแก้ตัว alibi
kawkidhen *n.* ข้อคิดเห็น tenet
kawklaoha *n.* ข้อกล่าวหา allegation
kawklaoha *n.* ข้อกล่าวหา charge
kawkwam *n.* ข้อความ note
kawkwamsansan *n.* ข้อความสั้นๆ jot
kawkwamtikadyanggan *n.*
ข้อความที่ขัดแย้งกัน antinomy
kawmeu *n.* ข้อมือ wrist
kawmmaijingjai *n.* ความไม่จริงใจ
insincerity
kawmoon *n.* ข้อมูล information
kawmoon *n.* ข้อมูล input
kawn *n.* ค้อน maul
kawn *n.* คอน perch
kawpidplad *n* ข้อผิดพลาด flaw
kawpisudtangkanitsat *n.*
ข้อพิสูจน์ทางคณิตศาสตร์ theorem
kawpukmad *n.* ข้อผูกมัด lien
kawpukmad *n.* ข้อผูกมัด obligation
kawpukmad *n.* ข้อผูกมัด pledge
kawrong *v.t.* ขอร้อง conjure
kawrong *v.t.* ขอร้อง request
kawsalub *n.* ข้อสรุป conclusion
kawsaneu *n.* ข้อเสนอ proposal
kawsaneu *n.* ข้อเสนอ proposition
kawsaneunae *n.* ข้อเสนอแนะ counsel
kawsangged *n.* ข้อสังเกต notice

kawsannitan *n.* ข้อสันนิษฐาน hypothesis
kawsiapriab *n* ข้อเสียเปรียบ drawback
kawsok *n* ข้อศอก ancon
kawsommud *n.* ข้อสมมุติ supposition
kawsongsai *n* ข้อสงสัย doubt
kawtan *n* ขอทาน beggar
kawtao *n.* ข้อเท้า ankle
kawtaw *n.* ข้อต่อ joint
kawtedjing *n* ข้อเท็จจริง fact
kawtod *v.i.* ขอโทษ apologize
kawtoklong *n.* ข้อตกลง accord
kawtoklong *n.* ข้อตกลง compact
kawtoklong *n.* ข้อตกลง covenant
kawtoklong *n.* ข้อตกลง pact
kawtoyang *n.* ข้อโต้แย้ง argument
kawyokwein *n* ข้อยกเว้น exception
kaya *n.* ขยะ garbage
kaya *n.* ขยะ litter
kaya *n.* ขยะ refuse
kaya *n.* ขยะ rubbish
kaya *n.* ขยะ trash
kayab *v. i. & n* ขยับ budge
kayai *v.t.* ขยาย amplify
kayai *v. t* ขยาย enlarge
kayai *v.t.* ขยาย expand
kayai *v. t* ขยาย extend
kayai *v.t.* ขยาย span
kayai-awk *v.t.* ขยายออก stretch
kayaikwam *v.t.* ขยายความ illustrate
kayaipab *v.i.* ขยายภาพ zoom
kayan *a* ขยัน diligent
kayan *a.* ขยัน strenuous
kayanrian *a.* ขยันเรียน studious
kayibta *v.i.* ขยิบตา wink
kwamlanlayjai *n.* ความลังเลใจ reluctance
kwamsokgaqprok *n.* ความสกปรก squalor
kwamtemjai *n.* ความเต็มใจ willingness
ked-amnadsan *n.* เขตอำนาจศาล jurisdiction
kedjangwat *a.* เขตจังหวัด provincial
kedpokkrong *n* เขตปกครอง canton

kesprokkrong *n.* เขตปกครอง county
kedron *n.* เขตร้อน tropic
kedsasana *n.* เขตทางศาสนา parish
keep *n* คีบ clamp
kem *a.* เข้ม intensive
kem *n.* เข็ม needle
kem *a.* เค็ม salty
kemkat *n* เข็มขัด belt
kem-nguad *a.* เข้มงวด ascetic
kem-nguad *a.* เข้มงวด rigorous
kem-nguad *a.* เข้มงวด stern
kem-nguad *a.* เข้มงวด strict
kem-nguad *a.* เข้มงวด stringent
kengkan *v. t* แข่งขัน contest
ket *n* เขต district
ket *n.* เขต zone
ketchumchon *a.* เขตชุมชน township
ketdan *n* เขตแดน border
ket-leuaktang *n* เขตเลือกตั้ง constituency
geuab *adv.* เกือบ almost
keuan *n* เขื่อน dam
keuan *n* เขื่อน embankment
keuan *n.* เขื่อนดิน rampart
keuangbanteuksiang *n.* เครื่องบันทึกเสียง recorder
keuangbod *n.* เครื่องบด grinder
keuanggamneudfiafa *n.* เครื่องกำเนิดไฟฟ้า generator
keuanggrasoon *n.* เครื่องกระสุน ammunition
keuanyaimaidai *a.* เคลื่อนย้ายไม่ได้ immovable
geudjak *v.i.* เกิดจาก stem
keun *v. t* ขึ้น board
keun *v.* ขึ้น rise
keuan-ai *v.i.* เขินอาย shy
keundi *v.t.* คืนดี reconcile
keunkreuang *adv* ขึ้นเครื่อง aboard
keunkreungbin *v. t* ขึ้นเครื่องบิน embark
keunkrongrat *v.t.* ขึ้นครองราชย์ throne
keunma *v.t.* ขึ้นม้า mount
keunna *adv.* ขึ้นหน้า ahead

keun-ngeunsod *v. t.* ขึ้นเงินสด cash
keunni *n.* คืนนี้ to-night
keunni *adv.* คืนนี้ tonight
keunpai *a.* ขึ้นไป upward
keunsanim *v.i* ขึ้นสนิม rust
keunweti *v.t.* ขึ้นเวที stage
keunyugab *a* ขึ้นอยู่กับ dependent
keunyugab *v.t.* ขึ้นอยู่กับ subject
keuy *adv* เคย ever
keuychin *a.* เคยชิน wont
kew *n* คิ้ว brow
kamtadsin *n* คำตัดสิน doom
ki *v.t.* ขี่ ride
ki-ai *a.* ขี้อาย bashful
ki-ai *a.* ขี้อาย sheepish
kian *v.t.* เฆี่ยน thrash
kian *v.t.* เฆี่ยน wallop
kian *v.t.* เขียน write
kiandeuydinsaw *v.t.* เขียนด้วยดินสอ
  pencil
kiandoey *v.t.* เขียนโดย ascribe
kiangkang *adv* เคียงข้าง abreast
kiankamnam *v.t.* เขียนคำนำ preface
kianprayokmai *v.t.* เขียนประโยคใหม่
  paraphrase
kianprogram *v.t.* เขียนโปรแกรม
  programme
kiantamlang *adj.* เขียนตามหลัง adscript
kianwatwat *v.t.* เขียนหวัดๆ scrawl
kianwatwat *v.t.* เขียนหวัดๆ scribble
kiaw *v. t* เคี้ยว chew
kiaw *a.* เขียว green
kiaw *v.t.* เคี้ยว masticate
kiaw *v.t.* เคี้ยว munch
kiaw *n.* เคียว scythe
kiaw *n.* เคียว sickle
kiaw *v.i.* เคี่ยว simmer
kiaw *v.t.* เคี่ยว stew
kiawcha-um *a.* เขียวชอุ่ม lush
kiawcha-umtalawdpi *a* เขียวชอุ่มตลอดปี
  evergreen
kiaw-eung *v.i.* เคี้ยวเอื้อง ruminate

kiawgabyingsao *a* เกี่ยวกับหญิงสาว
  maiden
kiawkaji *a.* เขียวขจี verdant
kiawkaji *n.* เขียวขจี greenery
kichamod *n.* ขี้ชะมด musk
kid *v.t.* คิด reckon
kid *v.t.* คิด think
kidkeunmai *v. t* คิดขึ้นใหม่ devise
kid-ngeunpaenggeunpai *v.t.*
  คิดเงินแพงเกินไป overcharge
kidsentai *v.t.* ขีดเส้นใต้ underline
kidwa *v.i.* คิดว่า deem
kigiad *a.* ขี้เกียจ indolent
kigiad *n.* ขี้เกียจ lazy
kigiad *n.* ขี้เกียจ slothful
kigiad *a.* ขี้เกียจ sluggish
kiglak *n.* ขี้กลาก ringworm
kiglua *a.* ขี้กลัว timorous
kigong *a.* ขี้โกง roguish
kihu *n* ขี้หู cerumen
kiklad *a.* ขี้ขลาด timid
kileum *a* ขี้ลืม forgetful
kim *n. pl.* คีม tongs
kimoho *a.* ขี้โมโห touchy
kimook *n.* ขี้มูก mucus
king *n.* ขิง ginger
kiniaw *a.* ขี้เหนียว niggardly
kiniaw *a.* ขี้เหนียว stingy
kipanawut *n.* ขีปนาวุธ missile
kipanawut *n.* ขีปนาวุธ projectile
kipeung *n.* ขี้ผึ้ง ointment
kipeung *n.* ขี้ผึ้ง wax
kipeung *n.* ขี้ผึ้ง balm
kipeung *n.* ขี้ผึ้ง balsam
kipeung *n.* ขี้ผึ้ง mote
kisao *a.* ขี้เซา sleepy
kiyae *a.* ขี้แย lachrymose
kladkleuan *a.* คลาดเคลื่อน inexact
klai *v. i.* คลาย cool
klai *prep.* ใกล้ nigh
klai *v.t.* คล้าย resemble
klai *a.* คล้าย similar

klai-awkpai *adv.* ไกลออกไป beyond

klaidao *adj.* คล้ายดาว asteroid

klaigan *a.* คล้ายกัน analogous

klaikan *a.* คล้ายกัน alike

klaikon *a.* คล้ายคน manlike

klaimai *a.* คล้ายไหม silken

klaimanud *adj.* คล้ายมนุษย์ anthropoid

klaimanud *a.* คล้ายมนุษย์ apish

klainakbun *a.* คล้ายนักบุญ saintly

klailookmai *a.* คล้ายลูกไม้ lacy

klam *v.t.* คลำ grope

kwamrew *n.* ความเร็ว velocity

klan *v. t* คลาน crawl

klan *v. i* คลาน creep

klang *a* คลั่ง crazy

klang a-wut *n.* คลังอาวุธ armoury

klang a-wut *n.* คลังอาวุธ arsenal

klangklai *a* คลั่งใคล้ fanatic

klangsinka *n* คลังสินค้า depot

klangsinka *n.* คลังสินค้า stock

klangsinka *n.* คลังสินค้า storage

glaoha *v.t.* กล่าวหา allege

glaoha *v. t* กล่าวหา blame

glaoha *v. t.* กล่าวหา charge

kleuab *v.t.* เคลือบ glaze

kleuab *v.t.* เคลือบ laminate

kleuabduaykipeung *v.t.* เคลือบด้วยขี้ผึ้ง wax

kleuab-ngao *v.t.* เคลือบเงา varnish

kleuabtong *v.t.* เคลือบทอง gild

kleuangamlang *v.t.* เคลื่อนกำลัง deploy

kleuanpaikangna *n.* เคลื่อนไปข้างหน้า advance

kleuantidai *a.* เคลื่อนที่ได้ movable

kleuantidai *a.* เคลื่อนที่ได้ removable

kleuantipaima *adj* เคลื่อนที่ไปมา ambulant

kleuantipenroobfanpla *v.i.* เคลื่อนที่เป็นรูปฟันปลา zigzag

kleuanwai *v.t.* เคลื่อนไหว move

kleuanwaidai *v.t.* เคลื่อนไหวได้ animate

kleuanwaipaipa *adv.* เคลื่อนไหวไปมา astir

kleuanyai *v.t.* เคลื่อนย้าย shift

kleuanyai *n* คลื่นใหญ่ billow

kleub-ngeun *v.t.* เคลือบเงิน silver

kleun *n.* คลื่น ripple

kleun *n.* คลื่น surf

kleun *n.* คลื่น wave

kleunkanadyai *n* คลื่นขนาดใหญ่ swell

kleuntalay *n.* คลื่นทะเล tide

kleuantidai *a.* เคลื่อนที่ได้ mobile

kleuandidai *v.t.* เคลื่อนที่ได้ mobilize

kleuantipaima *v.t.* เคลื่อนที่ไปมา shuttle

kleuanwai *v.i.* เคลื่อนไหว motion

kli *v.t.* คลี่ unfold

glibdawkmai *n.* กลีบดอกไม้ petal

kli-awk *v.t.* คลี่ออก sheet

klib *v.t* ขลิบ nip

glomgliaw *a.* กลมเกลียว harmonious

klon *n.* โคลน mud

klon *n.* โคลน silt

klon *n.* โคลน slush

klong *a.* คล่อง active

klong *n.* คลอง canal

klong *a* คล่อง fluent

klong *n.* โขลง horde

klong *adv* คล่อง pat

klong *n.* โคลง sonnet

klong *n.* โคลง verse

klongklaew *a.* คล่องแคล่ว agile

klongklaew *adj.* คล่องแคล่ว deft

klongklaew *a* คล่องแคล่ว facile

klongpuangmalai *v.t.* คล้องพวงมาลัย wreathe

glongsongtangglai *n.* กล้องส่องทางไกล telescope

glonpratu *n* กลอนประตู bolt

klontom *n.* โคลนตม slough

klukla *a.* ขรุขระ rough

glum *n* กลุ่ม bloc

klum *v.t* คลุม mantle

klum *v.t.* คลุม shroud

glumdao *n.* กลุ่มดาว asterism
klumkreua *a.* คลุมเครือ indistinct
klumkreua *a.* คลุมเครือ vague
klumkreua *a.* คลุมเครือ obscure
klumna *v.t.* คลุมหน้า veil
kluy *n* ขลุ่ย flute
knot *n.* น็อต knot
kob *n* ขอบ brim
kob *n.* ขอบ brink
kob *n* ขอบ edge
kob *n.* ขอบ margin
kob *n.* ขอบ rim
kobfa *n.* ขอบฟ้า horizon
kobfai *n.* คบไฟ torch
kobked *n* ขอบเขต dimension
kobked *n.* ขอบเขต scope
kobket *n* ขอบเขต boundary
kobket *n.* ขอบเขต extent
kobkun *v.t.* ขอบคุณ thank
kobnok *n.* ขอบนอก periphery
kobtang *n* ขอบทาง curb
kod-awd *v. i* กดออด buzz
kodkiaw *v.i.* คดเคี้ยว meander
kodkiaw *a.* คดเคี้ยว sinuous
kodkiaw *v.t.* คดเคี้ยว wind
kok *n.* โคก hillock
kok *n.* คอก pen
kok *n.* คอก stall
kokma *n* คอกม้า stable
kokmu *n.* คอกหมู sty
gognam *n.* ก๊อกน้ำ tap
kokwua *n* คอกวัว byre
kom *a* ขม bitter
kom *v.t.* ข่ม overshadow
komkeng *d* ข่มเหง mistreat
komheng *v.t.* ข่มเหง abuse
komheng *v.t.* ข่มเหง persecute
komkeun *v.t.* ข่มขืน rape
komku *v.t.* ข่มขู่ harass
kon *v.t.* โค่น hack
kon *n.* ค้อน hammer
kon *v.t.* โค่น hew

kon *v.t.* ค้น rifle
kon *n.* คอน roost
kon *v.i.* ค้น rummage
kon *n.* โคน stub
kon *v.i.* โค่น topple
kon-anglid *adj* คนอังกฤษ british
konba *n.* คนบ้า lunatic
konba *n.* คนบ้า maniac
konbab *n.* คนบาป sinner
konbai *n.* คนใบ้ mute
konbokbod *n.* คนบอกบท prompter
konchalad *n.* คนฉลาด genius
konchalad *n.* คนฉลาด sage
konchansoong *n.* คนชั้นสูง noble
konchantam *n* คนชั้นต่ำ boor
konchua *n.* คนชั่ว scoundrel
kondeuanlameu *n.* คนเดินละเมอ
   somnambulist
kondeuntanon *n.* คนเดินถนน pedestrian
kon-eun *pron.* คนอื่น other
konfaonaran *n* คนเฝ้าหน้าร้าน bouncer
konfaopratu *n.* คนเฝ้าประตู porter
konfarangsed *n* คนฝรั่งเศส French
konfoknang *n.* คนฟอกหนัง tanner
konfumfeuay *n.* คนฟุ่มเฟือย spendthrift
kong *v. t* โค้ง bend
kong *n.* ฆ้อง gong
kong *v.i.* โค้ง incline
kongae *n* ขนแกะ fleece
kongae *n.* คนแก่ senility
kongbantook *n.* ของบรรทุก load
kongborijak *n.* ของบริจาค alms
kongchaisuantua *n. pl* ของใช้ส่วนตัว
   paraphernalia
kongchan *pron.* ของฉัน mine
kongchan *a.* ของฉัน my
kongdong *n.* ของดอง pickle
kongebkaya *n.* คนเก็บขยะ scavenger
konggaerian *a.* คงแก่เรียน learned
konggaerian *a.* คงแก่เรียน scholarly
kongiadkran *n.* คนเกียจคร้าน idler
kongjon *n* ของโจร booty

kongkaeng *n* ของแข็ง solid
kongkaolaonan *a.* ของเขาเหล่านั้น their
kongkaopuchai *pron.* ของเขาผู้ชาย his
kongkaopuying *a* ของเขาผู้หญิง her
kongkrai *pron.* ของใคร whose
kongkwan *n.* ของขวัญ gift
kongkwan *n.* ของขวัญ present
konglahan *n* คนกล้าหาญ gallant
konglang *n.* คนกลาง middleman
kongleklek *n* ของเล็กๆ mite
konglen *n.* ของเล่น toy
konglew *n* ของเหลว fluid
konglew *n* ของเหลว liquid
konglomnoy *n.* คนกลุ่มน้อย minority
kongmeunmao *n.* ของมึนเมา intoxicant
kong-ngaw *a* โค้งงอ crook
kongniaw *n.* ของเหนียว paste
kongohok *n.* คนโกหก liar
kongong *n.* คนโกง trickster
kongprod *n* ของโปรด favourite
kongrao *pron.* ของเรา our
kongreek *n.* คนกรีก Greek
kongsia *n* ของเสีย spoil
kongsia *n.* ของเสีย waste
kongtawai *n.* ของถวาย offering
kongti *n.* คงที่ static
kongtijadsadaeng *n.* ของที่จัดแสดง exhibit
kongtiraleuk *n.* ของที่ระลึก keepsake
kongtiraleuk *n.* ของที่ระลึก souvenir
kongtiraleuk *n.* ของที่ระลึก token
kongtirareuk *n.* ของที่ระลึก memento
kongyu *v.i.* คงอยู่ remain
kongyu *v.i.* คงอยู่ last
konha *v.i* ค้นหา look
konha *v.t.* ค้นหา quest
konha *v.t.* ค้นหา search
konhuadeu *n* คนหัวดื้อ bigot
konhuaroonraeng *n* คนหัวรุนแรง extremist
konhuasoong *n.* คนหัวสูง snob
kon-italian *n.* คนอิตาเลียน Italian

konkab *n* คนขับ driver
konkabrod *n.* คนขับรถ chauffeur
konkabrodma *n* คนขับรถม้า coachman
konkabrodyon *n.* คนขับรถยนต์ motorist
konkai *n* คนไข้ invalid
konkai *n.* คนขาย seller
konkaidawkmai *n* คนขายดอกไม้ florist
konkaikanom *n* คนขายขนม confectioner
konkaikongcham *n.* คนขายของชำ grocer
konkaikreungkian *n.* คนขายเครื่องเขียน stationer
konkainangseu *n* คนขายหนังสือ bookseller
konkaineua *n* คนขายเนื้อ butcher
konkainok *n.* คนไข้นอก outpatient
konkaipa *n* คนขายผ้า draper
konkaipedploy *n.* คนขายเพชรพลอย jeweller
konkaisong *n.* คนขายส่ง wholesaler
konkaiwaenta *n.* คนขายแว่นตา optician
konkang *n* ขนแข็ง bristle
konkang *adv.* ค่อนข้าง quite
konkang *adv.* ค่อนข้าง rather
konkang *adv.* ค่อนข้าง somewhat
konkangdaeng *a.* ค่อนข้างแดง reddish
konkangkao *a.* ค่อนข้างขาว whitish
konkangleuang *a.* ค่อนข้างเหลือง yellowish
konkianpaenpab *n.* คนเขียนแผ่นพับ pamphleteer
konkigiad *n.* คนขี้เกียจ loafer
konkigiad *n.* คนขี้เกียจ sluggard
konkiklad *n.* คนขี้ขลาด coward
konkimao *n* คนขี้เมา bibber
konkiniaw *n.* คนขี้เหนียว niggard
kongong *n.* คนโกง trickster
konkrae *n* คนแคระ dwarf
konkrae *n.* คนแคระ midget
konkrae *n.* คนแคระ pigmy
konkrae *n.* คนแคระ pygmy
konkrengkrad *n.* คนเคร่งครัด prude
konkudloom *n.* คนขุดหลุม pitman

konkuiwo *n.* คนคุยโว windbag
konkwabkumtaofai *n.* คนควบคุมเตาไฟ stoker
konlalang *n.* คนล้าหลัง laggard
konlendontrichindiaw *n.* คนเล่นดนตรีชิ้นเดียว soloist
konlenpanan *n.* คนเล่นพนัน gambler
konlew *n.* คนเลว miscreant
konlianggae *n.* คนเลี้ยงแกะ shepherd
konliangsat *n.* คนเลี้ยงสัตว์ herdsman
konlob *n.* คนโลภ cormorant
konlokluang *n.* คนหลอกลวง impostor
konlokluang *n.* คนหลอกลวง swindler
konmainawaijai *n* คนไม่น่าไว้ใจ sneak
konmaiseutrong *n.* คนไม่ซื่อตรง jackal
konmao *n* คนเมา drunkard
konmilayliam *n.* คนมีเล่ห์เหลี่ยม sharper
konnawk *n.* คนนอก outsider
konneung *pron.* คนหนึ่ง one
kon-ngan *n.* คนงาน peon
kon-ngan *n.* คนงาน worker
kon-nganmeuang *n.* คนงานเหมือง miner
kon-ngo *n* คนโง่ dunce
kon-ngo *n* คนโง่ blockhead
kon-ngo *n* คนโง่ fool
kon-ngo *n.* คนโง่ idiocy
kon-ngo *n.* คนโง่ idiot
kon-ngo *n.* คนโง่ loggerhead
kon-ngo *n.* คนโง่ simpleton
konnok *n* ขนนก feather
konnawkkok *n.* คนนอกคอก outcast
konnokpradab *n* ขนนกประดับ aigrette
konnonlab *n.* คนนอนหลับ sleeper
konnuad *n.* คนนวด masseur
konnumsao *n* คนหนุ่มสาว young
konnumsao *n.* คนหนุ่มสาว youngster
kon-onkongpeud *n* ขนอ่อนของพืช nap
konpaireua *n.* คนพายเรือ oarsman
konpan *n.* คนพาล rascal
konpanya-on *n.* คนปัญญาอ่อน moron
konpateuan *n.* คนป่าเถื่อน barbarian
konpateun *n* คนป่าเถื่อน savage

konperokreuan *n.* คนเป็นโรคเรื้อน leper
konpewdam *n.* คนผิวดำ nigger
konpigan *n* คนพิการ cripple
konpigan *n* คนพิการ handicap
konplaek *n* คนแปลก cuckoo
konplaek *n.* คนแปลก coot
konplaekna *n.* คนแปลกหน้า stranger
konpleuay *n* คนเปลือย nude`
konplongtok *n.* คนปลงตก stoic
konpob *v. t* ค้นพบ discover
konprajobprajaeng *n.* คนประจบประแจง sycophant
konprajobsawplaw *n.* คนประจบสอพลอ courtier
konpralad *n.* คนประหลาด oddity
konpuay *n* คนป่วย patient
konrabchai *n* คนรับใช้ domestic
konrabjang *n.* คนรับจ้าง hireling
konrabchai *n* คนรับใช้ menial
konrabchai *n.* คนรับใช้ minion
konrabchai *n.* คนรับใช้ servant
konrabchaichai *n.* คนรับใช้ชาย lackey
konraek *a* คนแรก first
konraisinratam *n.* คนไร้ศีลธรรม libertine
konrak *n* คนรัก darling
konrak *n.* คนรัก lover
konramruay *n.* คนร่ำรวย nabob
konrangbaeb *a* คนร่างแบบ draftsman
konrekaikong *n* คนเร่ขายของ hawker
konreron *n.* คนเร่ร่อน rover
konrokjit *n.* คนโรคจิต psychopath
konronray *n.* คนร่อนเร่ vagabond
konroonlang *n.* คนรุ่นหลัง posterity
konsat *n.* ขนสัตว์ fur
konsat *n.* ขนสัตว์ wool
konscot *n.* คนสก็อต Scot
konseusat *n* คนซื่อสัตย์ stalwart
konsong-ekgasan *n.* คนส่งเอกสาร messenger
konsong-ekgasan *n.* คนส่งเอกสาร carrier
konspain *n.* คนสเปน Spaniard
konspain *n.* คนสเปน Spanish

konswiss *n.* คนสวิส swiss
konta *n* ขนตา eyelash
kontagla *n.* คนตะกละ glutton
kontaidin *n.* คนไถดิน ploughman
kontam-a-han *n* คนทำอาหาร cook
kontamkanompang *n.* คนทำขนมปัง
baker
kontamklod *n.* คนทำคลอด midwife
kontampidgodmai *n.* คนทำผิดกฎหมาย
outlaw
kontamsuan *n.* คนทำสวน gardener
kontichobkwamrunraeng *n.*
คนที่ชอบความรุนแรง sadist
kontidairabkwamcheunchomyangmak
n. คนที่ได้รับความชื่นชมอย่างมาก idol
kontigintaepak *n.* คนที่กินแต่ผัก
vegetarian
kontilongtang *n.* คนที่หลงทาง straggler
kontilongtang *n* คนที่หลงทาง stray
kontimi-a-
yurawangpaedsibtuangpaedsibgaopi
n. คนที่มีอายุระหว่าง 80 - 89 ปี
octogenarian
kontimikunsombattaotiamgan *n*
คนที่มีคุณสมบัติเท่าเทียมกัน equal
kontitawtangantaeng-gnan *n*
คนที่ต่อต้านการแต่งงาน agamist
kontitooksongglabprated *n*
คนที่ถูกส่งกลับประเทศ repatriate
kontiwaijaidai *n* คนที่ไว้ใจได้ confidant
kontiyud-nganpratuang *n.*
คนที่หยุดงานประท้วง striker
kontiyunaimeuangyai *n.*
คนที่อยู่ในเมืองใหญ่ metropolitan
kontooklok *n* คนถูกหลอก gull
kontrani *n.* คนตระหนี่ miser
kon-uad-ru *n.* คนอวดรู้ pedant
konyabkai *n* คนหยาบคาย churl
konyai *v.t.* ขนย้าย transfer
konyai *v.t.* ขนย้าย transport
konyaidai *a.* ขนย้ายได้ transferable
kon-yew *n.* คนยิว Jew

kosok *n.* โฆษก spokesman
koy *v. t* คอย bide
koy *v.i.* คอย wait
koykoylodlong *adj.* ค่อยๆ ลดลง
declivous
krab *n.* คราบ slough
krab *n.* คราบ stain
grachumgrachuay *a.* กระชุ่มกระชวย hale
krae *n.* แคร่ palanquin
krai *pron.* ใคร who
krai *pron.* ใคร whom
kraigawtam *pron.* ใครก็ตาม whoever
kwamjairew *n.* ความใจเร็ว impetuosity
kramklumkreua *n.* ความคลุมเครือ
vagueness
krang *v.i.* คราง groan
krang *v.i.* คราง moan
krangneung *adv.* ครั้งหนึ่ง once
krangraek *a.* ครั้งแรก premier
krangraekreum *a.* ครั้งแรกเริ่ม primeval
krao *n* เครา beard
kraokrao *a* คร่าวๆ cursory
kraokrao *a.* คร่าวๆ sketchy
krateub *v.t.* กระทืบ trample
krawgam *n.* เคราะห์กรรม adversity
krawrai *a.* เคราะห์ร้าย wretched
greinggai *a.* เกรงใจ considerate
kreingkrad *a.* เคร่งครัด austere
krengsasana *a.* เคร่งศาสนา pious
krengsasana *a.* เคร่งศาสนา puritanical
krengsasana *a.* เคร่งศาสนา religious
kreuabduaykipeung *adj.* เคลือบด้วยขี้ผึ้ง
cerated
kreuajaggapob *n.* เครือจักรภพ
commonwealth
kreuakai *n.* เครือข่าย network
kreuangbin *n.* เครื่องบิน aeroplane
kreuangbin *n.* เครื่องบิน aircraft
kreuangbin *n.* เครื่องบิน plane
kreuangchai *n.* เครื่องใช้ appliance
kreuangchai *n.* เครื่องใช้ utensil

kreuangchaipab *n.* เครื่องฉายภาพ projector

kreuangchang *n.* เครื่องชั่ง scale

kreuangdeum *n* เครื่องดื่ม beverage

kreuangdeum *n* เครื่องดื่ม drink

kreuangdeum *n.* เครื่องดื่ม refreshment

kreuangdinpao *a* เครื่องดินเผา earthen

kreuanggiawkao *n.* เครื่องเกี่ยวข้าว reaper

kreuanggidkwang *n.* เครื่องกีดขวาง barrier

kreuanggidkwang *n.* เครื่องกีดขวาง hurdle1

kreuanggwan *n.* เครื่องกว้าน winch

kreuangjaksan *n.* เครื่องจักรสาน wicker

kreuangkidlek *n* เครื่องคิดเลข calculator

kreuangkleuabdinpao *n.* เครื่องเคลือบดินเผา crockery

kreuangkreuabdinpao *n* เครื่องเคลือบดินเผา ceramics

kreuanglenpansiang *n.* เครื่องเล่นแผ่นเสียง gramophone

kreuangmai *n* เครื่องหมาย colon

kreuangmaidawkjan *n.* เครื่องหมายดอกจัน asterisk

kreuangmairabrongkunnapab *n.* เครื่องหมายรับรองคุณภาพ hallmark

kreuangmaisadaengtua *n.* เครื่องหมายแสดงตัว badge

kreuangmaiwakton *n.* เครื่องหมายวรรคตอน apostrophe

kreuangmaiwakton *n* เครื่องหมายวรรคตอน comma

kreuangmeu *η.* เครื่องมือ apparatus

kreuangmeu *n* เครื่องมือ device

kreuangmeu *n.* เครื่องมือ outfit

kreuangmeu *n.* เครื่องมือ tool

kreuangmeuwadkwamsoong *n* เครื่องมือวัดความสูง altimeter

kreuangmuandai *n.* เครื่องม้วนด้าย winder

kreuangnai *n.* เครื่องใน entrails

kreuang-ngeun *n.* เครื่องเงิน silver

kreuangnon *n.* เครื่องนอน bedding

kreuangnuadkao *n.* เครื่องนวดข้าว thresher

kreuangnunghom *n* เครื่องนุ่งห่ม clothing

kreuangpadgwad *n.* เครื่องปัดกวาด sweeper

kreuangpan *n.* เครื่องปั่น churn

kreuangpandai *n.* เครื่องปั่นด้าย spinner

kreuangpandinpao *n.* เครื่องปั้นดินเผา pottery

kreuangpandinpao *n.* เครื่องปั้นดินเผา ware

kreuangpim *n.* เครื่องพิมพ์ printer

kreuangpradab *n* เครื่องประดับ accessory

kreuangpradab *n.* เครื่องประดับ ornament

kreuangrang *n.* เครื่องราง talisman

kreuangron *n.* เครื่องร่อน glider

kreuangsakpa *n.* เครื่องซักผ้า washer

kreuangsam-ang *n.* เครื่องสำอาง cosmetic

kreuangsong *n.* เครื่องส่ง transmitter

kreuangtaenggai *n.* เครื่องแต่งกาย array

kreuangtaenggai *n.* เครื่องแต่งกาย attire

kreuangtaengtua *n.* เครื่องแต่งตัว garb

kreuangtawpa *n* เครื่องทอผ้า loom

kreuangted *n* เครื่องเทศ aniseed

kreuangted *n.* เครื่องเทศ spice

kreuangteuankwamjam *n.* เครื่องเตือนความใจ reminder

kreuangtuaycham *n.* เครื่องถ้วยชาม porcelain

kreuangwat-aun-hapum *n.* เครื่องวัดอุณหภูมิ thermometer

kreuangyon *n* เครื่องยนต์ engine

kreung *n.* ครึ่ง half

kreung *a* ครึ่ง half

kreungbaeb *n.* เครื่องแบบ livery

kreungbin-i-pon *n.* เครื่องบินไอพ่น jet

kreungbintingrabeud *n* เครื่องบินทิ้งระเบิด bomber

kreungdontri *n.* เครื่องดนตรี instrument

kreunggreung *n.* เครื่องกลึง lathe

kreunggrong *n* เครื่องกรอง filter

kreunghamlaw *n* เครื่องห้ามล้อ brake

kreungkayaisiang *n* เครื่องขยายเสียง amplifier

kreungkian *n.* เครื่องเขียน stationery

krengkreum *a.* เคร่งขรึม solemn

kreunglok *n.* ครึ่งโลก hemisphere

kreungmeu *n.* เครื่องมือ implement

kreungmeuwatkwamkonkongnom *n.* เครื่องมือวัดความข้นของนม lactometer

kreungpedploy *n.* เครื่องเพชรพลอย jewellery

kreungrang *n.* เครื่องราง amulet

kriad *a.* เครียด intense

kriad *a* เครียด serious

kriad *v.t* เครียด stress

kribpla *n* ครีบปลา fin

krisamat *n.* คริสต์มาส Xmas

krisasanigachon *n* คริสตศาสนิกชน Christian

kris-tajak *n.* คริสต์จักร Christendom

krob *v. t.* ครอบ cap

grob *v.t.* กรอบ frame

krobklum *a* ครอบคลุม comprehensive

krobklum *a.* ครอบคลุม inclusive

krobkrong *v.t.* ครอบครอง possess

krobkrua *n* ครอบครัว family

krob-ngam *v.t.* ครอบงำ obsess

krobrobroypi *adj.* ครบรอบร้อยปี centennial

krobrobsongroypi *adj* ครบรอบสองร้อยปี bicentenary

krobtuan *a.* ครบถ้วน integral

kronggradook *n.* โครงกระดูก skeleton

krongrang *n* โครงร่าง build

krongrat *v.i.* ครองราชย์ reign

krongsang *n.* โครงสร้าง structure

krongsangtikadpentarang *n.* โครงสร้างที่ขัดเป็นตาราง lattice

kru *n.* ครู pedagogue

kru *n.* ครู preceptor

kru *n.* ครู teacher

krua *n.* ครัว kitchen

kruangmoon *n.* เครื่องหมุน turner

kruangrabai-a-gad *n.* เครื่องระบายอากศ ventilator

kruankrang *v.i.* ครวญคราง whine

krukra *adj* ขรุขระ bumpy

krukra *a.* ขรุขระ rugged

krunkid *v.t.* ครุ่นคิด mull

krunkid *v.i.* ครุ่นคิด muse

krunkid *a.* ครุ่นคิด pensive

krunkid *v.t.* ครุ่นคิด ponder

krunkid *a.* ครุ่นคิด thoughtful

krupised *n.* ครูพิเศษ tutor

kruyai *n.* ครูใหญ่ principal

ku *v.t* ขู่ blackmail

ku *v. t.* ขู่ cow

ku *a* คู่ dual

ku *v.t.* ขู่ intimidate

ku *v.t.* ขู่ overawe

ku *n.* คู่ pair

gu *v.t.* กู้ retrieve

ku *n.* คู trench

kua *n.* ขั้ว polar

kua *a* คั่ว roast

kuabkum *v. t* ควบคุม conduct

kuabkum *v. t* ควบคุม curb

kuabkum *v. t* ควบคุม dictate

kuabkum *v.t* ควบคุม head

kuabkum *v.t.* ควบคุม rein

kuabkum *v.t.* ควบคุม superintend

kuabkum *v.t.* ควบคุม supervise

kuabkum-a-romdaidi *a.* ควบคุมอารมณ์ได้ดี temperate

kuabma *v.t.* ควบม้า gallop

kuad *n* ขวด bottle

kuadgaew *n* ขวดแก้ว flask

kuadgaew *n.* ขวดแก้ว phial

kuadlek *n.* ขวดเล็ก vial

kuan *v.t.* ข่วน scratch

kuangaeganyokyong *a.* ควรแก่การยกย่อง praiseworthy

kuchabab *n.* คู่ฉบับ counterpart

kud *v.t.* ขุด dig
kud *v.t* ขุด grate
kud *v.t.* ขุด rack
kud *v.t.* ขุด shovel
kud *v.t.* ขุด unearth
kuddin *v.t.* ขุดดิน spade
kudkon *v. t.* ขุดค้น excavate
kudku *v.t.* ขุดคู trench
kud-u-mong *v.i.* ขุดอุโมงค์ tunnel
kugorani *n.* คู่กรณี litigant
kugrun *v.i.* คุกรุ่น smoulder
kuha *n* คูหา booth
kui *v. i.* คุย chat2
kuiganyangsanidsanom *v. t*
  คุยกันอย่างสนิทสนม commune
kuk *n.* คุก prison
kukaeng *n.* คู่แข่ง rival
kukaengkan *n.* คู่แข่งขัน opponent
kukkam *v.t* คุกคาม menace
kukkao *v.i.* คุกเข่า kneel
kukrong *n* คู่ครอง mate
kukuan *a.* คู่ควร worthy
guli *n* กุลี coolie
kumeu *n.* คู่มือ handbook
kumeu *n* คู่มือ manual
kumeuan *n.* คู่เหมือน couplet
kumeuan *n* คู่เหมือน match
kumgan *v. t* คุ้มกัน escort
kumgan *v.i.* คุ้มกัน guard
kun *a* ขุ่น dense
kun *a.* ขุ่น milky
kun *v.t.* คูณ multiply
kun *a.* ขุ่น opaque
kunam *n* คูน้ำ ditch
kunamrobmuang *n.* คูน้ำรอบเมือง moat
kunatam *n.* คุณธรรม virtue
gung *n.* กุ้ง crevet
gungfoy *n.* กุ้งฝอย serge
kunka *n.* คุณค่า value
kunkeuy *a.* คุ้นเคย accustomed
kunkeuy *v.t.* คุ้นเคย acquaint
kunkeuy *a* คุ้นเคย conversant

kunkeuy *a* คุ้นเคย customary
kunkeuy *a* คุ้นเคย familiar
kunnalaksana *n.* คุณลักษณะ attribute
kunnapab *n.* คุณภาพ quality
kunnapabdi *n.* คุณภาพดี premium
kunnasombat *n.* คุณสมบัติ qualification
kunnasombat *n.* คุณสมบัติ trait
kunnasombatchapaw *n.* คุณสมบัติเฉพาะ
  peculiarity
kunnatam *n.* คุณธรรม merit
kunnatam *n.* คุณธรรม moral
kunon *n* คู่นอน lay
kunsombatkongchaomeuang *n.*
  คุณสมบัติของชาวเมือง urbanity
kunying *n.* คุณหญิง dame
kupong *n.* คูปอง coupon
kusamipanlaya *n* คู่สามีภรรยา couple
kusomrod *n.* คู่สมรส consort
kusongkram *n* คู่สงคราม belligerent
guyeum *v.t.* กู้ยืม loan
kwa *v.t.* คว้า grab
kwa *v.t.* คว้า snatch
kwabangkab *n.* ข้อบังคับ statute
kwabkum *v.t.* ควบคุม master
kwadlow *n.* ขวดโหล jar
kwaen *v.t.* แขวน hang
kwaenam *n.* แควน้ำ tributary
kwai *n.* ควาย buffalo
kwam *v. i.* คว่ำ capsize
kwam-ab-ai *n.* ความอับอาย humiliation
kwam-a-gatanyu *n.* ความอกตัญญู
  ingratitude
kwam-ai *n.* ความอาย shy
kwam-a-kat *n.* ความอาฆาต feud
kwamantarai *n.* ความอันตราย danger
kwam-aowjaisai *n.* ความเอาใจใส่ regard
kwambaklang *n.* ความบ้าคลั่ง frenzy
kwambang-eun *n.* ความบังเอิญ
  contingency
kwambanteung *n.* ความบันเทิง
  entertainment
kwambat *v. t.* คว่ำบาตร boycott

kwambeua *n* ความเบื่อ bore
kwambobbang *n.* ความบอบบาง subtlety
kwambokprong *n* ความบกพร่อง defect
kwamborisut *n.* ความบริสุทธิ์ purity
kwamborisut *n.* ความบริสุทธิ์ virginity
kwamcha *n.* ความช้า slowness
kwamchabchuay *n.* ความฉาบฉวย
  superficiality
kwamchadjen *n* ความชัดเจน clarity
kwamchadjen *n.* ความชัดเจน
  manifestation
kwamchalad *n.* ความฉลาด intelligence
kwamchalad *n.* ความฉลาด sagacity
kwamchalad *n* ความฉลาด smart
kwamchaliawjai *n.* ความเฉลียวใจ inkling
kwamchamnan *n* ความชำนาญ bent
kwamchamnan *n.* ความชำนาญ keenness
kwamchamnan *n.* ความชำนาญ mastery
kwamchamnanpised *n.*
  ความชำนาญพิเศษ specialization
kwamchenchom *n.* ความชื่นชม adoration
kwamcheua *n* ความเชื่อ belief
kwamcheuafang *n.* ความเชื่อฟัง
  obedience
kwamcheuamyong *n.* ความเชื่อมโยง link
kwamcheuareuangjitwinyan *n.*
  ความเชื่อเรื่องจิตวิญญาณ spirituality
kwamcheuay *n.* ความเฉื่อย inertia
kwamcheuaycha *n.* ความเฉื่อยชา
  inaction
kwamcheuayleau *n* ความช่วยเหลือ
  rescue
kwamcheuchoklang *n.* ความเชื่อโชคลาง
  superstition
kwamcheun *n* ความชื้น damp
kwamcheun *n.* ความชื้น humidity
kwamcheun *n.* ความชื้น moisture
kwamcheunchom *n.* ความชื่นชม
  appreciation
kwamcheuaycha *n.* ความเฉื่อยชา
  lethargy
kwamchob *n.* ความชอบ likeness

kwamchob *n.* ความชอบ liking
kwamchob *n.* ความชอบ preference
kwamchobtam *n.* ความชอบธรรม
  legitimacy
kwamchokdi *n.* ความโชคดี luck
kwamchuayleua *n* ความช่วยเหลือ aid
kwamchuayleua *n* ความช่วยเหลือ
  favourl
kwamchuk *n.* ความชุก prevalence
kwamchun *n.* ความฉุน pungency
kwamchunlamun *n* ความชุลมุน rout
kwamdaipriab *n.* ความได้เปรียบ
  advantage
kwamdenchad *n.* ความเด่นชัด
  prominence
kwamdeuaddan *n.* ความเดือดดาล fury
kwamdeudeung *n.* ความดื้อดึง obstinacy
kwamdeuran *n* ความดื้อรั้น bigotry
kwamdeuran *n.* ความดื้อดึง obduracy
kwamdeuran *n.* ความดื้อรั้น tenacity
kwamdi *n* ความดี good
kwamdi *n.* ความดี goodness
kwamdikwamchob *n.* ความดีความชอบ
  laurel
kwamdi-ngam *n.* ความดีงาม morality
kwamdodden *n* ความโดดเด่น distinction
kwamdodden *n* ความโดดเด่น eminence
kwamfumfeuay *n* ความฟุ่มเฟือย
  extravagance
kwamfumfeuay *n.* ความฟุ่มเฟือย luxury
kwamfumfeuay *n.* ความฟุ่มเฟือย
  prodigality
kwamfumfeuay *n.* ความฟุ่มเฟือย
  profligacy
kwamfumfeuay *n.* ความฟุ่มเฟือย
  profusion
kwamfun *n* ความฝัน dream
kwamgamguam *n.* ความกำกวม
  ambiguity
kwamgangwan *n.* ความกังวาล sonority
kwamgangwon *a* ความกังวล anxiety
kwamgangwon *n* ความกังวล concern

kwamgangwon *n.* ความกังวล solicitude
kwamgangwon *n.* ความกังวล worry
kwamgaona *n.* ความก้าวหน้า progress
kwamgaona *n.* ความก้าวหน้า prosperity
kwamgaona *n* ความก้าวหน้า stride
kwamgiadkran *n.* ความเกียจคร้าน idleness
kwamgiawdong *n* ความเกี่ยวดอง affinity
kwamgiawkong *n* ความเกี่ยวข้อง connection
kwamgiawkong *n.* ความเกี่ยวข้อง relation
kwamgiawpan *n.* ความเกี่ยวพัน implication
kwamgla *n* ความกล้า boldness
kwamgla *n* ความกล้า bravery
kwamgla *n.* ความกล้า courage
kwamglahan *n.* ความกล้าหาญ daring
kwamglahan *n.* ความกล้าหาญ gallantry
kwamglahan *n.* ความกล้าหาญ hardihood
kwamglahan *n.* ความกล้าหาญ intrepidity
kwamglahan *n.* ความกล้าหาญ mettle
kwamglahan *n.* ความกล้าหาญ prowess
kwamglahan *n.* ความกล้าหาญ valour
kwamglahan *n.* ความกล้าหาญ chivalry
kwamglaichid *n.* ความใกล้ชิด intimacy
kwamglaichid *n.* ความใกล้ชิด proximity
kwamgliad *n* ความเกลียด grudge
kwamgliad *n.* ความเกลียด hate
kwamgliadchang *n.* ความเกลียดชัง abhorrence
kwamgliadchang *n* ความเกลียดชัง animosity
kwamgliadchang *n.* ความเกลียดชัง antipathy
kwamgliadchang *n.* ความเกลียดชัง odium
kwamglomgliaw *n.* ความกลมเกลียว concord
kwamgrot *n.* ความโกรธ outrage
kwamglua *n* ความกลัว fear
kwamglua *n.* ความกลัว fright
kwamglua *n.* ความกลัว scare

kwamgoddan *n.* ความกดดัน pressure
kwamgrahai *n.* ความกระหาย thirst
kwamgrateureuron *n.* ความกระตือรือร้น alacrity
kwamgrateureuron *n.* ความกระตือรือร้น ardour
kwamgrateureuron *n* ความกระตือรือร้น enthusiasm
kwamgrateureuron *n.* ความกระตือรือร้น zeal
kwamgrot *n.* ความโกรธ anger
kwamgrodkreuang *n.* ความโกรธเคือง wrath
kwamgrot *n.* ความโกรธ indignation
kwamgrot *n.* ความโกรธ ire
kwamgrot *n.* ความโกรธ rage
kwamgwang *n.* ความกว้าง width
kwamhaenglaeng *n* ความแห้งแล้ง drought
kwamhaiyana *n* ความหายนะ disaster
kwamhaiyana *n.* ความหายนะ havoc
kwamhaiyana *n.* ความหายนะ scourge
kwamhaiyana *n.* ความหายนะ wrack
kwamhen *n* ความเห็น comment
kwamhen *n.* ความเห็น opinion
kwamhen *n.* ความเห็น remark
kwamhen *n.* ความเห็น view
kwamhen *n.* ความเห็น vista
kwamhenjai *n* ความเห็นใจ compassion
kwamhenjai *n.* ความเห็นใจ sympathy
kwamhew *n* ความหิว hunger
kwamhodrai *n* ความโหดร้าย atrocity
kwamhodrai *n* ความโหดร้าย cruelty
kwam-id-cha *v* ความอิจฉา envy
kwam-id-cha *n.* ความอิจฉา jealousy
kwamjaiboon *n* ความใจบุญ bounty
kwamjaiboon *n.* ความใจบุญ philanthropy
kwamjaidi *n.* ความใจดี generosity
kwamjaigwang *n.* ความใจกว้าง magnanimity
kwamjam *n.* ความจำ memory
kwamjampen *n.* ความจำเป็น necessary

kwamjampen *n.* ความจำเป็น necessity
kwamjampen *n.* ความจำเป็น need
kwamjamseuam *n* ความจำเสื่อม amnesia
kwamjaolay *n* ความเจ้าเล่ห์ cunning
kwamjaorabiab *n.* ความเจ้าระเบียบ purist
kwamjebpuad *n.* ความเจ็บปวด agony
kwamjebpuad *n.* ความเจ็บปวด ordeal
kwamjebpuad *n.* ความเจ็บปวด pain
kwamjebpuad *n.* ความเจ็บปวด poignacy
kwamjebpuad *n* ความเจ็บปวด sore
kwamjebpuad *n.* ความเจ็บปวด sting
kwamjebpuay *n.* ความเจ็บป่วย illness
kwamjebpuay *n.* ความเจ็บป่วย sickness
kwamjeudcheud *n.* ความจืดชืด insipidity
kwamjing *n.* ความจริง truth
kwamjingjai *n.* ความจริงใจ sincerity
kwamjongrakpakdi *n.* ความจงรักภักดี
   allegiance
kwamjongrakpakdi *n.* ความจงรักภักดี
   royalty
kwamju *n* ความจุ bulk
kwamkadklan *n* ความขาดแคลน dearth
kwamkadklan *n.* ความขาดแคลน lack
kwamkadklan *n.* ความขาดแคลน scarcity
kwamkadson *n.* ควมขัดสน paucity
kwamkadwang *n.* ความคาดหวัง
   expectation
kwamkadyaeng *n.* ความขัดแย้ง conflict
kwamkadyaeng *n* ความขัดแย้ง
   contradiction
kwamkadyaeng *n* ความขัดแย้ง
   controversy
kwamkadyaeng *n* ความขัดแย้ง dispute
kwamkaengraeng *n.* ความแข็งแรง
   stamina
kwamkanong *n.* ความคะนอง levity
kwamkaojai *n.* ความเข้าใจ apprehension
kwamkaojai *n* ความเข้าใจ
   comprehension
kwamkaojai *n.* ความเข้าใจ realization
kwamkaojaileukseung *n.*
   ความเข้าใจลึกซึ้ง insight

kwamkaorob *n* ความเคารพ esteem
kwamkaorob *n.* ความเคารพ respect
kwamkaorob *n.* ความเคารพ reverence
kwamkaorob *n.* ความเคารพ veneration
kwamkayan *n* ความขยัน diligence
kwamkemkaeng *n.* ความเข้มแข็ง strength
kwamkem-nguad *n.* ความเข้มงวด
   stringency
kwamkeuychin *n* ความเคยชิน wont
kwamkid *n* ความคิด conceit
kwamkid *n.* ความคิด idea
kwamkid *n.* ความคิด notion
kwamkid *n* ความคิด thought
kwamkidpeufan *n.* ความคิดเพ้อฝัน whim
kwamkidrireum *n.* ความคิดริเริ่ม
   originality
kwamkidtimaitooktong *n*
   ความคิดที่ไม่ถูกต้อง fallacy
kwamkigiad *n.* ความขี้เกียจ laziness
kwamkigiad *n.* ความขี้เกียจ sloth
kwamkiklad *n.* ความขี้ขลาด cowardice
kwamkiklad *n.* ความขี้ขลาด timidity
kwamklaigan *n.* ความคล้ายกัน analogy
kwamklaigan *n.* ความคล้ายกัน
   semblance
kwamklaigan *n.* ความคล้ายกัน similarity
kwamklaigan *n.* ความคล้ายกัน similitude
kwamklaigan *n.* ความคล้ายกัน
   verisimilitude
kwamklaikleung *n.* ความคล้ายคลึง
   resemblance
kwamklangklai *n* ความคลั่งไคล้ craze
kwamklangklai *n* ความคลั่งไคล้ mania
kwamklao *n* ความเขลา folly
kwamklongkleaw *n.* ความคล่องแคล่ว
   agility
kwamkluatilong *n.* ความกลัวที่โล่ง
   agoraphobia
kwamklumkreua *n.* ความคลุมเครือ
   obscurity
kwamklumkreua *n.* ความคลุมเครือ
   opacity

kwamkolahon *n.* ความโกลาหล
pandemonium

kwamkomkeun *n.* ความขมขื่น rancour

kwamkrengsanana *n.* ความเคร่งศาสนา
piety

kwamkreungkreum *n.* ความเคร่งขรึม
solemnity

kwamkriad *n.* ความเครียด intensity

kwamkriad *n.* ความเครียด stress

kwamkriad *n.* ความเครียด tension

kwamkunkeuy *n.* ความคุ้นเคย
acquaintance

kwamkwang *n* ความกว้าง breadth

kwamkwaojaipid *n.* ความเข้าใจผิด
misunderstanding

kwamlab *n* ความลับ confidence

kwamlab *n.* ความลับ secrecy

kwamlab *n.* ความลับ secret

kwamlaklai *n.* ความหลากหลาย
multiplicity

kwamlaklai *n.* ความหลากหลาย
multitude

kwamlaklai *n.* ความหลากหลาย variety

kwamlam-iang *n.* ความลำเอียง partiality

kwamlam-iang *n.* ความลำเอียง prejudice

kwamleuk *n* ความลึก depth

kwamleuk *n* ความลึก fathom

kwamleuk *n.* ความลึก profundity

kwamleuklab *n.* ความลึกลับ mystery

kwamlew *n.* ความเลว meanness

kwamlob *n.* ความโลภ avarice

kwamlob *adv.* ความโลภ avidity

kwamlob *n* ความโลภ cupidity

kwamlob *n.* ความโลภ greed

kwamlokluang *n.* ความหลอกลวง guile

kwamlomlew *n* ความล้มเหลว deadlock

kwamlomlew *n* ความล้มเหลว failure

kwamlomlew *n* ความล้มเหลว fiasco

kwamlonglai *n.* ความหลงใหล fascination

kwamlonglai *n.* ความหลงใหล infatuation

kwamlonglai *n.* ความหลงใหล passion

kwammaenyam *n.* ความแม่นยำ precision

kwammahoran *n.* ความมโหฬาร
immensity

kwammai *n.* ความหมาย meaning

kwammai *n.* ความใหม่ novelty

kwammai *n.* ความหมาย purport

kwammaiborisut *n.* ความไม่บริสุทธิ์
impurity

kwammaichob *n* ความไม่ชอบ dislike

kwammaihaigiat *n* ความไม่ให้เกียรติ
dishonour

kwammaihenduay *n.* ความไม่เห็นด้วย
disagreement

kwammaihenduay *n* ความไม่เห็นด้วย
disapproval

kwammaikaengraeng *n.* ความไม่แข็งแรง
infirmity

kwammaikaorob *n* ความไม่เคารพ
disrespect

kwammailongroygan *n*
ความไม่ลงรอยกัน discord

kwammaimankong *n.* ความไม่มั่นคง
insecurity

kwammaimankong *n.* ความไม่มั่นคง
instability

kwammaimawsom *n.* ความไม่เหมาะสม
impropriety

kwammaimawsom *n.* ความไม่เหมาะสม
misappropriation

kwammaimilaksanachapaw *n.*
ความไม่มีลักษณะเฉพาะ anonymity

kwammaimisinratam *n.*
ความไม่มีศีลธรรม immorality

kwammainaejai *n.* ความไม่แน่ใจ
indecision

kwammainaejai *n.* ความไม่แน่ใจ
quandary

kwammainaejai *n.* ความไม่แน่ใจ shilly-
shally

kwammainaenon *n.* ความไม่แน่นอน
vagary

kwammai-odton *n.* ความไม่อดทน
impatience

kwammaipawjai *n* ความไม่พอใจ
discontent

kwammaipawjai *n* ความไม่พอใจ
displeasure

kwammaipawjai *n* ความไม่พอใจ
dissatisfaction

kwammaipawjai *n* ความไม่พอใจ
malcontent

kwammaipawjai *n.* ความไม่พอใจ
resentment

kwammairobkob *n.* ความไม่รอบคอบ
imprudence

kwammairobkob *n.* ความไม่รอบคอบ
indiscretion

kwammairu *n.* ความไม่รู้ nescience

kwammaisabai *n* ความไม่สบาย
morbidity

kwammaisabaijai *n.* ความไม่สบายใจ fret

kwammaisaduaksabai *n*
ความไม่สะดวกสบาย discomfort

kwammaisamkan *n.* ความไม่สำคัญ
insignificance

kwammaisa-ngob *n* ความไม่สงบ disquiet

kwammaisa-ngobsuk *n* ความไม่สงบสุข
unrest

kwammaiseusat *n.* ความไม่ซื่อสัตย์
dishonesty

kwammaiseusat *n.* ความไม่ซื่อสัตย์
knavery

kwammaimitisinsud *n.* ความไม่มีที่สิ้นสุด
infinity

kwammaisomboon *n.* ความไม่สมบูรณ์
immaturity

kwammaisomboon *n.* ความไม่สมบูรณ์
imperfection

kwammaisonjai *n* ความไม่สนใจ
disregard

kwammaisupab *n.* ความไม่สุภาพ
immodesty

kwammaitaektang *n.* ความไม่แตกต่าง
indifference

kwammaiwaijai *n.* ความไม่ไว้ใจ mistrust

kwammaiwaijai *n* ความไม่ไว้ใจ distrust

kwammaiyutitam *n.* ความไม่ยุติธรรม
injustice

kwammangkang *n.* ความมั่งคั่ง opulence

kwammankong *n.* ความมั่นคง stability

kwammawsom *n.* ความเหมาะสม
propriety

kwammawsom *n.* ความเหมาะสม
suitability

kwammetti *n.* ความเมตตา mercy

kwammeud *n* ความมืด dark

kwammeud *n.* ความมืด gloom

kwammeudbod *n* ความมืดบอด ablepsy

kwammeudbod *n* ความมืดบอด blindness

kwammeuncheuy *n.* ความเมินเฉย
nonchalance

kwammi-amnad *n.* ความมีอำนาจ majesty

kwammi-atta *n* ความมีอัตตา egotism

kwammi-a-wuso *n.* ความมีอาวุโส
seniority

kwammicheusiang *n* ความมีชื่อเสียง
frame

kwammicheusiang *n.* ความมีชื่อเสียง
notability

kwammichiwitchiwa *n.* ความมีชีวิตชีวา
spark

kwammichiwitchiwa *n.* ความมีชีวิตชีวา
verve

kwammichiwitchiwa *n.* ความมีชีวิตชีวา
vivacity

kwammihedmipon *n.* ความมีเหตุมีผล
rationality

kwammihedpon *n.* ความมีเหตุผล validity

kwammilayliam *n.* ความมีเล่ห์เหลี่ยม
roguery

kwammimarayad *n.* ความมีมารยาท
courtesy

kwammiprasitipab *n* ความมีประสิทธิภาพ
efficacy

kwammiprasitipab *n* ความมีประสิทธิภาพ
efficiency

kwammiprasitipab *n.*
ความมีประสิทธิภาพ proficiency

kwammisanei *n.* ความมีเสน่ห์ glamour

kwammisati *n.* ความมีสติ sobriety

kwammungrai *n.* ความมุ่งร้าย malice

kwamnabeua *n.* ความน่าเบื่อ tedium

kwamnaenon *n.* ความแน่นอน certainty

kwamnaenon *n.* ความแน่นอน steadiness

kwamnaenon *n.* ความแน่นอน surety

kwamnagliad *n.* ความน่าเกลียด ugliness

kwamnaglua *n* ความน่ากลัว dread

kwamnaglua *n.* ความน่ากลัว horror

kwamnaglua *n.* ความน่ากลัว monstrous

kwamnagreingkam *n.* ความน่าเกรงขาม
awe

kwamnajapen *n.* ความน่าจะเป็น
probability

kwamnanaen *n* ความหนาแน่น density

kwamnaoyen *n.* ความหนาวเย็น chill

kwamnarak *n.* ความน่ารัก prettiness

kwamnasongsai *n.* ความน่าสงสัย
suspicion

kwamneuakwa *n.* ความเหนือกว่า pre-
eminence

kwamneuakwa *n.* ความเหนือกว่า
superiority

kwamneuy *n* ความเหนื่อย fatigue

kwam-ngam *n* ความงาม beauty

kwam-ngam *n* ความงาม belle

kwam-ngao *n.* ความเหงา loneliness

kwam-ngiab *n* ความเงียบ hush

kwam-ngiab *n.* ความเงียบ quiet

kwam-ngiab *n.* ความเงียบ reticence

kwam-ngiab *n.* ความเงียบ silence

kwam-ngiabsa-ngob *n.* ความเงียบสงบ
still

kwam-ngo *n.* ความโง่ stupidity

kwam-ngod-ngam *n.* ความงดงาม
splendour

kwam-nguangnon *n.* ความง่วงนอน
somnolence

kwam-ngud-ngid *n* ความหงุดหงิด
vexation

kwam-ngun-ngong *n* ความงุนงง daze

kwamning *n.* ความนิ่ง stillness

kwamniyom *n.* ความนิยม popularity

kwamnoy *n.* ความน้อย smallness

kwamnoyjai *n.* ความน้อยใจ petulance

kwamnum *n.* ความนุ่ม soft

kwam-ob-aom-ari *n.* ความโอบอ้อมอารี
liberality

kwam-ob-aun *n.* ความอบอุ่น warmth

kwam-ob-om-a-ri *n.* ความโอบอ้อมอารี
hospitality

kwam-odton *n.* ความอดทน patience

kwam-odton *n.* ความอดทน tolerance

kwam-odton *n.* ความอดทน toleration

kwam-od-ton *n.* ความอดทน fortitude

kwam-od-yak *n* ความอดอยาก famine

kwam-on-ae *n.* ความอ่อนแอ weakness

kwam-onlaweng *n.* ความอลเวง tumult

kwam-onnom *n.* ความอ่อนน้อม humility

kwam-onplia *n* ความอ่อนเพลีย debility

kwampaipae *n* ความพ่ายแพ้ defeat

kwampaklang *n.* ความบ้าคลั่ง uproar

kwampanya-on *n.* ความปัญญาอ่อน
retardation

kwampateuan *n.* ความป่าเถื่อน barbarism

kwampateuan *n* ความป่าเถื่อน barbarity

kwampateuan *n.* ความป่าเถื่อน savagery

kwampawdi *n* ความพอดี fit

kwampawjai *n* ความพอใจ content

kwampawjai *n* ความพอใจ contentment

kwampawjai *n.* ความพอใจ satisfaction

kwampawpiang *n.* ความพอเพียง
adequacy

kwampawpiang *n.* ความพอเพียง
sufficiency

kwampawpraman *n.* ความพอประมาณ
moderation

kwampayayam *n.* ความพยายาม attempt

kwampayayam *n* ความพยายาม effort

kwampayayam *n* ความพยายาม
endeavour

kwampayayam *n.* ความพยายาม
perseverance

kwampayayam *n.* ความพยายาม strife

kwampayayam *n* ความพยายาม try

kwam-payayam *n.* ความพยายาม essay

kwampen-ammata *n.* ความเป็นอมตะ
immortality

kwampen-anneung-andiawgan *n.*
ความเป็นอันหนึ่งอันเดียว unity

kwampenchai *n.* ความเป็นชาย manhood

kwampenchai *n* ความเป็นชาย manliness

kwampenchai *n.* ความเป็นชาย virility

kwampen-ekkated *n.* ความเป็นเอกเทศ
individuality

kwampenhunsuan *n.* ความเป็นหุ้นส่วน
partnership

kwampen-issara *n.* ความเป็นอิสระ
freedom

kwampen-issara *n.* ความเป็นอิสระ
independence

kwampenjaokong *n.* ความเป็นเจ้าของ
ownership

kwampenjing *n.* ความเป็นจริง reality

kwampenkonbannok *n.*
ความเป็นคนบ้านนอก rusticity

kwampenleud *n.* ความเป็นเลิศ excellence

kwampenmae *n.* ความเป็นแม่ maternity

kwampenmae *n.* ความเป็นแม่
motherhood

kwampenmit *n.* ความเป็นมิตร rapport

kwampenneungdiaw *n.*
ความเป็นหนึ่งเดียว oneness

kwampenpahupod *n.* ความเป็นพหูพจน์
plurality

kwampenpaidai *n.* ความเป็นไปได้
likelihood

kwampenpaidai *n.* ความเป็นไปได้
possibility

kwampenpaimaidai *n.* ความเป็นไปไม่ได้
impossibility

kwampenpeuan *n.* ความเป็นเพื่อน
amiability

kwampenpinong *n* ความเป็นพี่น้อง
brotherhood

kwampenpinong *n.* ความเป็นพี่น้อง
confraternity

kwampenpinong *n.* ความเป็นพี่น้อง
sisterhood

kwampenpit *n.* ความเป็นพิษ virulence

kwampenponlameuang *n*
ความเป็นพลเมือง citizenship

kwampenpunam *n.* ความเป็นผู้นำ
leadership

kwampenpuyai *n.* ความเป็นผู้ใหญ่
maturity

kwampenpuying *n.* ความเป็นผู้หญิง
womanhood

kwampenrabiab *n.* ความเป็นระเบียบ
tidiness

kwampensagon *n.* ความเป็นสากล
universality

kwampensattru *n* ความเป็นศัตรู enmity

kwampensattru *n.* ความเป็นศัตรู hostility

kwampensuantua *n.* ความเป็นส่วนตัว
privacy

kwampentad *n.* ความเป็นทาส slavery

kwampentad *n.* ความเป็นทาส thralldom

kwampentammachat *n.*
ความเป็นธรรมชาติ spontaneity

kwampeungpawjai *n.* ความพึงพอใจ
gratification

kwampiak *n.* ความเปียก wetness

kwampid *n* ความผิด fault

kwampid *n.* ความผิด guilt

kwampidpagati *n* ความผิดปกติ anomaly

kwampidpagati *n.* ความผิดปกติ
irregularity

kwampidplad *n* ความผิดพลาด error

kwampidplad *n.* ความผิดพลาด mistake

kwampidwang *n* ความผิดหวัง dejection

kwampigan *n* ความพิการ disability

kwampised *n.* ความพิเศษ speciality

kwamplabpleum *n.* ความปลาบปลื้ม rapture

kwamplaekjai *n.* ความแปลกใจ astonishment

kwamplaekjai *n* ความแปลกใจ wonder

kwampleudpleun *n* ความเพลิดเพลิน relish

kwampleumpiti *n.* ความปลื้มปิติ jubilation

kwamplodpai *n.* ความปลอดภัย safe

kwamplodpai *n.* ความปลอดภัย safety

kwamplodpai *n.* ความปลอดภัย security

kwampraladjai *n.* ความประหลาดใจ amazement

kwampramua *n* ความพร่ามัว blur

kwamprani *n.* ความปรานี lenience, leniency

kwampranipranom *n* ความประนีประนอม compromise

kwampranit *n.* ความประณีต nicety

kwampranit *n.* ความปราณีต refinement

kwamprapeud *n* ความประพฤติ conduct

kwamprapeud *n* ความประพฤติ behaviour

kwamprapeuddi *n* ความประพฤติดี decency

kwampratabjai *n.* ความประทับใจ expression

kwampratabjai *n.* ความประทับใจ impression

kwampratana *n.* ความปรารถนา aspiration

kwampratana *n* ความปรารถนา desire

kwampratana *n.* ความปรารถนา longing

kwampratana *n.* ความปรารถนา volition

kwampratana *n.* ความปรารถนา wish

kwampratana *n.* ความปรารถนา yearning

kwamprayad *n* ความประหยัด economy

kwamprayad *n.* ความประหยัด retrenchment

kwamprayad *n.* ความประหยัด thrift

kwamprom *n.* ความพร้อม readiness

kwamprompriang *n.* ความพร้อมเพรียง unison

kwampukpan *n.* ความผูกพัน affiliation

kwampumjai *n.* ความภูมิใจ pride

kwamrabpid *n.* ความรับผิด liability

kwamrabpidchob *n.* ความรับผิดชอบ responsibility

kwamraidiangsa *n.* ความไร้เดียงสา innocence

kwamraidiangsa *n.* ความไร้เดียงสา naivete

kwamraika *n.* ความไร้ค่า nullification

kwamraisamadtapab *n.* ความไร้สมรรถภาพ impotence

kwamraisara *n* ความไร้สาระ absurdity

kwamrak *n.* ความรัก affection

kwamrak *n* ความรัก amour

kwamrak *n* ความรัก love

kwamrakchat *n.* ความรักชาติ partiotism

kwamramadrawang *n.* ความระมัดระวัง precaution

kwamramkan *n.* ความรำคาญ annoyance

kwamramkan *n.* ความรำคาญ irritation

kwamramruay *n.* ความร่ำรวย affluence

kwamramruay *n.* ความร่ำรวย riches

kwamramruay *a.* ความร่ำรวย richness

kwamramruay *n.* ความร่ำรวย wealth

kwamrew *n.* ความเร็ว speed

kwamrengron *n.* ความเร่งร้อน vehemence

kwamreunreung *n.* ความรื่นเริง gaiety

kwamreunreung *n.* ความรื่นเริง joviality

kwamreunreung *n.* ความรื่นเริง mirth

kwamreunreungyindi *n.* ความรื่นเริงยินดี cheer

kwamrew *n.* ความเร็ว rapidity

kwamriab-ngai *n.* ความเรียบง่าย simplicity

kwamribreng *n.* ความรีบเร่ง haste

kwamribreng *n.* ความรีบเร่ง urgency

kwamrobkob *n* ความรอบคอบ deliberation

kwamrobkob *n.* ความรอบคอบ prudence

kwamrobru *n.* ความรอบรู้ omniscience
kwamron *n.* ความร้อน heat
kwamroonraeng *n* ความรุนแรง acrimony
kwamroonraeng *n.* ความรุนแรง rigour
kwamru *n.* ความรู้ knowledge
kwamruammeu *n* ความร่วมมือ
collaboration
kwamrungreuang *n.* ความรุ่งเรือง glory
kwamrunraeng *n.* ความรุนแรง severity
kwamrunraeng *n.* ความรุนแรง violence
kwamruseuk *n.* ความรู้สึก sentience
kwamruseuk *n* ความรู้สึก feeling
kwamruseuktawgansampat *n.*
ความรู้สึกต่อการสัมผัส sensation
kwamruseuktuamton *n* ความรู้สึกท่วมท้น
fervour
kwamsabai *n.* ความสบาย comfort
kwamsabai *a.* ความสบาย leisurely
kwamsabsawn *n.* ความซับซ้อน
sophistication
kwamsabsom *n* ความสับสน commotion
kwamsabson *n* ความสับสน confusion
kwamsabson *n.* ความสับสน frustration
kwamsabson *n.* ความสับสน perplexity
kwamsabson *n.* ความสับสน welter
kwamsaduak *n.* ความสะดวก convenience
kwamsamad *n* ความสามารถ ability
kwamsamad *n.* ความสามารถ capability
kwamsamad *n* ความสามารถ competence
kwamsamadnaiganchamrani *n.*
ความสามารถในการชำระหนี้ solvency
kwamsamadnaigangaepanha *n.*
ความสามารถในการแก้ปัญหา solubility
kwamsamadnaiganjadgan *n.*
ความสามารถในการจัดการ providence
kwamsamadnaigankaosangkom *n.*
ความสามารถในการเข้าสังคม sociability
kwamsamadnaiganmonghen *n.*
ความสามารถในการมองเห็น visibility
kwamsamadnaigannaenam *n*
ความสามารถในการแนะนำ advisability

kwamsamadrobtua *n.*
ความสามารถรอบตัว versatility
kwamsamadtangjidjai *n.*
ความสามารถทางจิตใจ mentality
kwamsamadtijarabdai *n.*
ความสามารถที่จะรับได้ capacity
kwamsamakki *n.* ความสามัคคี harmony
kwamsamakki *n.* ความสามัคคี solidarity
kwamsamamsameu *n.* ความสม่ำเสมอ
regularity
kwamsamkan *n.* ความสำคัญ importance
kwamsamkan *n.* ความสำคัญ significance
kwamsamkan *n.* ความสำคัญ signification
kwamsamneuknaiboonkun *n.*
ความสำนึกในบุญคุณ gratitude
kwamsamneukpid *n.* ความสำนึกผิด
compunction
kwamsampan *n.* ความสัมพันธ์ correlation
kwamsampan *n.* ความสัมพันธ์ relevance
kwamsampantimaimawsom *n.*
ความสัมพันธ์ที่ไม่เหมาะสม misalliance
kwamsamred *n* ความสำเร็จ feat
kwamsamred *n.* ความสำเร็จ
accomplishment
kwamsamred *n.* ความสำเร็จ achievement
kwamsamred *n.* ความสำเร็จ success
kwamsamsak *n* ความซ้ำซาก monotony
kwamsamsak *n.* ความซ้ำซาก redundance
kwamsandod *n* ความสันโดษ
monasticism
kwamsa-nga-ngam *n* ความสง่างาม
elegance
kwamsa-nga-ngam *n.* ความสง่างาม grace
kwamsa-nga-ngam *n.* ความสง่างาม
grandeur
kwamsa-ngob *n.* ความสงบ calm
kwamsa-ngob *n.* ความสงบ composure
kwamsa-ngob *n.* ความสงบ serenity
kwamsa-ngob *n.* ความสงบ tranquility
kwamsanook *n.* ความสนุก glee
kwamsanook *n.* ความสนุก joy

kwamsanooksanan *n* ความสนุกสนาน amusement

kwamsanooksanan *n* ความสนุกสนาน enjoyment

kwamsanooksanan *n.* ความสนุกสนาน frolic

kwamsanooksanan *n.* ความสนุกสนาน hilarity

kwamsanooksanan *n.* ความสนุกสนาน merriment

kwamsanooksanan *n.* ความสนุกสนาน revelry

kwamsanooksanan *n.* ความสนุกสนาน zest

kwamsao *n* ความเศร้า distress

kwamsao *n.* ความเศร้า melancholy

kwamsao *n.* ความเศร้า mourning

kwamsao *n.* ความเศร้า woe

kwamsaprow *n* ความสะเพร่า blunder

kwamsatjing *n.* ความสัตย์จริง veracity

kwamsatta *n* ความศรัทธา faith

kwamsawang *n* ความสว่าง brilliance

kwamsawang *n.* ความสว่าง lucidity

kwamsawang *n.* ความสว่าง radiance

kwamsawang *n.* ความสว่าง refulgence

kwamseplay *n* ความเสเพล debauchery

kwamseusat *n* ความซื่อสัตย์ fidelity

kwamseusat *n.* ความซื่อสัตย์ honesty

kwamseusat *n.* ความซื่อสัตย์ integrity

kwamseusat *n.* ความซื่อสัตย์ loyalty

kwamseutrong *n.* ความซื่อตรง naivety

kwamsiahai *n.* ความเสียหาย damage

kwamsiahai *n.* ความเสียหาย harm

kwamsiajai *n.* ความเสียใจ grief

kwamsiajai *n.* ความเสียใจ grievance

kwamsiajai *n* ความเสียใจ lament

kwamsiajai *n.* ความเสียใจ lamentation

kwamsiajai *n* ความเสียใจ regret

kwamsiajai *n.* ความเสียใจ sorrow

kwamsinwang *n* ความสิ้นหวัง despair

kwamsoongsong *n.* ความสูงส่ง nobility

kwamsobsao *n.* ความซบเซา stagnation

kwamsodklong *n.* ความสอดคล้อง conformity

kwamsodklong *n.* ความสอดคล้อง consonance

kwamsokgaprok *n* ความสกปรก dirt

kwamsokgaprok *n* ความสกปรก filth

kwamsomboon *n* ความสมบูรณ์ abundance

kwamsomboon *n.* ความสมบูรณ์ fullness

kwamsomboon *n.* ความสมบูรณ์ perfection

kwamsomboon *n.* ความสมบูรณ์ prefect

kwamsomdoon *n.* ความสมดุล balance

kwamsomhedsompon *n.* ความสมเหตุสมผล justification

kwamsommat *n.* ความสมมาตร symmetry

kwamsomwang *n.* ความสมหวัง fulfilment

kwamsomdun *n* ความสมดุล poise

kwamsongjam *n.* ความทรงจำ recollection

kwamsongjam *n.* ความทรงจำ remembrance

kwamsongjam *n.* ความทรงจำ reminiscence

kwamsongsai *n.* ความสงสัย misgiving

kwamsongsai *n.* ความสงสัย scepticism

kwamsongsan *n.* ความสงสาร pathos

kwamsongsan *n.* ความสงสาร pity

kwamsonjai *n.* ความสนใจ attention

kwamsonjai *n.* ความสนใจ interest

kwamsonjainaisingleklek *n.* ความสนใจในสิ่งเล็กๆ micrology

kwamsook *n* ความสุข bliss

kwamsook *n.* ความสุข happiness

kwamsook *a.* ความสุข happy

kwamsooksabai *n* ความสุขสบาย ease

kwamsoong *n.* ความสูง stature

kwamsoongsong *n.* ความสูงส่ง sublimity

kwamsoonsia *n.* ความสูญเสีย loss

kwamsook *n* ความสุข felicity

kwamsumsam *n* ความซุ่มซ่าม bungle

kwamsoong *n.* ความสูง altitude

kwamsoong *n.* ความสูง height
kwamsoongsud *n* ความสูงสุด extreme
kwamsupab *n.* ความสุภาพ pliteness
kwamtaekrao *n.* ความแตกร้าว rift
kwamtaektang *n* ความแตกต่าง contrast
kwamtaektang *n* ความแตกต่าง
  difference
kwamtaektang *n* ความแตกต่าง disparity
kwamtaektangleknoy *n.*
  ความแตกต่างเล็กน้อย nuance
kwamtaekteun *n.* ความแตกตื่น stampede
kwamtaekyaek *n.* ความแตกแยก schism
kwamtai *n* ความตาย death
kwamtai *n* ความตาย decease
kamtalaenggan *n.* คำแถลงการณ์
  statement
kwamtalokkanong *n* ความตลกคะนอง
  flippancy
kwamtamtoy *n.* ความต่ำต้อย lowliness
kwamtammada *n.* ความธรรมดา
  mediocrity
kwamtanad *n.* ความถนัด aptitude
kwamtangjai *n.* ความตั้งใจ aim
kwamtangjai *n* ความตั้งใจ animus
kwamtangjai *n.* ความตั้งใจ concentration
kwamtangjai *n.* ความตั้งใจ intent
kwamtangjai *n.* ความตั้งใจ intention
kwamtangjai *n.* ความตั้งใจ purpose
kwamtangjai *n.* ความตั้งใจ will
kwamtanong *n.* ความทะนง insolence
kwamtanongtua *n.* ความทะนงตัว
  vainglory
kwamtansami *n.* ความทันสมัย modernity
kwamtaotiam *n* ความเท่าเทียม equality
kwamtaotiam *n* ความเท่าเทียม equation
kwamtaotiam *n.* ความเท่าเทียม
  parallelism
kwamtaotiam *n.* ความเท่าเทียม parity
kwamtatai *n.* ความท้าทาย challenge
kwamtawneuang *n.* ความต่อเนื่อง
  consistency

kwamtawneuang *n.* ความต่อเนื่อง
  continuation
kwamtawneuang *n* ความต่อเนื่อง
  continuity
kwamtawon *n.* ความถาวร permanence
kwamtawraman *v.t.* ความทรมาน torment
kwamtayeutayan *n.* ความทะเยอทะยาน
  ambition
kwamtem-im *n.* ความเต็มอิ่ม satiety
kwamteunten *n.* ความตื่นเต้น thrill
kwamteunten *n.* ความตื่นเต้น twitter
kwamteuntranok *n.* ความตื่นตระหนก
  panic
kwamteuntua *n.* ความตื่นตัว alertness
kwamti *n.* ความถี่ frequency
kwamti *n.* ความถี่ frequent
kwamtoklong *n.* ความตกลง agreement
kwamtoktam *n* ความตกต่ำ downfall
kwamtonggan *n.* ความต้องการ appetence
kwamtonggan *n.* ความต้องการ
  requirement
kwamtonggan *n* ความต้องการ want
kwamtontan *n.* ความทนทาน endurance
kwamtook *n.* ความทุกข์ anguish
kwamtooktong *n.* ความถูกต้อง accuracy
kwamtooktong *n* ความถูกต้อง correction
kwamtooktong *n* ความถูกต้อง right
kwamtooktongtamgodmai *n.*
  ความถูกต้องตามกฎหมาย legality
kwamtooktoraman *n.* ความทุกข์ทรมาน
  martyrdom
kwamtookyak *n.* ความทุกข์ยาก hardship
kwamtookyak *n.* ความทุกข์ยาก misery
kwam-uan *n.* ความอ้วน obesity
kwam-u-domsomboon *n.*
  ความอุดมสมบูรณ์ luxuriance
kwam-u-domsomboon *n*
  ความอุดมสมบูรณ์ fertility
kwam-u-domsomboon *n.*
  ความอุดมสมบูรณ์ superabundance
kwamwaewwao *n.* ความแวววาว gloss
kwamwadglua *n.* ความหวาดกลัว terror

kwamwaiwangjai *n.* ความไว้วางใจ reliance

kwamwaiwangjai *n.* ความไว้วางใจ trust

kwamwan *n.* ความหวาน sweetness

kwamwang *n* ความหวัง hope

kwamwangplao *n.* ความว่างเปล่า void

kwamwigonjarit *n.* ความวิกลจริต lunacy

kwamwiparit *n.* ความวิปริต perversion

kwamwiparit *n.* ความวิปริต perversity

kwamwitokgangwon *n.* ความวิตกกังวล suspense

kwamwunwai *n* ความวุ่นวาย disorder

kwamwunwai *n.* ความวุ่นวาย fuss

kwamwunwai *n.* ความวุ่นวาย muddle

kwamwunwai *n.* ความวุ่นวาย turbulence

kwamwunwai *n.* ความวุ่นวาย turmoil

kwamwunwai *n.* ความวุ่นวาย upheaval

kwamyabkai *n.* ความหยาบคาย impertinence

kwamyabkai *n.* ความหยาบคาย indecency

kwamyabkai *n.* ความหยาบคาย vulgarity

kwamyablon *n.* ความหยาบโลน coprology

kwamyaito *n.* ความใหญ่โต gland

kwamyak *n* ความยาก difficulty

kwamyak *n.* ความอยาก appetite

kwamyak-a-han *n.* ความอยากอาหาร appetite

kwamyaklambak *n.* ความยากลำบาก tribulation

kwamyakru *n* ความอยากรู้ curiosity

kwamyamjon *n.* ความยากจน poverty

kwamyao *n.* ความยาว length

kwamyindi *n* ความยินดี delight

kwamyindi *n.* ความยินดี pleasure

kwamying *n.* ความหยิ่ง arrogance

kwamying *n.* ความหยิ่ง vanity

kwamyingyai *n.* ความยิ่งใหญ่ stateliness

kwamyingyai *n.* ความยิ่งใหญ่ supremacy

kwamyon *n.* ความหย่อน laxity

kwamyungyak *n.* ความยุ่งยาก complication

kwamyungyak *n.* ความยุ่งยาก stickler

kwamyungyeung *v. t* ความยุ่งเหยิง clutter

kwamyungyeung *n.* ความยุ่งเหยิง jumble

kwamyungyeung *n.* ความยุ่งเหยิง tangle

kwamyutitam *n.* ความยุติธรรม fair

kwamyutitam *n.* ความยุติธรรม justice

kwan *n.* ขวาน axe

kwan *n.* ขวาน hatchet

kwan *n.* ควัน smoke

kwanchang *n.* ควาญช้าง mahout

kwamchokrai *n.* ความโชคร้าย misadventure

kwamsuayleua *n.* ความช่วยเหลือ assistance

kwuandairab *v.t* ควรได้รับ merit

kwang *prep.* ขวาง athwart

gwang *a* กว้าง broad

kwang *v.t* ขว้าง fling

kwang *v.t.* ขว้าง hurl

kwang *v.t.* ขว้าง pitch

gwang *a.* กว้าง roomy

kwang *v.t.* ขว้าง throw

kwangpokkrongnai-anglid *n.* แขวงปกครองในอังกฤษ shire

gwangtuamia *n* กวางตัวเมีย doe

gwangyai *adj.* กว้างใหญ่ cosmic

kwam-odglan *n.* ความอดกลั้น repression

kwanpenglang *n.* ความเป็นกลาง impartiality

kwansanook *n.* ความสนุก fun

kwanwunwai *n.* ความวุ่นวาย chaos

kwaubkum *v.t* ควบคุม harness

kwuab-kum *v. t* ควบคุม control

L

la *interj.* ลา adieu

la *n* ลา donkey

la *v.t.* ล่า hunt

la *n.* หลา yard
la-ai *a.* ละอาย ashamed
la-awk *v.t.* ลาออก resign
lab *adj.* ลับ clandestine
lab *a.* ลับ confidential
lab *a.* ลับ secret
lab *v.i.* หลับ sleep
labhaikom *v.t.* ลับให้คม whet
lacha *adj.* ล่าช้า belated
lacha *adv.* ล่าช้า late
lactose *n.* แลกโตส lactose
lad-iang *v.i.* ลาดเอียง slope
ladtrawen *v.i.* ลาดตระเวน patrol
ladyang *v.t.* ลาดยาง tar
lae *conj.* และ and
la-iad *a* ละเอียด elaborate
laekplian *v. t* แลกเปลี่ยน exchange
laekplian *v.* แลกเปลี่ยน interchange
laem *a.* แหลม sharp
laen *n.* แหลน javelin
laengtima *n.* แหล่งที่มา resource
laenreuabai *v.i* แล่นเรือใบ yacht
lagon *interj.* ลาก่อน bye-bye
lagon *interj.* ลาก่อน farewell
lagon *interj.* ลาก่อน good-bye
lai *v.i* ไหล flow
lai *a.* หลาย multiple
lai *v.t.* ไล่ sack
lai *n.* ไหล่ shoulder
lai *v.i.* ไหล stream
la-iad-on *a* ละเอียดอ่อน delicate
la-iadtituan *a* ละเอียดที่ถ้วน thorough
lai-awk *v. t.* ไล่ออก dismiss
lai-awkjakglum *v. t.* ไล่ออกจากกลุ่ม excommunicate
laichalu *n.* ลายฉลุ stencil
laichiaw *a.* ไหลเชี่ยว torrential
laidan *a.* หลายด้าน multiplex
laimeu *n.* ลายมือ script
laimeuwat *n.* ลายมือหวัด scribble
lain *n.* เลน slime
laisen *n.* ลายเซ็นต์ autograph

laiseum *v.i.* ไหลซึม ooze
laitam *v. t.* ไล่ตาม chase1
laitam *v. t* ไล่ตาม dog
lak *v. t* ลาก drag
lak *v.i.* ลาก heave
lak *a* หลัก main
lakgan *n* หลักการ canon
lakgan *n* หลักการ discipline
lakgan *n.* หลักการ maxim
lakgan *n.* หลักการ principle
lak-godmai *n.* หลักกฎหมาย jurisprudence
lakkwamcheua *n* หลักความเชื่อ dogma
lakkwamcheua *n.* หลักความเชื่อ orthodoxy
laklaem *adj* หลักแหลม argute
laklaem *a.* หลักแหลม shrewd
laklai *a* หลากหลาย diverse
laklai *a.* หลากหลาย manifold
laklai *a.* หลากหลาย multifarious
laklai *a.* หลายหลาย sundry
laklai *a.* หลากหลาย varied
laklairoobsong *n.* หลากหลายรูปทรง multiform
laklobkakai *v.i.* ลักลอบค้าขาย traffic
laklobnamkao *v.t.* ลักลอบนำเข้า smuggle
lakon *n* ละคร drama
lakon *n.* ละคร play
lakonbai *n.* ละครใบ้ mime
lakonbai *n.* ละครใบ้ pantomime
lakontalok *n.* ละครตลก comedy
lakontalok *n* ละครตลก farce
lakpatua *v.t.* ลักพาตัว abduct
lakpatua *v.t.* ลักพาตัว kidnap
lakplian *v.t.* แลกเปลี่ยน barter1
laksanachapaw *n* ลักษณะเฉพาะ feature
laksanachapaw *n.* ลักษณะเฉพาะ identity
laksanachapaw *n.* ลักษณะเฉพาะ singularity
laksanapainok *n.* ลักษณะภายนอก guise
laksanatangteknik *n.* ลักษณะทางเทคนิค technicality

laksi *a.* หลากสี motley
laksut *n* หลักสูตร curriculum
laksut *n.* หลักสูตร syllabus
laktan *n* หลักฐาน evidence
laktan *n.* หลักฐาน testimony
lalai *v.t* ละลาย dissolve
lalai *v.i.* ละลาย melt
lalai *v.i* ละลาย thaw
laleuy *v.t.* ละเลย neglect
lam *n.* ล่าม interpreter
lam *a.* ล่ำ stout
lamang *n.* ละมั่ง antelope
lambak *a.* ลำบาก laborious
lamdabganbangkabbancha *n.*
 ลำดับการบังคับบัญชา hierarchy
lamdabkwamsamkan *n.*
 ลำดับความสำคัญ priority
lamdabtisam *n.* ลำดับที่สาม third
lamdabtisamsib *n* ลำดับที่สามสิบ
 thirtieth
lamdabtisibsong *n.* ลำดับที่สิบสอง
 twelfth
lamdabtisong *a.* ลำดับที่สอง secondary
lamdabtiyisib *n* ลำดับที่ยี่สิบ twentieth
lamduaycheuak *v.t.* ล่ามด้วยเชือก tether
lameudmaidai *a.* ละเมิดไม่ได้ inviolable
lameiang *a.* ลำเอียง partial
lamnamnitan *n.* ลำนำนิทาน ballad
lamok *a.* ลามก lewd
lamok *a.* ลามก obscene
lampang *a.* ลำพัง alone
lampang *a* ลำพัง sole
lamsaeng *n* ลำแสง beam
lamsai *n.* ลำไส้ bowel
lamsai *n.* ลำไส้ intestine
lamsaiyai *n* ลำไส้ใหญ่ colon
lamtan *n.* ลำธาร creek
lamtan *n.* ลำธาร rivulet
lamtan *n.* ลำธาร stream
lamton *n* ลำต้น stalk
lamton *n.* ลำต้น stem
lamton *n.* ลำต้น trunk

lan *n.* ล้าน million
lanban *n.* ลานบ้าน courtyard
lanbod *n.* ลานโบสถ์ churchyard
lanchai *n.* หลานชาย nephew
lang *prep.* หลัง after
lang *n.* หลัง back
lang *v.t.* ล้าง rinse
lang *v.t.* หลั่ง secrete
langbab *v.t.* ล้างบาป sanctify
langjak *a* หลังจาก after
langjaknan *adv.* หลังจากนั้น afterwards
langjaknan *adv.* หลังจากนั้น then
langka *n.* หลังคา roof
langkaglom *n* หลังคากลม dome
langlayjai *a.* ลังเลใจ reluctant
langlay *v.i.* ลังเล hesitate
langmai *n.* ลังไม้ crate
langmoranagam *a.* หลังมรณกรรม
 posthumous
langsanghon *n.* ลางสังหรณ์ hunch
lanjaknan *adv.* หลังจากนั้น thereafter
lankakong *n.* หลังคาโค้ง vault
lankamungjak *n.* หลังคามุงจาก thatch
lansao *n.* หลานสาว niece
lao *n.* เหล้า liquor
lao *n.* หลาว spear
lao *v.t.* เหลา whittle
lao-a-ngun *n.* เหล้าองุ่น malmsey
lao-a-ngun *n.* เหล้าองุ่น vintage
laomalt *n* เหล้ามอลต์ ale
la-onggesondawkmai *n.*
 ละอองเกสรดอกไม้ pollen
la-ongnam *n* ละอองน้ำ spray
laorum *n.* เหล้ารัม rum
laowaimai *n* เหล้าไวน์ใหม่ must
lasamai *a.* ล้าสมัย medieval
lasamai *a.* ล้าสมัย obsolete
lasamai *a.* ล้าสมัย outdated
lasamai *a.* ล้าสมัย outmoded
lating *v. t* ละทิ้ง abnegate
lating *v. t* ละทิ้ง discard
lating *v.t* ละทิ้ง forgo

lating *v.t.* ละทิ้ง forsake
lating *v.t.* ละทิ้ง omit
latoy *v.i.* ล่าถอย retreat
latti *n* ลัทธิ anabaptism
latti *n* ลัทธิ cult
latti *n* ลัทธิ doctrine
latti-a-natipatai *n.* ลัทธิอนาธิปไตย anarchism
lattigangawganrai *n.* ลัทธิการก่อการร้าย terrorism
lattigiawgabjitwinyan *n.* ลัทธิเกี่ยวกับจิตวิญญาณ spiritualism
lattijakgawatniyom *n.* ลัทธิจักรวรรดินิยม imperialism
lattikommunit *n* ลัทธิคอมมิวนิสต์ communism
lattikwamcheua *n.* ลัทธิความเชื่อ creed
lattiprajaokeujakkawan *n.* ลัทธิพระเจ้าคือจักรวาล pantheism
lattitongtin *n.* ลัทธิท้องถิ่น provincialism
lava *n.* ลาวา lava
lavender *n.* ลาเวนเดอร์ lavender
law *a.* หล่อ handsome
law *v.t.* หล่อ mould
law *n.* ล่อ mule
law *n.* ล้อ wheel
lawdawkyang *v.t.* หล่อดอกยาง retread
lawdchidya *n.* หลอดฉีดยา syringe
lawdfaifa *n.* หลอดไฟฟ้า bulb
lawdleuadhuajaitib *n* หลอดเลือดหัวใจตีบ angina
lawen *v.i.* ละเว้น abstain
lawjai *v. t.* ล่อใจ entice
lawddai *v.t.* ล่อใจ lure
lawk *a* หลอก bogus
lawkluang *v.t* หลอกลวง gull
lawkluang *v.t* หลอกลวง hoax
lawleun *v.t.* หล่อลื่น lubricate
lawlian *a.* ล้อเลียน mimic
lawlian *v.t* ล้อเลียน mimic
lawlian *v.i.* ล้อเลียน mock
lawlian *adj* ล้อเลียน mock

lawlian *v.t.* ล้อเลียน parody
lawkluang *v. t* ล่อลวง beguile
lawluang *v.t.* ล่อลวง tempt
lawluanghaitampid *v. t.* ล่อลวงให้ทำผิด debauch
lawmlalaidai *a.* หลอมละลายได้ molten
lawn *v.t.* หลอน haunt
bawlong *n.* เบาะรอง padding
lawyeua *v.t.* ล่อเหยื่อ bait
leakliang *v.t.* หลีกเลี่ยง shirk
leekliang *v.t.* หลีกเลี่ยง avoid
lew *a.* เลว bad
lewrai *a* เลวร้าย dire
lewsam *a* เลวทราม despicable
lewsam *a.* เลวทราม sordid
lek *n.* เหล็ก iron
lek *a.* เล็ก puny
lek *a.* เล็ก small
lek *n.* เหล็ก steel
lekanugan *n.* เลขานุการ secretary
lekkaeng *n* เหล็กแข็ง cast-iron
leklaem *n.* เหล็กแหลม spike
lekmak *a.* เล็กมาก miniature
lekmak *a.* เล็กมาก minuscule
lekmak *a.* เล็กมาก minute
leknoy *a* เล็กน้อย few
leknoy *a.* เล็กน้อย little
leknoy *a.* เล็กน้อย marginal
leknoy *a.* เล็กน้อย minor
leknoy *a.* เล็กน้อย petty
leknoy *a.* เล็กน้อย slight
leknoy *a.* เล็กน้อย some
leknoy *a.* เล็กน้อย tiny
leknoy *a.* เล็กน้อย trivial
lekpasom *n.* เหล็กผสม solder
lektisud *a.* เล็กที่สุด minimal
lem *v.t.* เล็ม nibble
lemya *v.i.* เล็มหญ้า graze
len *v.i.* เล่น toy
lengila *v.i.* เล่นกีฬา sport
lenhua *v.t.* เล่นหัว dandle
lenkam *v.i.* เล่นคำ pun

lenlakon *v.i.* เล่นละคร play

lenpaklenpuak *a* เล่นพรรคเล่นพรรค factious

lens *n.* เลนส์ lens

lensaget *v.t.* เล่นสเก็ต skate

lensanook *v.i.* เล่นสนุก frolic

leuacheua *a.* เหลือเชื่อ incredible

leuad *n* เลือด blood

leuad-awk *v. i* เลือดออก bleed

leuak *v. t.* เลือก choose

leuak *v.i.* เลือก opt

leuak *v.t.* เลือก pick

leuak *v.t.* เลือก select

leuakdai *a.* เลือกได้ alternative

leuaktang *v. t* เลือกตั้ง elect

leuaktangsom *n* เลือกตั้งซ่อม by-election

leuan *v.t.* เลื่อน adjourn

leuan *v.t.* เลื่อน postpone

leuk *a.* ลึก deep

leuk *v.t* ลึก fathom

leuk *a.* ลึก profound

leuk *v.t.* เลิก quit

leuklab *a.* ลึกลับ mysterious

leuklab *a.* ลึกลับ occult

leuklom *v.t* เลิกล้ม abolish

leum *v.t* ลืม forget

leun *a.* ลื่น greasy

leun *v.i.* ลื่น skid

leun *a.* ลื่น sleek

leun *v.i.* ลื่น slide

leun *v.i.* ลื่น slip

leun *a.* ลื่น slippery

luangta *v. t.* ลวงตา delude

leunpenman *a* ลื่นเป็นมัน slick

leuteu *a* เลอะเทอะ bulky

leuy *n.* เลื่อย saw

leuy *v.t.* เลื่อย saw

leuy *v.i.* เลื้อย snake

leuypan *prep.* เลยผ่าน past

lewrai *a.* เลวร้าย heinous

lewrai *n.* เลวร้าย woeful

lewsam *a.* เลวทราม vile

lia *v.t.* เลีย lick

liammoom *n* เหลี่ยมมุม facet

lianbaeb *v. t* เลียนแบบ emulate

lianbaeb *v.t.* เลียนแบบ imitate

lianbaeb *v.t.* เลียนแบบ impersonate

lianbaebmaidai *a.* เลียนแบบไม่ได้ inimitable

liangdu *v.t.* เลี้ยงดู mother

liangdu *v.t.* เลี้ยงดู nourish

liangdu *v.t.* เลี้ยงดู nurture

liangmaidai *a.* เลี้ยงไม่ได้ inevitable

liaw *v.i.* เลี้ยว turn

lift *n.* ลิฟต์ lift

lignite *n.* ลิกไนต์ lignite

lim *n.* ลิ่ม clot

lim *n* ลิ่ม colter

lim *n.* ลิ่ม wedge

lin *n.* ลิ้น tongue

linchak *n* ลิ้นชัก drawer

ling *n.* ลิง baboon

ling *n.* ลิง chimpanzee

ling *n.* ลิง gorilla

ling *n.* ลิง guerilla

ling *n.* ลิง monkey

linin *n.* ลินิน linen

linpidpeud *n.* ลิ้นปิดเปิด valve

litre *n.* ลิตร litre

lo *n.* โล่ shield

lob *adj.* โลภ avid

lob *v. t* ลบ delete

lob *v. t* หลบ dodge

lob *v. t* ลบ erase

lob *a.* โลภ greedy

lob *v.i.* หลบ lurk

lob *prep.* ลบ minus

lob *v.t.* หลบ shelter

lob-awk *v. t* ลบออก efface

lobby *n.* ล็อบบี้ lobby

lobliang *v.t.* หลบเลี่ยง shunt

loblik *v. t* หลบหลีก elude

loblik *v. t* หลบหลีก evade

loblikdai *a* หลบหลีกได้ elusive

lobni *v.i* หลบหนี escape
lobni *a.* หลบหนี fugitive
lobsanghan *v. t* ลอบสังหาร burke
lobster *n.* ล็อบสเตอร์ lobster
locker *n.* ล็อกเกอร์ locker
locket *n.* ล็อกเกต locket
lod *n.* หลอด tube
laddai *n.* หลอดด้าย reel
lawdgaew *n.* หลอดแก้ว cuvette
lodka *v. t* ลดค่า degrade
lodka *v.t.i.* ลดค่า depreciate
lawdleuaddaeng *n.* หลอดเลือดแดง artery
lawdleud *n.* หลอดเลือด vessel
lodlong *v. t* ลดลง decrease
lodlong *v. t* ลดลง diminish
lodlong *v. t* ลดลง dwindle
lodlong *v. i* ลดลง ebb
lodlong *v.t.* ลดลง reduce
lodlong *v.i.* ลดลง subside
lodlong *v.i.* ลดลง wane
lodtamlong *a* ลดต่ำลง downward
lodtamlong *v.t.* ลดต่ำลง lower
logarithm *n.* ลอการิทึม logarithm
loha *n.* โลหะ metal
lohapasom *n.* โลหะผสม alloy
lok *n.* โลก globe
lok *n.* โลก planet
lok *n.* โลก world
lawkkrab *v.i.* ลอกคราบ moult
lawkkrab *v.t.* ลอกคราบ slough
lawklaichalu *v. t* ลอกลายฉลุ cyclostyle
lawkluang *v. t* หลอกลวง deceive
lokmitchachib *n.* โลกมิจฉาชีพ underworld
lom *v. i* ล้ม collapse
lom *v.i.* ล้ม fall
lom *v.t* ล้ม fell
lom *v.t* ล้อม hedge
lom *n.* หล่ม mire
lom *v.t.* หลอม smelt
lom *v.i.* ล้ม tumble
lom *n.* ลม wind

lomfangsob *n.* หลุมฝังศพ grave
lomhaijai *n* ลมหายใจ breath
lomhaijai *n.* ลมหายใจ puff
lomkutawsu *v.t* ล้มคู่ต่อสู้ floor
lomraeng *n.* ลมแรง gale
lomraeng *a.* ลมแรง windy
lomlalai *n.* ล้มละลาย bankrupt
lomlalai *a.* ล้มละลาย insolvent
lomlang *v.t.* ล้มล้าง overthrow
lomlang *v.t.* ล้มล้าง subvert
lomlew *v.i* ล้มเหลว fail
lommoon *n.* ลมหมุน whirlwind
lom-on-on *n* ลมอ่อนๆ breeze
lompadbaobao *n* ลมพัดเบาๆ waft
lomraeng *n* ลมแรง blow
lomraeng *n.* ลมแรง gust
lomrob *v.t.* ล้อมรอบ begird
lomrob *v. t* ล้อมรอบ encircle
lomrob *v. t* ล้อมรอบ enclose
lomrob *v. t* ล้อมรอบ encompass
lomrob *v.t.* ล้อมรอบ surround
lomrobduaykunam *v.t.* ล้อมรอบด้วยคูน้ำ moat
lomrua *v.t* ล้อมรั้ว fence
lomrua *v.t.* ล้อมรั้ว picket
lomtawantok *n.* ลมตะวันตก zephyr
lomyen *n* ลมเย็น draught
long *v.t* ลง avale
longcheuraek *v.t* ลงชื่อแรก initial
longglon *v.t* ลงกลอน lock
longjod *v.i.* ลงจอด alight
longjod *v.i.* ลงจอด land
longkanaen *v.i.* ลงคะแนน vote
longkodsana *v.t.* ลงโฆษณา advertise
longlai *a.* หลงใหล passionate
longloy *v.t.* ล่องลอย waft
longnamruam *v. t* ลงนามร่วม countersign
longpaeng *v.t.* ลงแป้ง starch
longpai *prep* ลงไป down
longpid *v.t.* หลงผิด pervert
longprachatan *v.t.* ลงประชาทัณฑ์ lynch

longreua *v.i.* ล่องเรือ cruise
longtam *adv* ลงต่ำ downward
longtam *adv* ลงต่ำ downwards
longtang *adv.,* หลงทาง astray
longtang *v.t.* หลงทาง misdirect
longtang *v.i.* หลงทาง straggle
longtod *v. t.* ลงโทษ castigate
longtod *v.t.* ลงโทษ inflict
longtod *v.t.* ลงโทษ penalize
longtoon *v.t.* ลงทุน invest
longtod *v.t.* ลงโทษ sanction
longwanti *v. t* ลงวันที่ date
longwantichakwawanjing *v.t.*
ลงวันที่ช้ากว่าวันจริง post-date
longwantigonwanjing *n*
ลงวันที่ก่อนวันจริง antedate
lonlan *a.* ลนลาน frantic
loob *v.t.* ลูบ pat
look-anta *n.* ลูกอัณฑะ testicle
lookchai *n.* ลูกชาย son
lookdawk *n.* ลูกดอก dart
lookdok *a.* ลูกดก prolific
lookgae *n.* ลูกแกะ lambkin
lookged *n.* ลูกเกด raisin
lookgling *n.* ลูกกลิ้ง roller
lookgrong *n.* ลูกกรง bar
lookgwad *n.* ลูกกวาด sweetmeat
lookheb *n.* ลูกเห็บ hail
lookhebtok *v.i* ลูกเห็บตก hail
lookjang *n* ลูกจ้าง employee
lookka *n..* ลูกค้า client
lookka *n* ลูกค้า customer
lookkongai *n.* ลูกขนไก่ shuttlecock
lookkreungpewkaogabpewdam *n.*
ลูกครึ่งผิวขาวกับผิวดำ mulatto
lookku *n* ลูกคู่ refrain
lookkun *n.* ลูกขุน juror
lookgwad *n.* ลูกกวาด candy
looklan *n.* ลูกหลาน offspring
looklan *n.* ลูกหลาน progeny
lookmaew *n.* ลูกแมว kitten
lookmai *v.i* ลูกไหม้ flame

lookmai *n.* ลูกไม้ lace
looknawkgodmai *n.* ลูกนอกกฎหมาย
bastard
looknong *n.* ลูกน้อง henchman
look-om *n.* ลูกอม toffee
look-on *n.* ลูกอ่อน nestling
lookpad *n* ลูกปัด bead
lookpasom *a.* ลูกผสม hybrid
look-peach *n.* ลูกพีช peach
lookpear *n.* ลูกแพร์ pear
lookpenfai *a* ลูกเป็นไฟ fiery
lookpenfai *v.i* ลูกเป็นไฟ flare
lookpenfai *v.t.* ลูกเป็นไฟ inflame
lookplong *v.i* ลูกโพลง blaze
lookrabeud *n.* ลูกระเบิด grenade
lookrabeud *n* ลูกระเบิด bomb
lookreua *n.* ลูกเรือ crew
looksao *n* ลูกสาว daughter
looksat *n.* ลูกสัตว์ whelp
lookseua *n* ลูกเสือ scout
looksoob *n.* ลูกสูบ piston
looksunak *n.* ลูกสุนัข puppy
lookta *n* ลูกตา eyeball
looktao *n.* ลูกเต๋า dice
looktum *n.* ลูกตุ้ม pendulum
lookwua *n.* ลูกวัว calf
loom *n* หลุม hole
loom *n.* หลุม pit
loomlobpai *n* หลุมหลบภัย bunker
loomprang *n.* หลุมพราง pitfall
loong *n.* ลุง uncle
loop-lai *v.t* ลูบไล้ fondle
lopni *v.i* หลบหนี abscond
lopni *v. i* หลบหนี decamp
lord *n.* ลอร์ด lord
lotion *n.* โลชั่น lotion
lottery *n.* ล็อตเตอรี่ lottery
loy *adv.* ลอย afloat
loy *v.i* ลอย float
loynamdai *a.* ลอยน้ำได้ natant
luadnam *n.* ลวดหนาม barb
leuklab *a.* ลึกลับ mystic

luam *a.* หลวม lax
luam *a.* หลวม loose
luang *a* ลวง fictitious
luanglam *v. i* ล่วงล้ำ encroach
luanglam *v.i.* ล่วงล้ำ trespass
luanlam *v.t.* ลวนลาม molest
lukpenfai *adv.* ลุกเป็นไฟ aflame
lumfangsob *n.* หลุมฝังศพ tomb

ma *v. i.* มา come
ma *n.* ม้า horse
ma *n.* ม้า mount
ma *n.* ม้า pony
ma *n.* ม้า steed
mad *v.t* มัด bind
mad *n.* หมัด flea
mad *n.* หมัด louse
mad *n.* หมัด tick
madwai *n* มัดไว้ deligate1
madwat *n.* มาตรวัด gauge
madwatkwamrewlom *n*
    มาตรวัดความเร็วลม anemometer
mae *n* แม่ mother
mae *n* แม่ mum
mae *n.* แม่ mummy
maegranan *conj.* แม้กระนั้น yet
maegratang *adv* แม้กระทั่ง even
maegunjae *n* แม่กุญแจ lock
maelao *n.* แม่เล้า bawd
maelek *n.* แม่เหล็ก magnet
maemai *n.* แม่หม้าย widow
maemod *n.* แม่มด witch
maenam *n.* แม่น้ำ river
maenyam *a* แม่นยำ exact
maepim *n* แม่พิมพ์ die
maepim *n.* แม่พิมพ์ mould
maepim *n.* แม่พิมพ์ plate
maeraeng *n.* แม่แรง jack
maew *n.* แมว cat

maewa *conj.* แม้ว่า albeit
maewa *conj.* แม้ว่า although
maewnam *n.* แมวน้ำ seal
magok *n.* มะกอก olive
mahachon *n.* มหาชน public
mahadsajan *a.* มหัศจรรย์ wonderful
mahadsajan *a.* มหัศจรรย์ wondrous
mahadsajan *a.* มหัศจรรย์ marvellous
mahagab *n* มหากาพย์ epic
mahadsajan *a.* มหัศจรรย์ wonderful
mahadsajan *a.* มหัศจรรย์ wondrous
mahasamud *n.* มหาสมุทร ocean
mahasan *a* มหาศาล myriad
mahasedti *n.* มหาเศรษฐี croesus
mahadsajan *a.* มหัศจรรย์ marvellous
mahawitayalai *n.* มหาวิทยาลัย university
maheudmai *v.t.* มาเกิดใหม่ incarnate
mahoran *a.* มโหฬาร immense
mahuma *a* มหึมา mammoth
mai *adv.* ใหม่ afresh
mai *v. t* ไหม้ burn
mai *adv.* ไม่ nay
mai *a.* ใหม่ new
mai *a.* ไม่ no
mai *adv.* ไม่ no
mai *conj.* ไม่ nor
mai *a.* ใหม่ novel
mai *n.* ไหม silk
mai *n.* ไม้ wood
mai-awkpon *adj.* ไม่ออกผล acarpous
maiborisut *a.* ไม่บริสุทธิ์ impure
maichadjen *a.* ไม่ชัดเจน misty
maichalad *a.* ไม่ฉลาด injudicious
maichamnan *a.* ไม่ชำนาญ maladroit
maichennan *adv.* ไม่เช่นนั้น otherwise
maichennan *conj.* ไม่เช่นนั้น otherwise
maicheuafang *v. t* ไม่เชื่อฟัง disobey
maichob *v. t* ไม่ชอบ dislike
maichobtam *a.* ไม่ชอบธรรม illegitimate
maidaipon *a.* ไม่ได้ผล inoperative
maidairabganlongtod *a.*
    ไม่ได้รับการลงโทษ scot-free

maidaiyin *a.* ไม่ได้ยิน inaudible
maidi *adv.* ไม่ดี ill
maigangkaen *n.* ไม้กางเขน rood
maigayasit *n.* ไม้กายสิทธิ์ wand
maigiawkong *a.* ไม่เกี่ยวข้อง irrelevant
maiglua *a* ไม่กลัว dauntless
maigrabong *n* ไม้กระบอง cudgel
maigrachabgracheng *n* ไม้กระฉับกระเฉง
　fallow
maigradan *n.* ไม้กระดาน plank
maigwad *n* ไม้กวาด broom
maihaigiat *v. t* ไม่ให้เกียรติ dishonour
maihed *n.* หมายเหตุ notation
maihenduay *v. i* ไม่เห็นด้วย disagree
maihenduay *v. t* ไม่เห็นด้วย disapprove
maihengaetua *a.* ไม่เห็นแก่ตัว selfless
maikongai *n* ไม้ขนไก่ whisk
maijamgad *a.* ไม่จำกัด indefinite
maijamgad *a.* ไม่จำกัด limitless
maijamgad *a.* ไม่จำกัด measureless
maijampen *a.* ไม่จำเป็น needless
maijan *n.* ไม้จันทน์ sandalwood
maijawjong *a.* ไม่เจาะจง indiscriminate
maijingjai *a.* ไม่จริงใจ insincere
maikaehu *n.* ไม้แคะหู aurilave
maikaengraeng *a.* ไม่แข็งแรง infirm
maikam *n* ไม้ค้ำ strut
maikamneungteung *a.* ไม่คำนึงถึง
　irrespective
maikamyan *n.* ไม้ค้ำยัน prop
maikaoruam *v.t* ไม่เข้าร่วม absent
maikeuy *adv.* ไม่เคย never
maikeuy *adv.* ไม่เคย not
maikleuanwai *a.* ไม่เคลื่อนไหว
　motionless
maikoyja *adv.* ไม่ค่อยจะ hardly
maikleuanwai *a.* ไม่เคลื่อนไหว sedentary
maikuabkum *v.t.* ไม่ควบคุม decontrol
maikukuan *a.* ไม่คู่ควร matchless
maikukuan *a.* ไม่คู่ควร worthless
maila-ai-jai *a.* ไม่ละอายใจ shameless
mailalai *n.* ไม่ละลาย insoluble

mailam-iang *a.* ไม่ลำเอียง objective
mailawsom *a.* ไม่เหมาะสม undue
maileuay *n* ไม้เลื้อย creeper
maileuy *adv.* ไม่เลย none
maimagleua *n* ไม้มะเกลือ ebony
maimaikong *a.* ไม่มั่นคง insecure
maimak *adv.* ไม่มาก little
maimawsom *a.* ไม่เหมาะสม improper
maimawsom *v.t.* ไม่เหมาะสม
　misappropriate
maimeuan *a* ไม่เหมือน unlike
maimeuangan *a* ไม่เหมือนกัน dissimilar
maimi-a-rai *adv.* ไม่มีอะไร nothing
maimicheusiang *a.* ไม่มีชื่อเสียง infamous
maimichiwitchiwa *adv* ไม่มีชีวิตชีวา duly
maimichiwitchiwa *a.* ไม่มีชีวิตชีวา
　inanimate
maimigamlang *a.* ไม่มีกำลัง nerveless
maimika *a.* ไม่มีค่า null
maimikawpidplad *a.* ไม่มีข้อผิดพลาด
　infallible
maimikonyu *a.* ไม่มีคนอยู่ unmanned
maimikrai *pron.* ไม่มีใคร nobody
maimikunasombat *v. t.* ไม่มีคุณสมบัติ
　disqualify
maimikwammai *a.* ไม่มีความหมาย
　nonsensical
maimikwamruseuk *a.* ไม่มีความรู้สึก
　senseless
maimikwamsook *a.* ไม่มีความสุข
　unhappy
maimileuy *pron.* ไม่มีเลย none
maimimoonkwamjing *a.*
　ไม่มีมูลความจริง baseless
maiminamjai *a.* ไม่มีน้ำใจ inconsiderate
maimirodchat *adj.* ไม่มีรสชาติ bland
maimiroydang *a.* ไม่มีรอยด่าง spotless
maimisi *adj* ไม่มีสี achromatic
maimisi *a* ไม่มีสี pale
maimisilapa *a.* ไม่มีศิลปะ artless
maimisinratam *a.* ไม่มีศีลธรรม immoral
maimitipriab *a.* ไม่มีที่เปรียบ nonpareil

maimituaton *a.* ไม่มีตัวตน immaterial
maimituaton *a.* ไม่มีตัวตน impersonal
maimiwinai *a.* ไม่มีวินัย unruly
mainaejai *a.* ไม่แน่ใจ hesitant
mainaejai *v.i.* ไม่แน่ใจ shilly-shally
mainaejai *a.* ไม่แน่ใจ uncertain
mainaenon *adj.* ไม่แน่นอน astatic
mainanmani *a.* ไม่นานมานี้ recent
mainanmani *adv.* ไม่นานมานี้ recently
mainasonjai *a.* ไม่น่าสนใจ frivolous
maineukteung *a.* ไม่นึกถึง oblivious
mai-ngai *a.* ไม่ง่าย uneasy
mai-odton *a.* ไม่อดทน impatient
maipaeng *a.* ไม่แพง inexpensive
maipai *n.* ไม้ไผ่ bamboo
maipai *n.* ไม้พาย oar
maipai *n* ไม้พาย paddle
maipakati *a.* ไม่ปกติ irregular
maipawjai *v. t* ไม่พอใจ displease
maipawjai *v. t.* ไม่พอใจ dissatisfy
maipawjai *a.* ไม่พอใจ malcontent
maipawjai *v.t.* ไม่พอใจ resent
maipawjai *v.t.* ไม่พอใจ upset
maipawpiang *a.* ไม่พอเพียง insufficient
maipenmid *a.* ไม่เป็นมิตร inhospitable
maipenmid *a.* ไม่เป็นมิตร inimical
maipentanggan *a.* ไม่เป็นทางการ informal
maipentanggan *a.* ไม่เป็นทางการ casual
maipeudpei *a.* ไม่เปิดเผย underhand
maiponpan *a.* ไม่ผ่อนผัน relentless
maiprongdong *adj* ไม่ปรองดอง absonant
maipum *n.* ไม้พุ่ม wormwood
mairabpidchob *a.* ไม่รับผิดชอบ irresponsible
mairacket *n.* ไม้แร็กเก็ต racket
mairanaeng *n.* ไม้ระแนง lath
maireunreung *a* ไม่รื่นเริง cheerless
mairiak *n.* หมายเรียก summons
mairobkob *a.* ไม่รอบคอบ careless
mairobkob *a.* ไม่รอบคอบ imprudent
mairobkob *a.* ไม่รอบคอบ indiscreet

mairoonraeng *adj* ไม่รุนแรง benign
mairua *n.* ไม้รั้ว pale
mairujakpaw *a.* ไม่รู้จักพอ insatiable
mairunangseu *a.* ไม่รู้หนังสือ illiterate
mairuseukkobkun *a.* ไม่รู้สึกขอบคุณ thankless
mairutua *a.* ไม่รู้ตัว unaware
maisabai *a.* ไม่สบาย unwell
maisabaijai *v.t.* ไม่สบายใจ fret
maisaduak *a.* ไม่สะดวก inconvenient
maisaijai *a.* ไม่ใส่ใจ ignorant
maisaijai *v.t.* ไม่ใส่ใจ ignore
maisak *n.* ไม้สัก teak
maisamad *a.* ไม่สามารถ unable
maisamadtamdai *a.* ไม่สามารถทำได้ impracticable
maisamkan *a.* ไม่สำคัญ insignificant
maisamkan *a.* ไม่สำคัญ negligible
maisamkan *a.* ไม่สำคัญ paltry
maisan *n.* หมายศาล writ
maisa-nga-ngam *a.* ไม่สง่างาม ungainly
maisankongwaitayagon *n* ไม้สั้นของวาทยากร baton
maiseusat *a* ไม่ซื่อสัตย์ disloyal
maiseusat *a* ไม่ซื่อสัตย์ dishonest
maisiahai *a.* ไม่เสียหาย intact
maisinsud ~*a.* ไม่สิ้นสุด ceaseless
maisinsud *a.* ไม่สิ้นสุด infinite
maisinsud *a.* ไม่สิ้นสุด interminable
maisomboon *a.* ไม่สมบูรณ์ immature
maisomboon *a.* ไม่สมบูรณ์ imperfect
maisomboon *a .* ไม่สมบูรณ์ incomplete
maisongtuapukumkangmasan *n.* หมายส่งตัวผู้คุมขังมาศาล habeas corpus
maisonjai *v. t* ไม่สนใจ disregard
maisonjai *a.* ไม่สนใจ mindless
maisonjai *a.* ไม่สนใจ negligent
maisupab *a.* ไม่สุภาพ immodest
maisung *n.* ไม้ซุง timber
maisupab *a* ไม่สุภาพ discourteous
maisupab *a.* ไม่สุภาพ impolite

maisupab *a* ไม่สุภาพ unmannerly

maitaektang *a.* ไม่แตกต่าง indifferent

maitaitod *a. (verb)* ไม่ถ่ายทอด intransitive

maitangsongyang *conj.* ไม่ทั้งสองอย่าง neither

maitao *n.* ไม้เท้า cane

maitao *n* ไม้เท้า crutch

maitao *n.* ไม้เท้า stick

maitasi *n.* ไม้ทาสี maulstick

maitawka *n.* ไม้ต่อขา stilt

maitawneuang *v. t* ไม่ต่อเนื่อง discontinue

maitawneuang *a* ไม่ต่อเนื่อง fitful

maitawneuang *a.* ไม่ต่อเนื่อง incoherent

maiteung *v.t* หมายถึง mean

maitookgodmai *a* ไม่ถูกกฎหมาย bastard

maitooktong *adv.* ไม่ถูกต้อง amiss

maitooktong *a* ไม่ถูกต้อง erroneous

maitooktong *a.* ไม่ถูกต้อง inaccurate

maitooktong *a.* ไม่ถูกต้อง incorrect

maitooktong *a.* ไม่ถูกต้อง wrongful

maitrijit *n.* ไมตรีจิต goodwill

maitupeun *n.* ไม้ถูพื้น mop

maiwa-annaigawtam *pron* ไม่ว่าอันไหนก็ตาม whichever

maiwaijai *v. t.* ไม่ไว้ใจ distrust

maiwaja *conj.* ไม่ว่าจะ whether

maiwatinaigawtam *adv.* ไม่ว่าที่ไหนก็ตาม wherever

maiyeunton *n.* ไม้ยืนต้น perennial

maiyompae *a.* ไม่ยอมแพ้ inexorable

maiyu *adv.* ไม่อยู่ away

maiyutitam *a* ไม่ยุติธรรม unfair

maiyutitam *a.* ไม่ยุติธรรม unjust

maiyutrongglang *adj* ไม่อยู่ตรงกลาง acentric

majingjoktuamia *n.* หมาจิ้งจอกตัวเมีย vixen

mak *a* มาก abundant

mak *a.* มาก ample

mak *a.* มาก massive

mak *a.* มาก massy

mak *a* มาก much

mak *a.* มาก numerous

mak *adv.* มาก so

mak *a.* มาก very

makam *n.* มะขาม tamarind

makeuapraw *n* มะเขือเปราะ brinjal

makeuatet *n.* มะเขือเทศ tomato

makgeunpai *a* มากเกินไป excess

makgeunpai *adv.* มากเกินไป too

makkwa *a.* มากกว่า more

makkwa *adv* มากกว่า more

makmai *adv.* มากมาย galore

makmai *a.* มากมาย incalculable

makmai *a.* มากมาย many

makmai *a.* มากมาย substantial

makmai *a.* มากมาย voluminous

makrook *n.* หมากรุก chess

maktisud *a.* มากที่สุด most

malaeng *n.* แมลง insect

malaengsab *n* แมลงสาบ cockroach

malaengwan *n* แมลงวัน fly

malai *n.* ม้าลาย zebra

malaikrobsisa *n* มาลัยครอบศีรษะ anadem

malaeng *n.* แมลง bug

malaria *n.* มาลาเรีย malaria

maled *n.* เมล็ด seed

maledfai *n.* เมล็ดฝ้าย linseed

maledkao *n.* เมล็ดข้าว grain

maledpeudtigindai *n* เมล็ดพืชที่กินได้ pulse

mam *n.* ม้าม spleen

mamoon *n.* ม้าหมุน whirligig

mamuang *n* มะม่วง mango

man *v. t* หมั้น betroth

man *n* ม่าน curtain

man *v. t* หมั้น engage

man *pron.* มัน it

man *a.* มัน oily

manainiyai *n.* ม้าในนิยาย bayard

manang *n* ม้านั่ง bench

manao *n.* มะนาว lemon

manao *n.* มะนาว lime
manbod *n.* มันบด mash
manfarang *n* มันฝรั่งทอด fry
manfarang *n.* มันฝรั่ง potato
mangganese *n.* แมงกานีส manganese
mangkang *a.* มั่งคั่ง opulent
mangkon *n* มังกร dragon
mangmeun *v.t.* หมางเมิน alienate
maengmoom *n.* แมงมุม spider
mangpong *n.* แมงป่อง scorpion
manjai *a.* มั่นใจ confident
mankaeng *n.* มันแข็ง tallow
mankong *a.* มั่นคง stable
mankong *a.* มั่นคง steady
manmu *n.* มันหมู lard
manopab *n.* มโนภาพ imaginary
mansaku *n.* มันสาคู arrowroot
mansion *n.* แมนชั่น mansion
manudputuchon *n.* มนุษย์ปุถุชน
    worldling
manudsayachat *n.* มนุษยชาติ humanity
manudsayachat *n.* มนุษยชาติ mankind
mao *a.* เมา tipsy
mapa *n.* หมาป่า fox
mapa *n.* ม้าป่า mustang
mapa *n.* หมาป่า wolf
mapraw *n* มะพร้าว coconut
marathon *n.* มาราธอน marathon
marayat *n.* มารยาท manner
marayat *n* มารยาท decorum
marayat *n* มารยาท etiquette
mareng *n.* มะเร็ง cancer
mateung *v.i.* มาถึง arrive
matratan *n.* มาตรฐาน standard
matrix *n* เมตริก matrix
mattayad *a.* มัธยัสถ์ frugal
matuamia *n.* ม้าตัวเมีย mare
matuapu *n.* ม้าตัวผู้ stallion
matwadrayatang *n.* มาตรวัดระยะทาง
    furlong
maudulaimeu *n.* หมอดูลายมือ palmist
maw *a.* เหมาะ applicable

maw *adj* เหมาะ apposite
maw *n* หมอ doctor
maw *n.* หมอ medico
maw *n.* หมอ physician
maw-ai-nam *n.* หม้อไอน้ำ steamer
mawfin *n.* มอร์ฟีน morphia
mawgabreudugan *a.* เหมาะกับฤดูกาล
    seasonable
mawgabwela *a.* เหมาะกับเวลา well-timed
mawgaeganpawpruk *adj*
    เหมาะแก่การเพาะปลูก arable
mawk *n.* หมอก mist
mawnam *n* หม้อน้ำ boiler
mawpatad *n.* หมอผ่าตัด surgeon
mawpi *n.* หมอผี necromancer
mawsom *a.* เหมาะสม advisable
mawsom *a.* เหมาะสม appropriate
mawsom *a* เหมาะสม becoming
mawsom *a* เหมาะสม decent
mawsom *a* เหมาะสม expedient
mawsom *a.* เหมาะสม opportune
mawsom *a.* เหมาะสม proper
mawsom *adv* เหมาะสม right
mawsom *a.* เหมาะสม seemly
mawsom *a.* เหมาะสม suitable
mawsomgabgankai *a.* เหมาะกับการขาย
    salable
mawsonsasana *n.* หมอสอนศาสนา
    missionary
mawtisud *a* เหมาะที่สุด optimum
mayagon *n* มายากล trick
mayok *n.* ม้าโยก hobby-horse
medpong *n* เม็ดพอง bleb
medta *adv.* เมตตา kindly
meetsan *n.* มีดสั้น baslard
mek *n.* เมฆ cloud
mekfon *n.* เมฆฝน nimbus
melon *n.* เมลอน melon
men-ab *a.* เหม็นอับ musty
menu *n.* เมนู menu
meter *n.* เมตร meter
metre *n.* เมตร metre

metta *a.* เมตตา merciful
meu *n* มือ hand
meua *adv.* เมื่อ when
meu-a-chip *a.* มืออาชีพ professional
meuak *n.* เมือก mucilage
meuan-a-gad *adj.* เหมือนอากาศ aeriform
meuandekpuying *a.* เหมือนเด็กผู้หญิง girlish
meuang *n* เมือง city
meuang *n.* เหมือง quarry
meuang *n.* เมือง town
meuangan *a* เหมือนกัน duplicate
meuangan *a.* เหมือนกัน homogeneous
meuangan *a.* เหมือนกัน like
meuangluang *n.* เมืองหลวง capital
meuanglucern *n.* เมืองลูเซิร์น Lucerne
meuangrae *n* เหมืองแร่ mine
meuangwellington *n.* เมืองเวลลิงตัน wellington
meuangyai *n.* เมืองใหญ่ metropolis
meuankonchai *a.* เหมือนคนใช้ menial
meuanmae *a.* เหมือนแม่ motherlike
meuanmeuangan *conj* เหมือนๆ กัน both
meuanmichiwit *a.* เหมือนมีชีวิต animate
meuanpinong *a.* เหมือนพี่น้อง sisterly
meuanpuying *a.* เหมือนผู้หญิง womanish
meuansopeni *a.* เหมือนโสเภณี slatternly
meuantarok *a.* เหมือนทารก infantile
meuanyiaw *adj* เหมือนเหยี่ยว accipitral
meuayla *a.* เมื่อยล้า weary
meud *a* มืด dark
meud *v.i.* มืด darkle
meudmua *a.* มืดมัว gloomy
meuk *n.* หมึก ink
meumainanmani เมื่อไม่นานมานี้ lately
meuncheuy *a.* เมินเฉย nonchalant
meundao *a.* เหมือนดาว stellar
meungan *a.* เหมือนกัน identical
meuraigawtam *adv. conj* เมื่อไรก็ตาม whenever
meusamaklen *n.* มือสมัครเล่น amateur
meuwanni *n.* เมื่อวานนี้ yesterday

meuwanni *adv.* เมื่อวานนี้ yesterday
mi *n* หมี bear
mi *v.t.* มี have
mi-a-kati *v. t* มีอคติ bias
mi-ammad *a.* มีอำนาจ potent
mi-ammad *a.* มีอำนาจ powerful
mi-amnardtookyang *a.* มีอำนาจทุกอย่าง omnipotent
mianoy *n.* เมียน้อย mistress
mi-a-rayatam *v. t* มีอารยธรรม civilize
mi-a-romkan *a.* มีอารมณ์ขัน humorous
mi-a-romkunmua *a.* มีอารมณ์ขุ่นมัว morose
mi-a-yu *a.* มีอายุ aged
mi-a-yurawangpaedsibteungpaedsibgaopi *a.* มีอายุระหว่าง 80 - 89 ปี octogenarian
mi-a-yu-yeunkwa *v.i.* มีอายุยืนกว่า outlive
mipaedmoom *a.* มีแปดมุม octangular
michaichana *a.* มีชัยชนะ victorious
michancheung *a.* มีชั้นเชิง tactful
michayawa *adv.* มีฉายาว่า alias
micheusiang *a* มีชื่อเสียง famous
micheusiang *a.* มีชื่อเสียง notable
micheusiang *a.* มีชื่อเสียง renowned
micheusiangnaitangmaidi *a.* มีชื่อเสียงในทางไม่ดี notorious
michiwit *v.i.* มีชีวิต live
michiwitchiwa *a* มีชีวิตชีวา alive
michiwitchiwa *a.* มีชีวิตชีวา live
michiwitchiwa *a.* มีชีวิตชีวา sprightly
michiwitchiwa *a.* มีชีวิตชีวา vivacious
michiwityu *a.* มีชีวิตอยู่ living
michiwityudai *a.* มีชีวิตอยู่ได้ viable
microfilm *n.* ไมโครฟิล์ม microfilm
micrometer *n.* ไมโครเมตร micrometer
microphone *n.* ไมโครโฟน microphone
microwave *n.* ไมโครเวฟ microwave
mid *n.* มีด knife
midad *a.* มีแดด sunny

midantaogantookdan *a*
มีด้านเท่ากันทุกด้าน equilateral
midgon *n.* มีดโกน razor
midgon *n* มีดโกน shave
midmaw *n.* มีดหมอ lancet
mifontok *a.* มีฝนตก rainy
migamlang *a* มีกำลัง forceful
migamlang *adj.* มีกำลัง mighty
migamrai *a.* มีกำไร lucrative
migesonpetmianeung-an *a.*
มีเกสรเพศเมียหนึ่งอัน monogynous
migiled *a.* มีกิเลส voluptuous
migraine *n.* ไมเกรน migraine
mihedmipon *a.* มีเหตุมีผล rational
mihedmipon *a.* มีเหตุมีผล reasonable
mihedpon *a.* มีเหตุผล valid
mi-ittipontaw *v.t.* มีอิทธิพลต่อ influence
mi-ittipontaw *a.* มีอิทธิพลต่อ influential
mijaimetta *v.t.* มีใจเมตตา humanize
mijamnuanmakkwa *v.t.* มีจำนวนมากกว่า
outnumber
mika *a.* มีค่า precious
mika *a.* มีค่า valuable
mika *a* มีค่า worth
mikanadlek *a.* มีขนาดเล็กมาก
microscopic
mikanadyai *a.* มีขนาดใหญ่ sizable
mikanadyaipenpised *a.*
มีขนาดใหญ่เป็นพิเศษ outsize
mikawpidplad *a* มีข้อผิดพลาด faulty
mikobket *a* มีขอบเขต finite
mikoonnasombatpenya *a.*
มีคุณสมบัติเป็นยา medicinal
mikunka *v.t.* มีคุณค่า value
mikunkatangpochanagan *a.*
มีคุณค่าทางโภชนาการ nutritious
mikunkatangpochanagan *a.*
มีคุณค่าทางโภชนาการ nutritive
mikunnasombat *v.i.* มีคุณสมบัติ qualify
mikunnasombat *a.* มีคุณสมบัติ
qualitative
mikunnatam *a.* มีคุณธรรม moral

mikwamdikwamchob *a.*
มีความดีความชอบ meritorious
mikwammai *a.* มีความหมาย meaningful
mikwammai *v.t.* มีความหมาย signify
mikwammaimeuangan *a.*
มีความหมายเหมือนกัน synonymous
mikwampidtanluanggeun *a.*
มีความผิดฐานล่วงเกิน sacrilegious
mikwampratana *v.t.* มีความปรารถนา
aspire
mikwamrabpidchob *a* มีความรับผิดชอบ
accountable
mikwamsamad *a.* มีความสามารถ
competent
mikwamsampangan *v.t.*
มีความสัมพันธ์กัน correlate
mikwamsatta *a* มีความศรัทธา faithful
mikwamwang *a.* มีความหวัง hopeful
milaksanakongpedchai *a.*
มีลักษณะของเพศชาย virile
milayliam *a* มีเล่ห์เหลี่ยม crafty
milayliam *a.* มีเล่ห์เหลี่ยม shifty
milayliam *a.* มีเล่ห์เหลี่ยม sly
milayliam *a.* มีเล่ห์เหลี่ยม tricky
mile *n.* ไมล์ mile
mimagonna *a.* มีมาก่อนหน้า antecedent
mimanudsayatam *a.* มีมนุษยธรรม
humane
mimekmak *a.* มีเมฆมาก overcast
mimoonlaka *v.t.* มีมูลค่า cost
minaewnom *a* มีแนวโน้ม subject
minaewnomjaplianjai *a.*
มีแนวโน้มจะเปลี่ยนใจ capricious
minakom *n* มีนาคม march
minammak *a.* มีหนามมาก thorny
minamnakgeun *v.t.* มีน้ำหนักเกิน
outweigh
minamnakmak *a.* มีน้ำหนักมาก weighty
minamnakmakkwa *v.t.* มีน้ำหนักกว่า out-
balance
mineuatibanjudaimak *a.*
มีเนื้อที่บรรจุได้มาก capacious

minpramat v.t. หมิ่นประมาท libel
minpramat a. หมิ่นประมาท slanderous
mint n. มินท์ mint
mipaebpan a. มีแบบแผน methodical
mipatigiriyatobgladdoeytanti a
มีปฏิกิริยาตอบกลับโดยทันที reflex
mipayangdiaw a. มีพยางค์เดียว
monosyllabic
mipayulaeng a. มีพายุแรง tempestuous
mipedsampan v.i. มีเพศสัมพันธ์ copulate
mipeek adj. มีปีก aliferous
mipongamrai a. มีผลกำไร profitable
mipongratob a มีผลกระทบ effective
mipongratob a มีผลกระทบ efficient
miponlameungnanaen a.
มีพลเมืองหนาแน่น populous
miponnaitanglob a มีผลในทางลบ
adverse
miponsamred a มีผลสำเร็จ successful
miponsawan a. มีพรสวรรค์ gifted
mipontamma v.i มีผลตามมา ensue
miprasobgan v. t. มีประสบการณ์
experience
miprasobgan a. มีประสบการณ์ veteran
mipumkumgan a. มีภูมิคุ้มกัน immune
miradab a มีระดับ classic
miridra-ngabprasad adj
มีฤทธิ์ระงับประสาท calmative
mirod-a-roy a. มีรสอร่อย toothsome
mirodchat a. มีรสชาติ tasteful
mirom-ngao a. มีร่มเงา shadowy
miroobrangdi a. มีรูปร่างดี shapely
mirotchat v.t. มีรสชาติ savour
miroypeuan v.t. มีรอยเปื้อน taint
misakgayapab a. มีศักยภาพ potential
misamsuan a. มีสามส่วน triple
misanaedeungdud a. มีเสน่ห์ดึงดูด
magnetic
misati a มีสติ conscious
misati a. มีสติ sane
misheusiang a. มีชื่อเสียง prestigious
misidleuaktang a มีสิทธิ์เลือกตั้ง eligible

misilapa a. มีศิลปะ artistic
misongmoom adj. มีสองมุม biangular
mitakangdiaw a. มีตาข้างเดียว
monocular
mitaksa a. มีทักษะ skilful
mitamnaeng a. มีตำแหน่ง titular
mitaojamnuanmak n. มีเท้าจำนวนมาก
multiped
mitasanakatikaeb a. มีทัศนคติแคบ
insular
mitrapab n. มิตรภาพ amity
miwaijai v.t. ไม่ไว้ใจ mistrust
miwatasin a มีวาทศิลป์ eloquent
miyutem v.i. มีอยู่เต็ม teem
mo v.i โม้ boast
mo v. i โม้ brag
mobhai v. t มอบให้ bestow
mobhai v. t มอบให้ devote
mobmai v.t. มอบหมาย assign
mobmai v. t. มอบหมาย consign
mobmai v. t มอบหมาย delegate
mobrangwan v.t. มอบรางวัล award
mod n มด ant
mod-a-yu v.i. หมดอายุ expire
modgamlang a. หมดกำลัง prostrate
modlook n. มดลูก uterus
modlook n. มดลูก womb
modtua a. หมดตัว penniless
moho v.i. โมโห rampage
mok n หมอก fog
mokkwan n. หมอกควัน haze
mokkwan n. หมอกควัน smog
mokmoon v.t หมกมุ่น engross
mokmoon v.t. หมกมุ่น immerse
mokmuntangpet a. หมกมุ่นทางเพศ
sensual
molecule n. โมเลกุล molecule
momentum n. โมเมนตัม momentum
mon n หมอน pillow
monggut n มงกุฎ crown
monggut n. มงกุฎ tiara
monghendai a. มองเห็นได้ visible

mongkam *v.t.* มองข้าม slight
mongloknai-ngaedi *a.* มองโลกในแง่ดี optimistic
mongloknai-ngaedi *a.* มองโลกในแง่ดี roseate
mongloknai-ngaerai *a.* มองโลกในแง่ร้าย pessimistic
mongmaihen *a.* มองไม่เห็น invisible
monlapid *n.* มลพิษ pollution
modraeng *a.* หมดแรง worn
mooktalok *n.* มุขตลก banter
moom *n.* มุม angle
moom *n* มุม corner
moom *n.* มุม nook
moommong *n* มุมมอง angle
moommong *n.* มุมมอง aspect
moon *v.t.* หมุน pivot
moon *v.i.* หมุน spin
moon *v.t.* หมุน wheel
moon *n.i.* หมุน whirl
moonka *n.* มูลค่า worth
moonrob *v.i.* หมุนรอบ revolve
moonrob *a.* หมุนรอบ rotary
moonsat *n* มูลสัตว์ dung
moonwian *v. i.* หมุนเวียน circulate
moonwian *v.i.* หมุนเวียน rotate
moo-pa *n* หมูป่า boar
moradok *n.* มรดก heritage
moradok *n.* มรดก legacy
moradokkongbida *n.* มรดกของบิดา patrimony
mora-got *n* มรกต emerald
morasum *n.* มรสุม monsoon
mosaic *n.* โมเสค mosaic
motel *n.* โมเต็ล motel
mu *n.* หมู pig
mu *n.* หมู pork
mu *n.* หมู swine
mua *a* มัว dull
mua-a-han *n.* มื้ออาหาร meal
muad *n.* หมวด category
muad *n.* หมวด platoon

muak *n* หมวก coif
muak *n.* หมวก hat
muakgannok *n.* หมวกกันน็อค helmet
muaksatri *n.* หมวกสตรี milliner
muaktiprasai *n.* หมวกที่พระใส่ mitre
muan *v.t.* ม้วน furl
muan *v.i.* ม้วน reel
muan *n.* ม้วน roll
muan *v.i.* ม้วน roll
muangradat *n.* ม้วนกระดาษ scroll
muankaoduaygan *v.t.* ม้วนเข้าด้วยกัน convolve
muban *n.* หมู่บ้าน village
mubankanadlek *n.* หมู่บ้านขนาดเล็ก hamlet
mud *n.* หมุด peg
mud *n.* หมุด pin
mud *n.* หมุด rivet
muktalok *n.* มุขตลก gag
mummy *n* มัมมี่ mummy
munglangka *v.t.* มุงหลังคา roof
munglangkaduayjak *v.t.* มุมหลังคาด้วยจาก thatch
mungpaidannok *adv* มุ่งไปด้านนอก outwards
muntan *n.* มูลฐาน rudiment
mustard *n.* มัสตาร์ด mustard

N

na *n* หน้า face
na *a.* หนา thick
nab *v. t.* นับ count
nabeua *a.* น่าเบื่อ humdrum
nabeua *a.* น่าเบื่อ banal
nabeua *a.* น่าเบื่อ lacklustre
nabeua *a.* น่าเบื่อ tedious
nabeuanai *a.* น่าเบื่อหน่าย tiresome
nabkanaen *v.t.* นับคะแนน tally
nabmai *v.t.* นับใหม่ recount
nabmaituan *a.* นับไม่ถ้วน countless

nabmaituan *a.* นับไม่ถ้วน innumerable
nabmaituan *a.* นับไม่ถ้วน numberless
nabteu *v.t.* นับถือ admire
nachang *a* น่าชัง abominable
nacheuateu *a* น่าเชื่อถือ credible
nacheuateu *a* น่าเชื่อถือ creditable
nacheunchom *a.* น่าชื่นชม admirable
nadaeng *n* หน้าแดง flush
nadaeng *v.i* หน้าแดง blush
nadeang *adv* หน้าแดง ablush
nadeungdud *a.* น่าดึงดูด attractive
nadmai *v.t.* นัดหมาย appoint
naechad *a.* แน่ชัด categorical
naen *a.* แน่น tight
naenam *v.t.* แนะนำ advise
naenam *v. t* แนะนำ commend
naenam *v.t.* แนะนำ guide
naenam *v.t.* แนะนำ introduce
naenam *v.t.* แนะนำ recommend
naenam *v.t.* แนะนำ suggest
naenamdai *a.* แนะนำได้ suggestive
naenampid *v.t.* แนะนำผิด misguide
naenon *a* แน่นอน absolute
naenon *a* แน่นอน certain
naenon *a* แน่นอน definite
naenon *a.* แน่นอน steadfast
naenon *a.* แน่นอน sure
naenon *a* แน่นอน constant
naewkid *n* แนวคิด concept
naewnae *a.* แน่วแน่ adamant
naewnae *a.* แน่วแน่ resolute
naewnae *a* แน่วแน่ set
naewnom *n.* แนวโน้ม proclivity
naewnom *n.* แนวโน้ม tendency
naewnom *a.* แนวโน้ม tentative
naewnom *n.* แนวโน้ม trend
naewpatibat *n.* แนวปฏิบัติ course
naewpommai *n.* แนวพุ่มไม้ hedge
naewruam *n.* แนวร่วม alliance
naewtang *a.* แนวตั้ง vertical
naewtangpatibat *n.* แนวทางปฏิบัติ
  process

nagak *n.* หน้ากาก mask
nagliad *a.* น่าเกลียด ugly
naglua *a* น่ากลัว dread
naglua *a.* น่ากลัว fearful
naglua *a* น่ากลัว formidable
naglua *a.* น่ากลัว hideous
naglua *a.* น่ากลัว horrible
naglua *a.* น่ากลัว ghastly
nagradad *n.* หน้ากระดาษ page
nai *prep.* ใน in
nai *n.* นาย master
nai-a-nakod *a.* ในอนาคต future
naibeungton *adv.* ในเบื้องต้น primarily
naiboriwennan *adv.* ในบริเวณนั้น
  thereabouts
naichanton *a.* ในชั้นต้น preliminary
naichuangglangkeun *a* ในช่วงกลางคืน
  overnight
naichuangwelani *adv.* ในช่วงเวลานี้
  presently
na-idcha *a* น่าอิจฉา enviable
naijang *n* นายจ้าง employer
nailamdabsam *adv.* ในลำดับสาม thirdly
naimaicha *adv.* ในไม่ช้า soon
naina *n* นายหน้า broker
nainamkong *n* ในนามของ behalf
naiponreua *n.* นายพลเรือ admiral
naipraisani *n.* นายไปรษณีย์ postmaster
naipran *n.* นายพราน huntsman
nairakakaiplik *a* ในราคาขายปลีก retail
nairom *adv.* ในร่ม indoors
naitabian *n.* นายทะเบียน registrar
naitana *pron.* ในฐานะ as
naitanakan *n.* นายธนาคาร banker
naitangglabgan *adv.* ในทางกลับกัน vice-
  versa
naitanti *adv.* ในทันที instantly
naitanti *adv.* ในทันที suddenly
naitinan *adv.* ในที่นั้น wherein
naitiseung *conj.* ในที่ซึ่ง where
naitisud *adv.* ในที่สุด eventually
naitisud *adv.* ในที่สุด last

noytisud *a.* น้อยที่สุด least
naitooktookti *conj.* ในทุกๆ ที่ whereupon
naitungna *adv.* ในทุ่งนา afield
nai-u-domkati *a.* ในอุดมคติ idealistic
naiwanni *adv.* ในวันนี้ today
najodjam *a.* น่าจดจำ memorable
nak *n.* นาก otter
nakaeng *n.* หน้าแข้ง shin
nakam *a.* น่าขำ hilarious
nakam *a.* น่าขำ ridiculous
nakao *n.* นาข้าว paddy
nakaorob *a.* น่าเคารพ honourable
nakaorob *a.* น่าเคารพ respectful
nakaorob *a.* น่าเคารพ reverend
nakaorob *a.* น่าเคารพ reverent
nakbambadbaeb-ongruam *n.*
   นักบำบัดแบบองค์รวม homoeopath
nakbanchi *n.* นักบัญชี accountant
nakbanchi *n* นักบัญชี book-keeper
nakbin *n.* นักบิน aviator
nakbin *n.* นักบิน pilot
nakbin-a-wagad *n.* นักบินอวกาศ
   astronaut
nakbuad *n* นักบวช clergy
nakboon *n.* นักบุญ saint
nakchiwawittaya *n* นักชีววิทยา biologist
nakdarasat *n.* นักดาราศาสตร์ astronomer
nakdontri *n.* นักดนตรี instrumentalist
nakdontri *n.* นักดนตรี musician
nakduantang *n.* นักเดินทาง traveller
nakgaiyagam *n.* นักกายกรรม acrobat
nakgaiyagam *n.* นักกายกรรม tumbler
nakganmeuang *n.* นักการเมือง politician
nak-gan-nguen *n* นักการเงิน financier
nakgantut *n* นักการทูต diplomat
nakgawi *n.* นักกวี poet
nakgawichanlew *n.* นักกวีชั้นเลว
   poetaster
nakgawiying *n.* นักกวีหญิง poetess
nakgila *n.* นักกีฬา athlete
nakgila *n.* นักกีฬา sportsman
nakgodmai *n.* นักกฎหมาย jurist

nakgonrayut *n.* นักกลยุทธ์ tactician
nakgymnastic *n.* นักยิมนาสติก gymnast
nakhorasat *n.* นักโหราศาสตร์ astrologer
nakjitwittaya *n.* นักจิตวิทยา psychologist
nakkanidsat *n.* นักคณิตศาสตร์
   mathematician
nakkao *n.* นักข่าว journalist
nakkemi *n.* นักเคมี chemist
nakkian *n.* นักเขียน writer
nakkianbodlakon *n* นักเขียนบทละคร
   dramatist
nakkid *n.* นักคิด thinker
nakkodsana *n.* นักโฆษณา propagandist
naklanok *n.* นักล่านก fowler
nakleng *n.* นักเลง gangster
nakleng *n.* นักเลง ruffian
nakleng *n.* นักเลง thug
naklengon *n.* นักเล่นกล juggler
naklengon *n.* นักเล่นกล magician
nakmaenpeun *n.* นักแม่นปืน marksman
nakmanudsayatam *a* นักมนุษยธรรม
   humanitarian
nakmuayplam *n.* นักมวยปล้ำ wrestler
nakniruktisat *n.* นักนิรุกติศาสตร์
   philologist
nakpanjaggayan *n* นักปั่นจักรยาน cyclist
nakpayagon-a-gad *n.* นักพยากรณ์อากาศ
   meteorologist
nakphysic *n.* นักฟิสิกส์ physicist
nakpiano *n.* นักเปียโน pianist
nakpinkao *n* นักปีนเขา alpinist
nakpinkao *n.* นักปีนเขา mountaineer
nakprad *n.* นักปราชญ์ sophist
nakpradid *n.* นักประดิษฐ์ inventor
nakprasatwitaya *n.* นักประสาทวิทยา
   neurologist
nakpratya *n.* นักปรัชญา philosopher
nakprawatsat *n.* นักประวัติศาสตร์
   historian
nakpumisad *n.* นักภูมิศาสตร์ geographer
nakrian *n.* นักเรียน pupil
nakrian *n.* นักเรียน student

nakriannairoy *n.* นักเรียนนายร้อย cadet
nakrob *n* นักรบ combatant1
nakrob *n.* นักรบ warrior
nakrong *n.* นักร้อง singer
nakrong *n.* นักร้อง songster
nakrong *n.* นักร้อง vocalist
naksadaeng *n.* นักแสดง performer
naksadaenglakonbai *n.* นักแสดงละครใบ้
  mummer
naksadaengtalok *n.* นักแสดงตลก
  comedian
naksadeangchai *n.* นักแสดงชาย actor
naksadeangying *n.* นักแสดงหญิง actress
naksangkomniyom *n,a* นักสังคมนิยม
  socialist
naksasom *n* นักสะสม collector
naksatiti *n.* นักสถิติ statistician
naksattawawitaya *n.* นักสัตววิทยา
  zoologist
nakseub *n.* นักสืบ detective
nakseub *n.* นักสืบ spy
naksuksaradabparinyatri *n.*
  นักศึกษาระดับปริญญาตรี undergraduate
naksuwua *n .* นักสู้วัว matador
naktaengnawaniyai *n.* นักแต่งนวนิยาย
  novelist
naktewawittaya *n.* นักธรณีวิทยา
  geologist
nakted *n.* นักเทศน์ preacher
niyom *n.* นักเทววิทยา theologian
naktod *n.* นักโทษ captive
naktod *n* นักโทษ convict
naktod *n.* นักโทษ inmate
naktod *n.* นักโทษ prisoner
naktongtiaw *n.* นักท่องเที่ยว tourist
naktongtiaw *n.* นักท่องเที่ยว visitor
naktridsadi *n.* นักทฤษฎี theorist
nakturagid *n* นักธุรกิจ businessman
nak-u-domkati *n.* นักอุดมคติ idealist
nakviolin *n.* นักไวโอลิน violinist
nakwainam *n.* นักว่ายน้ำ swimmer
nakwaiyagon *n.* นักไวยากรณ์ grammarian

nakwannakadi *n.* นักวรรณคดี litterateur
nakwichagan *n.* นักวิชาการ scholar
nakwijan *n* นักวิจารณ์ critic
nakwikraw *n* นักวิเคราะห์ analyst
nakwing *n.* นักวิ่ง runner
nakwitayasat *n.* นักวิทยาศาสตร์ scientist
nakyongbao *n* นักย่องเบา burglar
nakyudtasat *n.* นักยุทธศาสตร์ strategist
nala-ai-jai *a.* น่าละอายใจ shameful
nalanggiad *a.* น่ารังเกียจ repulsive
naliga *n.* นาฬิกา clock
nam *v. t* นำ bring
nam *v.t.* นำ lead
nam *n.* หนาม thorn
nam *n.* น้ำ water
nam-a-suji *n.* น้ำอสุจิ semen
namcheuam *n.* น้ำเชื่อม syrup
namdi *n* น้ำดี bile
nameud *a* หน้ามืด faint
namgleua *n* น้ำเกลือ brine
namhom *n.* น้ำหอม fragrance
namhom *n.* น้ำหอม perfume
namkaeng *n.* น้ำแข็ง ice
namkang *n.* น้ำค้าง dew
namkangkaeng *n.* น้ำค้างแข็ง frost
namkao *v.t.* นำเข้า import
namkaokok *v.t.* นำเข้าคอก stable
namlai *n.* น้ำลาย saliva
namlai *n* น้ำลาย spittle
namlawliang *n.* น้ำหล่อเลี้ยง sap
namman *n.* น้ำมัน oil
nammanao *n.* น้ำมะนาว lemonade
nammanbensin *n.* น้ำมันเบนซิน petrol
nammandib *n.* น้ำมันดิบ tar
nammangad *n.* น้ำมันก๊าด kerosene
nammankleuab-ngao *n.* น้ำมันเคลือบเงา
  varnish
nammanlahoong *n.* น้ำมันละหุ่ง castor oil
nammanlawleun *n* น้ำมันหล่อลื่น grease
nammanpetroleum *n.* น้ำมันปิโตรเลียม
  petroleum
nammanson *n.* น้ำมันสน turpentine

nammatam *a* นามธรรม abstract
namnak *n.* น้ำหนัก weight
namnaktam-a-yu *n.* น้ำหนักตามอายุ weightage
namnong *n.* น้ำหนอง pus
namong *a.* น่ามอง sightly
namook *n.* หน้ามุข portico
nampakga *n.* นามปากกา pseudonym
nampeung *n.* น้ำผึ้ง honey
nampolamai *n* น้ำผลไม้ juice
namprungrod *n.* น้ำปรุงรส sauce
nampu *n.* น้ำพุ fountain
namsakun *n.* นามสกุล surname
namsalad *n* น้ำสลัด dressing
namsomsaichu *n.* น้ำส้มสายชู vinegar
namsomsaichujaklaomalt *n* น้ำส้มสายชูจากเหล้ามอลต์ alegar
namsoupkon *n* น้ำซุปข้น bisque
namta *n.* น้ำตา tear
namtammachatniyom *n.* นักธรรมชาตินิยม naturalist
namtan *n.* น้ำตาล sugar
namtang *v.t.* นำทาง steer
namtang *v.t.* นำทาง usher
namtanong *a.* น้ำตานอง tearful
namtok *n.* น้ำตก cascade
namtok *n.* น้ำตก waterfall
namtuam *n* น้ำท่วม flood
namtuam *n.* น้ำท่วม spate
namwan *n.* น้ำหวาน nectar
namwoan *n.* น้ำวน whirlpool
nan *a.* นั้น that
nanabteu *a.* น่านับถือ venerable
nanaen *a* หนาแน่น rank
nang *n.* หนัง leather
nang *v.t.* นั่ง seat
nang *v.i.* นั่ง sit
nangfa *n* นางฟ้า angel
nangmai *n.* นางไม้ nymph
nang-ngeuk *n.* นางเงือก mermaid
nangran *n.* นั่งร้าน girder
nangran *n.* นั่งร้าน scaffold

nangsat *n.* หนังสัตว์ hide
nangseu *n* หนังสือ book
nangseuchichuan *n.* หนังสือชี้ชวน prospsectus
nangseudeuntang *n.* หนังสือเดินทาง passport
nangseulemna *n.* หนังสือเล่มหนา tome
nangseupim *n.* หนังสือพิมพ์ gazette
nangseupimraiwan *n.* หนังสือพิมพ์รายวัน daily
nangseurabrong *n.* หนังสือรับรอง testimonial
nangseusadaenggammasittidin *n.* หนังสือแสดงกรรมสิทธิ์ที่ดิน muniment
nangseusuadmon *n.* หนังสือสวดมนต์ breviary
nangseuwian *n.* หนังสือเวียน circular
nangsisa *n* หนังศีรษะ scalp
nangtaileb *n* หนังใต้เล็บ quick
nangyongyong *v.i.* นั่งยองๆ squat
nao *a* หนาว chilly
nao *v.i.* เน่า rot
na-oak *n* หน้าอก breast
naosia *v.t.* เน่าเสีย spoil
napa *n.* หน้าผา cliff
napad *n.* หน้าปัด dial
napak *n* หน้าผาก forehead
napawjai *a.* น่าพอใจ satiable
napawjai *a.* น่าพอใจ satisfactory
napratabjai *a.* น่าประทับใจ impressive
narak *a.* น่ารัก lovely
narak *a* น่ารัก pretty
narak *adv.* น่ารัก pretty
naramkan *v.t.* น่ารำคาญ annoy
naramkan *a.* น่ารำคาญ irksome
naramkan *a.* น่ารำคาญ irritable
naranggiad *a.* น่ารังเกียจ loathsome
naranggiad *a.* น่ารังเกียจ nasty
naranggiad *a.* น่ารังเกียจ obnoxious
naranggiad *a.* น่ารังเกียจ odious
naranggiad *a* น่ารังเกียจ beastly

narikajabwela *n* นาฬิกาจับเวลา chronograph

narok *n.* นรก hell

narok *n.* นรก purgatory

nasangged *a.* น่าสังเกต noteworthy

nasao *a.* น่าเศร้า tragic

nasiajai *a.* น่าเสียใจ lamentable

nasongsai *a.* น่าสงสัย questionable

nasongsai *a.* น่าสงสัย sceptical

nasongsai *a.* น่าสงสัย suspect

nasongsai *a.* น่าสงสัย suspicious

nasongsan *a.* น่าสงสาร piteous

nasongsan *a.* น่าสงสาร pitiable

nasongsan *a.* น่าสงสาร pitiful

nasongsan *a.* น่าสงสาร sympathetic

nasonjai *a.* น่าสนใจ interesting

natamni *a* น่าตำหนิ culpable

natamni *a* น่าตำหนิ deplorable

natang *n.* หน้าต่าง window

nateung *a.* น่าทึ่ง remarkable

nateunten *a.* น่าตื่นเต้น adventurous

nateunten *a.* น่าตื่นเต้น spectacular

nati *n* หน้าที่ duty

nati *n.* หน้าที่ function

nati *n.* นาที minute

nati *n.* หน้าที่ mission

nati *n.* หน้าที่ onus

nawaijai *a.* น่าไว้ใจ trustworthy

nawaiwangjai *n.* น่าไว้วางใจ trusty

nawaniyai *n* นวนิยาย novel

nawattagam *n.* นวัตกรรม innovation

nawetana *a.* น่าเวทนา abject

nawetana *a.* น่าเวทนา pathetic

nawiggayotin *n.* นาวิกโยธิน mariner

nawingwian *a.* น่าวิงเวียน giddy

nawkjak *prep* นอกจาก outside

nawkjakni *prep* นอกจากนี้ besides

nawkjakni *adv* นอกจากนี้ besides

nawkneua *adv.* นอกเหนือ apart

nayindi *a.* น่ายินดี pleasant

nayobai *n.* นโยบาย policy

nayokrattamontri *n* นายกรัฐมนตรี premier

nayoktedsamontri *n.* นายกเทศมนตรี governor

nayoktedsamontri *n.* นายกเทศมนตรี mayor

nayokyong *a.* น่ายกย่อง commendable

neaukwa *v.i.* เหนือกว่า predominate

neauyang *n* เนื้อย่าง roast

nebnaem *a.* เหน็บแนม ironical

nebnaem *v.t.* เหน็บแนบ taunt

negro *n.* นิโกร negro

nen *v. t* เน้น emphasize

nenganpatibat *a.* เน้นการปฏิบัติ pragmatic

nenyam *v.t* เน้นย้ำ state

nerated *v.t.* เนรเทศ banish

nerated *v.t.* เนรเทศ deport

nerated *v. t* เนรเทศ exile

neua *n* เนื้อ flesh

neua *n.* เนื้อ meat

neua *a* เหนือ north

neua *prep.* เหนือ over

neua *adv* เหนือ over

neua *a.* เหนือ upper

neuadin *n* เนื้อดิน argil

neuagae *n.* เนื้อแกะ mutton

neuaha *n* เนื้อหา essence

neuaha *n.* เนื้อหา text

neuaha *n.* เนื้อหา content

neuakeunpai *adv.* เหนือขึ้นไป upwards

neuakwa *adv* เหนือกว่า above

neuakwa *prep.* เหนือกว่า beyond

neuakwa *a.* เหนือกว่า pre-eminent

neuakwa *v.i.* เหนือกว่า preponderate

neuakwa *a.* เหนือกว่า superior

neuamanud *a.* เหนือมนุษย์ superhuman

neuangjak *conj.* เนื่องจาก now

neuangjak *conj.* เนื่องจาก since

neungjak *conj.* เนื่องจาก for

neua-ngokbonpewnang *n.* เนื้องอกบนผิวหนัง wen

neua-ngwak *n.* เนื้องอก tumour

neuapa *n.* เนื้อผ้า texture

neuapa *n.* เนื้อผ้า woof
neuaponlamai *n.* เนื้อผลไม้ pulp
neuatae *a.* เนื้อแท้ intrinsic
neuatammachad *a.* เหนือธรรมชาติ supernatural
neuawua *n* เนื้อวัว beef
neuay *v. t.* เหนื่อย exhaust
neuayeua *n.* เนื้อเยื่อ tissue
neukkid *v.t.* นึกคิด imagine
neukpabnaijai *v.t.* นึกภาพในใจ visualize
neun *n.* เนิน mound
neung *a.* หนึ่ง a
neung *art* หนึ่ง an
neung *n* หนึ่ง first
neung *a.* หนึ่ง one
neunggammeu *n.* หนึ่งกำมือ wisp
neunglo *n* หนึ่งโหล dozen
neungpan *n.* หนึ่งพัน thousand
neungpan *a* หนึ่งพัน thousand
neungpanpi *n.* หนึ่งพันปี chiliad
neungtam *n* หนึ่งแต้ม ace
neutron *n.* นิวตรอน neutron
neuy *n* เนย butter
neuay *v.t* เหนื่อย fatigue
neuynamnak *n* หน่วยน้ำหนัก dram
neuywat *n.* หน่วยวัด inch
new *n* นิ้ว finger
newchi *n* นิ้วชี้ forefinger
newpong *n.* นิ้วโป้ง thumb
newtao *n.* นิ้วเท้า toe
neytiam *n.* เนยเทียม margarine
nga-chang *n.* งาช้าง ivory
nga-chang *n.* งาช้าง tusk
ngad *v.t.* งัด lever
ngaemyu *adv.* แง้มอยู่ ajar
ngai *a* ง่าย easy
ngai *a.* ง่าย simple
ngan *n.* งาน affair
ngan *n* งาน choir
ngan *n* งาน errand
ngan *n.* งาน job
ngan *n.* งาน task

ngan *n.* งาน work
ngan-a-direk *n.* งานอดิเรก hobby
ngan-a-direk *n.* งานอดิเรก pastime
ngan-carnival *n* งานคาร์นิวัล carnival
ngan-chalong *n.* งานฉลอง jubilee
nganchin-ek *n.* งานชิ้นเอก masterpiece
nganfansi *n.* งานแฟนซี masquerade
ngan-feemeu *n* งานฝีมือ craft
ngan-feemeu *n.* งานฝีมือ handicraft
ngan-feemeu *n.* งานฝีมือ handiwork
ngangawinipon *n.* งานกวีนิพนธ์ poetics
nganliang *n.* งานเลี้ยง banquet
nganliang *n* งานเลี้ยง feast
nganliang *n.* งานเลี้ยง party
ngan-mai *n.* งานไม้ carpentry
ngannak *n.* งานหนัก toil
ngan-reunreung *n* งานรื่นเริง festival
ngan-reunreung *n.* งานรื่นเริง revel
ngansob *n.* งานศพ funeral
ngantaeng-ngan *n.* งานแต่งงาน spousal
ngao *a* เหงา forlorn
ngao *a.* เหงา lonely
ngao *a.* เหงา lonesome
ngao *n.* เงา shadow
ngeua *n.* เหงื่อ sweat
ngeua *n.* เหงื่อ perspiration
ngeua-awk *v.i.* เหงื่อออก perspire
ngeuak *n.* เหงือก gum
ngeuakpennong *n.* เหงือกเป็นหนอง pyorrhoea
ngeuankai *n* เงื่อนไข condition
ngeu-awk *v.i.* เหงื่อออก sweat
ngeukchai *n.* เงือกชาย merman
ngeun *n.* เงิน money
ngeunchodcheuymeuleukjang *n.* เงินชดเชยเมื่อเลิกจ้าง severance
ngeunchuayleua *n* เงินช่วยเหลือ grant
ngeundeuan *n.* เงินเดือน stipend
ngeundeumpan *n* เงินเดิมพัน stake
ngeunkai *n.* เงื่อนไข proviso
ngeunkangchamra *n.pl.* เงินค้างชำระ arrears

ngeunleknoy *n.* เงินเล็กน้อย pittance
ngeunpenny *n.* เงินเพนนี penny
ngeunpisetjakgantam-ngannokwela *n*
  เงินพิเศษจากการทำงานนอกเวลา
  overtime
ngeunpound *n.* เงินปอนด์ pound
ngeunraidai *n* เงินรายได้ emolument
ngeunraipi *n.* เงินรายปี annuity
ngeunrangwan *n.* เงินรางวัล gratuity
ngeunrouble *n.* เงินรูเบิล rouble
ngeunrupi *n.* เงินรูปี rupee
ngeunsod *n.* เงินสด cash
ngeunsomanakun *n.* เงินสมนาคุณ
  honorarium
ngeunsterling *n.* เงินสเทอร์ลิง sterling
ngeuntib *n.* เงินทิป tip
ngeuntitongchamla *n* เงินที่ต้องชำระ due
ngeuntoon *n.* เงินทุน fund
ngeun-yen *n.* เงินเยน Yen
ngiab *a.* เงียบ quiet
ngiab *a.* เงียบ sedate
ngiab *a.* เงียบ silent
ngiabkreum *a.* เงียบขรึม staid
ngiabkreum *a.* เงียบขรึม taciturn
ngib *v.i.* งีบ nap
ngiblab *v.i.* งีบหลับ slumber
ngo *adj.* โง่ asinine
ngo *adj.* โง่ crass
ngo *adj.* โง่ daft
ngo *a* โง่ dumb
ngo *a* โง่ foolish
ngo *a.* โง่ idiotic
ngo *a.* โง่ silly
ngo *a* โง่ stupid
ngo *a.* โง่ witless
ngob-praman *n* งบประมาณ budget
ngod-ngam *a.* งดงาม gracious
ngod-ngam *a.* งดงาม magnificent
ngu *n.* งู serpent
ngu *n.* งู snake
nguang *adv.* ง่วง asleep
nguangnon *n.* ง่วงนอน somnolent

ngud-ngid *a.* หงุดหงิด moody
ngu-how *n* งูเห่า cobra
ngu-lam *n.* งูหลาม python
ngum-ngam *a.* งุ่มง่าม awkward
ngum-ngam *a.* งุ่มง่าม uncouth
ni *n* หนี้ debt
ni *v.i* หนี flee
niaw *a.* เหนียว sticky
niaw *a.* เหนียว tenacious
nickel *n.* นิกเกิล nickel
nicotine *n.* นิโคติน nicotine
nigai *n.* นิกาย sect
ning *a.* นิ่ง stagnant
ning *a.* นิ่ง still
ning-ngiab *a.* นิ่งเงียบ mum
nintalablang *v.t.* นินทาลับหลัง backbite
niranam *a.* นิรนาม anonymous
nirandon *n* นิรันดร eternity
nirooktisat *n.* นิรุกติศาสตร์ etymology
niruktisat *n.* นิรุกติศาสตร์ philology
nisai *n.* นิสัย habit
nisaitagla *n.* นิสัยตะกละ gluttony
nisoonglang *adj.* หนีศูนย์กลาง centrifugal
nitam *v. i* หนีตาม elope
nitan *n.* นิทาน fable
nitanfaengkati *n* นิทานแฝงคติ apologue
nitansonjai *n.* นิทานสอนใจ parable
nitayasanraideuan *n* นิตยสารรายเดือน
  monthly
nitayasanraisabda *n.* นิตยสารรายสัปดาห์
  weekly
nitrogen *n.* ไนโตรเจน nitrogen
nittayasan *n.* นิตยสาร journal
niyai *n* นิยาย fiction
niyai *n.* นิยาย tale
niyam *v. t* นิยาม define
nobnom *v. i.* นอมน้อม cringe
nobnom *a.* นอบน้อม meek
noen *rel. pron.* โน่น that
noimak *adv.* น้อยมาก barely
nok *n* นก bird
nokchanidneung *n.* นกชนิดหนึ่ง wren

nokchanidneung *n.* นกชนิดหนึ่ง jay
nokchanidneung *n.* นกชนิดหนึ่ง rook
nokgangken *n.* นกกางเขน magpie
nokgrajawk *n.* นกกระจอก sparrow
nokgrajib *n.* นกกระจิบ warbler
nokgrajokted *n.* นกกระจอกเทศ ostrich
nokgrasa *n.* นกกระสา stork
nokgrata *n.* นกกระทา quail
nok-insi *n* นกอินทรีย์ eagle
nokjakni *adv.* นอกจากนี้ withal
nokgaew *n.* นกแก้ว parrot
nokkaomaew *n.* นกเค้าแมว owl
nokkok *a* นอกคอก outcast
nokmeuang *a.* นอกเมือง suburban
noknang-an *n.* นกนางแอ่น swallow
noknangnuan *n.* นกนางนวล gull
nok-nightingale *n.* นกไนติงเกล
    nightingale
nokpirab *n* นกพิราบ dove
nokpirab *n.* นกพิราบ pigeon
nokraeng *n.* นกแร้ง vulture
nokramreua *adv.* นอกลำเรือ overboard
nokrong *v.i.* นกร้อง chirp
noksidam *n.* นกสีดำ raven
nokwelapakati *adv.* นอกเวลาปกติ
    overtime
nokyung *n.* นกยูง peacock
nokyungtuamia *n.* นกยูงตัวเมีย peahen
nom *n.* นม milk
nom-iang *v.i.* โน้มเอียง tend
nomkon *n* นมข้น curd
nomnan *a.* นมนาน immemorial
nomnow *v.t.* โน้มน้าว wheedle
nompriaw *n* นมเปรี้ยว buttermilk
non *n.* หนอน worm
nongnam *n.* หนองน้ำ swamp
nonkwam *a.* นอนคว่ำ prone
nonnangseu *n* หนอนหนังสือ book-worm
nonnangseu *n.* หนอนหนังสือ bookish
nonpak *v.i.* นอนพัก repose
nonpiseua *n* หนอนผีเสื้อ caterpillar
noomsod *n.* หนุ่มโสด bachelor

now *adj* เน่า addle
noy *a.* น้อย less
noy *adv.* น้อย less
noy *n.* น้อย low
noy *adv.* น้อย small
noyjai *a.* น้อยใจ petulant
noykwa *a.* น้อยกว่า lesser
nu *n.* หนู mouse
nu *n.* หนู rat
nu *n.* หนู rodent
nuad *v.t.* นวด massage
nuad *n.* หนวด moustache
nuad *n.* หนวด mustache
nuadkao *v.t.* นวดข้าว thresh
nuadkrao *n.* หนวดเครา whisker
nuay *n.* หน่วย unit
nuay-ngan *n.* หน่วยงาน agency
nuaywatkwamjukonglewtinoytisud *n.*
    หน่วยวัดความจุของเหลวที่น้อยที่สุด
    minim
nuaywatkwamron *a.* หน่วยวัดความร้อน
    centigrade
noommeungammayi *a.*
    นุ่มเหมือนกำมะหยี่ velvety
noommeunmai *a.* นุ่มเหมือนไหม silky
noomsao *a.* หนุ่มสาว youthful
noonmon *v.t.* หนุนหมอน pillow
nylon *n.* ไนลอน nylon

O

oak *n* อก chest
oasis *n.* โอเอซิส oasis
ob-aun *a.* อบอุ่น cosy
ob-aun *a.* อบอุ่น snug
ob-aun *a.* อบอุ่น warm1
ob-god *v. t.* โอบกอด embrace
ob-om-a-ri *a.* โอบอ้อมอารี hospitable
obpayob *v. t* อพยพ evacuate
obpayob *v.i.* อพยพ immigrate

obpayobpaipenglum *v.i.*
อพยพไปเป็นกลุ่ม swarm
obrom *v.t.* อบรม train
od-a-han *v.i* อดอาหาร fast
odglan *v.t.* อดกลั้น repress
odton *v.i* อดทน abide
odton *adj.* อดทน hardy
odton *a.* อดทน patient
odton *a.* อดทน tolerant
odton *v.t.* อดทน tolerate
o-gad *n.* โอกาส chance
o-gad *n.* โอกาส occasion
o-gad *n.* โอกาส opportunity
o-gadtipenpaidai *n.* โอกาสที่เป็นไปได้
odds
om *a.* อ้อม indirect
om *a.* อ้อม oblique
omyim *n.* อมยิ้ม lollipop
on *a.* อ่อน mild
on-ae *a.* อ่อนแอ rickety
on-ae *a.* อ่อนแอ vulnerable
on-ae *a.* อ่อนแอ weak
on-aen *a* อ่อนแอ้น effeminate
ongganfaitulagan *n.* องค์การฝ่ายตุลาการ
judicature
ong-gon *n.* องค์กร organization
ong-pragob *n* องค์ประกอบ element
ong-pragob *n.* องค์ประกอบ quorum
onla *a.* อ่อนล้า weary
on-nom *a.* อ่อนน้อม submissive
on-plia *v.t.* อ่อนเปลี้ย paralyse
on-raeng *a* อ่อนแรง feeble
on-raeng *a* อ่อนแรง flabby
on-raeng *v.i.* อ่อนแรง lag
on-raeng *v.i.* อ่อนแรง languish
on-raeng *v.i.* อ่อนแรง pine
on-wai *a.* อ่อนไหว sensible
on-wai *a.* อ่อนวัย young
on-waigwa *a.* อ่อนวัยกว่า junior
on-wawn *v.t.* อ้อนวอน implore
on-yon *a.* อ่อนโยน gentle
on-yon *a* อ่อนโยน tender

ooppagon *n* อุปกรณ์ equipment
opal *n.* โอปอล opal
opera *n.* โอเปร่า opera
oppatam *v.t.* อุปถัมภ์ patronize
oppayob *v.i.* อพยพ migrate
orchestra *n.* ออร์เคสตร้า orchestra
organlek *n.* ออร์แกนเล็ก harmonium
o-uad *a.* โอ้อวด pretentious
ounce *n.* ออนซ์ ounce
owl *n* อ่าว bay
owlchanamaidai *a.* เอาชนะไม่ได้
insurmountable
owlmeuloob *v.t.* เอามือลูบ palm
oxygen *n.* ออกซิเจน oxygen

P

pa *n.* ป้า aunt
pa *n* ผ้า fabric
pa *n* ป่า forest
pa *n.* ป่า jungle
pa *v.t.* ปะ patch
pa *v.t.* ปา stone
pab *v.t* พับ fold
pab *n.* ภาพ image
pab *n* ภาพ photo
pab *n.* ภาพ picture
pabai *n.* ผ้าใบ canvas
pabhedgan *n.* ภาพเหตุการณ์ scenery
pablawlian *n.* ภาพล้อเลียน caricature
pablon *n.* ภาพหลอน illusion
pabluangta *n.* ภาพลวงตา delusion
pabluangta *n.* ภาพลวงตา mirage
pabpayon *n* ภาพยนตร์ film
pabpayon *n.* ภาพยนตร์ movies
pabrang *n* ภาพร่าง draft
pabrang *n.* ภาพร่าง sketch
pabruam *n.* ภาพรวม overall
pabsaton *n.* ภาพสะท้อน reflex
pabtai *n* ภาพถ่าย photograph

pachanatam-a-han *n* ภาชนะทำอาหาร cooker

pachedna *n.* ผ้าเช็ดหน้า handkerchief

pachedna *n.* ผ้าเช็ดหน้า kerchief

pachedpak *n.* ผ้าเช็ดปาก napkin

pacheunna *v. t* เผชิญหน้า encounter

pacheunna *v.t* เผชิญหน้า face

pacheunna *v.t* เผชิญหน้า front

pad *v.t.* ปัด spurn

pad *v.t.* ปัด whisk

padedgan *a* เผด็จการ autocratic

padfoon *v.t.* ปัดฝุ่น dust

padjekbukkon *n.* ปัจเจกบุคคล individualism

padlom *n* พัดลม fan

padpong *v.t.* ปัดป้อง parry

pae *n.* แพะ goat

pae *v.t.* แปะ paste

paed *n* แปด eight

paed-siang *v. i* แผดเสียง bellow

paedsib *n* แปดสิบ eighty

paegrajai *v.t.* แผ่กระจาย pervade

paendinwai *n* แผ่นดินไหว earthquake

paeng *a.* แพง costly

paeng *a* แพง dear

paeng *a* แพง expensive

paeng *n* แป้ง flour

paeng *n.* แผง panel

paeng *n.* แป้ง starch

paengan *n.* แผนการ plan

paengan *n.* แผนการ scheme

paengankraokrao *n.* แผนการคร่าวๆ outline

paengkanompang *n* แป้งขนมปัง dough

paengkonkosat *n.* แผงขนคอสัตว์ mane

paenhin *n.* แผ่นหิน slab

paenhinneualumfangsob *n.* แผ่นหินเหนือหลุมฝังศพ ledger

paenkleuabchromium *n* แผ่นเคลือบโครเมียม chrome

paen-ngan *n.* แผนงาน project

paenpa *n* แผ่นปะ patch

paenpab *n* แผนภาพ diagram

paenpab *n.* แผ่นพับ pamphlet

paenpub *n* แผ่นพับ brochure

paensatonglab *n.* แผ่นสะท้อนกลับ reflector

paenti *n.* แผนที่ atlas

paenti *n* แผนที่ map

paerabbab *n.* แพะรับบาป scapegoat

paerangsi *v. i* แผ่รังสี beam

pafai *n.* ผ้าฝ้าย mull

pafai *n.* ผ้าฝ้าย muslin

pafai *n.* ผ้าฝ้าย poplin

paganpeuan *n.* ผ้ากันเปื้อน apron

pagarang *n* ปะการัง coral

pagati *a.* ปกติ normal

pagati *a.* ปกติ regular

pagati *a.* ปกติ usual

pagati *a.* ปกติ workaday

pagen *n.* ปะเก็น gasket

pahawsob *n.* ผ้าห่อศพ shroud

pahom *n* ผ้าห่ม blanket

pahupaki *a.* พหุภาคี multilateral

pai *v.i.* ไป go

pai *n.* ป้าย label

pai *v.i.* พาย paddle

pai *v.t.* พาย row

pai *n.* ป้าย sign

pai-antarai *n* ภัยอันตราย menace

pai-antarai *n.* ภัยอันตราย peril

paikangna *adv.* ไปข้างหน้า forth

paikangna *a.* ไปข้างหน้า onward

paikangna *adv.* ไปข้างหน้า onwards

pailang *adv* ภายหลัง after

painai *prep.* ภายใน inside

painai *a* ภายใน inside

painai *adv.* ภายใน inside

painai *a.* ภายใน interior

painai *a.* ภายใน internal

painai *a.* ภายใน inward

painai *prep.* ภายใน within

painai *adv.* ภายใน within

painai *n.* ภายใน within

painai-a-kan *a.* ภายในอาคาร indoor
painok *adv* ภายนอก outside
painok *a* ภายนอก external
paipicnic *v.i.* ไปปิกนิก picnic
paipragad *n.* ป้ายประกาศ placard
pairaw *a.* ไพเราะ melodious
pairummy *n.* ไพ่รัมมี่ rummy
paitangdannok *adv.* ไปทางด้านนอก
  outwardly
paiyuchonnabot *v.t.* ไปอยู่ชนบท rusticate
pak *v.t.* พัก lodge
pak *n.* ปาก mouth
pak *v.i.* พัก rest
pak *n.* ผัก vegetable
pakad-aew *n.* ผ้าคาดเอว waistband
pakati *a.* ปกติ ordinary
pakati *a.* ปกติ wonted
pakchi *n.* ผักชี coriander
pakganseuksa *n.* ภาคการศึกษา semester
pakirew *n.* ผ้าขี้ริ้ว rag
pakirew *n.* ผ้าขี้ริ้ว tatter
pakkom *n.* ผักขม spinach
paklumlai *n.* ผ้าคลุมไหล่ shawl
paklumna *n.* ผ้าคลุมหน้า veil
paklumtiang *n.* ผ้าคลุมเตียง coverlet
pakmud *v.t.* ปักหมุด pin
pagonggang *n.* ป่าโกงกาง groove
pakonnu *n.* ผ้าขนหนู towel
pakonsat*n.* ผ้าขนสัตว์ camlet
pakonsat *n* ผ้าขนสัตว์ woollen
pakpanuak *n.* ภาคผนวก appendix
pakpraw *v. t. & i* ปากเปราะ blab
pakpumjaijakchaichana *a.*
  ภาคภูมิใจจากชัยชนะ triumphant
pakraem *v.i.* พักแรม sojourn
paksadaeng *n.* ภาคแสดง predicate
paktangkaotaw *n.* ปากทางเข้าท่อ
  manhole
paktawan-awk *n.* ภาคตะวันตก occident
palamaw *n.* ป่าละเมาะ coppice
palang-ngan *n.* พลังงาน energy
palit *v.t.* ผลิต manufacture

palidtapanjaknom *n* ผลิตภัณฑ์จากนม
  dairy
palit *v.t.* ผลิต produce
palittapan *n.* ผลิตภัณฑ์ product
pamai *n.* ป่าไม้ woods
pamai *n.* ป่าไม้ woodland
pam-ngao *n.* ภาพเงา silhouette
pamrian *v.t.* ปั๊มเหรียญ mint
pan *n* พันธุ์ brood
pan *v. t. & i.* ปั่น churn
pan *v.t.* พัน gird
pan *v.t* พัน girdle
pan *v.i.* ผ่าน pass
panak-ngan *n.* พนักงาน staff
panak-nganrabfak-ngeun *n.*
  พนักงานรับฝากเงิน teller
panak-nganraksapamai *n*
  พนักงานรักษาป่าไม้ forester
panak-nganseubchai *n.*
  พนักงานเสิร์ฟชาย waiter
panak-ngantonrabbonkreuangbin *n.*
  พนักงานต้อนรับบนเครื่องบิน steward
panan *v.i* พนัน bet
panan *v.i* พนัน game
panan *v.i.* พนัน wager
panana *v. t.* พรรณนา depict
panatan *n* พณฯ ท่าน excellency
pan-ek *n.* พันเอก colonel
paneukgamlang *v. t.* ผนึกกำลัง
  consolidate
panglang *a* ปานกลาง medium
panglang *a.* ปานกลาง middling
pangpon *n.* พังพอน marten
pangpon *n.* พังพอน mongoose
panha *n.* ปัญหา problem
panha *n.* ปัญหา trouble
panjan *n* ปั้นจั่น crane
panjugrapong *v.t.* บรรจุกระป๋อง tin
pankaomaidai *a.* ผ่านเข้าไปไม่ได้
  impenetrable
panglang *a.* ปานกลาง moderate
panlan *n* พันล้าน billion

panpae *v.t* พันแผล bandage
panpai *v. t* ผ่านไป elapse
panpai *prep.* ผ่านไป through
panpaidai *a.* ผ่านไปได้ navigable
panpon *v.t.* ผ่านพัน surmount
panraya *n.* ภรรยา wife
panrayakunnang *n.* ภรรยาขุนนาง
  countess
panrayanoy *n* ภรรยาน้อย concubine
panta *n* พันธะ bond
pantamit *n.* พันธมิตร ally
pantanagan *n* พันธนาการ bondage
pantang *a* พันทาง mongrel
pantri *n* พันตรี major
pantugam *n.* พันธุกรรม heredity
panuak *v.t.* ผนวก annex
panuam *n.* ผ้านวม quilt
panya *n.* ปัญญา intellect
panya *n.* ปัญญา wisdom
panya *n.* ปัญญา wit
pao *v. t* เผา cremate
pao-awk *v.t.* เป่าออก winnow
paokluy *v.i* เป่าขลุ่ย flute
paomai *v. t* เผาไหม้ coke
paomai *n.* เป้าหมาย goal
paomai *n.* เป้าหมาย objective
paomai *n.* เป้าหมาย target
paotrae *v. i* เป่าแตร bray
paotrae *v.t.* เป่าแตร trump
paotrae *v.i.* เป่าแตร trumpet
papankaw *n.* ผ้าพันคอ scarf
papanpae ~*n.* ผ้าพันแผล bandage
papidta *v. t* ผ้าปิดตา blindfold
papoksisa *n.* ผ้าโพกศีรษะ turban
papoksisasatri *n.* ผ้าโพกศีรษะสตรี
  wimple
paputinon *n.* ผ้าปูที่นอน sheet
para *n* ภาระ burden
parad-eiw *n.* ผ้ารัดเอว girdle
paraffin *n.* พาราฟิน paraffin
param *n.* ปะรำ canopy
param *n.* ปะรำ pavilion

parasite *n.* ปาราสิต parasite
pared *n.* พาเหรด parade
pariman *n.* ปริมาณ quantity
pariman *n.* ปริมาณ volume
parimangeun *n* ปริมาณเกิน over
parimanmak *n.* ปริมาณมาก mass
parimanya *n* ปริมาณยา dose
parinya-ek *n* ปริญญาเอก doctorate
parod *n.* ปรอท mercury
parod *n.* ปรอท quicksilver
pasa *n.* ภาษา language
pasa-anglid *n* ภาษาอังกฤษ English
pasachapawglum *n.* ภาษาเฉพาะกลุ่ม
  jargon
pasachapawglum *n.* ภาษาเฉพาะกลุ่ม
  lingo
pasadi *n.* พัศดี warden
pasaglang *n.* ภาษากลาง lingua franca
pasakkarad *n* ผ้าสักหลาด flannel
pasasat *n.* ภาษาศาสตร์ linguistics
pasatichaiprajamwan *n.*
  ภาษาที่ใช้ประจำวัน vernacular
pasatin *n* ภาษาถิ่น dialect
pasatpailemya *v.t.* พาสัตว์ไปเล็มหญ้า
  agist
pasawa *n.* ปัสสาวะ urine
pasi *n.* ภาษี tax
pasi-a-gon *n* ภาษีอากร excise
pasipandan *n.* ภาษีผ่านด่าน octroi
pasiseunpeum *n.* ภาษีส่วนเพิ่ม surtax
pasit *n.* ภาษิต adage
pasit *n.* ภาษิต proverb
pasitigebpeum *n.* ภาษีที่เก็บเพิ่มเติม
  supertax
pasiyoi *n.* ภาษีย่อย tithe
pasom *v. t* ผสม blend
pasom *v. i* ผสม compound
pasom *v.t.* ผสม intermingle
pasom *v.t.* ผสม mingle
pasom *v.i* ผสม mix
pasomglomgleun *n* ผสมกลมกลืน
  assimilation

pasompan *v.t* ผสมพันธุ์ breed
pasompasan *n.* ผสมผสาน chord
pasusat *n.* ปศุสัตว์ cattle
pat *v.i.* พัด blow
patagan *v. i.* ปะทะกัน collide
patapisat *n.* ปฐพีศาสตร์ agronomy
pateuan *a.* ป่าเถื่อน barbarian
pateuan *a.* ป่าเถื่อน barbarous
patibaddai *a.* ปฏิบัติได้ practicable
patibat *v.t.* ปฏิบัติ practise
patibatdaijing *a.* ปฏิบัติได้จริง realistic
patibatniyom *n.* ปฏิบัตินิยม pragmatism
patiroob *v.t.* ปฏิรูป reform
patiroob *a* ปฏิรูป reformatory
patised *v. t.* ปฏิเสธ decline
patised *v. t.* ปฏิเสธ deny
patised *v.t.* ปฏิเสธ gainsay
patised *v.t.* ปฏิเสธ refuse
patised *v.t.* ปฏิเสธ refute
patised *v.t.* ปฏิเสธ repudiate
patised *v.t.* ปฏิเสธ overrule
patised *v.t.* ปฏิเสธ reject
patitin *n.* ปฏิทิน calendar
patitinhorasad *n.* ปฏิทินโหราศาสตร์
  almanac
patiwat *v.i.* ปฏิวัติ revolt
patjai *n* ปัจจัย factor
patjuban *a* ปัจจุบัน current
pattana *v. t.* พัฒนา develop
patu *v. i* ปะทุ erupt
patwanpraganprung *v.i.*
  ผัดวันประกันพรุ่ง procrastinate
paw *n* พ่อ dad, daddy
paw *n* พ่อ father
paw *n.* ปอ jute
pawajid *n.* ภาวะจิต conation
pawakadsan-a-han *n.*
  ภาวะขาดสารอาหาร malnutrition
pawamiprajamdeuan *n.*
  ภาวะมีประจำเดือน menses
pawamodprajamdeuan *n.*
  ภาวะหมดประจำเดือน menopause

pawa-ngeunfeud *n.* ภาวะเงินฝืด deflation
pawapagati *n.* ภาวะปกติ normalcy
pawapengrod *a* ภาวะเป็นกรด acid
pawaraiprajamdeuan *n*
  ภาวะไร้ประจำเดือน amenorrhoea
pawasaitasan *n.* ภาวะสายตาสั้น myopia
pawasa-ngobning *n.* ภาวะสงบนิ่ง lull
pawaseumsao *n.* ภาวะซึมเศร้า
  melancholia
pawa-songkram *n* ภาวะสงคราม
  belligerency
pawatiditisud *n.* ภาวะที่ดีที่สุด optimum
pawdi *a* พอดี fit
pawjai *adj.* พอใจ complacent
pawjai *a.* พอใจ content
pawjai *v.t.* พอใจ satisfy
pawka *n.* พ่อค้า merchant
pawka *n.* พ่อค้า monger
pawka *n.* พ่อค้า tradesman
pawkakaisong *n.* พ่อค้าขายส่ง jobber
pawkanaleud *n.* พ่อค้าหน้าเลือด profiteer
pawmai *n.* พ่อหม้าย widower
pawmod *n.* พ่อมด sorcerer
pawmod *n.* พ่อมด wizard
pawpawgan *adv.* พอๆ กัน as
pawpiang *a.* พอเพียง adequate
pawpiang *a* พอเพียง enough
pawpiang *adv* พอเพียง enough
pawpiang *a.* พอเพียง sufficient
pawpluk *v.t.* เพาะปลูก rear
pawprameunkadai *a.* พอประเมินค่าได้
  appreciable
pawpruk *v. t* เพาะปลูก cultivate
pawyudai *a.* พออยู่ได้ habitable
payaban *n.* พยาบาล nurse
payaban *v.t* พยาบาล nurse
payakna *v.i.* พยักหน้า nod
payakon *v.t* พยากรณ์ forecast
payan *n.* พยาน witness
payanchana *n.* พยัญชนะ consonant
payanchanasiangnasik *n*
  พยัญชนะเสียงนาสิก nasal

payang *n.* พยางค์ syllable
payanlaktan *n* พยานหลักฐาน affidavit
payayam *v.t.* พยายาม attempt
payayam *v.i* พยายาม endeavour
payayam *v.i.* พยายาม persevere
payayam *v.i.* พยายาม try
payok *n* ผ้ายก brocade
payu *n.* พายุ storm
payu *n.* พายุ tempest
payucyclone *n.* พายุไซโคลน cyclone
payuhima *n* พายุหิมะ blizzard
payumoon *n.* พายุหมุน tornado
payutewaniyom *n.* พหุเทวนิยม polytheism
payutyphoon *n.* พายุได้ฝุ่น typhoon
ped *n* เพชร diamond
ped *n.* เป็ด duck
ped *n.* เพศ gender
ped *n.* เพศ sex
pedan *n.* เพดาน ceiling
pedanpak *n.* เพดานปาก palate
pedploy *v.t.* เพชรพลอย jewel
pedron *a.* เผ็ดร้อน spicy
peek *n.* ปีก wing
peisachagon *n* เภสัชกร druggist
pen เป็น am
pen-ammapat *a.* เป็นอัมพาต paralytic
pen-ammata *a.* เป็นอมตะ immortal
pen-a-nanikom *a* เป็นอาณานิคม colonial
pen-anneung-andiawgan *a.* เป็นอันหนึ่งอันเดียวกัน unique
pen-antarai *a.* เป็นอันตราย noxious
pen-antarai *a.* เป็นอันตราย pernicious
pen-antarai *a.* เป็นอันตราย risky
penbab *a.* เป็นบาป sinful
penboonkun *a.* เป็นบุญคุณ grateful
penbuang *a.* เป็นบึง marshy
penchuangchuang *a.* เป็นช่วงๆ periodical
pen-ekgachan *a.* เป็นเอกฉันท์ unanimous
penfafaed *a* เป็นฝาแฝด twin
peng *v.t.* เพ่ง gaze
pengammagan *v.t.,* เป็นกรรมการ umpire

penganaenam *a.* เป็นการแนะนำ introductory
penganbanyai *a* เป็นการบรรยาย descriptive
pengandumin *a* เป็นการดูหมิ่น contemptuous
pengan-eng *a* เป็นกันเอง cozy
pengangwon *a.* เป็นกังวล solicitious
pengantamnai *a.* เป็นการทำนาย oracular
pengantriamprom *a.* เป็นการเตรียมพร้อม preparatory
pengiad *a.* เป็นเกียรติ honorary
penglang *a.* เป็นกลาง impartial
penglang *a.* เป็นกลาง neutral
pengliaw *a.* เป็นเกลียว spiral
pengloom *a* เป็นกลุ่ม collective
pengongna *v.t.* เป็นกองหน้า spearhead
pengrod *adj.* เป็นกรด citric
penhedhai *v.t* เป็นเหตุให้ occasion
pen-issara *a.* เป็นอิสระ independent
penjangwa *a.* เป็นจังหวะ rhythmic
penjaokong *v.t.* เป็นเจ้าของ own
penkarawat *a.* เป็นฆราวาส lay
penkatobtaen *a.* เป็นคำตอบแทน remunerative
pen-kong *v. i* เป็นของ belong
penkonglew *a* เป็นของเหลว fluid
penkonglew *a.* เป็นของเหลว liquid
penkrab *v.t.* เป็นคราบ stain
penkrangkrao *a.* เป็นครั้งคราว occasional
penkreuangtuan *a.* เป็นเครื่องเตือน monitory
penlabob *a.* เป็นระบบ systematic
penlaksanachapaw *prep* เป็นลักษณะเฉพาะ like
penlang *v.t.* เป็นลาง portend
penlangrai *a.* เป็นลางร้าย sinister
penlod *a.* เป็นหลอด tubular
penlom *v.i* เป็นลม swoon
penlookbat *a* เป็นลูกบาศก์ cubical
penloom *v.t* เป็นหลุม hole
penmai *v.t.* เป็นหม้าย widow

penman *a.* เป็นหมัน futile
penman-ngao *a.* เป็นมันเงา shiny
penmanwow *a.* เป็นมันวาว glossy
penmeuak *a.* เป็นเหมือก mucous
penmit *a.* เป็นมิตร amiable
penmit *adj.* เป็นมิตร amicable
penmit *a* เป็นมิตร cordial
penmoka *a.* เป็นโมฆะ invalid
penmongkon *a.* เป็นมงคล auspicious
penmoonhed *adj.* เป็นมูลเหตุ causal
penmoradoktoktod *a.* เป็นมรดกตกทอด
  heritable
pennai *a.* เป็นนัย implicit
pennai *a.* เป็นนัย tacit
pennamkaeng *a.* เป็นน้ำแข็ง icy
penneauyeua *a.* เป็นเนื้อเยื่อ pulpy
penneungdiaw *a.* เป็นหนึ่งเดียว
  incorporate
penni *v.t* เป็นหนี้ owe
penpagatiwisai *a.* เป็นปกติวิสัย inherent
penpaha *adj.* เป็นพาหะ borne
penpaidai *a* เป็นไปได้ feasible
penpaidai *a.* เป็นไปได้ likely
penpaidai *a.* เป็นไปได้ possible
penpaidai *a.* เป็นไปได้ probable
penpaimaidai *a.* เป็นไปไม่ได้ impossible
penpanha *a.* เป็นปัญหา troublesome
penpanta *a.* เป็นพันธะ obligatory
penpara *a* เป็นภาระ burdensome
penpatipak *v.t.* เป็นปฏิปักษ์ antagonize
penpatipak *a* เป็นปฏิปักษ์ belligerent
penpayan *v.i.* เป็นพยาน witness
penpeuan *v. t.* เป็นเพื่อน befriend
penpeuan *a.* เป็นเพื่อน neighbourly
penpeunkan *a.* เป็นผื่นคัน rash
penpeuntan *a.* เป็นพื้นฐาน rudimentary
penpid *a.* เป็นพิษ poisonous
penpised *a* เป็นพิเศษ extra
penpitigan *a.* เป็นพิธีการ ceremonious
penpon *v.i.* เป็นผล result
penpong *a.* เป็นผง mealy

penprachatipatai *a* เป็นประชาธิปไตย
  democratic
penpragai *v.i.* เป็นประกาย scintillate
penprajam *a* เป็นประจำ routine
penprapeni *a.* เป็นประเพณี traditional
penpratan *v.i.* เป็นประธาน preside
penprayod *a.* เป็นประโยชน์ advantageous
penprayod *a* เป็นประโยชน์ beneficial
penprayod *a.* เป็นประโยชน์ helpful
penprayod *a.* เป็นประโยชน์ informative
penprayod *a.* เป็นประโยชน์ useful
penprayod *a.* เป็นประโยชน์ wholesome
penprong *a.* เป็นโพรง hollow
penpudi *a.* เป็นผู้ดี urbane
penpuyai *a.* เป็นผู้ใหญ่ mature
penreungrao *v.i.* เป็นเรื่องราว matter
penrokdisan *v.t.* เป็นโรคดีซ่าน jaundice
penroobfanpla *a.* เป็นรูปฟันปลา zigzag
penroobsamliam *a.* เป็นรูปสามเหลี่ยม
  triangular
penroobsiliamjaturat *a.*
  เป็นรูปสี่เหลี่ยมจัตุรัส quadrangular
penroobsiliampeunpa *a.*
  เป็นรูปสี่เหลี่ยมผืนผ้า rectangular
pensamnuan *a.* เป็นสำนวน idiomatic
pensamtao *a.* เป็นสามเท่า triplicate
pensanim *a.* เป็นสนิม rusty
pensanyalak *v.t.* เป็นสัญลักษณ์
  symbolize
pensanyan *a.* เป็นสัญญาณ signal
pensattru *a.* เป็นศัตรู hostile
pensenyai *a.* เป็นเส้นใย webby
pensichompu *a.* เป็นสีชมพู pinkish
pensiliam *a* เป็นสี่เหลี่ยม square
pensuantua *a.* เป็นส่วนตัว secluded
pentahan *v.i.* เป็นทหาร soldier
pentamnan *a.* เป็นตำนาน legendary
pentanggan *a.* เป็นทางการ ceremonial
pentanggan *adv.* เป็นทางการ officially
pentangleuak *a.* เป็นทางเลือก optional
pentarang *a.* เป็นตาราง tabular

pentipeungpratana *a* เป็นที่พึงปรารถนา desirable

pentipeungpratana *a* เป็นที่พึงปรารถนา desirous

pentirak *a* เป็นที่รัก beloved

pentirak *a.* เป็นที่รัก lovable

pentirareuk *a* เป็นที่ระลึก memorial

pentirujakdi *a.* เป็นที่รู้จักดี well-known

pentiyomrab *a.* เป็นที่ยอมรับ welcome

pentuataen *a.* เป็นตัวแทน representative

pentuataen *a.* เป็นตัวแทน vicarious

pentuayang *v.t.* เป็นตัวอย่าง typify

pentuayangtipid *v.t.* เป็นตัวอย่างที่ผิด misrepresent

pen-oopagon *a.* เป็นอุปกรณ์ instrumental

penyeua *v.i.* เป็นเหยื่อ prey

peua *prep* เพื่อ for

peuakwambanteung *a* เพื่อความบันเทิง leisure

peuan *n* เพื่อน chum

peuan *n.* เพื่อน companion

peuan *v.t.* เปื้อน contaminate

peuan *v. t.* เปื้อน daub

peuan *n* เพื่อน fellow

peuan *n.* เพื่อน friend

peuan *n.* เพื่อน helpmate

peuan *n.* เพื่อน kith

peuan *n.* เพื่อน mate

peuan *n.* เพื่อน pal

peuan *n.* เพื่อน peer

peuanleuad *a* เปื้อนเลือด bloody

peuannamlai *v. t* เปื้อนน้ำลาย beslaver

peuanruam-ngan *n* เพื่อนร่วมงาน colleague

peud *n* พืช crop

peud *n* พืช flora

peud *a.* เปิด open

peud *v.t.* เปิด open

peud *n.* พืช plant

peudchanidneung *n.* พืชชนิดหนึ่ง beech

peudchanidneung *n.* พืชชนิดหนึ่ง nettle

peudchanidneung *n.* พืชชนิดหนึ่ง plantain

peudminam *n.* พืชมีหนาม thistle

peudpak *n.* พืชผัก produce

peudpak *n.* พืชผัก vegetation

peudpeuy *v. t* เปิดเผย disclose

peudpeuy *v. t* เปิดเผย expose

peudpeuykwamlab *v. t.* เปิดเผยความลับ divulge

peufan *a.* เฟ้อฝัน imaginative

peufan *a.* เฟ้อฝัน quixotic

peufan *a.* เฟ้อฝัน visionary

peukcheuy *a.* เพิกเฉย inattentive

peuktawn *v.t.* เพิกถอน revoke

peuktawndai *a.* เพิกถอนได้ revocable

peuktonsit *v.t.* เพิกถอนสิทธิ attaint

peum *v.t.* เพิ่ม add

peum *adj* เพิ่ม adscititious

peum *v.t.* เพิ่ม augment

peum *v.t.* เพิ่ม increase

peum *a.* เพิ่ม plus

peumkanad *v.t.* เพิ่มขนาด magnify

peumkeun *v.t.* เพิ่มขึ้น accrete

peumkeun *v.i.* เพิ่มขึ้น accrue

peumkeun *adv.* เพิ่มขึ้น further

peumkeun *a* เพิ่มขึ้น further

peumkeunsamtao *v.t.* เพิ่มขึ้นสามเท่า triplicate

peumkeunyangruadrew *v.i.* เพิ่มขึ้นอย่างรวดเร็ว surge

peumkwamgoddan *v.t.* เพิ่มความกดดัน pressurize

peumpam *v.i.* พึมพำ purr

peumpentawikun *v.t.* เพิ่มเป็นทวีคูณ redouble

peumrodchat *v.t.* เพิ่มรสชาติ season

peumteum *a.* เพิ่มเติม additional

peumteum *a.* เพิ่มเติม supplementary

peun *n* พื้น floor

peun *n.* พื้น ground

peun *n.* ปืน gun

peuanpan *n.* เพื่อนบ้าน neighbor

peundin *n* พื้นดิน earth

peung *n.* ผึ้ง bee

peung *n.* เพิง cote

peung *adv.* เพ่ง just

peung *n* เพิง shed

peung-pa *v. i.* พึ่งพา depend

peungpagan *a.* พึ่งพากัน interdependent

peungpawjai *a.* พึงพอใจ preferential

peunkabsila *n.* ปืนคาบศิลา musket

peunmeuang *a* พื้นเมือง aboriginal

peunmeuang *a.* พื้นเมือง native

peunmuang *a.* พื้นเมือง indigenous

peunpok *n.* ปืนพก pistol

peunpok *n.* ปืนพก revolver

peuntan *adj.* พื้นฐาน basal

peuntan *a.* พื้นฐาน basic

peuntan *a.* พื้นฐาน fundamental

peunti *n* พื้นที่ area

peunti *n.* พื้นที่ tract

peuntilad-iang *n.* พื้นที่ลาดเอียง slope

peuntipen-acre *n.* พื้นที่เป็นเอเคอร์ acreage

peunyai *n.* ปืนใหญ่ artillery

peunyai *n.* ปืนใหญ่ cannon

peunyao *n* ปืนยาว rifle

peuy *v.t.* เผย bare

peuyprae *v.t.* เผยแพร่ propagate

peuyprae *v.t.* เผยแพร่ publicize

pew *n.* ผิว skin

pewna *n.* ผิวหน้า surface

pewnang *n.* ผิวหนัง cutis

pewpak *v.i.* ผิวปาก whistle

pewpeun *a.* ผิวเผิน superficial

phosphate *n.* ฟอสเฟต phosphate

phosphorus *n.* ฟอสฟอรัส phosphorus

physics *n.* ฟิสิกส์ physics

pi *n* ผี bogle

pi *n.* ผี ghost

pi *n.* ผี wraith

piak *a.* เปียก wet

piakcheun *adj.* เปียกชื้น dank

piakcheun *a.* เปียกชื้น muggy

pianglampang *a.* เพียงลำพัง solo

piangpaw *v.i.* เพียงพอ suffice

piangtaonan *a.* เพียงเท่านั้น mere

piano *n.* เปียโน piano

pichakanid *n.* พีชคณิต algebra

picnic *n.* ปิกนิก picnic

pid *v. t* ปิด close

pid *a* ผิด false

pid *v.t.* ปิด shut

pid *a.* ผิด wrong

pid *adv.* ผิด wrong

pidbang *v. t* ปิดบัง benight

pidbang *v.t.* ปิดบัง obscure

pidbangkawtedjing *v.t.* ปิดบังข้อเท็จจริง whitewash

pidgalatesa *a.* ผิดกาละเทศะ inopportune

pidgodmai *a.* ผิดกฎหมาย illegal

pidgodmai *a.* ผิดกฎหมาย illicit

pidgodmai *a.* ผิดกฎหมาย lawless

pidpagati *a* ผิดปกติ abnormal

pidpagati *a.* ผิดปกติ morbid

pidplad *v.t.* ผิดพลาด mistake

pidprachum *v.t.* ปิดประชุม prorogue

pidsat *n.* พิษสัตว์ venom

pidtammada *a* ผิดธรรมดา anomalous

pidtammada *a.* ผิดธรรมดา extraordinary

pidwang *v. t* ผิดหวัง disappoint

pigan *a* พิการ disabled

pigan *a.* พิการ lame

pijarana *v. t* พิจารณา consider

pijarana *v. t* พิจารณา contemplate

pijarana *v.t.* พิจารณา view

pijaranakadi *v.i.* พิจารณาคดี proceed

pijaranakadi *v.i.* พิจารณาคดี testify

pilakrang *n.* ปีละครั้ง year

pileuk *a.* พิลึก grotesque

pim *v.t.* พิมพ์ print

pim *v.t.* พิมพ์ publish

pim *v.t.* พิมพ์ type

pimpid *v.t.* พิมพ์ผิด misprint

pimsam *v.t.* พิมพ์ซ้ำ reprint

pin *v.i* ปีน climb

pin *n.* พิณ lyre
pinaigam *n.* พินัยกรรม testament
pindauykwamlambak *v. i*
ปีนด้วยความลำบาก clamber
ping *v.t.* ปิ้ง toast
pinitpikraw *v.t.* พินิจพิเคราะห์ scrutinize
pinkeun *v.t.* ปีนขึ้น ascend
pipitapan *n.* พิพิธภัณฑ์ museum
pirakrang *adv.* ปีละครั้ง yearly
pireunongchai *n* พี่หรือน้องชาย brother
pireunongsao *n.* พี่หรือน้องสาว sister
pisad *n.* ปีศาจ demon
pisad *n* ปีศาจ devil
pisad *n* ปีศาจ evil
pisad *n* ปีศาจ fiend
pisad *n.* ปีศาจ monster
pisagot *n.* ปี่สก็อต bagpipe
pisad *n.* ปีศาจ spectre
pised *a.* พิเศษ special
pised *a* พิเศษ especial
pised *a.* พิเศษ singular
piseua *n* ผีเสื้อ butterfly
pisud *v.t.* พิสูจน์ prove
pisud *v.t.* พิสูจน์ substantiate
pisud *v.t.* พิสูจน์ verify
pisudwapid *v. t* พิสูจน์ว่าผิด disprove
pisudwatampid *v.t.* พิสูจน์ว่าทำผิด
confute
piti-eukgareuk *n.* พิธีเอิกเกริก pomp
pitigam *n.* พิธีกรรม rite
pitigam *n.* พิธีกรรม ritual
pitigan *n.* พิธีการ ceremony
pitikaorabtamnaeng *n.* พิธีเข้ารับตำแหน่ง
inauguration
pitilangbab *n.* พิธีล้างบาป baptism
pitirabkaopenchisasanigachon *n.*
พิธีรับเข้าเป็นคริสต์ศาสนิกชน sacrament
pla *n* ปลา fish
pla *n.* ปลา herring
plabpleum *a.* ปลาบปลิ้ม rapt
plabplian *v.t.* ปรับเปลี่ยน modify
plabplian *v.t.* ปรับเปลี่ยน modulate

pladlong *v.i.* พลัดหลง stray
pladpai *v.t.* พลาดไป overlook
plae *v.t.* แปล translate
plaek *a.* แปลก odd
plaek *a.* แปลก perverse
plaek *a.* แปลก queer
plaek *a.* แปลก strange
plaek *a.* แปลก uncanny
plaek *a.* แปลก weird
plaek *a.* แปลก whimsical
plaekjai *v.t.* แปลกใจ amaze
plaekjai *v.t.* แปลกใจ astonish
plaekjai *n.* แปลกใจ surprise
plaekjai *v.i.* แปลกใจ wonder
plaekplom *a* แปลกปลอม foreign
plaekpralad *a.* แปลกประหลาด outlandish
plaepeuy *n.* แผลเปื่อย ulcer
plaepid *v.t.* แปลผิด misconstrue
plaepupong *n* แผลพุพอง blister
plaewfai *n* เปลวไฟ blaze
plai *n.* ปลาย nib
plai *a.* ปลาย terminal
plai *n.* ปลาย tip
plaingchat *n* เพลงชาติ anthem
plaisud *n.* ปลายสุด apex
plaitang *n.* ปลายทาง terminus
plak *v.t.* ผลัก shove
plak *v.t.* ผลัก thrust
plam *v.i.* ปล้ำ wrestle
prang *n* แปรง brush
platapian *n.* ปลาตะเพียน bass
plawan *n.* ปลาวาฬ whale
plawkkaen *a* ปลอกแขน armlet
plawkkasoon *n.* ปลอกกระสุน cartridge
plawkkaw *n* ปลอกคอ collar
playdek *n* เปลเด็ก cradle
playdek *n.* เปลเด็ก crib
playham *n.* เปลหาม stretcher
pleng *n.* เพลง song
plengglomdek *n.* เพลงกล่อมเด็ก lullaby
plengsaeng *v.i* เปล่งแสง glare
plengsaeng *v.i.* เปล่งแสง glow

plengsuad *n* เพลงสวด carol

plengsuad *n.* เพลงสวด hymn

plengsuad *n.* เพลงสวด psalm

pleuak *n.* เปลือก peel

pleuak *n.* เปลือก shell

pleuakhoy *n.* เปลือกหอย conch

pleuangraeng *a.* เปลื้องแรง laboured

pleuay *v.t.* เปลือย denude

pleuaygai *a.* เปลือยกาย nude

pleuayplao *a.* เปลือยเปล่า bare

pleudpleun *v.t.* เพลิดเพลิน relish

pleumpiti *a.* ปลื้มปีติ jubilant

pleuay *a.* เปลือย naked

plewfai *n* เปลวไฟ flame

plewfai *n* เปลวไฟ flare

plewfairibri *n* เปลวไฟริบหรี่ flicker

plian *v. t* เปลี่ยน convert

plian *v.t.* เปลี่ยน switch

plianjai-ngai *v.i.* เปลี่ยนใจง่าย vacillate

plianpengrod *v.* เปลี่ยนเป็นกรด acetify

plianplang *v. t.* เปลี่ยนแปลง change

plianplang *v.* เปลี่ยนแปลง transform

plianplang *v.t.* เปลี่ยนแปลง vary

plianplangdai *a.* เปลี่ยนแปลงได้ variable

plianroob *v.t.* เปลี่ยนรูป transfigure

plikglabdai *a.* พลิกกลับได้ reversible

pling *n.* ปลิง leech

plo-awkma *v. i* โผล่ออกมา emerge

plobjai *v. t* ปลอบใจ console

plobjai *v.t.* ปลอบใจ solace

plod *v. t* ปลด discharge

plod-a-wut *v. t* ปลดอาวุธ disarm

plodpai *a.* ปลอดภัย safe

plodpai *prep* ปลอดภัย save

plodpai *a.* ปลอดภัย secure

plodpara *v.t.* ปลดภาระ unburden

plodploytad *v.t.* ปลดปล่อยทาส manumit

plod-umnad *v. t* ปลดอำนาจ dethrone

plokeunmatipewna *v.i*
    โผล่ขึ้นมาที่ผิวหน้า surface

plokmid *n.* ปลอกมีด scabbard

ploknew *n.* ปลอกนิ้ว thimble

plom *a.* ปลอม artificial

plom *a.* ปลอม counterfeit

plom *a.* ปลอม spurious

plomplaeng *v.t* ปลอมแปลง forge

plomplang *v.i.* ปลอมแปลง sham

plomplangdai *a* ปลอมแปลงได้ sham

plomtua *v. t* ปลอมตัว disguise

plon *v.t.* ปล้น depredate

plon *v.i.* ปล้น loot

plon *v.i.* ปล้น maraud

plon *v.t* ปล้น pirate

plon *v.t.* ปล้น plunder

plon *v.t.* ปล้น ransack

plon *v.t.* ปล้น rob

plongfai *n.* ปล่องไฟ chimney

ploy *v.t.* ปล่อย let

ploy *v.t.* ปล่อย loose

ploy *v.t.* ปล่อย release

ploy-ai-nam *v.i.* ปล่อยไอน้ำ steam

ploy-awkma *v. t* ปล่อยออกมา emit

ploygaw *v.t* ปล่อยเกาะ maroon

ployhaisatlemya *v.t.*
    ปล่อยให้สัตว์เล็มหญ้า pasture

ployhaiwang *v.t.* ปล่อยให้ว่าง vacate

ploypen-isala *v.t* ปล่อยเป็นอิสระ free

ploypen-isara *v.t.* ปล่อยเป็นอิสระ liberate

ploysinam-ngeun *n.* พลอยสีน้ำเงิน
    sapphire

ploytua *v.t.* ปล่อยตัว acquit

plua *n.* พลั่ว mattock

plua *n.* พลั่ว shovel

plua *n.* พลั่ว spade

plugfai *n.* ปลั๊กไฟ plug

pluk *v.i.* ปลุก rouse

plukfang *v.t.* ปลูกฝัง instill

plukfee *v.t.* ปลูกฝี inoculate

plukjai *v.t.* ปลุกใจ fortify

pluklonggratang *v.t.* ปลูกลงกระถาง pot

plukpan *v.t.* ปลุกปั่น agitate

plukpan *v.t.* ปลุกปั่น manipulate

plukplan *v. t* พลุกพล่าน bustle

pluktai *v.t.* ปลูกถ่าย transplant

pluktaineuayeua *v.t* ปลูกถ่ายเนื้อเยื่อ graft

pob *v.t* พบ find

pobhennaitookti *a.* พบเห็นในทุกที่ omnipresent

pobpa *v.t.* พบปะ meet

pochanagan *n.* โภชนาการ nutrition

pod *n* ปอด lung

pojananugrom *n* พจนานุกรม dictionary

pokklum *v.t* ปกคลุม engulf

pokklumduaymek *a* ปกคลุมด้วยเมฆ cloudy

pokklumduayra *a.* ปกคลุมด้วยรา mouldy

pokklumpaiduayhima *a.* ปกคลุมไปด้วยหิมะ snowy

pokkrong *v.t* ปกครอง dominate

pokkrong *v.t.* ปกครอง govern

pokkrong *v.t.* ปกครอง rule

pokkrongton-eng *a* ปกครองตนเอง autonomous

pokpid *v.t* ปกปิด bemask

pokpid *v.t.* ปกปิด conceal

pokpid *v.t.* ปกปิด cover

pokpleuak *v.t.* ปอกเปลือก peel

pokpleuak *v.t.* ปอกเปลือก shell

pokpong *v.t.* ปกป้อง protect

pokpong *a.* ปกป้อง protective

pom *n* ผม hair

pom *a.* ผอม slim

pom *a.* ผอม thin

pombang *a.* ผอมบาง trim

pomdoy *n* ปมด้อย complex

pomdoy *n.* ปมด้อย inferiority

pomkao *a.* ผมขาว grey

pomplom *n.* ผมปลอม wig

pompragan *n* ป้อมปราการ bulwark

pompragan *n.* ป้อมปราการ citadel

pompragan *n.* ป้อมปราการ fort

pompragan *n.* ป้อมปราการ fortress

pomsoong *a.* ผอมสูง lank

pomtiproknapak *n* ผมที่ปรกหน้าผาก forelock

pon *v.i.* ฟน spout

pon *v.i.* ฟน spurt

pong *n.* ผง powder

pongamnod *a.* พ้นกำหนด overdue

pongamrai *n.* ผลกำไร lucre

ponggan *v.t* ป้องกัน defend

ponggan *v.t* ป้องกัน fend

ponggan *v.t* ป้องกัน forestall

ponggan *v.t.* ป้องกัน prevent

ponggan *v.t.* ป้องกัน save

ponggan *v.t.* ป้องกัน shield

ponggan *v.t.* ป้องกัน ward

pongganmaidai *a.* ป้องกันไม่ได้ indefensible

pongratob *v.t.* ผลกระทบ affect

pongratob *n* ผลกระทบ effect

pongratob *n.* ผลกระทบ impact

ponhan *n.* ผลหาร quotient

ponhawk *n.* พลหอก lancer

ponjatawa *n* พลจัตวา brigadier

ponklai *v.t* ผ่อนคลาย ease

ponklai *a* ผ่อนคลาย laxative

ponklai *v.t.* ผ่อนคลาย relax

ponklai *v.t.* ผ่อนคลาย relieve

ponklai *v.t.* ผ่อนคลาย remit

ponkonggangratam *n.* ผลของการกระทำ repercussion

ponkun *n* ผลคูณ multiple

ponlab *n* ผลลัพธ์ consequence

ponlab *n.* ผลลัพธ์ outcome

ponlab *n.* ผลลัพธ์ result

ponlamai *n.* ผลไม้ fruit

ponlamaichae-im *n.* ผลไม้แช่อิ่ม preserve

ponlameuang *n* พลเมือง citizen

ponlareuan *n* พลเรือน civilian

ponlasat *n.* พลศาสตร์ dynamics

ponlawat *a* พลวัตร dynamic

ponmadeua *n* ผลมะเดื่อ fig

ponmak *n* ผลหมาก areca

pon-mulberry *n.* ผลมัลเบอรี่ mulberry

ponpalid *n.* ผลผลิต output

ponpanhai *a.* ผ่อนผันให้ indulgent

ponploydai *n* ผลพลอยได้ by-product
ponprayod *n* ผลประโยชน์ benefit
ponprayod *n* ผลประโยชน์ gain
ponprayod *n.* ผลประโยชน์ sake
ponpron *v.i.* ผ่อนปรน relent
ponruam *v.i* ผลรวม amount
ponruam *n.* ผลรวม total
ponsawan *n.* พรสวรรค์ talent
ponsudtai *n.* ผลสุดท้าย upshot
ponti-tamma *a* ผลที่ตามมา consequent
ponton-oak *n.* ผลต้นโอ๊ก acorn
pookmad *a* ผูกมัด binding
poomlang *n.* ภูมิหลัง background
poommai *n* พุ่มไม้ bush
poon *n.* ปูน cement
poonkao *n.* ปูนขาว lime
poonplaster *n.* ปูนปลาสเตอร์ plaster
pope *n.* โป๊ป pope
poster *n.* โปสเตอร์ poster
potassium *n.* โปแตสเซียม potassium
poypom *n.* ปอยผม ringlet
pra *n.* พระ minister
pra *n.* พระ monk
pra *n.* พระ priest
pra *n.* พระ vicar
prab *v.t* ปรับ fine
prab *v.t.* ปราบ subdue
prab *v.t.* ปราบ suppress
prabgae *v.t.* ปรับแก้ adjust
prabpram *v.t.* ปราบปราม subjugate
prabpram *v.t.* ปราบปราม vanquish
prabprung *v.t.* ปรับปรุง improve
prabprungmai *v.t.* ปรับปรุงใหม่ renovate
prabsihaiglomgleun *v.t.*
 ปรับสีให้กลมกลืน tone
prabtua *v.t.* ปรับตัว adapt
prachachon *n.* ประชาชน people
prachachonnaigrungmosco *n.*
 ประชาชนในกรุงมอสโก muscovite
prachakom *n.* ประชาคม community
prachakon *n.* ประชากร populace
prachakon *n.* ประชากร population

prachamati *n.* ประชามติ referendum
prachamati *n.* ประชามติ consensus
prachao *n.* พระเจ้า messiah
prachatipatai *n* ประชาธิปไตย democracy
pradab *v.t.* ประดับ ornament
pradabdoydawkmai *v.t.* ประดับด้วยลูกไม้
 lace
praden *n.* ประเด็น issue
praden *n.* ประเด็น point
prated *v.t.* ประดิษฐ์ invent
praelai *adv* แพร่หลาย abroad
praelai *a.* แพร่หลาย prevalent
praelai *a.* แพร่หลาย widespread
praepan *v.i.* แพร่พันธุ์ proliferate
praepruan *a* แปรปรวน fickle
praewpraow *a* แพรวพราว brilliant
pragad *v.t.* ประกาศ announce
pragad *v. t.* ประกาศ declare
pragad *v.t.* ประกาศ post
pragad *v.t.* ประกาศ proclaim
pragadgrisadiga *v. i* ประกาศกฤษฎีกา
 decree
pragaifai *n.* ประกายไฟ spark
pragan *v.t.* ประกัน warrant
pragantua *v. t.* ประกันตัว bail
pragasaniyabat *n.* ประกาศนียบัตร
 certificate
pragasaniyabat *n* ประกาศนียบัตร
 diploma
pragob *v.t.* ประกอบ assemble
pragob *v. t* ประกอบ concoct
pragob *v.t.* ประกบ sandwich
pragobduay *v. t* ประกอบด้วย compose
pragobduay *v. i* ประกอบด้วย consist
pragobduay *v. t* ประกอบด้วย constitute
pragobduaygleua *a.* ประกอบด้วยเกลือ
 saline
pragobduaysai *a.* ประกอบด้วยทราย
 sandy
pragod *v.i.* ปรากฏ appear
pragod *v.t.* ปรากฏ manifest
pragodgan *n.* ปรากฏการณ์ phenomenon

pragodgan *n.* ปรากฏการณ์ spectacle
prahan *v. t* ประหาร execute
prajae *n.* ประแจ wrench
prajamgan *v.t.* ประจำการ base
prajampi *a.* ประจำปี annual
prajamti *a.* ประจำที่ stationary
prajamwan *a* ประจำวัน daily
prajan *n.* พระจันทร์ moon
prajao *n* พระเจ้า divinity
prajao *n.* พระเจ้า godhead
prajao (chai) *n.* พระเจ้า(ชาย) god
prajao (ying) *n.* พระเจ้า(หญิง) goddess
prakob *v.t* ประคบ foment
pralad *adj* ประหลาด bizarre
pralad *a.* ประหลาด peculiar
praman *adv* ประมาณ about
praman *a.* ประมาณ approximate
praman *prep.* ประมาณ around
pramat *a.* ประมาท reckless
prameun *v.t.* ประเมิน appraise
prameun *v.t.* ประเมิน assess
prameun *v. t* ประเมิน evaluate
pramoon *v.t.* ประมูล auction
pramoon *v.t* ประมูล bid
pramua *a.* พร่ามัว hazy
pranam *v. t.* ประนาม condemn
pranam *v. t* ประนาม denounce
prani *a.* ปรานี lenient
pranipranom *v. t* ประนีประนอม
  compromise
prapeni *n.* ประเพณี custom
prapeni *n.* ประเพณี tradition
prapeudtuamaimawsom *v.i.*
  ประพฤติตัวไม่เหมาะสม misbehave
prapuyai *n.* พระผู้หญิง priestess
prarachakana *n.* พระราชาคณะ cardinal
prarachakana *n.* พระราชาคณะ prelate
prasad *n.* ปราสาท castle
prasai *v.t.* ปราศรัย address
prasajak *adv.* ปราศจาก without
prasajak *n* ปราศจาก without
prasajakcheua *a.* ปราศจากเชื้อ sterile

prasajakcheuarok *a.* ปราศจากเชื้อโรค
  antiseptic
prasangan *v.t.* ประสานกัน interlock
prasan-ngan *v. t* ประสานงาน co-ordinate
prasatsampat *n.* ประสาทสัมผัส sense
prasatwitaya *n.* ประสาทวิทยา neurology
prasitipad *a.* ประสิทธิภาพ proficient
prasob *v.t.* ประสบ undergo
prasobgan *n* ประสบการณ์ experience
pratab *v.t.* ประทับ imprint
pratabjai *a.* ประทับใจ expressive
pratabjai *v.t.* ประทับใจ impress
pratabtra *v.t.* ประทับตรา seal
pratan *n* ประธาน chairman
pratana *v.t.* ปรารถนา crave
pratana *v.t* ปรารถนา desire
pratana *v.i* ปรารถนา long
pratana *v.t.* ปรารถนา wish
pratana *v.i.* ปรารถนา yearn
pratanatibodi *n.* ประธานาธิบดี president
pratednaikreuajakgapob *n*
  ประเทศในเครือจักรภพ dominion
pratedtaebtawan-awk *n.*
  ประเทศแถบตะวันออก orient
prated *n.* ประเทศ country
pratedjeen *n.* ประเทศจีน china
pratibet *n.* พระธิเบต lama
pratu *n* ประตู door
pratu *n.* ประตู portal
pratuang *v. t* ประท้วง demonstrate
pratuang *v.i.* ประท้วง protest
pratulek *n.* ประตูเล็ก wicket
praturua *n.* ประตูรั้ว gate
pratya *n.* ปรัชญา philosophy
praw *a.* เปราะ brittle
praw *adj.* เปราะ crump
praw *a.* เปราะ fragile
praw *a.* เปราะ frail
prawatganpuay *n* ประวัติการป่วย
  anamnesis
prawatsat *n.* ประวัติศาสตร์ history
prawatyaw *n.* ประวัติย่อ profile

prawatyaw *n.* ประวัติย่อ resume

prawwa *conj.* เพราะว่า because

prayad *a* ประหยัด economical

prayad *a.* ประหยัด prudent

prayad *v.t.* ประหยัด retrench

prayad *a.* ประหยัด thrifty

pra-yesu *n.* พระเยซู Christ

prayok *n.* ประโยค sentence

prayokkamtam *n* ประโยคคำถาม interrogative

preuksakwamlab *v. i* ปรึกษาความลับ confide

priabsameuan *v.t.* เปรียบเสมือน liken

priabtiab *v. t* เปรียบเทียบ compare

priaw *a.* เปรี้ยว sour

prieng *n* เพรียง barnacles

prik *n.* พริก chilli

prikkinu *n* พริกขี้หนู capsicum

priktai *n.* พริกไทย pepper

prisana *n.* ปริศนา conundrum

prissana *n* ปริศนา enigma

prob *v.t.* ปลอบ appease

probmeu *v.t.* ปรบมือ applaud

probmeu *v. i.* ปรบมือ clap

prodpran *a* โปรดปราน favourite

proey *v. t* โปรย bestrew

program *n.* โปรแกรม programme

prom *n.* พรม carpet

prom *n.* พรม mat

prom *a.* พร้อม prompt

prom *adv.* พร้อม readily

prom *a.* พร้อม ready

prom *n.* พรม rug

prom *n.* พรม tapestry

promajan *n.* พรหมจรรย์ virgin

promchai-ngan *a.* พร้อมใช้งาน operative

promgan *adv.* พร้อมกัน jointly

promlikit *n.* พรหมลิขิต predestination

promtawsu *a* พร้อมต่อสู้ bellicose

promtijataeng-ngan *a.* พร้อมที่จะแต่งงาน nubile

prong *n* โพรง burrow

prong *n.* โพรง cavity

prong *n.* โพรง hollow

pronggratai *n.* โพรงกระต่าย warren

prongmai *n* โพรงไม้ muse

prongsai *a.* โปร่งใส transparent

protein *n.* โปรตีน protein

proy *v. t.* โปรย sprinkle

proy *v.t.* โปรย strew

prudsapakom *n.* พฤษภาคม May

pluk *v.t.* ปลูก plant

pruksasad *n* พฤกษศาสตร์ botany

prungni *n.* พรุ่งนี้ morrow

prungni *n.* พรุ่งนี้ tomorrow

prungni *adv.* พรุ่งนี้ tomorrow

prusajigayon *n.* พฤศจิกายน november

prutigamkonkonhuasoong *n.* พฤติกรรมของคนหัวสูง snobbery

pu *adj* ผุ carious

pu *n* ปู crab

puad *v.i.* ปวด ache

puadfan *n.* ปวดฟัน toothache

puadhua *n.* ปวดหัว headache

puakkao *pron.* พวกเขา them

pu-an *n.* ผู้อ่าน reader

puang *n* พวง bundle

puangmalai *n* พวงมาลัย festoon

puangmalai *n.* พวงมาลัย garland

puangrid *n.* พวงหรีด wreath

puapan *v. t* พัวพัน entangle

pu-awkgodmai *n.* ผู้ออกกฎหมาย legislator

pu-awkgodrabiab *n.* ผู้ออกกฎระเบียบ regulator

pu-a-wuso *n* ผู้อาวุโส elder

pu-a-wuso *n.* ผู้อาวุโส senior

puay *v.t.* ป่วย ail

puay *a.* ป่วย ill

puay *a.* ป่วย indisposed

puay *a.* ป่วย sick

pubaengpakbaengpuak *n.* ผู้แบ่งพรรคแบ่งพวก partisan

pubampentaba *n.* ผู้บำเพ็ญตบะ ascetic

pubanchagan *n* ผู้บัญชาการ commandant
pubanchagan *n* ผู้บัญชาการ commander
pubanteukhedganprajampi *n.*
 ผู้บันทึกเหตุการณ์ประจำปี annalist
pubanyai *n.* ผู้บรรยาย lecturer
pubanyai *n.* ผู้บรรยาย narrator
puborihan *n.* ผู้บริหาร administrator
puborijak *n* ผู้บริจาค donor
pubuadmai *n.* ผู้บวชใหม่ novice
pubukbeuk *n* ผู้บุกเบิก forerunner
pubukbeuk *n.* ผู้บุกเบิก pioneer
puchai *n* ผู้ชาย male
puchai *n.* ผู้ชาย man
puchairaeng-gnan *n.* ผู้ใช้แรงงาน
 labourer
puchaisamruay *n* ผู้ชายสำรวย dandy
puchamnandanboranwattu *n.*
 ผู้ชำนาญด้านโบราณวัตถุ antiquary
puchamnangan *n.* ผู้ชำนาญการ adept
puchamnangantampaenti *n.*
 ผู้ชำนาญการทำแผนที่ topographer
puchana *n.* ผู้ชนะ victor
puchana *n.* ผู้ชนะ winner
puchanaleud *n.* ผู้ชนะเลิศ champion
puchanaleud *n.* ผู้ชนะเลิศ medallist
puchao *n.* ผู้เช่า lessee
puchao *n.* ผู้เช่า tenant
pucheuareuangjitwinyan *n.*
 ผู้เชื่อเรื่องจิตวิญญาณ spiritualist
pucheulattiprajaokeujakkawan *n.*
 ผู้เชื่อลัทธิพระเจ้าคือจักรวาล pantheist
pucheunailatti-aktewaniyom *n.*
 ผู้เชื่อในลัทธิเอกเทวนิยม monotheist
puchiawchan *n* ผู้เชี่ยวชาญ expert
puchiawchan *n.* ผู้เชี่ยวชาญ specialist
puchiawchandanpasa *n.*
 ผู้เชี่ยวชาญด้านภาษา linguist
puchiawchannaitakgawittaya *n.*
 ผู้เชี่ยวชาญในตรรกวิทยา logician
puchiawchantangtechnology *n.*
 ผู้เชี่ยวชาญทางเทคโนโลยี technologist
puchidwaksin *n.* ผู้ฉีดวัคซีน vaccinator

puchobtaktang *n.* ผู้ชอบถากถาง satirist
puchom *n.* ผู้ชม spectator
puchuay *n.* ผู้ช่วย adjunct
puchuay *n.* ผู้ช่วย assistant
puchuay *n.* ผู้ช่วย seconder
puchuaybatluang *n.* ผู้ช่วยบาทหลวง
 deacon
puchuaychiwit *n.* ผู้ช่วยชีวิต saviour
puchuaytut *n.* ผู้ช่วยทูต attache
pud *v.t.* พูด mouth
pud *v.t.* พูด say
pud *v.i.* พูด speak
pud *v.i.* พูด talk
pud *v.t.* พูด utter
pud *v.t* พูด word
pudairab-a-nuyad *n.* ผู้ได้รับอนุญาต
 licensee
pudairabgansaneucheu *n*
 ผู้ได้รับการเสนอชื่อ nominee
pudairabmoradok *n.* ผู้ได้รับมรดก heir
pudairabrangwan *n* ผู้ได้รับรางวัล
 laureate
pudamneungan *n.* ผู้ดำเนินการ operator
pudamrongtamnaeng *n.* ผู้ดำรงตำแหน่ง
 incumbent
pudding *n.* พุดดิ้ง pudding
pudeuntang *n.* ผู้เดินทาง voyager
pudeuntang *n.* ผู้เดินทาง wayfarer
pudgeunjing *v. t.* พูดเกินจริง exaggerate
pudhairai *v.t.* พูดให้ร้าย slander
pudi *n.* ผู้ดี aristocrat
pudi *n.* ผู้ดี gentry
pudi *n.* ผู้ดี nobleman
pudibannawk *n.* ผู้ดีบ้านนอก squire
pudjapeudpeuy *a.* พูดจาเปิดเผย
 outspoken
pudkamyab *v.t.* พูดคำหยาบ profane
pudklumkreu *v.i.* พูดคลุมเครือ quibble
pudlen *v.i* พูดเล่น trifle
pudmaichad *v.t.* พูดไม่ชัด lisp
pudmaidai *a.* พูดไม่ได้ nefandous

pudmairureuang *v.t.* พูดไม่รู้เรื่อง maunder

pudnoy *a.* พูดน้อย reticent

pudoeysan *n.* ผู้โดยสาร passenger

pudpennai *v.i.* พูดเป็นนัย allude

pudpeujeu *v.i.* พูดเพ้อเจ้อ rave

pudpeumpam *n.* พูดพึมพำ purr

pudplam *v.i.* พูดพล่าม babble

pudplam *v.i.* พูดพล่าม gabble

pudplong *v. t* พูดโพล่ง blurt

pudpongpak *n.* พูดป้องปาก aside

pudraisara *v.i.* พูดไร้สาระ prattle

pudreuaypeuay *v. i* พูดเรื่อยเปื่อย blether

pudsam *v.t.* พูดซ้ำ reiterate

pudsam *v.t.* พูดซ้ำ repeat

pudsiang-u-i *v.i.* พูดเสียงอู้อี้ mumble

pudtakuktakak *v.i* พูดตะกุกตะกัก falter

pudtalok *v.t.* พูดตลก gag

pudtalok *v.i.* พูดตลก jest

pudtalok *v.i.* พูดตลก joke

pudtid-ang *v.i.* พูดติดอ่าง stammer

pudtokyam *v. t* พูดตอกย้ำ belabour

pudtorasab *v.t.* พูดโทรศัพท์ telephone

pudulae *n.* ผู้ดูแล guardian

pudulae *n.* ผู้ดูแล monitor

pudulae *n.* ผู้ดูแล superintendent

pudulae *n* ผู้ดูแล tender

pudulae-nganpainaiwang *n* ผู้ดูแลงานภายในวัง chamberlain

pudulaesabsin *n.* ผู้ดูแลทรัพย์สิน trustee

pudyaeng *v. t* พูดแย้ง counter

pudyawyei *v.i.* พูดเยาะเย้ย scoff

pufang *n.* ผู้ฟัง audience

pufang *n.* ผู้ฟัง listener

pufaodu *n.* ผู้เฝ้าดู invigilator

pufeuk-gnan *n.* ผู้ฝึกงาน apprentice

hongchut *n.* ห้องชุด suite

pufongrong *n.* ผู้ฟ้องร้อง suitor

pugamgab *n.* ผู้กำกับ director

pugawganrai *n.* ผู้ก่อการร้าย terrorist

pugawjarajon *n.* ผู้ก่อจลาจล rebel

pugawtang *n.* ผู้ก่อตั้ง founder

pugebgiaw *n.* ผู้เก็บเกี่ยว havester

puginneuakon *n.* ผู้กินเนื้อคน androphagi

puglaiglia *n.* ผู้ไกล่เกลี่ย mediator

puglaokamprasai *n.* ผู้กล่าวคำปราศรัย orator

pugliadchangkon-eun *n.* ผู้เกลียดชังคนอื่น misanthrope

pugodki *n* ผู้กดขี่ despot

pugodki *n.* ผู้กดขี่ oppressor

pugodki *n.* ผู้กดขี่ tyrant

pugrabeuang *v.t.* ปูกระเบื้อง tile

pugradan *v.t.* ปูกระดาน plank

pugratampid *n* ผู้กระทำผิด culprit

pugratampid *n.* ผู้กระทำผิด malefactor

pugratampid *n.* ผู้กระทำผิด offender

pugratampidgodmai *ns.* ผู้กระทำผิดกฎหมาย barrator

pugrateureuron *n.* ผู้กระตือรือร้น zealot

pugu-isarapab *n.* ผู้กู้อิสรภาพ liberator

puhaiganpenpayan *n.* ผู้ให้การเป็นพยาน deponent

puhaikampreuksa *n.* ผู้ให้คำปรึกษา mentor

puhaikanaen *n.* ผู้ให้คะแนน scorer

puhoi *n.* ฟูหอย frill

pui *n* ปุ๋ย fertilizer

puikok *n.* ปุ๋ยคอก manure

puikok *n.* ปุ๋ยคอก muck

pujadgan *n.* ผู้จัดการ manager

pujadgan *n.* ผู้จัดการ settler

pujadhahai *n.* ผู้จัดหาให้ supplier

pujaiboon *n.* ผู้ใจบุญ philanthropist

pujamnong *n.* ผู้จำนอง mortgator

pujatwang-ongpragob ผู้จัดวางองค์ประกอบ compositor

pujeraja *n.* ผู้เจรจา negotiator

pujodchawalek *n.* ผู้จดชวเลข stenographer

pujongrakpakditawgasat *n.* ผู้จงรักภักดีต่อกษัตริย์ royalist

puk *v.t.* ผูก affix

puk *v.t.* ผูก tie

puka *n* ผู้ค้า dealer
puka *n.* ผู้ค้า trader
puka *n.* ผู้ค้า vendor
pukaikawmoon *n.* ผู้ให้ข้อมูล informer
pukao *n.* ภูเขา hill
pukao *n* ภูเขา mount
pukao *n.* ภูเขา mountain
pukaofai *n.* ภูเขาไฟ volcano
pukaonamkaeng *n.* ภูเขาน้ำแข็ง iceberg
pukaorobroobpan *n.* ผู้เคารพรูปปั้น
  idolater
pukaoruam *n.* ผู้เข้าร่วม attendant
pukaoruam *n.* ผู้เข้าร่วม participant
pukaplik *n.* ผู้ค้าปลีก retailer
pukawkwamramkan *n.* ผู้ก่อความรำคาญ
  gadfly
pukcheuak *v.t.* ผูกเชือก rope
pukcheuak *v.t.* ผูกเชือก string
puki *n.* ผู้ขี่ rider
pukian *n.* ผู้เขียน author
pukianchiwaprawat *n* ผู้เขียนชีวประวัติ
  biographer
pukkad *v.t.* ผูกขาด monopolize
puklangklai *n* ผู้คลั่งใคล้ fanatic
puk-ngeuan *v.t.* ผูกเงื่อน knot
pukodsana *n.* ผู้โฆษณา publisher
pukpan *n.* ผูกพัน bound
pukpayabat *a.* ผูกพยาบาท revengeful
pukrawrai *n.* ผู้เคราะห์ร้าย wretch
pukrengnairabiab *n.* ผู้เคร่งในระเบียบ
  martinet
pukrengsasana *n.* ผู้เคร่งศาสนา puritan
pukrobkrong *n.* ผู้ครอบครอง occupant
pukrobkrong *n.* ผู้ครอบครอง occupier
pukuabkum *n* ผู้ควบคุม conductor
pukuabkum *n.* ผู้ควบคุม controller
pukuabkum *n.* ผู้ควบคุม supervisor
pukum *n.* ผู้คุม jailer
pukum *n.* ผู้คุม warder
pukumgan *n.* ผู้คุ้มกัน bodyguard
pukumgan ผู้คุ้มกัน guard
pukumkrong *n* ผู้คุ้มครอง custodian

pukwang *n.* ผู้ขว้าง pitcher
pula *n.* ผู้ล่า hunter
pulaklobnamkao *n.* ผู้ลักลอบนำเข้า
  smuggler
pulaktonpasusat *n* ผู้ลักต้อนปศุสัตว์
  abactor
pulawluanghaitampid *n*
  ผู้ล่อลวงให้ทำผิด debauchee
puleakliang *n.* ผู้หลีกเลี่ยง shirker
pulen *n.* ผู้เล่น player
pulianbaeb *n.* ผู้เลียนแบบ imitator
pulipai *n.* ผู้ลี้ภัย fugitive
pulipai *n.* ผู้ลี้ภัย refugee
pulongkanaen *n.* ผู้ลงคะแนน voter
pulongnamnaisanya *n.* ผู้ลงนามในสัญญา
  signatory
pulongtun *n.* ผู้ลงทุน capitalist
pumaicheuanai-prajao *n*
  ผู้ไม่เชื่อในพระเจ้า atheist
pumi-amnadsoongsud *n.* ผู้มีอำนาจสูงสุด
  sovereign
pumi-a-romkan *n.* ผู้มีอารมณ์ขัน
  humorist
pumi-a-yuroipikeunpai *n*
  ผู้มีอายุร้อยปีขึ้นไป centenarian
pumicheusamgabkon-eun *n.*
  ผู้ที่มีชื่อซ้ำกับคนอื่น namesake
pumicheusiang *n* ผู้มีชื่อเสียง celebrity
pumigiled *n.* ผู้มีกิเลส voluptuary
pumi-ittipon *n.* ผู้มีอิทธิพล magnate
pumikwampratana *n.* ผู้มีความปรารถนา
  aspirant
puminaewkid-a-nurakniyom *n*
  ผู้มีแนวคิดอนุรักษ์นิยม conservative
pumipak *n.* ภูมิภาค region
pumipalangjit *n.* ผู้มีพลังจิต telepathist
pumiprated *n.* ภูมิประเทศ landscape
pumisad *n.* ภูมิศาสตร์ geography
pumisatipanya *n.* ผู้มีสติปัญญา
  intellectual
pumisitleuaktang *n.* ผู้มีสิทธิเลือกตั้ง
  constituent

pumisinlatam *n.* ผู้มีศีลธรรม moralist

pumisitleuaktang *n* ผู้มีสิทธิเลือกตั้ง electorate

pumi-umnarddedkad *n* ผู้มีอำนาจเด็ดขาด autocrat

pumiwetmon *n* ผู้มีเวทมนตร์ mystic

pumjai *a.* ภูมิใจ proud

pumkumgan *n.* ภูมิคุ้มกัน immunity

pummaina *n.* พุ่มไม้หนา thicket

pumokmuntangpet *n.* ผู้หมกมุ่นทางเพศ sensualist

pumongloknai-ngaedi *n.* ผู้มองโลกในแง่ดี optimist

pumongloknai-ngaerai *n.* ผู้มองโลกในแง่ร้าย pessimist

punabteu *n.* ผู้นับถือ worshipper

punabteuprajao *n.* ผู้นับถือพระเจ้า deist

punabteuprajao *n.* ผู้นับถือพระเจ้า theist

punam *n.* ผู้นำ leader

punampitigan *n.* ผู้นำพิธีการ beadle

punamteam *n.* ผู้นำทีม skipper

punabteulattipahutewaniyom *n.* ผู้นับถือลัทธิพหุเทวนิยม polytheist

punamying *n.* ผู้นำหญิง matriarch

pung-awkpaidai *a* พุ่งออกไปได้ projectile

puniyom-latti-a-natipatai *n* ผู้นิยมอนาธิปไตย anarchist

pu-oppyob *n.* ผู้อพยพ immigrant

pu-ob-rom *n.* ผู้อบรม trainee

pu-oopatam *n.* ผู้อุปถัมภ์ patron

pu-oppyob *n.* ผู้อพยพ migrant

pupadedgan *n* ผู้เผด็จการ dictator

pupak-a-sai *n* ผู้พักอาศัย resident

pupalid *n* ผู้ผลิต manufacturer

pupatibat *n.* ผู้ปฏิบัติ practitioner

pupenglang *n* ผู้เป็นกลาง neuter

pupenpatipak *n.* ผู้เป็นปฏิปักษ์ antagonist

pupim *n.* ผู้พิมพ์ typist

pupipaksa *n.* ผู้พิพากษา judge

puplomplaeng *n.* ผู้ปลอมแปลง counterfeiter

puplon *n.* ผู้ปล้น marauder

puplongprachon *n.* ผู้ปลงพระชนม์ regicide

pupluktonmai *n.* ผู้ปลูกต้นไม้ grower

pupokkrong *n.* ผู้ปกครอง parent

pupokkrong *n.* ผู้ปกครอง ruler

pupokprongchansoongsud *n.* ผู้ปกครองชั้นสูงสุด paramount

pupokkrongying *n.* ผู้ปกครองหญิง governess

pupokpong *n.* ผู้ปกป้อง protector

pupragob *n.* ผู้ประกอบ compounder

puprahanchiwit *n.* ผู้ประหารชีวิต executioner

pupramoon *n* ผู้ประมูล bidder

puprasan-ngan *n.* ผู้ประสานงาน liaison

pupratiroob *n.* ผู้ปฏิรูป reformer

pupud *n.* ผู้พูด speaker

purab *n.* ผู้รับ addressee

purab *n.* ผู้รับ receiver

purab *n.* ผู้รับ recipient

purabbamnan *n.* ผู้รับบำนาญ pensioner

purabjamnong *n.* ผู้รับจำนอง mortagagee

purabmao *n* ผู้รับเหมา contractor

purab-ngeun *n.* ผู้รับเงิน payee

purab-ngeunprajampi *n* ผู้รับเงินประจำปี annuitant

purab-on *n.* ผู้รับโอน assignee

purabrong *n.* ผู้รับรอง warrantor

purai *n* ผู้ร้าย criminal

purai-ngan *n.* ผู้รายงาน reporter

purakchat *n.* ผู้รักชาติ nationalist

purakchat *n.* ผู้รักชาติ patriot

puraksa *n.* ผู้รักษา keeper

puraksagan *n* ผู้รักษาการแทน deputy

puramruayyangruadrew *n.* ผู้ร่ำรวยอย่างรวดเร็ว upstart

pureron *n.* ผู้เร่ร่อน nomad

pureumton *n.* ผู้เริ่มต้น originator

puriak *n* ผู้เรียก caller

puriakrong *n* ผู้เรียกร้อง claimant

puriakrong *n.* ผู้เรียกร้อง solicitor

purian *n.* ผู้เรียน learner
purianbaeb *n* ผู้เลียนแบบ ape
puriekprachum *n* ผู้เรียกประชุม convener
purongrian *n.* ผู้ร้องเรียน petitioner
pudrua *v.t.* พูดรัว jabber
puruamngan *n.* ผู้ร่วมงาน associate
puruamngan *n* ผู้ร่วมงาน co-partner
puruamnganreunreung *n.*
  ผู้ร่วมงานรื่นเริง reveller
puruampedtangtawannak *n.*
  ผู้ร่วมเพศทางทวารหนัก sodomite
purukran *n.* ผู้รุกราน aggressor
purulaipasa *n.* ผู้รู้หลายภาษา polyglot
pusadaengsoganatagam *n.*
  ผู้แสดงโศกนาฏกรรม tragedian
pusaengnawattagam *n.* ผู้สร้างนวัตกรรม
  innovator
pusamak *n.* ผู้สมัคร applicant
pusamakkaengkan *n.* ผู้สมัครแข่งขัน
  candidate
pusamredganseuksa *n* ผู้สำเร็จการศึกษา
  graduate
pusanabsanoon *n* ผู้สนับสนุน exponent
pusanabsanoon *n.* ผู้สนับสนุน sponsor
pusanabsanoonganbaengyaekdindaen *n.*
  ผู้สนับสนุนการแบ่งแยกดินแดน
  secessionist
pusandod *n.* ผู้สันโดษ recluse
pusang *n* ผู้สร้าง creator
pusanggedgan *n.* ผู้สังเกตการณ์ on-looker
pusanghan *n.* ผู้สังหาร assassin
pusaosok *n.* ผู้เศร้าโศก mourner
pusawaengboon *n.* ผู้แสวงบุญ pilgrim
pusawn *n.* ผู้สอน instructor
pusesaeng *n.* ผู้เสแสร้ง hypocrite
puseu *n.* ผู้ซื้อ buyer
puseubsagoon *n* ผู้สืบสกุล descendant
puseubtamnaeng *n.* ผู้สืบตำแหน่ง
  successor
puseukao *n.* ผู้สื่อข่าว correspondent
puseukao *n.* ผู้สื่อข่าว herald

puseuksaboranwattu *n*
  ผู้ศึกษาโบราณวัตถุ antiquarian
puseusat *n.* ผู้ซื่อสัตย์ loyalist
pusob *n* ผู้สอบ examiner
kusomrod *n.* คู่สมรส spouse
pusomruruamkid *n* ผู้สมรู้ร่วมคิด
  accomplice
pusomruruamkid *n.* ผู้สมรู้ร่วมคิด
  conspirator
pusongsai *n.* ผู้สงสัย sceptic
pusongsan *n.* ผู้ส่งสาร courier
pusongtoralek *n.* ผู้ส่งโทรเลข
  telegraphist
pusonsasana-islam *n.*
  ผู้สอนศาสนาอิสลาม mullah
pusoonsiakwammanjai *n*
  ผู้สูญเสียความมั่นใจ bottler
pusuksagiawgabrae *n.* ผู้ศึกษาเกี่ยวกับแร่
  mineralogist
putadsin *n.* ผู้ตัดสิน arbiter
putadsin *n.* ผู้ตัดสิน referee
putadsinchikad *n.* ผู้ตัดสินชี้ขาด
  arbitrator
putaen *n* ผู้แทน delegation
putaengpleng *n.* ผู้แต่งเพลง lyricist
putaenti *n.* ผู้แทนที่ substitute
putaipab *n.* ผู้ถ่ายภาพ photographer
putaktang *n* ผู้ถากถาง cynic
putam *n.* ผู้ทำ maker
putamhai-ngiab *n.* ผู้ทำให้เงียบ silencer
putamlai *n.* ผู้ทำลาย wrecker
putam-nganfeemeu *n* ผู้ทำงานฝีมือ
  craftsman
putampaktan *n.* ผู้ทำภาคทัณฑ์
  probationer
putamsongkram *n* ผู้ทำสงคราม militant
putamtarang *n.* ผู้ทำตาราง tabulator
putang *v.t.* ปูทาง pave
putannaihedgannai-anakot *n.*
  ผู้ทำนายเหตุการณ์ในอนาคต seer
putantanggantut *n* ผู้แทนทางการฑูต
  emissary

putaw *n.* ผู้ทอ weaver
putawrayod *n.* ผู้ทรยศ traitor
putawtanlattitewaniyom *n*
ผู้ต่อต้านลัทธิเทวนิยม antitheist
puteu-akgasit *n.* ผู้ถือเอกสิทธิ์ monopolist
putidtam *n* ผู้ติดตาม follower
putidya *n.* ผู้ติดยา addict
putilookbon *n.* ผู้ตีลูกบอล batsman
puti-on-ae *n.* ผู้ที่อ่อนแอ weakling
putiyomfaisai *n* ผู้นิยมฝ่ายซ้าย leftist
putodsob *n* ผู้ทดสอบ essayist
putongsongsai *n* ผู้ต้องสงสัย suspect
putongtiaw *n.* ผู้ท่องเที่ยว ranger
putontook *n.* ผู้ทนทุกข์ martyr
putookglaoha *n.* ผู้ถูกกล่าวหา accused
putookhammaihaideumlao *n.*
ผู้ถูกห้ามไม่ให้ดื่มเหล้า teetotaller
putookrabrong *n.* ผู้ถูกรับรอง warrantee
putooktodsob *n* ผู้ถูกทดสอบ examinee
putraudsob *n.* ผู้ตรวจสอบ overseer
putruadgae *n.* ผู้ตรวจแก้ censor
putruadgan *n.* ผู้ตรวจการ commissioner
putruadsob *n.* ผู้ตรวจสอบ inspector
putruadsobbanchi *n.* ผู้ตรวจสอบบัญชี
auditor
pu-u-tidtua *n* ผู้อุทิศตัว devotee
pu-u-tidtua *n.* ผู้อุทิศตัว votary
pu-u-ton *n.* ผู้อุทธรณ์ appellant
puwijan *n* ผู้วิจารณ์ commentator
puyai *n.* ผู้ใหญ่ adult
puyao *n* ผู้เยาว์ minor
puyeunkamrong *n.* ผู้ยื่นคำร้อง pleader
puying *n.* ผู้หญิง woman
puyingtanu *n* ผู้ยิงธนู archer
puyomrabkwamjing *n.* ผู้ยอมรับความจริง
realist
puyu-a-sai *n.* ผู้อยู่อาศัย inhabitant
puyuayuan *n.* ผู้ยั่วยวน tempter
puyunai-u-pagara *n* ผู้อยู่ในอุปการะ
dependant
puyutaibangkabbancha *n*
ผู้อยู่ใต้บังคับบัญชา subordinate

Q

quantum *n.* ควอนตัม quantum
quota *n.* โควต้า quota

R

rab *v.t.* รับ admit
rab *a* ราบ flat
rab *v.t.* รับ receive
rabai *v. t* ระบาย drain
rabailom *v.t.* ระบายลม ventilate
rabaisileaung *v.t.* ระบายสีเหลือง yellow
rabbamnan *v.t.* รับบำนาญ pension
rabchai *v.t.* รับใช้ serve
rabeud *v. i.* ระเบิด burst
rabeud *n* ระเบิด dynamite
rabeud *v. t.* ระเบิด explode
rabeud *v.i* ระเบิด blast
rabeud *v. t* ระเบิด bomb
rabeuddai *a* ระเบิดได้ explosive
rabiang *n.* ระเบียง balcony
rabiang *n.* ระเบียง corridor
rabiang *n.* ระเบียง porch
rabiang *n.* ระเบียง terrace
rabjang *a.* รับจ้าง mercenary
rabkonmai *v.t.* รับคนใหม่ recruit
rabliangpenbud *v.t.* รับเลี้ยงเป็นบุตร
adopt
rabma *v.t* รับมา fetch
rabob *n.* ระบบ system
rabob *n* ระบบ tract
rabobganjadgebpasi *n.*
ระบบการจัดเก็บภาษี taxation
rabobganpokkrong *n.* ระบบการปกครอง
polity
rabobganpokkrong *n.* ระบอบการปกครอง
regime

rabobgansongtoralek *n.*
ระบบการส่งโทรเลข telegraph
rabobpukkad *n.* ระบบผูกขาด monopoly
rabobraisai *n* ระบบไร้สาย wireless
rabobratchagan *n.* ระบบราชการ
Bureacuracy
rabobsaifai *n.* ระบบสายไฟ wiring
rabobtansong *adj* ระบบฐานสอง binary
rabobtorarat *n.* ระบบทรราชย์ tyranny
rabpara *v. t* รับภาระ burden
rabpara *v.t.* รับภาระ shoulder
rabpara *v.t.* รับภาระ undertake
rabparanakguenpai *v.t.*
รับภาระหนักเกินไป overburden
rabpidchob *a.* รับผิดชอบ liable
rabpidchob *a.* รับผิดชอบ responsible
rabpidchobtawnati *a* รับผิดชอบต่อหน้าที่
dutiful
rabrangwan *v.t.* รับรางวัล reward
rabrong *v.t.* รับรอง assure
rabrong *v. t.* รับรอง certify
rabrong *v.t* รับรอง guarantee
rabrong *v.t.* รับรอง insure
rabrong *v.t.* รับรอง recognize
rabrongkunnapab *v.i.* รับรองคุณภาพ
vouch
rabru *v. t* รับรู้ conceive
rabru *v.t.* รับรู้ perceive
rabrudai *a.* รับรู้ได้ perceptive
rabrudaiduaygansampad *a.*
รับรู้ได้ด้วยการสัมผัส tactile
rabsinjoom *v.t.* รับศีลจุ่ม baptize
rachagan *n* รัชกาล reign
rachawong *n* ราชวงศ์ dynasty
rachini *n.* ราชินี queen
radab *n.* ระดับ grade
radab *n.* ระดับ level
radab *n* ระดับ plane
radab *n* ระดับ degree
radabsoongsud *n* ระดับสูงสุด utmost
radabsoongsud *n.* ระดับสูงสุด utterance
radduaysainang *v.t.* รัดด้วยสายหนัง strap

radglao *n.* รัดเกล้า coronet
radkemkad *v.t* รัดเข็มขัด fasten
radomying *v.t* ระดมยิง volley
rae *n.* แร่ mineral
rae *n.* แร่ ore
raed *n.* แรด rhinoceros
raekreum *a.* แรกเริ่ม original
raemaelek *n.* แร่แม่เหล็ก loadstone
raemica *n.* แร่ไมกา mica
raengbandanjai *n.* แรงบันดาลใจ
inspiration
raengdanfaifa *n.* แรงดันไฟฟ้า voltage
raenggla *a* แรงกล้า fervent
raenggratoon *n.* แรงกระตุ้น impulse
raengjungjai *n.* แรงจูงใจ motivation
raengjungjai *n.* แรงจูงใจ motive
raengkab *n* แรงขับ drive
raeng-ngan *n.* แรงงาน labour
raengnomtuang *n.* แรงโน้มถ่วง
gravitation
raengnomtuang *n.* แรงโน้มถ่วง gravity
raengsiadtan *n.* แรงเสียดทาน friction
raesikiaw *n.* แร่สีเขียว serpentine
raeyaihin *n.* แร่ใยหิน asbestos
rahad *n* รหัส code
rahad *n.* รหัส watchword
raheuy *v. i* ระเหย evaporate
rai *n.* ไร mite
rai-a-rom *n.* ไร้อารมณ์ apathy
raichiwitchiwa *a.* ไร้ชีวิตชีวา lifeless
raichiwitchiwa *a.* ไร้ชีวิตชีวา listless
raidai *n.* รายได้ income
raidai *n.* รายได้ proceeds
raidai *n.* รายได้ revenue
raidai *n.* รายได้ salary
raidairuam *n.* รายได้รวม gross
raidiangsa *a.* ไร้เดียงสา childish
raidiangsa *a.* ไร้เดียงสา innocent
raidiangsa *a.* ไร้เดียงสา naive
raigad *a.* ร้ายกาจ baleful
raigan *n.* รายการ item
raigan *n.* รายการ list

raigan-ngeuntitookhakjakbanchi *n*
รายการเงินที่ถูกหักจากบัญชี debit

raihedpon *a.* ไร้เหตุผล illogical

raihua *adj.* ไร้หัว acephalous

raikrab *a.* ไร้คราบ stainless

raikwammai *a.* ไร้ความหมาย
meaningless

raikwamprani *a.* ไร้ความปรานี ruthless

raikwamruseuk *a.* ไร้ความรู้สึก insensible

raikwamsamad *a.* ไร้ความสามารถ
incapable

raikwamwang *a.* ไร้ความหวัง hopeless

raila-iad *n* รายละเอียด detail

rai-ngan *v.t.* รายงาน report

rai-ngan *n.* รายงาน report

raipak *adj.* รายปักษ์ bimonthly

raipak *adj* รายปักษ์ bi-weekly

raipak *adj* รายปักษ์ bimensuel

raiped *a.* ไร้เพศ neuter

raipi *a.* รายปี yearly

raipon *adv* ไร้ผล abortive

raiprasobgan *adj* ไร้ประสบการณ์ callow

raiprayod *a.* ไร้ประโยชน์ helpless

raiprayod *a.* ไร้ประโยชน์ vain

raiprayod *a.* ไร้ประโยชน์ waste

rairaeng *a.* ร้ายแรง grave

rairaeng *a* ร้ายแรง malign

rairaeng *a.* ร้ายแรง malignant

rairaeng *a.* ร้ายแรง virulent

raira-iad *n.* รายละเอียด particular

raira-iad *n.* รายละเอียด specification

raihedpon *a.* ไร้เหตุผล irrational

raisabda *a.* รายสัปดาห์ weekly

raisabda *adv.* รายสัปดาห์ weekly

raisai *a.* ไร้สาย wireless

raisamadtapab *a.* ไร้สมรรถภาพ
incompetent

raisara *a* ไร้สาระ absurd

raisilatam *a.* ไร้ศีลธรรม amoral

raisilatam *a.* ไร้ศีลธรรม licentious

raitetta *adj.* ไร้เมตตา merciless

raiwedmon *v.i.* ร่ายเวทมนตร์ conjure

rak *v.t.* รัก adore

rak *v.t.* รัก love

raka *n.* ราคา price

raka *n.* ราคา rate

rakaikeung *a.* ระคายเคือง irritant

rakkrai *a.* รักใคร่ affectionate

raksa *v. t.* รักษา cure

raksa *v.i.* รักษา heal

raksa *v.t.* รักษา keep

raksa *v.t.* รักษา maintain

raksa *v.t* รักษา remedy

raksa *v.t.* รักษา treat

raksadai *a* รักษาได้ curable

raksadai *a* รักษาได้ curative

raksadai *a.* รักษาได้ remedial

raksamaihai *a.* รักษาไม่หาย incurable

raktan *n.* รากฐาน basis

raleuk *v.t.* ระลึก recollect

raleukteung *v. t.* ระลึกถึง commemorate

ramadrawang *a.* ระมัดระวัง precautionary

ramadrawang *a.* ระมัดระวัง wary

ramkan *v.t.* รำคาญ irritate

ramleuktuang-a-dit *a.* รำลึกถึงอดีต
retrospective

ramruay *a.* ร่ำรวย wealthy

ramruay *a.* ร่ำรวย well-to-do

ran *n.* ร้าน shop

ran *n.* ร้าน store

ranab *a.* ระนาบ plane

ranad *n.* ระนาด xylophone

ran-a-han *n.* ร้านอาหาร restaurant

rang *v. t* ร่าง draft

rang *n.* รัง nest

rang *v.t.* ร่าง outline

rang *v.t.* ร่าง sketch

ra-ngab *v.i.* ระงับ lapse

ra-ngab *v.i.* ระงับ refrain

ra-ngab *v.t.* ระงับ withhold

ra-ngabchuakrao *v.t.* ระงับชั่วคราว
suspend

rangafae *n.* ร้านกาแฟ cafe

ranggae *v. t.* รังแก bully
ranggai *n* ร่างกาย body
ranggiad *a.* รังเกียจ averse
rangkae *n* รังแค dandruff
rangkaikongsatri *n.* รังไข่ของสตรี ovary
rangnam *n.* รางน้ำ gutter
rangnam *n.* รางน้ำ spout
rangpeung *n* รังผึ้ง alveary
rangpeung *n.* รังผึ้ง apiary
rangpeung *n.* รังผึ้ง beehive
rangpeung *n.* รังผึ้ง hive
rangpeung *n.* รังผึ้ง honeycomb
rangrodfai *n.* รางรถไฟ railway
rangsi *n.* รังสี ray
ra-ngub *v.t.* ระงับ quell
ra-ngub *v.t.* ระงับ quench
rangwan *n.* รางวัล award
rangwan *n.* รางวัล prize
rangwan *n.* รางวัล reward
rangwan *n.* รางวัล trophy
rangya *n.* รางหญ้า manger
rankaikanom *n* ร้านขายขนม
confectionery
rankaikanompang *n* ร้านขายขนมปัง
bakery
rankaikongcham *n.* ร้านขายของชำ
grocery
rankailao *n.* ร้านขายเหล้า tavern
rankaimuaksatri *n.* ร้านขายหมวกสตรี
millinery
rankaiya *n* ร้านขายยา dispensary
rankaiya *n.* ร้านขายยา pharmacy
rao *n.* ราว rail
raogabpayu *a.* ราวกับพายุ stormy
raogawsiangfarong *a.* ราวกับเสียงฟ้าร้อง
thunderous
raolookgrong *n.* ราวลูกกรง railing
raoron *a.* เร่าร้อน vehement
rareung *a.* ร่าเริง rosy
rareung *a.* ร่าเริง sanguine
rareuk *v.t.* ระลึก recall
rareung *a.* ร่าเริง shanty

rareung *a.* ร่าเริง sportive
rasami *n.* รัศมี radius
rasigoom *n.* ราศีกุมภ์ aquarius
rasimed *n* ราศีเมษ aries
rasising *n.* ราศีสิงห์ Leo
ratabanpasom *n* รัฐบาลผสม coalition
rataburut *n.* รัฐบุรุษ statesman
ratatammanoon *n* รัฐธรรมนูญ
constitution
rattaban *n.* รัฐบาล government
rattamontri *n.* รัฐมนตรี chancellor
rattasapa *n.* รัฐสภา parliament
raw *v.t.* รอ await
rawaedwawang *a.* ระแวดระวัง vigilant
rawang *prep* ระหว่าง between
rawang *v.i.* ระวัง beware
rawang *prep* ระหว่าง during
rawang *v.t.* ระวัง mind
rawangprated *a.* ระหว่างประเทศ
international
rawk *n.* รอก pulley
raya *n.* ระยะ range
rayatang *n* ระยะทาง distance
rayatangpenmile *n.* ระยะทางเป็นไมล์
mileage
rayawela *n* ระยะเวลา duration
rayawela *n.* ระยะเวลา period
rayawela *n* ระยะเวลา spell
rayawelasippi *n.* ระยะเวลาสิบปี
decennary
rayibrayab *v.i.* ระยิบระยับ glitter
ream *n.* รีม ream
reaunamtiaw *n* เรือนำเที่ยว cruiser
reum *v.t.* เริ่ม start
reng *v.t* เร่ง accelerate
rekaikong *n* เร่ขายของ hawk
rekakanit *n.* เรขาคณิต geometry
reng *v. t.* เร่ง expedite
reng *v.t* เร่ง urge
rengkwamreiw *v.i.* เร่งความเร็ว speed
rengrib *v.t.* เร่งรีบ hurry
reron *a.* เร่ร่อน nomadic

reu *v. t* เรอ belch
reua *n* เรือ boat
reua *n.* เรือ ship
reuabai *n.* เรือใบ yacht
reuabantook *n.* เรือบรรทุก barge
reuabantook *n.* เรือบรรทุก tanker
reuadamnam *n.* เรือดำน้ำ submarine
reuahapla *n.* เรือหาปลา smack
reuakamfak *n* เรือข้ามฟาก ferry
reuangbedtaled *n.* เรื่องเบ็ดเตล็ด miscellany
reuang-eu-chao *n* เรื่องอื้อฉาว scandal
reuang-kobkan *n.* เรื่องขบขัน funny
reuanglao *n.* เรื่องเล่า lore
reuanglao *n.* เรื่องเล่า narrative
reuanglawlian *n.* เรื่องล้อเลียน skit
reuangpraromlok *n.* เรื่องประโลมโลก melodrama
reuangraisara *n.* เรื่องไร้สาระ nonsense
reuangraisara *n.* เรื่องไร้สาระ rot
reuangraisara *n.* เรื่องไร้สาระ trifle
reuangrao *n.* เรื่องราว story
reuangraotawma *n.* เรื่องราวต่อมา sequel
reuangsaeng *a.* เรื่องแสง luminous
reuangsan *n.* เรื่องสั้น novelette
reuangtalok *n.* เรื่องตลก joke
reuangtangped *n.* เรื่องทางเพศ sexuality
reuangted *n* เรื่องเท็จ canard
reuano-a *n* เรือโนอา ark
reuarang *a.* เรื้อรัง chronic
reudubaimairuang *n.* ฤดูใบไม้ร่วง autumn
reudunao *n.* ฤดูหนาว winter
reuduron *n.* ฤดูร้อน summer
reukdi *n.* ฤกษ์ดี auspice
reum *v,* เริ่ม begin
reum *v. t* เริ่ม commence
reum *v.t.* เริ่ม launch
reumkeun *v. i.* เริ่มขึ้น dawn
reummai *a.* เริ่มใหม่ nascent
reumton *v.t.* เริ่มต้น originate
reuang *n.* เรื่อง matter

reuangrakkrai *n.* เรื่องรักใคร่ romance
reuanlanglek *n.* เรือนหลังเล็ก outhouse
reuanrang *n.* เรือนร่าง physique
reunreung *a.* รื่นเริง cheerful
reunreung *a.* รื่นเริง jolly
reunreung *a.* รื่นเริง jovial
reusi *n.* ฤษี hermit
reutawn *v.t.* รื้อถอน raze
rew *a* เร็ว fast
rew *adv* เร็ว fast
rew *a.* เร็ว quick
rew *a.* เร็ว rapid
rewgwasiang *a.* เร็วกว่าเสียง swift
rewgwasiang *a.* เร็วกว่าเสียง supersonic
riab *a.* เรียบ smooth
riab-ngai *a.* เรียบง่าย rustic
riabroy *adv.* เรียบร้อย already
riabroy *a.* เรียบร้อย neat
riabroy *a.* เรียบร้อย tidy
riak *v. t.* เรียก call
riak *v.t.* เรียก page
riakcheupid *v.t.* เรียกชื่อผิด miscall
riakkatai *v.t.* เรียกค่าไถ่ ransom
riakkwamsonjai *v.* เรียกความสนใจ advert
riakrong *v. t* เรียกร้อง claim
riakrong *v. t* เรียกร้อง demand
riakrong *v.t.* เรียกร้อง requisition
riakrong *v.t.* เรียกร้อง solicit
riakrongkeun *v.t.* เรียกร้องคืน reclaim
riaktua *v.t.* เรียกตัว summon
rian *n* เหรียญ coin
rian *v.i.* เรียน learn
rian *v.i.* เรียน study
lianbaeb *v.t.* เลียนแบบ ape
riangtamtua-akson *a.* เรียงตามตัวอักษร alphabetical
rianjob *v.i.* เรียนจบ graduate
rianshilling *n.* เหรียญชิลลิ่ง shilling
riantra *n.* เหรียญตรา medal
rlasamadtapab *a.* ไร้สมรรถภาพ impotent
ribgin *n.* รีบกิน gobble

ribreng *v.t.* รีบเร่ง rush
ribreng *v.i.* รีบเร่ง hasten
ribreng *a.* รีบเร่ง hasty
ribri *v.t* ริบหรี่ flicker
rid *v.t.* รีด iron
ridnom *v.t.* รีดนม milk
riekprachum *v. t* เรียกประชุม convene
riekprachum *v.t.* เรียกประชุม convoke
riew *n.* ริ้ว stripe
rim *n.* ริม verge
rimfeepak *n.* ริมฝีปาก lip
rin *v.i.* ริน pour
rireum *v.t.* ริเริ่ม initiate
rita *v.i.* หรี่ตา squint
robguan *v. t* รบกวน bedevil
robguan *v. t* รบกวน bother
robguan *v. t* รบกวน disturb
robguan *v.t.* รบกวน trouble
robkob *a* รอบคอบ careful
robkob *a.* รอบคอบ cautious
robkob *adj.* รอบคอบ circumspect
robkob *a* รอบคอบ deliberate
robkob *a.* รอบคอบ prudential
robnok *a.* รอบนอก outer
robru *adj.* รอบรู้ conversant
robru *v.t.* รอบรู้ sophisticate
rodbantook *n.* รถบรรทุก lorry
rodbantook *n.* รถบรรทุก truck
rodbus *n* รถบัส bus
rodchat *n* รสชาติ flavour
rodchat *n* รสชาติ smack
rodchat *n.* รสชาติ taste
rodchiwit *v.i.* รอดชีวิต subsist
rodchiwit *v.i.* รอดชีวิต survive
roddi *a.* รสดี tasty
rodduan *n* รถด่วน express
rodfai *n.* รถไฟ train
rodgeng *n.* รถเก๋ง saloon
rodgeng *n.* รถเก๋ง sedan
rodjad *a.* รสจัด piquant
rodkendektarok *n.* รถเข็นเด็กทารก perambulator

rodlak *n.* รถลาก cart
rodlak *n.* รถลาก rickshaw
rodlakpeunyai *n* รถลากปืนใหญ่ limber
rodma *n* รถม้า chaise
rodma *n* รถม้า chariot
rodmotersaikanadlek *n.* รถมอเตอร์ไซด์ขนาดเล็ก scooter
rodnam *v.t.* รดน้ำ water
rodpayaban *n.* รถพยาบาล ambulance
rodpuang *n.* รถพ่วง trailer
rodrahjang *n.* รถรับจ้าง cab
rodrang *n.* รถราง tram
rodtu *n.* รถตู้ van
rodyon *n.* รถยนต์ automobile
rodyon *n.* รถยนต์ car
rodyon *n.* รถยนต์ motor
rok *n* โรค disease
rok *n.* รอก tackle
rokbaimai *n* โรคใบไหม้ blight
rokbaowan *n* โรคเบาหวาน diabetes
rokbid *n* โรคบิด dysentery
rokdisan *n.* โรคดีซ่าน jaundice
rokgout *n.* โรคเกาต์ gout
rokgraduk-on *n.* โรคกระดูกอ่อน rickets
rokgungying *n.* โรคกุ้งยิง stye
rokhawb *n.* โรคหอบ asthma
rokhid *n.* โรคหิด scabies
rokjit *n.* โรคจิต psychosis
rokkaikaw-akseb *n.* โรคไขข้ออักเสบ rheumatism
roklohidjang *n* โรคโลหิตจาง anaemia
roklombamu *n* โรคลมบ้าหมู epilepsy
rokpai *n.* โรคภัย affliction
rokpitsunakba *n.* โรคพิษสุนัขบ้า rabies
rokpodbuam โรคปอดบวม pneumonia
rokprasat *n.* โรคประสาท hysteria
rokprasat *n.* โรคประสาท neurosis
rokpuadkaw *n* โรคปวดข้อ arthritis
rokrabad *n.* โรคระบาด plague
rokrai *n.* โรคร้าย malignancy
rokreun *n.* โรคเรื้อน leprosy

rokritsiduangtawan *n.* โรคริดสีดวงทวาร
  piles
roktidtawrairaeng *n.* โรคติดต่อร้ายแรง
  pestilence
rom *n.* ร่ม shade
rom *n.* ร่ม umbrella
romchuchib *n.* ร่มชูชีพ parachute
romkwan *v.i.* รมควัน smoke
rommai *n* ร่มไม้ bower
romreun *a.* ร่มรื่น sylvan
ron *v.t.* ร่อน glide
ron *a.* ร้อน hot
rong *n* ร่อง cleft
rong *v.t* ร่อง groove
rong *n.* รอง vice
rong *v.i.* ร้อง warble
rong-a-han *n.* โรงอาหาร canteen
rong-atiganwat *n* รองอธิการวัด prior
rongbaw *v. t* รองเบาะ cushion
rongdin *n.* ร่องดิน furrow
rongfeuk-ngan *n.* โรงฝึกงาน workshop
rongfoknang *n.* โรงฟอกหนัง tannery
ronggaga *v. i.* ร้องกาๆ caw
ronggasab *n* โรงกษาปณ์ mint
rongglan *n.* โรงกลั่น refinery
rongglanlao *n* โรงกลั่นเหล้า brewery
rongglansura *n* โรงกลั่นสุรา distillery
ronghai *v. i* ร้องไห้ cry
ronghai *v.i.* ร้องไห้ weep
ronghaikramkruan *v.i.* ร้องไห้คร่ำครวญ
  wail
rongkaw *v. t.* ร้องขอ entreat
rongkramkruan *v.i.* ร้องคร่ำครวญ
  whimper
ronglakon *n.* โรงละคร theatre
ronglakonsat *n.* โรงละครสัตว์ circus
ronglaw *n.* โรงหล่อ foundry
rongna *n.* โรงนา barn
rongnang *n.* โรงหนัง cinema
rong-ngan *n* โรงงาน factory
rongpayaban *n.* โรงพยาบาล hospital
rongpleng *v.i.* ร้องเพลง sing

rongraem *n.* โรงแรม hotel
rongraem *n.* โรงแรม inn
rongrian *v.t.* ร้องเรียน petition
rongrian *n.* โรงเรียน school
rongrianpolyrtechnic *n.*
  โรงเรียนโปลีเทคนิค polytechnic
rongrod *n.* โรงรถ garage
rongroy *n.* ร่อยรอย trace
rongroy *n.* ร่องรอย vestige
rongroy *n.* ร่อยรอย whiff
rongsi *n.* โรงสี mill
rongsianglaem *v. i* ร้องเสียงแหลม cheep
rongsianglaem *v.i.* ร้องเสียงแหลม squeak
rongsianglaem *v.i.* ร้องเสียงแหลม twitter
rongsiangtam *v.i.* ร้องเสียงต่ำ low
rongsob *n* โรงศพ coffin
rongtang *n.* ร่องทาง rut
rongtao *n.* รองเท้า shoe
rongtaosaget *n.* รองเท้าสเก็ต skate
rongtaotae *n.* รองเท้าแตะ sandal
rongtaotae *n.* รองเท้าแตะ slipper
rongtawboot *n* รองเท้าบู๊ต boot
rongtilek *n* โรงตีเหล็ก forge
rongtook *v. i* ร้องทุกข์ complain
rongyim *n.* โรงยิม gymnasium
ronjad *a.* ร้อนจัด torrid
ron-ob-aow *a.* ร้อนอบอ้าว sultry
ronray *a* ร่อนเร่ vagabond
roobbaeb *n* รูปแบบ format
roobfanpla *n.* รูปฟันปลา zigzag
roobhaliam *n.* รูปห้าเหลี่ยม pentagon
roobhuajai *adj.* รูปหัวใจ cordate
roobkon *n.* รูปคน portrait
roobkong *a* รูปโค้ง arch
roobpaedliam *n.* รูปแปดเหลี่ยม octagon
roobpahupod *a.* รูปพหุพจน์ plural
roobpan *n.* รูปปั้น statue
roobpatam *a* รูปธรรม concrete
roobpatam *a.* รูปธรรม tangible
roobrang *n* รูปร่าง figure
roobrang *n* รูปร่าง form
roobrang *n.* รูปร่าง shape

roobrangklaihu *adj.* รูปร่างคล้ายหู auriform

roobrangpombang *n.* รูปร่างผอมบาง slender

roobsiliam *a. & n.* รูปสี่เหลี่ยม quadrilateral

roobsiliamjaturat *n.* รูปสี่เหลี่ยมจัตุรัส quadrangle

roobsiliampeunpa *n.* รูปสี่เหลี่ยมผืนผ้า oblong

roobsongglom *n.* รูปทรงกลม sphere

roobsongpyramid *n.* รูปทรงปิรามิด pyramid

roobwongri *n* รูปวงรี oval

roonnong *n.* รุ่นน้อง junior

roonraeng *a* รุนแรง drastic

roonraeng *a.* รุนแรง severe

rotchat *n.* รสชาติ savour

rotma *n.* รถม้า barouche

roy *n.* ร้อย hundred

roy *n.* รอย mark

roybak *n.* รอยบาก nick

roybak *n.* รอยบาก notch

roybak *n.* รอยบาก scotch

roycham *n* รอยช้ำ bruise

roydai *v.t.* ร้อยด้าย thread

roydang *n.* รอยด่าง stigma

royfun *n* รอยฟัน slash

roygad *n* รอยกัด bite

roygridyao *n.* รอยกรีดยาว slit

roygaew *n.* ร้อยแก้ว prose

roykian *n.* รอยเขียน weal

roykuan *n.* รอยขวน scratch

royla *adv.* ร้อยละ per cent

roymalai *v.t.* ร้อยมาลัย garland

roypab *n* รอยพับ fold

roypab *n* รอยพับ ply

roypeuan *n.* รอยเปื้อน blot

roypeuan *n.* รอยเปื้อน smear

roypeuan *n.* รอยเปื้อน taint

royplaepen *n* รอยแผลเป็น scar

roypratab *n.* รอยประทับ imprint

roysak *n.* รอยสัก tattoo

roytaek *n* รอยแตก breakage

roytaek *n* รอยแตก crack

roytaek *n* รอยแตก fissure

roytaek *n.* รอยแตก fracture

roytaeng *n.* รอยแทง prick

roytao *n. & adj* ร้อยเท่า centuple

royto *n.* ร้อยโท lieutenant

royyeb *n.* รอยเย็บ stitch

royyim *n.* รอยยิ้ม smile

royyon *n* รอยย่น crease

royyon *n.* รอยย่น wrinkle

ru *v.t.* รู้ know

ru *n.* รู puncture

rua *n* รั้ว fence

rua *v.i.* รั่ว leak

rua *n.* รั้ว picket

ruabruam *v.t.* รวบรวม aggregate

ruabruam *v.t.* รวบรวม amass

ruabruam *v. t* รวบรวม compile

ruabruam *v. t.* รวบรวม embody

ruabruam *v.t.* รวบรวม muster

ruabruam *v.t.* รวบรวม piece

ruadrew *a.* รวดเร็ว speedy

ruam *v. t* รวม combine

ruam *v.t.* รวม include

ruam *v.t.* ร่วม join

ruamgamlang *v.t* รวมกำลัง marshal

ruamgan *v.t.* รวมกัน amalgamate

ruamgan *v.t.* รวมกัน incorporate

ruamgan *v.t.* รวมกัน merge

ruamgan *a.* ร่วมกัน mutual

ruamgan *adv.* รวมกัน together

ruamganpengon *v.i* รวมกันเป็นก้อน mass

ruamglum *v.t.* รวมกลุ่ม associate

ruamglum *v. i.* รวมกลุ่ม cluster

ruammeu *v. i* ร่วมมือ collaborate

ruammeu *v. i* ร่วมมือ co-operate

ruammeugan *a* ร่วมมือกัน co-operative

ruam-nganliang *v.t.* ร่วมงานเลี้ยง banquet

ruampen *v.* รวมเป็น amount

ruampengon *v.t.* รวมเป็นก้อน lump

ruamsamai *a* รวมสมัย contemporary
ruamtua *v.i* รวมตัว flock
ruamtua *v.t.* รวมตัว gather
ruamtua *v.t.* รวมตัว unite
ruamyod *v.t.* รวมยอด sum
ruamyod *v.t.* รวมยอด total
ruanreung *a.* รื่นเริง mirthful
ruaseum *v.i.* รั่วซึม seep
ruay *a.* รวย affluent
ruay *a.* รวย rich
ruaytangtaegeud *adj.* รวยตั้งแต่เกิด born rich
rudugan *n.* ฤดูกาล season
rudzip *v.t.* รูดซิป zip
rujaeng *v. t.* รู้แจ้ง enlighten
rujamook *n.* รูจมูก nostril
rukumkon *n.* รูขุมขน pore
rulaipasa *a.* รู้หลายภาษา poligot
ruluangna *v.t* รู้ล่วงหน้า foresee
rumantahod *n.* รูม่านตาหด myosis
rumlom *v. t* รุมล้อม besiege
runangseu *a.* รู้หนังสือ literate
rungchao *n* รุ่งเช้า dawn
rungreuang *a.* รุ่งเรือง glorious
rungreung *v.i* รุ่งเรือง flourish
rungrod *a.* รุ่งโรจน์ lustrous
roonraeng *a.* รุนแรง radical
roonraeng *a.* รุนแรง rampant
roonraeng *a.* รุนแรง violent
rura *a.* หรูหรา sumptuous
ruroycheuak *n* รูร้อยเชือก eyelet
ruseuk *v.t* รู้สึก feel
ruseukkobkun *a.* รู้สึกขอบคุณ thankful
ruseukla-ai-jai *v.t.* รู้สึกละอายใจ shame
ruseuknameud *v.i* รู้สึกหน้ามืด faint
ruseukpid *a.* รู้สึกผิด guilty
ruseukpid *v.i.* รู้สึกผิด repent
ruseukpumjai *v.t.* รู้สึกภูมิใจ pride
ruseuksonjai *a.* รู้สึกสนใจ interested
ruseuktuamton *v.t.* รู้สึกท่วมท้น overwhelm
rusuksiajai *v.t.* รู้สึกเสียใจ rue

S

sa-ad *a* สะอาด clean
sab *v. t* สับ chop
sab *v.t.* สับ mince
sabai *a* สบาย comfortable
sabaijai *a.* สบายใจ smug
saban *v.t.* สาบาน swear
sabanton *n.* สาบานตน oath
sabda *n.* สัปดาห์ week
sabiang-a-han *n. pl* เสบียงอาหาร victuals
sabpanamburudtineung *pron.* สรรพนามบุรุษที่หนึ่ง I
sabparod *n.* สับปะรด pineapple
sabplian *v.i.* สับเปลี่ยน shuffle
sabsawn *a.* ซับซ้อน sophisticated
sabsin *n.* ทรัพย์สิน asset
sabsin *n.* ทรัพย์สิน mammon
sabsin *n.* ทรัพย์สิน property
sabsombat *n.* ทรัพย์สมบัติ pelf
sabson *v. t* สับสน bewilder
sabson *a* ซับซ้อน complex
sabson *v.t.* สับสน frustrate
sabson *a.* ซับซ้อน intricate
sabson *v.t.* สับสน perplex
sabu *n.* สบู่ soap
sad *v.i.* สาด splash
sadaeng *v. t* แสดง display
sadaeng *v. t.* แสดง express
sadaeng *v.t.* แสดง perform
sadaeng *v.t.* แสดง show
sadaengbodbat *v.t.* แสดงบทบาท personify
sadaengconcert *v. t* แสดงคอนเสิร์ต concert2
sadaengkwamhen *v.t.* แสดงความเห็น opine
sadaengkwamrak *adj* แสดงความรัก amatory

sadaengkwamsiajai v. i. แสดงความเสียใจ condole

sadaengkwamyindi v. t แสดงความยินดี congratulate

sadaengkwamyindi v.t แสดงความยินดี felicitate

sadaenglakonbai v.i แสดงละครใบ้ mime

sadaenglodpon v.t. แสดงโลดโผน stunt

sadaengnam v.t. แสดงนำ star

sadaengtua v.t. แสดงตัว identify

sadaengtua v.t. แสดงตัว profess

sadgiawgabsiang n. ศาสตร์เกี่ยวกับเสียง acoustics

sadnaiganlamdabhedgan n. ศาสตร์ในการลำดับเหตุการณ์ chronology

sadsuan n สัดส่วน faction

sadsuan n สัดส่วน portion

sadsuan n. สัดส่วน proportion

sadsuan n. สัดส่วน ratio

sadtru n ศัตรู enemy

sadtru n ศัตรู foe

saduak a สะดวก convenient

saduak a. สะดวก handy

sadud v.i. สะดุด stumble

sadung v.t. สะดุ้ง startle

sadung v.i. สะดุ้ง wince

sae n. แส้ whip

saek v.t. แทรก insert

saek v.t. แทรก interrupt

saeksaeng v.i. แทรกแซง interfere

saeksaeng v.i. แทรกแซง intervene

saeksaeng v.t. แทรกแซง penetrate

saeng n. แสง light

saengfaiwab n แสงไฟวาบ flash

saengja n แสงจ้า dazzle

saengrayibrayab n แสงระยิบระยับ glitter

saengrayibrayab n. แสงระยิบระยับ twinkle

saengsawang n แสงสว่าง shine

saengtam v.t แสร้งทำ feign

saengwab n. แสงวาบ sparkle

saengwaewwao n แสงแวววาว glow

sa-euk-sa-euan a สะอึกสะอื้น maudlin

sa-eun v.i. สะอื้น sob

sagad v. t. สกัด chisel

sagad v.t. สกัด intercept

sagayapab n. ศักยภาพ potency

sagodjit v.t. สะกดจิต hypnotize

sagodjit v.t. สะกดจิต mesmerize

sagodkam v.t. สะกดคำ spell

sagodroy v.t. สะกดรอย track

sagon a. สากล universal

sagoon-ngeun n สกุลเงิน currency

sahai n. สหาย comrade

sahapab n. สหภาพ union

sahapan a สหพันธ์ federal

sahapan n. สหพันธ์ league

sahapantarat n สหพันธรัฐ federation

sahasawat n. สหัสวรรษ millennium

sahaseuksa n. สหศึกษา co-education

sahed n. สาเหตุ cause

sai a. ซ้าย left

sai v.t. ใส่ put

sai n. ทราย sand

sai-aek v.t. ใส่แอก yoke

sai-an v.t. ใส่อาน saddle

saicable n. สายเคเบิ้ล cable

saidaipawdi v.t ใส่ได้พอดี fit

saidud n. ทรายดูด quicksand

saifai n. สายไฟ wire

saigleua v.t ใส่เกลือ salt

saigoonjaemeu v. t ใส่กุญแจมือ cuff

saigoonjaemeu v.t ใส่กุญแจมือ handcuff

saigoonjaemeu v.t. ใส่กุญแจมือ shackle

saigrapao v.t. ใส่กระเป๋า pocket

saijai a. ใส่ใจ attentive

saijud v. t ใส่จุด dot

saikamnamna v.t. ใส่คำนำหน้า prefix

saikeuangtet v.t. ใส่เครื่องเทศ spice

saiglon v. t ใส่กลอน bolt

saikok v.t. ใส่คอก pen

saikwam v.t. ใส่ความ impute

saikwam v.t. ใส่ความ vilify

saileuan *n.* ไส้เลื่อน hernia
sailookprakam *n.* สายลูกประคำ rosary
sainagak *v.t.* ใส่หน้ากาก mask
sainamhom *v.t.* ใส่น้ำหอม perfume
sainamtan *v.t.* ใส่น้ำตาล sugar
saipriktai *v.t.* ใส่พริกไทย pepper
saipui *v.t* ใส่ปุ๋ย fertilize
saipui *v.t.* ใส่ปุ๋ย manure
sairad *n.* สายรัด strap
sairadtungtao *n.* สายรัดถุงเท้า garter
sairai *v.* ใส่ร้าย asperse
sairai *v. t.* ใส่ร้าย calumniate
sairai *v. t.* ใส่ร้าย defame
sairai *v.t.* ใส่ร้าย malign
sairao *v.t.* ใส่ราว rail
saitagiang *n.* ไส้ตะเกียง wick
saitakeb *v.t* ใส่ตะเข็บ fringe
saitasan *a.* สายตาสั้น myopic
saiting *n.* ไส้ติ่ง appendix
saiting-akseb *n.* ไส้ติ่งอักเสบ appendicitis
saitualek *v.t.* ใส่ตัวเลข number
saitung *v. i.* ใส่ถุง bag
saiwad *n.* สายวัด tape
saiyang *n.* สายยาง hose
sajjaniyom *n.* สัจนิยม realism
saka *n* สาขา branch
sakdai *a.* ซักได้ washable
sakgara *v.t.* สักการะ worship
sakgayapab *n.* ศักยภาพ potential
sakgayapab *n.* ศักยภาพ pontentiality
saklai *v.i.* สักลาย tattoo
saklang *v.t.* ซักล้าง wash
sakparakhakpang *n* ซากปรักหักพัง debris
sakparakhakpang *n.* ซากปรักหักพัง wreckage
sakreuataek *n.* ซากเรือแตก wreck
sakrid *v.t.* ซักรีด launder
saksit *a.* ศักดิ์สิทธิ์ godly
saksit *a.* ศักดิ์สิทธิ์ holy
saksit *a.* ศักดิ์สิทธิ์ sacred
saksit *a.* ศักดิ์สิทธิ์ sacrosanct

saksob *n.* ซากศพ remains
saktam *v.t.* ซักถาม interrogate
sala *v.t.* สละ relinquish
sala *v.t.* สละ renounce
salabgandai *a.* สลับกันได้ alternate
salad *n.* สลัด salad
salaitua *v. t.* สลายตัว decompose
salak *v. t* สลัก engrave
salao *a.* สลัว sombre
salasit *v.t.* สละสิทธิ์ waive
sala-umnad *v.t,* สละอำนาจ abdicate
salesman *n.* เซลส์แมน salesman
saloop *a.* สรุป brief
saloop *v. t* สรุป conclude
salua *a* สลัว dim
sam *n.* สาม three
sam *a* สาม three
samachik *n.* สมาชิก member
samachikkongnigai *a.* สมาชิกของนิกาย sectarian
samachikmai *n.* สมาชิกใหม่ recruit
samachikpakripublican *n* สมาชิกพรรคริพับริกัน republican
samachikratasapa *n.* สมาชิกรัฐสภา parliamentarian
samachiksahabab *n.* สมาชิกสหภาพ unionist
samachiksapa *n.* สมาชิกสภา councillor
samad *a* สามารถ able
samad *v.* สามารถ can
samad *a.* สามารถ capable
samad *v. t* สามารถ enable
samadchamranidai *a.* สามารถชำระหนี้ได้ payable
samadhadai *v.t.* สามารถหาได้ afford
samaiboran *n.* สมัยโบราณ antiquity
samaini *adv* สมัยนี้ adays
samainiyom *n.* สมัยนิยม vogue
samak *v.t.* สมัคร apply
samak *v. t* สมัคร enrol
samakom *n.* สมาคม association
samakom *n.* สมาคม fraternity

samakom *n.* สมาคม guild
samakpennaksuksa *v.t.* สมัครเป็นนักศึกษา matriculate
samakpensamachik *v.t.* สมัครเป็นสมาชิก subscribe
samakpentahan *v. t* สมัครเป็นทหาร enlist
saman *a.* สามัญ common
saman *a.* สามัญ commonplace
samanchon *n.* สามัญชน commoner
samawreua *n.* สมอเรือ anchor
sameu *adv* เสมอ always
sameu *adv.* เสมอ usually
sameuan *a* เสมือน virtual
sameugan *a* เสมอกัน level
sami *n* สามี husband
samian *n* เสมียน clerk
samitipanrayamichu *n.* สามีที่ภรรยามีชู้ cuckold
samkan *a.* สำคัญ capital
samkan *a.* สำคัญ cardinal
samkan *a.* สำคัญ chief
samkan *a* สำคัญ considerable
samkan *adj.* สำคัญ constituent
samkan *a* สำคัญ critical
samkan *adj.* สำคัญ crucial
samkan *a* สำคัญ emphatic
samkan *a* สำคัญ essential
samkan *a.* สำคัญ important
samkan *a* สำคัญ prime
samkan *a* สำคัญ principal
samkan *a.* สำคัญ significant
samkan *a* สำคัญ staple
samkan *a.* สำคัญ vital
samkantisud *a* สำคัญที่สุด foremost
samkrang *adv.* สามครั้ง thrice
samlak *n.* ลำลัก hiccup
samlak-a-han *v. t.* สำลักอาหาร choke
samliam *n.* สามเหลี่ยม triangle
samnakchi *n* สำนักชี convent
samnakchi *n.* สำนักชี nunnery
samnak-ngan *n.* สำนักงาน bureau
samnak-ngan *n.* สำนักงาน office

samnaksong *n.* สำนักสงฆ์ abbey
samnaktabian *n.* สำนักทะเบียน registry
samnakwichagan *n* สำนักวิชาการ academy
samnao *n* สำเนา copy
samnao *n.* สำเนา replica
samneukpid *a.* สำนึกผิด repentant
samniang *n* สำเนียง accent
samnuan *n* สำนวน diction
samnuan *n.* สำนวน idiom
samnuan *n.* สำนวน locution
samnuankwam *n* สำนวนความ file
samong *n* สมอง brain
samongcha *a.* สมองช้า backward
samoonprai *n.* สมุนไพร herb
samoson *n* สโมสร club
sampad *v. t.* สัมผัส caress
sampad *v.t.* สัมผัส touch
sampangantangsaileuad *adj* สัมพันธ์กันทางสายเลือด cognate
sampara *n.* สัมภาระ luggage
sakparakhakpang *n.* ซากปรักหักพัง ruin
sampat *v.t.* สัมภาษณ์ interview
sampat *v.t.* สัมผัส pet
sampat *v.t.* สัมผัส sense
sampatan *n* สัมปทาน concession
samprasit *n.* สัมประสิทธิ์ coefficient
samredkwamkraiduaytau-eng *v.i.* สำเร็จความใคร่ด้วยตัวเอง masturbate
samred *a* สำเร็จ accomplished
samred *v.i.* สำเร็จ succeed
samrong *v.t.* สำรอง alternate
samruad *v.t* สำรวจ explore
samruad *v.t.* สำรวจ survey
samruadkwamhen *v. t.* สำรวจความเห็น canvass
samruadkwamrusuktua-eng *v.i.* สำรวจความรู้สึกตัวเอง introspect
samsak *a.* ซ้ำซาก monotonous
samsak *a.* ซ้ำซาก redundant
samsi *a.* สามสี tricolour
samsib *n.* สามสิบ thirty

samsib *a* สามสิบ thirty
samudlongtabian *n.* สมุดลงทะเบียน register
samudrainam *n* สมุดรายนาม directory
san *n.* ศาล court
san *n.* สาร message
san *n.* สาร missive
san *v.i.* สั่น quake
san *v.i.* สั่น quiver
san *n.* สัน ridge
san *a.* สั่น shaky
san *v.i.* สั่น shiver
san *a.* สั้น short
san *adv.* สั้น short
san *v.i.* สั่น tremble
san *n.* ศาล tribunal
san *v.i.* สั่น vibrate
sanabsanoon *v.t.* สนับสนุน advocate
sanabsanoon *v. t.* สนับสนุน endorse
sanabsanoon *v.t.* สนับสนุน second
sanabsanoon *v.t.* สนับสนุน sponsor
sanabsanoon *v.t.* สนับสนุน support
sanabsanoon *v.t* สนับสนุน uphold
sanae *n.* เสน่ห์ charm1
sanambinlek *n* สนามบินเล็ก aerodrome
sanamgila *n* สนามกีฬา arena
sanamgila *n.* สนามกีฬา lists
sanamrob *n* สนามรบ battle
sanamya *n.* สนามหญ้า lawn
sanamya *n.* สนามหญ้า turf
sa-ngobsook *a.* สงบสุข peaceful
sanchanton *n* ศาลชั้นต้น chancery
sanchat *n.* สัญชาติ nationality
sanchattayan *n.* สัญชาตญาณ instinct
sandwich *n.* แซนด์วิช sandwich
saneu *v.t.* เสนอ offer
saneu *v.t.* เสนอ present
saneu *v.t.* เสนอ project
saneu *v.t.* เสนอ propose
saneu *v.t.* เสนอ propound
saneucheu *v.t.* เสนอชื่อ nominate

saneurakasungkwa *v.t.* เสนอราคาสูงกว่า outbid
sang *v.t.* สั่ง adjure
sang *v. t* สร้าง build
sang *v. t* สั่ง command
sang *v. t* สร้าง create
sang *v. t.* สร้าง establish
sang *v.t.* สร้าง found
sang *v.t.* สั่ง instruct
sang *v.t* สั่ง order
sa-nga *a.* สง่า lordly
sa-nga-ngam *n* สง่างาม august
sa-nga-ngam *n* สง่างาม dignity
sa-nga-ngam *adj* สง่างาม elegant
sa-nga-ngam *a.* สง่างาม imposing
sangansia *n.* สารกันเสีย preservative
sanggasi *n.* สังกะสี zinc
sangged *v.t.* สังเกต notice
sanghan *v.t.* สังหาร assassinate
sanghanmu *v.t.* สังหารหมู่ massacre
sangharimmasab *n.* สังหาริมทรัพย์ movables
sangja *n.* แสงจ้า glare
sangket *v.t.* สังเกต observe
sangkom *n.* สังคม society
sangkomniyom *n* สังคมนิยม socialism
sangkomsat *n.* สังคมศาสตร์ sociology
sanglua *v.i.* สั่นกลัว shudder
sangmao *a.* สร่างเมา sober
sangnaewket *v.t* สร้างแนวเขต border
sangnawattagam *v.t.* สร้างนวัตกรรม innovate
sa-ngob *a.* สงบ pacific
sa-ngob *a.* สงบ sedative
sa-ngob *a.* สงบ serene
sa-ngob *a.* สงบ tranquil
sa-ngobning *a.* สงบนิ่ง placid
sa-ngobsook *a.* สงบสุข peaceable
sangpumkumgan *v.t.* สร้างภูมิคุ้มกัน immunize
sangrachab *a.* สั้นกระชับ laconic
sangrading *v.t.* สั่นกระดิ่ง ring

sangsalua *n* แสงสลัว twilight
sangsan *a.* สร้างสรรค์ inventive
sangson *adj.* สร้างสรรค์ creative
sangsonsinlatam *v.t.* สั่งสอนศีลธรรม moralize
sangtong *n* แสงทอง aurora
sanim *n.* สนิม rust
sankemi *n.* สารเคมี chemical
sankleuabfun *n* สารเคลือบฟัน enamel
sanlalaigleua *n.* สารละลายเกลือ salinity
sanlawleun *n.* สารหล่อลื่น lubricant
sanlodgrod *adj.* สารลดกรด antacid
sannitan *v.t.* สันนิษฐาน presume
sannitan *v.t.* สันนิษฐาน presuppose
sannitan *v.t.* สันนิษฐาน surmise
sannu *n* สารหนู arsenic
sanook *n.* สนุก joyful, joyous
sanooksanan *v. t* สนุกสนาน enjoy
sanooksanan *v.i.* สนุกสนาน revel
sanpawit *n.* สรรพาวุธ ordnance
sanpragob *n* สารประกอบ compound
sanprakobcarbon *n.* สารประกอบคาร์บอน carbide
sansadaengnaiwelaklangwan *n.* การแสดงในเวลากลางวัน matinee
sansangkraw *n* สารสังเคราะห์ synthetic
sansebtid *n.* สารเสพติด narcotic
sanseun *v.t.* สรรเสริญ laud
sanchattayan *n.* สัญชาตญาณ intuition
santanagan *n.* สันทนาการ leisure
santangton *n.* สารตั้งต้น precursor
santichaikreubneuamai *n.* สารที่ใช้เคลือบเนื้อไม้ primer
santipab *n.* สันติภาพ peace
santitamhairakaikeuang *n.* สารที่ทำให้ระคายเคือง irritant
sangtridsadi *v.i.* สร้างทฤษฎี theorize
san-udfun *n* สารอุดฟัน amalgam
sanya *n* สัญญา contract
sanya *n.* สัญญา treaty
sanyalak *n* สัญลักษณ์ cachet
sanyalak *n.* สัญลักษณ์ carat

sanyalak *n* สัญลักษณ์ emblem
sanyalak *n.* สัญลักษณ์ symbol
sanyalakniyom *n.* สัญลักษณ์นิยม symbolism
sanyan *n.* สัญญาณ signal
sanyanfainamtang *n* สัญญาณไฟนำทาง beacon
sanyanteuanpai *n* สัญญาณเตือน alarm
sao *a* เศร้า blue
sao *adj* เศร้า melancholy
sao *n.* เสา pillar
sao *n.* เสา pole
sao *a.* เศร้า sad
sao-a-gad *n.* เสาอากาศ aerial
sao-a-gad *n.* เสาอากาศ antennae
saochai *n.* สาวใช้ maid
saogradongreua *n.* เสากระโดงเรือ mast
saoseub *n.* สาวเสิร์ฟ waitress
saosod *n.* สาวโสด maiden
saosok *v.t.* เศร้าโศก aggrieve
saosok *adj.* เศร้าโศก alamort
saosok *a.* เศร้าโศก melancholic
saosok *v.i.* เศร้าโศก mope
saosok *v.i.* เศร้าโศก mourn
saosok *n.* เศร้าโศก mournful
sapa *n.* สภา council
sapab *n.* สภาพ state
sapabpengrod *n.* สภาพเป็นกรด acidity
sapabrokroongrang *n.* สภาพรกรุงรัง mess
sapabtipidgodmai *n.* สภาพที่ผิดกฎหมาย illegibility
sapacongress *n* สภาคองเกรส congress
sapabkleunmaikaokaimai-awk *n.* สภาพกลืนไม่เข้าคายไม่ออก predicament
sapan *n* สะพาน bridge
sapanam *n.* สรรพนาม pronoun
sapanitibanyat *n.* สภานิติบัญญัติ legislature
sapansongnam *n* สะพานส่งน้ำ aqueduct
sapawalambak *n* สภาวะลำบาก dilemma
sapok *n* สะโพก buttock

sapok *n* สะโพก hip
sapom *v.t.* สระผม shampoo
sappa-ngok *v. i* สัปหงก doze
saprao *a.* สะเพร่า slipshod
saprao *v.i* สะเพร่า blunder
saranugrom *n.* สารานุกรม encyclopaedia
sarapab *v. t.* สารภาพ confess
sarasamkan *n.* สาระสำคัญ synopsis
saroob *v.t.* สรุป summarize
sasada *n.* ศาสดา prophet
sasan *n.* สสาร substance
sasana *n.* ศาสนา religion
sasanakrit *n.* ศาสนาคริสต์ Christianity
sasom *v.t.* สะสม accumulate
sasom *v. t* สะสม collect
sasomwai *v.t.* สะสมไว้ stock
sat *n.* สัตว์ animal
sat *n* สัตว์ creature
sataban *n.* สถาบัน institution
sataem *n.* สแตมป์ stamp
satan *n.* ซาตาน satan
satana *n.* สถานะ status
satanagan *n.* สถานการณ์ situation
satanaganchukcheuan *n*
สถานการณ์ฉุกเฉิน emergency
satani *n.* สถานี station
sataniplaitang *n* สถานีปลายทาง terminal
satanliangdekgampra *n.*
สถานเลี้ยงเด็กกำพร้า orphanage
satanpayaban *n.* สถานพยาบาล
sanatorium
satanrabliangdek *n.* สถานรับเลี้ยงเด็ก
nursery
satanti *n.* สถานที่ locus
satanti *n.* สถานที่ place
satanti *n.* สถานที่ venue
satantigeudhed *n.* สถานที่เกิดเหตุ locale
satantiprabprungkwampraprud *n.*
สถานปรับปรุงความประพฤติ
reformatory
satantitang *n.* สถานที่ตั้ง site
satantitipaiboy *n* สถานที่ที่ไปบ่อย haunt

satantut *n* สถานทูต embassy
satapanik *n.* สถาปนิก architect
satarana *a* สาธารณะ communal
satarana *a.* สาธารณะ public
sataranarat *n.* สาธารณรัฐ republic
sataranupapok *n.* สาธารณูปโภค utility
satawat *n.* ศตวรรษ century
sateunnamsateunbok *adj*
สะเทินน้ำสะเทินบก amphibious
satisampachanya *n* สติสัมปชัญญะ
conscience
satitisat *n.* สถิติศาสตร์ statistics
satjampuakjingjo *n.* สัตว์จำพวกจิงโจ้
marsupial
satkanbambatbaeb-ongruam *n.*
ศาสตร์การบำบัดแบบองค์รวม
homeopathy
satkiaw-eung *n.* สัตว์เคี้ยวเอื้อง ruminant
satleuayklan *n.* สัตว์เลื้อยคลาน reptile
satliang *n.* สัตว์เลี้ยง pet
satlianglookduaynom *n.*
สัตว์เลี้ยงลูกด้วยนม mammal
saton *v. t* สะท้อน echo
saton *v.i.* สะท้อนกลับ rebound
satonglab *v.t.* สะท้อนกลับ reflect
satpa *n* สัตว์ป่า brute
satpik *n.* สัตว์ปีก fowl
satpik *n.* สัตว์ปีก poultry
satrai *n* สัตว์ร้าย beast
satri *n* สตรี female
satsitao *n.* สัตว์สี่เท้า quadruped
satsongtao *n* สัตว์สองเท้า biped
sattasat *n.* สัทศาสตร์ phonetics
sattawawitaya *n.* สัตววิทยา zoology
sattirobguan *n.* สัตว์ที่รบกวน pest
sattru *n.* ศัตรู adversary
saw *n* ซอ fiddle
sawan *n.* สว่าน auger
sawan *n.* สวรรค์ heaven
sawan *n.* สวรรค์ paradise
sawan *n.* สว่าน wimble
sawang *adv.* สว่าง aglow

sawang *a* สว่าง bright

sawang *a* สว่าง light

sawang *a.* สว่าง lucent

sawang *a.* สว่าง lucid

sawangsawai *a.* สว่างไสว radiant

sawatdigan *n.* สวัสดิการ welfare

sawdrusawdhen *a.* สอดรู้สอดเห็น nosey

sawdrusawdhen *a.* สอดรู้สอดเห็น nosy

saweangha *v.t.* แสวงหา woo

somrob *v.i.* ซ้อมรบ manoeuvre

sawokkongprakris *n.* สาวกของพระคริสต์ apostle

say *v.t.* เซ tip

say *v.i.* เซ stagger

sedgaew *n.* เศษแก้ว cullet

sedkaya *n.* เศษขยะ junk

sedlek *n* เศษเหล็ก faggot

sedleklek *n.* เศษเล็กๆ scrap

sedleklek *n.* เศษเล็กๆ splinter

sedleksednoy *n* เศษเล็กเศษน้อย crumb

sedsuan *n.* เศษส่วน fraction

sedti *n.* เศรษฐี millionaire

seed *v. t. & i* ซีด blanch

sensoonsut *n* เส้นศูนย์สูตร equator

sell *n.* เซล cell

semha *n.* เสมหะ sputum

senbonpaenti-a-gad *n.* เส้นบนแผนที่อากาศ isobar

sendai *n.* เส้นด้าย yarn

sengaen *n.* เส้นแกน axis

sedhin *n.* เศษหิน rubble

senkob *n* เส้นขอบ contour

senkong *n* เส้นโค้ง curve

senleuaddam *n.* เส้นเลือดดำ vein

senpasoonglang *n* เส้นผ่าศูนย์กลาง diameter

senprasat *n.* เส้นประสาท nerve

senrobwong *n.* เส้นรอบวง circumference

senroong *n.* เส้นรุ้ง latitude

sensampad *n.* เส้นสัมผัส tangent

sentang *n.* เส้นทาง route

sentangchak *n.* เส้นตั้งฉาก perpendicular

senwaeng *n.* เส้นแวง longitude

senyai *n* เส้นใย fibre

seriniyom *n.* เสรีนิยม liberalism

sesaeng *a.* เสแสร้ง hypocritical

sesaeng *v.t.* เสแสร้ง pretend

setasad *n.* เศรษฐศาสตร์ economics

seu *v. t.* ซื้อ buy

seu *v.t.* ซื้อ purchase

seua *n.* เสือ leopard

seua *n.* เสือ tiger

seuachannaisatri *n* เสื้อชั้นในสตรี chemise

seuacoat *n* เสื้อโค้ท coat

seuagao *n.* เสื้อกราวน์ gown

seuagraw *n.* เสื้อเกราะ armour

seuaklum *n.* เสื้อคลุม cloak

seuaklum *n* เสื้อคลุม mantle

seuaklum *n.* เสื้อคลุม toga

seuaklum *n.* เสื้อคลุม wardrobe

seuamsom *a* เสื่อมโทรม decadent

seuanok *n.* เสื้อนอก frock

seuapa *n.* เสื้อผ้า apparel

seuapa *n* เสื้อผ้า cloth

seuapa *n.* เสื้อผ้า clothes

seuapa *n.* เสื้อผ้า costume

seuapa *n.* เสื้อผ้า garment

seuapa *n.* เสื้อผ้า shirt

seuapuying *n.* เสือผู้หญิง tomcat

seuaradroob *n* เสื้อรัดรูป bodice

seuasatri *n* เสื้อสตรี blouse

seuatuamia *n.* เสือตัวเมีย tigress

seub *v.i.* สืบ spy

seubha *v. t* สืบหา detect

seubpan *v.t.* สืบพันธุ์ reproduce

seubsuan *v.t.* สืบสวน probe

seubtaw *v.t.* สืบต่อ inherit

seubtawmajakbanpaburud *a.* สืบต่อมาจากบรรพบุรุษ ancestral

seubtod *v. i.* สืบทอด descend

seuadam *n.* เสือดำ panther

seuaglam *n.* เสื้อกล้าม jerkin

seuaglam *n.* เสื้อกล้าม vest

seuglang *n* สื่อกลาง medium

seukaidai *a.* ซื้อขายได้ marketable

seuglang *n.* สื่อกลาง intermediary

seuaklum *n.* เสื้อคลุม overcoat

seuaklumkongpra *n.* เสื้อคลุมของพระ vestment

seukong *v.i.* ซื้อของ shop

seuakotsan *n.* เสื้อโค้ทสั้น waistcoat

seum *a.* เสริม auxiliary

seum *v.t.* เสริม reinforce

seum *a.* เสริม subsidiary

seum *v.t.* เสริม supplement

seumgamlang *v. t.* เสริมกำลัง enforce

seuamsiatangped *a.* เสื่อมเสียทางเพศ lascivious

seungbaengpuak *a.* ซึ่งแบ่งพวก partisan

seungchamranidai *a.* ซึ่งชำระหนี้ได้ solvent

seunggeudsam *a.* ซึ่งเกิดซ้ำ recurrent

seungjeuajang *a* ซึ่งเจือจาง dilute

seunglomlang *a.* ซึ่งล้มล้าง subversive

seungmaihenduay *a.* ซึ่งไม่เห็นด้วย disagreeable

seungmikwamruseuk *a.* ซึ่งมีความรู้สึก sentient

seungmipid *a.* ซึ่งมีพิษ venomous

seungmi-um-nad *a.* ซึ่งมีอำนาจ authoritative

seungmodwang *a* ซึ่งหมดหวัง desperate

seungpenjaokong *a.* ซึ่งเป็นเจ้าของ proprietary

seungpen-ngeuankai *a* ซึ่งเป็นเงื่อนไข conditional

seungpladlong *a* ซึ่งพลัดหลง stray

seungpragobgan *a* ซึ่งประกอบกัน compound

seungtaidai *a.* ซึ่งตายได้ perishable

seungtamhaisomboon *a* ซึ่งทำให้สมบูรณ์ complementary

singtimaimikraitiabdai *n.* สิ่งที่ไม่มีใครเทียบได้ nonpareil

seungyinyom *adj.* ซึ่งยินยอม compliant

seungyuayuan *a* ซึ่งยั่วยวน seductive

seungyunaikansungsud *a.* ซึ่งอยู่ในขั้นสูงสุด superlative

seungyutainam *a* ซึ่งอยู่ใต้น้ำ submarine

seusan *v. t* สื่อสาร communicate

seusan *v. t.* สื่อสาร convey

seusat *a.* ซื่อสัตย์ honest

seusat *a.* ซื่อสัตย์ loyal

seusat *a.* ซื่อสัตย์ stalwart

seusat *a.* ซื่อสัตย์ staunch

seusat *a.* ซื่อสัตย์ truthful

seuasatri *n.* เสื้อสตรี smock

seutrong *a.* ซื่อตรง incorruptible

seuayeud *n.* เสื้อยืด jersey

sew *n.* สิว pimple

si *n* สี colour

si *n.* สี่ four

si *n.* สี paint

siajai *v. t* เสียใจ bewail

siajai *v.t.* เสียใจ grieve

siajai *v.i.* เสียใจ lament

siajai *v.i.* เสียใจ regret

siajai *a.* เสียใจ rueful

siajai *v.i.* เสียใจ sorrow

siajai *a.* เสียใจ sorry

siang *n.* เสียง noise

siang *v.t.* เสี่ยง risk

siang *n* เสียง sound

siang *n.* เสียง voice

siangbao *n.* เสียงเบา undertone

siangbon *n* เสียงบ่น bleat

siangdang *n.* เสียงดัง bam

siangdang *n.* เสียงดัง clink

siangdang *n.* เสียงดัง creak

siangdang *a.* เสียงดัง noisy

siangdang *n* เสียงดัง pop

siangdang *n.* เสียงดัง rumble

siangdangchae *n.* เสียงดังแฉ sizzle

siangdanggraheum *n.* เสียงดังกระหึ่ม whir

siangdangtub *n.* เสียงดังตุบ thud

siang-eukgateuk *v. i.* เสียงอึกทึก clamour

siang-eukgateuk *n* เสียงอึกทึก din
siang-eukkateuk *n.* เสียงอึกทึก hubbub
siangfarong *n.* เสียงฟ้าร้อง thunder
sianggong *n.* เสียงก้อง resonance
sianggring *n.* เสียงกริ่ง jingle
sianghaeb *a.* เสียงแหบ throaty
sianghaeb *a.* เสียงแหบ hoarse
sianghao *n.* เสียงเห่า bark
siangheung *n.* เสียงหึ่ง buzz
siangho *n.* เสียงโห่ hoot
sianghuaraw *n.* เสียงหัวเราะ laugh
sianghumpleng *n* เสียงฮัมเพลง hum
siangkamram *n* เสียงคำราม growl
siangkamram *n.* เสียงคำราม grunt
siangkamram *n.* เสียงคำราม bellows
siangkrang *n* เสียงคราง groan
siangku *n* เสียงขู่ hiss
siangku *n.* เสียงขู่ snarl
sianglan-iad-iad *n* เสียงลั่นเอี๊ยดๆ squeak
siangmaewrong *n.* เสียงแมวร้อง mew
siangnokrong *n* เสียงนกร้อง chirp
siangpaedku *n.* เสียงแปดคู่ octave
siangpai *v.t.* เสี่ยงภัย venture
siangpedrong *n* เสียงเป็ดร้อง quack
siangpewpak *n* เสียงผิวปาก whistle
siangpuempum *v.t.* เสียงพึมพำ murmur
siangrabeud *n.* เสียงระเบิด bang
siangrongkongga *n.* เสียงร้องของกา caw
siangrongkongma *n.* เสียงร้องของม้า
  neigh
siangrongkongnokkao *n*
  เสียงร้องของนกเขา coo
siangrua *n* เสียงรัว rattle
siangsara *n.* เสียงสระ vowel
siangsampadnaibodgawi *n.*
  เสียงสัมผัสในบทกวี rhyme
siangsan *n.* เสียงสั่น quiver
siangsanrua *n* เสียงสั่นรัว warble
siang-saton *n* เสียงสะท้อน echo
siangsuanyai *n.* เสียงส่วนใหญ่ majority
siangsudjamuk *n* เสียงสุดจมูก sniff
siangtoktod *n.* สิ่งตกทอด relic

siangtrae *n* เสียงแตร bray
siangwaedlom *n.* สิ่งแวดล้อม
  surroundings
siangwoywai *n.* เสียงโวยวาย row
siasara *v.t.* เสียสละ sacrifice
sib *n., a* สิบ ten
sib-ed *n* สิบเอ็ด eleven
sibgao *n.* สิบเก้า nineteen
sibha *n* สิบห้า fifteen
sibjed *n., a* สิบเจ็ด seventeen
sibpaed *a* สิบแปด eighteen
sibsam *n.* สิบสาม thirteen
sibsam *a* สิบสาม thirteen
sibsi *n.* สิบสี่ fourteen
sibsok *n., a.* สิบหก sixteen
sibsong *n.* สิบสอง twelve
sibsong *n* สิบสอง twelve
sichompu *n.* สีชมพู pink
sichompu *a* สีชมพู pink
sid *n* ศิษย์ disciple
sid *v.i.* ซีด pale
sid *a.* ซีด wan
sidaeng *a.* สีแดง red
sidaeng *n.* สีแดง red
sidaengkem *n* สีแดงเข้ม crimson
sidaengsod *n.* สีแดงสด vermillion
sidaengsod *a.* สีแดงสด vermillion
sidgaoying *n* ศิษย์เก่าหญิง alumna
sidiaw *a.* สีเดียว monochromatic
siengkui-eu-eung *n* เสียงคุยอื้ออึง babel
siew *n* สิว acne
siew *n* สิ่ว chisel
sifa *n* สีฟ้า blue
sijangjang *n.* สีจางๆ tinge
sikao *v.t.* สีข้าว mill
sikao *a.* สีขาว white
sikao *n* สีขาว white
sikiaw *n* สีเขียว green
sikram *n.* สีคราม indigo
sigrong *n.* ซี่กรอง baleen
sikrong *n.* ซี่โครง rib
silapa *n.* ศิลปะ art

silapaclassic *n* ศิลปะคลาสสิก classic

silapagankadlaimeu *n*
ศิลปะการคัดลายมือ calligraphy

silapaganwadpabkon *n.*
ศิลปะการวาดภาพคน portraiture

silapin *n.* ศิลปิน artist

silaw *n* ซี่ล้อ cog

silaw *n.* ซี่ล้อ rung

silawrod *n.* ซี่ล้อรถ spoke

sileuang *a.* สีเหลือง yellow

sileuang *n* สีเหลือง yellow

sileuang-omsom *a* สีเหลืองอมส้ม saffron

siliam *n.* สี่เหลี่ยม square

siliampeunpa *n.* สี่เหลี่ยมผืนผ้า rectangle

siliamroobkanan *n.* สี่เหลี่ยมรูปขนาน
parallelogram

simuang *adj./n.* สีม่วง purple

simuang *n.* สีม่วง violet

sina *n.* สีหน้า countenance

sina *n.* สีหน้า physiognomy

sinamtan *a* สีน้ำตาล brown

sinamtan *n* สีน้ำตาล brown

sinamtandeang *n.* สีน้ำตาลแดง maroon

sinamtandeang *a* สีน้ำตาลแดง maroon

sinamtan-om-leuang *n* สีน้ำตาลอมเหลือง
buff

sinbon *n* สินบน bribe

sincheung *adv.* สิ้นเชิง stark

singchodcheuy *n* สิ่งชดเชย offset

singdaidai *n.* สิ่งใดๆ aught

sing-eun *a* สิ่งอื่น another

si-ngeun *a* สีเงิน silver

singfumfeuay *n.* สิ่งฟุ่มเฟือย superfluity

singgidkwang *n* สิ่งกีดขวาง block

singgidkwang *n.* สิ่งกีดขวาง hitch

singgidkwang *n.* สิ่งกีดขวาง impediment

singgratoon *n.* สิ่งกระตุ้น goad

singgratoon *n.* สิ่งกระตุ้น spur

singgratoon *n.* สิ่งกระตุ้น stimulant

singhakom *n.* สิงหาคม August

singjampen *n.* สิ่งจำเป็น must

singjampen *n* สิ่งจำเป็น requiste

singjungjai *n.* สิ่งจูงใจ incentive

singkong *n.* สิ่งของ stuff

singkong *n.* สิ่งของ thing

singlaw *n.* สิ่งล่อ lure

singleknoy *n.* สิ่งเล็กน้อย little

singleknoy *n.* สิ่งเล็กน้อย slight

singmahadsajan *n.* สิ่งมหัศจรรย์ miracle

singmahatsajan *n.* สิ่งมหัศจรรย์ marvel

singmichiwit *n* สิ่งมีชีวิต being

singmichiwit *n.* สิ่งมีชีวิต organism

singmichiwit *n.* สิ่งมีชีวิต wight

singnamchok *n.* สิ่งนำโชค mascot

singnan *dem. pron.* สิ่งนั้น that

singpatigoon *n.* สิ่งปฏิกูล sewage

singpeumteum *n* สิ่งเพิ่มเติม
accompaniment

singpidpagati *n.* สิ่งผิดปกติ paradox

singponggan *n.* สิ่งป้องกัน safeguard

singpradagwaewwow *n.*
สิ่งประดับแวววาว tinsel

singsaksit *n.* สิ่งศักดิ์สิทธิ์ sanctity

singsudtai *n* สิ่งสุดท้าย last

singtaw *n* สิ่งทอ textile

singti *pron.* สิ่งที่ which

singtichaitamkruengmai *n.*
สิ่งที่ใช้ทำเครื่องหมาย marker

singtigeudjakganpasom *n*
สิ่งที่เกิดจากการผสม hybrid

singtigeudkeun *n.* สิ่งที่เกิดขึ้น occurrence

singtigeudkeunnaitanti *n.*
สิ่งที่เกิดในทันที sudden

singtigindai *n.* สิ่งที่กินได้ eatable

singtigukeun *n* สิ่งที่กุขึ้น figment

singtihaisaengsawang *n.* สิ่งที่ให้แสงสว่าง
luminary

singtikleuanwaidai *n.* สิ่งที่เคลื่อนไหวได้
mover

singtileuayu *n.* สิ่งที่เหลืออยู่ residue

singtimaisamkan *n.* สิ่งที่ไม่สำคัญ
nonentity

singtimakgeunpai *n.* สิ่งที่มากเกินไป
surfeit

singtimeuangan *n.* สิ่งที่เหมือนกัน ditto

singtipen-antarai *n.* สิ่งที่เป็นอันตราย hazard

singtipenkongkaotanglai *pron.* สิ่งที่เป็นของเขาทั้งหลาย theirs

singtipennamatam *n.* สิ่งที่เป็นนามธรรม abstraction

singtipenprayod *n* สิ่งที่เป็นประโยชน์ boon

singtipim *n* สิ่งตีพิมพ์ bulletin

singtiprajaopratanhai *n.* สิ่งที่พระเจ้าประทานให้ godsend

singtisoongsong *n* สิ่งที่สูงส่ง sublime

singtitawneuanggan *n.* สิ่งที่ต่อเนื่องกัน serial

singtitongmigon *n* สิ่งที่ต้องมีก่อน prerequisite

singtitronggankam *n.* สิ่งที่ตรงกันข้าม antithesis

singtiyaetisud *n.* สิ่งที่แย่ที่สุด worst

singto *n* สิงโต lion

singtongham *n.* สิ่งต้องห้าม taboo

singtotalay *n.* สิงโตทะเล walrus

singtotuamia *n.* สิงโตตัวเมีย lioness

singtrongkamgan *n.* สิ่งตรงข้ามกัน antipodes

sing-umnuaykwamsaduak *n* สิ่งอำนวยความสะดวก facility

singwaedlom *n.* สิ่งแวดล้อม environment

singwaedlom *n.* สิ่งแวดล้อม milieu

singwaedrom *n* สิ่งแวดล้อม circumstance

sinka *n.* สินค้า cargo

sinka *n.* สินค้า commodity

sinka *n.* สินค้า merchandise

sinkatikonsong *n.* สินค้าที่ขนส่ง freight

sinsod *n* สินสอด dowry

sinsud *v. t* สิ้นสุด end

sinsud *v.t.* สิ้นสุด terminate

sinsudlongdai *a.* สิ้นสุดลงได้ terminable

sintichob *n.* สิ่งที่ชอบ like

sinwang *v. i* สิ้นหวัง despair

si-on *n.* สีอ่อน tint

sipew *n* สีผิว complexion

siren *n.* ไซเรน siren

sisaw *v.i* สีซอ fiddle

sisib *n.* สี่สิบ forty

sisom *a* สีส้ม orange

sitaen *n., a.* สีแทน tan

sitao *a.* สี่เท่า quadruple

sitibat *n* สิทธิบัตร patent

sitipiset *n.* สิทธิพิเศษ privilege

sitong *a.* สีทอง golden

sittinaiganleuaktang *n.* สิทธิในการเลือกตั้ง suffrage

siyaek *n.* สี่แยก intersection

siyom *n* สีย้อม dye

slogan *n.* สโลแกน slogan

slum *n.* สลัม slum

so *n* โซ่ chain

sob *n* ศพ corpse

sob *v.i.* ซบ nestle

sobsao *v.i.* ซบเซา stagnate

sobsuan *v.t.* สอบสวน inquire

sobsuan *v.t.* สอบสวน investigate

sod *a.* สด fresh

sod *a.* โสด single

sodcheun *a.* สดชื่น lively

sodklonggan *a* สอดคล้องกัน coherent

sodklonggan *a* สอดคล้องกัน consistent

sodmakeuated *n.* ซอสมะเขือเทศ ketchup

sodnam *v.i* สอดแนม scout

sodrusodhen *v.i.* สอดรู้สอดเห็น pry

sodsaek *v.t.* สอดแทรก insinuate

sofa *n.* โซฟา sofa

soganatgam *n.* โศกนาฏกรรม tragedy

sokgaprok *a.* สกปรก squalid

sokgaprok *a.* สกปรก foul

soikaw *n* สร้อยคอ bracelet

soikaw *n.* สร้อยคอ necklace

soikaw *n.* สร้อยคอ necklet

sok *n* ศอก elbow

sokgaprok *a* สกปรก dirty

sokgaprok *a* สกปรก filthy

som *n.* ส้ม orange

som *v.t.* ซ้อม rehearse
som *v.t.* ซ่อม repair
sombat *n.* สมบัติ treasure
sombatsuantua *n.* สมบัติส่วนตัว belongings
somboon *adv.* สมบูรณ์ full
somboon *a.* สมบูรณ์ perfect
somboon *a.* สมบูรณ์ replete
somboon *a.* สมบูรณ์ sound
somdai *a.* ซ่อมได้ raparable
somhedsompon *a.* สมเหตุสมผล justifiable
somkuandairab *v. t.* สมควรได้รับ deserve
somkuanyokyong *a.* สมควรยกย่อง laudable
sommatgan *a.* สมมาตรกัน symmetrical
sommud *v.t.* สมมุติ suppose
sommutitan *n.* สมมติฐาน assumption
somruruamkid *v. i.* สมรู้ร่วมคิด conspire
somsaem *v.t.* ซ่อมแซม mend
somwang *v.t.* สมหวัง fulfil
son *v.t* ซ่อน hide
son *a.* ซน naughty
son *v.t.* สอน teach
song *pref* สอง bi
song *n* ช่อง brothel
song *v. t* ส่ง deliver
song *n* ซอง envelope
song *v.t* ส่ง hand
song *v.t.* ส่ง send
song *n.* สอง two
song *a.* สอง two
song-awk *v. t.* ส่งออก export
songglab *v.t.* ส่งกลับ remand
songglabprated *v.t.* ส่งกลับประเทศ repatriate
songglinmen *v.i.* ส่งกลิ่นเหม็น stink
songgrajok *v.t.* ส่องกระจก mirror
songjodmai *v.t.* ส่งจดหมาย mail
songkamfak *v.t* ส่งข้ามฟาก ferry
songglom *n.* ทรงกลม round
songkong *v.t.* ส่งของ consign

songkram *n.* สงคราม war
songkramsasana *n* สงครามศาสนา crusade
songkrang *adv.* สองครั้ง twice
songpan *v.t.* ส่งผ่าน transmit
songpantaw *v.i* ส่งผ่านท่อ pipe
songpasa *a* สองภาษา bilingual
songsabda *n.* สองสัปดาห์ fort-night
songsaeng *v.i.* ส่องแสง shine
songsaengrayib *v.i.* ส่องแสงระยิบ twinkle
songsai *v. i* สงสัย doubt
songsai *v.t.* สงสัย suspect
songsan *v.t.* สงสาร pity
songsanyanpansaicable *v. t.* ส่งสัญญาณผ่านสายเคเบิ้ล cable
songsanyanriak *v.t.* ส่งสัญญาณเรียก beckon
songsawang *v.t.* ส่องสว่าง alluminate
songsawang *v.t.* ส่องสว่าง illuminate
songseum *v. t* ส่งเสริม boost
songseum *v.t* ส่งเสริม further
songseum *v.t.* ส่งเสริม promote
songsiangchae *v.i.* ส่งเสียงแฉ sizzle
songsiangdang *v. t* ส่งเสียงดัง blare
songsiangdang *v.i.* ส่งเสียงดัง rumble
songsianggrunggring *v.i.* ส่งเสียงกรุ๋งกริ๋ง jingle
songsiangrua *v.i.* ส่งเสียงรัว rattle
songtao *a* สองเท่า double
songtao *a.* สองเท่า twofold
songtaw *v.t* ส่งต่อ forward
songtua *v.t.* ทรงตัว poise
sonjai *v.t* สนใจ focus
sonjai *a.* สนใจ mindful
sontana *v. i* สนทนา confer
sontana *v.t.* สนทนา converse
sontao *n.* สันเท้า heel
sontaya *n* สนธยา dusk
soob *v.t.* สูบ pump
sookapab *n.* สุขภาพ health
sookapabdi *a.* สุขภาพดี healthy
sooksan *a* สุขสันต์ merry

soomnaen *adv* สุมแน่น aheap
soompratukong *n.* ซุ้มประตูโค้ง arch
soon *n.* ศูนย์ cipher, cipher
soon *n.* ศูนย์ nought
soon *n.* ศูนย์ zero
soonganka *n.* ศูนย์การค้า mart
soongkeunpai *adv.* สูงขึ้นไป aloft
soonglang *n* ศูนย์กลาง center
soonglang *n* ศูนย์กลาง centre
soongsud *a.* สูงสุด maximum
soongwai *a* สูงวัย elderly
soonpan *a* สูญพันธุ์ extinct
soonsia *v.t.* สูญเสีย lose
soonsia *v. t.* สูญเสีย bereave
soonsong *a.* สูงส่ง sublime
soontariyasad *n.pl.* สุนทรียศาสตร์
aesthetics
soonyagad *n.* สูญญากาศ vacuum
sopeni *n.* โสเภณี courtesan
sopeni *n.* โสเภณี prostitute
sopeni *n.* โสเภณี slattern
sopeni *n.* โสเภณี slut
sopeni *n.* โสเภณี strumpet
sopeni *n.* โสเภณี wench
sopeni *n.* โสเภณี whore
sotruan *n* โซ่ตรวน fetter
soup *n* ซุป broth
soup *n.* ซุป soup
spray *n.* สเปรย์ spray
spring *n* สปริง spring
stadium *n.* สเตเดียม stadium
stew *n.* สตูว์ stew
sticker *n.* สติ๊กเกอร์ sticker
strawberry *n.* สตรอเบอรี่ strawberry
studio *n.* สตูดิโอ studio
style *n.* สไตล์ style
suad *v.i.* สวด pray
seuaklum *n.* เสื้อคลุม robe
seuakonmink *n.* เสื้อขนมิงค์ mink
suammonggut *v. t* สวมมงกุฎ crown
suannaisud *a.* ส่วนในสุด innermost
suamrongtao *v.t.* สวมรองเท้า shoe

suamsai *v.t.* สวมใส่ wear
suamseuapa *v. t* สวมเสื้อผ้า clothe
suamseua *v.t.* สวมเสื้อ vest
suamseuaklum *v.t.* สวมเสื้อคลุม robe
suamtagrawkrobpaksunak *v.t*
สวมตะกร้อครอบปากสุนัข muzzle
suan *n.* สวน garden
suan *n.* ส่วน part
suan *n.* ส่วน plantation
suan *n.* ส่วน sector
suangeun *n.* ส่วนเกิน surplus
suankong *n.* ส่วนโค้ง arc
suanlod *n.* ส่วนลด rabate
suannai *n.* ส่วนใน inside
suanpanuak *n.* ส่วนผนวก appendage
suanpasom *n.* ส่วนผสม ingredient
suanponlamai *n.* ส่วนผลไม้ orchard
suansamkan *n* ส่วนสำคัญ main
suansat *n.* ส่วนสัตว์ zoo
suansatarana *n.* ส่วนสาธารณะ park
suanse *v.i.* ซวนเซ lurch
suanseum *n* ส่วนเสริม appurtenance
suanseum *n.* ส่วนเสริม supplement
suantao *a.* ส่วนตัว individual
suantileuayu *n.* ส่วนที่เหลืออยู่ remainder
suantina *n.* ส่วนที่หนา thick
suantitabgan *n* ส่วนที่ทับกัน overlap
suantitaek-awk *n.* ส่วนที่แตกออก
fragment
suantitooktad-awk *n.* ส่วนที่ถูกตัดออก
lop
suantong *a.* ส่วนท้อง abdominal
suantongtin *a.* ส่วนท้องถิ่น municipal
suantua *a.* ส่วนตัว personal
suantua *a.* ส่วนตัว private
suantua *a.* ส่วนตัว subjective
suanyai *adv.* ส่วนใหญ่ mainly
suanyai *a.* ส่วนใหญ่ major
suanyai *n* ส่วนใหญ่ most
seuapapidkanad *n.* เสื้อผ้าผิดขนาด misfit
suay *a* สวย beautiful
suay *a.* สวย gorgeous

suay *a.* สวย picturesque
suay-ngam *a.* สวยงาม aesthetic
soobpom *a.* ซูบผอม haggard
subsintihamadai *n* ทรัพย์สินที่หามาได้
    acquest
sud *v.i.* ทรุด relapse
sud *v.i.* สูด sniff
sudglin *v.t* สูดกลิ่น nose
sudseung *a.* สุดซึ้ง inmost
sudtai *a* สุดท้าย conclusive
sudtai *a* สุดท้าย final
sudtai *a.* สุดท้าย last1
sudtaini *adv.* สุดท้ายนี้ lastly
sudtua *v.i.* ทรุดตัว slump
sook *a* สุก ripe
sukkalaksana *n.* สุขลักษณะ hygiene
suksawang *a.* สุกสว่าง resplendent
sukum *a.* สุขุม judicious
sumsam *v. t* ซุ่มซ่าม bungle
sumsam *a* ซุ่มซ่าม clumsy
sumsam *v.i.* ซุ่มซ่าม fumble
sumtuayang *v.t.* สุ่มตัวอย่าง poll
sumtuayang *a.* สุ่มตัวอย่าง random
sunak *n* สุนัข dog
sunak *n.* สุนัข greyhound
sunaklaneua *n.* สุนัขล่าเนื้อ hound
sunakpanneung *n* สุนัขพันธุ์หนึ่ง bulldog
sunakpanneung *n.* สุนัขพันธุ์หนึ่ง spaniel
sunakpanneung *n.* สุนัขพันธุ์หนึ่ง terrier
sunaktuamia *n* สุนัขตัวเมีย bitch
soong *a.* สูง high
soong *a.* สูง tall
soongsud *a.* สูงสุด ultimate
supab *a.* สุภาพ affable
supab *a.* สุภาพ courteous
supab *a.* สุภาพ mannerly
supab *a.* สุภาพ polite
supabburut *n.* สุภาพบุรุษ gentleman
supasit *n* สุภาษิต dictum
surao *n.* สุเหร่า mosque
suriyubparaka *n* สุริยุปราคา eclipse
surob *v. i.* สู้รบ battle

susan *n.* สุสาน cemetery
susan *n.* สุสาน mausoleum
susan *n.* สุสาน necropolis
susan *n.* สุสาน sepulchre
sut *n* สูตร formula
sut *n.* สูตร recipe
sutti *a* สุทธิ net
sweater *n.* สเวตเตอร์ sweater
switch *n.* สวิตช์ switch

T

ta *v. i.* ท้า dare
ta *n* ตา eye
tab *n.* ตับ liver
tabai *n* ตะไบ file
tabai *v.t* ตะไบ file
tabgan *v.t.* ทับกัน overlap
tablang *n.* ทับหลัง lintel
tabod *n* ตาบอด amauriosis
tabod *a* ตาบอด blind
tabongped *n.* ตะบองเพชร cactus
tabpi *n.* ทัพพี ladle
tabtim *n.* ทับทิม ruby
tad *v. t* ตัด cut
tad *v.t.* ตัด lop
tad *n.* ทาส serf
tad *v.t.* ตัด shear
tad *n.* ทาส slave
tad *n.* ทาส thrall
tad *n.* ถาด tray
tad-awk *v.t.* ตัดออก prune
tadeun *n.* ท่าเดิน gait
tadgamlang *v. t.* ตัดกำลัง enfeeble
tadgan *v.t.* ตัดกัน intersect
tadhua *v. t.* ตัดหัว behead
tadkad *v. t* ตัดขาด disconnect
tadkon *v.t* ตัดขน fleece
tadpai *adv.* ถัดไป next
tadredium *n.* ธาตุเรเดียม radium
tadsin *v.t.* ตัดสิน adjudge

tadsin *v. t.* ตัดสิน doom
tadsin *v.i.* ตัดสิน judge
tadsinchikad *v.t.* ตัดสินชี้ขาด arbitrate
tadsinjai *v. t* ตัดสินใจ decide
tadsinjai *v. t* ตัดสินใจ determine
tadsinjaipid *v.t.* ตัดสินใจผิด misjudge
tadsinwapid *v. t.* ตัดสินว่าผิด convict
tadsit *v. t.* ตัดสิทธิ์ debar
tadtae *n* ธาตุแท้ entity
tadtaeng *v.t.* ตัดแต่ง trim
tadton *v.t* ตัดทอน abridge
tadton *v. t* ตัดตอน extract
tadya *v.t.* ตัดหญ้า mow
tae *a.* แท้ authentic
tae *a* แท้ bonafide
tae *conj.* แต่ but
tae *a.* แท้ genuine
tae *conj.* แต่ only
taebjamai *adv.* แทบจะไม่ seldom
taebkwang *adj.* ถากกว้าง cultrate
taebpai *n.* ถากป้าย tag
taebucha *n.* แท่นบูชา shrine
taechao *adv* แต่เช้า early
taeduaynew *v.t* แตะด้วยนิ้ว finger
taegamneud *a* แต่กำเนิด congenial
taegon *adv* แต่ก่อน formerly
taek *v.t* แตก fracture
taek *v.i.* แตก split
taek-awk *adv.* แตกออก asunder
taek-awk *v.t.* แตกออก rupture
taekla-iad *v.t.* แตกละเอียด shatter
taeknaw *v.i.* แตกหน่อ germinate
taeknaw *v.i.* แตกหน่อ sprout
taekra-iad *v. t* แตกละเอียด crumble
taekrao *v. i* แตกร้าว crack
taektaeng *a* แตกต่าง distinct
taektang *v. t* แตกต่าง contrast
taektang *v. i* แตกต่าง differ
taektang *a.* แตกต่าง various
taektangjak *prep* แตกต่างจาก unlike
taekteun *v.i* แตกตื่น stampede
taela *a* แต่ละ each

taelakon *pron.* แต่ละคน each
taem-baseball *n.* แต้มเบสบอล innings
taemsi *v.t.* แต้มสี tincture
taemsijangjang *v.t.* แต้มสีจางๆ tinge
taemsijangjang *v.t.* แต้มสีจางๆ tint
taen *n.* แตน hornet
taen *n.* แท่น pedestal
taen *n.* แท่น rostrum
taeng *v.i* แท้ง abort
taeng *v.i* แทง lunge
taeng *v.i.* แท้ง miscarry
taeng *v.t.* แทง prick
taeng *v.t.* แทง stab
taengan *a* แทนกัน several
taenggai *v.t.* แต่งกาย apparel
taenggai *v.t.* แต่งกาย array
taenggai *v.t.* แต่งกาย attire
taengkwa *n* แตงกวา cucumber
taengmo *n.* แตงโม water-melon
taengnamkaeng *n.* แท่งน้ำแข็ง icicle
taeng-ngan *v.t.* แต่งงาน marry
taeng-ngan *v.t.* แต่งงาน mate
taeng-ngan *v.t.* แต่งงาน wed
taeng-ngandai *a.* แต่งงานได้ marriageable
taengprayok *v.t.* แต่งประโยค sentence
taengreuang *v.t* แต่งเรื่อง fabricate
taengtang *v.t.* แต่งตั้ง accredit
taengtang-asawin *v.t.* แต่งตั้งอัศวิน knight
taengtangpentanggan *n.* แต่งตั้งเป็นทางการ institute
taengtangputaen *v. t* แต่งตั้งผู้แทน depute
taengtua *v.t.* แต่งตัว bedight
taengtua *v. t* แต่งตัว dress
taengtua *v.t* แต่งตัว garb
taenti *v.t.* แทนที่ replace
taenti *v.t.* แทนที่ substitute
taew *n* แถว column
taew *n* แถว cue
taew *n.* แถว line
taew *n.* แถว row
taewtinang *n.* แถวที่นั่ง tier

tagiang *n.* ตะเกียง lamp

tagieng *n.* ตะเกียง lantern

tagla *a.* ตะกละ voracious

tagoan *v.i.* ตะโกน yell

tagon *n.* ตะกอน sediment

tagoan *v.i.* ตะโกน shourt

tagra *n.* ตะกร้า basket

tagraeng *n.* ตะแกรง grate

tagraeng *n.* ตะแกรง sieve

tagrawkrobpaksunak *n.*
 ตะกร้อครอบปากสุนัข muzzle

tagua *n.* ตะกั่ว lead

tahan *n.* ทหาร soldier

tahangongnoon *n.* ทหารกองหนุน militia

tahanma *n.* ทหารม้า cavalry

tahanma *n* ทหารม้า chevalier

tahanma *n.* ทหารม้า trooper

tahanpanseuk *n.* ทหารผ่านศึก veteran

tahanpeunkabsila *n.* ทหารปืนคาบศิลา
 musketeer

tahanrab *n.* ทหารราบ infantry

tahanreua *n.* ทหารเรือ sailor

tai *prep* ใต้ below

tai *a* ตาย dead

tai *v. i* ตาย decease

tai *v. i* ตาย die

tai *n.* ไต kidney

tai *v.i.* ตาย perish

tai *v.i* ไถ plough

tai *prep.* ใต้ under

tai *adv* ใต้ under

taipab *v.t.* ถ่ายภาพ photograph

taipabduayrangsi-x *v.t.*
 ถ่ายภาพด้วยรังสีเอ็กซ์ x-ray

taipabpayon *v.t* ถ่ายภาพยนตร์ film

taipasawa *v.i.* ถ่ายปัสสาวะ urinate

taireua *n.* ท้ายเรือ stern

taisamnao *v.t.* ถ่ายสำเนา xerox

taitod *v.i.* ได้โทษ atone

taitod *v.t.* ถ่ายทอด relay

taitoddueykampud *v.t.*
 ถ่ายทอดด้วยคำพูด phrase

taitodtoratat *v.t.* ถ่ายทอดโทรทัศน์
 televise

tajawdreua *n.* ท่าจอดเรือ moorings

tak *v.t.* ถัก knit

tak *n.* ตัก lap

tak *n.* ทาก snail

takab *n.* ตะขาบ centipede

takai *n.* ตาข่าย mesh

takai *n.* ตาข่าย net

takaw *a.* ตะขอ barbed

takaw *n.* ตะขอ crotchet

takaw *n.* ตะขอ grapple

takaw *n.* ตะขอ hook

takdoeytabpi *v.t.* ตักด้วยทัพพี ladle

takduaychon *v.t.* ตักด้วยช้อน spoon

takeb *n.* ตะเข็บ commissure

takeb *n.* ตะเข็บ fringe

takeb *n.* ตะเข็บ seam

takeb *n.* ตะเข็บ welt

takga *n.* ตรรกะ logic

takgataen *n.* ตั๊กแตน locust

takrainam *n.* ตะไคร่น้ำ moss

taksa *n.* ทักษะ skill

taksagantam-ngan *n.* ทักษะการทำงาน
 workmanship

taktai *v.t.* ทักทาย greet

taktai *v.t* ทักทาย hail

taktang *v.t.* ถากถาง lampoon

taktang *v.t.* ถากถาง satirize

takteuan *v.t.* ตักเตือน admonish

taktuang *v. t* ตักตวง exploit

talablookpeun *n* ตลับลูกปืน bearing

talabtape *n.* ตลับเทป cassette

talad *n* ตลาด market

talaenggan *n.* แถลงการณ์ manifesto

talang *n.* ตาราง chart

talaw *v.i.* ทะเลาะ quarrel

talaw *v.i.* ทะเลาะ wrangle

talawdchiwit *a.* ตลอดชีวิต lifelong

talay *n.* ทะเล sea

talaysab *n.* ทะเลสาบ lagoon

talaysab *n.* ทะเลสาบ lake

talaysai *n* ทะเลทราย desert
talod *adv.* ตลอด across
talod *pref.* ตลอด be
talod *a* ตลอด through
talodgan *a.* ตลอดกาล everlasting
talodkeun *adv.* ตลอดคืน overnight
talodpai *adv* ตลอดไป forever
talodpi *a.* ตลอดปี perennial
talok *a* ตลก comic
talok *a* ตลก comical
talok *a.* ตลก jocular
taloknang *v.t* ถลอกหนัง skin
talok-ngo-ngo *a.* ตลกโง่ๆ zany
tam *v.t.* ถาม ask
tam *n.* ถ้ำ cape
tam *n.* ถ้ำ cave
tam *n.* ถ้ำ cavern
tam *n* ถ้ำ den
tam *v. t* ทำ do
tam *conj.* ถ้า if
tam *n.* ถ้ำ lair
tam *a.* ต่ำ low
tam *adv.* ต่ำ low
tam *v.t.* ทำ make
tam *v.t* ถาม query
tamada *a.* ธรรมดา stereotyped
tam-a-han *v. t* ทำอาหาร cook
tambab *v.i.* ทำบาป sin
tambanchi *v.t.* ทำบัญชี account
tamcha *a.* ต่ำช้า base
tamhaisodcheun *v.t.* ทำให้สดชื่น refresh
tamduaykonsat *a.* ทำด้วยขนสัตว์ woollen
tamduaymai *a.* ทำด้วยไม้ wooden
tamduaytagua *a.* ทำด้วยตะกั่ว leaden
tamgamnodgan *v.t.* ทำกำหนดการ schedule
tamglang ท่ามกลาง midst
tamgodmai *a.* ตามกฎหมาย statutory
tamgwa *prep* ต่ำกว่า beneath
tamhai-ab-ai *v.t.* ทำให้อับอาย abash
tamhai-ab-ai *v.t.* ทำให้อับอาย mortify
tamhai-abpang *v.t.* ทำให้อับปาง wreck

tamhai-ai *v. t* ทำให้อาย embarrass
tamhai-ai *v.t.* ทำให้อาย humiliate
tamhaiba *v.t* ทำให้บ้า dement
tamhaibadjeb *v.t.* ทำให้บาดเจ็บ jeopardize
tamhaibang *v.t.* ทำให้บาง thin
tamhaibantao *v.t.* ทำให้บรรเทา temper
tamhaibeua *v.t.* ทำให้เบื่อ tire
tamhaibeuanai *v.t. & i* ทำให้เบื่อหน่าย weary
tamhaiborisut *v.t.* ทำให้บริสุทธิ์ purify
tamhaiborisut *v.t.* ทำให้บริสุทธิ์ sublimate
tamhaibud *v.t* ทำให้บูด ferment
tamhaicha *v.t.* ทำให้ช้า retard
tamhaicha *v.i.* ทำให้ช้า slow
tamhaichadjen *v. t* ทำให้ชัดเจน clear
tamhaichalad *v.i* ทำให้ฉลาด smart
tamhaicheuang *v.t.* ทำให้เชื่อง tame
tamhaicheun *v. t.* ทำให้ชื้น damp
tamhaicheun *v.t.* ทำให้ชื้น moisten
tamhaichum *v. t* ทำให้ชุ่ม drench
tamhaichum *v.t.* ทำให้ชุ่ม saturate
tamhaidaeng *v.t.* ทำให้แดง redden
tamhaidairabkwamniyom *v.t.* ทำให้ได้รับความนิยม popularize
tamhaidaisadsuan *v.t.* ทำให้ได้สัดส่วน proportion
tamhaidijai *v. t* ทำให้ดีใจ enrapture
tamhaidijai *v.t.* ทำให้ดีใจ gladden
tamhaidikeun *v. t* ทำให้ดีขึ้น better
tamhaidikeun *v. t* ทำให้ดีขึ้น enrich
tamhaidikeun *v.t.* ทำให้ดีขึ้น mercerise
tamhaigannam *v.t.* ทำให้กันน้ำ waterproof
tamhaigeud *v.t* ทำให้เกิด cause
tamhaigeud-antarai *v.t.* ทำให้เกิดอันตราย imperil
tamhaigeudfong *v.t* ทำให้เกิดฟอง foam
tamhaigeudrokrabad *v.t.* ทำให้เกิดโรคระบาด plague
tamhaigeudrom-ngao *v.t.* ทำให้เกิดร่มเงา shade

tamhaigeudsiang *v.i.* ทำให้เกิดเสียง pop

tamhaigeudsiang *v.i.* ทำให้เกิดเสียง sound

tamhaigeudsiangdangtub *v.i.* ทำให้เกิดเสียงดังตุ๊บ thud

tamhaigla *v. t.* ทำให้กล้า embolden

tamhaiglaichid *v.t.* ทำให้ใกล้ชิด intimate

tamhaigliad *v.t.* ทำให้เกลียด loathe

tamhaiglua *v. t* ทำให้กลัว daunt

tamhaiglua *v.t.* ทำให้กลัว frighten

tamhaiglua *v.t.* ทำให้กลัว horrify

tamhaiglua *v.t.* ทำให้กลัว terrify

tamhaiglua *v.t.* ทำให้กลัว terrorize

tamhaiglua *v.t.* ทำให้กลัว threaten

tamhaigrapeuam *v.t.* ทำให้กระเพื่อม ripple

tamhaigrot *v.t.* ทำให้โกรธ infuriate

tamhaigrot *v.t.* ทำให้โกรธ offend

tamhaigrot *v.t.* ทำให้โกรธ outrage

tamhaigwang *v.t.* ทำให้กว้าง widen

tamhaihaeng *v. i.* ทำให้แห้ง dry

tamhaihaeng *v.t.* ทำให้แห้ง parch

tamhaihaijaimai-awk *v.t.* ทำให้หายใจไม่ออก stifle

tamhaihob *v.t.* ทำให้หอบ smother

tamhaihodhu *v. t* ทำให้หดหู่ depress

tamhai-iang *v.i.* ทำให้เอียง tilt

tamhaijebpuad *v.t.* ทำให้เจ็บปวด pain

tamhaijebpuay *v.t.* ทำให้เจ็บป่วย afflict

tamhaijeuajang *v. t* ทำให้เจือจาง dilute

tamhaikaeb *v.t.* ทำให้แคบ narrow

tamhaikaeng *v.i.* ทำให้แข็ง freeze

tamhaikaeng *v.t.* ทำให้แข็ง harden

tamhaikaeng *v.t.* ทำให้แข็ง ossify

tamhaikaeng *v.t.* ทำให้แข็ง stiffen

tamhaikaengraeng *v.t.* ทำให้แข็งแรง toughen

tamhaikan *v.t.* ทำให้คัน tickle

tamhaikanan *v.t.* ทำให้ขนานกัน parallel

tamhaikao *v.t.* ทำให้ขาว whiten

tamhaikaogan *v.t* ทำให้เข้ากัน mesh

tamhaikaojaipid *v.t.* ทำให้เข้าใจผิด mislead

tamhaikemkaeng *v.t.* ทำให้เข้มแข็ง strengthen

tamhaikeuychin *v. t.* ทำให้เคยชิน habituate

tamhaiklaigan *v.* ทำให้คล้ายกัน assimilate

tamhaikled *v.t.* ทำให้เคล็ด sprain

tamhaiglom *v.t.* ทำให้กลม round

tamhaikomkeun *v. t* ทำให้ขมขื่น embitter

tamhaikong *v.t.* ทำให้โค้ง arch

tamhaikong *v. t* ทำให้โค้ง curve

tamhaikreungkreum *v.t.* ทำให้เคร่งขรึม solemnize

tamhaikriad *v.t.* ทำให้เครียด intensify

tamhaikrobtuan *v. t* ทำให้ครบถ้วน complete

tamhaikunkeuang *v.t.* ทำให้ขุ่นเคือง nettle

tamhaikunkeuy *v.t.* ทำให้คุ้นเคย accustom

tamhailacha *v.t. & i.* ทำให้ล่าช้า delay

tamhailaem *v.t.* ทำให้แหลม sharpen

tamhailambak *v.t.* ทำให้ลำบาก straiten

tamhaileuklab *v.t.* ทำให้ลึกลับ mystify

tamhailodlong *v.t* ทำให้ลดลง lessen

tamhailodlong *v.i.* ทำให้ลดลง taper

tamhailonglai *v. t* ทำให้หลงใหล enamour

tamhailonglai *v. t* ทำให้หลงใหล enchant

tamhailonglai *v.t* ทำให้หลงใหล fascinate

tamhailongsanae *v. t.* ทำให้หลงเสน่ห์ charm2

tamhailongsanae *v.t* ทำให้หลงเสน่ห์ bewitch

tamhailuam *v.t.* ทำให้หลวม loosen

tamhaimai *v.t.* ทำให้ไหม้ singe

tamhaimankong *v.t.* ทำให้มั่นคง stabilize

tamhaimankong *v.t.* ทำให้มั่นคง steady

tamhaimawsom *v.t.* ทำให้เหมาะสม suit

tamhaimeud *v. t.* ทำให้มืด blacken

tamhaimeunmao *v.t.* ทำให้มึนเมา intoxicate

tamhaimichiwitchiwa *v. t.* ทำให้มีชีวิตชีวา enliven

tamhaimichiwitchiwa *v.t.* ทำให้มีชีวิตชีวา vitalize

tamhaimipon *v.t.* ทำให้มีผล implement

tamhaimodgamlang *v.t.* ทำให้หมดกำลัง prostrate

tamhaimodgamrangjai *v. t.* ทำให้หมดกำลังใจ discourage

tamhaimodgamrangjai *v. t* ทำให้หมดกำลังใจ dishearten

tamhaimoho *v. t* ทำให้โมโห enrage

tamhaimua *v. t* ทำให้มัว blear

tamhaimua *v. t.* ทำให้มัว dull

tamhaimun-ngong *v.t.* ทำให้มึนงง stupefy

tamhaina *v.i.* ทำให้หนา thicken

tamhainadaeng *v.i* ทำให้หน้าแดง flush

tamhainaejai *v.t.* ทำให้แน่ใจ ascertain

tamhainaejai *v. t* ทำให้แน่ใจ ensure

tamhainaen *v.t.* ทำให้แน่น tighten

tamhainagliad *v.t.* ทำให้น่าเกลียด uglify

tamhaineuangnaen *v.t.* ทำให้เนืองแน่น throng

tamhai-ngai *v.t.* ทำให้ง่าย simplify

tamhai-ngawdai *v.t.* ทำให้งอได้ limber

tamhai-ngiab *v.i* ทำให้เงียบ hush

tamhai-ngiab *v.t.* ทำให้เงียบ quiet

tamhai-ngiab *v.t.* ทำให้เงียบ sedate

tamhai-ngiab *v.t.* ทำให้เงียบ silence

tamhai-ngod-ngam *v.t.* ทำให้งดงาม grace

tamhai-ngong *v.t* ทำให้งง astound

tamhai-ngong *v. t* ทำให้งง daze

tamhai-ngong *v.t.* ทำให้งง puzzle

tamhai-ngong *v.t.* ทำให้งง stun

tamhaining *v.t.* ทำให้นิ่ง still

tamhainoy *v.t.* ทำให้น้อย minimize

tamhainoom *v.t.* ทำให้นุ่ม soften

tamhai-ob-aun *v.t.* ทำให้อบอุ่น warm

tamhai-on-ae *v.t. & i* ทำให้อ่อนแอ weaken

tamhai-on-yao *v.t.* ทำให้อ่อนเยาว์ rejuvenate

tamhaipagati *v.t.* ทำให้ปกติ normalize

tamhaipawjai *adj.* ทำให้พอใจ complaisant

tamhaipawjai *v.t.* ทำให้พอใจ satiate

tamhaipawjai *v. t* ทำให้พอใจ content

tamhaipen-aeng *v.t.* ทำให้เป็นแอ่ง puddle

tamhaipen-ammata *v.t.* ทำให้เป็นอมตะ immortalize

tamhaipenbodgawi *v.t.* ทำให้เป็นบทกวี versify

tamhaipendekgampra *v.t* ทำให้เป็นเด็กกำพร้า orphan

tamhaipenglang *v.t.* ทำให้เป็นกลาง neutralize

tamhaipenjuddang *v.t.* ทำให้เป็นจุดด่าง spot

tamhaipenkongrat *v.t.* ทำให้เป็นของรัฐ nationalize

tamhaipenlon *v.t.* ทำให้เป็นลอน crimple

tamhaipenmatratan *v.t.* ทำให้เป็นมาตรฐาน standardize

tamhaipenmit *v.t.* ทำให้เป็นมิตร conciliate

tamhaipenmoka *v.t.* ทำให้เป็นโมฆะ annul

tamhaipenmoka *v.t.* ทำให้เป็นโมฆะ void

tamhaipenpa *v.t.* ทำให้เป็นป่า afforest

tamhaipenpid *v.t.* ทำให้เป็นพิษ pollute

tamhaipenplaepen *v.t.* ทำให้เกิดแผลเป็น scar

tamhaipenprong *v.t* ทำให้เป็นโพรง hollow

tamhaipenpum *v.t.* ทำให้เป็นปุ่ม stud

tamhaipenpuying *v.t.* ทำให้เป็นผู้หญิง womanise

tamhaipenrabob *v.t.* ทำให้เป็นระบบ systematize

tamhaipenriew *v.t.* ทำให้เป็นริ้ว stripe

tamhaipenroobrang *v.t.* ทำให้เป็นรูปร่าง form

tamhaipenroobrang *v.t* ทำให้เป็นรูปร่าง shape

tamhaipenroy *v.t.* ทำให้เป็นรอย line

tamhaipenru *v.t.* ทำให้เป็นรู perforate

tamhaipensam *v.t.,* ทำให้เป็นสาม triple

tamhaipensiliam *v.t.* ทำให้เป็นสี่เหลี่ยม square

tamhaipensitao *v.t.* ทำให้เป็นสี่เท่า quadruple

tamhaipentammachat *v.t.* ทำให้เป็นธรรมชาติ naturalize

tamhaipentirak *v.t* ทำให้เป็นที่รัก endear

tamhaipenyeua *v.t.* ทำให้เป็นเหยื่อ victimize

tamhaipeuan *v. t* ทำให้เปื้อน blot

tamhaipeuan *v.t.* ทำให้เปื้อน smear

tamhaipeuan *v.t.* ทำให้เปื้อน soil

tamhaipeuan *v.t.* ทำให้เปื้อนเขม่า soot

tamhai-peuan-clone *v. t* ทำให้เปื้อนโคลน bemire

tamhaipiak *v.t.* ทำให้เปียก wet

tamhaipidwang *v. t* ทำให้ผิดหวัง deject

tamhaipigan *v.t.* ทำให้พิการ handicap

tamhaipigan *v.t.* ทำให้พิการ lame

tamhaiplaekjai *v.t.* ทำให้แปลกใจ surprise

tamhaiplodpai *v.t.* ทำให้ปลอดภัย secure

tamhaipom *v.i.* ทำให้ผอม slim

tamhaipong *v.i* ทำให้พอง billow

tamhaipragod *v. t* ทำให้ปรากฏ evoke

tamhaipraladjai *v.t.* ทำให้ประหลาดใจ nonplus

tamhaiprasajakcheua *v.t.* ทำให้ปราศจากเชื้อ sterilize

tamhaipriaw *v.t.* ทำให้เปรี้ยว sour

tamhairaheuy *v.t.* ทำให้ระเหย vaporize

tamhairaika *v.t.* ทำให้ไร้ค่า nullify

tamhairaikwamsamad *v. t* ทำให้ไร้ความสามารถ disable

tamhairakatook *v. t.* ทำให้ราคาถูก cheapen

tamhairiab *v.t.* ทำให้เรียบ level

tamhairiab *v.t.* ทำให้เรียบ smooth

tamhairiabroy *v.t.* ทำให้เรียบร้อย tidy

tamhairok *v.i* ทำให้รก mess

tamhairon *v.t* ทำให้ร้อน heat

tamhairuamgan *v.t.* ทำให้รวมกัน conglutinate

tamhairusukmaimankong *v.t.* ทำให้รู้สึกไม่มั่นคง unsettle

tamhaisabson *v. t.* ทำให้สับสน baffle

tamhaisabson *v. t* ทำให้สับสน confuse

tamhaisabson *v. t* ทำให้สับสน bemuse

tamhaisaksit *v.t.* ทำให้ศักดิ์สิทธิ์ hallow

tamhaisalua *v. t* ทำให้สลัว dim

tamhaisan *v.t.* ทำให้สั้น shorten

tamhaisa-nga-ngam *v.t* ทำให้สง่างาม dignify

tamhaisa-ngob *v. t.* ทำให้สงบ calm

tamhaisa-ngob *v.t.* ทำให้สงบ pacify

tamhaisa-ngob *v.t.* ทำให้สงบ tranquillize

tamhaisanooksanan *v.t.* ทำให้สนุกสนาน amuse

tamhaisao *v. t* ทำให้เศร้า commiserate

tamhaisao *v.t.* ทำให้เศร้า sadden

tamhaisawang *v. t* ทำให้สว่าง brighten

tamhaisawang *v.i.* ทำให้สว่าง lighten

tamhaiseuam *v. t.* ทำให้เสื่อม debase

tamhaiseuam *v. t.* ทำให้เสื่อม demoralize

tamhaiseuamsia *v.t.* ทำให้เสื่อมเสีย tarnish

tamhaisia *v.t.* ทำให้เสีย vitiate

tamhaisiacheusiang *v.t.* ทำให้เสียชื่อเสียง scandalize

tamhaisiahai *v. t.* ทำให้เสียหาย damage

tamhaisiahai *v.t* ทำให้เสียหาย harm

tamhaisiahai *v.t.* ทำให้เสียหาย mar

tamhaisiajai *v. t* ทำให้เสียใจ distress

tamhaisipewkemkeun *v.i.* ทำให้สีผิวเข้มขึ้น tan

tamhaisomboon *v. i* ทำให้สมบูรณ์ compete

tamhaisomboon *v.t.* ทำให้สมบูรณ์ perfect

tamhaisomboon *v.t.* ทำให้สมบูรณ์ validate

tamhaisomdoon *v.t.* ทำให้สมดุล balance

tamhaisongsai *v.t.* ทำให้สงสัย misgive

tamhaisook *v.i.* ทำให้สุก ripen

tamhaisoong *v.t.* ทำให้สูง heighten

tamhaisoongsong *v. t.* ทำให้สูงส่ง ennoble

tamhaisoongsud *v.t.* ทำให้สูงสุด maximize

tamhaitaek *v.t.* ทำให้แตก splinter

tamhaitangkeun *v. t* ทำให้ตั้งขึ้น erect

tamhaitansamai *v.t.* ทำให้ทันสมัย modernize

tamhaitaogan *v. t.* ทำให้เท่ากัน equalize

tamhaitaogan *v. t* ทำให้เท่ากัน equate

tamhaitaogan *v. t* ทำให้เท่ากัน even

tamhaitaogan *v. t* ทำให้เท่ากัน equal

tamhaitapra *v. t.* ทำให้ตาพร่า dazzle

tamhaitaworn *v.t.* ทำให้ถาวร perpetuate

tamhaitawraman *n.* ทำให้ทรมาน torment

tamhaiteung *v.t.* ทำให้ตึง strain

tamhaiteungjudsungsud *v.i.* ทำให้ถึงจุดสูงสุด culminate

tamhaiteunten *v.t.* ทำให้ตื่นเต้น thrill

tamhaitidgab *v. t.* ทำให้ติดกับ entrap

tamhaitoklongma *v. t* ทำให้ตกลงมา down

tamhaitookgodmai *v.t.* ทำให้ถูกกฎหมาย legalize

tamhaitooktong *v. t* ทำให้ถูกต้อง correct

tamhaitooktong *v.i.* ทำให้ถูกต้อง rectify

tamhaitooktong *v.t.* ทำให้ถูกต้อง right

tamhaitrong *v.t.* ทำให้ตรง straighten

tamhaituam *v.t.* ทำให้ท่วม swamp

tamhaiwan *v.t.* ทำให้หวาน sweeten

tamhaiwang *v* ทำให้ว่าง empty

tamhaiwelapanpai *v.t.* ทำให้เวลาผ่านไป while

tamhaiwunwai *v.t.* ทำให้วุ่นวาย muddle

tamhaiyae *v.t.* ทำให้แย่ worsen

tamhaiyakjon *v.t.* ทำให้ยากจน impoverish

tamhaiyao *v.t.* ทำให้ยาว lengthen

tamhaiyawn *v.t.* ทำให้หย่อน slacken

tamhaiyod *v. i* ทำให้หยด drip

tamhaiyon *v.t.* ทำให้ย่น crankle

tamhaiyon *v.t.* ทำให้ย่น wrinkle

tamhaiyung *v. t* ทำให้ยุ่ง disrupt

tamhaiyungyak *v. t* ทำให้ยุ่งยาก complicate

tamhaiyungyeung *v.t.* ทำให้ยุ่งเหยิง tangle

tamhaiyutaibangkabbancha *v.t.* ทำให้อยู่ใต้บังคับบัญชา subordinate

tamhok *v.i.* ทำหก spill

tamhuang *v.t.* ทำห่วง noose

tamjai *v. t* ตามใจ cocker

tamjai *v.t.* ตามใจ indulge

tamjai *v.t.* ตามใจ pamper

tamjakconcrete *v. t* ทำจากคอนกรีต concrete

tamjaklaorum *a* ทำจากเหล้ารัม rum

tamjing *adv.* ตามจริง actually

tamkanaen *v.t.* ทำคะแนน score

tamkanompang *v. t. & i* ทำขนมปัง breaden

tamglang *prep.* ท่ามกลาง amid

tamglang *prep.* ท่ามกลาง among

tamglang *prep.* ท่ามกลาง amongst

tamkreuangmai *v.t.* ทำเครื่องหมาย sign

tamkreuangmai *v.i.* ทำเครื่องหมาย tick

tamkreuangmai *v.t* ทำเครื่องหมาย mark

tamkwa *a.* ต่ำกว่า nether

tamkwamsa-ad *v. t* ทำความสะอาด clean

tamkwamsa-ad *v. t* ทำความสะอาด cleanse

tamkwasoon *a* ต่ำกว่าศูนย์ minus

tamlai *v.t.* ทำลาย annihilate

tamlai *v.t.* ทำลาย decimate

tamlai *v. t.* ทำลาย demolish

tamlai *v. t* ทำลาย destroy
tamlai *v.t.* ทำลาย mangle
tamlai *v.t.* ทำลาย torpedo
tamlai *v.t.* ทำลาย waste
tamlailang *v.t.* ทำลายล้าง ravage
tamlakjariyatam *a* ตามหลักจริยธรรม ethical
tamlamdab *a.* ตามลำดับ respective
tamlay *n.* ทำเล location
tamlenlen *v. i.* ทำเล่นๆ dabble
tamlohamaepim *v.t.* ทำโลหะแม่พิมพ์ stereotype
tamtoy *a.* ต่ำต้อย lowly
tammachat *n.* ธรรมชาติ nature
tammada *a.* ธรรมดา mediocre
tammada *a.* ธรรมดา plain
tammada *a.* ธรรมดา prosaic
tammai *v.t.* ทำใหม่ renew
tammai *adv.* ทำไม why
tammakgeunpai *v.t.* ทำมากเกินไป overdo
tammeuanghin *v.i.* ทำเมืองหิน quarry
tamnabeung *v.i* ทำหน้าบึ้ง frown
tamnabeung *v.i.* ทำหน้าบึ้ง scowl
tamnaeng *n.* ตำแหน่ง position
tamnaeng *n* ตำแหน่ง post
tamnaeng *n.* ตำแหน่ง rank
tamnaeng *n.* ตำแหน่ง standing
tamnaengbatluang *n* ตำแหน่งบาทหลวง benefice
tamnaenggabtan *n.* ตำแหน่งกัปตัน captaincy
tamnaengkunnang *n.* ตำแหน่งขุนนาง lordship
tamnaengpanak-nganpokkrong *n.* ตำแหน่งพนักงานปกครอง magistracy
tamnaengpulencriket *n.* ตำแหน่งผู้เล่นคริกเกต mid-off
tamnaengpulencriket *n.* ตำแหน่งผู้เล่นคริกเกต mid-on
tamnaengpunam *n.* ตำแหน่งผู้นำ helm

tamnaengsantapapa *n.* ตำแหน่งสันตปาปา papacy
tamnaengtodsaniyom *a* ตำแหน่งทศนิยม decimal
tamnaengwang *n.* ตำแหน่งว่าง vacancy
tamnai *v.t* ทำนาย foretell
tamnai *v.t.* ทำนาย predict
tamnai *v.t.* ทำนาย prophesy
tamnan *adv.* ตามนั้น accordingly
tamnan *n.* ตำนาน legend
tamnan *n.* ตำนาน myth
tamnan *n.* ตำนาน mythology
tamnati *v.i* ทำหน้าที่ function
tamnati *v.i.* ทำหน้าที่ officiate
tamnatitaen *v.t.* ทำหน้าที่แทน represent
tam-ngan *v.t.* ทำงาน task
tam-ngan *v.t.* ทำงาน work
tam-ngannak *v.i.* ทำงานหนัก moil
tam-ngandai *a.* ทำงานได้ workable
tam-ngan-makgpai *v.i.* ทำงานมากไป overwork
tam-ngannak *v.i.* ทำงานหนัก slave
tam-ngannak *v.i.* ทำงานหนัก toil
tamni *n* ตำหนิ blemish
tamni *v. t* ตำหนิ cavil
tamni *v. t.* ตำหนิ censure
tamni *a.* ตำหนิ lash
tamni *v.t.* ตำหนิ reprimand
tamni *v.t.* ตำหนิ reproach
tamniampatibad *n.* ธรรมเนียมปฏิบัติ mannerism
tamnob *n.* ทำนบ weir
tamnong *n.* ทำนอง tune
tampaenti *v.t.* ทำแผนที่ map
tampakyon *v.t.* ทำปากย่น purse
tampensongtao *v. t.* ทำเป็นสองเท่า double
tampeunrongtao *v.t* ทำพื้นรองเท้า sole
tampid *v. i* ทำผิด err
tampid *v.t.* ทำผิด wrong
tampidgodmai *v.t* ทำผิดกฎหมาย outlaw
tampidplad *v. t* ทำผิดพลาด botch

tampitipeud *v.t.* ทำพิธีเปิด auspicate
tamplad *v.t.* ทำพลาด miss
tamrai *v.t.* ทำร้าย assault
tamrai *v.t.* ทำลาย ruin
tamlailang *v.t.* ทำลายล้าง sabotage
tamrang *v.t.* ทำรัง nest
tamreudugan *a.* ตามฤดูกาล seasonal
tamroy *v.t.* ตามรอย trail
tamruad *n* ตำรวจ constable
tamruad *n.* ตำรวจ police
tamruad *n.* ตำรวจ policeman
tamsam *v. t* ทำซ้ำ duplicate
tamsamati *v.t.* ทำสมาธิ meditate
tamsamnao *v. t* ทำสำเนา copy
tamsamred *v.t.* ทำสำเร็จ accomplish
tamsamred *v.t.* ทำสำเร็จ achieve
tamsanya *v. t* ทำสัญญา contract
tamsiangdang *v. t* ทำเสียงดัง brustle
tamsiangdang *v.t.* ทำเสียงดัง crackle
tamsiangdang *v. i* ทำเสียงดัง creak
tamsiangdang *v.i.* ทำเสียงดัง whiz
tamsiangku *v.i* ทำเสียงขู่ hiss
tamsianglaem *n. & v. i* ทำเสียงแหลม
    clack
tamsongkram *v.i.* ทำสงคราม war
tamtaengtiyuglai *n.* ตำแหน่งที่อยู่ไกล
    offing
tamtammachat *a.* ตามธรรมชาติ natural
tamtammachat *adv.* ตามธรรมชาติ
    naturally
tamtam-u-domkati *v.t.* ทำตามอุดมคติ
    idealize
tamtan *v.t.* ตามทัน overtake
tamtanbon *v.t.* ทำทัณฑ์บน parole
tamtau-awkson *a.* ตามตัวอักษร literal
tamtawan *v.t.* ทำตาหวาน ogle
tamtawneuang *v. i.* ทำต่อเนื่อง continue
tamtod *v.t.* ทำโทษ punish
tan *prep.* ต้าน against
tan *n.* แท่น altar
tan *v. t.* ทาน dine
tan *n.* ท่าน sir

tan-a-hankam *v.i.* ทานอาหารค่ำ sup
tanai *n* ทนาย advocate
tanai *n.* ทนาย attorney
tanai *n.* ทนาย barrister
tanai *n.* ทนาย counsellor
tanai *n.* ทนาย lawyer
tanakan *n.* ธนาคาร bank
tanamman *v.t.* ทาน้ำมัน anoint
tanbon *n.* ทัณฑ์บน parole
taneuy *v. t* ทาเนย butter
tang *n.* ทั่ง anvil
tang *n* ถัง bucket
tang *n.* ถัง pail
taeng *v.t.* แทง stick
tang *n.* ทาง way
tanganchang *n.* ทางการช่าง technical
tanganpaet *a.* ทางการแพทย์ medical
tangantahan *a.* ทางการทหาร military
tang-a-rom *a* ทางอารมณ์ emotional
tang-awk *n.* ทางออก exit
tang-a-ya *a* ทางอาญา criminal
tang-a-ya *a.* ทางอาญา penal
tangcamp *v. i.* ตั้งแคมป์ camp
tangchak *a.* ตั้งฉาก perpendicular
tangcheu *v. t.* ตั้งชื่อ entitle
tangcheu *v.t.* ตั้งชื่อ name
tangcheulen *v.t.* ตั้งชื่อเล่น nickname
tangdanjidjai *a.* ทางด้านจิตใจ mental
tangdao *a.* ต่างด้าว alien
tangdao *adj* ต่างด้าว alien
tangdeun *n.* ทางเดิน path
tangdeun *n.* ทางเดิน pavement
tangdeun *n.* ทางเดิน rote
tangdeun *n.* ทางเดิน trail
tangdeuntimilangkakong *n*
    ทางเดินที่มีหลังคาโค้ง arcade
tangdeunyao *n.* ทางเดินยาว nave
tangduayleklaem *v.t.*
    แทงด้วยเหล็กแหลม spike
tanggai *v. t* ตั้งใจ concentrate
tanggammapan *n.* ทางกรรมพันธุ์
    hereditary

tanggan *a* ต่างกัน different
tanggan *a.* ทางการ official
tanggangased *a* ทางการเกษตร
  agricultural
tangganka *a* ทางการค้า commercial
tangganmeuang *a.* ทางการเมือง political
tanggan-ngeun *a.* ทางการเงิน monetary
tanggan-nguen *a* ทางการเงิน formal
tang-gan-nguen *a* ทางการเงิน financial
tang-gan-nguen *a* ทางการเงิน fiscal
tanggantut *a* ทางการทูต diplomatic
tanggongai *a* ทางกลไก mechanic
tangjai *v.i.* ตั้งใจ aim
tangjai *v.t.* ตั้งใจ intend
tangjai *a.* ตั้งใจ intent
tangjai *a.* ตั้งใจ intentional
tangjai *v.t.* ตั้งใจ purpose
tangjit *a.* ทางจิต psychic
tangjitwittaya *a.* ทางจิตวิทยา
  psychological
tangkamtam *v.t.* ตั้งคำถาม question
tangkamtam *v.t.* ตั้งคำถาม quiz
tangkanadyai *n.* ถังขนาดใหญ่ tank
tangkanlaikrang *a.* ตั้งครรภ์หลายครั้ง
  multiparous
tangkao *n* ทางเข้า entrance
tangkao *n* ทางเข้า entry
tangkemi *a.* ทางเคมี chemical
tang-kong *n* ทางโค้ง bend
tangku *a* ทั้งคู่ both
tangku *pron* ทั้งคู่ both
tangleuak *n.* ทางเลือก alternative
tangleuak *n.* ทางเลือก option
tang-leuak *n.* ทางเลือก choice
tanglok *a.* ทางโลก mundane
tangluang *n* ทางหลวง causeway
tangluang *n.* ทางหลวง highway
tangmae *a.* ทางแม่ maternal
tangmai *n* ถังไม้ cask
tangmod *adv* ทั้งหมด all
tangmod *a* ทั้งหมด entire
tangmod *a* ทั้งหมด gross

tangmod *a.* ทั้งหมด total
tangmod *a* ทั้งหมด utter
tangmod *a.* ทั้งหมด whole
tangmod *n* ทั้งหมด whole
tangmod *adv.* ทั้งหมด wholly
tangnai *adv.* ทางไหน whither
tangnam *n.* ถังน้ำ tub
tangnasik *a.* ทางนาสิก nasal
tangneua *adv.* ทางเหนือ north
tangneua *a.* ทางเหนือ northerly
tangneua *adv.* ทางเหนือ northerly
tangni *adv.* ทั้งนี้ anyhow
tangnoan *a.* ทางโน้น yonder
tangnoan *adv.* ทางโน้น yonder
tangpan *n.* ทางผ่าน passage
tangpratya *a.* ทางปรัชญา philosophical
tangradodrom *n.* นักกระโดดร่ม
  parachutist
tangranggai *a* ทางร่างกาย bodily
tangranggai *adv.* ทั้งร่ายกาย bodily
tangraya *v.t.* ตั้งระยะ range
tangrekakanit *a.* ทางเรขาคณิต
  geometrical
tangsaiglang *n* ทางสายกลาง middle
tangsangkom *n.* ทางสังคม social
tangsanjon *n.* ทางสัญจร thoroughfare
tangsatiti *a.* ทางสถิติ statistical
tangsetagid *a* ทางเศรษฐกิจ economic
tangsiang *v.t.* ตั้งเสียง tune
tangtae *prep.* ตั้งแต่ since
tangtaenanma *adv.* ตั้งแต่นั้นมา since
tangtai *adv* ทางใต้ south
tangtalay *a.* ทางทะเล marine
tangtalay *a.* ทางทะเล nautic(al)
tangtawantok *a.* ทางตะวันตก
occidental
tangtawan *adj.* ทางทวาร anal
tangtawan-awk *a* ทางตะวันออก eastern
tangtechnology *a.* ทางเทคโนโลยี
  technological
tangtewaniyom *a.* ทางเทววิทยา
  theological

tangtidneua *a.* ทางทิศเหนือ northern
tangtidtai *a.* ทางทิศใต้ southerly
tangtidtai *a.* ทางทิศใต้ southern
tangtidtawan-awk *adv* ทางทิศตะวันออก east
tangtidtawan-awk *a* ทางทิศตะวันออก east
tangtidtawantok *a.* ทางทิศตะวันตก west
tangtidtawantok *adv.* ทางทิศตะวันตก west
tangtidtawantok *a.* ทางทิศตะวันตก western
tangtobtangan *a.* ต่างตอบแทนกัน reciprocate
tangtobtangan *v.t.* ต่างตอบแทนกัน reciprocate
tangton *n.* ทางตัน impasse
tangtoraniwittaya *a.* ทางธรณีวิทยา geological
tangtrong *a* ตั้งตรง erect
tangtrong *adv.* ตั้งตรง up
tangwaja *a.* ทางวาจา verbal
tangwaja *adv.* ทางวาจา verbally
tangwattanatam *a* ทางวัฒนธรรม cultural
tangwatti *v.t.* ทางวัตถุ materialize
tangwokwon *n.* ทางวกวน maze
tangyao *n.* ทางยาว strip
tangyu *v.t.* ตั้งอยู่ locate
tangyutangtawantok *a.* ตั้งอยู่ทางตะวันตก westerly
tanha *n.* ตัณหา lust
tanhailonglai *v.t.* ทำให้หลงใหล infatuate
tanhaipenkrabneow *v.t* ทำให้เป็นคราบเหนียว lime
tanhajad *a.* ตัณหาจัด lustful
tanhin *n* ถ่านหิน coal
tankrongsang *a.* ทางโครงสร้าง structural
tannamkaeng *n.* ธารน้ำแข็ง glacier
tanom-a-han *v. t* ถนอมอาหาร conserve
tanon *n.* ถนน avenue
tanon *n.* ถนน road
tanon *n.* ถนน street

tanong *a.* ทะนง haughty
tanraigan *v.t.* ทำรายการ list
tansamai *a* ทันสมัย fashionable
tansamai *a.* ทันสมัย modern
tansamai *a.* ทันสมัย up-to-date
tadseua *v.t.* ตัดเสื้อ tailor
tansuansamkan-awk *v.t.* ตัดส่วนสำคัญออก mutilate
tangtalay *a.* ทางทะเล maritime
tantanwai *a.* ต้านทานไว้ repellent
tantapaed *n* ทันตแพทย์ dentist
tanti *a* ทันที abrupt
tanti *adv.* ทันที anon
tanti *adv.* ทันที forthwith
tanti *a* ทันที immediate
tanti *a.* ทันที instant
tanti *a.* ทันที instantaneous
tanti *a.* ทันที intermediate
tanti *adv.* ทันที straight
tantiman *n.* ฐานที่มั่น base
tanu *n* ธนู arrow
tawainam *n.* ท่าว่ายน้ำ stroke
tanwakom *n* ธันวาคม december
tanyapeud *n.* ธัญพืช cereal
tao *n* เท้า foot
tao *n.* เตา stove
tao *n.* เต่า tortoise
tao *n.* เต่า turtle
taofai *n.* เตาไฟ hearth
taogan *a* เท่ากัน equivalent
taogan *a* เท่ากัน even
taogan *a.* เท่ากัน tantamount
taonan *a.* เท่านั้น only
taonan *adv.* เท่านั้น only
taonom *n.* เต้านม mamma
taonom *n.* เต้านม udder
tao-ob *n.* เตาอบ oven
taoping *n.* เตาผิง furnace
taosiab *n.* เต้าเสียบ socket
taotan *n.* เถ้าถ่าน ash
taotiam *a* เท่าเทียม equal
taotong *n* เต่าทอง beetle

tapob *v.t.* ตะปบ paw
tapu *n.* ตะปู nail
tapu *n.* ตะปู stud
tapugliaw *n.* ตะปูเกลียว screw
tarang *n.* ตาราง jail
tareua *n.* ท่าเรือ dock
tareua *n.* ท่าเรือ harbour
tareua *n.* ท่าเรือ port
tarodpai *a.* ตลอดไป perpetual
tarok *n.* ทารก babe
tarok *n.* ทารก baby
tarok *n.* ทารก bantling
tarok *n.* ทารก infant
tarokraihua *n.* ทารกไร้หัว acephalus
taroon *a* ทารุณ brutal
tasanakati *n.* ทัศนคติ outlook
tasanakati *n.* ทัศนคติ perspective
tasaniyababcheunggwang *n.*
  ทัศนียภาพเชิงกว้าง panorama
tasi *v. t* ทาสี colour
tasi *v.t.* ทาสี paint
tasanakati *n.* ทัศนคติ attitude
tatai *v. t.* ท้าทาย challenge
tatang *n.* ท่าทาง gesture
tatang *n.* ท่าทาง pose
tatang *n.* ท่าทาง posture
tauchanidneung *n.* ถั่วชนิดหนึ่ง lentil
tautalok *n* ตัวตลก buffoon
tautalok *n* ตัวตลก clown
tavon *a.* ถาวร permanent
taw *n.* ต้อ cataract
taw *prep.* ต่อ per
taw *n.* ท่อ pipe
taw *v.i.* ถ่อ shake
taw *n.* ตอ snag
taw *n.* ตอ stubble
taw *v.t.* ทอ weave
taw-ai-sia *n.* ท่อไอเสีย muffler
tawannak *n.* ทวารหนัก anus
tawhin *n.* ต้อหิน glaucoma
tawib *n* ทวีป continent
tawjakni *adv.* ต่อจากนี้ henceforth

tawjakni *adv.* ต่อจากนี้ henceforward
tawjakni *adv.* ต่อจากนี้ hereafter
tawktapu *v.t.* ตอกตะปู nail
tawma *conj.* ต่อมา after
tawma *a.* ต่อมา latter
tawmai *n.* ตอไม้ stump
tawn *v.t* ถอน abstract
tawn *v.t.* ถอน pluck
tawn *v.t.* ถอน withdraw
tawnamsia *n* ท่อน้ำเสีย sewer
tawnasan *a.* ต่อหน้าศาล subjudice
tawneuang *adj.* ต่อเนื่อง continual
tawneuang *a* ต่อเนื่อง continuous
tawneuang *adj.* ต่อเนื่อง consecutive
tawneuanggan *a.* ต่อเนื่องกัน serial
tawneuanggan *a.* ต่อเนื่องกัน successive
tawneuang *adv.* ต่อเนื่อง on
tawnhaijai *v.i.* ถอนหายใจ sigh
tawn-ngeun-geun *v.t.* ถอนเงินเกิน
  overdraw
tawntonmai *v.t.* ถอนต้นไม้ uproot
tawpa *v.i.* ทอผ้า loom
tawpai *a.* ต่อไป next
tawrabainam *n* ท่อระบายน้ำ drain
tawraman *v.t.* ทรมาน torture
tawraniwittaya *n.* ธรณีวิทยา geology
tawrayod *a.* ทรยศ treacherous
tawrong *v.t.* ต่อรอง bargain
tawrongraka *v.i.* ต่อรองราคา haggle
tawsaifai *v.t.* ต่อสายไฟ wire
tawsu *v. i* ต่อสู้ contend
tawsu *v.t* ต่อสู้ fight
tawsu *v.i.* ต่อสู้ militate
tawsu *v.i.* ต่อสู้ strive
tawsu *v.i.* ต่อสู้ struggle
tawsugab *prep.* ต่อสู้กับ versus
tawsugan-udtalud *v.i.* ต่อสู้กันอุตลุด
  scuffle
tawtai *v.t.* ต่อท้าย suffix
tawtaidin *n.* ท่อใต้ดิน culvert
tawtan *pref.* ต่อต้าน anti
tawtan *v. t.* ต่อต้าน combat

tawtan *v.t.* ต่อต้าน oppose

tawtan *a.* ต่อต้าน repugnant

tawtan *v.t.* ต่อต้าน resist

tawtan *a.* ต่อต้าน resistant

tawtan-a-gadsayan *a.* ต่อต้านอากาศยาน anti-aircraft

tawyod *v.t.* ต่อยอด top

taxi *n.* แท็กซี่ taxi

tayeutayan *a.* ทะเยอทะยาน ambitious

tay *v.t.* เตะ kick

team *n.* ทีม team

teb *n.* เทพ deity

tebniyai *n* เทพนิยาย fairy

technique *n.* เทคนิค technique

technology *n.* เทคโนโลยี technology

tedsaban *n.* เทศบาล municipality

teidsagan-easter *n* เทศกาลอีสเตอร์ easter

teknikgansongtoralek *n.* เทคนิคการส่งโทรเลข telegraphy

tem *a.* เต็ม full

teumcheuapleung *v.t.* เติมเชื้อเพลิง stoke

temchon *n.* เต็มช้อน spoonful

temjai *a.* เต็มใจ whole-hearted

temjai *a.* เต็มใจ willing

temmeu *n.* เต็มมือ handful

tempaidauybai *a.* เต็มไปด้วยใบ leafy

tempaiduay *a.* เต็มไปด้วย fraught

tempaiduay-ai *a.* เต็มไปด้วยไอ vaporous

tempaiduay-antarai *a.* เต็มไปด้วยอันตราย perilous

tempaiduaydawkmai *a* เต็มไปด้วยดอกไม้ flowery

tempaiduayduangdao *a.* เต็มไปด้วยดวงดาว starry

tempaiduayfongsabu *a.* เต็มไปด้วยฟองสบู่ soapy

tempaiduayhin *a.* เต็มไปด้วยหิน stony

tempaiduayklon *v.t.* เต็มไปด้วยโคลน silt

tempaiduaykwamsao *a.* เต็มไปด้วยความเศร้า woebegone

tempaiduaykwan *a.* เต็มไปด้วยควัน smoky

tempaiduaypukao *a.* เต็มไปด้วยภูเขา mountainous

tempak *n.* เต็มปาก mouthful

temti *a.* เต็มที่ sheer

tennis *n.* เทนนิส tennis

tenpenjangwa *v. t.* เต้นเป็นจังหวะ beat

tenpenjangwa *v.i.* เต้นเป็นจังหวะ pulsate

tenpenjangwa *v.i.* เต้นเป็นจังหวะ pulse

tenpenjangwa *v.i.* เต้นเป็นจังหวะ throb

tenram *v. t.* เต้นรำ dance

tenrua *v.t* เต้นรัว flutter

tenrua *v.i.* เต้นรัว palpitate

tent *n.* เต็นท์ tent

tesana *v.i.* เทศนา preach

tesana *v.i.* เทศนา sermonize

teu *a* ทื่อ blunt

teu *v.t* ถือ hold

teuakkao-alp *n.* เทือกเขาแอลป์ alp

teuan *v. t.* เตือน caution

teuan *v.t.* เตือน remind

teuan *v.t.* เตือน warn

teuanluangna *v.t* เตือนล่วงหน้า forewarn

teuanpai *v.t* เตือนภัย alarm

teubto *v.t.* เติบโต grow

teubto *v.i* เติบโต mature

teubtobonsing-eun *adj.* เติบโตบนสิ่งอื่น adnascent

teubtonaineuamai *a.* เติบโตในเนื้อไม้ xylophilous

teum *v.t* เติม fill

teum *a.* ทึ่ม obtuse

teum *v.t.* เติม replenish

teun *v.t.* ตื่น awake

teun *a.* ตื้น shallow

teunggamnod *a* ถึงกำหนด due

teungkriad *a.* ตึงเครียด tense

teungmaewa *conj.* ถึงแม้ว่า though

teungtai *a.* ถึงตาย mortal

teuntein *v. t* ตื่นเต้น excite

teunten *adj.* ตื่นเต้น agog

teuntua *a.* ตื่นตัว alert

teuntua *a* ตื่นตัว awake

teuntua *v.t.* ตื่นตัว wake

teuprayodpensamkan *a.*
ถือประโยชน์เป็นสำคัญ utilitarian

teuwa *v.t.* ถือว่า attribute

tewaniyom *n.* เทวนิยม theism

tewaniyom *n.* เทววิทยา theology

tewatipatai *n.* เทวาธิปไตย theocracy

ti *prep.* ที่ at

ti *v.t.* ตี hit

ti *v.i.* ตี smack

tiabfang *adv.* เทียบฝั่ง ashore

ti-adnaen *a.* ที่อัดแน่น compact

tiang *n* เตียง bed

tiang *v. t* เถียง brangle

tiangkeun *n.* เที่ยงคืน midnight

tiangpab *n.* เตียงพับ cot

tiangtam *a.* เที่ยงธรรม virtuous

tiangtrong *a* เที่ยงตรง equitable

tiangwan *n.* เที่ยงวัน noon

tiankai *n.* เทียนไข candle

tiankanadlek *n* เทียนขนาดเล็ก taper

tibangkab *a* ที่บังคับ compulsory

tibanglom *n.* ที่บังลม lee

tibongchi *a.* ที่บ่งชี้ indicative

tichaipradab *a.* ที่ใช้ประดับ ornamental

tid *v.t.* ติด addict

tid *v.i.* ติด adhere

tid *v.t.* ติด adjoin

tid *v.t.* ติด attach

tid *v.t.* ติด jam

tid-a-wut *v.t.* ติดอาวุธ arm

tidcheua *v.t.* ติดเชื้อ infect

tidcheua *a.* ติดเชื้อ septic

tideungdudtangped *a.* ที่ดึงดูดทางเพศ
  sexy

tidgab *v* ติดกับ abutted

tidgan *a.* ติดกัน adjacent

tidgan *adj* ติดกัน cohesive

tidgradoom *v. t.* ติดกระดุม button

tidin *n* ที่ดิน estate

tidin *n.* ที่ดิน land

tidin *n* ที่ดิน lot

tidkook *v.t.* ติดคุก imprison

tidlom *v.t.* ติดหล่ม mire

tidnaen *a.* ติดแน่น adhesive

tidnaen *a.* ติดแน่น ingrained

tidneua *n.* ทิศเหนือ north

tidni *a.* ติดหนี้ indebted

tidpai *v.t.* ติดป้าย label

tidpai *v.t.* ติดป้าย tag

tidplug *v.i* ติดปลั๊ก bog

tidsataem *v.i.* ติดสแตมป์ stamp

tidsinbondai *a.* ติดสินบนได้ venal

tidtai *n.* ทิศใต้ south

tidtai *a.* ทิศใต้ south

tidtam *v.t.* ติดตาม accompany

tidtam *v.t* ติดตาม follow

tidtam *v.t.* ติดตาม pursue

tidtam *v.t.* ติดตาม trace

tidtamdai *a.* ติดตามได้ traceable

tidtang *n* ทิศทาง direction

tidtang *v.t.* ติดตั้ง install

tidtangkreuangmeu *v.t* ติดตั้งเครื่องมือ
  outfit

tidtaw *v. t* ติดต่อ contact

tidtawan-awk *n* ทิศตะวันออก east

tidtawantok *n.* ทิศตะวันตก west

tidtawgandai *a* ติดต่อกันได้ contagious

tidtawtangwittayu *v.t.* ติดต่อทางวิทยุ
  radio

tifawonglom *v.i.* ตีฝ่าวงล้อม sally

tigambang *n.* ที่กำบัง shelter

tiganchiang *v.t.* ตีกรรเชียง stroke

tigao *a.* ที่เก้า ninth

tigaosib *a.* ที่เก้าสิบ ninetieth

tigebkong *n* ที่เก็บของ cache

tigebsob *n.* ที่เก็บศพ morgue

tigedkeunnaiprawatsat *a .*
  ที่เกิดขึ้นในประวัติศาสตร์ historic

tigiawgabsupasit *a.* ที่เกี่ยวกับสุภาษิต
  proverbial

tigiawkonggan *a.* ที่เกี่ยวข้องกัน relative

tiglong *v.i.* ตีกลอง drum

tigodki *a.* ที่กดขี่ oppressive

tihok *a.* ที่หก sixth
tihoksib *a.* ที่หกสิบ sixtieth
tijab *n.* ที่จับ handle
tijamateung *a.* ที่จะมาถึง forthcoming
tijed *a.* ที่เจ็ด seventh
tika *v.t.* ตีค่า treasure
tikadwangwai *a.* ที่คาดหวังไว้ prospective
tikannangseu *n.* ที่คั่นหนังสือ book-mark
tikasoonggeunpai *v.t.* ตีค่าสูงเกินไป overrate
tikleuanpenwongglom *a* ที่เคลื่อนเป็นวงกลม circular
tiklumsanamplaw *n* ที่คลุมสนามเพลาะ blindage
tikwaenkawnaktod *n.* . ที่แขวนคอนักโทษ gallows
tikwam *v.t.* ตีความ interpret
tilaipaiduaygan *adj.* ที่ไหลไปด้วยกัน confluent
tilangga *v.i.* ตีลังกา somersault
tilanoi *a.* ที่ละน้อย gradual
tileauyu *a.* ที่เหลืออยู่ residual
tilipai *n* ที่ลี้ภัย asylum
tilobpai *n.* ที่หลบภัย haven
tilobpai *n.* ที่หลบภัย refuge
tilobpai *n.* ที่หลบภัย sanctuary
tima *n.* ที่มา source
timaiginneuasat *a* ที่ไม่กินเนื้อสัตว์ vegetarian
timainajageudkeun *a.* ที่ไม่น่าจะเกิดขึ้น unlikely
timaisinsud ที่ไม่สิ้นสุด eternal
timan *n.* ที่มั่น post
timan *n.* ที่มั่น stronghold
timduayhawk *v.t.* ทิ่มด้วยหอก lance
timi-a-rompruanprae *a.* ที่มีอารมณ์ปรวนแปร temperamental
timiglinhom *a.* ที่มีกลิ่นหอม odorous
timikukronglaikon *a.* ที่มีคู่ครองหลายคน polygamous
timikwamwang *a.* ที่มีความหวัง promising

timilaksanasongped *adj.* ที่มีลักษณะสองเพศ bisexual
timipleuak *a.* ที่มีเปลือก husky
timiroobrangklailookbat *adj.* ที่มีรูปร่างคล้ายลูกบาศก์ cubiform
timonghendai *a.* ที่มองเห็นได้ outward
timungpaidannok *adv* ที่มุ่งไปด้านนอก outward
tinai *adv.* ที่ไหน where
tinai *adv.* ที่ไหน whereabout
tinan *adv.* ที่นั่น there
tinang *n.* ที่นั่ง seat
tineaukwa *a.* ที่เหนือกว่า predominant
ting *v.t.* ทิ้ง shed
tinghu *n.* ติ่งหู lobe
tingriarad *v.t.* ทิ้งเรี่ยราด litter
tini ที่นี่ here
tini *adv.* ที่นี่ hither
tinon *n* ที่นอน berth
tinon *n* ที่นอน bunk
tinon *n.* ที่นอน mattress
tintiyu *n* ถิ่นที่อยู่ domicile
tintiyu *n.* ถิ่นที่อยู่ habitat
ti-padfoon *n* ที่ปัดฝุ่น duster
tipai *v.t.* ตีพ่าย rout
tipak *n.* ที่พัก hostel
tipak *n.* ที่พัก lodge
tipak-a-sai *n.* ที่พักอาศัย residence
tipaktak-a-gad *n* ที่พักตากอากาศ resort
tipangantodsob *a* ที่ผ่านการทดสอบ proof
tipanma *adv.* ที่ผ่านมา ago
tipanma *a.* ที่ผ่านมา late
tipanpailaew *a.* ที่ผ่านไปแล้ว past
tipenjaokong *a.* ที่เป็นเจ้าของ own
tipenlang *a.* ที่เป็นลาง ominous
tipenmoka *a.* ที่เป็นโมฆะ void
tipenpanha *a.* ที่เป็นปัญหา problematic
tipenprayod *a.* ที่เป็นประโยชน์ salutary
tipenrae *a* ที่เป็นแร่ mineral
tipenroobsiliampeunpa *a.* ที่เป็นรูปสี่เหลี่ยมผืนผ้า oblong

tipensaiyoikongmaenam *a.*
ที่เป็นสายย่อยของแม่น้ำ tributary
tipensuanseum *adj.* ที่เป็นส่วนเสริม
component
tipoytipai *a.* ดีโพยตีพาย hysterical
tipramanganwai *a.* ที่ประมาณการไว้
notional
tirab *n* ที่ราบ flat
tirab *n.* ที่ราบ plain
tirabaitong *a* ที่ระบายท้อง purgative
tirabgwangyai *n.* ที่ราบกว้างใหญ่ steppe
tirabreun *a.* ที่ราบรื่น seamy
tirabsoong *n.* ที่ราบสูง plateau
tirak *n* ที่รัก beloved
tirak *a* ที่รัก darling
tiraka *v. t* ตีราคา estimate
tiraka *v.t.* ตีราคา rate
tirakang *v.t.* ตีระฆัง toll
tiraksawai *a.* ที่รักษาไว้ preservative
tiraksawai *a.* ที่รักษาไว้ retentive
tirang *n* ที่รั้ง brace
tirareuk *n.* ที่ระลึก memorial
tirobru *a.* ที่รอบรู้ omniscient
tirokrang *n.* ที่รกร้าง wilderness
tiruamgan *adj.* ที่รวมกัน conjunct
tisam *a.* ที่สาม third
tisampangan *a.* ที่สัมพันธ์กัน associate
tisamsib *a.* ที่สามสิบ thirtieth
tisantonglab *a.* ที่สะท้อนกลับ reflective
tisantonglab *a* ที่สะท้อนกลับ reflexive
tisasomwai *a.* ที่สะสมไว้ stock
tisedsin *a* ที่เสร็จสิ้น complete
tisibgao *a.* ที่สิบเก้า nineteenth
tisibjed *a.* ที่สิบเจ็ด seventeenth
tisibjed *a.* ที่เจ็ดสิบ seventieth
tisibsam *a.* ที่สิบสาม thirteenth
tisibhok *a.* ที่สิบหก sixteenth
tisibsong *a.* ที่สิบสอง twelfth
tisomhedsompon *a.* ที่สมเหตุสมผล
tenable
tisong *a.* ที่สอง second
tisonren *a.* ที่ซ่อนเร้น latent

tisuang *conj.* ที่ซึ่ง whereat
tisud *a* ที่สุด extreme
tisud *adv.* ที่สุด most
tisud *a.* ที่สุด supreme
titamgangased *a.* ที่ทำการเกษตร agrarian
titamganpraisani *n.* ที่ทำการไปรษณีย์
post-office
titamma *a.* ที่ตามมา subsequent
titangkeun *a.* ที่ตั้งขึ้น upright
titangsob *n* ที่ตั้งศพ bier
titeuntua *a.* ที่ตื่นตัว wakeful
titodsamawreua *n* ที่ทอดสมอ anchorage
titriamwaisamrab-a-nakot *a.*
ที่เตรียมไว้สำหรับอนาคต provident
titruan *v.t* ตีตรวน fetter
tiwang *n.* ที่ว่าง space
tiwised *a.* ที่วิเศษ heavenly
tiyaklambak *a.* ที่ยากลำบาก trying
tiyangraeng *v.t.* ตีอย่างแรง whack
tiyeudyao *a.* ที่ยืดยาว lengthy
tiyisib *a.* ที่ยี่สิบ twentieth
tiyu *n.* ที่อยู่ accommodation
tiyu *n.* ที่อยู่ address
tiyu-a-sai *n* ที่อยู่อาศัย dwelling
tiyu-a-sai *n.* ที่อยู่อาศัย habitation
tiyudannawk *a.* ที่อยู่ด้านนอก outside
tiyunaitamnaeng *a* ที่อยู่ในตำแหน่ง
incumbent
to *n* โต๊ะ desk
to *n.* โต๊ะ table
tob *v.t* ตอบ answer
tob *v.i.* ตอบ reply
tob *v.i.* ตอบ respond
tob *v.t.* ตบ slap
tobdai *a.* ตอบได้ answerable
tobprisana *v.i.* ตอบปริศนา riddle
tobsanong *v.i.* ตอบสนอง react
tobsanong *v.t.* ตอบสนอง requite
tobta *v.t.* ตบตา hoodwink
tobta *v.t.* ตบตา juggle
tobtaen *v.t.* ตอบแทน recompense
tobto *v.t.* ตอบโต้ counteract

tobtuan *v.t.* ทบทวน review
tod *v.t.* ทอด fry
todhui *v.i.* ทอดหุ่ย loiter
todnam *v.t.* ทดน้ำ irrigate
tod-ngao *v.t* ทอดเงา shadow
todprahan *n* โทษประหาร execution
todsob *v. t.* ทดสอบ essay
todsob *v. t* ทดสอบ examine
todsob *v.t.* ทดสอบ test
tidtawgandai *a.* ติดต่อกันได้ infectious
todting *v.t.* ทอดทิ้ง abandon
todting *v. t.* ทอดทิ้ง desert
todtawn *v. t* ถอดถอน depose
tok *v. i* ตก drop
tok *v.t* ตอก hammer
tok *v.t.* ตอก ram
tokduaylim *v.t.* ตอกด้วยลิ่ม wedge
tokjai *v.t.* ตกใจ scare
tokjai *v.t.* ตกใจ shock
tokjaiglua *v.i.* ตกใจกลัว cower
toklong *v.t.* ตกลง accord
toklong *v.i.* ตกลง agree
toklong *v.i.* ตกลง settle
tokmud *v.t.* ตอกหมุด peg
tokmud *v.t.* ตอกหมุด rivet
tokpla *v.i.* ตกปลา dap
tokpla *v.i* ตกปลา fish
tokployploy *v. i* ตกปรอยๆ drizzle
tokrang *v. t.* ตกราง derail
toktaeng *v. t* ตกแต่ง beautify
toktaeng *v. t* ตกแต่ง deck
toktaeng *v. t* ตกแต่ง decorate
toktaeng *v.t.* ตกแต่ง furnish
toktaeng *v.t.* ตกแต่ง panel
toktaeng *v.t.* ตกแต่ง retouch
toktaleung *adv.* ตกตะลึง aback
toktaleung *a.* ตกตะลึง aghast
toktaleung *v.i* ตกตะลึง marvel
toktaeng *v.t.* ตกแต่ง adorn
tokyam *v.t.* ตอกย้ำ inculcate
tokyunai-antarai *v. t.* ตกอยู่ในอันตราย endanger

tokyunai-antarai *v.t.* ตกอยู่ในอันตราย peril
tom *v.i.* ต้ม boil
tom *n.* ตม hag
tom *n.* ต่อม node
tomboy *n.* ทอมบอย tomboy
tomnamlai *v.i.* ถ่มน้ำลาย spit
tomtua *v.t.* ถ่อมตัว abase
tomtua *a.* ถ่อมตัว humble
tomtua *a.* ถ่อมตัว modest
ton *v.t* ทน bear
tawn *n* ตอน episode
tawn *v.t.* ตอน geld
ton *n.* ตัน ton
ton *n.* ตัน tonne
ton-a-ngun *n.* ต้นองุ่น vine
tonbaeb *n.* ต้นแบบ model
tonbaeb *n.* ต้นแบบ prototype
tonchabab *n.* ต้นฉบับ manuscript
tonchabab *n* ต้นฉบับ original
tondai *a.* ทนได้ tolerable
tong *n* ท้อง abdomen
tong *n.* ธง banner
tong *n* ท้อง belly
tong *n* ธง flag
tong *n.* ทอง gold
tong *v.* ต้อง must
tong *a.* ท้อง pregnant
tong *n.* ท้อง stomach
tong *n.* ธง streamer
tongafak *n.* ต้นกาฝาก mistletoe
tongamneud *n.* ต้นกำเนิด origin
tongdaeng *n. & adj* ทองแดง bronze
tongdaeng *n* ทองแดง copper
tongfa *n.* ท้องฟ้า sky
tongfeu *a.* ท้องเฟ้อ gassy
tonggan *v.t.* ต้องการ require
tonggan *v.t.* ต้องการ want
tonggan *v.t.* ต้องการ will
tongham *a* ต้องห้าม taboo
tongjam *v.t.* ท่องจำ recite

tonglangkongprated *n.*
ตอนกลางของประเทศ midland

tongleuang *n.* ทองเหลือง brass

tongmigon *a.* ต้องมีก่อน prerequisite

tongpuk *n.* ท้องผูก constipation

tongsamsi *n* ธงสามสี tricolour

tongsiapasi *a.* ต้องเสียภาษี taxable

tongtiaw *v.i.* ท่องเที่ยว tour

tongtiawpai *v.i.* ท่องเที่ยวไป roam

tongtin *a.* ท้องถิ่น local

tongtin *n.* ท้องถิ่น locality

tongtin *a.* ท้องถิ่น rural

tonhom *n.* ต้นหอม leek

tonhonreua *n.* ต้นหนเรือ navigator

tawnjob *n* ตอนจบ finish

tawnjob *n.* ตอนจบ omega

tonka *n.* ต้นขา thigh

tonkaw *n.* ต้นคอ nape

tonlew *n.* ต้นหลิว willow

tonmadeua *n.* ต้นมะเดื่อ sycamore

ton-mahogany *n.* ต้นมะฮอกกานี
mahogany

tonmai *n.* ต้นไม้ gooseberry

tonmai *n.* ต้นไม้ poplar

tonmai *n.* ต้นไม้ tree

tonmaichanidneung *n.* ต้นไม้ชนิดหนึ่ง
birch

tonmaichanidneung *n.* ต้นไม้ชนิดหนึ่ง
dandelion

tonmaidai *a.* ทนไม่ได้ insupportable

tonmaidai *a.* ทนไม่ได้ intolerable

tonmaidai *a.* ทนไม่ได้ intolerant

tonmai-on *n.* ต้นไม้อ่อน sapling

tonmaitia *n.* ต้นไม้เตี้ย shrub

tonmaitikiawcha-umtalodpi *n*
ต้นไม้ที่เขียวชอุ่มตลอดปี evergreen

ton-narcissus *n* ต้นนาซีซัส narcissus

tawn-ngeun *v.t.* ถอนเงิน demonetize

ton-oak *n.* ต้นโอ๊ค oak

ton-on *n* ต้นอ่อน bud

ton-on *n* ต้นอ่อน sprout

ton-palm *n.* ต้นปาล์ม palm

tonplum *n.* ต้นพลัม plum

tonsai *n.* ต้นไทร banyan

tonsil *n.* ทอลซิล tonsil

tonson *n.* ต้นสน cedar

tonson *n* ต้นสน fir

tonson *n.* ต้นสน pine

tontan *a* ทนทาน abiding

tontan *a* ทนทาน durable

tontan *v.t.* ทนทาน endure

tontan *a.* ทนทาน lasting

tontandai *a* ทนทานได้ endurable

tontaw *v.t.* ทนต่อ withstand

tontawganplianplang *v.t.*
ทนต่อการเปลี่ยนแปลง weather

tontook *v.t.* ทนทุกข์ suffer

tontoon *n.* ต้นทุน cost

toob *n.* ธูป incense

took *a* ถูก cheap

took *a* ทุก every

tookdeuan *a.* ทุกเดือน monthly

tookdeuan *adv* ทุกเดือน monthly

tookgakkang *a.* ถูกกักขัง captive

tookgata *n* ตุ๊กตา doll

tookgodmai *a.* ถูกกฎหมาย lawful

tookgodmai *a.* ถูกกฎหมาย legal

tookjai *a.* ทุกข์ใจ grievous

tookjamgad *a.* ถูกจำกัด limited

tookkeun *adv.* ทุกคืน nightly

tookkon *pron* ทุกคน all

tooknati *adv.* ทุกนาที minutely

tooksab *a.* ถูกสาป accursed

tooksamdeaun *a.* ทุกสามเดือน quarterly

tooksukkalaksana *a.* ถูกสุขลักษณะ
hygienic

tooksuklaksana *a.* ถูกสุขลักษณะ sanitary

tooktong *a.* ถูกต้อง accurate

tooktong *adv* ถูกต้อง aright

tooktong *a* ถูกต้อง correct

tooktong *a.* ถูกต้อง right

tookwan *adv.* ทุกวัน daily

tookwela *a.* ถูกเวลา timely

tookyak *a.* ทุกข์ยาก miserable

toon *n* ทุ่น buoy
toongansuksa *n.* ทุนการศึกษา scholarship
toot *n.* ทูต ambassador
topasawa *n.* โถปัสสาวะ urinal
torahod *a.* ทรหด indomitable
torajit *n.* โทรจิต telepathy
torakamanakom *n.* โทรคมนาคม telecommunications
torakong *n.* โทรโข่ง megaphone
toralek *n.* โทรเลข telegram
toranipratu *n.* ธรณีประตู threshold
torasab *n.* โทรศัพท์ phone
torasab *n.* โทรศัพท์ telephone
torasan *n* โทรสาร fac-simile
toratat *n.* โทรทัศน์ television
torayod *v.t.* ทรยศ betray
torewkwa *v.t.* โตเร็วกว่า outgrow
torpedo *n.* ตอร์ปิโด torpedo
tosamka *n.* โต๊ะสามขา tripod
tosawat *n* ทศวรรษ decade
totiang *v. t* โต้เถียง bicker
totiangganleknoy *v.t.* โต้เถียงกันเล็กน้อย skirmish
totob *v. i* โต้ตอบ correspond
totob *v.t.* โต้ตอบ retort
toy *v.t.* ต่อย jab
toy *v.t.* ต่อย smash
toy *v.t.* ต่อย sting
toyaeng *v. t.* โต้แย้ง debate
toyaengmaidai *a.* โต้แย้งไม่ได้ indisputable
toyang *v.t.* โต้แย้ง argue
toyglab *adv.* ถอยกลับ backward
toykam *n.* ถ้อยคำ phrase
toylang *v.i.* ถอยหลัง recede
toylang *v.i.* ถอยหลัง recoil
toylang *v.t.* ถอยหลัง reverse
toylooktao *v. i.* ทอยลูกเต๋า dice
tractor *n.* แทรกเตอร์ tractor
trae *n.* แตร trump
trae *n.* แตร trumpet
traeboran *n.* แตรโบราณ clarion

traediaw *n* แตรเดี่ยว bugle
traetongleuang *n.* แตรทองเหลือง cornet
tragoon *n.* ตระกูล kinship
tragoon *n.* ตระกูล pedigree
traitrong *v. i* ไตร่ตรอง deliberate
traitrongluangna *v.t.* ไตร่ตรองล่วงหน้า premeditate
tranak *a.* ตระหนัก aware
tra-ngan *v.i.* ตระหง่าน tower
trani *a.* ตระหนี่ miserly
Transliteration *Noun, Verb etc.* **Thai Meaning English words**
trapratab *n.* ตราประทับ seal
triam *v.t.* เตรียม prepare
triam-a-hanglangwan *v.i.* เตรียมอาหารกลางวัน lunch
triamprom *v.t* เตรียมพร้อม groom
triamtipawpluk *v.t.* เตรียมที่เพาะปลูก till
tridsadi *n.* ทฤษฎี theory
trimat *n.* ไตรมาส quarter
tripaki *a.* ไตรภาคี tripartite
trok *n.* ตรอก alley
trong *a* ตรง direct
trong *a.* ตรง straight
tronggankam *a.* ตรงกันข้าม reverse
trongglang *a.* ตรงกลาง median
trongkam *pref.* ตรงข้าม contra
trongkam *a* ตรงข้าม contrary
trongkam *a* ตรงข้าม cross
trongkam *a.* ตรงข้าม opposite
trongkam *a.* ตรงข้าม reactinary
tronglewa *a.* ตรงเวลา punctual
trongpaitrongma *a.* ตรงไปตรงมา straightforward
trongpraden *a.* ตรงประเด็น pertinent
trongwela *adv.* ตรงเวลา sharp
truadsob *v. t.* ตรวจสอบ censor
truadsob *v. t.* ตรวจสอบ check
truadsob *v.t.* ตรวจสอบ inspect
truadsob *v.t.* ตรวจสอบ oversee
truadsob *v.t.* ตรวจสอบ scan
truadsobbanchi *v.t.* ตรวจสอบบัญชี audit

tu *n.* ตู้ ambry
tua *n.* ถั่ว bean
tua *n* ถั่ว nut
tua *n.* ถั่ว pea
tua *n.* ตั๋ว ticket
tua-akson *n.* ตัวอักษร alphabet
tua-eng *n.* ตัวเอง self
tua-a-suji *n.* ตัวอสุจิ sperm
tuabongchi *n.* ตัวบ่งชี้ indicator
tuaduang *n.* ตัวด้วง weevil
tua-ein *n.* ตัวเอน italics
tua-ek *n.* ตัวเอก protagonist
tuagratoon *n.* ตัวกระตุ้น stimulus
tuahanjamnuantem *n.* ตัวหารจำนวนเต็ม
  aliquot
tuakongchan *pron.* ตัวของฉัน myself
tualek *n* ตัวเลข digit
tualek *n.* ตัวเลข number
tualok *a.* ทั่วโลก global
tuam *v.t* ท่วม flood
tuamtoan *v.i.* ท่วมท้น well
tuamtoan *v.t.* ท่วมท้น whelm
tuangtamnong *n.* ท่วงทำนอง melody
tua-on *n* ตัวอ่อน embryo
tuapai *a.* ทั่วไป general
tuapraeton *n.* ตัวแปรต้น antecedent
tuapragan *n.* ตัวประกัน hostage
tuarai *n.* ตัวร้าย villain
tuased *n.* ตัวเศษ numerator
tuataen *n.* ตัวแทน proctor
tuataen *n.* ตัวแทน proxy
tuataen *n.* ตัวแทน representative
tuatalok *n* ตัวตลก comic
tuatalok *n.* ตัวตลก joker
tuatalok *n.* ตัวตลก pantaloon
tuatamgan *n* ตัวทำการ agonist
tuatamlalai *n* ตัวทำละลาย solvent
tuatan *n* ตัวแทน agent
tuatangkun *n.* ตัวตั้งคุณ multiplicand
tuataw *n.* ตัวต่อ wasp
tuay *n.* ถ้วย cup
tuayang *n* ตัวอย่าง example

tuayang *n.* ตัวอย่าง instance
tuayang *n.* ตัวอย่าง sample
tuayang *n.* ตัวอย่าง specimen
tuayangtidileud *n.* ตัวอย่างที่ดีเลิศ
  paragon
tuayangtimimagon *n.* ตัวอย่างที่มีมาก่อน
  precedent
tub *v.t.* ทุบ thump
tubponrapab *a.* ทุพพลภาพ invalid
tubti *v.t* ทุบตี maul
tuchae *n* ตู้แช่ cooler
tudoeysanrodfai *n.* ตู้โดยสารรถไฟ
  carriage
tuenten *a.* ตื่นเต้น nervous
tugebkong *n.* ตู้เก็บของ cabinet
tugebkong *n* ตู้เก็บของ cupboard
tujarit *a.* ทุจริต corrupt
teuktak *v.t.* ทึกทัก assume
tuktuk *a.* ทุกๆ all
tulakom *n.* ตุลาคม October
tung *n.* ถุง bag
tung *n.* ถุง pouch
tungmeu *n.* ถุงมือ mitten
tungmeuyao *n.* ถุงมือยาว gauntlet
tungmeuyao *n.* ถุงมือยาว glove
tungna *n* ทุ่งนา field
tungnong *n.* ถุงน่อง stocking
tunglong *n.* ทุ่งโล่ง moor
teungtaidai *a* ถึงตายได้ deadly
tungtao *n.* ถุงเท้า sock
tungtaoyao *n.* ถุงเท้ายาว hosiery
tungya *n.* ทุ่งหญ้า lea
tungya *n.* ทุ่งหญ้า mead
tungya *n.* ทุ่งหญ้า meadow
tungyaliangsat *n.* ทุ่งหญ้าเลี้ยงสัตว์
  pasture
tupeun *v.t.* ถูพื้น mop
tupla *n.* ตู้ปลา aquarium
turagid *n* ธุรกิจ business
turagidtongtiaw *n.* ธุรกิจการท่องเที่ยว
  tourism
tusinkarodfai *n.* ตู้สินค้ารถไฟ wagon

tuyen *n.* ตู้เย็น fridge
tuyen *n.* ตู้เย็น refrigerator
typhoid *n.* ไทฟอยด์ typhoid

uad-di *a.* อวดดี insolent
uad-ru *a.* อวดรู้ pedantic
uay-pon *v. t* อวยพร bless
u-bai *n.* อุบาย artifice
u-bai *n.* อุบาย plot
u-bai *n.* อุบาย ruse
u-bai *n.* อุบาย wile
u-bathed *n.* อุบัติเหตุ casualty
u-bathed *n* อุบัติเหตุ accident
u-bathed *n.* อุบัติเหตุ mishap
ud *n.* อูฐ camel
ud *v.t.* อุด throttle
udjara *n.* อุจจาระ stool
u-domkati *n* อุดมคติ ideal
u-domkatiniyom *n.* อุดมคตินิยม idealism
udomsomboon *a.* อุดมสมบูรณ์ luxuriant
u-domsomboon *a* อุดมสมบูรณ์ fertile
u-domsomboon *a.* อุดมสมบูรณ์ fruitful
u-domsomboon *a.* อุดมสมบูรณ์ resourceful
u-domsomboon *a.* อุดมสมบูรณ์ superabundant
ud-ru *v.t.* อุดรู plug
udsaha *a.* อุตสาหะ painstaking
um-nad *n.* อำนาจ authority
umnuaykwamsaduak *v.t* อำนวยความสะดวก facilitate
um-nuaykwamsaduak *v. t* อำนวยความสะดวก comfort
u-mong *n.* อุโมงค์ tunnel
ungtao *n.* อุ้งเท้า paw
u-pama-u-pamai *a* อุปมาอุปไมย figurative
u-parad *n.* อุปราช viceroy
u-pasak *n.* อุปสรรค ado

u-pasak *n.* อุปสรรค obstacle
u-patan *n* อุปทาน supply
u-tan *v.i* อุทาน exclaim
u-thidtonhaigab *v.t.* อุทิศตนให้กับ consecrate
u-tidtua *v. t.* อุทิศตัว dedicate
u-ton *v.t.* อุทธรณ์ appeal
utsaha *a.* อุตสาหะ industrious
utsahagam *n.* อุตสาหกรรม industry

vaseline *n.* วาสลีน vaseline
violin *n.* ไวโอลิน violin
virus *n.* ไวรัส virus
vitamin *n.* วิตามิน vitamin
volt *n.* โวลต์ volt

wa *conj.* ว่า that
wab *v.t* วาบ flash
wachapeud *n.* วัชพืช weed
wad *v.t* วาด draw
wad *v.t* วัด measure
waddai *a.* วัดได้ measurable
wadkrongrang *v.t.* วาดโครงร่าง profile
wadpab *v.t.* วาดภาพ picture
wadpab *v.t.* วาดภาพ portray
waen *n.* แหวน ring
waentaganfoon *n.* แว่นตากันฝุ่น goggles
waentakangdiaw *n.* แว่นตาข้างเดียว monocle
wai *adj* ไว brisk
wai-a-lai *a.* ไว้อาลัย obituary
waidek *n* วัยเด็ก boyhood
waidek *n.* วัยเด็ก childhood
waifai *a.* ไวไฟ inflammable
waijai *v. t* ไว้ใจ entrust

waijai *v.i.* ไว้ใจ rely

waijai *v.t* ไว้ใจ trust

waijaidai *a.* ไว้ใจได้ reliable

waijaidai *a.* ไว้ใจได้ trustful

waijaimaidai *a.* ไว้ใจไม่ได้ unreliable

wainam *v.i.* ว่ายน้ำ swim

waipuyai *a* วัยผู้ใหญ่ adult

wairaekroon *n.* วัยแรกรุ่น puberty

wairoon *n.* วัยรุ่น adolescence

wairoon *n.* วัยรุ่น teenager

waisateuan *a.* ไหวสะเทือน seismic

waitarok *n.* วัยทารก infancy

waitawkwamruseuk *a.* ไวต่อความรู้สึก sensitive

waiyagon *n.* ไวยากรณ์ grammar

wajang *v.t.* ว่าจ้าง wage

waksin *n.* วัคซีน vaccine

walnut *n.* วอลนัท walnut

wan *n* วัน day

wan *v.t.* หว่าน sow

wan *a.* หวาน sweet

wanarok *n.* วัณโรค tuberculosis

wanasat *n* วนศาสตร์ forestry

wan-a-tit *n.* วันอาทิตย์ Sunday

wanchristmas *n* วันคริสต์มาส Christmas

wang *v.t.* หวัง hope

wang *v.t.* วาง lay

wang *v.i.* วาง lie

wang *n.* วัง palace

wang *v.t.* วาง place

wang *v.t* วาง set

wang *a* ว่าง spare

wang *a.* ว่าง vacant

wa-ngai *a.* ว่าง่าย malleable

wangbonchan *v.t.* วางบนชั้น shelve

wangbonto *v.t.* วางบนโต๊ะ table

wangdeumpan *v.t.* วางเดิมพัน stake

wangeunpai *a.* หวานเกินไป saccharine

wanggabdak *v.t.* วางกับดัก snare

wanggabdak *v.t.* วางกับดัก trap

wangkai *v.i.* วางไข่ spawn

wangmad *a.* วางมาด pompous

wangmad *a.* วางมาด snobbish

wangmadjam *v.t.* วางมัดจำ pledge

wangpaen *v.t.* วางแผน plan

wangpaen *v.t.* วางแผน plot

wangpaengan *v.i.* วางแผนการ scheme

wangpaenrai *v.t.* วางแผนร้าย intrigue

wangplao *a* ว่างเปล่า empty

wangplao *a.* ว่างเปล่า stark

wangplao *a* ว่างเปล่า blank

wangrabiab *v.t.* วางระเบียบ regulate

wangta *v.i.* วางท่า pose

wangtronggankam *v.t.* วางตรงกันข้าม contrapose

wangtua *v. i.* วางตัว behave

wangyapid *v.t.* วางยาพิษ poison

wanjan *n.* วันจันทร์ Monday

wanlom *adj.* หว่านล้อม cogent

wanmaled *v.t.* หว่านเมล็ด seed

wanmod-a-yu *n* วันหมดอายุ expiry

wannakadi *n.* วรรณคดี literature

wannarokpod *n* วัณโรคปอด consumption

wanni *n.* วันนี้ today

wanparuhasabori *n.* วันพฤหัสบดี Thursday

wanpragobpititangsasanakrit *n.* วันประกอบพิธีทางศาสนาคริสต์ sabbath

wanput *n.* วันพุธ Wednesday

wansanae *v. t.* หว่านเสน่ห์ captivate

wansao *n.* วันเสาร์ Saturday

wansook *n.* วันศุกร์ Friday

wanti *n* วันที่ date

wangpidti *v.t.* วางผิดที่ misplace

wanyud *n.* วันหยุด holiday

wao *adj.* เว้า concave

wara *n.* วาระ agenda

wara *n.* วาระ term

warasansat *n.* วารสารศาสตร์ journalism

warasanti-awktamgamnod *n.* วารสารที่ออกตามกำหนด periodical

wat *n.* วัด cloister

wat *n.* วัด monastery

wat *v.t.* วัด scale

wat *n.* วัด temple

watagam *n* วาทกรรม discourse
watkanad *v.t.* วัดขนาด size
watmaidai *a.* วัดไม่ได้ immeasurable
watt *n.* วัตต์ watt
wattanatam *n* วัฒนธรรม culture
wattu *n.* วัตถุ object
wattu *n* วัตถุ material
wattuboran *a.* วัตถุโบราณ antique
wattuniyom *n.* วัตถุนิยม materialism
watturabeud *n.* วัตถุระเบิด explosive
wattusongglom *n.* วัตถุทรงกลม orb
waw *n.* ว่าว kite
wedmon *n.* เวทมนตร์ sorcery
wedmonkata *n.* เวทมนต์คาถา witchcraft
wen *v. t* เว้น except
wela *n.* เวลา time
welachao *n.* เวลาเช้า morning
welagontiang *n* เวลาก่อนเที่ยง forenoon
welanon *n.* เวลานอน bed-time
welayen *n* เวลาเย็น evening
wenraya *v.t.* เว้นระยะ space
weti *n.* เวที dais
weti *n.* เวที forum
weti *n.* เวที stage
weung *n* เว้ง bight
whisky *n.* วิสกี้ whisky
wi *n* หวี comb
wichadulaimeu *n.* วิชาดูลายมือ palmistry
wichaganbin *n.pl.* วิชาการบิน aeronautics
wichaganchangkanaengneung *n.*
วิชาการช่างแขนงหนึ่ง statics
wichakemi *n.* วิชาเคมี chemistry
wichanatiponlameuang *n*
วิชาหน้าที่พลเมือง civics
wichawaduaymalaeng *n.*
วิชาว่าด้วยแมลง entomology
wigonjarit *n.* วิกลจริต insanity
wigrittagan *n* วิกฤตการณ์ crisis
wijai *v.i.* วิจัย research
wijan *v. t* วิจารณ์ criticize
wijanyangroonraeng *adj*
วิจารณ์อย่างรุนแรง censorious

wikraw *v.t.* วิเคราะห์ analyse
winati *n* วินาที second
wine *n.* ไวน์ wine
wing *v.t.* วิ่ง jog
wing *v.i.* วิ่ง run
winglen *v.i.* วิ่งเล่น romp
winglen *v.i* วิ่งเล่น scamper
wingrao *v.t.* วิ่งราว pilfer
wingrewkwa *v.t.* วิ่งเร็วกว่า outrun
wingtemfeetao *v.i.* วิ่งเต็มฝีเท้า sprint
wingyawyaw *v.i.* วิ่งเยาะๆ trot
winichairok *v. t* วินิจฉัยโรค diagnose
winyan *n.* วิญญาณ manes
winyan *n.* วิญญาณ soul
winyan *n.* วิญญาณ spirit
wiraburud *n.* วีรบุรุษ hero
wiragam *n.* วีรกรรม heroism
wirasatri *n.* วีรสตรี heroine
wisahagit *n* วิสาหกิจ enterprise
wised *a.* วิเศษ magical
wised *a.* วิเศษ splendid
witayanipon *n.* วิทยานิพนธ์ thesis
witayasat *n.* วิทยาศาสตร์ science
witi *n* วิธี means
witi *n.* วิธี method
witichai *n.* วิธีใช้ use
witigan *n.* วิธีการ mode
witikuabkum *n.* วิธีควบคุม rein
witiyaekloha-awjakrae *n.*
วิธีแยกโลหะออกจากแร่ metallurgy
witsawagon *n* วิศวกร engineer
wittayalai *n* วิทยาลัย college
wittayu *n.* วิทยุ radio
wiwattanagan *n* วิวัฒนาการ evolution
woiwai *a.* โวยวาย outcry
wokwon *adj* วกวน anfractuous
wongdontri *n.* วงดนตรี band
wongglom *n.* วงกลม circle
wonggonhoy *n.* วงก้นหอย spiral
wongjon *n.* วงจร circuit
wongkojon *n* วงโคจร cycle
wongkojon *n.* วงโคจร orbit

wongleb n. วงเล็บ parenthesis
wongri a. วงรี oval
wongsymphony n. วงซิมโฟนี symphony
wongtragoon n. วงศ์ตระกูล parentage
wongtragoon n. วงศ์ตระกูล ancestry
wongwaenlek n วงแหวนเล็ก annulet
wongwai a. ว่องไว nimble
wua n วัว bull
wua n. วัว cow
wua n. วัว ox
wuanoom n วัวหนุ่ม bullock
wuapa n. วัวป่า yak
wunwai adv. วุ่นวาย chaotic
wunwai v.i วุ่นวาย fuss
wunwai a. วุ่นวาย turbulent
wutisamachik n. วุฒิสมาชิก senator
wutisapa n. วุฒิสภา senate

ya v. t หย่า divorce
ya n ยา drug
ya n หญ้า grass
ya n. ยา medicament
ya n. ยา medicine
ya n. ยา pill
ya n. หญ้า sod
yab a หยาบ coarse
yab a หยาบ curt
yabamroong n. ยาบำรุง tonic
yabkai a. หยาบคาย impertinent
yabkai a. หยาบคาย indecent
yabkai a. หยาบคาย profane
yabkai a. หยาบคาย rude
yabkai a. หยาบคาย vulgar
yabyang v.t. ยับยั้ง restrain
yabyang v.t. ยับยั้ง veto
yad n. ญาติ kin
yad n. ญาติ relative
yadsai v.t. ยัดไส้ stuff
yae adv. แย่ badly

yae v.t. แหย่ banter
yae v.t. แหย่ poke
yae a. แย่ terrible
yaek v.t. แยก isolate
yaek v.t. แยก part
yaek-awk v. t แยกออก detach
yaek-awk v. t แยกออก exclude
yaek-awk v.t. แยกออก segregate
yaek-awkjakgandai a. แยกออกจากกันได้
    separable
yaek-awkjakgandai a. แยกออกจากกันได้
    separate
yaekgandai v.t. แยกกันได้ separate
yaekglum v.t. แยกกลุ่ม segment
yaekmaidai a. แยกไม่ได้ inseparable
yaekneuaponlamai v.t. แยกเนื้อผลไม้
    pulp
yaekpraped v.t. แยกประเภท assort
yaekpraped v. t แยกประเภท classify
yaekpraped v.t แยกประเภท sort
yaektua v.t. แยกตัว seclude
yaektua-awk v.i. แยกตัวออก secede
yaekyaekwamtaektang v. i
    แยกแยะความแตกต่าง distinguish
yaemak a. แย่มาก awful
yaengching v.t. แย่งชิง wrest
yaengmaidai a. แย่งไม่ได้ irrefutable
yangnoitisud adv. อย่างน้อยที่สุด least
yaetisud a แย่ที่สุด worst
yafaran n. หญ้าฝรั่น saffron
yaganyung n ยากันยุง repellent
yai a ใหญ่ big
yai a ใหญ่ enormous
yai a. ใหญ่ gigantic
yai a. ใหญ่ grand
yai a. ใหญ่ huge
yai a. ใหญ่ large
yai v.t. ย้าย remove
yai a. ใหญ่ vast
yaimaengmoom n ใยแมงมุม cobweb
yaimangmoom n. ใยแมงมุม web
yaimaprao n ใยมะพร้าว coir

yaito *a.* ใหญ่โต palatial

yaito *a.* ใหญ่โต stately

yaito *a.* ใหญ่โต stupendous

yaito *a.* ใหญ่โต titanic

yaito *a.* ใหญ่โต tremendous

yajok *n.* ยาจก pauper

yak *a* ยาก difficult

yak *n.* ยักษ์ giant

yak *a.* ยาก onerous

yakacheuarok *n.* ยาฆ่าเชื้อโรค antiseptic

yakacheuarok *n.* ยาฆ่าเชื้อโรค germicide

yak-a-han *adj.* อยากอาหาร appetent

yakamalaeng *n.* ยาฆ่าแมลง insecticide

yakamalaeng *n.* ยาฆ่าแมลง pesticide

yakdai *v.i.* อยากได้ hanker

yakdaikongpu-eun *v.t.* อยากได้ของผู้อื่น covet

yakgapen *a.* อยากจะเป็น would-be

yakjon *a.* ยากจน poor

yakkatuatai *a.* อยากฆ่าตัวตาย suicidal

yaklai *v.t.* ยักไหล่ shrug

yaklambak *a.* ยากลำบาก arduous

yakmak *a.* ยากมาก herculean

yakrobjakkawan *n.* ยาครอบจักรวาล panacea

yakru *a* อยากรู้ curious

yakruyakhen *a.* อยากรู้อยากเห็น inquisitive

yakumgamneud *n.* ยาคุมกำเนิด contraception

yam *n.* แยม marmalade

yam *n.* ย่าม satchel

yam *n.* ยาม sentinel

yam *n.* ยาม sentry

yam *v.t.* ย่ำ tread

yamed *n.* ยาเม็ด tablet

yamtao *v.i.* ย่ำเท้า plod

yanat *n.* ยานัดถ์ snuff

yang *v.t.* ย่าง roast

yangchacha *adv.* อย่างช้าๆ slowly

yangchadjen *adv* อย่างชัดเจน clearly

yangdaiyangneung *a.*, อย่างใดอย่างหนึ่ง either

yanggriam *v.t.* ย่างเกรียม scorch

yanghoeyhuan *a.* อย่างโหยหวน shrill

yangjingjai *adv.* อย่างจริงใจ heartily

yangkadklan *adv.* อย่างขาดแคลน scarcely

yangkamtawkam *adv.* อย่างคำต่อคำ verbatim

yangkong *adv.* ยังคง still

yangkong *adv.* ยังคง yet

yanglablab *adv.* อย่างลับๆ stealthily

yangleuakfen *a.* อย่างเลือกเฟ้น selective

yanglilab *a.* อย่างลี้ลับ ulterior

yanglookpuchai *a.* อย่างลูกผู้ชาย manly

yangmai *n.* ยางไม้ asafoetida

yangmaihom *n.* ยางไม้หอม myrrh

yangmairibron *adv.* อย่างไม่รีบร้อน leisurely

yangmairoonrang *adv* อย่างไม่รุนแรง benignly

yangmaitangjai *adv.* อย่างไม่ตั้งใจ unawares

yangmak *n.* อย่างมาก arrant

yangmak *adv* อย่างมาก much

yangmak *adv.* อย่างมาก substantially

yangmak *a.* อย่างมาก utmost

yangmawsom *adv* อย่างเหมาะสม appositely

yangmirabiab *a.* อย่างมีระเบียบ orderly

yangmisanay *a.* อย่างมีเสน่ห์ winsome

yangna *adv.* อย่างหนา thick

yangnaenon *adv* อย่างแน่นอน absolutely

yangnaenon *adv.* อย่างแน่นอน certainly

yangnaenon *adv.* อย่างแน่นอน surely

yangpenkwamlab *a.* อย่างเป็นความลับ secretive

yangpeudpeuy *adv.* อย่างเปิดเผย openly

yangpised *adv* อย่างพิเศษ extra

yangpised *adv.* อย่างพิเศษ singularly

yangponggandai *adv.* อย่างป้องกันได้ defensive

yangpramat *a.* อย่างประมาท slovenly

yangraek *adv* อย่างแรก first

yangrai *adv.* อย่างไร how

yangraigawdi *adv.* อย่างไรก็ดี however

yangraigawdi *conj* อย่างไรก็ดี however

yangraigawdi *conj.* อย่างไรก็ดี nevertheless

yangraigawdi *adv.* อย่างไรก็ดี nonetheless

yangraigawdi *prep.* อย่างไรก็ดี notwithstanding

yangraigawdi *adv.* อย่างไรก็ดี notwithstanding

yangraigawdi *conj.* อย่างไรก็ดี notwithstanding

yangraigawdi *adv.* อย่างไรก็ดี somehow

yangraigawdi *adv.* อย่างไรก็ดี though

yangraiprayod *adv.* อย่างไร้ประโยชน์ vainly

yangrak *v.i.* หยั่งราก root

yangrew *adv.* อย่างเร็ว apace

yangrengrib *adv.* อย่างเร่งรีบ headlong

yangrob *n.* ยางลบ rubber

yangrodtilawdawkmai *n.* ยางรถที่หล่อดอกใหม่ retread

yangruabrad *adv.* อย่างรวบรัด shortly

yangruadrew *adv.* อย่างรวดเร็ว speedily

yangsoongsud *adv.* อย่างสูงสุด ultimately

yangsoong *adv.* อย่างสูง highly

yangtad *a.* อย่างทาส slavish

yangtaejing *adv.* อย่างแท้จริง indeed

yangtaektang *adv* อย่างแตกต่าง else

yangtam *a* อย่างต่ำ minimum

yangtangjai *adv.* อย่างตั้งใจ purposely

yang-taw-neuang *adv* อย่างต่อเนื่อง consecutively

yangtemti *adv.* อย่างเต็มที่ fully

yangtisud *adv.* อย่างที่สุด utterly

yangtooktong *adv.* อย่างถูกต้อง aright

yangyeun *a.* ยั่งยืน imperishable

yangyeun *v.t.* ยั่งยืน sustain

yangyungyeung *adv* อย่างยุ่งเหยิง topsy turvy

yangyutitam *adv.* อย่างยุติธรรม fairly

yangyutitam *adv.* อย่างยุติธรรม justly

yanom *v. t* หย่านม ablactate

yanom *v.t.* หย่านม wean

yanpahana *n.* ยานพาหนะ vehicle

yangrod *n.* ยางรถ tyre

yao *a.* เยาว์ juvenile

yao *a.* ยาว long

yaonan *adv* ยาวนาน long

yaowachon *n.* เยาวชน youth

yapid *n.* ยาพิษ poison

yaquinine *n.* ยาควินิน quinine

yara-ngabprasat *n* ยาระงับประสาท sedative

yasalob *n.* ยาสลบ anaesthetic

yasalob *n* ยาสลบ chloroform

yasamanprajamban *n.* ยาสามัญประจำบ้าน nostrum

yasapom *n.* ยาสระผม shampoo

yasoob *n.* ยาสูบ tobacco

yat *n.* ญาติ cousin

yatai *n.* ยาถ่าย laxative

yatai *n.* ยาถ่าย physic

yatai *n.* ยาถ่าย purgative

yatawnpid *n.* ยาถอนพิษ antidote

yatawnpid *n.* ยาถอนพิษ mithridate

yatinger *n.* ยาทิงเจอร์ tincture

yaw *v. t* ย่อ condense

yaw *v. t* ย่อ curtail

yawd *n* ยอด crest

yawkam *v.t.* ย่อคำ abbreviate

yawkwam *n.* ย่อความ precise

yawn *a.* หย่อน slack

yawna *n.* ย่อหน้า paragraph

yawnglab *v.i.* ย้อนกลับ backslide

yawnglab *v.i.* ย้อนกลับ return

yawnroydeum *v.t.* ย้อนรอยเดิม retrace

yawyei *v.i.* เยาะเย้ย gibe

yawyei *v.t.* เยาะเย้ย ridicule

yawyei *a.* เยาะเย้ย sardonic

yeast *n.* ยีสต์ yeast
yeb *v.t.* เย็บ sew
yeb *v.t.* เย็บ stitch
yebtakeb *v.t.* เย็บตะเข็บ seam
yeiyan *v.i.* เย้ยหยัน jeer
yen *a* เย็น cold
yeua *n* เหยื่อ bait
yeua *n.* เหยื่อ prey
yeua *n.* เหยื่อ victim
yeuabupew *n.* เยื่อบุผิว membrane
yeuahoomlookta *n* เยื่อหุ้มลูกตา choroid
yeuahumsamong-akseb *n.*
　เยื่อหุ้มสมองอักเสบ meningitis
yeuak *n.* เหยือก jug
yeuak *n.* เหยือก mug
yeud *v.t* ยึด forfeit
yeudsab *v. t* ยึดทรัพย์ confiscate
yeudsab *v. t* ยึดทรัพย์ deprive
yeudsab *v.t.* ยึดทรัพย์ levy
yeudtid *v. i.* ยึดติด cling
yeudwela *v.t.* ยึดเวลา prolong
yeudyoon *a* ยืดหยุ่น elastic
yeudyoon *a* ยืดหยุ่น flexible
yeudyun *a.* ยืดหยุ่น inflexible
yeum *v. t* ยืม borrow
yeun *v.i.* ยืน stand
yeunduayplaitao *v.t.* ยืนด้วยปลายเท้า toe
yeunfong *v.i.* ยื่นฟ้อง file
yeungran *a.* ยืนกราน insistent
yeungran *v.i.* ยืนกราน persist
yeunpramoon *v.t.* ยื่นประมูล tender
yeunyan *v.t.* ยืนยัน affirm
yeunyan *v.t.* ยืนยัน assert
yeunyan *v.t.* ยืนยัน attest
yeunyan *v.t.* ยืนยัน avow
yeunyan *v. t* ยืนยัน confirm
yeunyan *v.t.* ยืนยัน corroborate
yeunyan *v.t.* ยืนยัน insist
yeunyan *v.t.* ยืนยัน ratify
yeunyan *v.t.* ยืนยัน reassure
yeunyanwajing *a* ยืนยันว่าจริง affirmative
yiabkanreng *v.t.* เหยียบคันเร่ง pedal

yiabyam *v.t.* เหยียบย่ำ conculcate
yiadyam *a* เหยียดหยาม abusive
yiam *a* เยี่ยม fabulous
yiam *a* เยี่ยม fantastic
yiam *a.* เยี่ยม terrific
yiam *v.t.* เยี่ยม visit
yiaw *n* เหยี่ยว falcon
yihaw *n* ยี่ห้อ brand
yik *v.* หยิก pinch
yim *v.i.* ยิ้ม smile
yimyaw *v.i* ยิ้มเยาะ sneer
yindi *v. t.* ยินดี delight
yindi *v. i* ยินดี exult
yindi *v.t.* ยินดี please
yindi *v.i.* ยินดี rejoice
yindi *a.* ยินดี triumphal
yinditonrab *v.t* ยินดีต้อนรับ welcome
ying *a.* หยิ่ง arrogant
ying *v.t.* ยิง shoot
ying *a.* หยิ่ง vainglorious
ying-a-romrai *n.* หญิงอารมณ์ร้าย shrew
yingkwanan *adv.* ยิ่งกว่านั้น moreover
yingmai-awk *v.i.* ยิงไม่ออก misfire
yingnegro *n.* หญิงนิโกร negress
yingpaedsaya *n.* หญิงแพศยา minx
yingprommajan *n.* หญิงพรมจรรย์ damsel
yingprommajari *n* หญิงพรหมจารี virgin
yingroobrangbaebbang *n.*
　หญิงรูปร่างแบบบาง sylph
yingsakrid *n.* หญิงซักรีด laundress
yingsao *n.* หญิงสาว lady
yingsod *n.* หญิงโสด spinster
yingtimisamilaew *n.* หญิงที่มีสามีแล้ว
　matron
yingyai *a.* ยิ่งใหญ่ almighty
yingyai *a* ยิ่งใหญ่ great
yingyai *a.* ยิ่งใหญ่ imperial
yingyai *a.* ยิ่งใหญ่ majestic
yingyai *a.* ยิ่งใหญ่ monumental
yinyom *v.t.* ยินยอม consent3
yinyom *v.t.* ยินยอม vouchsafe
yisib *a.* ยี่สิบ twenty

yisib *n* ยี่สิบ twenty
yod *v.i.* หยด trickle
yodmanud *n.* ยอดมนุษย์ superman
yodnam *n* หยดน้ำ drip
yodnamman *v.t* หยดน้ำมัน grease
yodnamman *v.t.* หยดน้ำมัน oil
yodyiam *a.* ยอดเยี่ยม excellent
yoan *v.t.* โยน toss
yodlangka *n.* ยอดหลังคา steeple
yoi *v. t.* ย่อย digest
yoisalai *v. i* ย่อยสลาย decay
yoiyak *a.* ย่อยยาก indigestible
yok *n.* หยก jade
yok *v.t.* ยก lift
yok *v.t.* ยก raise
yok *v.t.* โยก rock
yok *v.i* โยก wobble
yokkeun *v.t.* ยกขึ้น uplift
yokkreuang *v.t.* ยกเครื่อง overhaul
yokleuk *v. t.* ยกเลิก abrogate
yokleuk *v. t.* ยกเลิก cancel
yokleuk *v.t.* ยกเลิก countermand
yokleuk *v.t.* ยกเลิก repeal
yokleuk *v.t.* ยกเลิก undo
yokmoradokhai *v. t.* ยกมรดกให้ bequeath
yoknew *v.t.* ยกนิ้ว thumb
yokradab *v. t* ยกระดับ elevate
yokradab *v. t* ยกระดับ exalt
yoktod *v.t.* ยกโทษ assoil
yoktod *v.t.* ยกโทษ pardon
yoktodhaidai *a.* ยกโทษให้ได้ venial
yokwen *prep* ยกเว้น except
wokwen *v. t.* ยกเว้น exempt
yokwen *prep* ยกเว้น but
yokwen *conj.* ยกเว้น unless
yokyaw *v.t* ยกยอ flatter
yokyong *v. t.* ยกย่อง extol
yokyong *v.t.* ยกย่อง glorify
yokyong *v.t.* ยกย่อง praise
yokyong *v.t.* ยกย่อง repute
yom *v. t* ย้อม dye
yom *v.t.* ยอม render

yom *v.t.* ยอม submit
yom *v.t.* ยอม yield
yomdai *a.* ยอมได้ permissible
yomhaikao *v.t.* ยอมให้เข้า adhibit
yomjamnon *v.i.* ยอมจำนน succumb
yompae *v.t.* ยอมแพ้ surrender
yomrab *v* ยอมรับ accept
yomrab *v.* ยอมรับ acknowledge
yomrab *v.t.* ยอมรับ concede
yomrabchai *a.* ยอมรับใช้ subservient
yomrabdai *a* ยอมรับได้ acceptable
yomrabdai *a.* ยอมรับได้ admissible
yomrabdai *a.* ยอมรับใช้ servile
yomrabfang *a* ยอมรับฟัง amenable
yomrabmaidai *a.* ยอมรับไม่ได้
   inadmissible
yomtam *v.i.* ยอมตาม acquiesce
yomtam *v. t* ยอมตาม capitulate
yomtam *v. i* ยอมตาม comply
yomtam *a.* ยอมตาม supple
yomtamtam *v.t.* ยอมทำตาม accede
yongkaoglai *v.i.* ย่องเข้าใกล้ stalk
yonhaisoong *v.t.* โยนให้สูง sky
yu *v.t.* อยู่ be
yu *v.i* อยู่ exist
yu *v.i.* อยู่ stay
yu-a-sai *v.t.* อยู่อาศัย inhabit
yuayao *v.t.* ยั่วเย้า tantalize
yuayao *v.t.* ยั่วเย้า tease
yuayu *v.t.* ยั่วยุ aggravate
yuayu *v.t.* ยั่วยุ provoke
yuayuan *n.* ยั่วยวน seduce
yucheuy *a.* อยู่เฉย passive
yud *v. t* หยุด break
yud *v. i.* หยุด cease
yud *v. t.* หยุด halt
yud *v.t.* หยุด stop
yudai *a.* อยู่ได้ inhabitable
yudchuakrao *v.i.* หยุดชั่วคราว pause
yud-nganpratuang *v.t.* หยุดงานประท้วง
   strike
yudtawiti *n.* ยุทธวิธี strategy

yuk *n* ยุค era
yukangna *v.* อยู่ข้างหน้า precede
yukglang *a.* ยุคกลาง medieval
yukhinmai *a.* ยุคหินใหม่ neolithic
yuksamai *n.* ยุคสมัย generation
yuna *prep* อยู่หน้า before
yung *a* ยุ่ง busy
yung *n.* ยุง mosquito
yung *v.i.* ยุ่ง tamper
yungchang *n.* ยุ้งฉาง granary
yungyeung *v.t.* ยุ่งเหยิง jumble
yungyeung *adv.* ยุ่งเหยิง pell-mell
yungyeung *a.* ยุ่งเหยิง topsy turvy
yurawang *prep.* อยู่ระหว่าง pending
yurawangglang *a.* อยู่ระหว่างกลาง
meditative

yurim *v.t.* อยู่ริม skirt
yuruamgan *v. i* อยู่ร่วมกัน co-exist
yutaewni *adv.* อยู่แถวนี้ hereabouts
yutaibangkabbancha *a.*
อยู่ใต้บังคับบัญชา subordinate
yutaidin *a.* อยู่ใต้ดิน subterranean
yutitam *a* ยุติธรรม fair
yutitam *a.* ยุติธรรม just
yuttawiti *n.* ยุทธวิธี tact
yuyonghaitampid *v.t.* ยุยงให้ทำผิด abet
yonbatlongkanaen *v.i.*
หย่อนบัตรลงคะแนน ballot

Z

zip *n.* ซิป zip